W9-AEC-886
Arctic Ocean
ASIA
EUROPE
LEBANON
SYRIA
CYPRUS
MESOPOTAMIA
BALUCHISTAN
PALESTINE
EGYPT
AFRICA
FR. SOMALILAND
ADEN
ANGLO-EGYPTIAN SUDAN
HADRAMAUT
SOCOTRA (BR.)
BR. SOMALILAND
UGANDA
KENYA
N. RHODESIA
SOUTH WEST AFRICA
TANGANYIKA
COMORO IS. (FR.)
SEYCHELLES (BR.)
AMIRANTES (BR.)
PROVIDENCE
ALDABRA (BR.) (BR.)
CHAGOS ARCH. (BR.)
DIEGO GARCIA (BR.)
CARGADOS CARAJOS (BR.)
RODRIGUEZ (BR.)
MAURITIUS (BR.)
REUNION (FR.)
MADAGASCAR
NYASALAND
S. RHODESIA
BECHUANALAND
SOUTH AFRICA
NEPAL
BHUTAN
INDIA
BURMA
(FR.) PONDICHERRY
KARIKAL (FR.)
CEYLON
LACADIVE IS. (BR.)
ANDAMAN IS. (BR)
NICOBAR IS. (BR.)
MALDIVE IS. (BR.)
MALAYA
SINGAPORE (BR.)
COCOS (BR.)
CHRISTMAS (BR.)
WEIHAIWEI (BR.)
HONG KONG (BR.)
KWANGCHOW (FR.)
FR. INDOCHINA
N. BORNEO
SARAWAK
BR. NEW GUINEA
BISMARCK ARCH. (BR.)
SOLOMON IS. (BR.)
GILBERT IS. (BR.)
ELLICE IS.
SANTA CRUZ IS. (BR.)
NEW HEBRIDES (BR.)
FIJI IS. (BR.)
NEW CALEDONIA (FR.)
NORFOLK (BR.)
LORD HOWE (BR.)
AUSTRALIA
TASMANIA
NEW ZEALAND
Indian Ocean
AMSTERDAM (FR.)
ST. PAUL (FR.)
CROZET (BR.)
MARION (BR.)
KERGUELEN (BR.)
BOUNTY
ANTIPODES (BR.)
AUCKLAND (BR.)
CAMPBELL (BR.)
MACQUARIE (BR.)
British Empire
French Empire
palacios

Britain and France

BOOKS BY *René Albrecht-Carrié*

BRITAIN AND FRANCE:
Adaptations to a
Changing Context
of Power

ONE EUROPE:
The Historical Background
of European Unity

THE MEANING OF THE FIRST WORLD WAR

EUROPE SINCE 1815

FRANCE, EUROPE AND THE TWO WORLD WARS

A DIPLOMATIC HISTORY OF EUROPE SINCE
THE CONGRESS OF VIENNA

ITALY FROM NAPOLEON TO MUSSOLINI

ITALY AT THE PARIS PEACE CONFERENCE

RENÉ ALBRECHT-CARRIÉ

Britain and France

Adaptations to a Changing Context of Power

1970
DOUBLEDAY & COMPANY, INC.
Garden City, New York

Library of Congress Catalog Card Number 79–111139

Printed in the United States of America
First Edition

FOR

Philip E. Moseley

CONTENTS

PREFACE

An interest in the operation of power at the level of states has been the motivation of this book. Power we shall always have with us so long as man is man. The state is less inescapable, though not social organization in some form. At any rate, the state, especially the nation-state, happens to be the form that social organization at the political level has taken for some time, and the model toward which it is still tending. However much it may seem superseded, and whatever its shortcomings, the prospects are that the state will survive at least for a considerable time. Like any other living thing, the first care of the state is survival. The concept of the national interest will therefore be taken for granted without any attempt at closer definition, from which derives in turn the assumption that the defense and promotion of that interest is a "natural," or "normal," indeed, under existing conditions, a "legitimate" aspect of any national policy.

The problem of the operation of power at the level of states is a large and complex one. The present essay has purposely confined itself to a limited aspect of it, a case study if one will, both in place and in time. It proposes to do no more than to examine and compare the operation of the foreign policies of two states during the major part of the nineteenth century and our own. The two states are Britain and France, and the reasons for the choice of those two and for that of the time span likewise are two.

Their power and their place and their changing positions have been the reasons for the choice of Britain and France. That place has in considerable measure been due to the fact that they have been models for the shape of institutions that have come to extend throughout the world. "England the mother of parliaments" is a trite phrase, but no less true for that; likewise, the influence of the French Revolution from the time of its occurrence need hardly be expatiated upon. One may point to the fact that the bevy of new states which have proliferated in our time have usually begun their independent life by instituting the trappings of representative and democratic institutions, however well or poorly they may subsequently implement the operation of the initial model. Even that bugaboo of many good democrats, the Communist state, asserts its dedication to an ultimately more perfect democracy than that existing so far.

Great as this influence of example has been, that of sheer power counts for more from our standpoint. The Napoleonic episode is a convenient landmark, for it brought out two things. The primacy of British power, acknowledged by all, is one; that of the French on the continent is the other. Even though the image of the latter was in some degree a distortion owing to the intrusion of the ideological factor and of some related technical innovations—the nation in arms, the career open to talent—it was on the whole fair to rate France number one among the states of the European continent.

But here a change began to happen which becomes the reason for the choice of the time span. The continental primacy of French power remained acknowledged until the Franco-Prussian War. Actually, French power had been diminishing, in relative terms to be sure, throughout the first half of the century. The steepening curve of its subsequent decline hardly needs to be emphasized. While this was happening, the curve of British power seemed to be rising to ever greater heights. Yet if there was no equivalent to the Franco-Prussian War in the British case, the passing of little more than another decade found Britain embarked upon a path, more gradual and less clearly perceived at first, of also relative decline, even if Britain was still acknowledged first place in the world while France definitely held no comparable rank, even within the confines of continental Europe.

This points to the division of our analysis into three parts, following the chronological order. During the first, "Disparity and Divergence," Britain is rising and France declining; Britain can afford Gladstone's "follies of a strong man," but France cannot, and when she tries she comes to grief. The second, "Disparity and Convergence," is the transitional interval during which the power of the two states is very different, yet the challenge to the primacy of Britain gradually brings her in a position increasingly similar to the French; the 1904 Entente is the appropriate climax, expression of this convergence of positions. Finally, the twentieth century has found the two quite definitely "In the Same Boat," meaning by this, in a similar defensive position vis-à-vis the outside, satisfied "have" states, mainly concerned with the problem of holding their own, searching for their proper place in the world of states. The case of the 1956 Suez episode was hardly an instance of the "follies of strong men," but rather one of folly unqualified. The continued decline of Britain in contrast with the qualified French revival after the Second World War does not fundamentally alter the similarity of position.

The common element, which is the attempt at adaptation in circumstances of decline, lends particular interest to the comparative analysis. The purpose is not to give complete histories of British and French foreign policies, though inevitably much of that story will appear, but rather through a selective choice from the respective records to let the story tell itself. Out of it will appear the elements of similarity and difference. The island position of Britain in contrast with that of continental France is obvious; the influence of that difference on modes of development, be it the attitude toward and the use of commerce, empire, and naval power, or the shape and practice of domestic institutions, will emerge. Traditions are difficult to break, and the cultural difference between the British and the French milieus will appear as an important element in shaping their respective reactions in the face of similar conditions. So is the fact that culture in the more limited sense has been looked upon and used in very different ways by the two countries. The whole course of British affairs, whether domestic or foreign, has been far smoother than the French. The concept of defeat is alien to the British people; the French have been familiar with both victory and defeat. This difference has had deep consequences.

In the course of our story we shall often find Britain and France in contact, whether in rivalry or in pursuit of a common purpose. Relations between them will therefore frequently appear, but we wish to emphasize that this aspect is only incidental to the main purpose of the discussion. The stress is on *comparison* between the modes of operation of two states, *not* on their mutual relations.

The literature bearing on our subject is vast and there is no pretense at exhaustive coverage. Obviously also, there could be no question of an extensive use of archival sources over so long a stretch of time. While gaps exist in the analysis of those sources, much of this work has been done and the results of it have been drawn upon. Given the breadth of our scope, the main lines of development may be regarded as sufficiently established, however much historians may vary in the interpretation of specific episodes or policies, or even in the estimate of the residue of a period or the accomplishment and moral qualities of an individual statesman. Whether in the last analysis Bismarck served his country well or planted the seeds of her own and many other disasters, there can be little argument about the quality of his management, as there can be little dispute about the impact of German growth under his guidance and during the Wilhelmine period. Secondary works, not least memoirs, have therefore been depended upon in the main.

In the writing of this book the author gratefully acknowledges a number of debts. A grant from the John Simon Guggenheim Foundation, support from the European Institute of Columbia University, through a grant of the Ford Foundation to the research program of the European Institute, and a travel grant from the American Philosophical Society have provided the free time and the opportunity to visit Britain and France which have made possible the writing of this study.

The list of individuals who have contributed of their time in comparing notes with the author and discussing his views would be too lengthy for enumeration. But he wishes to express special thanks to the Royal Institute of International Affairs for the use of its facilities at Chatham House, and particularly for the kindnesses of its library staff. London, Oxford, and Cambridge have been the scene of many meetings, the pleasantness of which enhanced the value of their content. The same was true in Paris, where the facilities of the Fondation Nationale des Sciences Politiques were made available to the author. To be sure, the events of May 1968, while full of interest, had a certain disrupting effect, perhaps compensated in full by the opportunity to observe at first hand certain forces in action.

To Professor Philip E. Mosely I wish to express special thanks for the interest he has taken in this project from the time of its inception. Professor Thomas P. Peardon has read with care the entire manuscript. The observations and suggestions that he made have been as useful as they were gratefully received. Professor George Woodbridge has also given me the benefit of his comments on certain chapters. For the rest, and needless to say, I am solely responsible for the final product and for any errors or flaws that it may contain.

Cache Lake, August 1969 RENÉ ALBRECHT-CARRIÉ

This royal throne of kings, this sceptered isle,
This earth of majesty, this seat of Mars,
This other Eden, demi-paradise;
This fortress built by nature for herself
Against infection and the hand of war;
This happy breed of men, this little world
This precious stone set in a silver sea,
Which serves it in the office of a wall,
Or as a moat defensive to a house,
Against the envy of less happier lands;
This blessed plot, this earth, this England, . . .

Shakespeare, *Richard II* (II, 1)

Heureux qui comme Ulysse a fait un beau voyage,
Ou comme cestui-là qui conquit la toison,
Et puis est retourné, plein d'usage et raison,
Vivre entre ses parents le reste de son âge.

Quand reverrai-je, hélas! de mon petit village
Fumer la cheminée, et en quelle saison
Reverrai-je le clos de ma pauvre maison,
Qui m'est une province, et beaucoup davantage?

Plus me plait le séjour qu'ont bâti mes aïeux
Que des palais romains le front audacieux;
Plus que le marbre dur me plait l'ardoise fine,

Plus mon Loire gaulois que le Tibre latin,
Plus mon petit Liré que le mont Palatin,
Et plus que l'air marin la douceur angevine.

Joachim du Bellay, *Regrets,* XXXI

PART ONE

Disparity and Divergence

(1815–1870)

I

INTRODUCTION: TWO LANDS AND TWO PEOPLES

What the English expect in their hearts is a final victory when the more brilliant and professional armies have got tired and see by the rules of the game, as Ludendorff did in 1918 and Pétain in 1940, that all is lost. It is then that the English soldier gets his unprofessional revenge.

D. W. Brogan, *The English People,* p. 210

***Au moment le plus intense d'un débat animé, un parlementaire modéré s'écria: "Oui, messieurs, cela ne peut plus durer. Il faut agir, il faut frapper un grand coup. Je vais écrire un article dans la* Revue des Deux Mondes."**

Jacques Fauvet, *La France déchirée,* p. 38

The periodization of history has been the subject of extensive debate until there are now those who argue the validity of the study of contemporary events under the label traditionally reserved for the past.[1] The present essay will indeed concern itself with the present, but in consonance with the predilection and conditioning of its author, the approach to it will be through the past. In the period of history that is generally called the modern, in the shaping of the ways and institutions of the world in which we exist, it would be difficult to find two nations which have left a stronger imprint than those on the opposite shores of the English Channel. The record of their vicissitudes is long and varied, no less than that of their contacts; that is one reason they have been selected as the subject for an examination and a comparison of the courses that they have followed for some time.

People make history and history in turn conditions their behavior. It seems proper, therefore, by way of introduction, to devote some attention to the distinct characteristics of the two peoples in question as well as to take note of some of the salient events in their historic records.

The Imponderables

The subject of national characteristics is an elusive one, on the score of which much has been written, of highly diverse quality, ranging the gamut from shrewd perception to arrant nonsense. These characteristics, moreover, can alter in the course of time, and some would argue that the range of diversity is greater within any one group than between groups. Merry England is a product of the same soil in which flourished Victorian repression and prudery, in England also Cavalier and Roundhead coexisted; Pascal and Voltaire are both French, so are Balzac and Rimbaud. Yet the distinctions between peoples, even the widespread popular misconceptions of them, are not wholly devoid of foundation.

The fact that Britain is an island may be regarded as the root of British insularity. Even without going the length of the derogatory view that would see the lesser breeds as beginning across the Channel, the fact of insularity can hardly be denied. A sense of apartness, at times accompanied by one of superiority and special mission, is often found among the British people. Seen through foreign eyes this is arrogance, which indeed it is, yet not of an aggressive kind. The British can be quite modest about themselves while feeling at the same time that there is no need to broadcast or assert merits and qualities which are so glaringly obvious that the recognition of them cannot be a profitable subject of discussion.

Among these merits what is sometimes called the political genius of the English people stands out. That genius was not quite so obvious before the seventeenth century, when the strange governmental ways of the English people seemed evidence to many of their inability to govern themselves.[2] They ordered those things so much better in Louis XIV's France. Yet there is also no denying that the record since the Glorious Revolution has been such and of such duration as to have made the British people a rare model in the ways of orderly government, more important still in the ability to effect political change within the framework of stable continuity.

Order, therefore, and orderly change, to a degree unlimited, have become fundamental aspects of the political landscape of Britain. No one nowadays is surprised at a Labour peer, and the socialist has accepted the peerage without feeling that he has betrayed his kind; nor was the British monarchy shaken when Ramsay MacDonald became His Majesty's first Socialist Prime Minister. This attitude stems from a deeply rooted belief in the virtues of the English way, a great respect for the rule of law rather than the more arbitrary one of men. The value of this tradition would be difficult to deny, though some would contend that it may have shortcomings and that there are times when revolutions are needed in order to release energies that are suppressed or may have become atrophied or dormant.

The quality of British politics is often associated with a broader aspect of character, the pragmatic approach to circumstances and problems in contrast with the abstract, doctrinaire, or theoretical. This points to what may seem a paradox. Britain has produced a long roster of political thinkers and statesmen of a high order, but it is not only such a mediocrity as Stanley Baldwin who professed a distrust of the intellect; his was merely a rather extreme case of a not uncommon attitude.

This condition has been reflected in the nature of Britain's leadership and in her system of education, at the upper levels especially. The training given to the future leaders of the country has traditionally been in the classical and literary disciplines, calculated it was believed to produce broadly educated and well-rounded men, gifted amateurs, who could then with success turn their hand to a variety of tasks. Some of the best turned to politics, the rewards of which have been held in the highest esteem.[3]

The leadership of Britain has long been recruited from a narrow class, and the feeling of class distinction has been strong in the country; it has far from vanished in the egalitarian welfare state of our day, where its survival some think now most perceptible in the lower strata of society. But the restricted ruling élite has also shown flexibility in its ability and willingness to absorb in its ranks talent from other layers. For the description is also apt of Britain as a nation of shopkeepers. The shopkeeper, provided his shop was large enough, could with relative ease enter the upper ranks, and the aristocracy was thus ever renewed through the infusion of fresh blood.

These shopkeepers, merchants and industrialists, have contributed much to the power of England. They could be hard taskmasters, for themselves no less than for those who depended on them for their livelihood. The price that the English people have paid for their industrial primacy has been very high; it was in connection with the Boer War that the awareness was brought home of the physical deterioration of the slum-dwelling working class, whose contribution—labor—had long been regarded as a commodity subject like others to the merciless law of the market. Comparisons of human costs have been made between that record and the more recent Russian one of forced industrialization.

Much of the English development took place under the aegis of the doctrine of economic liberalism. It was logical, if brutal, to treat labor as a mere commodity; freedom could go the length of the freedom to starve. Here one may see an application, or a survival, or that unlovely Calvinistic view which would see in material success the earthly stamp of the Almighty's approval. England was spared the continental experience of the wars of religion; the political approach to matters religious in that respect served her well. It also had the effect of giving free scope to the seed of disintegration that was contained in the basic Protestant assertion of the supremacy of the individual's right of decision and judgment. Thus, for all that Henry VIII was the founder of a state church, which still exists much watered down, the non-conformist conscience flourished in England and left a powerful imprint upon her development and her people. There is no need to decide which was the causal factor between institutions and national character. The non-conformist tradition has been a powerful component of the Labour movement and its influence is not spent.

The results have to a point been divergent. The logical consistency of the school of liberal economics implied the insistence on the value of individual freedom; one may trace a continuous line of development from Hampton's denial of the king's right to levy ship money to Mill's essay *On Liberty*. This line of thought could lead to strange places; one might mention here the profitable slave trade in which Englishmen successfully engaged, followed by the nineteenth-century dedication to the abolition of slavery, the records of which fill so much space in the Parliamentary Papers.

For duty is the counterpart of right, which last need not be divorced from a humane outlook. Mid nineteenth-century entrepreneurs, and coal magnates as late as the 1920's, could be very harsh men, but there was also considerable agitation for the redress of clearly inhumane conditions, and not by the victims alone, who on the whole have displayed unusual moderation, if not meekness, in putting forward their demands.[4]

Again, the quality of imagination, often commingled with gentleness and humor, is a characteristic of the English people. The love of nature is profound among them, well suited to much of the soft English landscape. Who but an Englishman could have written *The Wind in the Willows,* a man whose profession was banking of all things? The author of *Alice in Wonderland* was a mathematician by trade. Withal, the anthropomorphic sympathy for animal life, carried at times to somewhat absurd lengths, goes hand in hand with fox hunting. English romantic poetry is sufficiently known and reputed; more broadly, English literature in general must be ranked with the best anywhere.

The Englishman is sometimes said to be inarticulate and will indeed often own to the validity of the charge. Within his home as his castle the tradition of the stiff upper lip is admired, emotional display and volubility are by him frequently equated with volatility and weakness, flimsiness of content. His own reticence is not to be translated into dearth of thought or feeling even if the results of these may be sluggish in their manifestations. But certainly tenacity and adherence to purpose, once a cause of sufficient validity has brought out these qualities, can fairly be listed as characteristic of the English people. Sometimes it has been put in the form of the quip that the strength of the British lies in their inability to recognize defeat. Later on in this book, in the concluding section, some further observations will be made about the possible impact of circumstances that it may be difficult for the English people, because of what their history and their tradition have made them, to absorb with promptitude and ease.

The British scene and people hold no monopoly of inconsistencies and contradictions, manifestations of which can be found among others as well. Not only does the French physical landscape offer a much greater variety than the British—it would be difficult to match such a range of diversity in a comparable area—but, correspondingly, the ethnic composition is also more diverse. France partakes of the Mediterranean as well as of the North, though by this time it might be difficult to choose between the degree of the unity of the two peoples and their respective consciousness of it.

Unlike Britain, France is no island, a fact as simple and obvious as its importance is capital. Since 1066 many a time has France been familiar with the presence of alien invaders. Gaul is ancient, of which Caesar spoke, but making France—the very name is of Germanic derivation—where Gaul was has not been a simple accomplishment. The possibility in fact existed at one time that the line of the Loire might roughly become the line of demarcation between what would now be acknowledged as two distinct national entities; the French "nation" was but one of several represented at the ancient university of Paris.

History decreed otherwise, but it is worth noting that allowing that Wales was conquered, in contrast with the final fusion of England and Scotland—the outcome of a constitutional accident—in France the North at one point subdued the South by force; some would claim that the effects of the Albigensian Crusade have never been fully undone. For the rest, the drive toward the Rhine and the Alps has been a long secular travail which has not succeeded in making the left bank of the Rhine wholly French. Nevertheless, France as one now thinks of her was made.

The process and its vicissitudes have left their mark, though here again the question might properly be raised about cause and effect, and undoubtedly interaction, between the people and their character on the one hand and circumstances on the other. France did not know the success of the Reformation though she had her wars of religion and it was touch and go at one point. A very large proportion of her dominant class was attracted to the doctrine of Calvin—a Frenchman himself—and Henvy IV's mot about Paris and a mass is familiar. In this respect his approach to religion was very much the same as that of his contemporary, Elizabeth of England; they were both *politiques*, but the outcomes were different on the two sides of the Channel.

Catholicism is by its very nature, if not necessarily intolerant, at least of an authoritarian cast. The French king might quarrel with the Pope—he often did in fact—but he remained His Most Christian Majesty, and since the seventeenth century at least the tradition has been strong in France of the centralized state. It has not been at all affected by the accident of a variety of régimes; in this respect, even the godless Third Republic merely continued the work of Louis XIV, the First Republic, and the first Napoleon.

This condition is presented sometimes as the necessary counterpart of the centrifugal tendencies of the individualistic French. The French equivalent of the quip that when three Englishmen meet in the desert their first care is to build a church and organize a club is that where there are two Frenchmen three opinions are found. To the French, France is a very solid and living reality, but it is also an abstraction, and they are very prone to disagree with other Frenchmen. Hence in their case as well, some at least seeming contradictions.

Perhaps precisely because of their individualistic diversity the French are enamored of order. But it is order of an intellectual kind, for which there is no need to blame or to credit Descartes. Be it in the drawing up of constitutions or in a learned treatise, the parts must fit with coherence and harmony; hence the great stress on logic, which becomes equated with the clarity necessary for understanding.

This is not a value that warrants looking down upon, for its merits are considerable; it makes for disciplined and clear thinking that will be alert in picking out flaws in someone else's reasoning. It has been properly said—by an Englishman—that, in order to understand German philosophy, it should be read in French translation. This characteristic has become embodied in the tradition of French education, where great stress has been put on the quality of the rational intellect rather than on the totality of the well-rounded social animal, and with special emphasis on the analytical aspect. The standards have been high and the weeding-out process very ruthless.

The results of the system have been diverse. It has undoubtedly selected an élite on which the impact of rigid discipline has been lasting. But there are other facets to the process. For one thing, the very clarity and order of the result can be misleading; the very neatness of it can be overconvincing, a result sometimes obtained at the cost of disregarding certain elements in the situation, thereby achieving a deceptively harmonious simplicity. There are things which are neither simple nor clear.

Another effect has been the tendency to squelch initiative. But as against this, those who succeed in surviving the rigid cast of iron discipline are likely to be the strong, among whom the incidence of revolt has been high. The result has often been curious, for the revolt finds expression within the framework of a permanently established mold. Rejection of a system may simply result in the adoption of another, equally comprehensive and clear, logically consistent and rigid. This is brought out to a nicety in the strong anti-clerical tradition of France, some of the manifestations of which have been quite as intrasigeant as the intransigeance it was rejecting. It is a notable fact that Communism has had great attraction in Catholic France; it answers the same intellectual needs, in not very dissimilar fashion, as does the Catholic doctrine itself. Thus some of the effects of the emphasis on orderly intellectual construction stand in contrast with those of British practicality. Once the conditions of a problem have been adequately understood and formulated, interest may slough off and shift to another domain, disregarding the meaner drudgery of implementation. The French have been credited, with a measure of justice, with being fertile in ideas, the working out and application of which they have neglected, leaving others sometimes to do this.

One manifestation of the fondness for abstraction is found in the political domain, characterized in France not only by a variety of doctrines, but by a multiplicity of political parties as well. The results have been two. The survival—and the respectability—of the revolutionary tradition and label is one. The Great

Revolution itself, in contrast with the Glorious one of Britain, went wrong, degenerating into excesses, partly because of the too rigid adherence to the doctrinaire approach of perfection. The numerous régimes since then—five republics, two monarchies, and two empires—bear witness to the pursuit of a will-o'-the-wisp; constitution making has been a very popular political sport in France. The other consequence has been that of governmental instability within the stability of a given régime, as under the Third and Fourth Republics, for example.

Yet there has also been stability of a different kind, the social, and even a large measure of conservatism in practice. While the working class has in large numbers adhered to the revolutionary tradition, under a variety of political dispensations the controls have remained in the hands of the bourgeois class. Thus, curiously, and in contrast with Britain, while class distinction has meant less in France, the society as a whole has not developed the same degree of homogeneous integration. At all levels the attitude toward the state has been very different in the two countries. The outwardly weak French state has actually been very strong, sustained through its vicissitudes by an all-pervading bureaucracy. By its nature bureaucracy tends to be conservative, *routinière,* and often petty, but at the upper levels the old tradition of the *grand commis* has on the whole functioned well. To be sure, with the passage of time, the growth of technology, and the increase in the complexity of the social organization, the tendency has been everywhere for the ranks of the bureaucracy to swell.

At all events there has been regard for the intellect in all quarters and the social standing of the intellectual and the artist has been correspondingly high in France. The spread and the defense of French culture have received marked attention from the state and one may indeed think of this as a consciously used tool, as cultural imperialism, in marked contrast with the far more casual British attitude in this domain. The quality of the achievements of this culture over an extended period has been outstanding; even if it is pointed out that there is no French Dante, Shakespeare, or Newton, one finds French representation at a high level in virtually all manifestations of culture.

The French tongue for a time became the universal language of civilized Western man, superseding Latin. Following the rise of French power to at least continental primacy, eighteenth-century France, even while drawing heavily on British contributions, was the acknowledged center of the Enlightenment; Frederick of Prussia wrote mainly in French, which also became the language of the Russian court. In passing, it may be noted that this cultural standing bears but poor relation to the fact of power. The classical French age is the Age of Louis XIV; the Enlightenment occurred in a period when French power was on the whole poorly managed; and the French primacy in the pictorial arts, simultaneous with high literary accomplishment, took place at a time of marked power decline after the Franco-Prussian War.

The subject touched upon in these opening pages is vast and the intention is no more than to point to some elements which emphasize the contrast between the two countries considered in this essay. Yet the contacts and the exchanges between them have been intimate and numerous over a long period of time. There has always been in Britain a category of people who have looked up to the cultural achievements of their neighbors across the Channel, who have even been willing to grant them a status of primacy; the British intellectual or artist sometimes finds more congenial the continental attitude than that of his own country, for much that has been said of the French milieu applies in this respect to the wider confines of continental Europe. On the French side there has been a continuing stream that has held English institutions and ways in the highest esteem, and some of the most perceptive and favorable appreciations of them have been penned by French writers.

Yet in both cases these represent thin streams, certainly not the popular image. When the two people come into contact with each other the mutual reaction has rather been one of puzzlement and incomprehension, from which it is an easy step for either to look down upon the other. This may be due to a common quality of insularity. That quality is easy to understand in the English case, and allusion has been made to it and to the forms that it takes. It may seem more surprising in the French instance. But, although in a different shape and with another stress, the tendency among the French has been strong to take for granted the primacy of their own culture, a fact, as in the English case, so obvious as not to be a worthwhile subject of discussion. Thus one comes to a point of convergence, for the French, too, thinking themselves models of good manners and taste, are apt to be surprised at what others consider their arrogance. But just because there is a similarity of attitudes, though attached to a different set of values, it becomes understandable that the British and the French should manifest deep reciprocal incomprehension and intolerance toward each other. And one is thus led to the curious paradox that what have been for a long time the two leading nations of the West should both find it easier to establish contact and understanding with third parties than with each other; think, for example, of the Anglo-French, the Franco-German, and the Anglo-German relationships, at all levels, over an extended period of time. These imponderables can carry great weight.

The Conditioning of History

The French have often pointed out that, within the span of the past century, their country has been invaded three times by the Germans. This is a simple fact, but it disregards the earlier record and has a distorting effect. Many in France and perhaps even more outside, have come to think of Franco-German enmity as one of the established facts of nature. True as it is that, since the making of united Germany, the record has been one of dissension and wars—and of French fear—allowing also that the rivalry was but a continuation of the relationship between France and whatever power existed in mid Europe, whereas in contrast Britain and France have not been at war since Napoleon, the longer record of Anglo-French contention should not be ignored, especially as an important part of the background. A few things are worth recalling in this connection.

Since the assimilated-into-France Normans conquered England, that country has not known the tread of foreign armies. Threats and alarums have recurred, but the Channel moat has frustrated them all. It would be difficult to overemphasize the impact of so unique an experience; as far as the people of Britain are concerned, invasion is outside the domain of practical reality.

The aftermath of the Norman Conquest was, however, a long legacy of continental involvement, of which it may suffice to say that it ended with the complete eviction of England from the Continent. Calais, the last foothold, was finally lost in 1556.

By that time England had already begun to look to and across the ocean, even though she was slower than some continental states, Spain, Portugal, and even France, in pursuing the new possibility in earnest; more than a century elapsed between Cabot's voyage and the first hesitant attempts at settlement in Virginia and in Massachusetts. But that seed prospered, as well as other seeds elsewhere; in the seventeenth and eighteenth centuries England was engaged in a grandiose struggle for world-wide empire.

The French had started a little earlier and they too went to the New World and to India. But the French had another concern, which in their case must have priority, the land. Had it not been for the extent of their resources, domestically greater than England's, they might not have been able to pursue simultaneously the drive toward natural frontiers, mainly the Rhine, and a world-wide imperial policy. As it was, they might have used their resources to better effect than they did in the latter domain. They were a mere handful on the St. Lawrence and in North America in general, as well as in India; in both places they relied in considerable measure on native allies, in which endeavor they fared rather well, meeting in this respect better success than their English rivals. But the one thing they failed to do above all was to invest sufficiently in sea power.

England and France were not alone in the competition, but in the eighteenth century they became the two outstanding contestants. By that time a clear British policy had evolved which consisted in maintaining supremacy at sea while preventing the continental equilibrium from being upset, the main threat to it being French. Thus a series of parallel wars were fought simultaneously overseas and in Europe, truly world wars.

In the former quarter the British relied primarily on their own power, especially at sea.[5] In the latter they chiefly depended on the fostering of alliances, content to supply these with the sinews of war, intervening themselves directly only when that contribution proved insufficient, as in the War of the Spanish

Succession, for example. We know the outcome that was the Treaty of Paris of 1763: France was evicted from the North American mainland[6] as well as essentially from India. The revolt of the American colonies was an important footnote in the story of the British imperial evolution, but it did nothing to restore the French position.

It contributed instead to, though it can hardly be said to have caused, the explosion that was the revolution in France. That episode in its initial stages was, after all, the result of the financial plight of the French state, a plight to which the involvement in the War of American Independence made an appreciable contribution.

The French Revolution and its Napoleonic sequel loom large in modern annals. Initially, the revolution aroused no special fear or opposition in Britain, where it could even be regarded in the light of the compliment of imitation. But, perhaps owing to some of the French characteristics alluded to before, the revolution early went off the rails; France became a Republic and executed her king, an action which by this time no longer had any aura of respectability in Britain, the corresponding English performance being more than a hundred years old. Even more serious, France had become embroiled in continental war, in which England joined in 1793.

The conflict which had begun in 1792 did not come to a close until almost a quarter of a century had elapsed; during that time, where England and France were concerned, it was uninterrupted save during the one-year uneasy truce that was the Peace of Amiens. In France, through a variety of constitutional essays, from that of 1791 to that of 1799, out of the revolution came Napoleon. France fought all Europe, and conquered or overran much of it, from Gibraltar to Moscow; the various continental states again and again made peace with her, some of them at various times in willing or reluctant alliance.

The unity of Europe under French control Britain under any conditions would not have. Call it selfish dislike of the unitary European ideal, or the defense of the liberties of Europe, it was in either case defense of the British interest. Again and again coalitions were raised, of which Britain was the staunchest backbone, and to which she gave the usual financial support; her own direct contribution was at sea, where matters may be said to have been conclusively settled at Trafalgar, after which episode the French no longer seriously attempted to challenge Britain on the water.

As economic warfare proved to be inconclusive and Napoleon repeatedly got the better of continental coalitions, England was again driven to participate herself in the warfare on land. This she did with success; at Waterloo, allowing for Blücher's timely arrival, Wellington was in command. The Russian contribution should also be noted, though it must not be forgotten that what impelled Napoleon to go to Moscow was, indirectly, the fact that he was fighting England, which must be totally isolated first. In any case, the two peripheral states of Europe, Britain and Russia, were the main architects of Napoleon's ultimate downfall. The freedom of disunity would be restored to Europe, and so it was, at Vienna, where with seeming success the clock was set back.

Two aspects, or lessons, of the episode must be emphasized, which are central to the aim of this entire treatment. British tenacity had won, and the value of that asset should not be underrated. Yet it would have been insufficient without the more tangible one of British resources, sea power, and wealth. In any case, the primacy of British power could not be denied, and it was suitable that Britain should play the dominant role that she did in the settlement of 1815. Castlereagh, the quality of whose statesmanship ranks high, with the adequate representative of the British status of power.

But the Napoleonic episode furnished convincing evidence of the magnitude of French power as well. To be sure, that power had to a point been distortedly magnified by the fact that the revolution in France had changed the rules of the game through the ideological and practical innovations—the nation in arms, for example—that it had introduced into the classical operation of the relationships of power. Napoleon made use of these to good effect and it took a long time for his adversaries to learn and to apply the lesson, hampered in doing this as they were in addition by the limitations imposed by the nature of the social order which they were striving to uphold. Nevertheless, allowing for this distorting factor, in the French case as in the British, the importance of the concrete fact of material resources should not be minimized or underrated.

Thus we may say that, in 1815, *the primacy of British power and the magnitude of the French both stood out.* Defeated France was properly acknowledged first rank on the continent. Talleyrand's place stands high in the roster of statesmen; but, able as he was, he could hardly have accomplished as much as he did had not the extent of French power been what it was, and recognized as such, as was the British, by all. Just as it was wholly suitable that Castlereagh should represent Britain at Vienna, so likewise Talleyrand was the proper representative of France.

The details and the making of the settlement of Vienna do not belong in this discussion, but one or two aspects of them are worth retaining for the significance they take on in regard to later developments. The English interest lay not so much in the defeat of France as such. This was a necessary prerequisite, yet also a secondary accomplishment to the larger purpose that was the preservation of the continental equilibrium of power, the *real* British interest. To that end, the preservation of French power—within suitable limits, of course—was a necessity. Castlereagh strongly resisted the understandable vengefulness and the pettiness of others who took a less far-sighted view of the possibilities offered by momentary advantage. Even for the Hundred Days but minor retribution was exacted: an indemnity, substantial but not unmanageable, minor frontier changes, and the occupation of some territory.

To have diminished France too much, even apart from weakening the none-too-popular restored Bourbons and arousing French national feeling, would have merely opened the door to other influences, the Russian for example, and thus been tantamount to a defeat of the main British purpose. The alliance contracted between Britain, Austria, and France herself in January 1815 was Castlereagh's work in large measure. It was designed to contain Russian ambitions and thus illustrates to perfection the nature of the British outlook and mode of operation.

Reference has just been made to the possible risk of exasperating French national feeling. This was a real factor, perhaps most marked in the French case, for the French Revolution, initiated with a universalistic outlook, had had the seemingly inconsistent effect of giving a great fillip to the national consciousness of the French[7]; that revolution is often, and on the whole quite correctly, credited with having initiated the modern nationalistic aberration. Yet that situation was very different at the beginning of the nineteenth century from the state of affairs with which we have become familiar since. This is what made it possible at Vienna to barter peoples about in callous fashion in one view, to handle conflicting interests with detached reasonableness in another interpretation.

One more thing may be mentioned at this point which has special bearing on the Anglo-French relationship. In the context of that relationship the outcome of 1815 was but another instance of the fact that, over a long period, be it in checking the continental extension of French power or in the imperial domain, in a succession of encounters the balance of success had undeniably been Britain's. Whether or not this was a desirable outcome for others—for Europe as a whole, for example—does not matter; it was undoubtedly a good result from the British standpoint. Nor does it matter whether or not the condition was the result of better management of British power than of French, or of a combination of adventitious circumstances. What must be borne in mind is the fact that, in certain French quarters at least, notably the Navy, for one, a tradition was confirmed that rankled. As the British put it sometimes, the French have never forgotten Trafalgar, not to mention Agincourt. To think in such terms in the second half of the twentieth century may seem out-of-date parochialism. It is perhaps not irrelevant to mention the fact none the less and there will be occasion to revert to it in our concluding pages.

For, apart from containing French power within appropriate limits—Britain to be the judge of these—Britain had no special quarrel with France. And since 1815 the two countries, if they have often been at odds, have never been at war with each other, though both, sometimes together, have been at war with other Powers. However, we must insist that the focus of this treatment is not on Anglo-French relations, but rather on a comparative analysis of the manner in which the two Powers have reacted, adapted, or failed to adapt, themselves to the changing vicissitudes of their respective positions.

Diplomacy, foreign relations, and war are all of them in the last resort exercises in the manipulation of power. For that reason, and still by way of general background and introduction, before entering into the details of our story it seems desirable to attempt some definition and assessment of

The Components of Power

"Power tends to corrupt, and absolute power corrupts absolutely," said Lord Acton, a maxim of which many earlier and later variants have been given and which has been the subject of considerable debate. Be it evil or not, power *is,* and all the deprecations of the great moral teachers of mankind have at best mitigated its operation. Also, the wielders of power are men, and not always necessarily evil men, in some respects a complicating factor. It is generally preferable when they are realistic men, for no more pain and bloodshed have been brought to mankind than by the well-intentioned, starry-eyed upholders of impossibly high ideals—withal an indispensable breed; high as their price may come, prophets are worth their salt. We are at any rate concerned with power, the components of which may be classified under two comprehensive heads, the material or physical on the one hand, those that may be broadly lumped under the "moral" label on the other, Bismarck's imponderables. The former are more amenable to quantification, the latter far more elusive of measurement, and the appraisal of them is subject to the virtues of understanding perceptivity and to the limitations of personal prejudice and judgment.

As indicated before, our interest is focused on two peoples, nations, or states. But, obviously, for purposes of comparative appraisal of their standing in the world, it will be necessary to say something of others as well; the changing place of Britain and of France would be seen in a meaningless vacuum if reference were not made to Germany and to the United States, for example. Also, among the three predicates used at the beginning of this paragraph, the word "states" will be retained as the most relevant. For in the period under consideration the nation-state is the fundamental political entity. Much of the energy and of the story of nineteenth-century Europe, of the twentieth century elsewhere, has been absorbed by the endeavor to create such entities. Not until 1870 for Germany and for Italy, until 1919 for the east central region, was the political map of Europe drawn on the basis of nationality; but in this evolution Britain and France, along with some other Atlantic communities, had led the way. By Napoleon's time, Englishmen had for quite some time known that they were English and the experience of the French has been similar; the added accent given to this development by the French Revolution has been mentioned before.

It did not matter very much whether the state found its symbolic expression in a monarch, be he absolute or constitutional, or whether it derived its legitimacy from the nation. For quite some time, since the Peace of Westphalia let us say, the states of Europe had evolved in their mutual relations certain codes of behavior which had served to establish a measure of order in the chaos and anarchy that are the logical concomitants of the claim of sovereignty. Sovereigns, being none of them subject to any higher authority, were equal in a sense; they generally subscribed to the doctrine of the equal right of all to existence. In effect they were not equal, for their power varied over a very wide range. The contrast between abstract theory and existing reality was compromised in the effective acknowledgement of differences. There were the great and the smaller, the latter having presumably limited and circumscribed interests only, the former having "general" interests, meaning that they acknowledged to each other the right to a say in all matters, in more homely parlance, the right to have a finger in every pie. The Concert of Europe, a loose yet far from meaningless reality, was the characteristic expression of this state of affairs, which implied the legitimacy of the pursuit of the national interest. It implied also moderation and a sense of responsibility for the orderly, preferably peaceful, operation of the European family as a whole.

That situation was but temporarily disturbed by the intrusion of the French revolutionary ideology. From the standpoint of the state system of Europe, the universalistic aspect of that ideology was defeated. The earlier framework of sovereign states functioned throughout the nineteenth century, and one may say that it still does, though subject to some serious challenges—it has proved so inadequate—in our own. That is why mention of it is made, for, to repeat, sight must never be lost of the fact that this entire analysis centers on the power of two states in particular.

Whatever success may attend the current endeavors in the conquest of space, should they even lead to the acceptance by mankind of the unity of the planet earth, so far the simple facts of geography have been of paramount importance. There is no need to emphasize again the significance of the island position of Britain. Once the political unity of Great Britain had been realized, the whole island could act as a unit vis-à-vis the outside. Since that event roughly coincided with the outburst of energy that sent Europeans to the four quarters of the earth, the outward-looking approach and the preference for the wide seas were increasingly and consciously asserted, until naval supremacy became a fundamental tenet of British foreign policy, even allowing for occasional lapses in keeping up the naval establishment either in terms of size or of modernity.[8]

The sea has served the British well. Not only did it act as a protection from invasion, it became the great avenue of commercial and imperial expansion. But it also gave that expansion, as in the case of other European states, the peculiar character of separating the central motive core from its acquisitions. In some quarters, relatively empty ones, the British people themselves swarmed; in others, where the conditions of climate, existing populations and cultures precluded substantial immigration, they merely went to trade and often rule. The fact of physical separation between the mother country and the colonies is important, and the effects of it have been fully registered in the contrast between the British case and those of the United States and Russia.[9]

Sea power thus became the mainstay and the symbol of Britain's world position and eventual primacy. The role of it was perceptively brought out by Captain Mahan in the 1890's. Sea power has always made far more limited demands on the human resources of a country than does land power; Britain was enabled to maintain the tradition of not depending on land armies. In the period preceding the one under discussion in this book, sea power also made relatively smaller demands on the exchequer. This may be regarded as Britain's good fortune rather than any special merit of the British people; it goes a long way toward explaining how and why a relatively small country, not overendowed with resources, came to play the role that it did and to rank on a par with the greatest. The realization of the possibilities of the sea can hardly be regarded, however, as merely an accident of geography, though it is well to bear in mind the lateness of this realization.

In this connection passing mention should be made of the role of the Irish situation. Ireland, too, is an island, and if one bears in mind that, as late as the beginning of the nineteenth century, her population was of a comparable order of magnitude to the British, it becomes easier to understand the high priority given by Britain to the control of Ireland, which must not be allowed to be an independent enemy or a possible base of enemy action. This same condition goes some distance toward explaining the nature, unduly harsh at times and a departure from the norm adopted elsewhere, of the British rule of Ireland. Things began to change when the discrepancy between the two islands became enormous; the necessities of defense and the impulse of political liberality could accommodate to each other where Ireland was concerned.

Geography has given France a totally different set of conditions. The harmony of the hexagon of which the French speak is broken in the northeast, where there is no equivalent of the clear and solid barriers that are the sea on three sides, the Pyrenees and the Alps on two others. The plain that stretches with but minor interruptions from the Pyrenees to Kamtchatka has facilitated the movement of peoples, whether as migrant hordes or as armies. The gap of the northeast has been repeatedly breached. The French response has been the *Drang nach Osten* that has been the attempt to secure the "natural" frontier of the Rhine. That drive has been going on since the collapse of Charlemagne's empire and the creation of the impossible middle kingdom of Lothair.

Once the English continental ambition had been eliminated—the real meaning of the Hundred Years' War—France could focus on the Central European Habsburg threat. For a time, the first half of the sixteenth century, when Spain and Central Europe were joined, France was dangerously encircled—as she was to be again after 1936. The separation of Spain from Central Europe, the decline of the former, then the advent of the Bourbons in that country, resulted in, or were manifestations of, the rise of French power to continental primacy; simultaneously an attempt was made to pursue a policy of world empire. All the while, as indicated before, Britain maneuvered with skill, and ultimately with success, in checkmating French ambitions by fostering the continued fragmentation of Europe. The French counterpart of this British policy may be seen as founded on the principle that our neighbors are our enemies, but the neighbors of our neighbors are our friends. France cultivated in turn the Turkish, the Swedish, and the Polish alliances, even the Prussian at one point when Prussia was East European; later on she would join hands with Russia.

In resisting Habsburg encirclement, then seeking to establish her own primacy, apart from the advantage of geography—a central position and good frontiers save on one side—France enjoyed certain other advantages. We are alluding to the fundamental components of power that are numbers and material resources.

We have become only too familiar with the destructive power of weapons; even a few machine guns can effectively hold a mob in abeyance. These are relatively recent innovations, before the advent of which the individual, or at least the individual with a spear or a gun, counted for more. So likewise, before the advent of mass production and of automation, the individual hand counted for more. Numbers have in the past had greater importance as a component of the power of the state than they have in our present mechanized society, for all that their significance is far from having disappeared; backward as it may still be, the sheer weight of the Chinese mass cannot be ignored.

The fact therefore must be emphasized that for a long time France had been the most populous state of Europe, not excluding vast Russia.[10] At the turn from the eighteenth to the nineteenth century her population, numbering some 27,000,000, was two and a half times the British. There were altogether in Europe more German-speaking people than there were French, but they were divided among a number of political units, some of them engaged in competition. The French numbered 50 per cent more than the Italians, who were also disunited at this time.

Until the French Revolution the rulers had relied on professional armies, the dimensions of which depended on their policies and their resources. The relative overinvestment of Prussia in her armed forces—with a fifth of the French population she maintained an army of equal size to the French—had given that state a position out of proportion to its dimensions and resources, justifying the characterization of war as its national industry. The introduction of conscription was calculated to restore the proportionate influence of numbers, and the fact has been mentioned of the role of that innovation when revolutionary France confronted Europe. The reservoir of French manpower, in combination with the use of the forces of willing or coerced allies, goes a long distance toward explaining the Napoleonic performance, even while not detracting from the credit due his own military competence.

Even Napoleon's armies were, however, dependent on guns and ammunition. The wealth, the resources, the totality of the economic potential that stood behind his armies was thus a major consideration. Where France was concerned the state of her economy compounded the advantage of numbers in Napoleon's time. For, save for the Austrian Netherlands, future Belgium, France was the most advanced state of the continent in terms of economic development, and of such industry as there was.

But this is also where economic resources, in addition to the factor of her geographic position, compensated in the English case for the deficiency of numbers. England is the home of the industrial revolution; from roughly the middle of the eighteenth century she began to outdistance all others. Much smaller and less populated than France, her wealth was of the same order of magnitude toward the end of the century. This and the sound management of her finances is what enabled her to keep financing the anti-French coalition while maintaining the supremacy of her own sea power. English wealth was derived in substantial measure from commercial activity, the eighteenth-century growth of her trade far outdistancing that of her population.

These relative positions were destined to undergo modification in the nineteenth century, during the first half of which the change was advantageous to Britain and detrimental to France.[11] Europe as a whole set about disproving the validity of the gloomy Malthusian forecast.[12] The population of the United Kingdom doubled during the first fifty years of the century and increased another 30 per cent in the next thirty years. The French increase was much smaller, reaching 36,500,000 by 1850, with less than another 3,000,000 added by 1880. By 1870 the German total was about the same as the French. The great increase in Europe's population was made possible by drawing upon the resources of the outside world, the potential of which was in part developed by Europeans and the products of which were exchanged for those of Europe. The correlation is close between the rise in numbers and the expansion of industry and of commercial exchanges. A few indices bring this out quite convincingly. Iron and coal are the basic materials for the creation of industry. The following table of iron production sums up a telling story:

	United Kingdom	*France*	*Germany*	*U.S.A.*	*World*[13]
1830	680,000	270,000	45,000	180,000	1,600,000
1850	2,250,000	400,000	215,000	560,000	4,470,000
1870	5,960,000	1,180,000	1,400,000	1,690,000	12,260,000

It shows the overwhelming preponderance of the British position, maintaining itself at about half the world total during this period. It shows likewise the relative decline of the French place and the vigor of the German rise. By 1870, France and Germany were roughly on a par in the domain of industrial production. The same picture is conveyed by the extent of railway mileage, 17,500 and 20,000 kilometers respectively. The railway, like other machines, was born of the union of iron and steam; in this field also, England was well in advance of others.

It was logical that England should take the leadership in breaking the fetters of the old mercantilistic view. The controversy that raged over free trade won the day with the repeal of the Corn Laws in 1846 and of the Navigation Acts three years later. Not having the English advantage of prior start others were reluctant to follow the English example. France was highly protectionist until Napoleon III inaugurated a new economic policy, of which the Cobden-Chevalier treaty of 1860 was a manifestation. So likewise was the German Zollverein protectionist vis-à-vis the outside.

Free trade was but one aspect of a more encompassing philosophy. The doctrine of free enterprise asserted the virtues of competition unfettered in all domains of economic activity. The battle of free trade won after 1846, England became firmly wedded to the merits of that policy until it took on the attributes of "sacred cow" in the British milieu. The slogan that "that state governs best that governs least" did not achieve the same popularity on the Continent. The role of the state in the construction of the French railway system always remained important even though the railways were mainly built by private companies. Under the dispensation of open competition England fared well, the primacy of her economic position, of her power in general, being universally acknowledged. The Great Exhibition of 1851 was a suitable manifestation and index of her standing at the time of its occurrence.

The bases of the great outburst of German energy and power were being laid during this time, but the results would not appear until the political problem of unity had been resolved. All the while, though still granted general primacy of continental position, France was gradually falling behind in terms at least of relative growth.

Without seeking to unravel its deep causes, the fact is undeniable of a more limited horizon in the French economic practice; the phrase economic Malthusianism comes to mind in her case. There were large banking houses and financial interests in France, which also had not forgotten her imperial tradition. Yet the feebleness of her activity stands in contrast with the British, for all that in that country, too, the drive of imperial expansion operated at an attenuated tempo in this period. But it was the British who first went to China, the French following in their footsteps. While London was becoming the financial capital of the world, and profiting thereby, French enterprises continued to a far greater degree to remain family undertakings content with small size. The growth of the factory takes place in France definitely later than in Britain. The French economy remained more self-contained—and better balanced—than the British. France was largely self-supporting, while Britain, consistently accepting the implications of free trade, allowed the virtual destruction of her agriculture; cheaper corn could be had from the new world in exchange for British manufactures. The workshop of the world prospered under this dispensation, at least during these early stages. The subsequent story, but not for quite some time, would appear in a different light; it will be traced in later chapters.

Thinking therefore of the economic situation during the first half of the nineteenth century, until 1870, the picture that emerges is that of the unchallenged supremacy of Britain, where the rhythm of growth was very rapid. There was growth in France too, especially during the earlier part of the Second Empire, but if one leaves aside shorter-term fluctuations and thinks of the half century as a whole, the impression is rather of a plateau of stability, not to say of stagnation, being reached. Coming from behind, Germany had, by 1870, reached a position of rough parity with France, of somewhat greater advance in some respects, in the domain of economic development. We shall note later on the changed rates of growth after that date.

Tocqueville for one had perceived the great possibilities contained in the vast American and Russian complexes. Neither of these, however, was to have a very significant impact until a later time. American energies were overwhelmingly absorbed by the task of internal development, while Russia was hampered by the backward nature of her institutions.

The role of institutions can be of the highest importance, and in this case again the fact of interaction between them and circumstances may be observed. The free trade agitation in England was fostered by the demands of growing industry and trade; once successful, the emphasis on free enterprise itself gave an impulse to further growth. One must here bear in mind the ways and attitudes that prevail in a whole society, the imponderable, elusive elements that set its tone, give it cohesion, and thus themselves constitute a component of its power when it comes to dealing with others.

Napoleon had modernized France and released an untapped reservoir of energies. Bureaucratic and centralized as it was, the administration with which he endowed the country represented modernity and progress, as did the civil code and the agrarian and social changes already initiated by the revolution. He was aware of the importance of education, technical education in particular, especially at the higher levels; such an institution as the *École Polytechnique* bears witness to this.[14] Actually, in France the state showed greater interest in this domain than was the case in England, where Oxford and Cambridge fell to a rather low estate. In both countries, however, whether in or outside the universities, a number of gifted individuals made vital contributions of a scientific nature. This was still a time, in contrast with our own, when the individual scientist could operate with limited resources and research was not dependent on vast means and when the role of organized co-operative work was minimal. It was the heyday of the gifted amateur, a characteristic English product.

Germany was not laggard in this respect, this being in fact the great age of German scholarship, the accomplishments of which were acknowledged by all. There was also greater care, and higher quality, at the level of secondary education, in Prussia or in Holland than in France. If one thinks of education in a broad sense, the role of increasing literacy and of the press must not be forgotten. Here England led the way, be it in terms of less stringent control of the freedom of expression or, equally important, of making a cheap press available to an increasingly large section of the people.

Such freedom may be thought to have divisive effects. Indeed the discussion of political and social issues reached at times a high pitch of intensity in England, while the French preferred the revolutionary method of change. But be it the great Reform Bill in England or the upheavals of 1830 and 1848 in France, these did not yet seriously affect the cohesion of society. Although France adhered to universal manhood suffrage after 1848, the impact of such things as the Higher Criticism, of which Germany was the prime home, or of English Darwinian ideas remained confined to a very thin layer of society. There is an inevitable lag between the initial propounding of seminal ideas and their diffusion at the popular level; the lag was greater a hundred years ago, when the printed word, more controlled than it is now for that matter, was the only available instrument of that diffusion. The same phenomenon can be observed in the case of the continuing hold of religion.

But perhaps most important of all, especially in the context of the present discussion, is the intensification of national feeling, a contribution of the French Revolution which will not be stressed again. In the cases of Germany and of Italy, and granting ancient roots, the Napoleonic conquest lies unquestionably at the origin of the movement that resulted in the making of the two unitary states. The revival of national consciousness among the subject Slavic peoples of East Central Europe, Czechs, Serbians, and others, was not long in following, initiated in part by the work of German grammarians.[15]

England and France needed no such prodding to create a deep sense of national consciousness. In both countries we shall have occasion to observe instances of the demagogic appeal of political leaders to the patriotic emotion of the mass, an appeal which on the whole found an easy and ready response. There were indeed differences among the leaders and at times intensive debate, but the validity of the national ideal was not yet challenged in the way that it would be later on in the century or in our own time. Marx's ringing appeal, which set class allegiance above the national, was premature in 1848. There will be occasion to note the intensity of national reactions at the time of the crisis of 1840 or in connection with the Franco-Prussian War, to take but random examples. It would take the holocausts of twentieth-century wars in combination with the spread of the Marxist doctrine to induce the revulsion toward war and the questioning of the supremacy of the national value that are characteristic of our time. The nineteenth century, especially the first half of it, was not significantly disturbed by these problems; also, the wars that it witnessed were, by comparison with our own, gentle, short-lived, and limited affairs.

If it is true that war and diplomacy are but different methods of pursuing the same fundamental ends, exercises in the manipulation of power, the fact remains that in order to be effective, power must remain credible. The concrete components of it, numbers, wealth, economic resources, those on the basis of which calculations can be made, will be wasted assets unless there is the will to make full use of them. The use of them in action, when they are put to use, is also qualified by the nature of their management. The competence of military leadership, or conversely the lack of such competence, can at specific points become crucial in determining the outcome of a campaign or a war. The condition of the military establishment therefore ranks high once recourse is had to the ultimate test of force. But one must never lose sight of the role of the more elusive imponderables, such elements as national cohesion.

This last-mentioned factor may be related to that of institutions, and here we may point to both similarity and difference between the two states with which we are concerned. The British record presents the fortunate condition that the great problems which have faced many states in modern times have come to Britain in succession rather than in conjunctive complication. The story of the medieval English monarchy is hardly one of smoothness, but since the advent of the Tudors on only one occasion has a British ruler met with a violent end, Charles I paying the price of his head in the course of the seventeenth-century national turmoil. Yet that struggle did not affect national unity accomplished long before his time. Nor had that unity been significantly threatened by the religious issue of the preceding century; Henry VIII and his daughter Elizabeth managed to escape the bane of religious wars that created so much havoc on the Continent. More recently, in the period covered in the present book, religious and constitutional issues having been disposed of, Britain could proceed to put to good use the tradition of orderly and gradual reform in dealing with the social question.

The French record in contrast has been far less smooth down to the very present. The price of national unity was the harsh suppression of the South by the North in medieval days and the long struggle, fought in France, for the elimination of English continental ambitions. The Reformation tore the country asunder, and the ultimately tolerant settlement of that problem by

Henry IV initiated the institution of the strong, centralized, absolute monarchy. That institution served its purpose for a time; it was widely believed by contemporaries that Louis XIV's France was better governed than Stuart England. But the price of this success came high. Instead of a Glorious Revolution the French had their own version, the sequel of which stands in sharpest contrast with the British experience. Hence the jerkiness of the French political record—two monarchies, two empires, and five Republics—since the French Revolution. Even the Third Republic, which for a time seemed to have entered on the path of stability, led a very troubled existence, constitutional, religious, and social issues intertwining in divisive fashion.

Yet it is also proper to point out that in the case of both countries the fact of national unity prevailed. To it may be credited the steadiness and continuity of foreign policy characteristic of both states; whatever deviations and vagaries have occurred have not affected the main line of development, which has been the pursuit of a clearly defined and understood national interest. The Cromwellian interlude in England did not mark discontinuity in the commercial and imperial policy of England, just as the Second Empire and the Third Republic in the last analysis join hands in the pursuit of fundamentally similar aims.

The Period 1815–30

After the long turmoil which had come to an end in 1815 it is not surprising that the desire for tranquillity should have been widespread and deep. France herself shared it, where weariness with Napoleon's everlasting warfare and the demands which that warfare made on the French people and the resources of the country had contributed to the alienation of much of the support on which he had depended. Till mid century, until another Napoleon sat upon the French throne, there was peace in Europe, peace in the sense at least that no major conflict broke out involving the Great Powers with each other.

That peace was not synonymous with total quiescence, for the past cannot be undone, and the leaven of 1789 continued at work. France remained the home and the standard bearer of the revolutionary ideal, a condition the significance of which was ambivalent. It was the fact of French power which made the possibility of revolution in France a matter of international concern; conversely, the possibility of exploiting the appeal of revolution abroad could itself become an asset of French power. It followed quite naturally that the domestic politics of France, Parisian events in particular, were closely watched in foreign chancelleries.

The period between the first and the second French empires falls into two roughly equal segments, conveniently separated by the events of 1830. The second one of these, the period of the July Monarchy and the Second Republic, will form the subject of a separate chapter for the reason that, although France on the whole continued to "behave," meaning that she adhered to the policy of not upsetting the applecart of European peace, certain things happened, a more detailed discussion of which is relevant to our purpose. By way of introduction to them it will be useful at this point to make a brief survey of the period that ends in 1830, always bearing in mind that the focus of interest lies in the comparative analysis of British and French foreign policies. It will be convenient to examine each of these separately, even if this may entail some repetition.

Britain, 1815–30

The point has been made that the final outcome of the Napoleonic episode had been to make clear the primacy of the British position of power. It was the steadfastness of British purpose which, again and again, revived and sustained the anti-French coalitions, stood firm in the face of the Tsar's ambiguities and of Metternich's failing purpose. It was fitting expression of this state of affairs that Castlereagh's role should have been the dominant one that it was at Chaumont[16] and at Vienna. To be sure, this may be seen as no more than outward registration of existing British power, yet the point is worth emphasizing, for it marked also the beginning of the period during which Britain's primacy was most outstanding and least questioned, roughly the three quarters of a century after the Congress of Vienna.

Secure and confident, Britain could elevate the manipulation of circumstances into a conscious expression of long-term policy, not to say permanent attitude. Pitt's expression of it, as early as 1805, may be recalled, which was contained in his communication to the Russian ambassador. According to Pitt, Britain's purpose was:

> 1st. To rescue from the Dominion of France those countries which it had subjected since the beginning of the Revolution, and to reduce France within its former limits, as they stood before that time.
>
> 2ndly. To make such an arrangement with respect to the territories recovered from France, as may provide for their Security and Happiness, and may at the same time constitute a more effectual barrier in future against Encroachments on the part of France.
>
> 3rdly. To form, at the Restoration of Peace, a general Agreement and Guarantee for the mutual protection and Security of different Powers, and for reestablishing a general System of Public Law in Europe.

More significant still, the accomplishment of this purpose required

> . . . the most effectual measures for giving Solidity and Permanence to the System which shall thus have been established. Much will undoubtedly be effected for the future repose of Europe by these Territorial Arrangements, which will furnish a more effectual Barrier than has before existed against the ambition of France. But *in order to render this Security as complete as possible, it seems necessary,* at the point of a general Pacification, *to form a Treaty to which all the principal Powers of Europe should be Parties,* by which their respective Rights and possessions . . . shall be fixed and recognized, *and they should all bind themselves mutually to protect and support each other,* against any attempt to infringe them—It should re-establish a general and comprehensive system of Public Law in Europe, and provide, as far as possible, for repressing future attempts to disturb the general Tranquillity, and above all, for restraining any projects of Aggrandizement and Ambition similar to those which have produced all the Calamities inflicted on Europe since the disastrous era of the French Revolution.[17]

These were not empty words. Castlereagh made use of them before Parliament in May 1815; Pitt's program was precisely what he had successfully striven to achieve at Vienna. But one must look a little deeper, for it is at this point that a misunderstanding arose, a divergence of interpretation which others have sometimes seen as the ambiguity, not to say the duplicity, of British policy.

There was, on Britain's part, no duplicity of intent. Britain, like other states, was pursuing the defense of her own interest, but just because of her power she felt that she was in an arbitral position and saw that interest as lying most of all in the preservation of the balance of power. There was on her part no pathological fear, or hatred, of France, which indeed in her view constituted an indispensable element of the equilibrium of Europe. Castlereagh had fought hard on France's behalf at Vienna, a France reduced to be sure to adequate proportions. This is the point at which the misunderstanding arose.

Considerations of power equilibrium were anything but alien to the Metternichian outlook—witness his alliance with Britain and France in January 1815 designed to check Russian ambitions. Nevertheless, he put a different emphasis on the phrase "they should bind themselves mutally to protect and support each other" from that given to it by Castlereagh or British statesmen in general. In the eyes of the latter the aspect of ideology was minimal; a constitutional France was in fact closer to their own domestic practice than the autocracy of other European states. It was France *qua* France, as a state among states, hence French power, which was their main concern. But to Metternich—and increasingly to the Tsar—the social order assumed equal importance if not priority of care.

The cleavage was not long in appearing. Revolution in Naples or Spain, under the aegis of the constitutional banner, was to Britain largely a matter of indifference, even to a degree of some sympathy. Not so to Metternich. From his standpoint Austrian intervention in Italy was wholly logical.[18] Britain did not effectively object and in 1821 Metternich had his way. The simultaneous Spanish situation was different.

If one thinks primarily of the issue between Liberalism and conservation, it was not actually different, and the Tsar was the most consistent of all who would have sent his armies across

Europe to help the king of Spain. The meetings that took place at Troppau and Laibach at the turn from 1820 to 1821 dealt with the Neapolitan situation alone. But it is of interest to consider the position expounded by Castlereagh in the state paper bearing the date of May 5, 1820.[19] Formally dealing with the Spanish situation only—trouble did not break out in Naples until July—it was a broad exposition of the British position on the subject of intervention in general. Some brief extracts will suffice:

> It [the Alliance] was never intended as an Union for the Government of the World, or for the Superintendence of the Internal Affairs of other States. . . .
>
> . . . it was the Revolutionary Power *more particularly in its Military Character actual and existent within France against which it intended to take Precautions, rather than against the Democratic Principles* . . .

No sharper contrast could be found than between this assertion and the following words in the preliminary protocol of Troppau:

> States which have undergone a change of Government due to revolution, the results of which threaten other states, *ipso facto* cease to be members of the European Alliance. . . . If, owing to such situations, immediate danger threatens other states, the Powers bind themselves, by peaceful means, or if need be by arms, to bring back the guilty state into the bosom of the Great Alliance.[20]

Castlereagh did not deny the possibility of the spread of the revolutionary infection, which, however, remained a hypothetical matter. He adduced various arguments, authentic or tinged with sophistry, in favor of inaction. Thus,

> The King of Great Britain . . . has . . . all his means to acquire through Parliament, and He must well know that if embarked in a War, which the Voice of the Country does not support, the Efforts of the strongest Administration which ever served the Crown would soon be unequal to the prosecution of the Contest.

More important still was this summation:

> The principle of one State interfering in the internal affairs of another . . . is always a question of the greatest possible moral as well as political delicacy. . . . It is only important on the present occasion to observe that to generalize such a principle and to think of reducing it to a System, or to impose it as an obligation, is a Scheme utterly impracticable and objectionable. . . . No Country having a Representative System of Government could act upon it—and the sooner such doctrine shall be distinctly abjured as forming in any degree the basis of our Alliance, the better. . . .
>
> . . . .
>
> We shall be found in our place when actual danger menaces the System of Europe, but this Country cannot, and will not, act upon abstract and speculative Principles of Precaution.

There were other—unstated—reasons of a less lofty character. Liberal régimes anywhere might be advantageous to British trade, as could the success of the rebellion of Spain's American possessions. There was the likelihood that a European intervention in Spain would in effect be a French intervention,[21] a prospect highly distasteful to Britain.

Nevertheless, allowing for these qualifications, the fact remains that we find here the assertion of some long-term fundamental principles of British foreign policy. The preference for dealing with situations as they arise rather than on the basis of broad principle may be put down as characteristic of the national temperament. That for allowing others to arrange their domestic affairs as they wish is more closely related to the fact that no threat might arise therefrom, and if by chance a threat arose, Britain had sufficient power to deal with it. Hence a genuine preference for non-intervention.

To push the devotion to this policy to the point of using force to prevent others from intervening may seem a paradox. Yet this is just what happened in the matter of the rebellious colonies of Spain. The legitimacy of the Spanish title could hardly be questioned, but the Monroe Doctrine is sufficiently familiar. Its name derives from that of the American President who proclaimed it, but the British role in its formulation is equally well known.[22] Having made sure of at least passive French assent

Britain could proceed to dangle the threat of the interposition of her own naval power. Canning's boast, if unduly grandiloquent in its form, was in essence not unwarranted, especially in retrospect.

In defense of what she considered a fundamental interest Britain had shown that she would fight. She would do so again if needed, but the preference for the avoidance of the use of force was strong, undoubtedly made easier by the confidence in her own power and the knowledge that others were aware of the extent of that power.

Mediterranean affairs during the twenties furnish another illustration of the mode of operation and of the use of British power.

One consequence of the Napoleonic wars, more particularly of the French expedition to Egypt, had been to bring to Britain greater awareness of the whole Mediterranean. Her retention of Malta and the protectorate of the Ionian Islands were the concrete manifestations of this realization in 1815. But this interest ran into two others, the Russian and the French.[23] The first was, as it had already been for some time, focused on the Straits; the importance to Russia of the control of the passage through them hardly needs explanation. The French interest centered on Egypt, secondarily on Syria. The decadence of the Ottoman Empire, with the possibility of its demise and consequent partition, is the heart of the Eastern Question, the long story of which fills the nineteenth century. Imperial and naval Britain stood for two things, which came to be fixed cardinal principles of her policy: prevention of Russian control of the Straits; likewise prevention of a French establishment at the nodal point of Suez, an area to which the growth of trade with the East gave increasing importance. The simplest answer to both desiderata was the defense of Ottoman integrity, since no agreement could be reached for the division of spoils in the event of the collapse of the Turk, which therefore would in all likelihood have resulted in a conflict among the Powers.

There will be many occasions to examine the unfolding of the Eastern Question in this book. What may be regarded as the opening stage of it will be considered at this point, or at least some significant aspects of the British behavior will be.

What brought matters to a head was the Greek rebellion during the 1820's. It was no use taking Metternich's view that the Sultan was the legitimate ruler of Greece, which he undoubtedly was, and that the whole episode was taking place beyond the pale of civilization. The Greeks, though not Slavs, were Eastern Christians. The temptation was strong for the Tsar to exploit the situation for the promotion of Russian advantage, and the Greek rebellion had in fact been engineered, in part at least, on Russian soil.

In the three-cornered Anglo-Franco-Russian competition, keeping Russia out of the Mediterranean was a common Anglo-French interest. It was logical Russian policy to endeavor to separate her opponents, a possibility to which other sources of Anglo-French difference gave particular point.

As the Greeks failed to secure a European hearing at the Congress of Verona, Tsar Alexander came to reconcile his conflicting emotions—upholding legitimacy and the promotion of Russian interest—by suggesting the creation of autonomous Greek provinces. Nothing came of this project at first, but, after Alexander's demise, Canning sent the Duke of Wellington to St. Petersburg on a successful mission. The Anglo-Russian Protocol of April 4, 1826[24] provided for joint mediating action between the Porte and the Greeks. This was England's way to avoid outright opposition while retaining control of developments. Note that France was left out of this arrangement. But not for long. As the Sultan refused the proffered mediation, a year later, on July 6, 1827, all three Powers joined in repeating the proposal, adding this time the hint of joint action. Here was the Concert of Europe, or at least the relevant part of it in this case, at work.

Action very soon followed in fact, though it was unexpected in its nature. An allied fleet, mainly Anglo-French, destroyed the Turco-Egyptian[25] in Navarino Bay in October. The accidental and unintended victory was cause for intense dismay in London. It was suspect to Russia, which went to war the following April, while a French expeditionary force cleared the Morea of Egyptians, although it did not come to formal war between the Western Powers and Turkey.

These events placed a great strain on the continued agreement of the three signatories of the treaty of 1827, yet in the end agreement was maintained, expression of their common preference for peace. The Russians defeated the Turks, though not with ease; not until September was the Treaty of Adrianople signed. In the face of defeat and of the continuing agreement of the three European Powers involved, the Sultan could do nothing but yield.

In February 1830 there opened in London a conference of these Powers where the issue was finally settled. A fully independent Greece was born; its frontiers and the choice of its future ruler, the second son of the King of Bavaria, were the result of their decisions. This outcome may be seen as a success of British policy, which had contrived to preserve peace among the major Powers through an agreement that they could jointly underwrite. Although three Powers only, rather than all five Great Powers, were involved, the episode may properly be regarded as an instance of the successful operation of the European Concert, functioning in the limited fashion in which Britain envisaged its role. It was a premature judgment to speak of the demise of the Concert when Britain had parted company with the rest at Verona eight years before.

The full Concert also met in London, again in 1830, to deal with another European disturbance. The question of Belgian independence will be discussed in the next chapter, in which the Egyptian aftermath of Greek independence, the Anglo-French confrontation that grew out of it, will likewise be considered. Before doing this, it is relevant to make some observations on the score of French policy during the period which has just been under review.

France, 1815–30

The French part of our tale can be brief, for, inevitably, some of it has been touched upon in connection with the British story. There are important differences nevertheless.

That there should have been widespread respect for French power after 1815 needs no explanation in the light of the Napoleonic performance; to acknowledge that power first rank among continental states was no more than fair appraisal. But the point has already been made that the image of French power was magnified out of proportion to its true dimensions by the changes introduced by the French in the rules of the game of competition of power; mobilization of the entire manpower of the nation was perhaps more significant in this respect then Napoleon's military genius. Neither of these were permanent assets.

Despite the widespread weariness with war in France the martial spirit and the appeal of glory remained strong, of which the Hundred Days had been a telling demonstration. The other asset in France's armory, a prior, not to say monopolistic, and proprietary claim to the revolutionary idea, the impact of which was to be long-lasting, has also been mentioned. But this was a double-edged weapon, available to a revolutionary régime, to Napoleon even, but hardly to the restored Bourbons.

In concrete and objective terms France had been defeated, put on probation, and subjected to the disability of foreign occupation. There was in France, then and for a long time thereafter, much talk about the "iniquitous" peace. Apart from the injury to the national pride, the "iniquity" was hard to perceive, at most reduced to relatively minor haggling over details of the northeastern frontier. The complaint was a talking point, good ground for demagogic appeal, but actually not seriously entertained by the responsible members of successive French governments.

Nevertheless, in view of the defeat and the disabilities, the broad aim of French policy could be one thing alone, the recovery of position and the acknowledged acceptance by others that France was entitled to play a role commensurate with what might be described as that to which the "objective" measure of her power entitled her.

The fragility of the Grand Alliance, its immediate purpose accomplished, could be counted upon. Yet doubts about France persisted; any show of aggressiveness on her part would have been the best way to revive the coalition. No such intentions were part of Louis XVIII's policy. But at home he must be careful lest he open himself to the charge of being too amenable to foreign dictation; twice, after all, he had returned in the baggage of invading armies and his initial popularity was not great. Sensible man that he was, he sought, successfully on the whole, to navigate between the domestic Charybdis and Scylla of frustrated hopes and blind vengeful reaction. He achieved his modest ambition of having put an end to his travels and of dying peacefully in Paris.

Thus France "behaved," and in 1818 was granted the international certificate of good behavior that was the significance of the Congress of Aix-la-Chapelle. With the help of British bankers in the main, the remaining part of the indemnity was funded and an end put to an occupation that some of the occupiers at least had come to fear as a possible corrupting influence on their own forces. England was entirely willing to have France rejoin the European Concert in full and good standing, and France could even join the Alliance, though it is of interest to note that Castlereagh took the precaution of procuring a secret renewal of the Quadruple Alliance on the same occasion.

The internal ordering of France was not very different from that of Britain; both countries may properly be called constitutional monarchies, for all that the French Charter had been "granted" by, rather than forcibly extracted from, the king. A minuscule electorate in both cases, even smaller in France than in Britain, and political methods that our supposedly more virtuous time would label corrupt, nevertheless gave in both countries to "opinion" a significance and an influence that it did not have elsewhere.

Another point of affinity may be mentioned between the two "liberal" states of Western Europe. For both, the issue of the nation-state had long since been resolved. There was much sympathy in both countries for the desire of self-determination on the part of others, the stuggle for which was to constitute such a large part of the nineteenth-century story of mid Europe.

But one should not be misled by these very real affinities, the effect of which was, to a point, a confusing, rather than a significant factor in the operation of power. Talleyrand, for all his opportunistic shifts and vagaries, may be said to have consistently represented in France the British orientation of policy. But Talleyrand was in retirement. Britain and France had too long been the traditional enemies, and both were still too powerful, for the weight of the past to be suddenly undone or forgotten. The France of 1815, unlike that of 1919, was not obsessed by fear for her security—why should she be? Yet British primacy, if not openly recognized, was somehow felt by France. The failure—perhaps the impossibility—to develop sea power of the British class persisted; after Trafalgar there was to be no serious French naval challenge to the British, even though they at times, largely as a result of their own negligence in keeping up their naval establishment, chose to take alarm.

Thus, as already indicated, the French position in regard to intervention was, unlike the British, characterized by ambiguity. The Spanish situation brought out the difference very sharply. A successful intervention would redound to the credit of the régime and enhance its respectability in the eyes of the conservative courts. But, even apart from some doubts on the score of the reliability of the Army, in which the Napoleonic tradition was strong, intervention would elicit British opposition, mainly on the grounds of suspicion of the aims of French power. France decided to intervene in the end, derived some little prestige from the action, and British fears were set to rest when the French Army, its task accomplished, went home, having even tried to mitigate the vengefulness of the Spanish king. France was ostensibly content with playing the role of the agent of Europe.

But the aftermath of the rebellion of the American colonies of Spain was again cause for ambiguity. Like Britain, France was little concerned with upholding Spanish legitimacy across the ocean. But, whereas the British interest was in large part commercial, the French had in addition political overtones for which, needless to say, there was little sympathy in either Britain or in the United States. The prospect of an independent Argentina under the rule of a French prince, for example, was rather toyed with than seriously pursued. Such possibilities nevertheless were not unrelated to the proclamation of the Monroe Doctrine.

For combined commercial and ideological reasons the United States was sympathetic to Latin American emancipation under republican forms of government, differing in this last respect with Britain. Once the matter of the acquisition of Florida from Spain had been settled, the United States felt freer to express its predilections. It was Britain which mainly dealt with the French aspect of the problem. Having made it clear that no French interference would be brooked in the Americas, Canning had little difficulty in obtaining the acquiescence—or submission—of

Villèle and Polignac, after which the road was clear for President Monroe's declaration.

Sufficient has been said of what happened at the eastern end of the Mediterranean during the 1820's, the tortured and tortuous tale of the achievement of Greek independence. Most of the episode unfolded while reaction was in the saddle in France under the sympathetic eye of the last of the Bourbons, Charles X, whom the charge of inability to either learn or forget fits so well.

It was the vicissitudes of the Eastern Question, specifically the defeat of Turkey by Russia, which furnished Polignac with the occasion for the proposal of his grand design for the disposition of that problem through the radical device of partitioning the Ottoman state in combination with European readjustments that would undo the "iniquities" of the settlement of 1815. A Greater Greece was to be created that would include Constantinople and the rule of which would be given to King William of the Netherlands. The way would thus be opened for a disposition of the Netherlandish kingdom subject to a three-way partition: the colonies to Britain, Holland to Prussia,[26] and Belgium to France. That this piece of romantic fantasy received no serious hearing hardly needs explanation. It is of some significance nevertheless as a manifestation of the persistent French effort to reach to the "natural" boundaries of the country. It was also calculated to convey to others the image of a diplomacy that the epithet *brouillon* best describes.

A constant line of French endeavor manifested itself in another direction. Though for the time defeated, the quest for empire had played a large part in the foreign policy of France; it had not been abandoned and the interest in the Near East was its current expression. Allowing that there were no clearly formulated grandiose plans of imperial expansion, it is not unfair to place in this context the expedition to Algiers in 1830. A small enough, not to say petty, matter in itself, motivated in considerable measure by the wish to divert attention from domestic difficulties, undertaken without any deliberate plan of conquest in North Africa, the episode inserts itself nevertheless into the stream of a continuing tradition; even if inadvertently planted, it was a seed that was to grow, for a time at least, into a mighty oak and a consistent policy.

It is of interest that the English reaction to the Algerian episode was minimal. Other than some cautioning about the probable consequences of involvement and about the desirable limits of its extent, Britain did not object to the French expedition. In some degree, as was to be the case with Bismarck, a diversion of French interest and forces away from Europe could have its merits from the British standpoint at this time.

The capture of Algiers was almost simultaneous with the fall of Charles X. The 1830 revolution in Paris brought Louis Philippe to the throne. Rather embarrassed than pleased by the Algerian expedition, and without any future plans on that score, the new government yet did not withdraw.

The upheaval of 1830 in France raised far more serious prospects for the chancelleries of Europe, the specter of revolutionary France again. Such fears were soon set to rest by the moderate and unaggressive policy of the new régime; how it was shortly brought into close co-operation with Britain will be examined in the following chapter.

Taking the period of the fifteen years between the settlement of Vienna and the events of 1830 as a whole, the impression is conveyed of a clearer line of British policy than of French. The first also appears more assertive and dominant when compared with the hesitancies of the second. If Europe insisted on intervention against British wishes, let others intervene, but only to the point where a sufficiently important British interest was involved, when Britain would interpose a clear veto. To be sure, certain British distinctions may have appeared inconsistent or casuistic to others, as that between the cases of Naples and Spain. From the British standpoint they were not, for while Spain was regarded as a fully independent entity, Castlereagh was prepared to acknowledge that Naples fell within Austria's domain. He could even advise Metternich to proceed with expedition, hoping thereby to short-circuit the concerted action of Europe, precisely the opposite of what Metternich wished. Neither Britain nor France put its signature to the Troppau protocol, and when it came to Spain, no more than strong British objection was registered. For the rest Britain could simply wait for events to unfold, an attitude justified in the test.

It may not be amiss to point out also the significant role played by individuals. Canning and Castlereagh were of highly different temperaments, the reserve and aloofness of the latter in sharp contrast with the energetic flamboyance of his successor. Castlereagh knew how to play on the chord of national sentiment and pride, in a manner which in some way may be described as a preview of Palmerston. Different as they were, the two men nevertheless pursued a remarkably consistent policy; the British interest did not take on different colors with the change of the foreign office incumbent.

At the level of personality there was in France no counterpart in the corresponding office to these brilliant Englishmen. It certainly would be a distortion to read into this difference a measure of the position and power of the two countries; only in long retrospect may one speak of the initiation of a French decline while the British star was still in the ascendant. Yet it is also true that the deliberate avoidance of the possibilities of playing the revolutionary card constituted a diminution of this particular asset of French power. Britain was in no need of such an adventitious asset. If France was bent on "behaving," the leadership and dominance of England was all the more unchallenged. The following two decades, the period of the July Monarchy and of the Second French Republic, furnish some good illustrations of the continuing, in fact growing, discrepancy between the respective positions of British and French power.

NOTES ON *Chapter I*

1. See, for example, the discussion of this issue in Barraclough, Geoffrey, *An Introduction to Contemporary History* (1964). This is also available in paperback as a Pelican Book (1967), from which edition references are made here.

2. The record of orderly political transformation since the seventeenth century is what has given rise to the "legend" of continuity of development traced back to Magna Charta.

3. This condition has been changing with the increasing complexity of modern life and society and the growing role of technicians. But, despite a changing attitude, one can still find English intellectuals hankering for the more congenial continental atmosphere.

4. This is true despite a measure of violence which accompanied labor agitation, especially in the earlier part of the century. The Chartist move-

ment, despite its failure at the time, is more characteristic of the British method.

5. Cf. Barraclough, op. cit., p. 113

6. Louisiana, obtained from Spain and held by France for a time, was finally sold to the United States by Napoleon in 1804.

7. This was the consequence of substituting the nation for the monarch as the basis of the legitimacy of the state. Thus the French "people" became involved in war, and by repercussion, other peoples, Germans, Italians, Spaniards, eventually came to stress the "national" character of their struggle to rid themselves of French control.

8. Thus, for example, the British were laggard in comparison with the French in converting their Navy to the use of steel.

9. The United States, following the achievement of independence, may fairly be said to have embarked on a course of imperial expansion. But the nature of the continental growth of the United States made it possible to emphasize national unity while adhering to an anti-imperial ideology. The Russian expansion in Asia, especially in Siberia, bears considerable resemblance to the western growth of the United States.

10. The Russian population passed the French during the last decade of the eighteenth century.

11. After the Franco-Prussian War the picture becomes more complex. For that reason it will be dealt with in a later chapter, the present discussion remaining confined to the period before 1870.

12. Malthus' *Essay on Population* was first published in 1798.

13. *The New Cambridge Modern History,* Vol. X (1960), p. 29. The figures are in tons. "Germany" is taken here to include the area that was brought together in 1861.

14. The *École Polytechnique* was actually founded in 1794, but it is fair to credit Napoleon with the cast of the French system of education, the university especially, since his time.

The fact is also of interest that, in the case of France, the products of her excellent institutions of higher learning tended to gravitate toward public rather than private employment.

15. The Greek and the Belgian successful assertions of national distinctness are considered in the last section of this chapter and in Chapter II, respectively.

16. It was at Chaumont, while the campaign of France was still being waged, that Castlereagh procured the conclusion of the treaty of the Quadruple Alliance.

17. *British Diplomacy 1813–1815: Selected Documents Dealing with the Reconstruction of Europe,* Webster, C. K., ed. (1921), Appendix I. A convenient documentary source is Joll, James, *Britain and Europe, Pitt to Churchill, 1793–1940* (1950), which is also available as an Oxford paperback (1967). The italics are mine.

18. The purely Austrian state interest entered into the Italian situation, thereby clouding the issue to a point.

19. Ward, A. W. and G. P. Gooch, eds., *The Cambridge History of British Foreign Policy,* 3 vols. (1923), Vol. II, pp. 623–33. Hereafter referred to as *CHBFP*. See also, Albrecht-Carrié, R., *The Concert of Europe* (1968), p. 48. The italics are mine.

20. Quoted in Phillips, W. A., *The Confederation of Europe* (1914), p. 222.

21. As it actually was when it eventually took place in 1823. At the Congress of Verona, where this decision was made, Britain parted company with the Concert of Europe. Canning had expressed the strongest opposition, but as he committed suicide just before the meeting of the congress, it fell to Wellington to voice Britain's opposition at Verona.

22. See below, pp. 42–43.

23. Austria, at the time and for some time thereafter, adopted a passive attitude toward the Eastern Question. Of Prussian interest there was none.

24. Albrecht-Carrié, op. cit., Document 16, pp. 104–6.

25. The Egyptian presence was due to the fact that the Sultan had called upon his vassal, Mehemet Ali, the governor of Egypt, for assistance in putting down the Greek rebellion.

26. In addition, Prussia would acquire Saxony as compensation for her relinquishment of her Rhenish possessions, which would be erected as a buffer state between France and Prussia. By way of completing the scheme and in order to preserve the equilibrium of compensations, Russia would acquire the Principalities and some Asiatic territory, while Austria would absorb Serbia.

II

THE REIGN OF PALMERSTON, 1830–51

Hat der Teufel einen Sohn
So ist er sicher Palmerston

It should be little cause for surprise that the quarter century of war precipitated by the French Revolution was followed by a period of peace. Not that the traditional rivalries of power were suspended, as the proceedings at Vienna themselves had conclusively shown, but a compromise was achieved and there was a common bond among all in the desire to maintain the restored social order. Metternich's Carlsbad decrees, England's Six Acts, French reaction, may all be seen as different manifestations of the same fear felt by the ruling class or order. The fifteen years that followed the downfall of Napoleon had seen the logical application, in Naples and in Spain, of Metternich's belief in the solidarity of the thrones, and the Ottoman disturbance that was the Greek revolt was taking place beyond the pale of civilized Europe.

Yet rifts could also be seen in the system. Britain had objected to the French intervention in Spain, and the Greek problem had seen the active intervention of three major Powers, who, to be sure, had in that case contrived to preserve a measure of agreement among themselves. Moreover, the ferment of change, if for a time set back, had not been stilled. The continental turmoil had not affected British constitutional arrangements; the excesses of the revolution had to a point helped arrest the evolutionary trend of political change in that country, but it was resumed in the twenties. Talk of reform was again in the air, and the end of the decade, following the long tenure of the Liverpool ministry, witnessed a rapid turnover in office which calls to mind the later French Republic.[1] There were no well-organized and disciplined parties in England at this time, but a splintering, instead, where personal following loomed important. The Tory allegiance of the Canningite group was fragile and there was, after 1829, an Irish contingent as well as a Radical group. The passage of Catholic Emancipation in 1829 was indication that measures of liberal intent could be enacted. More serious was the talk of the need of electoral reform, for which various forces were pressing.

Restoration France was quite different from the France of the *ancien régime*, a necessity that Louis XVIII understood. The advent of his less tractable brother mainly served to increase the pressure of suppressed discontent; the unwise measures of repression to which he had resorted in 1830 finally precipitated the explosion which put an end to Bourbon rule in France. In the light of not long distant precedent, revolution in Paris inevitably had European repercussions. But intervention in France was not to be contemplated with frivolity; it had taken all Europe many years to check Napoleonic France, while England, which was least ideologically committed, more than any one had been the mainstay of the anti-French coalition.

Two things contributed to preserve the peace of Europe at this point. In France herself the July days were quickly over, and the new king, Louis Philippe, strove to reassure all of his peaceful intent, which was indeed quite authentic. The English role was equally important. For the 1814 Alliance, confirmed at Aix-la-Chapelle in 1818—mainly at England's urging—provided for consultation in precisely such a situation. But once it appeared that order would be preserved in France, the tendency in England was rather to welcome the change; as in the early stages of the Great Revolution, France might be regarded as paying England the compliment of imitation in the choice of her political ordering. Though extreme in its form, Palmerston's comment bears quoting:

> Well what a glorious event this is in France! How admirably the French have done it! What energy and courage in the day of trial: and what wisdom and moderation in the hour of victory! Who that remembers the excesses and outrages and horrors and insanity of 1792 and 93, could have expected to see in so short a time, a nation of maniacs and assassins converted into heroes and philosophers?[2]

Despite some grumblings, not least from the Tsar, the new French régime was shortly recognized by all. The Parisian revolution in fact, where England was concerned, proved a boon to reformers. This is precisely the time when the agitation came to a head which two years later resulted in the passage of the great Reform Bill of 1832. The English operation, revolutionary as it may have been in its implications, and though performed through what some would regard as a sleight of hand, was even more orderly than the French, thus constituting a powerful contribution to the English tradition of absorbing unlimited political change without resort to violence.

One consequence of these events was to create a favorable climate in Anglo-French relations and to emphasize what nowadays would be called the ideological cleavage of Europe between the liberal West and the conservative Center and East. This in itself is important, which is why it is mentioned, but the accent of the present discussion is not on that aspect of things. To be sure, if France and England, the two most powerful states of Europe, agreed, the combination of the rest against these two would be ineffectual. But Anglo-French rivalry and difference was a far older story than Anglo-French agreement; grounds for possible divergence appeared very soon.

The Independence of Belgium

When Palmerston wrote the above-quoted passage he could not know that within a week the standard of revolt would successfully be raised in Brussels. The local background of that episode can be described very briefly.

The Kingdom of the Netherlands was a creation of the Vienna settlement and had been purposely intended as an anti-French bulwark, a fact clearly expressed by the provision of a series of fortresses along the French frontier to the upkeep of which Britain contributed. The British interest in the new state as a barrier to possible French aggressive designs was second to none. The difficulty lay in the fact that the former Austrian Netherlands were quite different from Holland. Religion, as much as anything, was a source of division, a Protestant prince being disliked as such by the Catholics, who were particularly strong in the Flemish section. That prince, the King of Holland, was moreover deficient in tact, using too many Dutch administrators, who helped convey to the Belgians the sense of being treated as a conquered people; a majority as they were in the total population, constitutional arrangements virtually insured for them a minority position. Liberal elements in future Belgium, more prominent in the Walloon French-speaking section, also had grievances against the rule of King William. It was in fact the difficulty in reaching agreement between the two factions, Catholic and Liberal, which had prevented the issue from coming to a head before.[3]

French influence, emphasized by twenty years of integration in the French state, was strong in Belgium. The July days in Paris had repercussions in Brussels, where the intransigeance of the Dutch king in refusing moderate concessions caused the outbreak of August 25. The failure of Dutch force the following month resulted in the Belgian proclamation of complete independence on October 4.

Here was without a doubt a European problem. According to the existing law of Europe King William was unquestionably the legitimate ruler of Belgium. His appeal to his brother rulers for assistance in putting down rebellious subjects was based on precedent; it fell on responsive ears in the eastern courts, especially the Russian. England had a common stake with those Powers in maintaining the international order of Europe, but this in English eyes was confined to the equilibrium of power; England did not at all share Metternich's desire to maintain the internal social order of states. Castlereagh's paper of 1820 and his behavior at Verona, when he had sought to expound the principle of non-intervention, have been mentioned before.[4] What mattered for England at this juncture was France and French action.

There was in France, especially in the more radically inclined party of movement, much ideological sympathy for the rebellious Belgians, to whom some would have given armed assistance. But, more broadly, thinking of France as a state among states, the possibility of undoing one aspect of the "iniquitous" settlement of 1815 was an attractive prospect, which even Louis Philippe must endorse. Beyond this it could be a small step to the entertaining of annexationist ambitions. These Britain would oppose; she would even revive the Quadruple Alliance, though her preference was definitely not for war. Neither did the newly installed French king want war, though his position was still insecure and he could not take too determined a stand against the party of movement. His way out of the dilemma was to espouse the principle of non-intervention—France would stay out of Belgium provided others did likewise—by doing which he established common ground with the English position. The appointment of Talleyrand as ambassador to the Court of St. James was calculated to promote this policy.

Talleyrand was by now in his seventy-sixth year and had been mainly in retirement since his great work at the close of the Napoleonic adventure. If not always well liked or fully trusted, his reputation as the dean of European diplomats stood justifiably high; his urbane wit, his talent for intrigue, his sane willingness to compromise, combined with his awareness and acceptance of unavoidable change, are what accounted for his extraordinary feat of survival in service to all the régimes that France had seen since the *ancien*. His appointment was welcome in England; his own account of his reception in that country, in contrast with his first visit thirty-five years before, makes interesting reading.[5] Talleyrand remains a controversial figure, the object of the most diverse judgments; but on the score of his ability there can only be consensus. That he was in favor of cooperating with England is also not open to doubt.

Even to have reached this point represented a French advantage, for it meant in all probability a breach in the 1815 arrangements. At the same time England was placed in an arbitral position most congenial to her. Should France attempt to obtain territorial advantage, or even undue influence in Belgium, the coalition of the Quadruple Alliance could easily be revived; England need only indicate her assent to the three conservative Powers. But if it came to using outside force in aid of the Dutch king, thereby precipitating French counteraction and with it war, Britain could stand with France. How Britain used her arbitral position to preserve peace and insure her own desiderata, and how France endeavored to extract the greatest possible advantage from the situation is what we wish to examine.

The proposal that the Powers meet in conference with a view to resolving the problem in agreement was an obviously sensible one which all accepted. It did already constitute a success for the forces of change, for, unless the Dutch king could restore his control by his own means, Belgian independence was likely to be the result. The uncertainties that still surrounded the situation in Paris, the arbitral position of England, the fact that the Powers had already been discussing for some time in London the settlement of the Greek problem, all pointed to that city as the logical seat of the meeting.[6] Even Talleyrand agreed, though he went through the motions of attempting to have the conference meet in Paris, as he was instructed to do by his government.[7] Relations between himself and Wellington—they knew each other well from earlier collaboration—were cordial.

Very soon the Belgians scored a further point; the proposal of an armistice in itself created a strong presumption in favor of the fulfillment of their wishes. But, clearly, the most pressing requirement was the cessation of hostilities, which always hold in them the danger of external intervention. Specifying the armistice line as that of the possessions of King William in 1792 had also the effect of a mortgage on the future final decision on boundaries. What this meant in effect was that Britain was reconciled to the independence of Belgium, a position eminently acceptable to France. To be sure, at this stage the proposal was made more palatable, especially to the Tsar, by the suggestion that the future crown of Belgium should go to the son of King William of Holland.

At this point some important events took place which in the reckoning proved favorable to a solution of the problem.

The Tsar had been collecting troops on the Polish border for possible use in the West, but from November was faced with rebellion in Poland, a rebellion for which there was much sympathy in both England and France. The chief effect of this occurrence was to lessen the possibility of action on his part, for his forces found themselves occupied for the better part of a year in putting down the Polish rising. This situation was comparable to Metternich's concern with the disturbances in Italy, a similarly restraining factor in his case.

In Paris Louis Philippe was struggling to pursue a middle course of moderation and in this was achieving success. Through the changes in the composition of his government he exercised a strong directing hand, nowhere more than in the domain of foreign affairs, where he and Talleyrand worked in close agreement.[8] To the uncertainties of the French scene there was an English counterpart. For when Parliament met at the beginning of November, the Wellington administration was shortly defeated and resigned. The crisis was promptly resolved with the formation of the Whig ministry of Earl Grey. But in the context of the factional divisions of British politics the Grey cabinet was in effect a coalition, in which, from the present standpoint, the most significant aspect is the participation of Canningite elements. Lord Palmerston was at the foreign office. In view of the large role that he was destined to play in questions which are the main concern of this book, something may appropriately be said of the man at this point.

When Palmerston acceded to the foreign office, in November 1830, he had not been Grey's first choice for that post, a fact which is indicative of his political standing. He had long been in office, however, holding the secretaryship for war from 1809 to 1828, achieving cabinet rank only toward the end of his tenure. At the war office he had displayed the competence, the organizing ability, and the capacity for thoroughness characteristic of his whole career. Withal he had not made a very marked impression, being widely thought to attach greater importance to the amenities of social life, to which his antecedents gave him easy entrée. Typical product of the ruling class of England, whose prerogatives he took for granted, he was yet open to the thought of change, in many respects of liberal inclination. His party allegiance was as a consequence weak, and he was associated with the small Canningite faction. Thus he continued under Wellington until his break with him in 1828.

Far from unprincipled, he was yet capable of flexibility. He had been a strong advocate of Catholic Emancipation and likewise favored liberalization of the Corn Laws. For political reform he had little sympathy, yet perceived the inescapability of some changes in the existing practice of the time; but he would have preferred piecemeal, limited tampering with existing conditions precisely in order to avoid a broader and more sweeping modification of the system. It was consequently not very difficult for him to join Grey's Cabinet and when the time came he gave his support to the great Reform Bill.

With foreign affairs he had had relatively little to do so far, not coming to the foreign office until he had reached middle life. But to the conduct of these affairs he brought the qualities of self-confidence and managerial skill. His robust health enabled him to carry the burden of intense activity and minute care, down to details, of which his good memory gave him the advantage of mastery. Though he could charm, he generally preferred to be blunt and outspoken, showing little regard for age, position, or repute. Thus he made for himself the name of an *enfant terrible,* caring little for the sensibilities of others, whether his countrymen or foreigners. Among the many judgments that have been passed upon him, that of Talleyrand is worth quoting:

> Lord Palmerston is certainly one of the most skilful, if not the most skilful man of affairs whom I have met in my career. He has all the aptitudes and all the abilities which contribute to make up such a man in England; an extensive and varied knowledge, an indefatigable energy, iron health, inexhaustible resources of mind, a great facility of expression in parliament; without being what is called in England a good debater, his type of eloquence is biting and satirical; he knows better how to crush an adversary with his irony and sarcasm than how to persuade his audience; finally he has social grace and elegant manners. But a trait of his character spoils all these advantages and prevents him, in my view, from being rated a statesman: he is so impassioned in public affairs that he will sacrifice the greatest interests to his resentments; almost every political question is complicated in his case by a personal

question; and, while seeming to defend the interests of his country, it is almost always those of his hatred or his revenge that he is serving; he uses great skill in concealing this secret motivation under appearances that I might call patriotic; this is the act which always enables him to influence a large portion of public opinion in the service of his own passion. I shall have more than once in these recollections occasion to note the correctness of this observation, which explains, I believe, how Lord Palmerston has always maintained a certain popularity while changing parties and bringing his great talents in turn to the camps of the tories, the whigs, and even the radicals. Few Englishmen know as well as he how to strike the patriotic chord in John Bull.[9]

Talleyrand was a shrewd, if hardly an unprejudiced, observer, and though his judgment is colored by later differences with Palmerston, the fact is that Palmerston was in many respects an adequate personification of the self-confident power that was Britain's in his time. In any case Talleyrand's further statement that "we proceeded in perfect agreement during the first months of the conference, and this agreement is the source of the excellent results that were obtained,"[10] while an oversimplification, is also not an unfair summation of what happened.

It was, on the French side, reasonable to expect that in view of the great Whig sympathy for the July revolution relations would be easier with the new English Cabinet. Palmerston himself, though not a Whig, shared the favorable view of the new French régime; his policy may be summed up as one of close collaboration with France—with the important proviso that France should seek no more than was acceptable to England, a truly independent Belgium.

Ostensibly, the conference had gathered in response to the appeal of the Dutch king under the provisions of the settlement of Vienna. But it was soon clear that the makers of that settlement had the power, collectively, to effect changes in it. Quite early, on December 20, the implications of the armistice were realized with the virtual recognition of Belgium as a separate entity.[11] This crucial decision was not, however, the end of the story, for there remained a number of specific matters to be settled, the disposition of which gave rise to differences which at times even threatened the possibility of conflict.

Such questions as the sharing of the national debt between Holland and Belgium and the navigation of the Scheldt, with all that this implied for the economic viability of Antwerp, gave rise to lengthy, laborious, and often tedious discussions. These were relatively secondary matters,[12] however; certainly they had less importance in the eyes of the Powers than the issue of frontiers and that of the bearer of the future Belgian crown, to say nothing of the related problem of the enforcement of the collective decisions of Europe. Something must be said of each of these questions, bearing in mind that they were intertwined and considered simultaneously.

The protocol of January 27, accepted by King William, was objected to by the Belgians, largely for territorial reasons, since it left both Limburg and Luxembourg in the former's hands.[13] Having earlier excluded the House of Nassau from the Belgian crown, the Belgians now proceeded to elect for their king the second son of Louis Philippe, the Duke of Nemours, at the beginning of February 1831. This Palmerston would not accept and made his position quite clear to Talleyrand, stating that the acceptance of the offer by Nemours would result in a European war. There was a delicate passage, for French intrigues in Brussels had not been unconnected with the offer.[14] Talleyrand did not press the matter though he sought to extract some concessions for yielding. Palmerston was adamant and had his way; Louis Philippe declined the offer for his son and the conference could proceed to register in the case of Belgium the same self-denying ordinance to which the Powers had resorted in the case of Greece: the crown could not go to a member of the ruling family of any of the major Powers.

While Belgium organized herself under a regency the search for a candidate for her crown went on. An Austrian archduke was excluded for the same reason that the Duke of Nemours had been, and France objected to the Duke of Leuchtenburg because of his Napoleonic connections. The scarcity of possibilities among Catholic princes finally led to the choice of Prince Leopold of Saxe-Coburg, whose connection with the English royal house—he was the future Queen Victoria's uncle—was sufficiently remote to make him acceptable to all the Powers. Prince Leopold, who had earlier turned down a similar offer of the

Greek crown, was hesitant and his candidacy evoked at first little enthusiasm in either Belgium or France; this last country had still not abandoned the thought of extracting additional advantage from the situation. Thoughts of a partition of Belgium in which Holland and Prussia might join were never a serious consideration, though they caused Palmerston some uneasiness. The effort to dismantle the border fortresses was more insistently pursued by France, but here again Palmerston was quite firm.

An important step in the resolution of these various issues was taken in June. Prince Leopold was accepted by all, the Belgians and the Powers, and the conference then proceeded to draw up a scheme of partition more favorable to Belgium—the Eighteen Articles—which might expect to acquire Luxembourg. It was the turn of the Dutch king to raise objections, but he made the mistake of resorting to the use of force. Denouncing the armistice, he sent into Belgium an army against which the Belgians fared poorly. Prince Leopold was anxious for assistance, which the French furnished with promptitude and eagerness. The fact pointed to an important question for the future: would Belgium, a weak state, become a dependent of France, a prospect to which the marriage of Prince Leopold to a daughter of Louis Philippe gave added point? However, the uneasiness felt by all, not least by Palmerston, at the French intervention was set to rest with the prompt withdrawal of the French Army once it had accomplished its mission.

The episode had the effect of strengthening Anglo-French cooperation. When despite some concessions—the Twenty-Four Articles of October—King William still proved recalcitrant, the result was a joint Anglo-French intervention under the cover this time of enforcing the collective decision of Europe. King William was compelled to accept a new and indefinite armistice on the basis of the existing situation. A final attempt by the French to bargain their withdrawal for some concessions in the matter of the fortresses was successfully resisted, and though it took another seven years before King William would formally acknowledge the inevitable, by 1832 Belgium could definitely take her place in the community of European states.[15]

The creation of Belgium was an instance of the successful operation of the Concert of Europe: the final decisions had been taken by the Powers in conference and they had in the end used armed force to enforce these collective decisions. But it is also significant that the force had been English and French; the conservative Powers would at most tolerate this action but would not join in coercing a legitimate brother ruler. In the process the principle of non-intervention had been at once supported and breached, justifying Talleyrand's quip that *"la non intervention est une formule diplomatique et énigmatique qui signifie à peu près la même chose qu'intervention."*[16] Palmerston, who was above all a practical man, had no difficulty in taking an elastic view. It is indeed difficult to conceive of the principle being rigidly adhered to in any and all circumstances, as developments down to our time have shown.

From the French point of view the emergence of Belgium was undoubtedly a gain, representing as it did a breach in the 1815 arrangements, and there is no question that the initial French position was of crucial importance in insuring the success of the Belgian revolution. That France should have attempted to push her advantage as far as she could is not surprising and explains a measure of tortuousness in the implementation of French policy. France to a point was hampered by the uncertainties of her domestic arrangements, a fact which in turn made her a universal object of suspicion; the possibility was ever in the background that the anti-French coalition of the Quadruple Alliance might be revived.

To allow this to happen would, from the French point of view, have been a mistaken appraisal of the possibilities of French power. Louis Philippe was not the man to launch into so rash an adventure. Talleyrand's analysis, early in the proceedings, is sound:

> Europe is certainly, at this moment, in a state of crisis. England is the only power which, like ourselves, sincerely wants peace; the other powers acknowledge some sort of divine right, France and England alone no longer consider this the basis of their political systems. The principle of non-intervention is equally adopted by both countries; I shall add, and I attach importance to this,

that there is today a measure of sympathy between the two countries.

My opinion is therefore that we should make use of all these common factors to give Europe the tranquillity that she needs. If certain states are not disposed to peace, France and England must declare that they want it, and let this determination, in the two strongest and most civilized countries of Europe, be heard with the authority which derives from their power.

Some of the governments who still hold up the banner of divine right incline, at this moment, to form a coalition; they can come to an understanding because they have a common principle; this principle to be sure is weakening in certain places, but it still exists; thus when these cabinets speak with each other they soon find common ground. They uphold their divine right with cannon; England and ourselves will sustain public opinion with principles; principles always spread whereas the reach of cannon has known limits.

Europe finds herself thus divided between these two modes of government: they are those which rule today. The balance of forces is about equal between the principle which moves the Russian and the Austrian armies and that which, acting through opinion, is certain to move at least equal forces. The latter principle will find numerous allies in the countries opposed to it, whereas the contrary one can hardly count on more than the faubourg St. Germain. If there is equilibrium, the balance must be tilted on our side, and this can be accomplished by attracting Prussia toward ideas which are less alien to her than to the other northern countries. These must, it seems to me, be the views of the cabinet of London and of that of Paris.[17]

But, clearly also, the ultimate key to the whole situation was in London, which it is no exaggeration to characterize as the diplomatic capital of Europe at this time, the seat of the European conferences that disposed of both the Belgian and the Greek problems. To some degree England was, like France, hampered by the unfolding of an internal situation; the issue of the Reform Bill created a constitutional crisis whose vicissitudes were keenly followed in the conservative courts; there were even in England elements that may be seen as the counterpart of the Parisian faubourg St. Germain; but the English crisis was resolved in the manner that is familiar and only fettered Palmerston to the same degree that Louis Philippe was hampered by the opposite extremes of the French political spectrum.

The conservative states, concerned as they were by the appeal of the liberal principle in their own respective domains—Metternich in Italy and in the German states, where Prussia also had an interest, the Tsar in Poland—would hesitate to become entangled in war with France alone; to consider a clash with France supported by Britain was for them utterly out of the question. And England *would* act jointly with France, provided always, as indicated before, that France adhered to the English solution. Palmerston's patience, never a commodity in very large supply, was sorely tested at times and he could be quite sharp with Sébastiani, the French foreign minister, as well as blunt with Talleyrand. Bell's judgment expresses well the spirit of Palmerston's outlook and methods:

> He [Palmerston] concluded by accusing Sébastiani of pursuing "a course of miserable intrigue." The device he used for administering this unofficial reproof was by no means new; but such roughness was, to say the least, unusual. He was making the great game of diplomacy a game not only of the chessboard but of the professional football field. It was a pity that the other great courts could not appreciate rough-and-tumble play—combined, of course, with plenty of strategy—but why concern himself greatly over that? England was not afraid of any or all of them. In fact the more numerous her opponents, the more did her superiority become evident. And she was always right.[18]

The role of the two countries in procuring Belgian independence is aptly summed up by de Lannoy:

> . . . France and England have both contributed powerfully to the achievement of our independence. The former prevented Europe from placing us again under the yoke, by protecting us against the Prussian intervention and by defending us at the time of the Dutch invasion. The latter safeguarded our autonomy, which she had helped establish, by opposing with indefatigable energy the annexationist views of France as well as any scheme of partition.[19]

He strengthens this judgment with the observation that "it was she [England] who saved our country from dismemberment."[20] The English interest, expressed in 1814 through the formation of the Kingdom of the Netherlands, could accept the dissolution of that state, but French encroachment on any part of it was unacceptable. There was none.

This survey of the Belgian episode may be concluded with a final observation which illustrates one of the fundamental and long-term components of British policy. It is best brought out in Palmerston's own words in Parliament:

> . . . the independence of constitutional states, whether they are powerful, like France or the United States, or of less relative political importance, such as the minor states of Germany, never can be a matter of indifference to the British Parliament, or, I should hope, to the British public. Constitutional states I consider to be the natural allies of our country; and . . . no English Ministry will perform its duty if it be inattentive to the interests of such states.[21]

Altogether, the episode of Belgian independence offers a very nice illustration of the position, power, and mode of operation of the two countries. The important factor of ideological affinity between the two regimes cannot be ignored; yet it takes second place to the national interest. The French position of power was universally acknowledged, and that power was still engaged in the ancient pursuit of its "natural boundaries"; the acquisition of Belgium, or of a segment of it, is reminiscent of Louis XIV's patient and persistent gnawing attempts in that direction. England was quite content, in fact vastly preferred, to preserve the peace—on the basis of the equilibrium of power, which meant, for one thing and as usual, the containment of French territorial designs toward the North Sea and the Rhine. She had her way, through the agency of Palmerston's direction at this point, which adequately expressed the assurance—even to a degree the arrogance—of her confident power.

MEDITERRANEAN PROBLEMS

The emergence of an independent Belgium, serving French interest and acceptable to the British, had made possible cooperation between these two Powers, even to a degree against the rest. The subsequent record of Belgium seemed to justify the confidence of her sponsors; endowed with a liberal constitution, one often used by others as a model, in the lead of economic development, governing herself in orderly fashion, Belgium helped confirm the validity of the liberal view of self-determination, however small the political unit that might wish for separate existence. Set up in neutral status, Belgium created no problems for her neighbors, or for Europe in general, which in turn respected her status until 1914.

The Greeks finally achieved separate political existence at the same time as the Belgians. But, apart from the important difference that many Greeks were still outside Greece, the Greek situation stands in marked contrast with the Belgian, being more typical of the normal instability of the Mediterranean world. Except for France, a well-established state and a Great Power despite her domestic uncertainties, a circuit of the rest of the Mediterranean shores presented an uninterrupted scene of unresolved turmoil: be it the Iberian peninsula, or the fragmented Italy of the Risorgimento, or most of all the domain of the Turk, everywhere problems abounded, domestic situations whose unfolding was inescapable cause for active interest and, in one form or another, frequent intervention by the Powers. The intention is not to survey all the issues that arose around the Mediterranean basin in the decade following the emergence of Greece to independence, but only to consider those which gave rise to especially intense international activity. The British and French roles, though others were involved, were of primary importance and at this particular point had in addition the effect of seriously impinging on the course of Anglo-French relations.

By far the most important problem was that of the Near East as a whole, though matters at the opposite end of the Mediterranean also attracted attention and at one point the two problems became somewhat interrelated. Something will be said first of Iberian affairs.

That paragon of retrograde and blind reaction, King Ferdinand VII, whom French arms had assisted in 1823, ruled Spain for another decade. His approaching end—it finally took place in 1833—left the country saddled with the issue of succession.[22] What made the situation one of special difficulty, apart from considerations of law, was the identification of divergent political tendencies with the rival claimants to the Spanish throne. The king's brother, Don Carlos, was standard bearer of the reactionary forces, while liberals, the range of whose views was quite broad, favored the regent, Queen Maria Cristina. The immediate result was civil war in Spain, the Carlist wars, which lasted until almost the end of the decade. In neighboring Portugal a similar situation had existed for some time, the rival claimants, Maria and Dom Miguel, being correspondingly associated, as in Spain, with the liberal and conservative tendencies respectively. The advent of the Whig ministry in England in 1830 made that country more sympathetic to Queen Maria's cause, a position in which France could join after the July revolution. The two Powers even gave her some material assistance. The outbreak of civil war in Spain raised the possibility of the two civil wars merging, or even leading to a larger war. The British and the French governments tended to see eye to eye in these matters.

But Belgium had been the more pressing international problem. British and French force was being used in Belgium in 1832 to enforce the decision of Europe on the recalcitrant Dutch king when war flared up at the opposite end of the Mediterranean, in the Ottoman Empire. It could hardly be called civil war, being a clear contest between a vassal and his suzerain. War it was, nonetheless, which drew the attention of Europe.

The trouble that arose between Mehemet Ali, Pasha of Egypt, and Sultan Mahmoud was a legacy of Greek independence. For the Sultan in his efforts to put down the Greek rebellion had called upon his vassal for assistance, an assistance which—for a price—was given. Ibrahim, Mehemet's son, was achieving success in the Morea, and the bargain between Mehemet Ali and the Sultan could have been carried out had it not been for Europe's interference. Navarino and the French force that went to the Morea disposed of the Egyptian threat to the Greeks, but the result was a dispute between Mehemet Ali and the Sultan, for the former wanted his price for services rendered, which the Sultan was understandably reluctant to deliver for results not accomplished. The dispute came to focus on the Pashalik of Syria, whither Egyptian forces moved in 1832. At the end of the year, in December, at Koniah, Ibrahim totally defeated the Turkish Army, the road across Anatolia henceforth open to him.

Here was a situation wholly different from that which had developed in Greece. To speak of Arab, or Egyptian, nationalism would be premature at this time, feudal conditions and relationships being a more accurate characterization of the state of affairs. The governor of Egypt was himself no Egyptian. This unlettered barbarian of Albanian origin had risen in the Turkish service to his present position; personal power was his goal, for which Egypt was to provide the base. His rise had been accompanied by methods familiar to the milieu in which he was functioning: his treacherous riddance of the Mamelukes in 1811 and Mahmoud's massacre of the Janissaries in 1826 bear comparison.

Be that as it may, Mehemet Ali was an able man, one who could understand the modern world. The Napoleonic performance in Egypt had been to him a useful object lesson. The conclusions he drew were of two kinds: the bases of his political power would remain the familiar ones of unfettered despotism; Western political thought, representative institutions, had no significance for him. But the technical sources of Western effectiveness he would and did adopt. This meant the creation of a modern military force, a naval establishment, and economic development. The test in 1832 adequately demonstrated the soundness of his judgment, in the short term at least, and certainly the effectiveness of his reforms.

His victory widened the horizon of his ambition. He might contemplate either of two possibilities: displacing the Sultan himself and extending to the whole Ottoman Empire the rejuvenating reforms he had instituted in Egypt; alternately, using Egypt as a base, build around it an Arab empire of his own. The latter would destroy the Ottoman state, the future fate of which in either case was raised. The Powers could not but be highly concerned.

Their oft repeated dedication to the preservation of Ottoman integrity had not yet at this time become a clearly formulated policy. The Greek problem had been solved on the basis of creating an independent state of limited dimensions. Might not the same be done in Egypt? Such a solution would especially appeal to the French, the focus of whose interest in the Near East had been intensified and sharpened by the Napoleonic excursion. There was in France appreciable public interest in Egyptian affairs, and Mehemet Ali had made large use of French individuals in instituting his reforms; the original name of Soliman Pasha was Colonel Sèves.[23] Syria added to Egypt could in French eyes constitute a wholly acceptable, not to say desirable, base of French influence in the Levant.

The English view of such a possibility was quite different. The Napoleonic episode had had, among other things, the effect of intensifying the British interest in the Mediterranean. Especially with the growth of industrial development, the importance of the route to India and the Far East became emphasized, which meant the Isthmus of Suez, and even the possibility of the Euphrates route was considered. A strong Arab state astride these avenues of communication, especially if beholden to another European state, had no appeal for England, which preferred in its stead the preservation of the Turkish state as it was. Also, Palmerston was rather sanguine about the possibilities of reform in the Ottoman Empire.

A revived Turkish state did not fit Russian calculations at all. The final demise of the Sick Man, a partition of his possessions, would be acceptable to Russia, provided she could secure her desired share, control of the Straits holding the greatest interest for her. Otherwise Russia would prefer to preserve the Sultan's domain in a state of (to her) suitable and dependable decadence and weakness. But the prospect of Russian naval power in the Mediterranean met with an adamant English opposition, in which France was generally disposed to join.

These are fundamental and long-term considerations which must be borne in mind when examining what happened at this point. It was not at all what might have been expected and it may be described as an instance of both English and French oversight and negligence. At the turn of the year from 1832 to 1833 General Muraviev appeared in Constantinople with the mission of offering assistance to the Sultan. The appearance of a Russian squadron before Constantinople in February caused alarm in the West, though France already adopted at this point the policy to which she would adhere for some time of seeking to mediate between the Sultan and Mehemet Ali on the basis of securing advantageous terms for the latter. The Convention of Kutayah in April 1833[24] is an example; but continuing disagreement brought Russian troops to the Bosphorus to counter, if necessary, Mehemet Ali's threats.

Tension increased with the appearance of British and French squadrons in the Levant. However, a compromise was reached and peace was restored between Mehemet Ali and the Sultan. The Russians, abiding by their professed intentions, left the Straits. Their performance seemed rather puzzling until it appeared that there was to be some price for their services, though the form of the price was perhaps unexpected. The Treaty of Unkiar Skelessi, of July 8, 1833, was a Russo-Turkish alliance. As such, the significant part of it was the provision that, in case of Turkish need,

> His Majesty the Emperor of all the Russias . . . engages to furnish, by land and by sea, as many troops and forces as the two high contracting parties may deem necessary. It is accordingly agreed, that in this case the land and sea forces, whose aid the Sublime Porte may call for, shall be at its disposal.

The obligation of assistance was reciprocal, but on the possible value of positive Turkish assistance in the event of Russian need there is little necessity to enlarge. Yet Turkey could be very useful in a negative way, and this indeed was provided for in the "separate and secret article," the real heart of the alliance, appended to the treaty, which stipulated that

> . . . as His Majesty the Emperor of all the Russias, wishing to spare the Sublime Ottoman Porte the expense and inconvenience which might be occasioned to it, by affording substantial aid, will not ask for that aid if circumstances should place the Sublime Porte under the obligation of furnishing it. The Sublime Porte . . . shall confine its action in favor of the Imperial Court of Russia to closing the Straits of the Dardanelles, that is to say, to not allowing any foreign vessel of war to enter therein under any pretext whatsoever.[25]

The unilateral advantage thus secured by Russia was highly unwelcome to the Western Powers; but they confined their action to protest at this time, and the tension between them and Russia shortly evaporated. The effect was also, however, to confirm the community of their interest, as recently manifested in the case of Belgium. Palmerston had been taken by surprise; the Tsar's success was an expression of his irritation with both states, with France especially, of whose bourgeois king he took an unfavorable view.

The Russian success, the manner of it in particular, was also displeasing to Metternich, who might be thought to have in this matter a similar view to that of the British and French. There had been a brief period when both he and Palmerston had considered a meeting of the Powers, but the latter's proposal that the meeting should take place in London only aroused Metternich's suspicion that Palmerston was trying to enlarge the scope of the conference into that of a permanent institution, "in which the representatives of the three continental powers would be reduced to the role of accomplices of the reforming policy of the two maritime courts."[26]

Metternich would have liked to make Vienna the center of negotiations, which, for geographical reasons, would have seemed as justifiable in this case as was the holding in London of the Belgian discussions. Yet, displeased as he was with the Tsar, who on his side was distrustful, Metternich swallowed his pride, for he set considerable store by the continuing agreement of the three conservative courts. By September he had accepted the Tsar's reassurances, and the Münchengrätz agreement of that month was a declaration of common policy vis-à-vis the Ottoman Empire.

But the English regarded that agreement as an attempt to revive the Holy Alliance[27] and this is where the connection appears with events at the opposite end of the Mediterranean, giving grounds for the judgment that "international relations were for a time based on a community of institutions, a phenomenon which does not recur to the same degree at any other period of the century."[28] Be it in Italy, where Palmerston was satisfied with Casimir Périer's explanation of the occupation of Ancona[29] and took a generally sympathetic view of liberal aims in the whole peninsula, or in the matter of the Polish rebellion, there was appreciable common ground between the two governments.

The situation in the Iberian peninsula lent itself to a similar identity of views, hence to a common policy, while offering at the same time a measure of Palmerston's methods of operation and of their limitations. Combining the assistance to both liberal movements, to Queen Isabella in Spain and Queen Maria in Portugal, for all that the assistance was to remain "indirect" and that lip service continued to be paid to the principle of non-intervention, was a logical move. That he should ignore France at first in this attempt, then as an afterthought bring her into his calculations, may have been a sign of his "rashness and immaturity"[30]; it brought objections from Talleyrand, still in charge of the London embassy, and the final outcome was the so-called Quadruple Alliance of April 1834, which joined the two western liberal states in support of the legitimate constitutional claimants to the Spanish and Portuguese thrones respectively against the reactionary pretenders.

Non-intervention had become largely a fiction, with the suspension of the Foreign Enlistment Act in England and the use of the largely French-manned Spanish foreign legion, but greater significance attaches to the fact that the Quadruple Alliance was widely regarded as an answer to the "Triple Alliance" of Münchengrätz. Both views represent an overstatement; on the one hand the fundamental difference between Russian and Austrian interests in the Near East persisted[31]; on the other, Anglo-French co-operation in Spain was never quite wholehearted. Mutual suspicion, British especially, also persisted in this case, as it appeared that the government of Louis Philippe, growing more confident in the domestic basis of its power, was becoming correspondingly more conservative. Metternich's characterization of the Western combination as a "phantom" was not far off the mark.

Changes in the French Government, the termination of Talleyrand's embassy in London, the six-month interlude of Peel's first ministry in England, during which Wellington held the foreign office, were but passing incidents which had little impact on the course of events or on the fundamental attitudes of the governments. In April 1835 Melbourne returned to the prime ministership and Palmerston to the foreign office. It is of interest that in the election of 1834 Palmerston was the only minister to be defeated; but the combination of his competence and of his methods of operation had made him "both unmanageable and indispensable."[32] The "first Entente Cordiale," also an overstatement, continued in some measure to function during the second half of the thirties, until Palmerston was presented with an opportunity to retrieve the oversight of 1833, one of which he made brilliant use. Something must be said of the Near Eastern crisis of the years 1839 to 1841.

The Crisis of 1839–41

The settlement which the Egyptian Pasha had extracted from his suzerain was in reality but a truce. Mehemet Ali had not given up his ambitions, while Sultan Mahmoud was bent on revenge. He went about preparing for it in two ways. This was one of the eras of attempted reforms in the Ottoman state, in which Reshid Pasha exerted a strong influence; simultaneously, reforms and reorganization were undertaken in the more limited military field. Nothing of substance came of the political program; the military was about to be tested.

By 1838 Mehemet Ali was showing signs of restiveness and giving indications of a desire for complete independence from the Porte, while the Sultan thought he had adequately rejuvenated his armed forces. This is the background of the open clash that took place in April 1839, the initiative of which was Turkish. Sultan Mahmoud had obviously miscalculated, for the battle of Nesib was a repetition of that of Koniah seven years earlier. To compound the Turkish difficulty, the Turkish fleet, sent to Alexandria, went over to Mehemet Ali, and finally the Sultan died. Within a week Turkey had lost her Army, her fleet, and her ruler, whose successor was a youth of sixteen. Had the issue been contained within the Ottoman milieu the prospects would have been auspicious for Mehemet Ali to make good his desires; these consisted of the hereditary rule of Egypt, that of Syria, and the further concession of Adana.[33]

But Near Eastern affairs were by this time a well-established concern of Europe. The Treaty of Unkiar Skelessi provided Russia with a legal basis for intervention. Opposition to this might as usual seem a common Anglo-French interest, in the support of which Austria might join, but another question was that of the degree of French support for Mehemet Ali, a possible source of divergence between England and France. This was also the very time during which England had been exploring the above-mentioned possibility of the Euphrates route to the Persian Gulf, and hence felt an increased interest in the Syrian access to that route.[34]

Since Austria, on this occasion as on others, adhered to a timid policy of non-commitment, the field was pre-empted by the relations among three states, Britain, Russia, and France. The hope of avoiding a clash among these was shared by all the major Powers. Since their ambassadors were meeting in conference in London in connection with the final stages of the Belgian question, that capital seemed a logical place in which to consult over the newly arisen problem, and in fact throughout the episode London remained the center of diplomatic activity.

The first action of the Powers was the collective note which they sent to Constantinople on the fifteenth of July, which was tantamount to the assertion of their supervisory right of decision in the matter. The Russian position was at this point the key to an unexpected realignment. The Tsar, aware that any action on his part under the terms of Unkiar Skelessi stood in danger of precipitating a conflict with the Western Powers, turned instead to another possibility, that of driving a wedge between them. Moved in part by dislike of the French régime, he turned to England for an accommodation. On the basis of a joint agreement for the closure of the Straits, in place of the unilateral Russian position, a prospect appealing to England, a common Anglo-Russian position could be established. Brunnow, sent to London for the purpose of conducting the negotiation, proved to be a most amenable negotiator.

The French made at this point a serious error in judgment. They clung to the possibility of a direct Turco-Egyptian settlement, contradicting to a point the position they had taken by joining in the collective note of July; at the same time they discounted the possibility of an Anglo-Russian understanding, despite repeated warnings from Sébastiani, the French ambassador in London. As the latter reported to Soult in September:

> I asked Lord Palmerston if he did not find cause for reflection in the ease with which Russia accepted the English system; it is a very ephemeral alliance, I added, a too fortuitous coincidence

> of views to warrant sacrificing to it an alliance founded on principles and sentiments.—We know full well, answered Lord Palmerston, that it only applies to the occasion and that it will not prevent the two policies from resuming subsequently their normal courses; but how could we refuse it when it assists the interests we are defending . . . and seems to abdicate the exclusive protectorate and the almost preponderant influence which we are combating? . . . I do not doubt that the Russian cabinet . . . is mainly moved by the desire to bring our differences into the open and to espouse our view against yours.[35]

The warning was not heeded, France persisting in the hope of a direct settlement which would give Mehemet Ali the control of Syria. Syria was in fact the specific point of Anglo-French divergence, but by her insistence France was maneuvering herself into a position of isolation, since Metternich and Prussia were giving indications of following the Anglo-Russian leadership. Negotiations thus dragged on through the autumn, while support of Mehemet Ali was being increasingly asserted in France, where popular opinion was strongly in his favor. At the end of February 1840 domestic affairs resulted in a change in the French ministry, Thiers becoming Prime Minister just after Guizot had been appointed to the London embassy.[36] The two men, both in the tradition that has often wedded literature and scholarship with politics in France, represented diverse tendencies of opinion, even though they had for a time collaborated in the government. Guizot was the more conservative, which fitted well the gradualist approach of British politics; he was, not surprisingly, sympathetic to English ways. His pro-British leanings might be expected to augur well for the resumption of Anglo-French cordiality, and he found indeed a friendly reception in London, where he soon had a frank discussion with Palmerston, whom he reports as saying:

> You have the regency of Algiers; between you and your Egyptian ally what would be left? Almost nothing, only those poor states of Tunis and Tripoli. The whole African coast and part of the Asiatic coast on the Mediterranean, from Morocco to the Gulf of Alexandretta, would thus be in your power and under your influence. This we cannot accept.[37]

Guizot was faced with an impossible task.[38] For, favorable as he himself was to Anglo-French understanding, he yet had to defend a policy that was essentially not his own and of which he was not even completely informed. What happened in effect, during the spring of 1840, may be described as a duel between Palmerston and Thiers. Ignoring warning signals from London, Thiers persisted in his endeavor to contrive a direct understanding between Constantinople and Alexandria, which could then be presented to Europe as a *fait accompli* whereby peace was restored in the Near East. Self-assured Palmerston was fully capable of matching these tactics, even though he had not an easy task of it; he found not a little difficulty in imposing his views on some of his cabinet colleagues who were alarmed by and opposed to the growing Anglo-French rift. The outcome was in the nature of a *coup de théâtre,* the quadripartite treaty of July 15, 1840, by which the four Powers, without France, decided to impose their views. Mehemet Ali was to receive an ultimatum which would give him ten days in which to accept the relinquishment of Syria; after the lapse of a further ten days even his position in Egypt would no longer be assured to him.[39]

The Eastern Question had had its full European impact. The Sultan and the Pasha were at this point secondary figures, their quarrel of less moment than that produced by the isolation of France and the revival of the anti-French coalition of Napoleon's time. Guizot was genuinely hurt and thought that Palmerston had gone too far. But Palmerston's self-confidence was complete, as some of his statements at the time clearly show. To Melbourne he expressed himself in the following fashion:

> If the French attempt to bully and intimidate us as they have done, the only way of meeting their menaces is by quietly telling them we are not afraid, and by showing them, first, that we are stronger than they are, and, secondly, that they have more vulnerable points than we have.[40]

and to Lord Granville in Paris:

> . . . if Thiers should again hold to you the language of menace . . . convey to him in the most friendly and inoffensive manner

possible, that if France . . . begins a war, she will to a certainty lose her ships, colonies and commerce before she sees the end of it; that her army of Algiers will cease to give her anxiety, and that Mehemet Ali will just be chucked into the Nile.[41]

The bluntness of these judgments was in the end to prove sound Palmerston's willingness to call the French bluff. Yet he was also gambling, for the French reaction, at all levels, was very violent, and Thiers' tactics at this point were hardly deliberate bluff. As he wrote to Guizot on the sixteenth,

I find very serious the news that you send me; but one must not be moved and hold fast. The English are embarking on a dangerous undertaking; to separate themselves from France will have for them greater consequences than they imagine.[42]

There was point to this judgment also, for however correct Palmerston's assessment of potential and forces, others besides England were not so certain about the merits of war with France. Both Palmerston and Thiers stood their ground, the French proceeded to increase their armaments, and for a time the scene of possible conflict seemed to have shifted from the Nile to the Rhine.[43] Pressures on Palmerston were considerable. There was in England much opposition to his tactics and his ways, both in the Cabinet and in the press. Greville's account of the cabinet meeting of September 29 is worth quoting for the variety of things it illustrates:

I went to Clarendon's House on Monday evening, but He did not come home till 7 o'clock, the Cabinet having sat so long. His account of what passed was to the last degree amusing, but at the same time *pitoyable*. It must have been à payer les places to see. . . . At length Melbourne, trying to shuffle off the discussion, but aware that He must say something, began: 'We must consider about the time to which Parliament should be prorogued.' Upon this John took it up and said, 'I presume we must consider whether Parliament should be called together or not, because, as matters are now going on, it seems to me that we may at any moment find ourselves at war, and it is high time to consider the very serious state of affairs. I should like,' he added, turning to Melbourne, 'to know what is your opinion upon the subject.' Nothing, however, could be got from Melbourne, and there was another long pause, which was not broken till somebody asked Palmerston, 'What are your last accounts?' On this Palmerston pulled out of his pocket a whole parcel of letters and reports . . . and began reading them through, in the middle of which operation Clarendon happened to look up, and perceived Melbourne fast asleep in his Armchair. At length Palmerston got through his papers, when there was another pause; and at last John, finding that Melbourne would not take the lead or say a word, went at once into the whole subject. He stated both sides of the case with great precision, and in admirable, though very artful speech. . . . After some little talk, Palmerston delivered his sentiments the other way, made a violent philippic against France, talked of her weakness and want of preparation, of the Union of all the Powers of Europe against her, said that Prussia had 200,000 men on the Rhine, and (as Ld. Holland said) exhibited all the violence of '93. John was then asked, since such were his opinions, what course he would advise? He said he had formed his opinion as to what it would be advisable to do, and he produced a piece of paper on which he had written two or three things. The first was, that we should immediately make a communication to the French Government, expressing our thanks for the efforts France had made to induce the Pacha to make concessions for the purpose of bringing about a settlement; and next, to call together the Ministers of the other Powers, and express to them our opinion that it would be desirable to re-open negotiations for a settlement of the dispute in consequence of the effects produced by the mediation of France. There then ensued a good deal of talk (in which, however, the Prime Minister took no part), Minto espousing Palmerston's side and saying (which was true enough), that though Ld. Holland and Clarendon, who had all along opposed the Treaty, might very consistently take this course, he did not see how any of those could do so who had originally supported and approved it; to which John quietly and briefly said, 'The events at Alexandria have made all the difference.' This was in fact no answer, especially as John had taken his line before the events at Alexandria were known. Of the Ministers present besides Minto, Macaulay seemed rather disposed to go with Palmerston, and talked blusteringly about France, as he probably thought a Secretary at War should. Labouchere was first one way and then the other, and neither the Chancellor nor Chancellor of the Exchequer said one word. The result was an agreement, that it would be disrespectful to Lord Lansdowne, considering his position, to come to any resolution in his absence; and as he could not arrive before this day, the discussion should be adjourned till Thursday. . . . They were all to dine with Palmerston, and a queer dinner it must have been.[44]

Queen Victoria, with whom Palmerston's initial relations had taken place under favorable auspices, herself had doubts, which the advice of her uncle was calculated to strengthen. King Leopold of Belgium was distressed at the prospect of an Anglo-French clash, and even the Tsar was content with the degree of falling out which had occurred. The German Powers were favorable to an accommodation; Bülow, the Prussian minister in London, Guizot found especially understanding. Guizot's consideration that French participation was necessary to the proper functioning of Europe—this had after all been Castlereagh's idea in 1814—was itself an asset which made it possible, to a degree at least, for France to remain in expectation of concessions from others.

Syria remained the real bone of contention, and the execution of the treaty of July 15 was proceeded with, mainly by English force. It was the British fleet which conveyed there Turkish troops and which was instrumental in the fall of Acre in November. Interestingly, the French fleet had been called back to Toulon, and the defeats of Ibrahim in Syria revealed another French miscalculation. The degree of England's control of the situation may be judged from the action of Commodore Napier at Alexandria, where he took it upon himself to arrange political terms with the Pasha. This was indeed extracurricular, for Napier had no power to make such commitments, Mehemet Ali being by now ostensibly a mere rebel subject of the Sultan, who had decreed his dismissal.[45]

The complete destruction of Mehemet Ali was an unreasonable aim, but a European war to insure his control of Syria was no less so. This is how Guizot analyzed the situation:

Should France go to war in order that the Pasha of Egypt might keep Syria?

Obviously, this is not a sufficiently large interest to become a cause of war. France, which did not go to war to liberate Poland from Russia and Italy from Austria, cannot reasonably do so in order that Syria should be in the hands of the Pasha rather than of the Sultan.

The war would be either oriental and naval, or continental and general. If naval, the disparity of forces, damages and risks is undeniable. If continental and general, France could only sustain it by giving it a revolutionary character, that is by abandoning the honest, wise and useful policy which she has followed since 1830, thus herself transforming the alliance of the four powers into a European coalition.[46]

His lengthy analysis of the whole episode so far did not, however, exclude the possibility of war in the event of too great an intransigeance on the part of the signatories of the treaty of the preceding July, but he rather expected that France might rejoin the European Concert in some larger arrangement that would deal with Ottoman affairs as a whole.

It is at this juncture that Guizot himself assumed the direction of French affairs. Thiers, more inflexible, rather the counterpart of Palmerston, had prepared for the opening of the Chamber a speech of belligerent tone, of which Louis Philippe would not approve. The result was his resignation, Guizot taking his place.[47]

The accession of Guizot to the prime ministership of France might be thought to augur well for the resolution of the Eastern crisis. Such indeed was the final outcome, but not until some further time had passed during which not always easy negotiations took place. Palmerston had obviously scored, Thiers' dismissal being outward evidence that France's bluff had successfully been called. Guizot himself judged his predecessor's tactics to have been mistaken, but he was now in charge of the French interest and mere surrender was no part of his intentions. The treaty of July 1840 he looked upon as a gratuitous offense and was banking on the calculation that Europe would find it more comfortable to work with France than to keep her in isolation. One problem in the situation was the degree to which Palmerston would seek to push his advantage.

The speech he delivered to his constituents at Tiverton at the end of June 1841 is indication of what may be regarded as irresponsibility on his part:

> We brought within British influence, in one campaign, a vast extent of country larger than France, almost as big as half of Europe; and the way in which this was done and the results which have followed are well deserving of the people of England. There is a contrast of which we may have reason to be proud, between the progress of our arms in the East and the operations which a neighboring power, France, is now carrying on in Africa. The progress of the British army in Asia has been marked by a scrupulous reference to justice, an inviolable respect for property, an abstinence from anything that could tend to wound the feelings and prejudices of the people. . . . The different system pursued in Africa by the French has been productive of very different results; there the French army, I am sorry to say, is tarnished by the character of their operations. They sally forth unawares on the villagers of the country; they put to death every man who cannot escape by flight, and they carry off into captivity the women and children (shame, shame!). They carry away every head of cattle, every sheep, and every horse, and they burn what they cannot carry off. . . . They professed to colonize Algeria; but they are only encamped in military forts; and while in India we have the feelings of the people with us, in Africa every native is opposed to the French, and every heart burns with desire of vengeance (hear, hear!). I mention these things because it is right you know them; they are an additional proof that, even in this world, the Providence has decreed that injustice and violence shall meet with their appropriate punishment, and that justice and mercy shall also have their reward. . . .[48]

The point is not the accuracy of the description, but rather the fact that Palmerston was Britain's foreign minister, dealing with another Great Power whose view of its own contributions to civilization, rightly or wrongly, was that they are second to none. Guizot had every reason to be deeply wounded.

Yet France must pay a price for her miscalculation. The agreement contrived by Commodore Napier with Mehemet Ali—the hereditary Pashalik of Egypt alone—seemed to Guizot and to others a reasonable compromise. But in the course of the negotiations that took place among the Powers Guizot endeavored to inject the Syrian issue again. This he did in the form of suggesting—to Metternich—that the Powers obtain from the Porte guarantees for the Christian population of Syria, as well as the insurance of equal access for all to the commercial route between the Mediterranean and the Persian Gulf.

There is no cause to dwell on some oriental haggling between the Sultan and Mehemet Ali, in the course of which Ponsonby took a highly unco-operative stance. In the face of the agreement of the other Powers Palmerston finally consented to compromise. On the plea that the terms of the treaty of July 1840 had been fulfilled, hence that it was superseded, a new arrangement, in which France joined, was signed in London on July 13, 1841. It simply provided for closure of the Straits to ships of war so long as the Porte was at peace.[49]

With this the two-year crisis, during the course of which the possibility of war had at times been quite real, was finally resolved and the Concert of the Powers restored. How is one to appraise the significance of the episode for Britain and for France?

For the first it represented a success of the first magnitude, for which the credit must in full measure go to Palmerston; even against much domestic opposition he had had his way. His methods and his personality, important as they were in the details of implementation, dwindle into secondary significance by comparison with the accomplishment. Britain considered it her national interest not to let anyone establish too large a position in the Near East. The threat to her desires came from two quarters, the Russian and the French.

The French had been establishing an increasingly solid base of influence in Egypt and for that reason were willing to support the expansive ambitions, especially in Syria, of their protégé. But they miscalculated on several scores. They held too high an opinion of the strength of Mehemet Ali, who had shown himself capable of dealing with a Turkish army but proved unexpectedly ineffectual when confronted with British force; and Britain *was* willing to use force in the defense of what she deemed a sufficiently important interest. Palmerston was not a priori anti-

French and Guizot's judgment of him may be taken as fair appraisal:

> I attach great value to the quality of his mind. His method of procedure, although somewhat narrow and mischievous, I find acceptable; it is clear, prompt and firm. I do not believe in his hatred for France or her king, nor in his perfidies; and as to the difficulties, I might say the unpleasantness, that his passion for argumentation, his tendency to adhere to his thesis without his being able to see anything above, beyond, or in addition, intrude into the conduct of affairs, I am neither shocked by it, nor do I complain of it. It is the very nature of his mind; one must accept it, and accept it with good grace when dealing with him.[50]

The Russian position was unexpected by both Britain and France. But if the Tsar was unduly moved by anti-French emotion, it was also good policy on his part to liquidate the position established vis-à-vis the Ottoman Empire in 1833, for that position was a standing source of conflict with England. The Convention of the Straits of July 1841 created a situation acceptable to Russia and satisfactory to England. It was also acceptable to France, and in fact was the door through which she re-entered the Concert of the Powers. But in the process she had been isolated and, through the defeat of her Egyptian protégé, herself suffered a major setback to what were, especially in English eyes, too far-reaching Mediterranean ambitions. Palmerston had thus managed to achieve far more than he might have originally expected, killing two birds with one stone, the Russian position of privilege and the attempted French one. His exploitation of the opportunity enhanced his credit, even if his tactics were at certain points unnecessarily blunt and harsh. Palmerston did not want war but he was willing to face the possibility of it, gambling —correctly as it turned out—on the likelihood that in the test of wills his would prove stronger than that of the French, be it Thiers' or Louis Philippe's. In the process he knew how to exploit the nationalistic appeal, one of his sources of strength against his own domestic opposition.

Yet there was warrant for his gamble. For on the basis of an objective appraisal of the forces involved, Guizot's above-cited judgment was correct, hence likewise the decision to yield—provided things were not pushed too far. There was considerable belligerent talk in France and much national excitement, but a war against a European coalition would obviously have been folly. The prospect of exploiting the revolutionary factor opened indeed certain possibilities, to which the conservative continental Powers were not insensitive. But in this France was also hampered, for the spreading of revolution was the last thing Louis Philippe desired; he himself might be one of its victims. On the other hand, be it on the score of pure material power, or because of revolutionary possibilities, France must not be driven to exasperation. Thus a compromise was achieved, in which it was suitable that Metternich should play an important role, and which was accurate expression of the equilibrium of forces, material as well as ideological. On balance, nevertheless, it represented for France a marked setback, a very different outcome from the Belgian situation; the main difference lay in the fact that she had parted company with England, the chief controller of the destinies of Europe at this time.[51] English prestige and Palmerston's stood justifiably high in the eyes of all at this point.

The Last Phase of Palmerston at the Foreign Office

Yet, to a point, though less than France, England was also hampered by internal considerations. Had it not been for Palmerston's determination, the life of the Melbourne Cabinet might have ended even sooner than it did. Parliament was dissolved before the Convention of the Straits was signed and, in August, Peel took over the reins of government, with Aberdeen at the foreign office. In France Guizot was firmly established in the confidence of the king, whose chief minister he was to remain to the end of the July Monarchy.

The Anglo-French alliance, such as it was, had been a policy of the Whigs, of which the Tories had tended to be critical. The Egyptian crisis might have put an end to it, yet, interestingly, it seemed to revive in even more prosperous form, a fact due in considerable measure to the successful courting of the English queen by Louis Philippe, who behaved with considerable skill. Her visit to Eu in 1843, and again in 1845, she found wholly enchanting, and to the new relationship her uncle, King Leopold, son-in-law of Louis Philippe, gave every possible encouragement. Matching this honeymoon, Aberdeen and Guizot found each other highly congenial; they even went the length of an understanding, albeit an unwritten one, over Spanish affairs. The rivalry between England and France in Spain, which France tended to look upon as belonging in her sphere of influence, was coming to focus on the issue of a suitable husband for the young Spanish queen, soon to come of age. Palmerston's observations in Parliament on the score of Britain's foreign policy were marked by rancor and, even for him, unusual acerbity.[52]

For the better part of the decade European affairs were relatively quiescent. Britain's world-wide imperial and commercial activity impinged relatively little on European relationships, but she encountered as usual the Russian and the French interests. The beginning of her penetration of China was not yet cause of intense competition and rivalry,[53] and the squabble with France over Tahiti was small coin.[54] Domestic issues growing out of economic development, the free trade agitation and that of the laboring man, the Chartist movement, absorbed much of the English people's attention.[55] Correspondingly, in France the increasing conservatism of the July Monarchy, of which Guizot's administration was the expression, had the effect of increasing political tension. The bourgeoisie, the upper ranks of it especially, prospered in France, following the advice *"enrichissez-vous,"* but there was also drabness in the bourgeois king's régime, reflected in the observation that *"la France s'ennuie."*

The Tory administration of Peel came to an end in July 1846, when Lord John Russell was called upon to form a new ministry. The resolution of the problem was attended by some difficulty; it is of interest that Queen Victoria, a number of Whig leaders, and virtually all foreign governments, were all strongly opposed to the return of Palmerston to the foreign office. But he was still apparently "indispensable" and for the next five years remained in that position. Between himself and Guizot there was by this time no love lost and little trust, yet a sober appraisal of his intent may be found in this statement:

> Of course it is our object and our interest to be upon good terms with France. England and France have many interests,

> commercial and political, all over the world, which are perpetually coming into contact; and a good understanding between Paris and London is necessary, in order to prevent that contact from degenerating into collision. But as to trusting the French Government . . . I think everybody in England have now had their eyes sufficiently opened to prevent them from falling into mistake,[56]

which may be qualified by this other broad expression of policy that may in fact be said to express a long-term British view, rather than a merely Palmerstonian:

> Influence abroad is to be maintained only by the operation of one or other of two principles—hope and fear. We ought to teach the weaker Powers to hope that they will receive the support of this country in their time of danger. Powerful countries should be taught to fear that they will be resisted by England in any unjust acts either towards ourselves or towards those who are bound in ties of amity with us.[57]

The first of these statements was made at the beginning of 1847 after Palmerston had had his fingers burnt in Spain. The involved, sordid affair, not devoid of some comical element, of the Spanish marriages, alluded to before, is a minor episode that does not warrant much attention in the present discussion.[58] In the long-drawn-out contest for influence between England and France in Spain, Guizot had undoubtedly scored. Distrustful of Palmerston, who, upon his return to the foreign office, had taken up the problem where it had been left by Aberdeen, Guizot managed to confront his English rival with a *fait accompli:* in October 1846 the marriage of Queen Isabella to the Duke of Cadiz took place simultaneously with that of her sister to the Duke of Montpensier, one of Louis Philippe's sons.[59] The reaction at all levels in England, including Queen Victoria, was strong at what was taken as treachery, and the episode is generally considered to have put an end to the first Entente Cordiale.

Without going into the details of whose treachery, or into the moral aspect of the issue, this is to take too narrow a view of the disagreement. It must be considered in the larger context of Anglo-French rivalry, especially as this rivalry was focused on the unstable Mediterranean, over the whole of which French designs were suspected in England. The French establishment in Algeria was steadily expanding and showing signs of spilling over into neighboring Morocco[60]; in one form or another French influence threatened to become too strong in the whole western Mediterranean, hence must be checked in that quarter as it had been earlier at the eastern end of that sea.

If Mediterranean dominance was indeed the aim of French policy, it was a short-lived and empty success that had been achieved in Spain. To be sure Palmerston received little comfort from the rest of the Powers; there was no talk this time of a renewed Quadruple Alliance, with the consequence that both England and France remained isolated. The simple fact is that there was no real basis at this point for a solid Anglo-French connection.

It was not long before Palmerston had his revenge, reminiscent, on a minor scale, of his earlier encounter with Thiers. Switzerland provided the occasion for it, where tensions had been growing between the larger group of Protestant, and generally more liberally inclined, cantons and the smaller group of the more conservative Catholic ones. The formation by the latter of a league, the Sonderbund, for their mutual protection, led, on grounds of unconstitutionality, to a vote in the Diet demanding its dissolution in July 1847. This was the prelude to the Sonderbund war, a civil war, in which, because of their greater resources, the Protestant cantons could expect the victory that they won.

But the Swiss situation caused alarm among the conservative courts, who saw in it, as well as in the liberal Swiss practice of giving generous asylum to political malcontents from other countries, the usual specter of revolutionary plotting. The uncertain quantity was France, the standard-bearer of liberalism in many continental eyes, yet where Guizot was rather sympathetic to the Metternichian view of the situation. The usual proposal of consultation by the Powers, combined with French hesitancy and hedging, was used by Palmerston with skill as a delaying device which made it possible to isolate the Swiss problem until the outcome of the victory for the Protestant cantons.[61]

1848

The Swiss disturbance was in itself a small enough affair. Palmerston had no objection to a setback being inflicted on the Metternichian system, but the episode also had larger implications, for it tended to bring out the ideological cleavage of Europe, both among and within states, and was to a point the forerunner of the events which began to shake much of the continent of Europe to its very foundations in the year 1848.

The 1848 revolutions were, in the immediate sense, undoubtedly failures, a judgment warranted if one considers the state of Europe at the close of the following year. Metternich had misjudged when he abandoned the ship in March 1848; it was not long before his place was taken by a worthy successor in the person of Prince Schwarzenberg. England and Russia, the two peripheral states of Europe, were the ones that were not affected by the revolutions, and Russia at one point played an important role through her intervention in Hungary. But the English and the French roles are the ones we wish to examine; they furnish material for some interesting observations.

Though the first signs of disturbance occurred in Sicily, it was the February revolution in Paris that counted and was the spark that seemed to set much of Europe on fire. The new régime in France—the very name of which, Republic, is significant, no less than the institution of universal manhood suffrage in that country—was immediately faced with the dilemma of whether or not to assist revolution elsewhere; there were not a few, in Italy, in the Germanies, in the Habsburg domain, who, as half a century before, would have welcomed French armies in the guise of liberators. And, correspondingly, there were many in France, the more ideologically motivated radical elements, ready to give assistance to brother revolutionaries abroad.

But this is precisely where the French dilemma appeared, for the issue of the national interest arose. The fact that there was a strong nationalistic component in the Central European revolutions compounded the difficulty for the French, especially where Italy and Germany were concerned. It was a long-established, and quite logical, French policy to maintain the fragmentation of the Central European world; the emergence of a united

Italy, and even more of a united Germany, was definitely not a French national interest. To be sure, the possibility might exist of deriving some limited concrete advantage from such an outcome, or at least in connection with it, along the Rhine and the Alps, the everlasting aim of the "natural boundaries." A first French reaction was not long in coming. On March 5, the foreign minister in the provisional government, Lamartine, proclaimed a policy of non-intervention.

But the precise meaning of such a declaration remained open to interpretation, dependent upon the domestic course of French events and on that of unforeseeable external complications. It was not long before there was clarification on the score of the former; by June, a second revolution, or counterrevolution, though it did not restore Louis Philippe, made clear that the center of control had shifted but little.

Other things had happened meanwhile, and England from the very beginning had keenly watched continental events. As early as 1846 Palmerston had expressed the following view:

> Italy is the weak part of Europe, and the next war that breaks out in Europe will probably arise out of Italian affairs. . . . Outbreaks and insurrection and conspiracies have followed each other in rapid succession. . . . Leave things as they are, and you leave France the power of disturbing the peace of Europe whenever she chooses. . . . The ascendancy of the Liberal party at Paris, whenever it may happen . . . will soon be followed by an outbreak in Italy. That is the point to which the French liberals look; they know that if they tried to get back to the Rhine they would have against them all Germany united, Russia and more or less England; but in supporting an insurrection in Italy against Papal misgovernment, they would stand in a very different position.
>
> . . . .
>
> But Austria *would* interfere, and could scarcely help doing so. . . . France and Austria would then fight each other in Italy, and France would have all the Italians on her side. But the war, begun in Italy, would probably spread to Germany, and at all events, we can have no wish to see Austria broken down and France aggrandized, and the military vanity and love of conquest of the French revived and strengthened by success.[62]

Thus Palmerston was hardly unprepared for what happened in 1848, but his Italian policy suffered from what amounted to an attempt to manage at once, as the French say, both the goat and the cabbage. Where the Italian states were concerned it was consistent to favor reform as the best way to prevent revolution. This had in fact been an important aspect of Lord Minto's mission to the peninsula in 1847. But this effort ran counter to the very essence of Metternichian policy,[63] in whose eyes Lord Minto's activity was merely subversive. What is more, from the English standpoint, Austria represented an indispensable element of the European equilibrium, especially against either Russia or France, hence her position should not be diminished.

The reconciliation of these seemingly inconsistent aims Palmerston did not consider beyond his capacity. When revolution spread to virtually the entire Italian peninsula, and, worse, when Sardinia took against Austria the initative of a war which for a moment assumed the aspect of a war of national liberation for the whole of Italy, his solution consisted in the eviction of Austria from Italy and the formation of a Kingdom of Northern Italy, made up of Sardinia, Lombardy, and Venetia, which would have the possibility of maintaining itself in independence from both Austria and France.

A clash between these two powers was the thing that he wished above all to prevent. Though King Charles Albert had little desire for French assistance, when the fortunes of war turned sharply in June, the likelihood of such assistance, or even of an appeal for it, was obviously vastly increased. A common policy with France was, in the circumstances, the best way for England to prevent a single-handed French intervention. By September, Austria agreed to Anglo-French mediation, but it was by this time an empty gesture; why should Austria, successful in war, make any concessions? Palmerston may have succeeded in forestalling French action and a Franco-Austrian clash; his stock, understandably, did not stand very high at the Austrian court. It was, interestingly, higher in Turin, for the equally understandable reason that there was in that capital suspicion of mixed French motives, while there was no cause to question the British. If Britain had at this time a not altogether unselfish interest in the commercial possibilities that liberal régimes might offer, she certainly could not be suspected of territorial covetousness.

It may be pointed out—reason for all the more credit to him—that Palmerston carried out his policy in the face of strong domestic opposition. Apart from the conservative elements in England who sympathized with the victims of subversion, many of whom had taken refuge in that country, Queen Victoria was wholly incapable of understanding Palmerston's Italian policy. Reforms and constitutions she could accept to a point, even though they seemed little suited to Southern countries, but a cavalier view of legitimacy seems to have been beyond her comprehension; that the subjects of the Duke of Modena, for example, should have a say in the choice of their allegiance was to her a shocking idea. Though in the end she bowed to British constitutional practice, she certainly would have been glad to be rid of Palmerston and even tried to procure his departure from office. She had indeed legitimate grounds for complaint; in his self-confident impatience Palmerston behaved in rather cavalier fashion, informing the Queen of some of his actions after the event and tampering with despatches. His effrontery went the length of lecturing foreign governments, the Spanish and the Austrian, for example, in highly undiplomatic language. The retort he brought upon himself from Prince Schwarzenberg, no less proud and determined a man, is worth quoting:

> In truth . . . Lord Palmerston is a little too much inclined to consider himself the arbiter of the destinies of Europe. For our part we are not in the least disposed to attribute to him, in our own affairs, the role of Providence. We never pressed on him our advice concerning the affairs of Ireland. . . . I must frankly confess that we are tired of his eternal insinuations, of his tone now protective and pedantic, now insulting, but always unbecoming. . . . I do not know whether Lord Palmerston applies to himself the phrase of Louis XIV, and thinks that *l'Angleterre, c'est lui.*[64]

This may seem like personal trivia. Actually, there was not a little foundation to the charge, which corresponded to a reality. Leaving aside the idiosyncrasies of Palmerston's manner, there was considerable validity in ascribing to England an arbitral position; Palmerston certainly considered it to be such. In any case he had his way.

It took some time before the revolutionary fever spent itself. The flare-up of 1849, when Sardinia repeated the mistake of the preceding year, ended essentially in the same fashion of confirmation of the *status quo ante* in Italy, including the Austrian position in the peninsula. The Hungarians made more trouble for the Habsburg emperor; their inconsistency in denying to others, the Croats, for example, the benefits of national recognition, upon which they insisted for themselves, rendered their own position more difficult. But they fought well and did not finally surrender until a Russian army intervened. That intervention did not, however, result in complications; the Russians, their mission accomplished, went home. The French, too, intervened, but also in a very limited way and without causing larger repercussions; ironically, it was the Second Republic which helped restore and maintain the reactionary Pope.

The Frankfort assembly exhausted itself in verbose and futile discussions until what possibilities existed of its becoming an organ of substantial change had vanished. The Prussian intervention in the Danish Duchies, which Frankfort underwrote, also remained a limited affair.[65] By the end of 1849 order was fully restored in Central Europe. The Prussian king, fearful of Austrian opposition, had rejected the offer of the crown "from the gutter," and the following year his own fumbling attempts merely resulted in the humiliation that Schwarzenberg inflicted upon him at Olmütz.

The verdict is fundamentally correct that by her action, or rather her failure to act, France saved the peace at the cost of betraying the revolution, or at least not responding to the hopes of revolutionary Europe. The fundamental reason for this French behavior lay in the fact that in France herself the revolution was to a large extent frustrated. The election of a National Assembly gave evidence of the moderate mood of the majority of the French people—universal suffrage is not to be equated with the success of political extremism—and the election of Louis Napoleon to the presidency of the Republic at the end of 1848 was added confirmation of the state of French opinion.

So long as France "behaved," meaning by this, did not choose to exploit the possibility of assuming the revolutionary leadership of Europe, there was no cause for Britain to take alarm and for herself to intervene. There was in England considerable sympathy, not least at the court, for the victims of the continental revolutions; Queen Victoria could even forget her indignation at Louis Philippe's role in the affair of the Spanish marriages. But at the same time British policy did not contemplate assisting the forces of reaction. Palmerston's own sympathy, as usual, leaned toward constitutional governments; he would go as far as encouraging the Sultan to abide by his initial decision, in the face of Austrian and Russian pressure, not to surrender Hungarian refugees. His letter to Lord Russell verged on impertinence vis-à-vis the Queen, who was opposed to such interference:

> . . . the Hungarian leaders may certainly be called revolutionists, but they are revolutionists in the same sense as the men to whose measures and acts at the close of the seventeenth century it is owing that the present Royal Family of England, happily for the nation, are seated on the throne of these realms . . .[66]

Palmerston was, in the last analysis, England's foreign minister, and the English interest demanded peace and the preservation of the European equilibrium. Favorable as he may have been to Austrian concessions in Italy, the preservation of Austria was of greater importance:

> . . . if it [Austria] did not exist, it would have to be invented . . . it was an European necessity, and the natural ally of England in the East; he therefore counselled us [the Hungarians] to reconcile ourselves with Austria, because in the face of the European State-system it would be impossible to replace Austria by small states.[67]

Impressed as he had been by the quality of Prussia's accomplishments at the time of his visit to Berlin in 1844, he presciently foresaw some of the possible consequences of German unity, for the achievement of which he evinced little interest.

Don Pacifico and Louis Napoleon

Thus the revolutions of 1848, in the domain of the relations among the states of Europe, unfolded with a minimum of impact.

But Palmerston did not long survive them at the foreign office. The Don Pacifico affair in 1850, of small significance in itself, is yet worth mentioning as the occasion of one of his greatest parliamentary successes. Having taken up the defense of this somewhat dubious character,[68] the might and will of Britain were not to be defied with impunity. Annoyed as he had been with the Greek Government for some time, Palmerston ordered the squadron which had been standing at the Dardanelles—ready to support the Sultan against the above-mentioned Austro-Russian pressure—to proceed to Piraeus and exact retribution. Even the Greek acceptance of French mediation was bypassed. This was a typical manifestation of Palmerstonian high-handedness at its worst and earned him widespread condemnation, abroad and even at home. It furnished the occasion for a great debate in the House of Commons, in the course of which, on June 25, 1850, Palmerston delivered a lengthy and telling, if in part specious, defense of his policy over a long period of time. A passage of it ran as follows:

> The country is told that British subjects in foreign lands are entitled . . . to nothing but the protection of the laws and tribunals of the land in which they happen to reside. The country is told that British subjects abroad must not look to their own country for protection, but must trust to that indifferent justice which they may happen to receive at the hands of the Government and tribunals of the country in which they may be.
>
> . . . .
>
> I maintain that the principles which can be traced through all our foreign transactions, as the guiding rule and directing spirit of our proceedings, are such as to deserve approbation. I therefore fearlessly challenge the verdict which this House, as representing a political, commercial, and constitutional country, is to give on the question now brought before it; whether the principles on which the foreign policy of Her Majesty's Government has been conducted, and the sense of duty which had led us to think ourselves bound to afford protection to our fellow subjects abroad, are proper and fitting guides for those who are charged with the Government of England; and whether, as the Roman, in days of old, held himself free from indignity, when he could say *Civis Romanus sum;* so also a British subject, in whatever land he may be, shall feel confident that the watchful eye and the strong arm of England, will protect him against injustice and wrong.[69]

That the standards of Greek justice were not those of the British was true, but the fact might have been irrelevant had it not been for "the strong arm of England," quite comparable indeed to the Roman in its day. One is tempted to think of the contrast presented by more contemporary situations.

The speech was a resounding success; Palmerston knew how to appeal to the emotion of national pride. Yet both his policies and his overbearingness served to increase the tension between himself and the Queen.[70] The memorandum which she drew up, assisted by Prince Albert and Baron Stockmar, raised in the last analysis the important constitutional question of her right to dismiss ministers.[71] Palmerston bowed for the moment, but French events raised the problem again a year later.

The election of Louis Napoleon to the presidency of the Second Republic had undoubtedly to a degree been due to the prestige of the Napoleonic name and legend, which the successful candidate had known how to exploit with skill. Louis Napoleon, of whom more will have to be said, endeavored to be all things to all men, but on balance he represented the forces of order. The growing control exercised by these forces, despite some notable opposition, became more marked with the passage of time. The French intervention in Rome in 1849 on behalf of the Pope, the Falloux laws in 1850,[72] the stricter electoral law, all pointed in the same direction. The final outcome is reminiscent of 1799; the coup d'état of December 2, 1851, was a return to personal power, a prelude to the formal restoration of the empire a year later.

There were those in England, Palmerston among them, who were not at all shocked by the French coup d'état, taking a dim view of the existing constitution of France. His haste in expressing approval to Walewski, the French ambassador in London, and to his representative in Paris, was the last straw. The position taken by him obviously called for cabinet consultation and knowledge of the Queen. Palmerston had been too incautious, and his approval of Louis Napoleon robbed him of liberal and radical support, which had been one of his domestic elements of strength. He had to be disavowed and his own defense in the House was weak. On December 19, 1851, his tenure of the foreign office, though by no means of office, came to an end.

An episode in 1850 may be cited as apt summation of the man and his policy. On the observation of the Prussian minister, Baron Bunsen, that "he [Palmerston] has no principle, and he has no heart," the Duke of Argyll in his memoirs, comments as follows:

> In the sense in which these words were spoken they were founded on truth; but they were wrong in the sense they conveyed in our language. Palmerston was not, in the ordinary meaning of the word, an unprincipled politician. He was honest in his purposes, and truthful in his prosecution of them. That 'honesty is the best policy' was his favorite adage in diplomacy; but what Bunsen meant was true—he had no ideals for the future of the world, and had a profound distrust of those who professed to be guided by such ideals. To them he seemed to be, and he really was, heartless and unsympathetic.[73]

Allowing for his idiosyncrasies, his unnecessary high-handedness at times, but given the power of England, it was safe even to be high-handed. It was even possible to afford the luxury of principle that the support of constitutionalism expressed, all the more so that the extension of the English way to other states in no way constituted a threat to England in most cases. This was itself one of the assets of England, the fact that, in a later phrase, she was open to the winds of change.

The winds of change had blown harder in France, whose domestic record since the Great Revolution stands in contrast with the orderly English way of political transformation. Of ideals there was no dearth among French revolutionaries, as among revolutionaries in general. Yet the combination of unresolved domestic differences and of the ever present consideration of the interest of a state among states made for confusion and unexpected results. From the very beginning of their own revolution in 1848 the French had declined to assist revolution abroad, a position that went a long way toward making possible the restoration of the old order in mid Europe.

But now the Second Republic, like the first, was giving way to an emperor, the very heir himself of the Napoleonic tradition. Inevitably a question mark was raised for Europe. Napoleon III had no dearth of ideas, where either France or Europe were concerned. To the impact of some of these at least it is now suitable to turn.

NOTES ON *Chapter II*

1. Canning (April–August 1827), Goderich (August 1827–January 1828), Wellington (January 1828–November 1830).

2. Palmerston to Grant, August 17, 1830. Cited in Webster, Charles K., *The Foreign Policy of Palmerston,* 2 vols. (1951), Vol. I, p. 80.

3. Belgium had been prospering economically with the coming of the beginnings of industry. This created a divergence between the Belgian economy, increasingly oriented toward manufacture, and the more commercially oriented Dutch. On the other hand, the desire to retain unimpeded access to the Dutch market, both domestic and colonial, caused Belgian industrialists to be lukewarm in the cause of complete separation.

4. See above, pp. 33–34.

5. *Mémoires du Prince de Talleyrand,* ed. by Duc de Broglie, 5 vols. (1891–92).

6. The London meeting was to be a conference of ambassadors, not of heads of state or their chief ministers, as earlier congresses had been. This signalizes a change in the mechanism of the Concert of Europe.

7. *Mémoires de Talleyrand,* Vol. III, pp. 347–48.

8. Talleyrand and the foreign ministers in Paris, Molé, then Sébastiani, often did not see eye to eye. But the connection between Talleyrand and the king was close, especially through the intermediary of Madame Adelaïde, the king's sister, to whom Talleyrand reported extensively on the proceedings in London.

9. *Mémoires de Talleyrand,* Vol. III, pp. 406–7.

10. Ibid., p. 407.

11. This was spelled out in subsequent protocols of the conference, of January 20 and 27, 1831, which established the "*Bases de séparation*" of the two countries.

The trial of the ministers of Charles X, and the outcome of that trial, which showed the moderation of the new French régime, made a favorable impression in England and helped the tendency to Anglo-French co-operation.

12. They may be followed in the above-mentioned work of Charles Webster, as well as in Bell, Herbert C. F., *Lord Palmerston,* 2 vols. (1936), and Lannoy, Fleury de, *Histoire diplomatique de l'indépendance belge* (1930). Also in Bindoff, S. T., *The Scheldt Question* (1945).

13. The question of Luxembourg presented a special complication. King William III was its ruler, but the territory, distinct from the rest of his possessions, was part of the German Confederation, the city of Luxembourg itself being garrisoned by Prussia. Not contiguous to Holland proper, Luxembourg had been represented in the Belgian assembly, as had Limburg for that matter, hence the dispute over these two provinces.

14. French intrigues and intriguers had been active in Belgium even before the revolution in that country and in France. See *CHBFP,* Vol. II, pp. 121 ff.

15. In the final outcome both Limburg and Luxembourg were divided. The part of the latter not incorporated into Belgium continued to be under the personal rule of the Dutch king, part of the German Confederation, its capital city garrisoned by Prussia, a status under which it continued until 1867. One important decision of the London conference was to declare the perpetual neutralization of Belgium, a provision useful in meeting the French desire for the dismantlement of the border fortresses.

16. Cited in de Lannoy, op. cit., p. 15, n. 2.

17. Talleyrand to Sébastiani, November 27, 1830. Pallain, G., *Correspondance diplomatique de Talleyrand, Ambassade de Talleyrand à Londres 1830–1834* (1891), pp. 99–100.

18. Bell, op. cit., Vol. I, p. 98.

19. De Lannoy, op. cit., p. 308.

20. Ibid., p. 201.

21. Cited in Bell, op. cit., Vol. I, p. 103. This statement of Palmerston's suggests an interesting comparison with the analysis of the bases of British foreign policy contained in the Crowe memorandum of January 1, 1907. See below, pp. 360–61.

22. King Ferdinand had made various arrangements for dealing with his succession, finally deciding in favor of his daughter, Isabella, for whom, pending her reaching age, her mother was to be regent.

23. One of the chief military organizers used by Mehemet Ali, but there were many others.

24. France was instrumental in inducing the Sultan to grant to Mehemet Ali the control of all Syria and Adana.

25. Hurewitz, J. C., *Diplomacy in the Near and Middle East,* 2 vols. (1956), Vol. I, pp. 105–6. The alliance was concluded for eight years. It was not long before these terms became known to others.

26. Metternich to Neumann, June 9, 1833. Cited in Webster, C. K., "Palmerston, Metternich, and the European System 1830–1841," in *Proceedings of the British Academy,* 1934, Vol. 20, pp. 135–36.

27. Prussia had no interest in Eastern affairs but was generally a willing supporter of Metternich's reactionary policy.

28. Webster, "Palmerston, Metternich . . . ," p. 126. Metternich was also irritated by Palmerston's policy in regard to the German states and to Italy.

29. When the Austrians moved into the Legations, France occupied Ancona by way of demonstrating her insistence on the balance of power. Palmerston on his side was anxious to avoid a Franco-Austrian clash.

30. Webster, "Palmerston, Metternich . . . ," p. 138.

31. Guizot gives an apt estimate of the Ottoman situation: "The Porte was faced with two authentic allies [Austria and Great Britain], a hypocritical protector [Russia] and a friend whose heart was divided [France]. Guizot, François, *Mémoires pour servir à l'histoire de mon temps,* 8 vols. (1858–67), Vol. IV (1861), p. 44.

32. Bell, op. cit., Vol. I, p. 257.

33. The significance of this last was the control of the mountain barrier to Anatolia.

34. Exploration of that route had been taking place since 1835 while Mehemet Ali was extending his control in Arabia proper. In January 1839 Aden was occupied by the British, in part to forestall a French es-

tablishment. These developments pointed to the growing British interest, largely commercial in motivation, in the region intervening between the Mediterranean and the Persian Gulf, the Arab world. Britain's consequent concern over Mehemet Ali's activity was matched by her interest in Russian activity toward Persia.

35. Guizot, op. cit., Vol. IV, pp. 361–62.

36. Though he had never been to England before, he had devoted much attention to the study of British history and politics.

37. Guizot, op. cit., Vol. V (1862), pp. 42–43. The French had occupied Algiers in 1830. Following some years of uncertainty, by 1837 they moved to make their establishment in North Africa permanent and were engaged in the process of extending and organizing it.

38. "*Rendez-vous compte de ma situation: tout le monde est aux pieds de l'Angleterre; tout le monde offre de faire ce qui lui plaît; nous seuls nous disons non, nous qui nous disons des amis particuliers. Et c'est au nom de notre amitié, pour maintenir notre alliance que nous lui demandons de ne pas accepter ce que lui offrent tous les autres. Nous avons raison; mais ce n'est pas commode.*" Guizot to de Broglie, April 7, 1840. Guizot, op. cit., Vol. V, p. 53.

39. The text of the Treaty of London and of the proposed ultimatum to Mehemet Ali may be found in Hurewitz, op. cit., Vol. I, pp. 116–19.

40. Quoted in Bell, op. cit., Vol. I, p. 303.

41. Ibid., pp. 303–4.

42. Guizot, op. cit., Vol. V, p. 220.

43. Some indication of continuing Anglo-French relations may be seen in the successful French mediation of the Anglo-Neapolitan dispute over Sicilian sulphur and in Palmerston's gracious consent to the transfer to France from St. Helena of Napoleon's remains, which took place in Paris in December 1840 in a generally quiet and dignified atmosphere.

The German reaction to the turn of events, somewhat to French surprise, was an extremely strong and nationalistic one, memories of the Napoleonic performance and of its ultimate defeat for a while hurled back and forth across the Rhine. The *Wacht am Rhein* was composed in 1841.

44. *The Greville Memoirs,* edited by Lytton Strachey and Robert Fulford, 8 vols. (1938), Vol. IV, pp. 299–301.

45. The government in Constantinople sought to press this point, in doing which it was abetted by Ponsonby, the English representative, and even Palmerston for a while adhered to a legalistic position.

46. Guizot to de Broglie, September 23, 1840. Guizot, op. cit., Vol. V, p. 371.

47. The differences between the two, despite their limited co-operation, were considerable, in matters of domestic quite as much as of foreign policy. Guizot, a deputy, obtained leave from his ambassadorial post in order to participate in the opening debates in the Chamber.

48. Guizot, op. cit., Vol. VI (1864), pp. 412–13, from the *Morning Chronicle* of June 30, 1841.

49. Text in Hurewitz, op. cit., Vol. I, p. 123.

50. Guizot, op. cit., Vol. VI, pp. 131–32. The judgment, if anything, is kind. It may be contrasted with this other: "Nor was Palmerston in a much better position to accuse Thiers of swaggering and bullying than Louis-

Philippe of dealing underhand, for these were habits in which he himself excelled all Foreign Secretaries who have been before him and all who came after him." Cecil, Algernon, *British Foreign Secretaries, 1807–1916,* (1927), p. 153.

51. The dominant and arbitral position of English power, mentioned on various occasions in this treatment, cannot be emphasized too much. It rested on the combined pre-eminence of industrial and naval power, enabling England to exercise a controlling influence in European affairs while dealing with Central Asian and Chinese situations.

52. Witness for example his comments in the matter of Anglo-American relations, the Webster-Ashburton Treaty in particular. See Bell, op. cit., Vol. I, pp. 333 ff.

53. Others followed in the British wake in China, the French, the Dutch, and the Americans, but the intense competition over that country belongs to a later period.

54. Anglo-French rivalry, manifested in part through missionary activity, gave rise to some recriminations in the 1840's, until compensation was paid by France and the French protectorate was recognized.

55. The Corn Laws were abolished in 1846 and the Navigation Acts in 1849. The Chartist movement, based on a political approach to economic and social questions, collapsed in 1848.

56. Palmerston to Bloomfield (in St. Petersburg), January 1847. Quoted in Bell, op. cit., Vol. I, p. 388.

57. Quoted in Bell, op. cit., Vol. I, p. 354. This was said in the course of an attack in Parliament on Aberdeen's policy, when Palmerston was out of office.

58. The episode has been analyzed by Parry, E. J., *The Spanish Marriages* (1936).

59. This was the very thing that England had been trying to prevent. For if, as suspected, there was to be no issue from Isabella's marriage, an issue from that of her sister might become heir to the Spanish crown. This created an objectionable (to England) situation because of the too close connection which would be the result between the Spanish and the French crowns.

60. The bombardment of Tangier by a French fleet had brought a strong English reaction. It was an episode in the French conquest of Algeria, designed to bring pressure on Morocco, owing to the assistance from that country to Abd-el-Kader, the leader of the resistance to the French conquest.

61. The episode may be followed in *CHBFP,* Vol. II, pp. 296–97, and in Renouvin, Pierre, *Histoire des relations internationales,* Vol. V, Part I (1954), pp. 187–89. See also, Greer, D. M., *L'Angleterre, la France et la révolution de 1848* (1925). Following the Sonderbund war Switzerland was reorganized by the constitution of 1848.

62. Palmerston to Russell, June 30, 1846. Bell, op. cit., Vol. I, pp. 412–13.

63. It is of interest that Lord Minto's mission to Italy was simultaneous with an exploratory one of Ficquelmont, Metternich's envoy. Metternich was willing to consider certain administrative changes but no political reforms.

64. Schwarzenberg to Baron Werner, December 4, 1848. Quoted in Bell, op. cit., Vol. I, p. 442.

65. This aroused opposition from England, Russia, and Sweden. The London protocol of 1850 disposed for the time being of the problem of the Danish Duchies.

66. Palmerston to Russell, September 12, 1849. Quoted in Bell, op. cit., Vol. II, p. 20. According to Bell, a copy of this letter seems to have reached the Queen.

67. Ibid., p. 14. This judgment may be juxtaposed to the discussion of the merits of the disruption of Austria-Hungary after the First World War.

68. Of Portuguese Jewish origin, but born in Gibraltar, Don Pacifico was a British subject. During his residence in Athens as Portuguese consul general his house was sacked in the course of an anti-Semitic riot. This was the basis of his claim, which Britain supported, against the Greek Government.

69. Hansard's *Parliamentary Debates,* Third Series, Vol. CXII, pp. 381 and 444.

70. His behavior in connection with the visits to England of Haynau and of Kossuth was the object of considerable criticism.

71. The claim to her right to be informed and not to have decisions arbitrarily modified seemed hardly questionable; the sanction of dismissal was a different question however.

72. These were designed to strengthen the Catholic control of education.

73. Quoted in Bell, op. cit., Vol. II, p. 2.

III

THE FAILURE OF FRENCH LEADERSHIP

L'Empire, c'est la paix

Napoleon III, 1852

She [England] is really more an Asiatic Power than a European

Disraeli, 1868

"The man whom Victor Hugo branded as *Napoleon the Little* had greatness thrust upon him: without the magic of his name, he would never have become, and have remained for twenty years, the master of France and the arbiter of Europe. Yet he was not merely, as his enemies called him, 'Napoleon's cocked hat with no brains under it.' He had to achieve greatness: an adolescent dream slowly matured, realized at last not through luck alône, but through pertinacity, shrewdness, and daring. The dream was not ignoble; indeed, it was more generous than the sheer love of personal power which impelled Napoleon I."[1]

The overwhelming endorsement Louis Napoleon had received in his election to the presidency in 1848 was a free and authentic expression of the desires of the French people; so were on the whole, despite official pressure, the subsequent plebiscites. The fact is worth noting, however, which is characteristic of his whole tenure of office, that his support came in the main from the conservative forces in the country, the peasantry and the small bourgeoisie. This is well brought out by the voting pattern in the elections, which shows a majority opposed to him and his candidates in the urban centers; at this time France was not yet a developed industrial country, but still a primarily agricultural society. There is not a little irony in the fact that the Second Empire was a period of rapid industrial expansion in France—and of prosperity on the whole—a development strongly encouraged by the government. Napoleon III himself may fairly be described as a St. Simonian; his awareness of and interest in the social question was authentic; his writings, *Napoleonic Ideas* (1839) and *The Extinction of Pauperism* (1844), cannot be simply dismissed as window dressing propaganda.

But his record also bespeaks an ambiguity which ever remained unresolved and goes a long way toward explaining the riddle which he has remained to his interpreters. Had it not been for the disaster of 1870, the result of a war on which he himself had little taste for embarking, it is not unreasonable to speculate that his régime might have evolved into something surprisingly similar to that which succeeded his downfall; the "liberal Empire" certainly seemed launched in such a direction.

The man was not lacking in intelligence, his urbanity and personal charm were considerable. Within three years of his accession to the imperial dignity he could visit England and wholly capture both Queen Victoria and the Prince Consort, congenially exchanging with the latter memories of German student days, while his own consort was even more successful with the English queen. Yet Victoria never fully trusted him in affairs of state. He was also endowed with physical courage, but the sight of the battlefield revolted his humane instincts; Napoleon III was least of all a military man. Unresolved ambiguity, the mark of an indecisive personality, on occasion passing for profound design, expresses best his character.

This trait applied in the domain of foreign policy, which is what matters here. His official title of "Emperor of the French by the grace of God and the will of the people" was apt; it fitted the Napoleonic tradition in which the equation *vox populi, vox dei* is an important strand, hence the resort to the plebiscite and the dislike for parliamentary institutions where the idle talk of factions has full vent. The second French empire was not undemocratic, but it was Caesarian democracy.

What is more, despite the by now intimate identification of the first Napoleon with France, Napoleon III was in some respects even less French than his uncle. Much of Napoleon's family after 1815 resided in Rome, and Prince Louis Napoleon's education had been, as much as anything, Germanic, a legacy apparent in the accent he retained in speaking the French language. There is point to Guérard's characterization of him as "of Corsican and Creole descent, a Dutch prince at birth, always an Italian at heart, a German in thought, thoroughly at home in British society, married to a Spaniard, he was far more European than French."[2]

Yet he was after all Emperor of the French. However much he might see things in a European context, his position created an inescapable identity between his own, whether personal or dynastic, interest and the national French. Given the international standing of France in his time, it could be an easy step to conceive of reconciling the two under the guise of a European order under French leadership, leaving the precise meaning of that term not too clearly defined. Henry IV, too, had had a Grand Design, which has been variously appraised but which to some appeared to suffer from the vice of being a disguise for hegemonic intent. In the age of nationalism that was the nineteenth century, and especially in Napoleon III's hands, here was an unmatched opportunity for ambiguity and confusion.

The settlement of 1815 had undoubtedly been designed with a view to the containment of France. In addition to some minor territorial losses, of strategic significance, imposed by the second Treaty of Paris and not contained in the first, the extension of Prussia in the Rhineland and the creation of the Kingdom of the Netherlands were clearly anti-French provisions. Yet, considering the power of France and the Napoleonic performance, that settlement was not ungenerous in the totality of its terms. But it rankled, and it had been ever since common practice in France to refer to it as "iniquitous." The observation is apt that "this was the great dilemma of French statesmen in the nineteenth century. They proclaimed in general terms their complete hostility to the Congress settlement; but when they descended to particulars they found it difficult to say what they would have altered."[3] Given his own personality and the fact that he took the standard French position on the score of the settlement of Vienna, the advent of Louis Napoleon to the rule of France was bound to raise some questions, however peaceful his proclaimed intent may have been. The episode may be recalled of the visit of the Tsar's envoy, General Jomini, in the spring of 1852, on which occasion Napoleon, not quite emperor yet, expounded to his astonished guest far-reaching ideas for the redrawing of the map of Europe.[4] As things were to turn out, his reign coincided with a substantial revision of that settlement, though not perhaps in the manner that might have been foreseen and expected by him. One may see humor in the Tsar's willingness to acknowledge the new Emperor of the French, yet balking at the addition of a numeral to his name.[5] It was precisely with the Tsar, though hardly for that reason, that Napoleon was shortly at war.

The Mediterranean a French Lake

Among the Powers with Mediterranean interests various issues had appeared and various combinations had occurred. Three of those Powers had acted jointly as midwives to the birth of Greece to independence; all the European Powers, Russia and Britain especially, had joined to check the inordinate ambitions of France's Egyptian protégé in 1840, but France had rejoined the Concert a year later. Britain was the staunchest defender of Ottoman integrity.

The Crimean War

There is no need to rehearse the quarrel of the monks in Jerusalem.[6] It was a small point of prestige on the part of Napoleon III to reassert the ancient French claim to the protection of the Western or Latin (Catholic) Christians in the Sultan's domain, especially in the Holy Places. The Tsar responded with the assertion of a comparable claim in regard to the Eastern (Orthodox) Christians. Thus the Sultan was placed in an awkward position, not sure at first that differences among the Powers would have the usual effect of constituting his best guarantee of survival. This was in 1852.

This is the point at which things went wrong and began to

get out of control. As far back as 1844, as an aftermath of the earlier Anglo-Russian co-operation in checking France, Count Nesselrode had given to the British Government a memorandum that pointed to the possibility of far-reaching rearrangements in the Near East.[7] He found little response in Aberdeen, the British foreign minister at the time. But the project was now revived in the form of discussions with the British ambassador in St. Petersburg and with Aberdeen, now Prime Minister. Things were not made wholly clear and Tsar Nicholas seems to have drawn incorrect inferences about the British position.

The mission of Prince Menshikov to Constantinople, from February to May 1853, intended to overawe the Turks, had the effect of raising a general alarm and of transferring the initial petty issue to the higher plane of the future of the Ottoman Empire. Menshikov's mission was a total failure, for the Sultan felt by now confident of Western support, an impression for which the British representative at the Porte, Lord Stratford de Redcliffe, who reached his post in April, bears a measure of responsibility. De Redcliffe, well acquainted with the East from long residence and enjoying high prestige in Constantinople, was a determined exponent of the Palmerstonian view where Ottoman affairs were concerned.[8]

Irritated by the rebuff to Menshikov, the Tsar responded by occupying the Principalities in June, and this in turn led to the appearance of an Anglo-French squadron at Besike Bay, outside the Dardanelles. In Vienna, ever indecisive and relatively neutral, negotiations were proceeding which resulted in the so-called Vienna Note in July. The note, on which the five Powers had agreed, was of French draft and merely dealt with the initial issue of the protection of the Christians; but by this time the dispute had become a primarily Anglo-Russian confrontation with France relatively in the background.

Encouraged by de Redcliffe, the Sultan proposed certain amendments, which the Tsar in turn declined to accept, and finally, in October, the Turks, quite aroused by this time, took the initiative of a declaration of war. They had judged correctly in their reliance on Western support, which the Tsar on his side had miscalculated; like France in 1840 it was now Russia's turn to be isolated. But there was not in this instance the same desire to find a way for her to rejoin the Concert as had been shown toward France in 1840, while on his side Tsar Nicholas failed to emulate the accommodating behavior of Louis Philippe. Even so it was not until March 1854 that England and France declared war upon Russia. Austria did not join the war, but her threatening abstention was evidence to the Tsar of the fulfilment of Schwarzenberg's prediction that "Austria would astound the world with her ingratitude."[9]

Of the Crimean War itself it will suffice to say two things. As a military operation it furnished occasion for heroic and flamboyant behavior,[10] but it may also be summed up as a contest in comparative incompetence, the Russian proving greater than that of the Western Powers. The seas were less of an obstacle to the supplying of their forces than the quagmire of Russia was to hers. The fall of Sebastopol in September 1855, following the death of the Tsar in March, made it easier for his successor to acknowledge defeat. The other aspect of the war, the diplomatic, was marked by its urbane gentleness. Russia participated in the 1855 exposition in Paris, and the representatives of the belligerents were never out of contact in Vienna, where negotiations were carried on throughout the war.

Having gambled and lost, Russia must pay some price. The proposal of the four other Powers, the Four Points of Vienna, of August 1854, initially considered too humiliating by Russia, became the basis of agreement. Palmerston, not surprisingly in view of his past record, was the most intransigeant element in England, but Napoleon was anxious for peace; his hints of enlarging the issue, by raising the Polish question, for example, had on the whole a quieting effect. Also there was the fact that the English Government was none too happy over the fact that the British contingent in the war amounted to between a third and a half of the French.[11]

The congress which met in Paris from the middle of February to the middle of March 1856 was a convivial affair; the Russians were no criminal outlaws and it can be contended that the Congress of Paris is a good illustration of the Concert of Europe successfully restored after a passing accident of limited significance. There is no need to go into the details of the terms of the Treaty of Paris. In her mistaken attempt to extend her influence, Russia suffered a definite setback, losing access to the Danube and the right to maintain a naval establishment in the Black Sea; Europe, collectively rather than Russia alone, asserted a veiled right of protectorate over the Ottoman Empire, which, with unintended humor perhaps, was formally accepted as a member of the Concert at the same time. The outcome was at least as much a success of British as of French policy. France, and more particularly Napoleon III, could enjoy the asset of prestige, of which the Congress was confirmation; he could hardly thereafter be regarded as a usurper, and the whole episode redounded to his domestic popularity no less than to French standing abroad.

One interesting consequence was the friendly state of Franco-Russian relations thereafter. It reflected the fact that France continued to be a revisionist power—more evidence of this will be seen presently—while the setback of the Crimean War brought Russia into the same camp. That the bases for this common outlook were at this time very flimsy would not be long in appearing; yet for a while the association lasted.

Other Mediterranean Developments

Apart from prestige France derived no concrete gains from the war, yet the provisions of the Treaty of Paris offered some opportunities, small as they may have been, for the assertion and enhancement of French influence in the Near East. In the Principalities, still under Turkish suzerainty, the collective supervision of Europe had also been substituted for the exclusive influence of Russia. Following their evacuation by the Austrians in 1857, what took place during the following decade may be summed up as another instance of the successful assertion of nationalism, a cause ever congenial to the French emperor. He had his way against the British-supported Porte in procuring new elections,[12] which were a marked success for the unionist tendency. England and Europe gradually gave way, reasserting at first the separateness of the "United" Principalities, then acknowledging the de facto union that was the election of Alexander Couza in both, finally sanctioning the formal union in 1864. The emergence of Roumania was on the whole a minor success of French policy.[13]

Roumania is not a Mediterranean country though she is in the Balkans and was still formally part of the Ottoman domain. Syria was unquestionably Mediterranean. The rivalries which centered on the control of that Turkish province, Turco-Egyptian, Anglo-French at one remove, have been mentioned.[14] Following the restoration of Turkish control after 1840, the existence in Syria of an appreciable number of Christians furnished cause for Europe's continuing interference. Various unsatisfactory arrangements[15] failed to prevent an explosion of violence, Christian massacres in the Lebanon and in Damascus in 1860. The Powers met in Paris to discuss the situation and again the Anglo-French rivalry appeared, focusing in respective support of Moslem Druzes and Christian Maronites. The outcome was intervention in the form of a French expedition going to Syria to re-establish order. But France was acting on the basis of an international mandate, and the French force, its task accomplished, withdrew. There was all the while not a little English suspicion and England only grudgingly agreed to a brief extension of the stay of the French force. Again, this was a small affair though it, too, went to confirm the international standing of the second French empire and the continuity of French policy in the eastern Mediterranean.

At the opposite end of that sea, in Algeria, the French establishment was definitely confirmed. The development of Algeria during the Second Empire did not proceed with complete smoothness, continuing the groping efforts of the preceding period. Mistaken policies were adopted for a time, which gave way to a change of orientation, into the details of which there is no need to enter. The location of Algeria, a steady influx of settlers from France—some 200,000 by 1860—made it a special case of colonization. Algeria was increasingly taking on the appearance of an extension of metropolitan France, thus firmly installed astride the western Mediterranean.[16]

The observation that "the keys of the Mediterranean lie in the Red Sea" is of Italian origin. It is of later vintage and was, at the time it was made, an expression of frustration. Yet the importance of the Mediterranean-Red Sea route, especially in an age of expanding commercial activity and for England most of all, is obvious. The English had taken control of Aden in 1839, in part to forestall a French establishment. It was in 1862 that the French laid the bases of the small colony that was to become French Somaliland. Small as it was, the importance of it was considerable: a base on the route to the Far East, it was a counterpart to Aden at the opposite side of the southern entrance to the Red Sea; in the opposite direction it was a gateway to Abyssinia and opened up possibilities of East African expansion. Its importance was further enhanced by what was taking place at the northern end of the Red Sea.

The idea of cutting a water connection between the Mediterranean and the Red Sea has an ancient history. In the mid nineteenth century, if it was to be undertaken at all, logic pointed to England as the obvious candidate for the task. But there was in England scepticism of the possibility, for technical reasons in part: cost and problems of construction, railway as a better solution. However that may be, one thing was clear, a French canal was, from the English point of view, definitely an undesirable undertaking. In England, during nearly the entire decade from 1855 to 1865, Palmerston held the prime ministership.[17] Although the foreign office was in gentler hands, mainly Clarendon's and Russell's, Palmerston's long previous tenure of the post, plus his present position, gave his views unusual importance. What is more, Palmerston was well versed in Near Eastern affairs and in French designs in that quarter where he had worsted Thiers.

Among the many things he said on the score of the Suez enterprise, the following statement is a good expression of his views:

> But if the canal could be made, it would open to the French in the event of war a short cut to India, while we should be obliged to go round the Cape. The first thing the French would do would be to send a force from Toulon or Algeria to seize the canal. An expedition, naval and military, would steam away through the canal to India, sweep our commerce, take our colonies, and perhaps seize and materially injure some of our Indian seaports, long before our reinforcements, naval and military, could arrive by long sea voyage; and we might suffer in this way immense loss and damage.[18]

By this time, in 1860, the Suez Canal was no longer in the domain of Utopian speculation. The initiative of its building belonged, appropriately, to a St. Simonian, Ferdinand de Lesseps, who, in the course of an earlier consulship in Alexandria, had established relations of influential friendship with the Khedive. The initial concession was granted in November 1854.[19] Although the undertaking was a purely private enterprise, the need of the Sultan's assent made it at once an international question. Palmerston's action may fairly be described as an attempt at sabotage; pressure was put on the Sultan and the participation of English capital discouraged. When shares were issued on the international money market, the overwhelming majority of them was subscribed in Paris, insuring French control of the company.[20]

Napoleon III was very reticent at first, mainly because he did not wish to create an issue with England. But as time passed and active work on the project began—in 1859—he turned to a more positive attitude of support. England had let an opportunity pass, for, once it had become clear that she could not prevent the building of the canal, she might at least, through financial participation, have secured an important voice in the company. She finally withdrew her unrewarding opposition, reassured by promises that the French operation was devoid of political implications, and in May 1866 the Sultan approved the concession. The costs of construction went substantially beyond the initial estimates, but the necessary additional capital was forthcoming; in November 1869, to the accompaniment of suitably lavish ceremonies and in the presence of a galaxy of European royalty, the canal was formally inaugurated. It was not long before its financial success, exceeding the most sanguine expectations, set to rest any doubts about the soundness of the undertaking. Needless to say, British shipping was by far the greatest user of the canal.

For all that it had been, and remained, a private enterprise, the building of the Suez Canal represented an extension of French influence in a quarter where it had long been active. To regard it as an intentionally anti-British operation would be a false interpretation; in this as in other matters Napoleon III was desirous of co-operation with England. But it would be equally erroneous to deny the inevitable political implications of the canal as a French company.

Again, to interpret the various Mediterranean activities which have been indicated as part of a deliberate, conscious, and well-thought-out plan to establish French dominance in the whole of that sea would be an oversimplification for which there seems to be no adequate warrant. It may be pointed out that Bismarck, describing a meeting with Napoleon III in March 1857, reports that "he did not exactly contemplate making the Mediterranean a French lake, *mais à peu près.*"[21] This need not be taken in a literal sense, but policies are often the result of events as much as they can be sources of specific actions. In the light of both preceding and subsequent activity, the factor of continuity appears as a striking aspect of France's Mediterranean policy during the Second Empire.

The Reorganization of Europe

The Italian peninsula is certainly Mediterranean, but Italy was still in the mid nineteenth century no more than a geographical expression. The transformations that it underwent, and in the effecting of which the French role was decisive, were of even greater significance than those which have just been rehearsed around the rest of the Mediterranean basin. Also, the case of Italy inserts itself primarily in the mainstream of continental happenings rather than in a Mediterranean framework, an observation even more obviously true in the Germanic case.

The Crimean War, accidental though it may have been, nevertheless fits properly as an episode in the long tale of the Russian drive toward the open sea and of the resistance, British above all, to that Russian endeavor. In this contest the decadent Ottoman Empire plays an almost passive role; no doubt Russian encroachment, pinpointed at the Straits, was for it a matter of life and death, yet the decisive influence in the outcome was not its own deficient power but that of the Western states, plus Austria's to a point.

Seen from another standpoint, the Crimean War was the first breach in the European order created in 1815. To be sure, there had been some earlier modifications of that order, but the Belgian case, for example, could also be interpreted as confirmation of the successful operation of the Concert of Europe. The Crimean War could not. And if the Congress of Paris can be seen as a reaffirmation of the Concert, the clash which had involved three major Powers signified a failure and may also be seen as the opening of a period by the end of which the Concert was devoid of reality and the shape of Europe had been radically altered. Once Germany was made, it was not long before the focus of international affairs would be on a system of alliances rather than upon a continuing Concert.

The political reorganization of Europe which was effected during the brief span of a decade is a prime illustration of the successful assertion of the national factor. This is not in any sense to minimize the skill and the accomplishments of Cavour and Bismarck—the role of individuals and of specific events looms large in the short term and it is wholly appropriate to give it adequate recognition—but in the larger context of the whole nineteenth-century evolution the simple and overwhelmingly important fact is that there were such things as an Italian and a German people, which the House of Habsburg, regrettable as that may be, stood for an impossible attempt of the past to survive.[22]

The War with Austria and the Making of Italy

No attempt will be made to retell the often told tale of the Italian Risorgimento or of the corresponding romantic movement in Germany from its eighteenth-century beginnings through the War of Liberation and the subsequent agitation. Both were initially and primarily cultural developments which overflowed into and were annexed by political forces.[23] Despite the presence of some hard-headed men, Louis Blanc for example, the revolutions of 1848 on balance showed two things: the strength of the challenge to the established order was one; the innocence of romantic revolution was the other.

The focus at this point is on the French role in these affairs. If happenings in France had such widespread repercussions and were watched with so much interest in 1848, it was no doubt because of the proprietary claim that France had on the revolutionary idea; but it was also because of the stage of France's economic development and in the last resort because of the extent of French power. When Prince Louis Napoleon Bonaparte emerged on the French scene, first as President of the Republic then as Emperor of the French, the ambiguity of his position mentioned before must be recalled and emphasized. Napoleon III was now inextricably identified with the interest of a definite political entity, the French state; Napoleon III was also a nationalist and a European.

The synthesis of this ambiguity, not to say contradiction, was something in the nature of a Grand Design in which the French interest, but other desiderata as well, would be served by a revision of the order of 1815, a revision to be effected through an orderly and peaceful procedure. Napoleon III was ever ready to propose the calling of a European congress to effect needed changes in agreement and peace. But since such a gathering would be an inevitable challenge to a number of other existing interests, it is perhaps not very surprising that there were several wars instead. Nor should the vitiating fact be ignored that there was on the part of others a not unwarranted suspicion that the proposal was essentially a screen for the enhancement of the French position. It was not quite as simple as that; Napoleon III was not a Machiavellian, but rather an imaginative, often well-intentioned, as well as an irresolute man.

The Italian case offers a good illustration. Things Italian were ever close to the mind and the heart of both Napoleons, and the second of them had himself taken part in Italian conspiratorial activity before the larger French field became the main focus of his interest. The European congress which met in Paris in 1856 provided an excellent opportunity for Europe to consider any problems of general concern to its members besides the limited and concrete one of re-establishing peace among the belligerents. The general state of affairs in the peninsula, the festering sore of the backward maladministration of the States of the Church and of the Kingdom of the Two Sicilies, were matters of public knowledge, as well as the general prevalence of the anti-Austrian feeling in Italy. In its immediate domain, Lombardo-Venetia, the generally good quality of the Austrian administration was inadequate compensation for the fact of its foreignness. The Kingdom of Sardinia, where Austrian and French influences neutralized each other, was the only truly independent state in the whole of Italy. After its failure in 1848, and despite that failure, it had become the focus of Italian nationalist hopes.[24]

But Piedmont was a small and weak state, and the events of 1848 had also shown the futility of the slogan *Italia farà da sè*. Palmerston's idea of a Kingdom of Northern Italy,[25] quite sensible in many respects, had had no appeal for Austria, whose military success destroyed what momentary hopes there may have been of its realization. Austria was, in English eyes, an essential part of the structure of the European equilibrium, and Palmerston would go no further than offer his mediating offices while she was in difficulty. During the Crimean War, when the Western Powers had sought to enlist Austria's assistance, they had guaranteed her Italian possessions. The Sardinian intervention was to a point a lever to procure her own, but it proved ineffectual; Napoleon III even toyed with the idea of a transfer of the Principalities to Austria in exchange for her relinquishment of Lombardo-Venetia, but that project, too, was stillborn. It is worth noting, in passing, that his willingness to entertain such a possibility, when juxtaposed with his subsequent support of Roumanian nationalism, was calculated to raise doubts about the authenticity of his devotion to the nationalist cause in general.

Thus, where Italy was concerned, when Napoleon wished to do something for Italian nationalism, he found himself confronted with several problems, most of all by the fact that the creation of a unitary Italian state ran counter to the traditional French preference for Central European fragmentation; more narrowly, the French contingent in Rome, the solid guarantee of papal independence, had to be looked upon in the context of his desire for the support of his domestic Catholic opinion.

At Paris, in 1856, the Italian question had indeed been mentioned, though little more than that. Cavour had skillfully taken the position that reforms in Italy were the most effective counter to revolutionary agitation, but he had had to be content with Clarendon's presentation of the case; even Walewski, personally antagonistic, had only underwritten this position because of the specific instructions of the emperor. Matters lay dormant for a while.

Cavour, whose name stands high in the roster of statesmanship and diplomacy, was another consequence of 1848, or at least his accession to the prime ministership of Sardinia was. A typical mid nineteenth-century liberal, he was most attracted to England for two reasons: because of the nature of English institutions, political and economic, and because of his suspicion, based on an awareness of ambiguity, of French assistance. But beggars can't be choosers. Cavour well understood that Sardinia, or even Italy alone, was incapable of ousting Austria; in addition, good student and practicer of *Realpolitik* that he was, he soon came to realize that from England he would get sympathy, kind words, cultural appreciation, but no bayonets. If force was to be brought into use—and how else could anything be accomplished?—who but France could supply it?

Cavour was an abler man than Napoleon, whose irresolution was alien to his temperament. The combination of his skill and of Napoleon's hopes and desires is what produced a concrete plan of action, which Signor Benso[26] and the French emperor elaborated in secrecy in July 1858 at Plombières. Cavour could be counted on to provoke war with Austria in such a way as to bring into play an ostensibly defensive alliance. The outcome of a successful conflict would be a far-reaching reorganization of the political structure of Italy: the Austrian possessions would pass to the King of Sardinia to form a Kingdom of Northern Italy—remember Palmerston's proposal of 1848; to the south of it various small entities would be merged into a central kingdom—with a French prince perhaps; the rest would be left undisturbed, and the four segments would then join into a confederation under the nominal presidency of the Pope, but of which the House of Savoy would furnish the effective leadership.[27]

What was there of French advantage in this scheme, besides the satisfaction of Italian nationalism, a questionable asset at best? The eviction of Austrian influence, while still leaving Italy a weak state, could open the door to its replacement by French predominance. As Napoleon put it, in February 1859, "a great nation is like a planet, it cannot exist without satellites . . .

without states whose interests are directly tied to its own, whose existence depends on its own."[28] There would also be the concrete advantage of the acquisition of Savoy, the realization of natural frontiers in the southeast.[29]

How things developed, how the plan went wrong, and the final outcome, can be recalled very briefly. Walking into Cavour's trap, Austria obligingly took the initiative of an ultimatum to Sardinia and found herself at war, in April 1859, with the Franco-Sardinian combination. In the military operations, in part as a result of Austrian dilatoriness, the Franco-Sardinian forces were successful, although it is worth noting that Magenta was a near thing and a costly engagement, and Solferino little better. Worsted, but not destroyed, the Austrians withdrew to the shelter of the Quadrilateral fortresses, the reduction of which promised to be a lengthy operation.

But at this point the French and the Austrian emperors, meeting at Villafranca on July 11, agreed to put an end to hostilities. The plan which they outlined was only a partial fulfilment of the original Franco-Sardinian scheme: Austria would yield Lombardy but retain Venetia, and the Italian princes in the Duchies would be restored. By the time these arrangements were written into the Treaty of Zurich in November, intervening events had already rendered them obsolete.

For in the Duchies and Romagna representative assemblies of sorts had decreed union with Piedmont, a decision ratified by plebiscites in March 1860, and with which no one interfered. A new treaty between France and Sardinia, the Treaty of Turin, was tantamount to a modification of the earlier agreement, North Central Italy taking in it the place of Venetia. But even this was but a stage in a fast-developing situation. The picturesque Garibaldian expedition to Sicily in May 1860 within four months resulted in the collapse of the Neapolitan kingdom. Rome itself was saved but not most of the papal domain. In March 1861 the Kingdom of Italy was proclaimed, which reached from Sicily to the Alps, and in which Rome and Venice alone were still missing.

Here was a large modification of the existing European order. The ease with which it was accomplished may be credited to the lack of support for the previously existing structure; put in a different way, Italian nationalism, though still largely confined to the literate class, had come of age.[30] But the reconstruction of Italy was also a legitimate concern of the rest of the Powers. The reason for the Villafranca truce lay in the fear of Napoleon III lest larger complications arise; in simplest form, he did not feel, and quite rightly, that France was capable of sustaining war simultaneously on the Po and on the Rhine. Because of the war in Italy the eastern frontier of France had been left unprotected, and Prussia was mobilizing. To be sure, Napoleon had sent Morny to Russia and had secured from the Tsar a somewhat ambiguous reassurance. The Tsar had no objection to an Austrian defeat repaying Austria's ingratitude in the Crimean War; he even went so far as issuing warnings to Prussia, though he did this unbeknown to Napoleon, whom he preferred to keep in uncertainty. The burden of the Russian influence was in favor of a prompt restoration of peace.

When the Italian situation was getting out of hand, at the very time of the Franco-Austro-Sardinian negotiations in Zurich, Napoleon insisted on the fulfilment of the terms of Villafranca. Yet at the same time he interposed what was tantamount to a veto on any Austrian action in Italy, himself refusing to interfere in the Duchies, while the French representatives went on discussing a plan for an Italian federation of which Austria, in possession of Venetia—it would have in the federation a place comparable to that of Luxembourg in the German Confederation—would be a member.[31] The negotiations were in part a stalling device, which allowed time for Italian events to unfold and create a *fait accompli;* one can well understand Napoleon's advice to Cavour in 1860, *"faites vite."*[32] Napoleon was understandably embarrassed vis-à-vis his Sardinian ally; in all Italy Villafranca was looked upon as a betrayal, little redeemed by the above-mentioned Treaty of Turin, as the result of which Napoleon could, in better conscience, collect the price of Nice and Savoy.[33]

One significant aspect of the appearance on the map of Europe of the Kingdom of Italy was that so extensive a breach of the order instituted in 1815 took place without the intrusion of Europe in Concert. Clearly, the crucial factor had been the war between Austria and France, which was no doubt a French success, albeit a qualified one, whether in purely military terms or because of the restraining effect of the possibility of additional interference. France, or Napoleon—in this respect the two are one at this point—had succeeded in bringing about a wide breach in the "iniquitous" settlement, rather more far-reaching in fact than initially planned.

Yet it was also one of Napoleon's favorite devices to propose the holding of a European congress to deal with such situations as the Italian. Actually, before the war broke out and with a view to its avoidance, the proposal of a congress had come from Russia, and Napoleon had responded to it. The obstacle at that point had been mainly Austria, which had thus incidentally extricated Cavour, but in reality both at Villafranca and at Zurich French policy was more inclined to the making of bilateral arrangements.

The final stages of the making of Italy provide an excellent example of the methods, and the deficiencies, of the Napoleonic mode of operation. To say nothing of the unfavorable repercussions at home of the final outcome, especially where Rome was concerned, the French role in the unification of Italy earned him little gratitude in that country because of the specific manner in which the task had been accomplished. Napoleon was in many respects quite a reasonable man. Even the prospect of Rome in the new Italy he could envisage; the Pope and his nuncio in Paris had reason to feel increasingly betrayed[34] while remaining dependent on the permanence of a French force in Rome. The suspicions of all had to a point been aroused, not least, quite naturally, of England.

England's Abstention

The unfolding of Italian events was naturally closely watched in England, but her role is perhaps best summed up in the observation that, in this instance as in the case of the other Mediterranean developments which have been outlined, "French initiatives are decisive: they threaten the interests of Britain which however resigns herself."[35] There is therefore no need to examine at length the shifts in the British reaction.[36] The prospect of the entire peninsula falling under French influence, with all that this could entail in terms of Mediterranean position, was clearly one that England could not contemplate with indifference; but on the other hand an Italy united might have sufficient weight to resist French dominance, even become a counterweight to it. That is the view which came to prevail and which the future would prove to be justified. If after her unification Italy can be described as anyone's satellite, it was certainly England's rather than France's.

The reasons for this British passivity were to a large extent domestic, the preoccupation with internal issues such as political reform; but it can also be attributed to a certain lack of unity in British counsels. Palmerston's career after his fall from grace in 1851 belied the prognostications of those who thought his role in English politics was finished. To be sure, he never held the foreign post again, but in February 1855 he re-emerged in the role of Prime Minister, a place he was to retain for nearly a decade.[37] Clarendon at the foreign office, though of quieter temperament, generally saw eye to eye with him, but Russell, who was foreign minister during his last administration, did not provide strong leadership, with the consequence that foreign affairs continued in considerable measure to be Palmerston's preserve.

The impression conveyed in this period is, however, of a different Palmerston, in this domain at least, from the Palmerston of the forties. Not that his energy was less—he could outlast many a younger man in the long sittings of the House—and he could be as blustering and as sharp as of old. It would be easy to supply quotations from him that could be used to illustrate a variety of positions, yet the sum total adds up to a picture of almost vacillating indecision. This was in part because, where it came to Italian affairs, he, Russell, and Gladstone constituted a group, sometimes dubbed the *italianissimi,* strongly at odds with the Court, especially with Queen Victoria herself, who did not find the Palmerstonian cross easier to bear than she had earlier.

To complicate matters, in the case of defense, Palmerston and Gladstone were at odds with each other, while the Court influence rather leaned toward the Palmerstonian view. The issue of defense loomed important in 1859. The advent of steam raised doubts in many English minds about the value of the Channel moat, a concern that was compounded by the adoption of armor in the French Navy. As usual, when a new technical development occurs in the domain of armaments, it tends to threaten the advantage of existing superiority. The French Navy, especially if assisted by some other, might constitute a serious threat to the English dominance of the sea, not to mention the safety of the British Isles themselves.

If in retrospect it is clear that the likelihood of an Anglo-French conflict was very small at this time, that was not the way it universally appeared in England, where there was serious discussion of the deficiencies of the defense establishment. On the French side, Napoleon, however tortuous his policy might appear, was unquestionably desirous of preserving good relations with England, a policy to which Persigny, his ambassador to that country, was, if anything, even more dedicated. His acquiescence in the withdrawal of the French force from Syria, which gave the lie to English suspicions in that quarter, his co-operation with England in China, were evidences of his preference, and the same can be said of the Cobden-Chevalier treaty of January 1860. This French espousal, to a degree at least, of the English predilection for free trade, was much criticized in France, where it could only be enacted by Napoleon's resort to his treaty-making prerogative.

Yet the suspicion of the French emperor would not die, and there is little difficulty in understanding how his efforts to deal with the Italian situation, in which he had indeed been the prime mover but of which he had lost control, conveyed across the Channel a picture of tortuous insincerity rather than of the mere fumbling that in large measure they were. His declaration in November 1863 that the treaties of 1815 were dead, coupled with the proposal he sent to Queen Victoria that a European congress meet in Paris, was better designed to cause alarm than to lead to a solution of the problems of Europe in orderly fashion. It met with a polite but non-committal answer. Napoleon raised too many questions at once and no one could foresee the consequences of opening Pandora's box.[38]

That there were problems and unresolved difficulties could hardly be denied. The Poles had revolted again. There was considerable sympathy for them in the Western states and the Tsar had undoubtedly treated in high-handed fashion his obligations to the Poles. But who could expect him to submit the issue to the arbitration of Europe? The remonstrances that were the subject of individual parallel communications from the British, the French, and the Austrian governments merely created irritation; where Napoleon was concerned they put an end to the era of Franco-Russian co-operation that followed the Paris Congress of 1856.

There was trouble in Denmark as well, or at least in the Duchies of Schleswig and Holstein, where the integrating attempts of the Danish king gave rise to a dispute with the German Confederation. There is no need to go into the complexities of that extremely involved situation.[39] In London in 1852 the Powers had dealt with the problem; it was therefore quite suitable that they should meet to consider it again. The quip credited to Palmerston that only three men in Europe had ever understood the question—the Prince Consort, now dead; a Danish statesman, currently in an insane asylum; and he himself, who had now forgotten it—seemed to apply at least in the last part. Bismarck, who understood the question very well, had found him uninformed when discussing it with him.

It is sufficient to recall the outcome. The Danes, misled by loudly expressed English sympathy, became involved singlehanded in a war against both Prussia and Austria, the latter skillfully entangled in the operation by Bismarck. Bismarck had correctly judged the English temper; he had no fear of that country "which now always ran away from war and profited by having others pull her chestnuts from the fire," and whose "Premier was an old and toothless lion."[40] Napoleon was talking European congresses, but made no attempt to pull his own or England's chestnuts from the fire. As no one acted and as the Powers did not meet, the war proceeded in isolation to its inevitable end of Danish defeat and eviction from the Duchies.

In itself this was a small enough episode, although there is significance in the failure of Europe to take collective action; as in the case of Italy, the *fait accompli* was simply accepted. But the incident has even greater meaning as the first act in a long and intricate play, the various parts of which are steps in the decline of the Second Empire and of the French position, the story of which can now be resumed.

France and the Making of Germany

If Cavour was an abler man than Napoleon III, Sardinia was a small state and in the last resort he must defer to French power and wishes, even accept Villafranca. In regard to quality of statesmanship Cavour may be ranked as high as Bismarck, but even apart from the asset of longevity granted to the latter and denied to the former, Bismarck commanded the resources of a state which had great power rank, though at this time not rated first on the Continent. The story of the making of united Germany is best told around Bismarck as a center, but the focus of the present treatment lies in the French position. Because of the dramatic turn that the making of Germany signalized for the latter—not so much the specific event that was the Franco-Prussian War as the sharp readjustments of which that war was the initiation—some consideration must be given to the last stages of the accomplishment of German unity.

The tale may also be regarded as in considerable degree that of a contest between two men, Napoleon III and Bismarck. The rivals have been vividly portrayed by de la Gorce:

> In the growing shadow of the years these two figures will emerge from among the secondary ones, and such will be the contrast between them that never will a more striking one have been seen. On one side will appear the hard Chancellor, in the full vigor of his body at the time, in the full ripeness of years, straightly laced in his uniform as befits even the civilian councillors of a military monarchy, conveying in his very features strength, resolution, activity, realistic in his conceptions, even more so in his actions, by turns dissembling to the point of deceit or frank to that of indiscretion, and equally dangerous in his outbursts of sincerity as in the refinement of his craft, equally skillful in invoking right, as in circumventing or transgressing it, and transgressing it with ostentation, contemptuous of larger considerations and sensitive to advantage alone, not a humanitarian, rather narrowly patriotic, more Prussian than German, but also a great Prussian, conveying in a word the full picture of the man who engages in the struggle for life solely concerned with victory for himself, his master and his country. On the other side will appear, in a misty perspective, the weary and worried physiognomy of the feeble yet powerful Emperor, already subject to the first infirmities of decline, already

> troubled lest the results of his long successful errors should not endure, incapable of either adhering to a loyal course or to consistent deception, putting off, whether from fatigue or from indolence, firm resolutions, viewing all things with half-closed eyes that do not penetrate the thoughts of other men nor yet reveal his own, basking in a sort of indifferent impartiality as of a judge or a witness, hovering over the empire instead of governing it.[41]

Such were the men about to engage in a contest for very high stakes.

There is no need to go into the question of whether and how far Bismarck from the beginning envisioned a united Germany, or whether he was above all an opportunistic Prussian bent on the enhancement of Prussian power. A corresponding charge has been made in the case of Cavour. The simple fact remains that the one made Italy, the other Germany. Bismarck was not yet in charge of Prussian affairs at the time of the Franco-Austrian war, but he had counseled caution in the matter of coming to Austria's assistance lest her victory strengthen her hold on the entire Germanic world. Austro-Prussian rivalry had by this time a quite respectable background.

When Bismarck was called to become Minister President of Prussia in 1862, almost in desperation and as a last resort, the reason for that decision was primarily domestic, a clash between the king and the diet over the issue of military appropriations. The cavalier manner in which he dealt with the problem, his simple disregard of the constitution, may be taken as typical measure of the man. For the rest Bismarck was a staunch believer in the existing social order, if by no means a blind and inflexible reactionary when circumstances demanded; his experience so far had mainly been in the diplomatic service, in Frankfort, in St. Petersburg, and in Paris, in which last place in particular he had had an opportunity of taking the measure of the Emperor of the French. Bismarck was also a believer in politics as the art of the possible, in dealing with situations as they arose, though far from incapable of creating opportunities. Bismarck has also, and quite rightly, been associated with the "blood and iron" phrase that he used upon his assumption of office to express his judgment of the course to be adopted in future in contrast with his view of the ineffectualness of 1848.

The Danish war and its outcome had redounded to both French and British discredit. The passive role of England in continental affairs, to a point her abdication, largely continued during the rest of the decade of the sixties and even for some years thereafter under Gladstone's prime ministership.[42] Domestic and imperial affairs—about which more presently—tended to be the focus of English preoccupations. England's abstention gives all the more importance to the role of France; that role, too, albeit in a different way and with highly different consequences, was a role of abstention which left effective leadership in other hands.

There is no question that for all Europe the capital event of the decade was the accomplishment of German unity, clearly in turn the work of Bismarck. The existence of a German people is a simple fact of the European ethnic landscape, and from this point of view German unity may be seen as an inevitable outcome. But in the context of power relationships the emergence of a united German state could not but have incalculable repercussions. On the basis of what constitute the components of power, numbers and resources in the first place, it was bound to create a challenge to the primacy of continental position that had for a long time been France's, while it would also radically affect the position of others.

France's traditional opposition to German unity was a natural and logical policy that all French régimes had pursued, but, given the nineteenth-century force of nationalism, the problem was situated in a novel context. Taking the long-term view, it may be said that the deep underlying reason for the German success and the corresponding French failure was registration of the fact that German unity inserted itself into the mainstream of historic evolution, opposition to which is futile in the last resort. But we are concerned at this point with acts and policies over a brief span. At a particular point of time nothing is fated, and the role of individuals assumes considerable meaning; neither Bismarck nor the third Napoleon were inevitable events.

That the challenge to the French position could be successfully carried out without war did not seem probable to Bismarck.

To be sure, France might have bowed to the long-term inevitable, though it is not the way of power so easily to yield, and even those elements in France generally sympathetic to the national force—they included the emperor himself—found the prospect of German unity far more distasteful than the Italian.

Bismarck may be said to belong to the Frederickian tradition expressed in the observation that war is Prussia's national industry. Certainly that tradition had served Prussia well. Submerged for a time, even disliked and feared by many German nationalists among whom there was little love lost for Prussia, it was Bismarck's task to revive it. To initiate the process with a challenge to France would have been unwise; the inner complexities of the Germanic world must first be resolved.

These complexities derived from the existence of two rival centers of possible leadership, a continuation of the ancient Habsburg-Hohenzollern feud. In the long term again, and in the nineteenth-century context, it is clear that in this case also the advantage lay with Berlin, for Prussia could authentically pose as German while the very nature of Austria was to be antinational. But in the shorter term, that very situation could be a French asset; France, too, could associate herself with the view that Austria ought to have been invented had it not existed. A Franco-Austrian alliance might eventually have suffered from the same vice that was to make the Austro-German so disastrous to the second partner in it, the association with and the hampering commitment to a decadent entity; but this is not the type of long-term consideration which is likely to affect decisions of the moment. The Sick Man of Europe took a whole century to die, and the prospect of Austria's demise did not enter the practical calculations of the international politics of the sixties.

Napoleon III himself had chosen to humble the Habsburgs, to a point yielding to that other, though by this time out-of-date, tradition of French policy which continued to think in terms of rivalry with their house, on that occasion revealing the fundamental vice of the ambiguity of his policy. As to Bismarck, neither did he contemplate Austria's demise, rather agreeing with the view that Austria was a necessary element of Europe, in particular a useful defender of larger Germandom against the disintegrating pressure of various Slavic elements. Bismarck was a *kleindeutscher* who would leave intact the Habsburg domain proper, including German Austria. But in the rest the Gordian knot must be resolutely cut and Austria be made to acknowledge her eviction. This meant undoing the German Confederation.

The above-mentioned Danish war was but an episode in a much larger plan. From the Treaty of Vienna, which put an end to that war, through the deliberately intricate Convention of Gastein in 1865, to the Austro-Prussian War of 1866, the line of development is quite clear as is the skill of Bismarckian direction, for which one can only express high regard. Since wars are fought with armies, adequate preparations and reforms were instituted in Prussia in order to create a tool of appropriate superiority. Bismarck, with reason as the event was to prove, had confidence in this tool, but, of no less importance, the tool must be allowed to operate under favorable circumstances. That was the task of diplomacy, which may be said to have begun with the skillful exploitation of the Polish rising of 1863 and the consequent restoration of amicable relations with the grateful Tsar, to whom Napoleon instead gave irritating moral advice; Bismarck knew how to exploit opportunity, not a very difficult thing in this instance since Prussian and Russian interests ran parallel in Poland. One may note in contrast the Austrian action, similar to the French, with even less foundation.

The main thing was to isolate the coming conflict. Of England there was not too much cause to feel concern. Palmerston to be sure was no longer in office and the foreign secretaryship was now in Clarendon's hands, a man well versed in European affairs and whose stock in the diplomatic community stood high. England no doubt preferred peace and would indeed work for its preservation; she might even offer her mediating services, but the surmise was correct that she would not go the length of direct involvement, especially to prevent a final outcome—German unity—to which English opinion was by this time becoming reconciled, seeing in it no threat to the English position. Clarendon himself fully understood the situation, but he took no positive action, and to make matters easier, his tenure terminated at the crucial final moment, in July 1866. His successor, Stanley, was a far weaker man.

What really mattered was France. Napoleon, too, understood the situation and its future implications. He made a pardonable error of judgment in thinking that an Austro-Prussian conflict could develop in such a fashion as to leave him in an arbitral position: the European balance would be preserved and in the process some advantage might accrue to France. Had not Bismarck thrown out the hint to his (Napoleon's) ambassador that France might expand "Wherever French was spoken in the world"?[43] Thus, when Bismarck went to see Napoleon in Biarritz, in October 1865, he encountered little difficulty. The meeting was a cat-and-mouse game in which the common desire of the participants to avoid making firm commitments made possible a dubious understanding full of reservations on both sides. Bismarck could come away from the interview with reasonable confidence in French neutrality in the initial stages at least.

The ineptitude of French policy, only surpassed by that of Austria, played into his hands after this. It is more credit to Napoleon's heart than to his head that he had on his conscience his failure to have secured Venetia for Italy in 1859. Thus the Venetian question intruded, the complexities of which will not be considered. The outcome, with Napoleon's blessing, was the Prusso-Italian alliance of April 1866.[44]

Yet to the last uncertainties persisted which put to a severe test Bismarck's patience and skill. The vague reassurances given at Biarritz were no formal commitment, and it was clear, from discussions with the Prussian ambassador in Paris, for example, the able Von der Goltz, that if Napoleon acquiesced in Prussian wishes, he expected to receive some reward for his consent. As Napoleon put it at one point to the Prussian envoy, "if only you had a Savoy!"[45] But there was no French-speaking territory in Prussian possession and Bismarck must continue to dangle the prospect of compensations without coming to a precise definition of them.

The drift of things was sufficiently clear to cause alarm in various quarters in France. In the Corps Législatif, on May 3, the discussion of an increase in the armed forces was used by Thiers as occasion for expressing highly critical views. After a lengthy review of the empire's foreign policy and of the problems facing Europe at the moment, he had the following to say:

> What is certain is that, if she [Prussia] is successful in the war, she will absorb some of the northern German states; the rest will have representation in a Diet under her influence.
>
> She will therefore have a part of the German people under her direct authority, and exercise indirect control over the rest, after which Austria will be admitted as a *protégé* in this new order of things.
>
> And then, allow me to say it to you, will be accomplished a great transformation, toward the realization of which things have been moving for a century: we shall witness the making of a new Germanic empire, that empire which was once centered in Vienna, and which now would be focused in Berlin . . . and to complete the parallel, this empire of Charles V, instead of being attached to Spain, as in the fifteenth and sixteenth centuries, would be connected with Italy.

Thiers proceeded to pour scorn on the mean and inconsistent policy which would extract for France some limited territorial compensations, thereby putting his finger on one of the chief weaknesses of the emperor's endeavors, and went on to state the case for the preservation of the European equilibrium, which would be disturbed by the formation of a solid block that would unite all the German people,

> The European equilibrium, said Thiers, consists in the constant care of all nations, in modern times, in watching one another . . . in preventing any one of them from assuming proportions disquieting to the independence of all, and in joining to resist it for the sake of the preservation of an equilibrium of the European forces.[46]

The specific problem of the Duchies, initial source of the dispute, had by now been reduced to secondary importance; Austria was confronted with a Prussian-suggested reorganization of the German Confederation, which amounted to the loss of her influence in that body, as well as with her total eviction from the Italian world. By the time she sought to avoid the war on two fronts it was too late; in exchange for her willingness to yield Venetia she could obtain no more than a French promise of neutrality. She put the final nail in her coffin by taking the initiative of mobilization; this measure, justified by technical considerations, nevertheless played into Bismarck's hands vis-à-vis both German and outside opinion.

Bismarck's diplomacy had succeeded in isolating the conflict, in doing which he had been aided by divergences among the Powers.[47] In producing this condition the turbulent activity of the French emperor bore a fair share of responsibility, a crucial factor being the distrust of his intentions which he had managed to arouse in England: his far-reaching schemes of European reorganization raised the prospect of too many uncertainties, despite his own wholly sincere desire to work in accord with that country. It must be borne in mind that any accretion of French power—a possibility never divorced from other rearrangements—was regarded as undesirable in England, to the extent that the prospect of a united and strong Germany could for the future be regarded as a contribution to stability, a counter to excessive French ambitions.

Once war had broken out, Bismarck's other tool, the military, adequately performed its share of the plan. Events occurred at such speed that the South German states, favorable to Austria despite the advantages that were accruing to them from the Prussian-sponsored economic integration of Germany, the Zollverein, never had an opportunity to make their weight felt. The battle of Sadowa on July 3 was not an easy victory, but in the end it was a victory, and a decisive one. Austria sued for peace.

Bismarck was not insensitive to the wisdom of moderation, just as he could on occasion appreciate the value of truthfulness. At Nikolsburg, where the terms of peace were discussed, it was he who staunchly resisted the king and his generals, who wished to impose humiliating demands upon Austria. The gist of what he asked was very simple, though substantial enough: the dissolution of the Confederation, the non-Habsburg part of which he would proceed to reorganize. Defeated Austria acquiesced, but since the Confederation had been a creation of Europe in 1815 the change contemplated was proper cause for the intrusion of the rest of the Powers in the situation.

This meant three Powers, Britain, Russia, and France, since Italy had not existed in 1815.[48] The first two did not want above all an extension of the war. Gorchakov entertained the idea of joint representations in Berlin on the score of dissolving the Confederation, but a French query, after Sadowa, as to the Russian willingness to use force, brought a wholly negative answer. It was a case of nothing succeeding like success, a fact perhaps best shown by the English reaction, which may be summed up as one of realistic acceptance of the inevitable, at the level of both public and parliamentary opinion. From the lengthy debate on foreign policy in the House of Commons on July 20, the following passage of Stanley's reply to the various opinions that had been expressed may be quoted:

> The Italian question I look upon as not being distant from a fair settlement; and with regard to the other possible results of the war, and especially as to the establishment of a strong North German Power—of a strong compact Empire, extending over North Germany—I cannot see that, if the war ends, as it very possibly may, in the establishment of such an Empire—I cannot see that the existence of such a Power would be to us any injury, any menace, or any detriment. It might be conceivable enough that the growth of such a Power might indeed awaken the jealousy of other Continental States, who may fear a rival in such a Power. That is a natural feeling in their position. That position, however, is not ours, and if North Germany is to become a single great Power, I do not see that any English interest is in the least affected.[49]

France, after all, had been the traditional rival, and England did not feel a threat in the rising Prussian power. It certainly would be unreasonable to expect the England of 1866, powerful and self-confident, to foresee 1914 half a century in advance.

Thus France again was left in a crucial position. Although the emperor was already a sick man, a fact tending to emphasize his congenital tendency to indecision, neither did France in 1866 foresee 1914. There was in fact initially, though only for a very brief time, a not unfavorable reaction to Sadowa in French opinion. Yet Thiers' observation that it was France which had been defeated at Sadowa aptly sums up the situation, as does the judgment: "It is in Bohemia that Prussia had achieved her great military victory: it is with us that she would achieve her great diplomatic victory."[50] The thought of armed intervention was indeed entertained in France after that battle, but only briefly so.[51] There was instead a continuation of what Bismarck properly characterized as the inept and undignified *"politique des pourboires."* Mention has been made of the fact that, already before the outbreak of hostilities, Napoleon had sought to bargain for some compensation toward the Rhine, which Bismarck had finally refused so far as German territory proper might be involved.

The outcome of the war had naturally strengthened Bismarck's position and correspondingly weakened Napoleon's. Still Bismarck must be cautious and avoid larger complications while he proceeded with the implementation of his plan in mid Europe; he lent a willing ear to the proposals of the French ambassador, Benedetti, while he was negotiating with Austria at Nikolsburg. The traditional French policy of preserving the fragmentation of Central Europe might derive some comfort from the terms of the Treaty of Prague, which seemed to create a viable balance of power in that region, since the Habsburg domain was left intact and the independence of the German states south of the Main was assured. Napoleon did not know that treaties of alliance had already been concluded between these states and Prussia; in procuring this result Bismarck could make good use of Napoleon's Rhenish ambitions as evidence of the insincerity of his professed devotion to the continued independence of those states.[52]

In the circumstances of Nikolsburg, and in view of recent precedent, for Benedetti to suggest compensation in the German Rhineland may seem wholly egregious. But if that possibility was excluded others might not necessarily be so. Belgium was hinted at, in connection with which even the possibility of a Franco-Prussian alliance was mentioned;[53] one need only think of the likely English reaction! But a more modest compensation was perceived in Luxembourg; even that might satisfy Napoleon's increasing need to retrieve the glaring failures of his policy, which had by now become apparent to French opinion.

Luxembourg, a possession of the Dutch king, had been part of the German Confederation, a Prussian garrison established in its capital. The reorganization of which the creation of a North German Confederation in 1867 was the expression seemed suitable occasion for a revision of the status of Luxembourg; negotiations between Napoleon and the Dutch king for the purchase of Luxembourg led to an understanding. The latter wished, however, to have the prior consent for the transaction of King William of Prussia. Bismarck had insisted on secrecy, but when the question was raised in the Reichstag he pretended impotence in the face of aroused German national feeling; the Dutch king withdrew from the bargain.

There was a delicate passage, for the incident threatened to take on the color of an affair of honor in which Napoleon was personally involved. But as he had no desire for war, which Bismarck also did not want at this time, face was saved all around by discovering that the Powers in Congress could proceed to a modification of the treaties of 1815. Following the precedent of 1830, King William III of Holland issued an invitation to a congress which met in London in May 1867. Luxembourg, of which King William III continued to be ruler, would no longer be associated with Germany, its Prussian garrison would be withdrawn, instead of which the Grand Duchy would be neutralized. Ostensibly, French honor had been saved, but there were few illusions anywhere about who, in effect, had endured another setback.

Bismarck had no wish for war with France for its own sake, but he had few illusions about the likelihood of completing German unity without such a confrontation, for France would probably not tolerate passively so great a challenge to her own position and interest. His general strategy was the same as in the Austrian case: adequate military preparations on the one hand, while the task of diplomacy would be to isolate the conflict. His plan worked to perfection, aided by luck and by the fact that, in the last stages, France, like Austria four years earlier, played into his hands. Before outlining the story of two years something must be said of the English position; England was aware of continental developments and she was in addition the upholder *par excellence* of the preservation of the European equilibrium.

How European Is England?

That the Franco-Prussian relationship was the main European problem of the time was universally realized and the other

Powers were anxious to avoid a conflict the extension of which might be difficult to prevent. This was especially true of England, but the English role of relative passivity throughout the second half of the sixties, certainly not one of leadership commensurate with what her power could command, has already been mentioned. Gladstone, who became Prime Minister in December 1868, adequately expressed this reticent behavior, while explaining what should, in his view, be the broad bases of English foreign policy:

> I do not believe that England ever will or can be unfaithful to her great tradition, or can forswear her interest in the common transactions and the general interests of Europe. But her credit and her power form a fund which, in order that they may be made the most of, should be thriftily used . . .
>
> . . . .
>
> . . . England should keep entire in her own hands the means of estimating her own obligations upon the various states of fact as they arise; that she should not foreclose and narrow her liberty of choice by declarations made to the Powers . . . that it is dangerous for her to assume alone an advanced and therefore an isolated position, in regard to European controversies; that, come what may, it is better for her to promise too little than too much; that she should not encourage the weak by giving expectations of aid to resist the strong, but should rather seek to deter the strong by firm but moderate language from aggression on the weak; that she should seek to develop and mature the action of a common, or public or European opinion, as the best standing bulwark against wrong, but should beware of seeming to lay down the law of that opinion by her own authority, and thus running the risk of setting against her, and against right and justice, that general sentiment which ought to be, and generally would be, arrayed in their favour.[54]

The stress must be placed on the words "thriftily used." Gladstone may be characterized as a "little Englander," primarily concerned with domestic affairs; it was symbolic and appropriate that he should have come to power as a result of the election which took place after the passage of the Reform Bill of 1867. The discussion of that enlargement of the British electorate, like its predecessor of 1832, had largely filled the horizon of British political interest in this period.

But apart from this emphasis on domestic concerns there is another reason for the relative passivity of Britain's role in Europe's affairs. It was given conscious expression by Gladstone's great rival, himself no "little Englander." After serving in Derby's Cabinet, Disraeli himself became Prime Minister for a brief time, from February to December 1868. It was during the electoral campaign that he expressed the following views:

> The abstention of England from any unnecessary interference in the affairs of Europe is the consequence, not of her decline of power but of her increased strength. England is no longer a mere European Power; she is the metropolis of a great maritime empire, extending to the boundaries of the furthest ocean. It is not because England has taken refuge in a state of apathy that she now almost systematically declines to interfere in the affairs of the Continent of Europe. England is as ready and as willing to interfere as in old days when the necessity of her position requires it. There is no power, indeed, that interferes more than England. She interferes in Asia, because she is really more an Asiatic Power than a European. She interferes in Australia, in Africa, in New Zealand, where she carries on war often on a great scale. Therefore, it is not because England does not recognize her duty to interfere in the affairs of the Continent of Europe that persons are justified in declaring that she has relinquished her imperial position, and has taken refuge in the *otium cum dignitate* which agrees with the decline of life, of power, and of prosperity. On the contrary, she has a greater sphere of action than any European Power, and she has duties devolving upon her on a much larger scale.[55]

Granting that matters imperial were far more congenial to Disraeli than to Gladstone, the judgment nevertheless constitutes a fair appraisal of the dominant orientation of British policy during the period under discussion. There is no need to go into the details of Britain's imperial activity, which would take us too far afield for that matter; a mere mention of its chief accomplishments will suffice. The Crimean War and other Near Eastern developments which have been mentioned are indications of the degree of interest and of a clear and consistent line of action, even though a misjudgment had been made in the case of the

Suez Canal. The Indian Mutiny dates from 1857, followed by the great reorganization of the Indian domain. That event was simultaneous with the difficulties that arose over China and which did not reach a momentary settlement until the Anglo-French occupation of Peking in 1860.[56]

The adjective Anglo-French is worth noting, for it points to an especially important aspect of this discussion. France, unlike England, was first and foremost a continental power, but she, too, had an imperial tradition. In her spreading world-wide commitments England met France and Russia most of all. But whereas opposition to Russia is a fairly stable component of British policy—attempts at understanding either tended to fail or to end in misunderstanding—the Anglo-French relationship has a far more ambivalent character. French power in mid century may no longer have been what it was at its opening, but it was still sufficient to give ample cause for concern, even to the extent of discussing the need to guard against the possibility of French invasion.[57] But that very concern with France and French power also had the contrary effect of creating a desire for non-violent accommodation. That desire was, if anything, even stronger on the French side of the Channel; both Louis Philippe and even more Napoleon III were definitely in favor of a British orientation of French policy. Specific instances are many, of which some have been cited, as well as the good personal relations between Queen Victoria and the two successive French rulers.

Yet on balance these attempts were failures and the emphasis continued to be on difference and rivalry, as it had been for a long time before. Perhaps it may be put this way: both Powers were still too strong to find a common interest, which it would take several more decades to create and to make clear vis-à-vis the rest of the world. From this standpoint the Franco-Prussian War is extremely important because of what it did to French power and to the image of French power. Before returning to it mention may appropriately be made, however, of certain happenings on the American continent.

The French interest in that continent was quite small, certainly by comparison with the British. The Mexican adventure of Napoleon III must be seen as essentially a deviating aberration, and a very ill-advised one at that.[58] England as well as Spain had been involved in the initial stages of the dispute with Mexico, but France was left alone to pursue the conquest of the country. The adventure coincided in time with, and to a point was made possible by, the occurrence of the Civil War in the United States.

The United States at this time had still much to accomplish by way of even internal settlement and did not yet rank with the Great Powers of the day. But others besides Tocqueville, appropriately in England in particular, had developed awareness of the American potential. Both English and French interests had been active in Texas before that territory drifted from Mexico, through independence, finally into the Union. The possibility of fragmentation of North American power was, from the point of view of both England and France, an attractive prospect. Indeed that tended to be the view of the foreign offices which gave sympathetic consideration to recognition of the southern Confederacy. But the English evinced on balance in this case a better understanding than the French.

The combination of French intervention in Mexico and of Napoleon's offer of mediating services between the two American factions had the effect that might be expected. After the defeat of the South, French popularity in Washington reached a low point. British behavior was in contrast characterized by greater caution. There was some friction over happenings at sea: the high-handed American abduction of two representatives of the South from the British vessel *Trent* gave rise to sharp protests and was resolved by an American surrender; the privateering activities of southern raiders fitted out in England resulted in the *Alabama* claims, but these were eventually settled through a British acknowledgment of error and the payment of damages.[59]

This last episode inserts itself into and is an illustration of a major aspect of English policy, long and consistently pursued, which can only be described as a wise, perceptive, and in the end highly rewarding line of conduct. The Wars of Independence and of 1812 had the effect of making an anti-British stance a stock-in-trade of American politics. But this was a misleading view; the Monroe Doctrine is a better expression of the nineteenth-century Anglo-American relationship. At the time of its making that unilateral declaration was not an accurate expression of the possibilities of American power, and the often-made observation that for a long time the reality behind it was the British Navy is correct. The arrangement suited the purposes of English imperial policy. There were indeed points of contact and some friction between England and the United States—the northern boundary of the latter, rivalry of influence around the Central American isthmus—but the emphasis must be on the relative ease with which these issues were settled. It is in fact worth noting the extent to which powerful England proved accommodating, to the point that Palmerston himself was charged with remissiveness in the defense of the British interest in his own Parliament.[60] More will have to be said about the evolution of the Anglo-American relationship which made Canning's bombastic-sounding claim in 1823 no more, in the long term, than perceptive prescience.[61]

The British North America Act, the birth certificate of modern Canada, dates from 1867. It is an important landmark in the development of England's imperial policy, of which again it showed the consistent liberal flexibility. By creating the Dominion of Canada and launching it on the path of self-government, a model to be followed on later occasions and in other cases, England was planting the seeds of an evolutionary process full of the most promising possibilities. For a long time the result was success, accompanied by legitimate and understandable pride; the twentieth-century failures of the endeavor cannot in any way detract from its merits.

But in any event these preoccupations with imperial issues go some distance toward explaining the relative passivity of English policy when it came to continental affairs. To the Continent we must return, and to the closing of a highly important chapter in the French record.

The Franco-Prussian War and Its Significance

The occasion for the final showdown came from an unexpected quarter. In 1868, unstable and ill-governed Spain was the scene of revolution which put an end to the reign of Queen Isabella II. The decision of the constituent Cortes in 1869 to retain the monarchical institution resulted in the search for a candidate to the Spanish crown, the choice finally falling on Prince Leopold of Hohenzollern-Sigmaringen, whose brother Napoleon and Bismarck had jointly aided in attaining the rule of Roumania. But Spain, unlike Roumania, is contiguous to France, and Prince Leopold, though but distantly related to the Prussian king, was a member of the Hohenzollern clan. Again, the nineteenth century was not the sixteenth, and to envisage a revival of the empire of Charles V did not correspond to reality. Nevertheless, dynastic connections still counted, and French objections to the Hohenzollern candidacy were generally considered to be warranted.[62]

These objections did not come until very late, for negotiations had been conducted in understandable secrecy. But the secret was out on July 2, 1870; Bismarck had been no stranger to the whole transaction.[63] It is not unfair to say that Bismarck was by this time desirous of a showdown with France; in contrast, Napoleon III did not want war. A very sick man, he was more concerned with the domestic problem of insuring the continuance of the empire and of his dynasty in France.[64]

The French response to the news of the Hohenzollern candidacy was quite violent, the foreign minister, the Duke de Gramont, delivering in the French Chamber, on the sixth of July, an unnecessarily belligerent speech; there *were* belligerent elements in France. The abandonment of the candidacy might have salved French pride—it was, after all, in the eyes of the world a French diplomatic victory of sorts—had there not been a party which insisted on a further humiliation of Prussia. This was the mission entrusted to the French ambassador, the same Benedetti, whose task it was to extract from King William, vacationing at Ems, a blanket commitment for the future. While the encounters were courteous, the king would not commit himself, reporting to Bismarck in Berlin. That is what gave Bismarck his chance.

The story of the Ems despatch is familiar. It had the predictable effect on both sides of the Rhine. That Bismarck had provoked war is true; yet it is also true that France, like Austria on earlier occasions, had allowed herself to be outmaneuvered, acted with unnecessary intransigeance, and in the end put herself technically in the position of being the aggressor since it was she who took the initiative of a declaration of war, on July 19, 1870.

The war was settled very quickly in its essentials, though it went on for some time owing to the French unwillingness to acknowledge the inevitable. By the time a large French army with the emperor in its midst surrendered at Sedan the fate of arms was decided. The fall of the empire, a provisional government which sought to continue resistance, the siege of Paris, the tragic episode of the Commune, are in the present context but incidents. The Treaty of Frankfort, on May 10, 1871, restored peace. It was an imposed peace—France had no choice—in marked and interesting contrast with the Treaty of Prague, which closed the war of 1866. France was saddled with a heavy, punitive indemnity, though not an impossible one—it was discharged in three years. This was secondary to the territorial annexation which, because of its future consequences, has suitably been characterized as worse than a crime, a blunder. Meantime, as if by way of rubbing salt into the wound, on January 18, 1871, in the great palace of Versailles, King William was proclaimed German Emperor. Bismarck's plan had worked to perfection, though the wisdom of the terms of peace and of the Versailles performance is another question again.

Bismarck's achievement had been once more the fruit of his skill in isolating the conflict. But in doing this he had received considerable assistance from the indecisive ineptitude of French policy. It was entirely logical that, after 1866, France and Austria should seek to make a connection; attempts at an alliance were made. They failed for a variety of reasons, the divergence of interests being one, the internal condition of the reconstructed Dual Monarchy, for example, in which the Magyars found the consequences of the Austrian defeat wholly satisfactory to themselves, with the consequence that when Paris said "Rhine" Vienna tended to reply "Balkans." But there was also the fact that Austria's desire for reassurance on the Italian side ran into a difficulty that was in considerable measure of French making. Italy was not averse to entering a tripartite connection, but her price for it was Rome. One may recall Napoleon's earlier statement that what was needed was "a solution which makes it possible for *me* to claim that you have renounced Rome, while it makes it possible for you [Italians] to claim that you have not,"[65] or Gramont's more pompous way of putting it after the war had already begun, to the effect that "France cannot defend her honor on the Rhine and sacrifice it on the Tiber."[66] There are limits to the value and the possibilities of obfuscating pretense.

This same aspect of French policy had not a little to do with England's abstention, a congenial stance in any event, but strengthened by the distrust of that policy. Designs on the Rhine, even worse on Belgium, were viewed with anxiety in England, and Bismarck skillfully made suitable disclosures in regard to the latter.[67] Even a relatively innocuous scheme for the purchase of Belgian railways had aroused sufficient suspicion in England to cause its abandonment by France in 1869. If the French opposition to the Hohenzollern candidacy in Spain was considered legitimate, by the English and by others, the attempt to push the advantage beyond its relinquishment was not, and, as indicated before, the French initiative in the declaration of war had put France in the wrong.

Once war had broken out these abstentions continued. The initial military defeats effectively disposed of what possibilities there might have been of Austrian and Italian intervention. England was primarily concerned with the neutrality of Belgium, and, in the light of the recent French record, the focus of her suspicions was French rather than Prussian.[68] Napoleon had too successfully conveyed the impression of being a meddler, and his ever recurring proposals of European reorganization raised too many troublesome possibilities, fishing in troubled waters being one. Let Germany unite and constitute thereby a stronger element of stability.[69]

When France found herself isolated and defeated she quite understandably looked abroad for possible assistance. The prospect of other interventions, or even of mediating efforts by a league of the neutrals greatly concerned Bismarck; it was the reason for his annoyance at the French dilatoriness in acknowledging defeat. Thiers' tour of the neutral capitals of Europe met a negative response everywhere; in London he was confronted with a view which may best be summed up as "you were the ones to get yourselves into this situation after all."

French defeats and information about the intended Prussian terms of peace caused in England some shift of feeling,[70] of which Gladstone may be regarded as a spokesman. He was strongly opposed to the territorial annexation without at least a consultation of the people and would have joined in a protest by the neutrals. But he found no support for that position in his Cabinet and, clearly, armed intervention was out of the question. For the rest, any prospects of joint action by the neutrals were destroyed by the raising of an Anglo-Russian issue. In October 1870 the Russians denounced the demilitarization provisions of the Black Sea which had been imposed upon them by the Treaty of Paris. Who but England could say them nay? And England had no inclination to resist by force. Russia therefore had her way, and the most that could be done in the circumstances was to save the face of legality by ratifying in conference a modification of the Treaty of Paris, which was done in London in March 1871.

Bismarck was entirely willing to underwrite Russia's wishes—this was part of the price for her neutrality—which had the advantage of constituting an obstacle to the possibility of Anglo-Russian understanding. But he made it quite clear that he would not allow any other questions, the current war above all, to be brought up at the conference, participation of a French representative in which, he opposed.[71] The British role in the episode was essentially one of acquiescence.

For the major part of the duration of the second French empire, certainly after the Crimean War, the English role in European affairs had been one of relative effacement, certainly if one thinks of the primacy of power that was England's. The reasons for this abstention were various, domestic and imperial in large measure, to a degree reflection of the personalities in charge of the direction of English policy; Bismarck took the correct measure of England and of her probable failure to respond to his own initiatives. As a consequence, one may speak of a certain decrease of British influence in Europe. But in a sense this may be said not to have mattered, for no one entertained any doubts about the ultimate reserves of British power. It would not be long before Britain, deciding to assert herself, had her way.[72]

Actually, the real leadership of Europe, especially during the sixties, was neither British nor French. Berlin, where Bismarck was in control, rather than London or Paris, was the true directing center of the international politics of Europe. But the English case is very different from the French, for two reasons: because of the intense, even if misdirected, activity of the French emperor, in combination with the place of power that was acknowledged to France; because that very activity terminated in a significant displacement of the French position and had the consequence of opening an entirely new chapter for Europe as a whole. The Franco-Prussian War had no particular effect on the British position, in the record of which the date 1870, in the immediate sense, has no special significance.

Thus the French role remains, even in failure, a leading, or at least a crucial, one. The judgment of the place of Napoleon III must be severe, however good his intentions; Professor Renouvin has summed it up well:

> It [French policy] contributed directly to the eclipse of Russia. By its role in the Italian question it weakened Austria and encouraged a German national movement to the advantage of Prussia. It allowed the Prussian victory in 1866. Is it possible to perceive in these actions a coherent line, a calculated design?
>
> Up to July 1859 the policy of the Emperor seems to have a program the various aspects of which have a logical connection with each other: to weaken Russia and Austria was to remove obstacles to a "revisionist" policy; collaboration with Britain, or treating her with caution, was, in the mind of the Emperor, the way to neutralize a possible opposition to this policy.
>
> But between the end of July 1859 and the end of 1863 does Napoleon III have a plan? He allows the development of the Italian national movement, thinking however of checking it without letting it reach its normal objective, which is Rome. By the commercial treaty of 1862 he strengthens the economic weapon of which Prussia disposes in the German question; but he does not want German unity, which he would stop at the Main. How does he expect to remain in control of these movements which he had encouraged? On the other hand he abandons, in part, his regard for British interests: while giving Great Britain a satisfaction from the economic point of view with the commercial treaty of 1860, he embarks upon extra-European expansion, threatens English preponderance in the Mediterranean, takes position in favor of

an independent Poland, which would be a client of France, raises the prospect of vast territorial rearrangements on the continent. Thus the government of London is led to regard the danger of a French hegemony as the more serious one. Finally, in connection with the Polish question, the Emperor threatens directly Russian interests. Yet at no time does he have an armed force adequate to the implementation of such vast schemes, for he does not attempt to impose the necessary sacrifices upon a public opinion of the critical attitude of which he is aware.

In 1866 he gathers the fruit of his imprudence: in the face of an eventuality he had not foreseen—the Prussian victory of Sadowa—he is helpless. To aid Austria with armed force would be to deny all his policy so far and to acknowledge that he has been mistaken. The abstention of Great Britain and that of Russia which are, in considerable measure the result of his own initiatives, does not make it possible for him to exert an effective pressure on Prussia. Thereafter the Emperor's policy is one of drift at the mercy of events . . .[73]

The point made in this assessment, of the insufficiency of military power, is worth stressing. Clearly, the resources of France were not equal to those of the rest of Europe combined, even without taking England into account. But they were considerable, and Napoleon III's feeling that he held an arbitral position was not wholly devoid of warrant. What France would do was a question of the highest importance for all. Bismarck was fully aware of this; as he put it to the Italian envoy in Berlin, just before the conclusion of the Prusso-Italian alliance in April 1866, "all our arrangements are, it is understood, only valid if France agrees to them, for if she showed opposition nothing could be done."[74]

To make full and effective use of French power, to use that power in order to induce others to comply with its wishes—the ultimate test of the effectiveness of power—two things would have been necessary. First, Napoleon should have emulated Bismarck's policy in Prussia insofar as that policy aimed at the mobilization of the country's potential, in the last resort the creation of an adequate armed force; secondly, that armed force should be under competent leadership.

But the first possibility was always circumscribed by the physical limitations of national resources, numbers, and wealth, above all. In addition, the sword is of little value unless used by competent hands. This is where the task of diplomacy comes into its own. The second French empire, especially during the second decade of its existence, furnishes a prime example of power inadequately used, of the degree of importance that must be attached to the political aspect of international relations. Diplomacy cannot create power that does not exist, though it can go an appreciable distance toward nullifying the asset of concrete resources. Given a set of what one might call objective conditions, the material bases of power, the range remains considerable of the possibilities of its accomplishments, whether in the positive form of enhancement or in the negative one of detrimental results.

France was diminished and displaced as a consequence of the Franco-Prussian War; she was not destroyed any more than Germany was to be half a century later. How she endeavored to adapt herself to the changed circumstances, by what means, and with what success, will be examined in the next section of this book.

The end of this particular tale has been told. For Europe as a whole, the relations among its component parts, the Franco-Prussian War was the capital event of the century enclosed between the conclusion of the first Napoleonic episode and the outbreak of the First World War. Though the quip is apt that Europe gained a master at the cost of losing a mistress, the war had this significance not so much because of the defeat and attendant fall of the French stock as because Europe saw a new body appearing in its midst which was destined to be launched upon a course as unforeseen by itself as by others at the time of its birth. That central fact was to determine in the end the positions and the relations of others to it and to each other. The continued decline of the French position, to be followed before long by a beginning awareness in Britain that the British position was no longer what it had been, will also be examined next; Britain's position for a time was very different from France's. But before looking at the record of these two states it is worth pausing to examine the changes taking place over an extended period in some of the fundamental components of their respective power.

NOTES ON *Chapter III*

1. Guérard, Albert, *Napoleon III; a Great Life in Brief* (1955), p. 2.
2. Ibid., p. 20.
3. Taylor, A. J. P., *The Italian Problem in European Diplomacy 1847–1849* (1934), p. 6. The persistent attempt to recover the losses imposed by the second Treaty of Paris of 1815, at the time of Belgian independence, for example, as well as on subsequent occasions, was an expression of the French discontent. It may be pointed out that the creation of Belgium itself amounted to a significant revision of the anti-French provisions of the settlement of 1815 and that in any event the real substance of the French grievances was small.
4. Reported in Senior, Nassau W., *Conversations with MM. Thiers, Guizot and other Distinguished Persons,* 2 vols. (1878), Vol. II, p. 288.
5. The implication of the numeral was the assertion of the legitimacy of the Napoleonic claim to the rule of France. The Tsar refused to adopt the customary form of address among rulers, "my brother," with Napoleon III, using instead "my dear friend." Napoleon had no desire to make an issue of the matter and deftly turned the slight aside with the quip that one does not choose one's relatives but can choose one's friends.
6. The literature on the Crimean War is extensive. Convenient treatment of it in English may be found in *CHBFP,* Vol. II, Ch. VIII; Marriott, J. A. R., *The Eastern Question* (1940), Ch. X; Temperley, H. W. V., *England and the Near East: the Crimea* (1936), and Henderson, G. B., *Crimean War Diplomacy* (1947). In French, Guichen, Eugène de, *La Guerre de Crimée (1854–1856) et l'attitude des puissances européennes* (1936), may be cited.
7. The text of the Nesselrode memorandum may be found in Albrecht-Carrié, op. cit., pp. 154–57.
8. British opinion in the Cabinet was divided, Aberdeen, Clarendon, the foreign minister, and Palmerston, now home secretary, representing different tendencies, a situation which contributed to a lack of clarity in the British position. This, and Lord Stratford de Redcliffe's decisive stand in Constantinople, is what gave rise to Russian charges of British duplicity as well as to intra-British accusations, mainly directed at de Redcliffe.
9. Austria never participated in hostilities though she joined the Western alliance in December 1854 and went the length of an ultimatum to Russia a year later. Her restraint was partly due to fear that Prussia might take advantage of her involvement. As a concession to her, Russia evacuated the Principalities, into which Austrian forces moved, and this situation in turn, separating the belligerents, had the effect that the Crimea became the battleground.
10. The charge of the Light Brigade is sufficiently familiar. General Bugeaud's observation, "It is magnificent, but it is not war," may also

be cited, as well as MacMahon's, *"J'y suis, j'y reste,"* at the capture of the Malakoff tower.

11. One reason why the Sardinian intervention was favored by England.

12. The initial election had been admittedly attended by gross abuses.

13. When Couza ran into difficulty the Powers found a new ruler for Roumania in the person of Prince Charles of Hohenzollern-Sigmaringen, a choice essentially arranged between Napoleon III and Bismarck. Prince Charles received his formal investiture from the Sultan, and the last remaining servitudes were not removed from Roumania until 1878.

14. See Chapter II.

15. In 1842 the Sultan had accepted a scheme, drafted by Stratford de Redcliffe, which gave administrative autonomy to the various religious communities. After 1845 direct Turkish control was restored, Turkish policy being largely one of divide and rule among these groups. The Statute of the Lebanon, agreed upon between the Powers and the Sultan in 1861 provided peace and good administration thereafter until 1914.

16. It is too early to speak at this time of the West African empire, which it would be the task of the Third Republic to create. The seeds of it nevertheless were planted, as witnessed by the southern extension of the Algerian conquest and by activity in Senegal. See Julien, C. A., *Histoire de l'Afrique du Nord* (1913), and Bernard, A., *Algérie* (1930).

17. Except for the interval between February 1858 and June 1859 during which Derby was Prime Minister.

18. Bell, op. cit., Vol. II, p. 357. It should be borne in mind that this statement was made in the context of increasing French naval armaments, of the Italian situation, and also of the conclusion of the Cobden-Chevalier treaty, not to mention the recent Indian Mutiny and the consequent reorganization of India.

19. Talk of a canal had been in the air for some time. Mehemet Ali was on the whole opposed to it, for fear of international complications, and so was his successor, Khedive Abbas (1848–54), but Khedive Mohammed Said, who came to power in 1854, was more amenable to Western penetration.

20. Out of an issue of 400,000 shares 86,000 were reserved for the Khedive and for Egyptians. Of the remainder, only 219,000 shares were initially bought, 207,000 of them in France. There were still genuine doubts about the financial soundness of the undertaking. On the story of the Suez Canal, see Hallberg, Charles W., *The Suez Canal. Its History and Diplomatic Importance* (1931), and Wilson, Arnold T., *The Suez Canal* (1939).

21. *Bismarck, the Man and the Statesman; being The Reflections and Reminiscences of Otto, Prince von Bismarck,* 2 vols. (1898), Vol. I, p. 213.

22. It is all very well to assert, as Palmerston and others have done, that if Austria had not existed it should have been invented; and it may even be granted that the Habsburg state stood for a higher and in some respects more civilized concept than the crude one of self-determination. This is essentially as irrelevant as would be bemoaning the rising of the mass. In political terms, the nineteenth-century spread of democracy and of nationalism in Europe both stem from the assertion

of the Rights of Man, the deeper roots of which should perhaps be seen in the scientific and technological development of the preceding age.

23. The rise of these movements may be followed in some of the general treatments of the history of the period. Among a wealth of works the following may be indicated for the convenience of the interested reader: Bourgin, Georges, *La Formation de l'unité italienne* (Paris, 1929); Smith, D. Mack, *Italy* (Ann Arbor, 1959); Pinson, Koppel S., *Modern Germany* (New York, 1954); Taylor, A. J. P., *The Course of German History* (New York, 1946).

24. 1848 killed the prospects of either papal or Mazzinian leadership as a possible road to unity, leaving the field clear for the Piedmontese solution. The Statuto of 1848 in Piedmont confirmed this tendency, especially in view of the close alliance between liberalism and nationalism in Italy.

25. See above, p. 87.

26. The alias used by Cavour on his trip to Plombières.

27. The Plombières scheme was transformed into formal alliance in December.

28. Cited in Pingaud, Albert, "La Politique extérieure du second Empire," *Revue Historique,* 1927, Vol. CLVI, p. 47. This article incidentally constitutes an interesting analysis of Napoleon III's foreign policy throughout his reign.

29. Savoy being of French speech, its incorporation into France fitted the application of the principle of nationality. The case of the county of Nice, which for that matter was not initially included in the proposed territorial cession, was less clear. The annexation was ratified by plebiscites in both cases.

30. The phrase subsequently coined, "we have made Italy, all that remains to do is to make Italians," is apt summation of the problems of the future Italy. But it must also be recognized that, if much of the population were passive bystanders to these events, once they had happened no significant support was to be found for a return to the *status quo ante.*

31. The French side of the Zurich negotiations may be followed in *Le Conferenze e la Pace di Zurigo nei documenti diplomatici francesi,* Serie 3, 1848–1860, Vol. I (11–12 luglio 1859–24 giugno 1860), edited by Armando Saitta (Rome, 1965).

32. After Villafranca Cavour had resigned in high dudgeon but he resumed the prime ministership the following January. He thus guided the final stages of Italian unification, and had been no stranger to all the developments that led to it.

33. In March 1860, after the above-mentioned plebiscites.

34. The vicissitudes of the efforts of papal diplomacy can be followed in the *Carteggio Antonelli-Sacconi (1858–1860)*, 2 vols., edited by Mariane Gabriele (Rome, 1962). Just because he was dependent on French force the Pope had no choice but to yield to French pressure for increasing concessions on his part. The pamphlet *Le Pape et le Congrès,* which appeared in December 1859 and created a considerable sensation at the time, was good indication of the direction of Napoleon III's wishes and policy, he himself having been the inspirer of it.

35. Renouvin, op. cit., Vol. V, Part I, p. 315.

36. English policy in this matter may be followed in *CHBFP,* Vol. II,

Ch. X. See also, Seton-Watson, R. W., *Britain in Europe, 1789–1914* (1937), Chs. X, XI.

37. Until October 1865, except for the interval of the Derby ministry.

38. The same happened in 1860, when Lord Russell expressed alarm and strong opposition to a similar suggestion set forth in a pamphlet thought to have been inspired by Napoleon III. See the above-cited article of Pingaud, p. 26.

39. The episode may be followed in Steefel, L. D., *The Schleswig-Holstein Question* (1932). Bismarck made good use of it, just as he skillfully exploited the subsequent occasion of the Polish rebellion. See below, p. 124.

40. Bell, op. cit., Vol. II, p. 365.

41. La Gorce, Pierre de, *Histoire du Second Empire,* 7 vols. (1895–1905), Vol. IV (1899), p. 598.

42. The Prime Ministers after Palmerston were: Russell (Nov. 1865–Jun. 1866), Derby (Jul. 1866–Feb. 1868), Disraeli (Feb.–Dec. 1868), Gladstone (Dec. 1868–Feb. 1874). The foreign office was held in succession by Clarendon (Nov. 1865–Jul. 1866), Stanley (Derby) (Jul. 1866–Dec. 1868), Clarendon (Dec. 1868–Jul. 1870), Granville (Jul. 1870–Feb. 1874).

43. Cited in Taylor, A. J. P., *The Struggle for Mastery in Europe* (1954), p. 158.

44. As there was no excess of trust on the part of the Italians, Napoleon III went the length of reinsuring Italy in the event that she should be left to face Austria alone.

45. La Gorce, op. cit., Vol. IV, p. 601.

46. Thiers, A. *Discours parlementaires de M. Thiers,* publiés par M. Calmon, 16 vols. (1879–89), Vol. X (1881), pp. 617–21.

47. On the score of the problem of the Duchies, Bismarck's action should have created a common front between Russia, Britain, and France, but Franco-Russian divergence over Poland prevented this.

48. Militarily, Italy did poorly in the war, suffering defeats both on land and at sea, but her diversion of Austrian force had been an important factor at Sadowa.

49. Hansard's *Parliamentary Debates,* Third Series, Vol. CLXXXIV, p. 1256.

50. La Gorce, op. cit., Vol. V (1901), p. 34.

51. The concentration of Prussian forces in Bohemia at this point would have made a French intervention a highly dangerous thing for Prussia. One consideration on the French side was the current French involvement in Mexico.

52. Incautiously, Benedetti had written to Bismarck indicating the possibility of some French acquisition in the Rhineland, a document of which Bismarck made skillful use.

53. In this case also, Benedetti gave Bismarck a draft project of a treaty between France and Prussia (La Gorce, op. cit., Vol. V, pp. 68–69). That, too, was put to good use by Bismarck when the time came.

54. Gladstone's memorandum for the Queen, April 17, 1869, cited in *CHBFP,* Vol. III, p. 21.

55. Ibid., pp. 9–10.

56. Much of the decade of the fifties, the time of the Tai Ping Rebellion, was filled with haggling and disputes between China and the

Powers, degenerating into hostilities at certain points. The refusal to admit foreign diplomats in Peking led to the occupation of that city by an Anglo-French force.

57. See above, note 18.

58. Certainly the description of it as *La grande pensée de Napoléon III*, the title of Christian Schefer's book (1939), presents an indefensible view.

59. The bases for the settlement of this and various other Anglo-American disputes were laid in the Treaty of Washington in May 1871. The specific issue of the *Alabama* claims was settled in 1872 through the award, by an international commission that met in Geneva, of a payment of $15,000,000 by Britain for the damages inflicted by Confederate raiders.

60. Palmerston, out of office at the time, was highly critical of the Webster-Ashburton Treaty of 1842, which settled the northeastern frontier of the United States. He was countered by Peel with the rejoinder that his own [Palmerston's] earlier concessions were responsible for the nature of the treaty. Cf. Bell, op. cit., Vol. I, p. 335.

61. The importance of the Anglo-American relationship, which would assume particularly great significance in connection with the decline of British power in the twentieth century will be examined in Chapter VI.

62. Independently of the specific issue of the candidacy to the Spanish crown, Franco-Prussian tension had been mounting. In February 1870 Clarendon had sought to induce Bismarck to reduce Prussia's armaments, arguing France's pacific intentions and likely willingness to follow suit. Nothing came of his efforts.

63. Prince Leopold had been hesitant and in the failure of endorsement by King William, who was desirous of avoiding the foreseeable complications, declined the offer at first, but in July was induced to change his mind.

64. Yielding to growing opposition Napoleon III instituted significant constitutional changes in 1869 and 1870, which were widely endorsed in a plebiscite in May of the latter year, tantamount to giving the liberalized empire a new lease on life.

65. Renouvin, op. cit., Vol. V, Part I, p. 330.

66. Ibid., p. 388.

67. The draft treaty dealing with Belgium and the possibility of a Franco-Prussian alliance, which Benedetti had given to Bismarck in 1866, was published in *The* [London] *Times* on July 25, a week after the outbreak of war.

68. Gladstone's first care was to procure treaties with both France and Prussia in regard to Belgium, whose neutrality was respected by the belligerents.

69. The view that it was Germany's role to prove "a light to lighten the Gentiles, and to have a future more beautiful than any other nation's past," as Sir Robert Morier wrote to Baron Stockmar, expresses a widespread feeling in England at the time. Wemyss, Rosslyn, *Memoirs and Letters of the Right Honorable Sir Robert Morier*, 2 vols. (1911), Vol. I, p. 162.

70. An interesting and enlightening account is that given in the just cited memoirs of Sir Robert Morier. Morier's descriptions of conditions

and feelings in Alsace, which he visited during the war, is an excellent report on that much-debated problem. He himself, highly sympathetic to Germany and things German in general, came to the conclusion that the annexation was a mistake.

71. As a signatory of the Treaty of Paris France was obviously entitled to be represented at its revision. A French representative attended the last two meetings of the conference, but to the end Bismarck interposed difficulties in his reaching England.

72. For the Near Eastern crisis of the seventies, see below, pp. 189 ff.

73. Renouvin, op. cit., Vol. V, Part I, pp. 396–97.

74. La Gorce, op. cit., Vol. IV (1899), p. 597.

PART TWO

Disparity and Convergence

(1871–1904)

IV

TAKING STOCK

A general indication was given in the opening chapter of the components which go into the making of that elusive resultant, power. The reader may be reminded that the central focus of this entire analysis lies in the observation of the operation of that factor, specifically of its manifestations in the foreign policies of two states, Britain and France. As a consequence, a minimum of attention has been, and will be, given to tracing in detail the variations of those underlying elements on which the power basis rests. Nevertheless, that aspect of the problem, a crucial one since power is not an abstraction, ever remains in the background and must therefore be borne in mind. The less easily measurable components of power, the "imponderables," will also be given attention. That is the reason for the present chapter, the purpose of which is briefly to call attention to certain fundamentals. It is desirable to do this in order to retain a proper perspective and an adequate sense of proportion.

If we think of the power of our two principals in the period that has been surveyed so far, the first half of the nineteenth century, as represented by two curves, these would appear to follow paths of divergence, made especially clear by the advantage of the perspective that the passage of a century has furnished. The general acknowledgment of the primacy of British power was no more than sound appraisal of a fact. That condition found suitable expression in the British feeling of self-confidence, of which Palmerston may be regarded as the most flamboyant embodiment; usually moderate in its aims and in the mode of its behavior, British power could at times resort to arrogant manifestations. The Great Exposition of 1851 was a fitting display of the standing of Britain in the world, and the curve of British power continued in the ascendant thereafter. If the period of the second French empire was one during which British policy seemed relatively passive, often leaving initiatives in French hands, this meant no diminution or consciousness of decline on Britain's part, but was rather due to the generally pro-British orientation of the policy of the French emperor and to the supreme confidence that Britain felt in herself, no less than to the fact that much of her attention was diverted toward the wide world outside of Europe. The Franco-Prussian War had no perceptible impact on Britain or her standing; in her eyes there could even be some merit in the humbling of France, while the new Germany was not regarded as a threat, either actual or potential.

The curve of the French power position followed a different course during the same period. If the acknowledgment of the continental primacy of France after 1815 was also sound appraisal, the impression of French power was an exaggeration. This has been pointed out, and Guizot's judgment in 1839[1] was a more correct estimate of the possibilities of that power; the asset of the revolutionary ideology was a very special, and a transitorily distorting, condition. Thus we may speak at best in the French case of a plateau of power, though in effect there was relative decline; Napoleon III also judged correctly when he decided that the capabilities of French power did not warrant its contemplating the possibility of war simultaneously on the Po and the Rhine.

The Franco-Prussian War laid bare the deficiencies of French power, yet its outcome again produced a distorted image. By the objective criterion of material assets the war was a fair match, and to understand its outcome one must resort to an examination of the momentary deficiencies of French power, the faulty management of it by comparison with the superior quality of the German performance, in other words, to the special circumstances of the conflict. It is only because of later developments that the mistaken tendency is often found to read back into 1870 the conditions of 1914, not to mention those of 1940.

That the new Germany should displace France in the place of continental primacy after 1870 was a natural result of the outcome of the confrontation. But if there was in that year no catastrophic decrease of the concrete elements of French power, the Franco-Prussian War nevertheless did two things: it exploded, for one, the image of French primacy; for another, it initiated a period at the end of which, by 1914, the curve of French power had indeed suffered a very sharp decline.

Until 1914 Britain would generally have still been granted first place of power standing by others. But in relative terms the picture had considerably altered in the British case as well as in the French. Britain's primacy no longer seemed beyond challenge, the margin of British power over some others having been very seriously eroded. The consciousness of altered position, inevitably sharper at the directing level than in the British mass, was but reluctantly acknowledged; yet we shall have occasion to examine the British attitude toward the United States, the alliance with Japan, and most of all the understanding with France, all of which are properly to be interpreted as registrations of the British decline.

Thus if we return to our graphs of the power positions, the period of the second half of the century, from the Franco-Prussian War to the First World War—1880 might be a better date to choose in the British case if a specific date must be chosen—is one during which both curves follow parallel downward trends, the declivity being markedly sharper in the French than in the British case. The curves would not yet intersect, but the similarity of their directions warrants speaking of convergence, a tendency even more marked after the First World War, until after the Second a case could be made for the achievement of rough parity of positions.

The relativity of these positions must be borne in mind, for in absolute terms, numbers or wealth, there was everywhere increase. For that reason, therefore, and since we are concerned with the standing of two countries in the world community of states rather than with the Anglo-French relationship alone or as such, the place of others must be brought into the picture. Essentially this means no more than two others, Germany and the United States, the former above all, for the latter was still basking in the comparative innocence of isolation, involved in but minimal fashion in the broad scheme of world affairs. Japan and Russia were still waiting in the wings, only beginning to lay the foundations for the roles and positions which the mid twentieth century would make theirs. Returning once more to our graph of power curves, both the German and the American, be it in absolute or in relative terms, would appear to be characterized by steeply ascending gradients.

We are not concerned here with an analysis of causal factors, being content to register results. In observing these manifestations of change, as in the earlier discussion, it will be convenient to divide our survey under the two rubrics of the concrete, the material and measurable first, to be followed by some consideration of the imponderables, meaning by this those elements that do not lend themselves to quantitative measurement.

The Measurable Components of Power

Other things being equal, a larger fighting force may be expected to defeat a smaller. In actual fact those "other things" are seldom equal. Nevertheless the importance of numbers, be it as fighting men or as units of productive labor, can never be ignored. Something therefore must be said of the changes in the populations of the countries of Europe and some others.

The numbers of the Germany about to be made in connection with the Franco-Prussian War were not significantly larger than those of the French when that conflict broke out. The correlation has often been pointed out between the long-term record of the French position in Europe and the fact that, until the closing decade of the eighteenth century, France had the largest population of any European country. Throughout the following century the rate of the French growth shows a steady decline, and this became especially marked during the second half of the period, in which respect the French case is unique, a uniqueness reflected in the age distribution of the population that is a consequence of stagnant numbers. The French were increasingly an older people than others.

Where numbers are concerned France was successively passed by Germany, by Austria-Hungary, and by Britain; by the time of the First World War it was a safe prediction that before long there would be more Italians than Frenchmen. The appended table sums up these changes; the Russian and the American growths were markedly greater than any of the European countries.

POPULATION IN MILLIONS[2]

	1850	*1880*	*1890*	*1900*	*1910*
France	36.5	39.2	40.0	40.7	41.5
United Kingdom	22.3	31.1	34.3	38.2	42.1
Germany	31.7	40.2	44.2	50.6	58.5

The discrepancy would be even more marked if one should take account of emigration. Substantial numbers went abroad from both Britain and Germany, many to the United States, where by the end of the century the stream of European emigration was increasingly fed from southern and eastern Europe as well. France stood in sharp contrast with the rest, her native rate of reproduction hardly sufficient to maintain her numbers, which kept their level owing in part to the influx of outsiders. The situation was correspondingly reflected in the density of her population, markedly lower than the British, the German, or the Italian.

Under the practice of universal military service the impact of this state of affairs became a source of increasing concern to the French people. They managed to maintain an Army of comparable size to the German, but only at the cost of resorting to such devices as lower physical standards. This condition of growing numerical inferiority makes easy to understand the satisfaction with which the Russian alliance was contemplated in France, offering as it did the prospect of vast manpower resources, the famous Russian steam-roller; it also explains the emphasis put by France on the use of colonial recruits. Likewise it explains why the reversal of the demographic trend after the Second World War takes on so considerable a significance where France is concerned.

The British case was different. As a consequence of the accident of geography, Britain was able to dispense with conscription; volunteers and native recruits amply sufficed to meet the demands of even imperial expansion. A navy makes relatively small demands on numbers and Britain was content with maintaining her naval supremacy, even if on occasion she allowed herself to become somewhat negligent in that respect. Instances have been, and will be, mentioned of occasional invasion scares in England.

These were generally induced by French action, until Germany, at the very end of the century, decided that her future lay on the water. Ten years earlier Britain had adopted the two-power standard, but she was mainly thinking at the time of the possibility of having to confront the combined navies of France and Russia.

Military and naval establishments are expensive, and the improvements of technology have had the effect of ever raising their costs. Increasingly therefore the power of a nation becomes in the long run dependent upon its economic resources and the degree of their development, especially the level of its industry. Here lay the ultimate key to Britain's power, in her ability to finance wars and coalitions, the reason, for example, why she, more than any other single Power, had been the instrument of the downfall of Napoleon. The advantage that Britain enjoyed from the priority of her development will not be emphasized again. By 1870, if Britain was by far the prime industrial state in the world, industry was well launched on its eastward and southward course of expansion outside the British Isles; the period of the second French empire may be regarded as that of the industrial "take off" of continental Europe.

The second half of the nineteenth century is often spoken of as the time of the second industrial revolution. The characterization is warranted by the rate of growth of the existing industries as well as by the appearance of new ones, be it in the use of new materials or the advent of novel sources of power. The overall effect of these changes may be summed up as an increasingly serious challenge to the British position of primacy and a very real decline in France's position, somewhat comparable in her case to that of her demographic stagnation.

A few illustrations will suffice to bring out in concrete form the alteration of relative positions. Iron and coal had been the basic materials of industry. Their importance continued in the Age of Steel and in spite of the other developments just indicated. The following table sums up the record between 1870 and 1914:

PRODUCTION OF COAL
(*millions of metric tons*)[3]

	United Kingdom	*France*	*Germany*	*United States*	*World*
1871	117.4	12.9	29.3	42.5	230.0
1913	292.0	40.8	190.1	571.1	1,214.4

The continuing importance of the British position, still the first in Europe, stands out no less than the relative decline of that position and the extent to which France was falling behind the rest of the industrialized world. One is impressed likewise by the absolute figures, and even more by the rates of the German and the American growths. A similar picure is conveyed by the figures for iron and steel:

PRODUCTION OF PIG IRON
(*thousands of metric tons*)[4]

	United Kingdom	*France*	*Germany*	*United States*	*World*
1870	6,060	1,198	1,391	1,692	12,259
1890	8,033	1,970	4,637	9,353	27,630
1910	10,380	4,032	14,793	27,636	66,210

PRODUCTION OF STEEL
(*thousands of metric tons*)[5]

	United Kingdom	*France*	*Germany*	*United States*	*World*
1870	286	83	169	68	703
1890	3,637	566	2,161	4,346	12,096
1910	6,374	3,506	13,698	26,512	58,656

That German steel production should pass the British at the turn of the century was apt symbolic expression of the shifting positions of the two countries. One will note in passing the gigantic dimensions of the American expansion and the proportion of the world's total production accounted for by the four countries listed.

The textile, especially the cotton, industry is one that usually appears among the first manifestations of industrial development.

It was, along with coal and iron, one of the fundamental bases of the British standing. Between 1867 and 1913 the number of cotton spindles in that country grew from 34,000 to 55,576. During this interval, against a nearly static condition in France—an increase from 6,800 to 7,400—there stood a German expansion from 2,000 to 11,000.[6] Between these last two countries the discrepancy is smaller in the growth of the use of power, rising during the three decades between 1875 and 1907 from 949,000 to 6,500,000 hp in the German case, from 401,000 to 2,474,000 in the French.[7]

Britain was well established in the nineteenth century as the prime trading nation in the world, increasingly and more than any other concerned with and dependent on the whole world, both as a source of raw materials, wheat and cotton, for example, and as a market for her manufactures. World trade expanded greatly during the second half of the century in keeping with the indices of growth just indicated. Between 1860 and 1900 the total of world commerce nearly tripled, from $7,200,000,000 to $20,100,000,000, and doubled again in the remaining years before the war. It is revealing to note the changing proportions of that trade that went to different countries:

DISTRIBUTION OF WORLD TRADE IN PERCENTAGE[8]

	United Kingdom	*France*	*Germany*	*United States*
1860	25	11		9
1880	23	11	9	10
1900	21	8	12	11
1913	17	7	12	15

Economic growth meant increasing wealth. Between 1875 and 1914 the national income of the United Kingdom roughly doubled, that of Germany growing by a factor of three. This wealth was, to be sure, unequally distributed though the standard of living shows a generally rising trend everywhere. The accumulation of wealth caused capital to seek further outlets for its profitable employment. A considerable portion of the American growth was financed by British capital, which, however, flowed to other parts of the world as well. From 1870 to 1900 British investments abroad grew by a factor of three, from four to twelve billion dollars; they had increased by a further 50 per cent by 1914, about one third of the total being in the British Empire.

The French case in this respect is interesting. Though France fell to the rank of a poor fourth among industrial states before 1914, the French capacity for saving seemed considerable. The payment of the indemnity of 1871 was managed with relatively little difficulty and without injury to French credit. The government was surprised at the success of the loans that it launched, that of 1872, for 3,000,000,000 francs, being oversubscribed thirteen times.[9] By 1914 the French foreign investment amounted to some $9,000,000,000, a quarter of it having gone into Russia. Germany was comparatively laggard in this respect, her situation, if on a smaller scale, resembling the American, where internal growth absorbed much of the available capital. But by 1914 Germany had achieved the respectable total of $6,000,000,000 in foreign investment.

Here again the case of France presents some special aspects. The point has often been made that France's failure to develop her domestic industrial potential to the same degree as other industrial states has been for her a source of weakness. Whatever the reasons for this French behavior, rooted in social and psychological conditions in the last analysis, the fact that one fourth of France's foreign investment went to Russia against a mere tenth to her colonies bespeaks political direction, which was indeed the case. In any event there is no doubt that French wealth was an important component of French power, a factor in her case that went to compensate in part at least for other deficiencies.

The French badly neglected their maritime development though not the construction of railways.[10] French merchant tonnage amounted to 1,000,000 tons in 1870, about equal to the German, when the British was six times that figure, and only one third of the shipping in French ports was under the French flag. Despite some efforts to build a larger merchant marine, the figure had risen a bare 50 per cent by the eve of the war, while the British figure had doubled and the German increased by a factor of three.[11] French building costs could not compete with the British.

Britain's very large carrying trade was an important source of revenue and went along with the fact that, as the prime trading nation in the world, Britain also became the main center in which a large proportion of the world's commercial transactions were settled. Before 1914 London had truly become the financial capital of the world, a convenience to all and an additional source of income to Britain.

It was indicated a moment ago that France's foreign lending was subject to strong governmental direction, a point of contrast with the British practice. But this did not mean that the state itself was the lender, the matter being left to private institutions instead. For this was everywhere the heyday of private and free enterprise, in a broad sense adhering to the view that that government is best which governs least. Yet this statement stands in need of some qualification. It applied best in Britain and especially in the domain of trade. The great controversy of the earlier part of the century had resulted in a clear victory of the free trade doctrine, under the auspices of which Britain prospered. The advantage accruing from the priority of industrial development fitted well the free trade practice but also had the effect of obscuring the relative shares of credit that should have gone to that condition against those that could be credited to the doctrine as such.

It seemed for a time, especially during the period of the second French empire, as if the free trade view might prevail on the Continent as well. But in the late seventies matters began to take a different turn. That the Zollverein had served Germany well was not to be denied, but the view was not extended to the world outside the Zollverein, allowing for a tentative passage, instead of which the opposite tendency prevailed that nascent industry needed protection, a view not devoid of validity in the initial stages of development at least. Unlike Britain, Germany was not willing to sacrifice her agriculture, and there ensued "the marriage of steel and rye," the industrial interests of the West joining hands with the agricultural ones of the East in favor of protection for both. The German tariff of 1879 is sometimes regarded as initiating a new era in economic practice.

The American view was to a large extent similar to the German, in the sense at least that, enjoying within its own vast confines the advantages of a large free trade area, under the proddings of a fast-growing industry, the United States as a whole espoused the protectionist view.[12]

Something of a similar nature happened in France, where the strong agricultural interest succeeded in securing protection for itself, even though that meant less efficient methods of production and a price for French wheat higher than the world price. French industry accepted this condition, and after essays at tariffs in the eighties, the Méline tariff of 1892 definitely launched France on the protectionist path. To a point this had the effect of abetting French laggardness, yet the fact is worth bearing in mind that the French economy remained in better balance than the British, for example; France was to a much larger degree self-sufficient,[13] hence better sheltered from the accidents of uncontrollable fluctuations in the world economy and prices. This condition was not without certain merits, as developments in a more recent period have shown.

The success of the protectionist tendency, in combination with a sharpening competition from a variety of quarters, the German above all, had the consequence of eroding the advantages that Britain had derived from her priority of industrial development. It is not surprising in the circumstances that the merits of free trade should be questioned in Britain. It is enlightening to read the *Report of the Royal Commission to Inquire into the Depression of Trade and Industry,* dating from 1886, and itself a response to the economic crisis of the time. The following quotations will suffice:

> We think also that the severity of the competition of foreign countries is a matter deserving more serious attention than it has received at the hands of our commercial and industrial classes. We cannot, perhaps, hope to maintain, to the same degree as heretofore, the lead which we formerly held among the manufacturing nations of the world. Various causes contributed to give us a position far in advance of other countries, which we were well able to hold for many years; but those causes could not have been expected to operate permanently, and our supremacy is now being assailed on all sides.

While the report was content with expressing the hope that

> we have still the same physical and intellectual qualities which gave us so commanding a lead; and we see no reason why, with care, intelligence, enterprise, and thoroughness, we should not be able to continue to advance,

it may be noted that a minority view advocated a change in Britain's commercial policy. Ten years later a book entitled *Made in Germany* attracted considerable attention, focusing as it did on the chief single source of the threat to the British position.

It was a logical development in the circumstances that the views largely associated with the name of Joseph Chamberlain should become the focus of a sharp debate in Britain.[14] These views may be seen as an attempted compromise, for Chamberlain would have retained the free trade practice within the imperial structure as a whole following the German and the American examples in protecting it, again as a whole, from the outside, even though the empire accounted for only about one third of Britain's foreign trade. It was logical likewise that the same Chamberlain should be an advocate of imperial expansion, which indeed occurred at an impressive rate toward the end of the century, even if the economic factor cannot be seen as the exclusive motivation of that activity.[15]

The agitation was intense during the first decade of our century, when Chamberlain gave it clear and conscious expression, but the free trade practice had struck too deep roots in the British mind; it had achieved the standing of a "sacred cow," and protection was rejected by the electorate in the election of 1906. The focus of rivalry was increasingly by this time coming to center on the more limited aspect of naval competition, in which Germany was again the chief rival.

Germany's naval policy constituted a gamble. If the gamble was successful in so far as no attempt was made to destroy the nascent German naval power, it failed in the expectation that Britain might experience difficulty in meeting the challenge. British resources, her wealth in the last analysis, were equal to the task, and she was even capable of building enough ships to maintain her superiority, even if on a diminishing scale, while launching the beginnings of Lloyd George's war on poverty. Not only were the material resources adequate, but, of no less importance, the will to use them existed.

THE IMPONDERABLES

This last aspect cannot be given too much emphasis and leads into some considerations of the imponderables that go into the constitution of power. A few things must be said about the internal conditions of both the British and the French milieus. This is most easily observed in their domestic politics.

Mention has been made of the problems of trade and empire, both of them vital, especially the first, to the general state of the British economy. There was in the British case a particular problem which constituted a large part of the stuff of British politics in the prewar decades. We are referring to the Irish question.

By way of general summation and over a long period it may be said that the broad British tendency of liberal and flexible accommodation eventually came to prevail where Ireland was concerned as it had in other quarters. But Ireland was a special case, for geographical reasons among others, which therefore partook of both the domestic and the imperial aspects of British policy.

The Irish agitation came to center around the issue of Home Rule, toward which Gladstone and the Liberal Party were more sympathetic than the Tories and which concretely intruded in British politics in the form of a block of Irish members in the Parliament at Westminster. The result was at various points a coalition between the Liberals and the Irish group, but the alliance itself had the effect of creating a split within the Liberal party. It was the same Joseph Chamberlain who, in 1885, led the Liberal Union faction in opposition to Home Rule, thereby insuring its defeat. His just mentioned advocacy of expanding empire and imperial preference or protecton, even though it came somewhat later, represented consistency and eventually properly led the Liberal Unionists into the Conservative fold.

Another issue intruded at this point which became intermingled with the Irish, adequate reflection of changing conditions, in response to what may broadly be described as the social question. Under the impact of it the earlier Liberal tendency to espouse all aspects of freedom, be it at the level of individual political rights or in the various aspects of free enterprise and economic competition, underwent a change. Liberals, while still adhering to free trade, came to be the advocates of the increasing intervention of the state in social problems, the roots of the tendency which was to blossom into the welfare state of our day.

Matters came to a head in the first decade of the century and took the concrete form again of a Liberal-Irish alliance. It was thus possible to do two things: enacting Lloyd George's budget, the war on poverty, was one; the passage of an Irish Home Rule Bill was the other. There is no need to dwell on the spilling over of the issue into the constitutional domain.[16] The Home Rule Bill of 1912 would become effective within two years at the latest, even if the Lords maintained their opposition.

Such was the stuff of British politics on the eve of the war. Feeling was understandably intense and could easily convey abroad the impression of Britain as a house divided. Nor was the impression lessened by the aftermath of the situation in 1912. For the effect of the Home Rule Bill was to produce a division in Ireland, where the northeastern section, largely of British Protestant settlement, would not accept its provisions. It was long since the likelihood of civil war had been a reality among the British people, but matters went the length of doubts about the reliability of the armed forces should the worst come to pass. Was Britain under such circumstances in a position to take a strong stand and to make her weight felt in European and world councils? The difficulties of the British domestic scene were well known in Berlin.[17]

At the same time the demands of the war on poverty did not interfere with those of the naval establishment. If Germany insisted on building ships, Britain, though she would rather have preferred accommodation, would outmatch her. The *Dreadnought* made its appearance in 1906 and the naval race continued unabated.

Yet one can already perceive in the British milieu the seeds which would finally flower in our day. The episode of the Boer War is revealing in this respect. The well-nigh world-wide unpopularity of that war had the effect of stiffening the British purpose, and so had on the whole the local difficulties encountered on the South African terrain. The relief of Mafeking brought forth an outburst of nationalistic emotion in Britain. It might therefore seem that, on balance, the effect of the challenge was to bring out the solidity of the British nation and to silence the critics of the whole enterprise. And it may also be pointed out that, in part at least under the impact of the deficiencies brought to light by the Boer War, a reorganization took place in the machinery of defense. The institution of the Committee of Imperial Defense, and the reorganization of the Army, especially during Haldane's tenure of the war office, not to mention the formulation of military plans with the French and the Belgians, were manifestations of this changed approach; insufficient as they may have been, they would stand Britain in good stead in 1914.

Nevertheless, the criticism had been substantial in Britain. Already in 1895 the episode of the Jameson Raid[18] had given rise to some sharp questioning, even though a parliamentary commission exonerated Chamberlain, suspected of collusion. The initial setbacks suffered by the British forces in the South African War also were cause for criticism while they brought home the nature of the issue to the British public. Most of all, the brutality of the methods used by the military in an effort to cope with the tactics of guerrilla warfare adopted by the Boers, gave rise to some questioning that found expression even in Parliament. The Boer War had made unexpected demands, be it in terms of costs or of the number of troops that had to be raised. If there was little difficulty in meeting both requirements, and if imperial Britain in the end had her way, in the face of both world-wide sympathy for the Boers and of a surge of the nonconformist tradition at home, the Boer War constituted a crisis, both in the evolution of the empire and for the British conscience.[19]

But it would take time, and two world wars, before the acceptance of demotion, of quiet surrender, would become the prevailing mood of the British milieu, a mood of which the policy of appeasement of the 1930's is but another facet. Whether such a reaction be regarded as a manifestation of civilized sophistication or not, in a world of competing nation-states and empires it can hardly be regarded as other than an element of weakness —decadence is the word that some would prefer. It constitutes without a doubt a weakening of the moral fiber that is an important component of the power of a national entity. To repeat, the seeds alone of such a transformation can, especially in the light of retrospect, be detected before 1914, when the prevailing tone was still one of confident strength.[20]

Much has been heard, especially in the more recent decades, about the decadence of democracy in general. Among the states in which the democratic ideology and practice was either making headway or already established, the France of the Third Republic was in the eyes of many the most advanced and the most radical. France was a republic, for one thing, in a world where monarchy was still the norm; and even if the form of the executive has but secondary significance, France had since 1848 adhered to the practice of universal manhood suffrage. The talk of French decadence was heard in many quarters before 1914.

Demographic stagnation and economic retardation could be cited as concrete evidence, more solid bases than the licence of expression in speech or press and the popular legends about the fleshpots of Paris. Yet in the operation of the French body politic as a whole one could find cause for some doubts about its solidity. France absorbed the impact of the defeat of 1870 with relative ease and seemed to recover with success, to the extent that Bismarck wondered whether he ought not to have further exploited the defeat and would let rumors spread about the possibility of a preventive war.[21] Here a condition must be mentioned, the manifestations of which were in a sense misleading, for they pointed in what might seem to be contradictory directions.

On the score of the "iniquity" of the settlement of 1871 French sentiment may be regarded as unanimous, a wrong to be sometime redressed. Increasingly with the passage of time the more intransigeant aspects of French nationalism would come to be associated with the Right in politics, which is why Bismarck claimed to be republican in France. To a point this French tendency was misleading, for the Jacobin tradition was strong in France, which joined intense patriotism with social views more generally associated with the Left in politics. The more vigorous advocates of a continuation of the war, even after it had become a hopeless cause, had found their leader in Gambetta.

Apart from reconstruction, the issue of the constitutional reorganization of the state absorbed at first much of the political attention of the country. This was the central problem of the seventies, and may be said to have been essentially settled with the failure of the *16 mai*, MacMahon's attempt to assert the power of the executive.[22] But if the Republic had won, the question of the powers of the executive continued at the center of French politics. It reappeared under successive forms. The *ligue des patriotes*, Déroulède, General Boulanger, Barrès, Maurras, and many others, may be lumped together as representing in France the combination of the revanchist outlook with a generally conservative orientation in domestic affairs.

They were all defeated in the end and the men who came to rule the Third Republic were moderate bourgeois in the main. They could hardly be charged with deficient patriotism—witness Clemenceau for example—but on the score of revanche they took a realistic view of its possibilities. But the image of intense divisions did not become less sharp. The bubble that the Boulanger agitation proved to be had barely been pricked before Captain Dreyfus came to the center of the stage. The essence of that famous episode, which attracted world-wide attention at the time of its occurrence, is the contest for which it became the occasion and the focus, the place of the Army in the republican state. Not many knew—and how could they have known?—or for that matter cared, about the innocence or guilt of Captain Dreyfus: he was innocent if one was a good republican; he was guilty in the opposite case, or at least if one stood for a strong executive power and for the honor and intangibility of the Army. The Republic won that battle again, but the bitterness of division that was its legacy to the French body politic was hardly calculated to convey the image of a united country in other respects.

To keep up the tradition of violent divergences, the issue of the Church versus the Republic arose next. It was the same issue at bottom, the Church, the Army, the forces of conservation on one side, the lay Republic on the other, the Left in brief, moderate as it may have been, by later standards especially, on the score of the social question.

This last problem, in France as elsewhere for that matter, was emerging with increasing intensity. Among continental states a rough measure of its growing significance may be gathered from the progress of socialism. In both France and Germany the Socialist party, dedicated to the Marxist ideology with varying shades of tactical interpretation, was making steady progress, until in the latter country the Social Democrats had by 1914 become the largest single group in the Reichstag. The Socialists were internationalists, and the strike could be a powerful weapon.[23] Everywhere among the governments there were those who felt qualms about the direction of the aims of guns that would be put in the hands of the workers. There was great fear, and correspondingly hope, of the possibilities of the Socialist movement in preventing a European conflagration. It was thus in a sense appropriately symbolic that the murder of the French Socialist leader Jaurès, even if the deed of an unbalanced individual, should take place on August 31, 1914. Jaurès could not go to Brussels, where he would have met his German counterparts, even though there is no reason to believe that the meeting would have had any effect on the course of events. In the face of aroused nationalist emotion the Second International collapsed, while Socialists everywhere among the initial belligerents rediscovered their respective national allegiances.

Suspicion of the Army, fear of the man on horseback, ran deep among good French republicans, placing them to a point in a dilemma, for they also claimed to be heirs to the patriotic Jacobin tradition. The case of Jaurès himself may be cited, at once a Socialist and a patriot, and the first decade of the century was the time of the *réveil national.*[24] The demographic situation was the chief reason for the Army law of 1913 which extended the term of military service to three years. The law was enacted to the accompaniment of intense debate, which its passage did not still; the Socialists were opposed to it and the fate of the decision was uncertain in the Chamber of 1914.

These sharp divisions of the French milieu could easily convey an impression of weakness, just as their counterpart did in the British case, and their existence might be thought to affect the ability to conduct a coherent foreign policy. Up to 1914 domestic differences did not in either Britain or France have the effect of interfering with the demands of the requirements of defense. But the role of diplomacy was no less important. The function of that activity is obviously facilitated, it can seem almost superfluous, when superior strength stands behind it. Able as he may have been, Palmerston had little difficulty in, hence in a sense deserves relatively little credit for, having his way. Fifty years later the position of Britain had undergone substantial change and a correspondingly higher premium attached to skill and craft. We shall examine in detail in the following chapters the operation of British diplomacy and the uncertainties by which it is characterized in the effort to adapt itself to the changing circumstances of the British position.

The French decline was more catastrophic than the British and more clearly perceived by all, the French included. There are obvious limitations to what diplomatic skill can accomplish in the absence of sufficient force to support it. To a degree it may be said that French diplomacy supplied a substitute for the deficiencies of the concrete aspects of French power, though only to a degree, yet this itself was one of the elements of that power. This, too, will be examined in detail, being in fact one of the central purposes of the entire discussion.

The German case stands in contrast, where it is not unfair to say that diplomacy, the manipulation of power, had the contrary effect of minimizing, countering, and wasting, in fact, the asset of the more concrete components of German power. Of necessity some aspects of the German performance, too, will be part of our story.

In any case, and without a doubt, what happened in 1914 disposed of a number of questions, or myths, that had achieved wide currency before that date. Clearly, those who had contended that it was inconceivable that the great civilized Powers of Europe should resort to so crude a device as the test of physical force were proved wrong. So likewise were those who had felt qualms about the solidity of the national purpose, the national spirit, or the possible role of the anti-militaristic, internationalistic Socialist masses of workers.

The First World War and Its Impact

There was another myth that had wide currency in 1914. It was commonly believed that, should the inconceivable—war among the Great Powers—occur, technical reasons alone would preclude the possibility of a protracted struggle. Along with the highest achievements of civilization, the Great Powers of Europe were possessed of the most powerful guns that had ever existed. The unleashing of these engines of destruction would threaten the very fabric of civilization, the destruction of which was also inconceivable.

The war turned out instead to be protracted, and the havoc that it wreaked was enormous, but it did not entail the end of European civilization. Nevertheless, the outcome was also unexpected in that the climate of 1919 was very different from that of five years earlier. Some observations may be introduced at this point on the impact of the war on the British and the French positions of power. In summation it may be said that while both countries emerged from the conflict as victors, for both the victory was ashes and resulted in further marked decline. How and why is what we briefly wish to examine.

Consider first the material effects of the war. The human loss was very large, especially for France. She had managed to mobilize some 8,000,000 men, a fifth of her total population, during the course of the war; of these, 1,360,000 were killed, to which must be added another 4,000,000 wounded, who suffered from negligible to total disability. When one considers that the toll was exacted from the manpower of the nation in the most productive and vigorous years of its life, it is no exaggeration to speak of a process of biological selection in reverse; the phrase "bled white" seems totally appropriate. The British loss in dead, at some 900,000, if smaller, was also quite impressive. Much has been made of the significance of this bloodletting as an explanation for a great deal of what subsequently happened in both Britain and France. While the contention seems plausible, the validity of it must remain in question in the light of the fact that a comparable holocaust in the German and the Russian cases failed to have similar effects if we think of the policies and performances of those countries after a lapse of twenty years, a generation. Whatever may be said of these two instances, certainly lack of vigor or listlessness does not apply to them.

The material cost of the war was astronomical, but the effects of this damage were diverse. Save for very substantial shipping losses Britain suffered no physical damage in her homeland. She suffered in other ways, however, and the war had for her the effect of accelerating a process already under way before the conflict had begun. Mention has been made of the challenge to the British position of commercial primacy that had arisen from various quarters before 1914. Had there been no war, the process would undoubtedly have continued and there is no way of knowing how Britain would have adjusted herself to the changing situation.

The war in fact had for the time being eliminated the German aspect of the challenge, but only for a time, for it soon reappeared. Where Germany was concerned Britain was faced with the dilemma that the elimination of her chief rival meant at the same time that of her best customer. This is what explains the British tendency to leniency where the economic terms of the German peace were involved. But a more serious consequence of the war was the loss of much British export trade. The hope of "business as usual" soon had to be abandoned in the face of the insatiable demands of the war machine. Britain's place in many foreign markets, South America for example, was taken by others, the United States, most of all. But Japan too, and even India to a point, used the opportunity to develop their respective textile industries. Textiles, together with coal, became in fact after the war the sick industries of Britain, an illness from which there would be no recovery and which found expression in the dismal surroundings of depressed areas, where unemployment became the correspondingly demoralizing way of life and a specter hovering over the operation of British politics.

The endeavor to recover lost trade was naturally one of the chief concerns of British efforts, equally manifested in attempts to revive the German and the Russian markets and in the recrudescence of the prewar controversies over the merits of free trade versus imperial preference. These efforts met with but qualified success at best, and the problem of the balance of trade, still unresolved today, has thus continued to bedevil all attempts to recover a lost, if not an irretrievable position.

These problems were dealt with within the compass of orthodox financial practice, for it would be some time before the Keynesian outlook would achieve its subsequent standing of acceptance and respectability at the level of governmental direction. When it came to matters financial, be they German reparations or inter-Allied debts, the soundest and most realistic thinking was to be found in the British milieu, as the 1922 Balfour Note clearly showed.[25] But others would not see the merits of enlightened selfish generosity, and the futile attempt to perform the impossible was for a time pursued under the concealing shield of the outflow of American capital.

The world had been Britain's debtor before 1914 and had discharged its obligation through the device of an unfavorable British balance of trade. Much of Britain's investment abroad had been consumed during the war though Britain still remained a creditor on balance. But her overall balance of payments left but a small margin available for investment overseas, hence made it difficult to re-establish the pre-existing equilibrium. Nevertheless it proved possible in 1925 to bring the pound back to the 1914 gold parity. This was a matter of prestige rather than of sound economic thinking, Churchill's accomplishment, not one of those that have gone to the ultimate enhancement of his credit. The effect was to render even more difficult the British competitive position in world trade, aggravating Britain's difficulties, and a mere six years sufficed to prove that the old parity was untenable. When that happened, in 1931, the whole postwar financial structure of indebtedness was collapsing, evidence that the war-induced dislocation of the world's economy had not been made good. The illusion had only been sustained for a few years.

While the economy was limping, the Liberal party in politics was going through the agonies of disappearance.[26] For the first time in 1923 Labour's representation in Parliament was larger than the Liberal and as a consequence, likewise for the first time, a Labour Prime Minister presided over the destinies of

Britain. No disaster ensued, Ramsay MacDonald fitted easily into the traditional mold, and Labour no more than the Conservatives was able to produce a cure for Britain's economic ills; broadly speaking and in a fundamental sense, the malady persists half a century after 1914, Britain still pursuing the search of an elusive equilibrium.

The French case offers in many respects a markedly different picture from the British. If France's foreign trade is far from insignificant, that activity in her case has not the place it has for Britain, reflection of her economic retardation in part, in part also of the more balanced and self-contained nature of the French economy. Unlike Britain, France had furnished the battleground in the West, wherein the devastation was appalling. Reconstruction was unquestionably the first need and France set about the task, which was essentially accomplished by 1927. In the French case, as in others, this was evidence of unexpected recuperative capacity and of the validity of the phrase that "there is much ruin in a nation." One of the consequences was the asset of a modernized industrial plant.

The task of reconstruction had been enormously expensive, and since France had come out of the war with a large burden of debt, both domestic and foreign, the additional cost of reconstruction made the load of her indebtedness truly crushing. For some years after the war this was not too great a cause for concern, for the happy thought prevailed that, in time, Germany would pay it all. The episode of the occupation of the Ruhr in 1923,[27] if it succeeded in breaking Germany's will to resistance, also justified the quip that bayonets are unsuitable for the digging of coal.

Despite the temporary normalization of the reparations problem that was the Dawes Plan, French finances were in a sorry state by the mid twenties, a condition reflected in the flight from and the fall of the international value of the franc, a vicious circle of cumulating interaction of cause and effect. A Left coalition had been in control of the government since 1924, but in the emergency Poincaré was appealed to and given the opportunity to earn the title of "savior of the franc." This he did do in fact, and without too great difficulty, but also by resorting to the simple device of stabilizing the currency at one fifth of its 1914 gold parity. Thus the entity France may be said to have shown itself capable of absorbing the major part of the cost of the war and reconstruction,[28] even though this was done through the resort to repudiation of the major part of her internal obligation, which was the real meaning of devaluation. There was no counterpart in France of the great German inflation; nevertheless, the dimensions of the repudiation were such as to be far from negligible in their social consequences, a consideration that is worth bearing in mind.

Just as the too high value of the pound hampered the recovery of British trade, so conversely the low value of the Poincaré franc constituted a boon for the French. France prospered during the last years of the decade and even contrived to accumulate a surprisingly large share of the world's gold; she could even for a brief spell bask in the illusion that she might be exempt from the impact of the world's economic illness. Like Britain, France had lost a considerable portion of her foreign investment during the war, the Bolshevik repudiation of debt being the largest single item in the ledger; she, too, was unable to re-establish her former position in this respect, although she more than ever adhered to the practice of giving political direction to whatever lending she made.

The Third Republic had successfully come through the ordeal of war, a fact which on the whole redounded to the credit of the régime, in contrast with the challenge that defeat entailed in the states of Central and Eastern Europe, where the result was a spate of new constitutional arrangements. Thus French politics continued in the established grooves, confronted, however, with the legacy of the conflict in the form of two predominant preoccupations: a domestic one—reconstruction, with all its ramifications; the other foreign—how to achieve security for the long term.

The election of 1919 produced in France the blue horizon Chamber, counterpart of the outcome of the British khaki election of a year before. Both were reflections of the war-induced emotion followed by victory. Such reactions were not the most useful approach to the hard realities that must be faced in the form of dealing with the aftermath of the war. The election of

1924 may be seen as a return to normality, the resumption of the customary tendency toward *sinistrisme,* characteristic pattern of the French electorate; the Cartel des Gauches, under the leadership of Herriot, assumed the reins of government. But Left or Right, or more accurately Left Center or Right Center, the fundamental problems that must be dealt with were the same.

Thus Poincaré came back in the circumstances and for the reasons that have been indicated, the crisis of the franc. The result was a tacit compromise represented by the association in the government of Poincaré, the exponent of financial orthodoxy, with Briand, the advocate of a softer policy of reconciliation vis-à-vis Germany. When in 1928 the Right was rewarded by the verdict of the electorate for its accomplishment of having saved the franc, Briand remained in charge of foreign policy. He was to remain at the foreign office almost until his death in 1932, a long tenure comparable to that of Delcassé, lasting through the vicissitudes of a number of governmental changes. Even in 1932 conditions seemed sufficiently close to normality—the impact of economic difficulties and of developments across the Rhine had not sufficiently registered—to produce again a victory of the moderate Left.

Normality in fact had not returned for good, for Britain and for France any more than for others, as the economic crisis of the thirties would show. Without accepting the too limited view of exclusively economic interpretation, the overwhelming impact of the economic situation on the course of political evolution cannot be overlooked or minimized. The effects of it on such concrete matters as budgets, resources available for armament, are easy to perceive and fall indeed in the domain of the measurable.

But at this point the imponderables also intrude and the two sets of factors intermesh. It is no exaggeration to say that after the First World War the body politic of both Britain and France were victims of an illness. For both the victory had meant frustration and had induced an inward-looking reaction. This was even more marked in the French case than in the British, manifested in the paradox that France, a victor, suffered from a psychology of defeat. The obsession with security, which to many outside appeared as merely pathological, was not unjustified. The

French people in their mass would have liked nothing better than to be allowed to cultivate their own garden in peace, oblivious of the outside world. But this France cannot do, any more than Britain can, or for that matter the United States, although in the case of the last the factors of distance and power made it possible to cling to the illusion awhile longer.

Such conditions constitute a considerable handicap to the conduct of foreign policy. The difficulty was compounded by the fact of victory itself, for this had the effect of nurturing illusions and a distorted picture of reality. Neither Britain nor France was in control of much that happened elsewhere, certainly to a much lesser degree than they had been hitherto. That both were most sincerely desirous of peace is not to be denied; these were also the days when the old maxim *si vis pacem para bellum,* honored again after another war, had fallen in high disrepute.

More than ever, therefore, it is clear that the two countries were in the same boat, the same defensive position vis-à-vis the outside. Whether jointly they had sufficient power to cope with the task of the reorganization of Europe, the reintegration of Germany and of Bolshevik Russia into the comity of nations, the problems resulting from the Balkanization of much of mid Europe, those of a dislocated world economy, the manifestations of the deep twentieth-century malady that were the totalitarian systems of Italy and of Germany, is doubtful at best. In any case it was easier to find fault with each other. There was much criticism of French militarism in Britain, at the time of the Ruhr occupation, for example, and the French obsession with security was viewed with considerable suspicion. Conversely, in French eyes, Britain, and others for that matter, were ungrateful and unappreciative of the sacrifices that France had made in the common cause.

These may seem like futile details and meaningless recriminations, the importance of which has receded to secondary place with the passage of time. Even if there is warrant for this interpretation, they constitute an important element of the postwar landscape of international relations that goes some distance toward explaining the floundering which in different ways is so characteristic of the foreign policy of both countries between the two world wars. That is why this background has been mentioned, for the influence of the common illness must ever be borne in mind when one seeks to understand and unravel the specific performances of those policies, the object of the following chapters.

NOTES ON *Chapter IV*

1. See above, pp. 76–77.
2. *The Cambridge Economic History of Europe,* Vol. VI, Part I (Cambridge, 1965), p. 61. Of particular relevance to this entire chapter the following two works should be cited: Kindleberger, Charles P., *Economic Growth in France and Britain, 1851–1950* (1964), and Clough, Shepard B., *France, A History of National Economics, 1789–1939* (1939).
3. Clough, S. B., *European Economic History* (1968), p. 409.
4. Clough, S. B. and Cole, C. W., *Economic History of Europe* (Boston, 1941), p. 538.
5. Ibid. In considering the figures in this and the preceding tables in the cases of France and Germany account should be taken of the annexation of 1871, the significance of which became particularly important after the discovery in 1878 of a process which made possible the utilization of the Lorraine iron ore.
6. *The Cambridge Economic History of Europe,* Vol. VI, Part I, p. 443.
7. Ibid., p. 517. If other sources of energy are included, the figures for 1907 are 8,008,000 and 3,191,500 respectively. Loc. cit.
8. Clough, *European Economic History,* pp. 338 and 419. The composition of general trade should of course be borne in mind, for it is a very imperfect indication of growth. The large internal market of the United States, for example, long absorbed the bulk of the American production, a situation totally different from the British. The more specialized nature of French trade, dependent in considerable measure on luxury goods, should likwise be taken into consideration.
9. Clough, *France, A History of National Economics,* p. 204.
10. The basic network of French railways had been built by 1870, when it amounted to 18,500 kilometers. Construction thereafter brought it to 49,500 kms. by 1913. The German figures are very similar.
11. *The Cambridge Economic History* . . . , Vol. VI, Part I, p. 269.
12. Bearing in mind that, in contrast with Germany, the United States was an exporter of food and raw materials, wheat and cotton in particular. As a consequence the agricultural interests in the United States were generally in favor of low tariffs but their views did not prevail.
13. But only to a much larger degree, for France remained an importer of wheat, in varying quantities depending upon the quality of her own harvests. For example, in 1879, a particularly bad year, these reached the figure of 29,000,000 hectoliters. Clough, op. cit., p. 214.
14. On the evolution of Chamberlain's views from the primarily imperial to the imperial-protectionist, see Court, W. H. B., *A Concise Economic History of Britain* (1964), p. 333.
15. For a discussion of imperial activity, see Chapter VI.
16. The opposition of the Lords led to the enactment in 1911 of the Parliament Act, which curbed the powers of the upper house, its veto on legislation being reduced to delaying possibilities under certain conditions.

17. Actually, the Irish situation, while a source of concern, did not give rise to any difficulties at the time of the outbreak of the war. The implementation of Home Rule was put off for the duration and there was no dearth of Irish enlistments in the British forces. Apart from the 1916 Easter rising, the Irish problem was no source of difficulty during the war itself, but the issue reappeared in acute form after its termination.

18. An ill-contrived filibustering attempt to overthrow the government of the Transvaal which turned into an anti-climax, but in which the connivance of higher British authorities was not unjustly suspected.

19. The episode may be followed in *The Cambridge History of the British Empire,* 8 vols. in 9 (1929–59), Vol. III (1959), pp. 354–79.

20. As a relatively secondary, yet not insignificant, indication of the moral climate of Britain on the eve of the war mention may also be made of the feminist agitation. Humorous and relatively innocuous as some of its manifestations were, it, too, contributed to create an atmosphere of uncertainty and malaise. An account of it may be found in Dangerfield, G., *The Strange Death of Liberal England* (1935).

21. On the war scare of 1875, see below, p. 207.

22. President MacMahon's attempt to appoint his own Cabinet and his dissolution of the Chamber, regarded by many as in the nature of a coup d'état, was rebuffed by the electorate. Thereafter no President of the Third Republic sought to interfere with the supreme control of the legislature.

23. Also important was the syndicalist agitation, heir to the anarchist movement. A rival of the Socialist tendency in some respects, syndicalism had a strong influence among the unions and laid much stress on the revolutionary possibilites of the general strike, in doing which its influence converged with that of Socialism. An abortive attempt at a general strike took place in 1910.

24. A recrudescence of national feeling which occurred alongside the progress of Socialism, and of which the advent of Poincaré to the prime ministership, then to the presidency, of the country may be regarded as a symbolic expression.

25. This was a proposal for wiping the slate clean of the financial obligations due Great Britain if a general settlement of the international financial obligation resulting from the war could be effected. The American insistence on refusing to acknowledge any connection between reparations and the inter-Allied debts was largely responsible for the failure of Balfour's proposal.

26. The seeds of Liberal decline antedate the First World War, but the registration of that decline in parliamentary representation only began after that conflict. Thereafter it continued until the virtual disappearance of the Liberal party by the time of the Second, when its place in the scheme of British politics was taken by the Labour party.

27. See below, p. 429.

28. French receipts from German reparations, especially if set against France's debts to her allies, covered but a small fraction of the cost of reconstruction, not to mention other costs, such as pensions, resulting from the war. For an analysis of the French balance of payments in these respects, see Haig, R. M., *The Public Finances of Post-War France* (1929).

V

THE HEYDAY OF BISMARCK, 1871–87

Territorial questions are not to be disposed of by arbitrary limits; we cannot enjoy the luxury of taking Egyptian soil by pinches. We may seize an Aden or a Perim, where there is no already formed community of inhabitants, and circumscribe a tract at will. But our first site in Egypt, be it by larceny or by emption, will be the almost certain egg of a North African empire, that will grow and grow until another Victoria and another Albert, titles of the lake-sources of the White Nile, come within our borders; and till we finally join hands across the equator with Natal and Cape Town, to say nothing of the Transvaal and the Orange River on the south, or of Abyssinia or Zanzibar to be swallowed by way of viaticum on our journey.

Gladstone, 1877

Whatever you do, never let go of Egypt.

Thiers to Gambetta

Think of it [the loss of 1871] always, speak of it never.

Gambetta

Europe After 1871

Some question might be raised about the use of a German rubric for a section of a book concerned with the discussion of British and French policies. The justifying reason is not far to seek. The foreign policies of the two states with which we are primarily concerned will indeed remain the central focus of our analysis, but for the three quarters of a century following the Franco-Prussian War and the emergence of the second Reich, that entity, more than any other single one, was the central core and mover of events on the international scene. Our story, to be sure, will not be told from the standpoint of German policy, but the direction of that policy, its initiatives, must ever remain present in the mind when considering the actions, often the reactions, of the principals in our tale. The preceding chapter has shown the solid and concrete realities that underlay German power. Eventually, when it came to the ultimate test, the resort to armed force, the German performance would command the highest respect. These more recent occurrences, their enormous and disastrous impact—not least on Germany herself—will be considered later. What we wish to do at this point is to examine the initial stages of the tale, the period during which Germany was led, and Europe's policy in large measure directed, by one of the outstanding statesmen of all time. That period and the one immediately following, the three decades after 1871, is of particular importance in the present discussion; for Britain and for France it provides a study in adaptation to changing circumstances, albeit with considerable differences between the two. It may be put this way: the French defeat registered an important landmark in the decline of French power, a decline uninterrupted and seemingly irretrievable until perhaps our own time, and even and if so in totally different conditions; Britain in contrast still rode the crest for a time, but not for very long, and she, too, had to find ways of mitigating the effects of uncontrollable diminution. Britain and France therefore will be seen to offer both contrast and similarity. But we must not anticipate our story, and, to repeat, we wish first to examine the time of the heyday of Prince Bismarck.

The German Chancellor we have already met, and sufficient has been said of his character. The Franco-Prussian War found him at the height of his power and fame; the success Germany achieved was deserved, in terms of competence at least, and credit for the accomplishment belongs to Bismarck in full measure. The two succeeding decades, during which he continued in office, enabled him to mold and guide his creation.

Harsh as he may have been, uncouth and brutal on occasion,

Bismarck's chief title to greatness rests most of all on his adherence to rational moderation, even allowing for the mistaken annexation of 1871. Bismarck had no unlimited aims, in contrast with some of his German successors; his Germany was satisfied, and like all satisfied victors, Bismarck, the man of war, turned after 1871 into the man of peace based on the preservation of the status quo. But this did not imply an idle resting on laurels; to the extent that he could, he would seek to prevent the quarrels of others from degenerating into open conflict in which Germany might be unable to avoid involvement.

France recovered too fast for his taste. He thought at times she had not been sufficiently diminished[1] and he never regarded her as a negligible quantity. The possibility that she would become reconciled to her demotion and to her territorial loss was not great, and Bismarck never thought it such, though he made some efforts to normalize Franco-German relations. Should it come to the worst, he felt he could deal with France again, but on one condition: the specter of the war on two fronts remained his nightmare. That possibility was remote so long as relations with Russia continued as they had been for some time; the nineteenth-century record of Franco-Russian co-operation was a spasmodic one, of little substance in comparison with that of Russo-German relations.

Austria comes into the picture at this point. In the war of 1866 Russia had played vis-à-vis Prussia a role comparable to that which she played in the conflict of 1870. Moreover, with the decline of the Ottoman power, the old tradition of Austro-Russian co-operation against the Turk had been turning to a relation of rivalry over the spoils. That situation stood to be exacerbated by Austria's concern with the problem of her own Slav population, attracted by the existence of Balkan Slavs and by the example of their successful struggle for emancipation; support of this emancipation had an appeal for Russia, be it on sentimental grounds of religious and ethnic affinity or in the pursuit of expansion toward the Straits. In this situation Bismarck was an authentic neutral, Germany having no direct interest in the Near East at this time. Having defeated Austria but treated her with gentleness, Bismarck looked to the day of reconciliation, when the hybrid state would fill the role of an extension of

Germanic predominance throughout Middle Europe. In this aim he was served by the reorganization of the Dual Monarchy, itself a consequence of the defeat of 1866; for if the memory of that episode rankled, the desire of redressing it was enfeebled and impeded by the satisfactory outcome which it procured for Magyar nationalism. The substitution of the Hungarian Andrássy for the Saxon Beust at the head of Austro-Hungarian affairs served Bismarck's purpose well; the Dreikaiserbund of 1873 was the expression of the success of his efforts. For Bismarck the Dreikaiserbund represented the union of the socially and politically conservative states, a modernized version of the Metternichian alignment. Where foreign affairs were concerned it meant the confirmation of France's isolation and the composition of the Austro-Russian rivalry in the Balkans. Why should not the contestants accept the eminently reasonable solution of dividing the apple of discord in two, each acknowledging the complete freedom of action of the other in his own sphere?

The totality of power represented by the alliance of the three emperors meant in addition the likelihood of a controlling voice in the affairs of Europe, precisely Bismarck's intent. But it was also that aspect of it which could be irksome to England, whose arbitral position and whose interest were best served by the fragmentation of power on the continent of Europe. Whatever equilibrium of forces may have existed *within* the Dreikaiserbund, for Europe as a whole the association rather represented the denial of equilibrium.[2]

Yet there seemed to be initially neither objection nor concern in England. As indicated before, the rise of Germany had been entirely acceptable to that country; some criticism of Bismarck, his methods and the terms of the French peace, were voiced, but no counterpart was heard of the above-cited dire predictions of Thiers.[3] Moreover, Gladstone ruled England at this time, an anti-imperialist little Englander by preference, the prime focus of whose interest correspondingly lay in domestic affairs. This did not mean imperial abdication on the part of England, but an accommodating stance in settling the aftermath of the American Civil War, for example, the *Alabama* claims, finally disposed of in 1872,[4] and in the case of India a policy which the Viceroy himself described as one of "masterly inactivity." The steady Russian advance in Central Asia was observed with understanding rather than concern; the professedly temporary occupation of Samarkand, followed instead by the further acquisition of Khiva in 1873, rather than by withdrawal from the former place, was cause for neither alarm nor protests. England was after all well placed to appreciate the necessities of "defensive" expansion, and the Tsar's declarations of intent, if belied by events, need not be insincere.[5] At most Afghanistan would be watched, on the neutrality of which England and Russia could agree.

This was about to change, for the election of 1874 brought Disraeli to the prime ministership of Britain. The contrast between the personalities of Disraeli and Gladstone is matched by that between the foci of their respective interests. Disraeli had conclusively shown that he could play domestic politics with the best and had given ample evidence of the capacity for opportunistic adaptation; his intelligence could hardly be denied. It was the quality which, as much as any other, had caused him to rise to the position that he had achieved and to which he had risen against a sea of original handicaps. At all events Disraeli was no little Englander, though it may be appropriate to recall his statement about England being more Asiatic than European.[6] If he was not necessarily overwell informed about the details of European affairs, the Dreikaiserbund elicited from him an instinctive dislike, and he would not have been loath to see it disrupted. The defense and promotion of the imperial interest, an undertaking closer to his heart, had, though incidentally and hardly owing to his own initiative, precisely that effect at one point, as the following story will show.

The Defense of the British Route to the East

In the new British ministry Lord Derby, whose disposition did not make for decisiveness or the prosecution of a vigorous policy, was in charge of foreign affairs. More significant in many respects was the appointment of Lord Salisbury to the secretaryship of India.[7] A cultivated man of broad and firm views, long subject to the handicap of unreliable health, quite un-English in his deficient interest in sports, Salisbury was yet the embodiment of some fundamental aspects of the English patrician tradition, the assumption of the unquestioned right to rule being one, together with a profound awareness of the obligations that go with the assumption of that right. We shall often meet him again in the following pages.

The importance attached to India, more generally to the route to the East, is brought out by three episodes. The English mistake, or missed opportunity, that the construction of the Suez Canal under French auspices represented, has been explained in an earlier chapter. Given the circumstances of the Egyptian milieu, it is little cause for surprise that Khedive Ismail, despite many useful accomplishments in furthering the modernization of his country, should have found himself involved in financial difficulties. In 1875 he decided to sell his block of 175,000 shares in the Canal Company. But the difficulties he encountered in dealing with French bankers are what furnished the opportunity for Disraeli's purchase of these shares with the assistance of the English Rothschild, who, incidentally, sustained no loss in the transaction. Irregular as the proceeding may have been in the context of British constitutional practice, it was a brilliant coup, which Parliament endorsed, thus making England qua England an important shareholder in, though not giving her control of, the Canal Company. To a degree a past mistake had been retrieved, and we shall soon observe the unfolding of the Egyptian story thereafter.

The following year, despite some parliamentary opposition, Disraeli secured legislation the effect of which is best expressed in the *Punch* cartoon of the time showing him presenting Queen Victoria with an imperial crown instead of the hitherto merely royal one that she had worn. On January 1, 1877, throughout India, she was proclaimed *Kaisar-i-Hind,* Empress of India. It was no more than a gesture, which affected little the reality of things, but Disraeli regarded it as a significant and appropriate symbol, arguing the importance of external display in the world of the East.[8] It was in any case a clear assertion, to the English people themselves no less than to the outside world, of the significance attached by Britain to empire.

This last-mentioned evidence of emphasis on the imperial interest was almost simultaneous with the resumption of a more "forward" policy on the periphery of India, especially in the northwest, where in Afghanistan British and Russian influences met. The appointment of Lord Lytton as Viceroy to India in 1876 signalized the initiation of this more aggressive policy, the detailed and specific manifestations of which there is neither space nor need to trace in this discussion.[9] It is worth mentioning, however, as indication of an important and persistent strand in Anglo-Russian relations, the observation of Lord Northbrook, Lytton's predecessor, in January 1875: "I go heartily with Lawrence [Northbrook's predecessor] against fuss and interference, but there is one point upon which I would fight, and I should let the Russians understand this very clearly."[10] Lack of precision, reluctance to be clear on either side, hence ambiguity and reciprocal misunderstanding, recur again and again in the dialogue between the two countries, reflection perhaps of the deep differences in the respective outlooks and modes of operation of the two societies and milieus. The second Afghan War at the end of the decade is but an episode in the long and continuing story of Britain's defensive expansion on the Northwest frontier.

Britain as a Mediterranean Power

Imprecise as the formulation of British policy in Asia may have been, the items just mentioned add up to a clear line of action. With growing trade and imperial expansion in Asia the importance of the Mediterranean as the life line of empire took on increasing clarity. Athwart that avenue of communication still lay the decadent but large Ottoman state. We have seen the manifestations in the earlier part of the century of the Palmerstonian policy of preserving that state, based on the hope that it could be reformed and rejuvenated, hence stand on its own feet. There was in England a body of opinion—it may be described as the Turcophile—which believed in the possibilities of Turkey; Stratford de Redcliffe had been one of its most ardent representatives and agents. But the internal story of Turkey during the two decades following the Treaty of Paris was calculated to belie these British expectations; by the mid seventies even de Redcliffe felt discouraged. The Palmerstonian hope could hardly longer be persisted in, though the Turkish tendency to rely on

British support, even to an unwarranted degree, was not diminished.

This Turkish failure to reform is the fundamental background of the crisis of the second half of the seventies, in which again Britain was to be a prime mover and which we wish to examine primarily from the standpoint of the role played by her in it, all the more so as there was essentially no French role. The revolt which broke out in Bosnia and Herzegovina in the middle of 1875 was but another instance of the oppressively ineffectual rule of the Turk. The occurrence was hardly a novelty and there was ample precedent for action by the Powers, especially as the revolt, instead of being promptly put down, spread the next year to Bulgaria, where Turkish methods of suppression were unusually brutal, even by the standards of the Balkan milieu.

But the constellation of Powers in 1875 was different from that of the early fifties. France had not psychologically recovered from the impact of her defeat; her behavior throughout the episode was one of abstentious effacement, with the consequence that her role is virtually negligible and may essentially be ignored. Germany had taken her place as the active director of continental affairs, but Bismarck had no interest in the Near East, other than the negative one of avoiding its becoming a cause of disruption of his cherished Dreikaiserbund. Russia was very interested, but divided in her counsels. Apart from the unsatisfactory state of her finances and of her military establishment, there was on the one hand the very real and aggressive sympathy of the Pan-Slav movement, sharply manifested in the Moscow Benevolent Society. When Serbia went to war in 1876, many Russian volunteers—quite genuine ones in this instance—flocked to the Serbian ranks; one may recall the description in the closing pages of *Anna Karenina.* The Tsar himself was more moderate and in fact rather irritated with the Serbs.

To Andrássy the episode was an unwelcome annoyance, for he felt an equal dislike for the prospect of Russian gain and for having his country become more involved with, perhaps even having to incorporate additional, South Slavs. The Dreikaiserbund could furnish an answer which Bismarck would gladly assist in producing, through consultation with a view to elaborating a common policy; his own later description of his role in the episode as that of "honest broker" is essentially correct and applies from the very beginning. Proposals jointly endorsed by all three members of the alliance of the Eastern Powers would stand a good chance of being accepted by Europe.

The Andrássy Note of December 30, 1875, was an adequate response in the circumstances. It proposed a scheme of reforms which the Powers and even the Sultan accepted, but which the insurgents did not. The issue remained unresolved. There was no marked British reaction in the early stages of the disturbance, though it is interesting to recall the purchase of the Suez Canal shares and the assumption of the Indian imperial title at this time.[11] There was, however, guarded suspicion directed in varying degrees toward all three members of the Dreikaiserbund. Disraeli felt a certain personal jealousy of Bismarck for the position the latter had achieved in Europe, but more serious was a genuine distrust of his aims, which the war scare[12] earlier in the year had tended to accentuate. Bismarck, quite objective where Turkey herself was concerned, did not believe in her continued viability, hence was indifferent to the prospect of her demise and partition, a solution that might furnish an answer to his desire for continued Austro-Russian understanding.

His influence on Andrássy was considerable, but the latter was hesitant and might even respond to the British desire to stress the common bond of anti-Russian interest. Andrássy's ways proved tortuous in the event, not made easier by his distrust of Beust, his predecessor in office and currently his ambassador in London, whom he sometimes bypassed. Thus a possibility existed of either Anglo-German or Anglo-Austrian understanding, though on wholly different bases, hence of driving a wedge in the Austro-German combination. But Bismarck's approaches to England in 1876 foundered on the shoal of Derby's invincible distrust; the English attempt to establish a common policy with Austria was persisted in but it ran likewise into Austrian distrust: was not England attempting to have Austria pull the chestnuts out of the fire for her? The reverse possibility was precisely that which Bismarck entertained, at this time as on later occasions; though his preference was for general peace, an Anglo-Russian clash was the least unpleasant prospect from his own point of view.

In the delicate and complex game of playing for position, the Dreikaiserbund, if it could maintain its cohesion, would obviously carry great weight. The failure of the original Andrássy proposal resulted in another, the Berlin memorandum in May, an expanded and more specific version of the earlier Andrássy Note; it was the work of Bismarck, Andrássy, and Gorchakov, the respective leaders of the three Eastern Powers. For that very reason, hardly a cogent one in itself, it was rejected by England, where Disraeli yielded to his pique for not having been consulted. Even Queen Victoria was at this stage quite moderate in her views; as she put it in a letter to her Prime Minister: "The Queen's dislike of our separating ourselves from the rest arises from the fear that Turkey will look to us to help her against the rest of Europe and that we shall precipitate rather than prevent the catastrophe."[13] It was to be some time before Disraeli would convert her to his own uncompromising belligerency.

The Queen's point was indeed well taken, and here one is reminded of the tragicomedy that resulted in the Crimean War, the failure of communication between England and Russia. For the Tsar was not moved by aggressive intent, but rather bent on resisting the proddings of his own bellicose Pan-Slavs, quite powerful even at court. That influence hampered his freedom of action, for he could not, beyond a certain point, run counter to or even ignore a feeling that had deep roots in the Russian milieu. This is where a fundamental source of misunderstanding arose. Seen from England, the Russian concern for coreligionist Balkan Slavs easily took on the guise of hypocritical pretense; yet the authenticity of the Russian feeling was no different from the Gladstonian indignation at the doings of the "unspeakable" Turk. These feelings might be thought to have provided the basis of common understanding, but precisely in this fact lay the comedy of errors. Whatever the feeling in England, the possibility of Russia being the agent of Christian Europe in evicting the Turk ran into the English interest expressed in the view that the key of the road to India lay in Constantinople, for all that English opinion was divided on this point. Disraeli, partly because misinformed at first, played down the reports of Turkish behavior and, as indicated, was alone in Europe in refusing to accept the Berlin memorandum.

The Anglo-Russian Confrontation

Though popular opinion was a larger factor in England than in Russia, the ultimate control of foreign policy rested in few hands.[14] Of the Queen, whose role was not decisive, yet not devoid of importance, it may suffice to say that she was thoroughly under the influence of her Prime Minister, who knew so well how to cajole her womanly and royal feelings. A quotation will illustrate what came to be her state of mind. In January 1878, at the climax of the crisis, she wrote to Disraeli as follows: "She feels she cannot, as she said before, remain the sovereign of *a country that is letting itself down to kiss the feet of the great barbarians,* the retarders of all liberty and civilization that exists. . . . She is utterly ashamed of the Cabinet . . . *Oh, if the Queen were a man, she would like to go and give those Russians, whose word one cannot believe, such a beating!*"[15]

Disraeli said many things and can easily be quoted to varying purpose. Though not particularly well informed, yet willing to take a position, his guiding thought where matters imperial were concerned was consistently assertive and aggressive. In November 1876, when further things had happened which will be explained in a moment, justifying his policy, which had been the object of severe attacks, he used the following words on the occasion of the Lord Mayor's banquet at the Guildhall:

> . . . though the policy of England is peace, there is no country so well prepared for war as our own. If she enters into a conflict in a righteous cause . . . if the contest is one which concerns her liberty or her Empire, her resources are, I feel, inexhaustible. She is not a country that, when she enters into a campaign, has to ask herself whether she can support a second or a third campaign. She enters into a campaign which she will not terminate till right is done.[16]

Allowing for the somewhat exaggerated boast, echoes can be heard of Palmerston asserting the warranted self-confidence of British power. Like Palmerston earlier, Disraeli, as we shall presently see, would have his way in the end.

Lord Derby, though technically foreign secretary, played but a relatively minor role in the whole episode. What influence he had was thrown in the direction of passivity and inaction, and even in his own domain decisions were taken at times by others rather than by himself. It was fitting that he should resign at the nearing climax of the crisis, in January 1878, precisely on the issue of the use of force, and that his post should be taken by Salisbury, a more important figure altogether in this whole affair. The impression created by Salisbury's actions and words throughout is one of sane reasonableness and solid information, in which respects judgment can only be far more favorable than in the case of the Prime Minister. Salisbury thought that the Crimean War had been a blunder, the repetition of which he would do his utmost to prevent. His own views of the Eastern situation, detached and realistic, with perhaps a touch of cynicism, were clearly expressed as early as January 1876:

> Peace on this side of the world would be in no particular danger if only Turkey could be persuaded to stop crumbling to pieces. But if the process is to go on as fast as it has been going on for the past twelve months, the time will come when something must be done. A government of some kind or other must be formed for all those wretchedly oppressed multitudes. It cannot be left as a no-man's land. But the division of that kind of jetsam is peculiarly difficult. If the Powers quarrel over it, the calamities of a gigantic war must be undergone. If they agree, people call it a partition and denounce it as immoral.[17]

Mention must also be made of the situation in Constantinople, where it is no exaggeration to speak at this time of a tradition of dominant English influence. This was the result of the Turkish reliance on British opposition to Russian designs, an opposition most effectively implemented through the defense of Ottoman integrity, a policy to which Britain was more dependably wedded than any other European Power. There was foundation for this Turkish belief, encouraged even beyond the degree to which it was warranted by Britain's representatives at the Porte. The role and influence of Stratford de Redcliffe may be recalled, who believed in the possibilities of authentic Turkish reform and rejuvenation. Salisbury's scepticism on those scores has just been indicated, but the current British envoy, Sir Henry Elliot, was

Turcophile to an extent which caused him to report misleadingly to his own government on Bosnian and Bulgarian happenings, for instance.[18] His influence in Constantinople was as a consequence very great and to a point in turn misled the Turks into unwarranted assumptions of English support. His replacement by Layard, for similar reasons, did little to change the situation; the resulting misunderstanding is one of the basic components of the crisis, for it induced the Turks to take positions in the belief that, no matter what the consequences might be, they would, in the final outcome, always be rescued by Britain. Salisbury's comment is apt on the confusing effects of Britain's behavior: "The character of our ambassador has no doubt done something to ruin our influence, but the character of our policy has done more."[19]

The English representatives in Constantinople had to contend with their Russian counterpart. General Ignatiev represented the power of Russia at its most aggressive; far from devoid of ability, intrigue came to him easily and he could have been a good candidate for the distinction of being the greatest liar in Christendom. He could even be quite brazen about it.[20] Count Shuvalov, the Russian ambassador in London, was a rather different man, who gained British trust, worked for understanding and peace, and also played an important role in the story. These were the principals; under their guidance, and outside of it, matters drifted during 1876.

The British rejection of the Berlin memorandum in May of that year to a degree placed Britain in an isolated position, but it also had the effect of encouraging the Turkish belief in the dependability of British support. This was the year in which trouble spread to Bulgaria, the harsh suppression of which had among other effects that of introducing a further element of confusion in the English position. With the advent of the Tory administration in 1874 Gladstone went into relative retirement, even formally abdicating the Liberal leadership. Balkan events roused his moral indignation and prompted him to write, in September, the famous pamphlet on *The Bulgarian Horrors and the Question of the East,* in which he unmercifully castigated the Turks, advocating their eviction "bag and baggage" from Bulgaria—just from Bulgaria, incidentally, be it noted. The phrase caught on and the pamphlet was an enormous and immediate success, giving expression as it did to a widespread feeling in England, naturally a source of embarrassment to the Turcophile and anti-Russian—the two not necessarily identical—tendencies. At any rate British opinion was sharply divided, a division from which even the Cabinet was not immune, a condition in turn needless to say hardly conducive to clarity of policy.

Meantime Serbia had gone to war, soon to be joined by Montenegro, a development the Tsar reproved despite the flocking of Russian volunteers previously indicated. The spreading of the Balkan disturbance was proper cause for consultation among the members of the Dreikaiserbund. Instead of this, however, just two of its members, Austria and Russia, the most immediately concerned, laid between them the bases of a common policy, leaving Bismarck out of their counsels. The Reichstadt agreement of July 1876[21] was, as far as it went, a sensible move since it was calculated to avoid an Austro-Russian conflict, but it left out of account Turkish and British views and wishes, the former to a point dependent on the latter.

Serbia's defeat simplified matters in some degree, though it took a Russian ultimatum in October to induce Turkish acceptance of an armistice. Russia's belligerent preparations meantime had aroused Disraeli's concern and there was discussion of far-reaching possibilities of action ranging from Constantinople to the Persian Gulf and Suez.[22] Yet the Tsar had no wish for a confrontation with England. Though sceptical of the likelihood of Turkish reforms, he accepted the meeting of a conference of the Powers in Constantinople.

The fact that Salisbury was the English delegate at that meeting is measure of the importance attached to it by his government. He was well chosen for he took a moderate and sensible view of the whole situation. His observation to Disraeli in the preceding September is a good indication of his approach: "It is clear enough that the traditional Palmerstonian policy is at an end. We have not the power, even if we had the wish, to give back any of the revolted districts to the *discretionary* government of the Porte."[23] This could easily furnish the basis of an understanding with Russia. Salisbury went to Constantinople well briefed, for he proceeded in leisurely fashion by way of Paris,

Berlin, Vienna, and Rome. The Constantinople conference was a failure, and the details of it[24] need not be gone into. The failure was in part the result of what may be described as Turkish "shenanigans," the proclamation of a liberal constitution for Turkey under the influence of Midhat Pasha; reformed Turkey need not submit to any advice or interference from the Powers. Leaving aside the authenticity of the Turkish reforming zeal and the prospects of its future implementation, subjects on which scepticism was highly warranted, mention is worth making of the divided British counsels in Constantinople, a divergence most sharply focused on Salisbury and Layard respectively, and of which the Turks were highly aware. The conference disbanded on January 20, 1877, and the summation of Salisbury may be quoted:

> Our business here is, I imagine, pretty well over. I think it is time we concluded. If any further negotiations are possible to prevent the outbreak of war they will have a better chance elsewhere. . . . Your future policy will require the gravest consideration. You will have to choose between (1) Helping to coerce; which would give you a voice in the ultimate disposal,—but that you will not do.
>
> (2) Allowing Russia to do her worst, and if she attacks and wins, coming in to regulate her demands when peace is talked of. This would be the easiest way, if practicable. But it is very possible that she may refuse to let you have your word at the end—and that you may have to content yourself with writing a pathetic despatch on the model of Lord Aberdeen's after the peace of Adrianople.
>
> (3) You may come to terms with Andrassy and Gortchakoff for a regulated occupation of Bulgaria and Bosnia; providing for evacuation after a certain date—and securing an indemnity to the occupying Powers out of the revenue of the provinces of which Bulgaria at least is very rich. This could only end in the creation of two tributary States, but I believe it to be the safest course. That the machine here can stand very long I believe to be impossible. Even if Russia does not invade it will crumble of itself; and the Russian Embassy has in its hands the threads of a vast network of intrigue, by which it can, if it will, aggravate enormously any natural causes of anarchy.[25]

The final outcome is here outlined but it took another year and a half before it was achieved, and the climax of the crisis was reached during this interval. In England there was heated debate in Parliament,[26] which reflected in full the effects of the divided public feeling and where Disraeli defended his policy. To the traditional policy of defending the integrity of the Ottoman Empire England must adhere; allowing for the depth of the humanitarian feeling that moved the English people, like Palmerston of old, he ended on the note of appeal to the nationalist emotion; "the determination to maintain the empire of England" was a still deeper emotion. Put in another way, Disraeli considered it a vital British interest to veto too great a southward extension of the Russian influence.

This still left room for negotiated compromise. The Russians on their side, having made further arrangements with Austria,[27] finally cut the Gordian knot of futile haggling with the Turks by issuing a declaration of war on April 24. The situation was increasingly reminiscent of that of 1853, especially if one bears in mind the failure of the attempt to reach an Anglo-Russian understanding during the interval between the Constantinople conference and the Russian declaration of war. Yet the discussion went on, Derby attempting to clarify the precise nature of the British interest in a note to Russia in May, after which Shuvalov went to Russia. He himself, a moderate man, was exasperated by his failure to obtain a favorable response to the proposals he brought back from St. Petersburg. He squarely placed the blame for this failure on the Queen and on Disraeli, which in the last resort meant the latter, and a measure of his feeling may be gathered from his comment that "the other ministers do not look favorably on *this conspiracy of a half-mad woman with a minister who once had genius but had degenerated into a political clown.*"[28] Exaggerated though the language was, there was point to the observation, for divided counsels continued to prevail in London. While Layard in Constantinople complained of being "without general instructions for my guidance," later in the year, in November, Disraeli in a letter to the Queen bemoaned that "in a Cabinet of twelve members there are seven parties or policies"; with characteristic unction he went on to explain, after describing six of these policies, that "the seventh policy is that of Your Majesty, and which will be introduced and enforced to its utmost by the Prime Minister."[29]

The fact of war and the attendant uncertainties of its fortunes introduced a novel element in the situation. If tension subsided during the second half of 1877, it was because of Russian technical miscalculations. Instead of an easy march through the Balkans the Russians found themselves checked by the spirited resistance that Osman Pasha put up at Plevna, which they proceeded to besiege. There is some warrant for the view that Osman Pasha saved the peace of Europe at this point by furnishing an opportunity for the cooling of tempers and for further diplomatic discussions, the details of which need not be considered here.[30]

However, Plevna fell in December, after which Turkish resistance totally collapsed. As the Russians neared Constantinople there was panic in the Turkish Government; the outburst of the Grand Vizier to Layard early in January,[31] charging England with faithlessness and treachery, is wholly understandable. For Layard had encouraged unwarranted hopes among the Turks, hopes which English action seemed to belie. Despite Disraeli's brave words in private that "the critical time has arrived when we must declare the emergency. *We are drifting into war,*"[32] divisions in the Cabinet persisted. The fleet was ordered to enter the Straits, but the order was countermanded. The motion for military credits precipitated a five nights' debate in Parliament and on that issue Derby resigned, his place being taken by Salisbury, also a moderate but not an indecisive man. The Russians were profuse with reassurances about the ultimate fate of Constantinople, but would not commit themselves about its occupation, while London debated whether sending the fleet to that city would frighten the Russians into staying out or irritate them into coming in. Layard's observation that "our ships were sent up to protect the lives and property of British subjects which needed no protection. But we gave the Russians a pretext for entering the capital and causing the very danger apprehended"[33] had point.

Feeling left to themselves the Turks surrendered, accepting first an armistice at the end of January, then on March 3 signing the Treaty of San Stefano. The detailed terms of that arrangement need not be specified here[34]; it will suffice to say that it constituted another Russian mistake, specifically in the form of creating a very large (by Balkan standards) Bulgarian state which would reach from the Black Sea to Albania and abut on the Aegean. It was generally taken for granted that the Greater Bulgaria would be a Russian satellite, and this extension of Russian dominance almost to the gates of Constantinople is what Britain would in no circumstances allow. Nevertheless, though others too, Austria for example, might have reason to object, England remained isolated[35]; this is what precipitated the final crisis, which was an Anglo-Russian confrontation. Something must be said of its course and of its final resolution.

There is no need to dwell on the discussion of raising an English land force, or on the unimpressive gesture of moving a few thousand troops from India to Malta; without a continental ally—unwilling Austria was the only possible candidate since the Turks were defeated and demoralized—the prospect of land war with Russia was unpromising. Nor was the thought of attacking Russia from the rear, marching an expedition from India to the Caspian Sea, seriously entertained. Sea power could ensure control of Constantinople and inflict serious damage on Russia, whose exhausted forces and financial difficulties were an inducement to moderation.

The circumstances pointed to a rational compromise, but wars are often the result of blunder, misunderstanding, false pride taking a rigid stand on matters of prestige. The Crimean episode offered a good precedent for this sort of occurrence, and Salisbury's view of that conflict has been mentioned. The Tsar remembered it, too, the opening episode of his reign. Reason carried the day in the end, but the spring of 1878, during which unavoidably complex and delicate negotiations were carried on, was a period of uncertainty and crisis. That the Russians had put themselves at a disadvantage by their unilateral action[36] gave considerable strength to the English contention that the whole Treaty of San Stefano should be submitted to the arbitrament of Europe, which alone and collectively was entitled to entertain a revision of the existing international instruments—

mainly the 1856 Treaty of Paris—which regulated Eastern affairs. Salisbury was adamant on this point, which he made clear in his circular of April 1.[37] This document was generally well received, whether by the opposition at home, or by those abroad who had been irked by and concerned over what seemed confused purpose in England. At the same time Salisbury's position was not one of fundamental intransigeance; he was perfectly willing to accept that, having fought a successful war, Russia could hardly be expected merely to accept a restoration of the *status quo ante*. From this point on it was essentially a matter of finding common ground on the extent of the Russian advantage. This is what the Salisbury-Shuvalov protocol of May 30 accomplished, upon the latter's return from another visit to St. Petersburg. The ground was laid for the meeting of a European congress which, appropriately, was called by Bismarck and met in Berlin.[38]

England and the Congress of Berlin: "Peace with Honour." The importance of the Congress of Berlin of 1878 may be judged from the ranks of the personalities who attended its proceedings. Some aspects of it lend themselves to humorous treatment. Three old men stood at the apex. Bismarck, the youngest of them, was troubled by his usual ailments, but his interest in the situation brought him out in full vigor. He presided effectively, knowing how to dose deference with brutality, of which the Turks were the chief victims.[39] Gorchakov, vain and failing, jealous of both Bismarck and his own able second, Shuvalov, had to be carried to some of the meetings. Disraeli did not have to endure that indignity, content to hobble on his cane. The view of him expressed in confidence by Salisbury is worth quoting: "What with deafness, ignorance of French, and Bismarck's extraordinary mode of speech, Beaconsfield has the dimmest idea of what is going on—understands everything crossways—and imagines a perpetual conspiracy."[40] Yet Bismarck, suspicious and sceptical at first, came to appreciate the qualities of mind that *"der alte Jude"* displayed in private meeting.

On a more serious level, the congress, which lasted just one month—previous diplomacy had laid the ground—produced agreement with a relative modicum of difficulty. The guiding basis was the Anglo-Russian compromise, expressed in the formation of a much reduced Bulgaria that would not extend south of the Balkan range.[41] From this other things followed, mainly derived from the application of the principle of equilibrium, expressed in the form of compensatory gains for others: Bosnia and Herzegovina were turned over, save in formal title, to Austria, whose additional occupation of the Sandjak of Novi Bazar would prevent Serbo-Montenegrin contiguity; Germany wanted nothing for herself, France and Italy were too timid and did not push any claims of their own.[42] Within the Balkans proper, Serbia and Montenegro made some territorial gains, and so did Greece, although it took three years to implement the definition of her share.[43]

This left England. The guiding line of her policy is well expressed in an earlier communication from Salisbury to Layard:

> The more I think of the future destiny of the Porte, the more I am convinced that any return to the position of the Treaty of 1856, with its diminished boundaries and weakened force, could only lead to the dissolution of the whole Ottoman empire, followed by endless anarchy. The time is passed for talking about "independence and integrity." It was something of a sham in 1856,—as events have proved. But it would be a pure mockery now. The Porte must recognize that it needs protection; that that protection must be given by some Power that has an interest in avoiding the anarchy which would follow on its fall; and must be facilitated by a willingness on the part of the Porte itself to make the necessary arrangements.
>
> . . . .
>
> The mere presence of the Russians at Kars will cause Persia, Mesopotamia and Syria to turn their faces northward. Then a Russian party will arise,—and consequent disorder—and the languid administrative powers of the Porte will be overtaxed, and a chaos will follow of which, in some form or other, the Russians will take advantage to reduce the Porte to impotence, and to turn its provinces into Russian satrapies. *The presence of England is the only remedy which can prevent this process of destruction from going forward.* I think that we might very properly enter into a defensive alliance with the Porte, undertaking to join in defending her Asiatic Empire from any attacks of Russia. . . .

But, to give any strength or value to such an undertaking, some port in the Levant would be an absolute necessity.[44]

The italicized sentence is the key; the form which it finally took was Cyprus.[45] What mattered was to contain the southward advance of Russia, and since the Russian (or Bulgarian) withdrawal to the Balkan range had for its counterpart the British consent to Russian gains in Armenia, the Porte itself must in turn consent to a British presence in the Near East. An Anglo-Turkish Convention was signed on June 4. There is an interesting footnote, for the convention was secret and the question remained of its disclosure, which raised that of the reaction of the other Powers as well as that of domestic opinion. Some awkwardness was to be expected, especially as the secret was leaking out in the *Daily Telegraph*.[46] Salisbury was annoyed, though not unduly upset. The following quotation brings out several factors in the situation, as well as his own sense of humor:

My idea of the course of events may be expressed in the following calendar, of which, of course, the figures are imaginary:

June 25. Congress reaches end of 18th article.

June 25. Night. Mr. Layard is directed to get firman from Sultan and send it to Lord John Hay [the British admiral in the Mediterranean].

June 26. Congress discusses 19th article. British P.P. make earnest, but unavailing, attempts to persuade Russia not to take Kars. Then, at the end of the day, they reserve to themselves to state at the next sitting the course which will be imposed on England in consequence. Same day fleet is ordered to rendezvous near Cyprus.

June 27. British P.P. communicate the Convention: Waddington [the French representative] tears his hair, and telegraphs wildly to Toulon.

June 27. Same day, Lord John Hay anchors before Famagosta.

June 28. Sir Stafford Northcote [leader of the House of Commons] lays despatch and Convention on the table of Parliament. Mr. Gladstone makes a speech four hours long on the selfishness of England and the purity of Russian motives. French admiral arrives with three ships off Famagosta,—but finds he is too late.

June 29. *Daily News* conclusively proves that the idea of taking

Cyprus could only have occurred to the Semitic instincts of the Prime Minister.[47]

It was not a bad anticipatory summation of the course of events.

With the signature of the Treaty of Berlin on July 13, 1878, the three-year disturbance essentially came to a close and a thirty-year period of at least comparative stability was inaugurated in the Near East. How is the episode to be appraised, especially in the context of the focus of interest of the present discussion?

In the conclusion of his excellent study of the question[48] R. W. Seton-Watson gives a sharp analysis and redresses a balance. In moral terms the Russians were open to the same charge of duplicity, or deserving of an equal credit for sincerity, as the British. Backward as they themselves were by British standards, their advance in Central Asia was a civilizing activity. The difficulty and the reciprocal suspicions arose from the confusion of two levels of operation: sentiment and statecraft. The response to Gladstone's strictures was as genuine in England as the motivation of Russian volunteers in the Balkans. The factor of opinion is an important one, which governments must appease, but are also not backward in exploiting, misleading, and arousing. Neither side had a way of knowing for certain which in the opposite was authentic response or machiavellian calculation. Granting the far greater freedom of the English milieu, the contrast between the response to *The Bulgarian Horrors* and the popular jingle of 1878 could, to say the least, be puzzling as seen from St. Petersburg. Correspondingly, on the British side there was no way of disentangling the role of the various forces at work in the more secretive Russian milieu. In both cases, as in most human cases, explanations in terms of the forces of evil found readier acceptance than the opposite interpretation. At the level of statecraft naïveté is a forbidden commodity.

Leaving aside the moral aspect of the question and its effects, important as these were, and looking at the British side of the case, a distinction must be made between what may be called fundamental and long-term policy on the one hand and mode of implementation on the other. The Turkish failure was what gave rise to the issue at this particular time, as on other occasions. To get rid of the Turk, share his domain among the Powers, the great of Europe and the small Balkan ones, was a wholly rational solution in the context of the day. Bismarck thought it so, but the simplicity of his approach was to a large extent the result of his own lack of involvement. If the demise of the Turk was ruled out, or even his eviction "bag and baggage" from Bulgaria alone, what remained was the necessity of checking Russian expansion, a policy to be understood in the larger imperial context.

In the European sector a case could be made for what may broadly be described as the Gladstonian policy of underwriting the desires of all Balkan nationalisms, whose fierce attachment to independence could constitute a more solid barrier against Russian designs than the decadent Ottoman state. This would have been a long-term gamble, perhaps a shrewd act of self-interested broad-minded generosity, one by no means alien to the British tradition inimical to forcible prolonged suppression of the popular will. What counts in politics is results, and the merits of such a policy can only be appraised in the light of subsequent developments. No doubt the Balkan peoples were destined to become independent, and the strength and durability of the nationalist emotion is not to be denied. That particular story is not yet finished and we must remember that we are dealing with the eighteen seventies.

It is easy to take a cynical view of the Cyprus Convention, England's *"pot de vin,"* as Bismarck described it, and about which a variety of unflattering observations were made.[49] The fear, expressed in the above-cited communication of Salisbury to Layard, about the attraction of Russian power in the Asiatic domain of the Sultan may seem exaggerated; it, too, may be reflected on in the light of later developments. Given the fact of the British imperial establishment, the validity of which few questioned, a clear and logical policy is revealed. Such it appeared to Salisbury, desirous of peace and often critical of the ways of his chief; that is why he had accepted the succession of Derby in the Cabinet. Of course one can dismiss the whole proceedings as a sordid illustration of the wicked ways of imperialism. Such a view is as relevant as the true enough observation that the ways of power are evil, and as useful as the conclusion therefrom that the use of it must be eschewed. As a group, the directors of British policy were not especially evil men, no more than those in other occupations; the right to rule they did indeed take for granted, but the idea of service was also not alien to them. The world had not yet found a way to function without rulers.

Certainly the whole episode belies at this point the view of absent-mindedness where the imperial interest was concerned. The Palmerstonian tradition was upheld, which is not the same thing as saying that the method of operation deserves commendation for its technical quality. If Salisbury was a moderate and careful man, and Derby timid, Disraeli was neither. His casualness, the deficiencies of his information, caused him to act at times with irresponsibility. Yet it is also a measure of the power that England still commanded that carelessness could be afforded. Should it come to the test of force, England could still face it with confidence, even in the awkward absence of a continental ally. But this again is not to say that the handling of policy was of high quality. The "peace with honour" that Disraeli brought back from Berlin was a cheap phrase which meant little more than that Britain had had her way. His boast in a Guildhall speech in 1879 that "one of the greatest of Romans, when asked what were his politics, replied, *Imperium et Libertas*. That would not make a bad program for a British Ministry," recalls Palmerston's *civis romanus sum* discourse. It also had a somewhat hollow ring, though there was sound basis for the more sober sequel:

> If . . . one of the most extensive and wealthiest empires in the world . . . from a perverse interpretation of its insular geographical position, turns an indifferent ear to the feelings and fortunes of continental Europe, such a course would, I believe, only end in its becoming an object of general plunder. So long as the power and advice of England are felt in the councils of Europe, peace, I believe, will be maintained, and for a long period.[50]

England, like others, would defend, if need be fight for, what she regarded as the national interest, a matter on which agreement was closer than the divisions of popular opinion or the violence of parliamentary debates might seem at times to indicate. It was England's good fortune that her interest could easily accommodate itself with such basic components of the continental scene as the nationalistic force. This is in large measure what gave English policy the quality of fair and open-minded reasonableness which is one of its characteristics. Just as Palmerston was in favor of Austria surrendering her increasingly untenable position in Italy, and even allowing that there was point to Schwarzenberg's reminder about Ireland, so likewise Salisbury recognized that Bulgaria should not be put back under Turkish control. But then again this did not prevent the upholding of either Austria or Turkey, who, to be sure, should grant overdue reforms and concessions. To object that the Greater Bulgaria of San Stefano did violence to the Greek nationality happened to be a true observation; it also happened to fit to a nicety the wish to contain the expansion of Russian influence toward the Straits. That element of reasonableness, the ability to move with, instead of against, the active forces of the time, was a valuable asset of British policy, not available in the same measure to others. It was not, for that matter, adhered to with blind consistency where other interests were at stake, and we shall have occasion to observe presently Gladstone's own handling of British foreign affairs.

In any case the settlement of Berlin was undoubtedly a British success and it gave peace to the Near East for a time while providing a reprieve for the incorrigibly unreforming Turk. There is no need to go into the local details on its aftermath, be it the laborious implementation of the Greek share of compensation, or even the 1885 union of Eastern Roumelia with Bulgaria, a logical outcome of the decisions of 1878, and to a degree and for that reason not the occasion for a major crisis. One aspect of the aftermath of that incident must at least be mentioned, however, the disruption of the Dreikaiserbund as a consequence of Russian discontent, focused largely on luckless Bismarck. But even that, in the present context, does not assume undue importance. The Austro-German alliance of 1879 had been Bismarck's response to the first breakdown of the tripartite association, and two years later the Dreikaiserbund had been revived. When it broke down again over the same Balkan apple of discord, the episode just mentioned of Bulgarian aggrandizement and its repercussions, Bismarck contrived in 1887 the delicate, ambiguous solution that was the Reinsurance Treaty with Russia. Broadly speaking, and even if with increasing difficulty, from the standpoint of Europe as a whole, England included, it may be said that so long as he held office Bismarck dominated the international scene on the basis of the co-operation of the three Eastern Powers; whatever difficulties he encountered did not prevent the continuance of his good relations with England or the continued isolation of France.

But in Britain, shortly after the events of 1878, there was also an aftermath that must be mentioned. To put it succinctly, it may be said that Disraeli committed the error of failing to capitalize on the asset of the emotional welcome that greeted his return from Berlin, whence he brought back "peace with honour." The English scene, whether in Parliament or in the press, was little calculated to convey abroad the fundamental unity of purpose which was far better expressed in the actual operation of foreign policy. The glamor of Disraeli's achievement had long evaporated when a general election was called in March 1880. Gladstone had fully come out of retirement, leading his party with a vigor that found full vent in the intensity of his attacks on the policies of his rival, both domestic and foreign. The Midlothian campaigns are a landmark in British political annals. Leaving aside the domestic aspects of the debate, the definition given by Gladstone of what should in his view be the guiding principles of British foreign policy is worth recalling, even if in brief form, especially in view of his approaching resumption of office. In a speech at West Calder on November 27, 1879, these principles were stated as follows:

1. "To foster the strength of the Empire . . . and to preserve it for great and worthy occasions."
2. "To preserve to the nations . . . the blessings of peace."
3. "To cultivate to the utmost the Concert of Europe" in order to "neutralise and fetter the selfish aims of each."

4. "To avoid needless and entangling engagements."
5. "To acknowledge the rights of all nations."
6. Foreign policy "should always be inspired by love of freedom."[51]

Allowing for the high moral tone, which this extract fails to convey in full, one will observe that the fundamentals express broad continuity of purpose rather than substantive divergence. There was, however, enough of this divergence, in details of implementation especially, to make the debate a genuine discussion. As a result of the election the respective strengths of the parties were almost exactly reversed: the 351 Conservatives against 250 Liberals became 349 Liberals against 243 Conservatives.[52] In April 1880 Gladstone became for the second time, and to Queen Victoria's chagrin, her Prime Minister, to remain in that office for the next five years. The record of his administration, in which the foreign office again went to Granville, furnishes some interesting light on the operation of British foreign policy, the consistent continuity of which it serves to accent. We shall come back to it after, and in connection with, some other matters, having for the most part to do with French affairs.

The French Dilemma: Revanche or Empire?

French Retrenchment After 1871—Tunis

In the story that has just been recounted the name of France barely appears. The defeat of 1870 had had a very deep impact on the French body politic. Defeat in war can be a passing episode, retrievable in future if the means for it are at hand. It has been pointed out before that, from the standpoint of the objective components of power, France and Germany in 1870 were not unfairly matched. Bismarck thought so, even after the war, and ever watched with great care French internal developments, a matter largely outside of his control, as well as French diplomacy, an activity which his own could in considerable measure counter. His success in the latter domain, so long as he lasted in office, will not be repeated. By 1890 the relationship of power between the two countries was no longer the same as it had been twenty years earlier. The significance and the consequences of that fact will be examined in a later chapter.

On the score of the Treaty of Frankfort French sentiment may be regarded as unanimous: it was a wrong to be redressed. But in any event France must first put her own house in order. Much of this task was accomplished with both expedition and effectiveness. Native French wealth made it possible to discharge the war indemnity ahead of schedule, and the Army was reorganized. Bismarck was concerned over the rapidity and the extent of French recovery.

But, apart from the deserved respect that German power inspired, insofar as domestic affairs impinged upon foreign policy, in the French case their influence was a restraining factor. For the unanimity which prevailed in regard to the territorial loss did not extend to the view of future domestic political arrangements. The circumstances of the downfall of the empire effectively destroyed the prospects of a return of that régime; the upholders of Bonapartist legitimacy never commanded a dangerously large following. But monarchist legitimacy was a different matter; its advocates controlled in fact a majority in the National Assembly, and had it not been for the legacy of 1848 France might well have had a king after 1871.[53] More fundamentally, the issue which divided the French electorate, the same issue which had prevailed since the Great Revolution, was that of the power of the executive. In broad terms, the Republic came to stand for popular power, opposition to any form of dictatorship, watchfulness against the danger of the man on horseback. A weak executive therefore, an all-powerful legislature, was the republican answer; the debate of that issue absorbed much of the energy of French politics during the decade of the seventies till the Republic won.[54] While this was going on, the men in charge of foreign policy, from Thiers to Gambetta, through Freycinet and Ferry, were generally moderate men who entertained no grandiose illusions of the possibilities of French power. Revanche, if revanche there was to be, must be put off to more suitable times and circumstances, if not to the Greek kalends, which, however, does not mean that the idea was abandoned. French patriotism and nationalism was no withering plant.

For a time, rather than nourishing aggressive intent, it was the negative fear of renewed German aggression that dominated the cares of French policy. The war scare of 1875 may be mentioned in passing, though it warrants little more than that.[55] What is of interest about the incident is the use that was made of it by Decazes, the French foreign minister, to test the international climate. The matter was taken with sufficient seriousness in both St. Petersburg and London to cause those capitals to send cautioning warnings to Berlin: a further diminution of France would be injurious to the equilibrium of Europe. Bismarck, somewhat annoyed, especially at boastful Gorchakov, pretended innocence; there is little reason to believe that he seriously contemplated a preventive war against France at this time. France on her side could derive some small consolation from feeling that she had a measure of support, but fundamentally neither the Dreikaiserbund nor the satisfactory state of Anglo-German relations was seriously affected.

Whether justified or not, the French concern over German intentions was real. The hypnotic concentration on "the blue line of the Vosges" was an inhibiting limitation to the exercise of an influence and a policy which had encompassed the whole world. This condition went to the heart of a fundamental dilemma which was central to the orientation of French policy and which was to become the subject of intense debate. In a growing and expanding Europe, should France focus her attention on the Rhine to the exclusion of all other interests? The extension of the Southeast Asian establishment to the protectorate of Annam in 1874 and exploratory activity in the Red River delta were small things. In the Near Eastern crisis which has been discussed in the first part of this chapter the passivity of the French was tantamount to abdication. Yet the French interest in the Near East was both old and substantial; consideration of it by Britain in electing the Cypriote option rather than a mainland base has been indicated.

Since the fundamental criterion adopted in the Treaty of Berlin was that of equilibrium based on equivalent compensations, it would have been logical that France should gain some corresponding advantage in connection with that settlement. It was Salisbury who took the initiative, upon informing Waddington of the Cyprus Convention, of suggesting the impossibility of "leaving Carthage in the hands of the Barbarians."[56] Bismarck gave hints to the same purpose. Yet nothing was done at the time, partly in order to avoid difficulties with the Italians, to whom Bismarck held out the same bait. Both Italy and France came away from Berlin with clean but empty hands, the criticism addressed to Cairoli in the former country.

The Tunisian situation bears some resemblance to the Egyptian insofar at least as similar financial difficulties beset a native potentate; European intrusion into Tunisian finance went back to 1868. For the rest, Tunis constituted a logical extension of the Algerian possession. But, looking across the mid-Mediterranean passage, Tunis was similarly regarded by Italy as a logical extension of herself; climate and other conditions suggest affinity rather than difference between the Italian South and Tunisia. There had in fact been some Italian emigration into Tunisia, larger in numbers than the French; however, because of its nature, it did not carry the weight that French economic influence did. England, too, was interested in Tunisia though in a different way. The English interest was essentially strategic; possessed of Malta, England would find it preferable, now that Italy had become united, that the two sides of the mid-Mediterranean passage should not be in the same hands. A French occupation of Tunis would suit England's imperial calculations best.

The intense activity of French and Italian local representatives in Tunis[57] after the Congress of Berlin was indication that the days of Tunisian independence might be counted; there was mutual suspicion between France and Italy but neither country wished to raise an issue with the other. In 1880, while he was Prime Minister, Freycinet had told the Italian ambassador, "I promise you not to make any decision without consulting you."[58] But Freycinet fell in September, and Jules Ferry, his successor, did not abide by the promise. Using the pretext—a true condition though hardly a novel one—of tribal raids across the Algerian frontier, the appearance of a French naval force and a land expedition induced the Dey to sign in May 1881 the Treaty of Bardo, which turned Tunisia into a French protectorate. The Italian reaction was violent and was one of the factors which induced Italy to join the Triple Alliance the following year. Ferry's statement that "M. Cairoli was disappointed and surprised; he was not deceived,"[59] is a correct, if rather legalistic, appraisal, but the matter could have been handled with more deftness where Italy was concerned. However, neither in London nor in Berlin did Italy find support, for the French action was acceptable in both those capitals. In the latter especially, Franco-Italian divergence suited Bismarck's purpose to perfection; he was genuinely sympathetic toward French imperial activity which could serve the twin related purposes of diverting French energies and attention away from Europe, more specifically from the Rhine, while possibly embroiling her with others, and not with Italy alone. The French were not unaware of these possibilities, and the establishment of the Tunisian protectorate was not without its critics.[60] The affair was in part responsible for the bare majority that Ferry received in the Chamber after the elections and which led to his resignation in November.

The Struggle for the Nile (I)

Whether the establishment of the Tunisian protectorate was a passing and isolated episode or the inauguration of a new policy of imperial expansion was anything but clear at this point. In retrospect one can see that the latter was to be the case, but the result was tortuously achieved and in the face of persistent domestic opposition. Within a year of the Tunisian episode a more important issue had to be faced. Something must be said of the opening of the chapter, the close of which sixteen years later was the formal French surrender in Egypt.

The long-standing French interest in that still nominally Ottoman province and the vicissitudes of it since Palmerston's days have been explained.[61] So has the partial retrieval of an English oversight that was the purchase of the Khedive's shares in the Canal Company in 1875. It is worth recalling the warning issued by Derby at the time when the sale of the shares was being considered:

> You know what is my opinion of the French Company. It has taken the risks of the undertaking; it deserves all the credit for it and I have no wish to question any of its claims to the

> gratitude of all. But you must acknowledge that we are the country most interested in the Canal . . . ; the preservation of this passage has become for us a capital question. . . . The guarantee resulting from the control of the Porte is no longer sufficient today; if we should lose that provided to us by the participation of the Khedive, we should be wholly at the mercy of M. de Lesseps. . . . The Company and the French shareholders already own 110 millions out of the 200 which represent the capital of the shares; that is enough.[62]

This may be juxtaposed to Derby's communication to Lord Lyons, the British ambassador in Paris, "I sincerely hope we may not be driven to the expedient. The acquisition would be a bad one financially, and the affair must involve us in disagreeable correspondence both with France and the Porte."[63] Derby's customary caution, or timidity, would have been content to keep the status quo unaltered, meaning no increased French control of the company. We know the sequel. Disraeli was bolder; he, or England, purchased the shares. It is well to remember that this was 1875, the year of the war scare, when France was especially desirous of England's support, hence anxious not to antagonize her.

The course of Egyptian events during the next seven years can be briefly summarized.[64] Following the purchase of the Suez shares, the mission of Sir Stephen Cave to investigate the condition of Egyptian finances marks the beginning of the significant British intrusion in the affairs of that country. Suspension of debt payments in 1876, following the Ottoman example of the preceding year, led the Khedive to institute the *Caisse de la dette publique* to supervise the service of the debt. Though Austria-Hungary and Italy were represented in that body, the Anglo-French condominium which emerged is what mattered.

Further difficulties in 1877, a new inquiry, Anglo-French this time, brought suggestions for radical reforms that reached into the constitutional domain and out of which the beginnings of constitutional government might have developed for Egypt; in the ministry of Nubar Pasha, Rivers Wilson held the ministry of finance, that of public works going to the French de Blignières. Khedive Ismail was not co-operative, and under Anglo-French pressure the Sultan was induced to depose him in favor of his son, Tewfik, in some respects no improvement, for Tewfik was a weak and irresolute man.

The crisis of the second half of the seventies which has been recounted in the first part of this chapter is conclusive indication of the importance England attached to the protection of her communications with the East. For all that the Suez Canal had been a French undertaking and that the Canal Company was French, free passage from the Mediterranean to the Red Sea was inevitably a first care of British policy. That is why the Russians must be blocked at the Straits, lest they intrude too significantly into Mediterranean affairs; the control of Cyprus must in part be seen as a strategic move in the protection of Suez. Disraeli realized this full well, no less than Salisbury; his statement in Parliament in defense of his purchase of the Khedive's shares may be recalled: "I have always and do now recommend it [the purchase] to the country as a *political* transaction, and one which I believe is calculated to strengthen the empire."[65] It is well to remember, however, that this purchase did not give England control of the company any more than the occupation of Cyprus gave her control of Egypt.

The Egyptian focus of British interest was very clear and very consciously realized. The role of British officers in the Egyptian service, Baker Pasha (Valentine Baker), for example, in the early seventies, in confirming Egyptian control over the Sudan, is also to be borne in mind. The governor-generalship of the province by General Gordon during the second half of the decade fits into the same pattern of growing interest. Indeed the idea of British control of Egypt is one that in the circumstances must inevitably occur; Bismarck himself had suggested it, in part for motives of his own. But so far the idea was rejected, one reason being the complications to which it would give rise.

The French role in the development of modern Egypt, from the days of Mehemet Ali, has been mentioned before. French influence had not diminished under the reign of Khedive Ismail, and the canal had been built. Remembering his own encounter with Palmerston, Thiers' advice to Gambetta,[66] cited at the head of this chapter, may also be recalled. The unwillingness to face a confrontation with France, one for which the initiative would have had to be British, thus led in the Egyptian case to the same negative policy as in the case of Russia, a policy which found expression in the attempt to preserve Ottoman integrity, at least so far as it still had meaning in Egypt. The desire to avoid difficulties with France was likewise one of the reasons for choosing the Cypriote base instead of one on the mainland, for Syria, too, was a sphere of French interest. Salisbury had been careful to prepare the ground with Waddington before the disclosure of the Cyprus Convention, suggesting the possibility of the Tunisian compensation for France.[67] The establishment of the French protectorate over Tunis three years after the Congress of Berlin has been recounted.

The case of Egypt presented certain special features, for if the country was still formally part of the Ottoman Empire, that allegiance was little more than nominal. The fiction of the Sultan's power could be used in forcing the removal of Khedive Ismail, but that action was in effect the result of an Anglo-French decision. The Egyptian story in addition has special relevance in the present discussion, for Egypt was the locale where French and British influences met, and where we are about to record the opening of the last chapter in the contest between the two. That chapter is particularly instructive as an illustration of a difference in power and of the manner in which power was handled. The opening phase of the chapter alone will be considered at this point.

The difficulties in Egypt were of two kinds. The nature of the more narrowly financial is perhaps best expressed in Lord Cromer's words:

> The maximum amount of harm is probably done when an Oriental ruler is for the first time brought in contact with the European system of credit. He then finds that he can obtain large sums of money with the utmost apparent facility. . . . This is what Ismail Pasha did. During the early years of his rule, Egypt must have been an earthly paradise for all who had money to lend at usurious rates of interest, or third-rate goods of which they wished to dispose at first-rate prices.[68]

The rates of interest on some loans, effectively reaching 20 per cent, were indeed usurious, calculated to kill the goose that laid the golden eggs.

The other difficulty may be called psychological. Europeans enjoyed the privilege of extraterritoriality, for which indeed there was warrant. But the multiplicity of jurisdictions—seventeen of them—and the crass abuses to which their application had led, resulted in understandable xenophobia. This was particularly felt in Army circles, given the additional inducement of having been the victims of financial retrenchment. This is the background of a rising at the beginning of 1881, in which Ahmed Arabi played a leading part.[69]

By this time Gladstone and Granville had replaced Disraeli and Salisbury in England while Jules Ferry held power in France. Ferry was in turn replaced by Gambetta and his *grand ministère* in the middle of November. The Egyptian situation was explosive, and Gambetta was more determined than Gladstone on the score of possible intervention in Egypt. The result was the Gambetta Note of January 7, 1882. It was an Anglo-French instrument, intended to strengthen the position of Tewfik, and stated that

> The two governments closely united in their determination to anticipate by their common efforts all possible complications . . . do not doubt that the publicly given assurance of their formal intent in this regard will contribute to forestall the dangers that the government of the Khedive might have to fear, *dangers which,* for that matter, *would certainly find France and England united in meeting them* . . .[70]

Here was an attempt at French leadership, but it raised a number of questions. The declaration of Anglo-French agreement did not, for one, correspond to the facts; England was at this point far less sanguine than France about the prospect of intervention hinted at in the note. Secondly, although all acknowledged the primacy of the French and of the British interests, Egypt was in law Ottoman domain, hence an international question. Bismarck's views on the subject, even though Egypt was not a primary German concern, were not to be ignored;

Freycinet, soon to succeed Gambetta, was fully conscious of the weight they would carry.[71] On January 26 Gambetta's ministry was overthrown, on a domestic issue to be sure, though uneasiness over his foreign policy was in the background of the vote.

The struggle between Tewfik and the military was coming to a head. In support of the former an Anglo-French squadron appeared before Alexandria, while an ultimatum[72] from those Powers forced the resignation of the nationalist ministry. The inability of the Khedive to resolve the ensuing stalemate, save by recalling Arabi, was measure of the confused and explosive atmosphere which prevailed and which erupted into rioting in Alexandria on June 11, rioting in the course of which some fifty Europeans, many of them Greeks, were killed.

The response was not long in coming though it was not quite immediate. Just a month later, Alexandria was bombarded by the British fleet, the French dissociating themselves from this action. The reason for the English action was ostensibly self-defense, the raising of land fortifications and batteries by the nationalists.[73] There had taken place by this time almost a complete reversal of the French and English positions in regard to the manner of dealing with Egypt; Gladstone, even if reluctantly, was reaching a point of stronger resolution. While discussions were going on between the two countries on the scope and nature of the prospective intervention (shades of 1956!) Gladstone put the British position in the following terms on July 22 in the Commons:

> We should not fully discharge our duty, if we did not endeavour to convert the present interior state of Egypt from anarchy and conflict to peace and order. We shall look during the time that remains to us to the co-operation of the Powers of civilized Europe, if it be in any case open to us. But if every chance of obtaining co-operation is exhausted, the work will be undertaken by the single power of England.[74]

On the French side, Freycinet, though he might differ with the British on details, was fully aware of the consequences of the French abstention. On July 18 he obtained from the Chamber, by an overwhelming majority, a credit of 6,000,000 francs. Gambetta supported the motion, as well as the necessity of continued understanding with England, Clemenceau taking the opposite stand.[75] But only a few days later, on July 29, the request for an additional grant, though a modest enough one—only 9,000,000 francs—for contingent operations in Egypt, led to an intense debate. The earlier majority was almost exactly reversed, the motion was defeated, and the government fell. It was a crucial turning point, and the debate had been dramatic, adequate reflection of the uncertainties that troubled France. The opposing tendencies in the domain of foreign policy are well illustrated by two statements. In support of the motion Gambetta said:

> Let not France be shorn of her heritage; it is not for the sake of the Egyptian national party that we ought to go to Egypt; it is for the sake of the French nation. What I dread more than anything is that you may hand over to England, for good and all, territories, rivers, and rights of way where your title to live and to trade is no less valid than hers.[76]

With no less sincerity and conviction Clemenceau argued thus:

> Truly, there seems to be somewhere a fate which is preparing a terrible explosion in Europe. Who here will dare assume the responsibility for that which is impending? Who will dare say that on the day of the diplomatic settlement of the Egyptian question, it will be better for France to be alone with England in a quarrel with Europe than to be with all Europe claiming her legitimate share of influence in Egyptian territory? . . . Gentlemen, the conclusion of what is happening is this: Europe is full of soldiers; everybody is expecting them, all the powers are reserving their freedom of action for the future; reserve the freedom of France.[77]

In other words: the future is uncertain; do not scatter your forces; keep your powder dry—with an eye on the Rhine!

There is no denying that Gambetta's words were prophetic. There was no English plot to evict France from Egypt; as

Salisbury quite correctly had already summed it up a year earlier:

> As to our policy—the defense of it lies in a nutshell. When you have got a neighbour and faithful ally who is bent on meddling in a country in which you are deeply interested—you have three courses open to you. You may renounce—or monopolise—or share. Renouncing would have been to place the French across our road to India. Monopolising would have been very near the risk of war. So we resolved to share.[78]

Gladstone and Granville were quite willing to share, as far as immediate action at least was concerned, for Gladstone was strongly opposed to any joint permanent position in Egypt, foreseeing the difficulties and bickerings to which such an arrangement was likely to give rise.[79] The immediately preceding few years had already furnished sufficient evidence on that score.

In any case the French decision, registered in the overthrow of Freycinet at the end of July 1882, may be regarded as the turning point; Ferry's characterization of it, *"ce fut le grand naufrage!"*[80] seems apt. Ferry was a convinced imperialist, whose breadth of perception may in retrospect be judged quite justified; the opponents and critics of his policy, men like Clemenceau, for example, were not impelled by a dearth of patriotic emotion or by the moralistic view of imperial activity, but their judgment of the possibilities of French power, hence of the dangers implicit in the dispersal of native resources, was different.

Thus the British proceeded alone. Having brought up an adequate contingent, they landed in Egypt. Arabi's forces, offering no more than token resistance, were routed at Tel el-Kebir on September 13; two days later Cairo was entered. An important chapter in the story of Egypt, in that of the Anglo-French rivalry in the Near East, had been brought to a close and a new one opened. From this standpoint, the Fashoda confrontation sixteen years later is no more than a footnote, the larger significance of which will be examined in the next chapter.

The work of reorganization undertaken by Lord Cromer does not fall within the scope of this discussion; it is an interesting, enlightening, and by no means inglorious, page in the British imperial record. Suffice it to mention that in November the dual Anglo-French control was abolished. There was natural irritation and disgruntlement in France, but no effective opposition; the price of abdication must be paid. Beyond the immediate task of restoring order in Egypt there was no far-reaching, clearly thought-out plan of action. The statement in Granville's circular to the Powers of January 3, 1883, that British forces would be withdrawn "as soon as the state of the country and the organization of proper means for the maintenance of the khedivial authority will admit of it," can be taken at face value rather than as an expression of calculated insincerity.

Yet it is also difficult to refrain from a smile. The inner logic of empire was too strong, and it seems more appropriate to recall Gladstone's prophetic view of 1877 quoted at the head of this chapter. The just mentioned statement of Granville may be contrasted with the almost simultaneous plan drawn up by Lord Dufferin for the reorganization of Egypt. It was a statesmanlike document, expression of the English imperial approach at its best, looking to the day when Egyptians would be capable of governing themselves in the same civilized and effective manner as Englishmen did—perhaps a limited and naïve touch, some would say. But, obviously, that day lay in the future, and England's guiding hand could be quite firm in the meantime. This was aptly expressed in the Khedive's reply to some directions from the Sultan: *"Le véritable Khédive c'est Lord Dufferin. C'est de lui qu'émanent tous les ordres, et le Khédive n'en est que l'instrument de transmission."*[81] From the time he was appointed British agent and consul general in Cairo, Lord Cromer—still Sir Evelyn Baring at the time—may be regarded as the uncrowned king of Egypt. Put side by side, Granville's circular and Dufferin's almost simultaneous report furnish a perfect illustration of the English mode of operation, in its own eyes high-minded and straightforward while furnishing to outside onlookers food for the image of crafty duplicity.

Desirous though she may have been to leave Egypt, England soon found out that the attempt to re-establish order in that country could not be confined to financial advice and control.

For Egypt meant the Nile, and the political issue of the range of Egyptian control of that river could not be ignored. This meant in turn the Sudan, a vast region of somewhat vague definition, where Egyptian control was ever loose and now especially challenged by a local chieftain, the Sheik of Dongola, better known as the Mahdi, a fanatical religious leader in addition.

General Hicks led an Egyptian force that met defeat in November 1883. His expedition, though condoned, had been discouraged in London where the half-hearted policy of reluctant commitment continued to prevail. With a view to curtailing the extent of involvement, the Egyptian Government was compelled to accept the abandonment of the Sudan. Yet, feeling a degree of responsibility, General Gordon, who had earlier acquaintance with the region, was entrusted with the task of evacuating the Egyptian garrisons from it. The instructions given him were imprecise and Gordon had ideas of his own. Undertaking to dispose of the Mahdi, he found himself instead besieged in Khartoum. There were awkward, painful, and inconclusive discussions in the British Cabinet on the score of whether or not to relieve the reliever. Tergiversation turned into a case of too little and too late. When the expedition finally sent out approached Khartoum it found that the city had fallen, its garrison, including Gordon, having been massacred. This was in January 1885.

The episode was humiliating and there were recriminations in England. Yet the degree of the setback to the English position, and to the English imperial development as a whole, is perhaps best summed up in Gladstone's own words, though written in a different context:

> If England commits follies they are the follies of a strong man who can afford to waste a portion of his resources without greatly affecting the sum total. . . . She has a huge free margin, on which she might scrawl a long list of follies and even crimes without damaging the letterpress.[82]

The directors of French policy, even those who, like Freycinet and Ferry, favored imperial expansion, did not think that France could risk committing "the follies of a strong man." Ferry was again Prime Minister in February 1883 and took charge of the foreign office the following November. He was desirous of retrieving the French position in Egypt, but was unable to escape the consequences of the preceding July. For France to have expressed her disgruntlement by resuming her freedom of action was, in the circumstances, little more than a petulant gesture[83]; it amounted in effect to underwriting Britain's freedom of action, a far more meaningful thing, since Britain was in effective possession. There was otherwise no marked French reaction to the above-mentioned British circular of January 3.

The difficulties in which Britain became involved on the Nile made the prospects of her departure from Egypt more remote. Another British circular, of April 19, 1884, seemed a firmer commitment. Britain would withdraw her forces at the beginning of 1888, but more importance attaches to the qualification "on condition that the powers will then be of the opinion that the evacuation can be effected without compromising peace and order in Egypt."[84]

The condominium could not be revived, and Ferry fell back on the attempt to internationalize the question, a policy of which he made a somewhat strained defense in his own parliament. The issue of the debt gave him a useful lever, others tending to agree with the French position on that issue. Capitalizing on Britain's isolation and her Sudanese troubles, at the beginning of 1885 he took an initiative which, with the support of the other Powers, led to the meeting in Paris which produced an international convention in regard to Egyptian finances.[85] But more to the point is the summation that he had made a year before:

> . . . from the day . . . when the Chamber of Deputies refused to underwrite in any fashion an armed intervention in the valley of the Nile, it was evident that the arrangements, partly political, partly financial, of 1876 and of 1879, were fundamentally undermined, that they were fated to be soon inevitably ruined. The dual control, destroyed in fact, was soon to become abolished in law.[86]

The Paris meeting was also to deal with the question of the neutralization of the Suez Canal. The discussion opened on the morning of March 30 with an Anglo-French exchange of amenities. But on the afternoon of the same day Ferry's government was overthrown, though over a wholly unrelated issue; France was having some difficulties in Tonkin. Yet in a broader sense it was the same fundamental issue of the validity, or lack of validity, of French colonial enterprise. What happened on March 30, 1885, is very reminiscent of what had taken place on July 29, 1882; more will be said about this presently.

As to Egyptian matters, they may be dismissed at this point for the time being. A Suez Canal Convention was finally produced in 1888. France could not undo the controlling British position in Egypt; a policy which has been described as one of pinpricks was, with the passage of time, to become increasingly futile and unrewarding, and only served to confirm the British hold. It would take another decade, and a major Anglo-French confrontation, before France would decide to cut her losses. That episode will be examined in the next chapter. Much happened in between, of which something will now be said.

The Impact of the Revival of Imperial Activity (I)

The judgment of Gladstone which has been quoted,[87] if it had validity at the time it was penned, in 1889, would have seemed questionable to many on the morrow of the Sudanese setback. The last days of Gladstone's administration were beset by other troubles as well, and the accumulation of problems must be considered in the larger context of European politics.

French influence may have been effectively evicted from Egypt after 1882, but the ambiguity of the English position made it a hostage which others could exploit, France not the least. The first reaction to Khartoum, shared by the Queen herself, was to retrieve the setback; this was rejected by the Cabinet. As Rosebery later explained to Ponsonby:

> Every nation could do as it liked with us. . . . In all probability we should have embarked in one of the greatest wars of the century; and with both our arms bound, one to Afghanistan, the other to Central Africa, we should be exposed to endure what

any Power might choose to lay upon us, and be compelled to forgo all voice or share in the destinies of the world.[88]

The panicky tone of the statement was not wholly unwarranted. Salisbury's observations in the House of Lords expressed a calmer view and the policy to which England adhered:

> With Mediterranean politics, as such, we have no great reason to concern ourselves . . . but Egypt stands in a peculiar position. It is the road to India. The condition of Egypt can never be indifferent to us, and . . . we have a right, and it is our duty to insist upon it, that our influence shall be predominant in Egypt.[89]

The Sudan could be abandoned, for the time being at least, but not the control of Egypt, though Salisbury did not "care by what technical arrangements this result is obtained."

Gladstone survived the setback and the criticism, though only for a while longer. "Every nation," in Rosebery's statement, in effect meant three, France, Russia, and Germany. Russia mattered very much at the moment, for the long-standing competition in Central Asia flared up again at this point. Afghanistan as usual was its focus, where the Russian occupation of Pendjeh at the end of March was regarded in England as a breach of previous understandings and provoked a strong reaction. It almost looked like war for a moment—all the more reason for curtailing the Sudanese commitment—though it proved possible to reach eventual accommodation. The Tsar did not want war and he could both disavow and exploit the somewhat independent action of his generals.

The role of Germany must be mentioned here. Of Bismarck's attachment to the Dreikaiserbund sufficient has been said; the association had been revived and was effective at this time. It was Bismarck's desire to cater to Russian good will which caused him, when an Anglo-Russian war seemed a possibility, to advise the Porte to abide by existing arrangements, denying, by force if necessary, passage to British vessels through the Straits. The Western aspect of Bismarckian policy was equally distasteful to England. For if he would on occasion suggest that she take Egypt, he gave even greater encouragement to French imperial ambitions. Where Egypt was concerned he had supported the French in blocking the English proposal for a scheme of financial reorganization in 1884.

In fact, for roughly a decade, from 1875 to 1885, he adhered consistently to this policy, seemingly desirous and hopeful that it might lead to the abandonment of French revanchist hopes. His expectations on that score were deceived, and the French were on guard lest complications ensue in other quarters, suspicious of the Bismarckian encouragement, seen as possible duplicity, yet also welcoming it all the more, as their resentment over Egyptian developments had brought a cloud in their relations with England. To speak of an end of the Anglo-French alliance in 1882 is an overstatement, but it is nonetheless true that Ferry contemplated a limited measure at least of co-operation with Germany. For this he was violently attacked in his own country.

It would be no less an exaggeration to speak of a Franco-German alliance. Yet it is also true that the call for the colonial conference which met in Berlin in November 1884 was an expression of co-operation between those two countries and had an anti-British point. The Berlin congress ended in harmony—it dealt largely with the Congo—and endeavored to put some order in the process of colonization and the staking out of claims, but it also confirmed the French position on the banks of the Congo.

Bismarck's earlier opposition to imperial activity by his own country had been overcome by this time, and Germany was participating in the scramble for Africa, even if in relatively moderate fashion as a latecomer. Yet even in this early phase some friction with England appeared, Bismarck taking exception to what he referred to as a British Monroe Doctrine for Africa.[90] In any case Gladstone's policy had the effect of producing the isolation of England where there was some suspicion of the possibility of a continental combination. Bismarck was not anti-British and certainly wanted no quarrel with England, but, as he put it, "Mr. Gladstone knew nothing of foreign affairs and was impossible to do business with,"[91] a judgment confirmed by Queen Victoria's that "Mr. Gladstone has alienated all other countries from us, by his very changeable and unreliable policy."[92]

Remote as the possibility of anti-British continental coalition may have been, there was some reason for concern over the condition of England's first line of defense, naval supremacy. While the British Navy was the largest of all, by 1882, at a time of rapid technical transition, the English margin of superiority was hardly impressive.[93] The sum total of these circumstances is aptly expressed in Professor Langer's judgment:

> The British government that was responsible for this turn of events pursued a policy more disastrous than it could know, for the year 1885 marks the end of England's unquestioned preeminence in the colonial field. She was no longer the one real world power. The others had acquired extra-European interests, and the new colonies were born under the evil omen of antagonism to England. With new footings abroad the other powers were in a better position than ever to bring pressure upon England. She was more exposed to attack than before. From this time on, the policy of splendid isolation was already *passé*. For some time yet the policy was maintained, at least in theory, but if the isolation remained, the splendour was gone.[94]

It is difficult indeed to change a course and the methods which duration and success have endowed with the attribute of hallowed tradition, and we shall presently observe the slow and at times fumbling English search for adaptation, which some would say has not yet ended.

France had no cause to entertain similar illusions, or delusions, of power; the caution of her policy verged in fact at times on timidity. Yet there were those in France who advocated a bolder course, especially where matters imperial were concerned. The view expressed by Leroy-Beaulieu in his *De la colonisation chez les peuples modernes* that colonization "is for France a question of life and death: either France will become a great African power, or in a century or two she will be no more than a secondary European power; she will count for about as much in the world as Greece and Roumania in Europe,"[95] may be taken as their text. Gambetta and Ferry accepted this view, as the latter's analysis shows:

> The policy which would sacrifice the acquisitions which should be made at the present moment for the sake of future revindications is a policy of self-deception and improvidence. Such a policy would be suited to an impetuous people, ready to stake all on a throw of the dice, not to a peaceful and thoughtful France, which has never ceased to believe in the ultimate triumph of justice, but which can and must wait for the hour to strike on the clock of destiny. No one knows that hour, no one would dare set it. We only know that France will not seek deliberately to precipitate it. And yet the outside world moves on, interests shift, positions change, new groupings of forces are taking shape and organizing themselves. Should we have, for the sake of an unbridled but short-sighted chauvinism, cornered French policy in a blind alley, and our eyes fascinated by the blue line of the Vosges, allowed everything to happen, commitments to be made, issues resolved without us in the world around us? The policy of clean hands would have meant, without a doubt, Italy in Tunis, threatening our flank, Germany in Cochin China, England in Tonkin, both of them in Madagascar as well as in New Guinea, in a word the bankruptcy of our rights and of our hopes, a new treaty of 1763, without the alibi of Rossbach and of Madame de Pompadour. How could those who have spared the Republic and France such a humiliation not have deserved the gratitude of the Republic and the country?[96]

The penetration into the Red River region, out of which developed war with China in 1884,[97] was vigorously pushed by Ferry. Inadequate means and some military blunders resulted in a setback at Langson at the end of March 1885. The setback was easily retrieved, as shown by the conclusion in June of the Treaty of Tientsin, by which China recognized the French position. But the news of the setback produced a strong reaction in Paris; on the thirtieth of March a bitter debate took place in the Chamber, where Ferry defended his policy in connection with the request for an additional military appropriation of 200,-000,000 francs.

The debate is worth reading. Ferry's chief attacker, Clemenceau, proposed the following motion:

> *La Chambre, résolue à voter tous les crédits nécessaires pour venir au secours des soldats engagés dans l'Extrême-Orient et condamnant le ministère, passe à l'ordre du jour.*

It is also worth noting that in defense of his motion Clemenceau had the following to say:

> To open a credit of 200 millions means, I suppose, sending an expeditionary force of 50,000 men. Where are they to be sent? To send 50,000 men to China is the equivalent, bearing proportions in mind, of sending 5,000 men to Tonkin. That is precisely to continue the policy which we must no longer pursue. When these 50,000 men will have clashed, at any point of the Chinese empire, with the innumerable masses which may confront them, when they will be in danger, as are today our soldiers in Tonkin, we shall be asked other hundreds of millions, we shall be asked to furnish additional forces. And we shall not be able to deny them. And from appropriation to appropriation, from millions to millions, from additional forces to additional forces, we shall reach the exhaustion of the resources of France.
>
> Gentlemen, we must stop on this road, the time has come to face the situation. We must make a clear assessment of the risk, it must not be exaggerated, the situation is already sufficiently serious. It must be examined with coolness, and we must take with firm resolution the steps which it dictates. But to commit blindly the future of this adventurous expedition, to make at this moment a final commitment that France may be compelled to uphold, whatever the cost may turn out to be, Gentlemen, you could not think of taking such a step, and there will be no one here to suggest it.[98]

It may be pointed out, in passing, that this was France in 1885, not the United States in the 1960's. Clemenceau withdrew his motion after that of the government, limited to the request for credits, had been defeated by a vote of 306 to 149. The bitterness of feeling is evidenced by another motion which "*déclare le ministère solidairement responsable et demande sa mise en accusation.*"[99] This was defeated by 287 votes against 152.

The reason why this episode, minor in itself, has been dwelt upon at some length is because it brings out a number of important things. Given the situation in Tonkin, even Clemenceau agreed that French honor must be upheld, but for the rest the sharp confrontation between Ferry and himself is the nicest expression of the divisions of French opinion. On the score of patriotic devotion one could hardly choose between the two men; their difference was on the uses to which French power should be put, and this in turn implied a judgment on the extent and capabilities of that power; where the one saw frittering dispersion, the other perceived in the imperial endeavor the possibility of ultimate enhancement of that power. In the context of the day and with the advantage of perspective, it is difficult to dissent from Ferry's judgment; to refrain from participating in the imperial competition would have been tantamount to another abdication, a diminution of the position of world power, without furnishing any accretion to domestic French power or to the French position in Europe. Where economic motivation is concerned, French imperialism had weaker foundations than either the German or the British; apart from the elusive, yet not wholly empty of substance, factor of prestige, France derived comparatively little economic advantage from her imperial activity; her capital, of which there was an ample supply, did not flow in large quantities to her newly acquired African possessions, and it may even be contended that some at least of the large flow of foreign investment—to Russia, for example—could have been put to better use in developing a domestic economy which, among the advanced ones, remained relatively backward, in fact did not keep up with the rate of progress of others, the German most of all.

At this point another consideration intrudes. At the time of the Franco-Prussian War the population of France was almost equal to the German. But, for reasons the consideration of which exceeds the bounds of the present discussion, after 1870 France's numbers remained virtually unchanged, constituting in this respect an outstanding exception to the pattern of the rest of the world. With the passage of time the significance of the demographic deficiency, compounding the economic, was to become an increasing source of concern. Was France to follow in the footsteps of Spain, and how much and how long could she, in the circumstances, maintain her place among the Powers of first rank? Adjustments of this nature, as the Spanish case again shows, are slow of registration, yet their fundamental significance and effect cannot forever be denied.

Empire could to a point be an answer. To say nothing of the far from negligible use that France was to make of colonial contingents in mitigating her own manpower deficiency, the fact of cultivating world interests, of maintaining a presence in all quarters of the planet, could, for a time at least, also mitigate the effects of domestic relative decline. But only for a time perhaps. This is what lends especial interest to the efforts made by the directors of French policy to achieve through imperial development and diplomatic maneuver what concrete and material native resources might prove inadequate to do.

The further operation of this endeavor will be observed in the following chapters, but another component of the French situation may be mentioned at this point. Alsace-Lorraine, the wrong of 1871 to be redressed, had in French politics the status of a sacred cow. To advocate acceptance or renouncement—Bismarck's hope for a time—would in the French milieu have been tantamount to political suicide. Yet many at least, not to say most, of the French political leaders were sensible, realistic, and moderate men who did not entertain unwarranted illusions about the relative dimensions of, and about the growing discrepancy between, French and German power.

Brave speeches could be made, but even Clemenceau was not a rash man, while Boulanger was to prove an empty bubble and Déroulède provided an innocuous sop to feelings that need not be translated into action. France after all was a republic, alone among major European states endowed with universal suffrage. The fact is not without significance, for all that has been written—some of it with justice—about the deficiencies of French democracy. The French peasant and the French petit bourgeois—between them they accounted for a substantial majority—were in a fundamental sense a property-loving species, hence of conservative inclination, not to say even timid, hardly an adventurous breed. Patriotic they were indeed, and the nature of education, the manner in which history was taught in the schools, at the elementary and secondary levels especially, was a powerful instrument in instilling the nationalistic emotion and in cultivating the belief in the superiority of the national culture. But this is not the same as producing a widespread desire for adventure.

This moderation was reflected in the political domain; the overthrow of Ferry over a minor Tonkinese misadventure is suitable expression of this unadventurous mood. Taken as a whole, the French milieu was such as to constitute a hampering factor on the pursuit of a bold foreign policy; those in charge of that policy must operate with caution, ever aware of the limitations imposed by the mood of domestic opinion, no less than by the concrete components of French power, two elements not unrelated to each other. The cultivation of the possibilities of empire, an operation which it was generally possible to carry out with a small expenditure of resources and with a minimum of public attention, is one consistent aspect of French policy during this period; the exploitation of the possibilities offered by the relations of the European Powers among themselves is another, the operation of which we shall have occasion to observe.

NOTES ON *Chapter V*

1. On the idea of preventive war, and particularly on the war scare of 1875, see below, p. 207.

2. "There is no balance, and unless we go out of our way to act with the three Northern Powers, they can act without us, which is not agreeable for a state like England." Disraeli to Lady Bradford, Monypenny, William F. and Buckle, George E., *The Life of Disraeli, Earl of Beaconsfield,* 6 vols. (1913–20), Vol. VI (1920), p. 23.

3. See above, p. 126.

4. See above, p. 134.

5. The lack of proper co-ordination in the direction of Russian policy was to a point responsible for the seeming unreliability of Russian declarations. General Kaufmann, directing operations in Central Asia, acted with considerable independence.

6. See above, p. 99.

7. Lord Salisbury had broken with Disraeli at the time of the passage of the Reform Bill, but the quarrel was patched up and he retained office throughout the second Disraeli ministry, first as Secretary for India, then as foreign secretary. He supported and implemented Disraeli's foreign

policy though by no means always in agreement with him on specific matters or moves.

8. There had been hesitations and objections owing to the evil days upon which the imperial dignity had recently fallen, as shown by the fate of Napoleon III, not to mention that of the unfortunate Maximilian in Mexico.

9. A brief and convenient summary of this activity may be found in *CHBFP*, Vol. III, pp. 72–90.

10. Ibid., p. 77.

11. This is not to imply a causal connection between these various events, but it nicely underlines the contrasting interests and approaches.

12. See below, p. 207.

13. Queen Victoria to Disraeli, May 16, 1876. Cited in Seton-Watson, R. W., *Disraeli, Gladstone and the Eastern Question* (1935), p. 34. There was subsequently severe criticism of this rejection of the Berlin memorandum in England itself.

14. It is of interest to recall in this connection the views expressed by Lord Salisbury in an article in the *Quarterly Review* of January 1866: "Our system is constructed to carry out in the policy of the Government the actual opinion, at the moment, of the million and a quarter of electors by whom the nation is ruled. It is a machine of the most exquisite delicacy. The conduction from the electors, who are the source of power, to the Ministers, is so perfect that while Parliament is sitting they cannot govern for ten days in opposition to the public will." Cecil, Lady Gwendolen, *Life of Robert Marquis of Salisbury*, 4 vols. (1921–32), Vol. I (1921), p. 139.

15. Seton-Watson, op. cit., p. 267. (From Monypenny and Buckle, op. cit., Vol. VI, p. 216.)

16. Cited in Seton-Watson, op. cit., p. 104, and *CHBFP*, Vol. III, p. 108, from *The* [London] *Times* of November 10, 1878.

17. Salisbury to Sir Louis Mallet, January 14, 1876. Cecil, op. cit., Vol. II (1921), p. 80.

18. See Seton-Watson, op. cit., p. 29 and *passim*.

19. Salisbury to Lord Carnarvon, January 11, 1877. Cecil, op. cit., Vol. II, p. 122.

20. As when caught red-handed by Salisbury in the falsification of a map, an incident which he passed off smilingly with a compliment to Salisbury's finesse of perception.

21. It envisioned two alternatives: restoration of the *status quo ante* in the event of Turkish victory; extensive Balkan reforms and rearrangements, making Constantinople a free city among them, in the opposite eventuality.

22. Summarized in Seton-Watson, op. cit., pp. 95–101.

23. Salisbury to Lord Beaconsfield, September 23, 1876. Cecil, op. cit., Vol. II, p. 85. Disraeli had become Lord Beaconsfield in August.

24. Seton-Watson, op. cit., Ch. IV; Cecil, op. cit., Vol. II, Ch. IV; *CHBFP*, Vol. III, pp. 107–15.

25. Salisbury to Lord Derby, January 19, 1877. Cecil, op. cit., Vol. II, p. 124.

26. This may be followed in Hansard's *Parliamentary Debates*, Series III, Vol. CCXXXII.

27. The Budapest Convention in January, when the failure of the Constantinople conference had become apparent, and an extension of that convention in March.

28. Cited in Seton-Watson, op. cit., p. 203.

29. Disraeli to the Queen, November 8, 1877. Ibid., p. 237.

30. The persistent British attempt to enlist Austrian support was based on unfounded hopes of its possibility, for the Austro-Russian understanding continued during this phase of the war.

31. Layard to Lord Derby, January 8, 1878. *CHBFP,* Vol. III, p. 124.

32. Seton-Watson, op. cit., p. 364. This was the time of the popularity of the jingle: "We don't want to fight, but by jingo, if we do, we've got the men, we've got the ships, we've got the money too."

33. Seton-Watson, *Britain in Europe,* p. 532, n. 65. At one point the Turks opposed the coming of the British fleet for fear it would have precisely the effect of leading to a Russian occupation of Constantinople. Eventually, the fleet came but anchored some distance from the city, British naval and Russian land forces facing each other across a short stretch of water, an adequate expression of the degree of tension but also of the continuing reluctance of both countries to bring matters to the test of force.

34. The terms of the treaty may be found in a variety of places, for example, in Hertslet, D., *The Map of Europe by Treaty,* 4 vols. (1875–91), Vol. IV (1891), pp. 2672–96.

35. Continued English attempts to procure an alliance or at least an understanding with Austria were subject to the same frustrations as they had been before.

36. This was compounded by their dilatoriness in disclosing the terms of the treaty to the British. When these became known they produced the violent outburst of indignation that might have been expected.

37. This important statement of the British position is discussed in *CHBFP,* Vol. III, pp. 130–31. Also in Seton-Watson, *Disraeli . . . ,* pp. 379–83. The circular essentially embodied the views expounded by Salisbury in a letter of March 21 to Disraeli, with whom he had discussed the problem. See also Cecil, op. cit., Vol. II, p. 226.

38. Bismarck was none too happy over the situation, fully aware of the thanklessness of the role of the "honest broker." At the same time, Germany was the most authentic neutral in the Near Eastern imbroglio while highly concerned with the Austro-Russian relationship. France, too, had been a neutral but her self-effacing role still reflected the aftermath of her demotion of 1870. Berlin had indeed replaced Paris as the center of European diplomacy in 1878.

39. He seems to have felt special animus, to which he gave unmerciful vent, toward Mehmed Ali Pasha, a renegade Prussian, both nationally and religiously.

40. To Lady Salisbury, June 23, 1878. Cecil, op. cit., Vol. II, p. 287.

41. Russia secured in addition gains in the Armenian Caucasus—Kars, Ardahan, and Batum—and acquired the Southern Dobrudja for the purpose of exchanging it with Roumania for her Bessarabian loss of 1856.

42. The French abstention, especially in view of France's long-standing interest in the Near East, is particularly noteworthy. The significance of it is discussed below, p. 207.

43. Roumania gained no territory, apart from the just-mentioned ex-

changed with Russia, but her last remaining servitudes toward the Porte were removed.

44. Salisbury to Layard, May 2, 1878 (my italics). Cecil, op. cit., Vol. II, pp. 266–67.

45. There was discussion of various possibilities, but in deference to French susceptibilities Cyprus was elected in preference to a mainland base in Syria.

46. Just as the contents of the Anglo-Russian Protocol of May 30 had been revealed by the *Globe*. The sources of these leakages were Constantinople and London, the indiscretions of a foreign office clerk in the latter city.

47. Salisbury to Sir Stafford Northcote, June 6, 1878. Cecil, op. cit., Vol. II, pp. 276–77.

48. *Disraeli, Gladstone and the Eastern Question.*

49. For example, that of St. Vallier, the French ambassador in Berlin, quoted in Seton-Watson, ibid., p. 477, and the English quip of the day about "the peace that passeth all understanding and the honour that is common among thieves" (ibid., p. 490), a commentary about Disraeli's phrase "peace with honour," used to describe his achievement at the Congress of Berlin.

50. Cited in Seton-Watson, ibid., p. 544.

51. Summarized from Seton-Watson, *Britain in Europe*, p. 547.

52. The Irish group increased its membership from fifty-one to sixty.

53. After 1848 there were two rival claimants to the French crown, the heirs of Charles X and of Louis Philippe respectively. For his statement favoring the acceptance of the Republic, Thiers was ousted from the provisional presidency in 1873, to be replaced by the monarchist MacMahon. Not until 1875 was a constitutional amendment adopted which formalized the republican form of government.

54. The *16 mai*, President MacMahon's attempt to assert the executive power, and the defeat of that attempt, may be regarded as the turning point. To be sure, the issue of the powers of the executive is still unresolved in France, as a long roster of names, ranging from Boulanger to de Gaulle, attests. But the record of French domestic politics does not belong in this discussion save where it affects foreign policy. By the end of the seventies the Republic was essentially securely established and other issues thereafter constituted the main stuff of French domestic politics.

55. This episode, still somewhat controversial, the real or pretended fear of a preventive war by Germany, may be followed in detail in a variety of treatments, for example, in Langer, William L., *European Alliances and Alignments* (1931), Ch. II, where an extensive bibliography is also given.

56. Seton-Watson, *Disraeli* . . . , p. 457.

57. For a discussion of this, see Langer, op. cit., pp. 217–25. The position of the Powers in Morocco had been defined by the Act of Madrid of July 1880.

58. Freycinet, C. de, *Souvenirs 1878–1893* (1913), p. 169

59. Robiquet, P., ed., *Discours et opinions de Jules Ferry*, 7 vols. (1893–98) Vol. V (1897), p. 533. This statement appears in the preface, written by Ferry in 1892, of Narcisse Faucon's *La Tunisie.*

60. Especially as it proved necessary to send for a time larger forces to quell a revolt in the South.

61. See Chapter II.

62. Freycinet, C. de, *La question d'Egypte* (1905), pp. 151–52.

63. Derby to Lord Lyons, November 19, 1875. Cited in *CHBFP,* Vol. III, p. 157, n. 1.

64. It can be followed in *CHBFP,* Vol. III, pp. 154–76; Renouvin, *Histoire des relations internationales,* Vol. VI, Part II (1955), pp. 81–87. For more immediate accounts, see the above-cited works of Freycinet and Cromer, E. Baring, Lord, *Modern Egypt,* 2 vols. (1909).

65. Langer, op. cit., p. 256.

66. Cited in Deschanel, P., *Gambetta* (1920), p. 304.

67. See above, pp. 207–8.

68. Cromer, op. cit., Vol. I, pp. 58–59.

69. In 1880, following yet another investigation, a law of liquidation had provided new arrangements for the liquidation of the Egyptian debt. The English and the French commissioners had also become irremovable save with the consent of the Powers involved. It would be an oversimplification, however, to equate a nascent Egyptian nationalism exclusively with an anti-foreign reaction.

70. Freycinet, *La question d'Egypte,* p. 210 (my italics). See ibid., p. 212 on the French military preparations.

71. Especially as they would be endorsed by Austria as well as probably by Russia, and Italy in 1882 was ill disposed toward France.

72. On May 25.

73. Rambaud, A., *Jules Ferry* (1903), p. 262. The conference of the Powers which met in Constantinople during this interval turned out to be but another exercise in futility.

74. Morley, Lord John, *Life of William Ewart Gladstone,* 3 vols. (1903), Book VIII, Ch. V, p. 82.

75. The whole debate can be followed in the record of the session of the Chamber of Deputies for the date. *Journal Officiel, Chambre, Débats, Séance du 18 juillet 1883.*

76. *CHBFP,* Vol. III, p. 171.

77. Freycinet, *La question d'Egypte,* p. 311, and *Souvenirs 1878–1893,* p. 238. A full account is, of course, the official record of the debate in the Chamber.

78. Salisbury to Sir Stafford Northcote, September 16, 1886. Cecil, op. cit., Vol. II, pp. 331–32.

79. Morley, op. cit., Book VIII, Ch. V, *passim.*

80. Rambaud, op. cit., p. 263.

81. *CHBFP,* Vol. III, p. 176.

82. "The Triple Alliance and Italy's Place in it." *Contemporary Review,* October 1889. Cited in Morley, op. cit., Vol. III, p. 561.

83. *"Notre intime conviction . . . est que le* consortium *de la France et de l'Angleterre est nécessaire pour assurer les résultats désirés par tous . . . Le gouvernement britannique en juge autrement, et nous met dans l'obligation de reprendre en Egypte notre liberté d'action."* Duclerc to Tissot, January 4, 1883. Cited in Rambaud, op. cit., p. 264, n. 1.

84. Rambaud, op. cit., p. 266; Langer, op. cit., p. 299.

85. The colonial congress which met in Berlin at the turn from 1884 to

1885 (see p. 222) was in part related to the Egyptian question, the congress being the result of a Franco-German initiative.

86. In the Chamber on June 24, 1884. Freycinet, *La question d'Egypte*, pp. 331–32.

87. See above, p. 218.

88. Langer, op. cit., p. 313.

89. On February 26, 1885. Cecil, op. cit., Vol. III (1931), p. 257.

90. Particularly in regard to South Africa, but a similar feeling applied to England's position in the Pacific.

91. Report of a conversation with Bismarck by Sir Philip Currie, September 28–30, 1885. Cecil, op. cit., Vol. III, p. 257.

92. Cited in Langer, op. cit., p. 317. To similar effect may be cited the imaginary exchange given in *Punch:* "Prince Bismarck: 'We have helped you in Egypt, why not oblige us in Fiji?' Lord Derby: 'We can't do it.' Lord Granville: 'We won't do it.' Prince Bismarck: 'But you *must* do it.' Lord Granville: 'Very well, we will then.'" Ibid., p. 301.

93. Twenty first-class ships against sixteen for France and nine for Germany. Following discussion of this situation and agitation in the press, reminiscent of the scare in the early sixties, an extraordinary credit of £5,500,000 for naval construction was voted by Parliament in December 1884.

94. Langer, op. cit., p. 318.

95. This is in the preface of the 1882 edition of Paul Leroy-Beaulieu's book, which originally appeared in 1874.

96. From the preface to *Le Tonkin et la mère-patrie* (1890), a documentary collection published by Léon Sentupéry. Cited in Robiquet, op. cit., Vol. V, p. 562.

97. French interest in Southeast Asia had a long background. Following penetration in Cochin China and Cambodia, Hanoi was first seized in 1873. A treaty with Annam in 1883 which, following a new occupation of Hanoi, extended the French protectorate to Tonkin, in disregard of Chinese claims, is what precipitated hostilities.

98. *Journal Officiel, Chambre, Débats, Séance du 30 mars 1885*, pp. 704–5.

99. Ibid., p. 706.

VI

THE CONVERGENCE OF THE BRITISH AND THE FRENCH POSITIONS

Nations may roughly be divided between the living and the dying. . . . For one reason or another . . . the living nations will gradually encroach upon the territory of the dying. . . . Undoubtedly we shall not allow England to be at a disadvantage in any rearrangement that may take place. On the other hand, we shall not be jealous if desolation and sterility are removed by the aggrandisement of a rival in regions to which our arms cannot extend.

Salisbury, 1898

Comme notre voisin de Valençay, M. de Talleyrand, je pense que l'alliance de l'Angleterre et de la France est aussi nécessaire que celle du cavalier et du cheval. Mais, comme lui, je pense qu'il faut tâcher de ne pas être le cheval.

Paul-Boncour, J., *Entre deux guerres.*
Vol. III (1946), pp. 83–84

The importance has been stressed in the preceding chapter of the place of Germany on the international scene since her emergence into unity in connection with, in considerable part as a consequence of, the Franco-Prussian War. The place filled by Germany during this period is the result of two factors: the more objective one of her development, economic especially, hence of her real power; the less tangible, but no less important one, of the personality of Bismarck.

The British and the French reactions to this situation were

naturally quite different. Again in the objective, measurable terms of power, Germany was forging ahead: the margin of British supremacy was diminishing, and France, despite her recovery, rather than regaining ground was falling farther behind. She did not succeed in escaping from isolation, and Bismarck could feel decreasingly concerned about the prospects of revanche so long as her isolation persisted. The best that France could do was to seek the compensatory gains of imperial aggrandizement upon which she embarked under the guidance of some of her leaders, though to the accompaniment of much domestic objection, such as Clemenceau so forcefully voiced in parliament.

The changing position of Britain was less clearly apparent. We may recall nevertheless the above-cited judgment of Rosebery in 1885 and the later one of Professor Langer.[1] Perhaps the first was premature, and both somewhat overstated the impact of a momentary situation. But the fundamental fact of the continued rate of German growth, hence of the changing differential in positions of power between herself on the one hand, and Britain and France on the other, persisted. To attribute to this change the radical transformation of European relationships that was the composition of differences between the hereditary enemies, Britain and France, and the substitution of Germany for England in that role in the French scheme of things, the crystallization of Anglo-German rivalry in place of the contrary tradition in the two countries' relations, is not unjustified as a summation. During Bismarck's time and after him Germany was the dominant guide, then the problem, of European relations. The transformation was not accomplished easily, but rather through a tortuous and elaborate set of events, replete with unexpected, not to say unforeseeable, happenings. That is the tale with which the present chapter will deal. Beginning with the seeds of disintegration of the Bismarckian structure, the sprouting of which becomes in retrospect already clear during the last years of his own tenure of office; through the first phase of the collapse of his system that was the emergence of France from the ring he had forged around her; then through the involved repercussions of imperial activity, which activity itself provided the occasion for the convulsion that was the shift of Anglo-French relations from the verge of war to the verge of alliance, the story will be traced. As a whole it is sufficiently known; the emphasis of this treatment lies on the manner in which the two principals in our tale reacted and managed.

The difference in the mode of operation of the British and the French milieus will be apparent as we proceed, yet external appearances can also be misleading. In the case of the former country the fact of continuity is emphasized by the long tenure of Salisbury, who was in charge of affairs, either as Prime Minister or as foreign secretary, much of the time combining the two offices, for most of the period. He was Prime Minister from August 1886 to August 1892, taking charge of the foreign office in January 1887. After a three-year Liberal interlude, first under Gladstone, then under Rosebery, Salisbury resumed both the prime ministership and the foreign secretaryship in June 1895, relinquishing the latter post to Lansdowne from November 1900 until the end of his own tenure in July 1902. Lansdowne retained his place thereafter under Balfour until December 1905, by which time the just mentioned transformation in the Anglo-French relationship had taken place. Especially after the passing of Bismarck from the scene, Salisbury was the nearest thing to anyone filling Bismarck's place in Europe.

A far larger number of names would have to be mentioned in the French case, many of them largely and properly forgotten. Professor Dawson's judgment comes to mind that "a distempered France never returns to a normal condition until she has upset a Government,"[2] but this is also misleading. Certainly the French domestic scene, from Boulanger to the Dreyfus affair, through Panama scandals and other incidents, offered an outward picture of at times near chaotic instability. Yet, as will also appear, French foreign policy was on balance pursued with remarkable continuity and steadiness of purpose. We may recall that Delcassé was foreign minister without interruption for seven years, from June 1898 to June 1905, while such names as those of Hanotaux and Freycinet, whatever their particular office, recur with frequency in leading governmental positions. The role of the permanent civil servants should neither be minimized nor forgotten in either Britain or France, perhaps of greater significance for the latter owing to the frequently shorter duration of governments. Nor should the ambassadorial role be overlooked, which in days of rapid communications but slower transportation than our own, had greater importance than it has now. Lord Lyons in Paris, Waddington and Paul Cambon in London are but illustrations.

The End of Bismarck's Reign, 1887–90

When Salisbury resumed the direction of British affairs in 1886 he had to deal with the legacy of the Liberal administration.[3] His return to office was welcome to Bismarck, who had already voiced his satisfaction at the prospect of Liberal defeat in 1885; the opinion expressed to Sir Philip Currie has been cited before.[4] His desire for co-operation with England was not unrelated to his dissatisfaction with the manner in which France had failed to reciprocate his advances; "he washed his hands of France." An expression of his interest in cultivating England was the replacement in the London embassy of the too easygoing Münster by Hatzfeldt, whom he held in high regard.

In 1887 Salisbury's reaction to German advances may be described as cautiously responsive. He had no wish to quarrel with France, but the Egyptian issue, on which there was little room for compromise, stood in the way. French policy, which he regarded as one of unnecessary pinpricks, was taxing his patience, as may be gathered from the expression of his irritation to his ambassador in Paris:

> The French are inexplicable. One would have thought that under existing circumstances it was not necessary to *make* enemies, —that there were enough provided for France by nature just now; but she seems bent upon aggravating the patient beast of burden that lives here by every insult and worry that her ingenuity can devise.
>
> . . . .
>
> It is very difficult to prevent oneself from wishing for another Franco-German war to put a stop to this incessant vexation.[5]

He did not quite mean this, and the statement is all the better measure of the degree of irritation of a usually calm man. To a point, the legacy of Gladstone's policy had been to isolate

England, a condition that Salisbury would change if he could. Independence but not isolation may be described as the guiding thought of his efforts.

The year 1887 was one which witnessed considerable diplomatic activity, owing to the beclouded and uncertain international climate. The active agents of possible trouble were two, Russia and France, at the opposite ends of Europe. The roots of the Russian dissatisfaction lay in the usual Balkan locale. After the change of which Bulgaria had been the scene in 1885, two things occurred. The Tsar and the Bulgarian prince fell out with each other, and the issue was ultimately resolved by the establishment of a new ruler in Bulgaria, Alexander of Battenberg, Russia having meantime high-handedly interfered in Bulgaria's domestic affairs. But in connection with these difficulties—Serbia had gone to war against Bulgaria and been rescued from the consequences of defeat by Austria's diplomatic intervention—the Dreikaiserbund was again a casualty as it had been after the Congress of Berlin.

The French situation was of a different kind. Bismarck could overlook Déroulède and the *Ligue des Patriotes,* but had otherwise become convinced of France's intractability. In 1887 the agitation centering around General Boulanger was gathering momentum. Although, as it turned out, the episode was to prove froth and the solid bourgeois leaders of republican France would dispose of Boulanger with little difficulty in the end, and despite the quieting, sober appraisal of his ambassador in Paris, Bismarck was, or professed to be, alarmed.[6] In any case the nightmare of the war on two fronts was no pretense with Bismarck, and the possible conjunction of Russian and French discontents was not to be completely ignored.

With Russia he managed to deal, at least to a point, through the intricate tightrope walking act that was the Reinsurance Treaty of June 1887. In exchange for his own commitment not to assist Austria in aggression against Russia, though not in the reverse case, he obtained a corresponding Russian commitment of neutrality in the event of French aggression. His giving encouragement to Russian hopes toward the Straits—England could be counted on to check these—has been variously interpreted as duplicity and as an illustration of the fine art of preserving equilibrium within balance. It was Holstein, thinking mainly of Austria, who described the Reinsurance Treaty as political bigamy.

In any case Russia and France might broadly be described as revisionist powers in contrast with the rest who preferred to maintain the status quo. This was the fundamental common ground between England and the Triple Alliance, whose aims in these broad terms Salisbury could underwrite. This is the general background of the Mediterranean Agreements, an interesting episode in British policy.

As early as February 1, 1887, Count Corti, the Italian ambassador in London, had a meeting with Salisbury, on which the latter reported to the Queen as follows:

> Yesterday Count Corti came to see Lord Salisbury. He was the bearer of propositions from the Italian Government for a closer understanding between Italy and England. He left a memorandum . . . of which the effect was to offer an alliance in case of war against France. . . .[7]
>
> Salisbury's immediate reaction was to tell Count Corti that England never promised material assistance in view of an uncertain war of which the object and cause were unknown; and, secondly, that any promise, even of diplomatic co-operation, could not be directed against any single Power such as France. But that on the other hand . . . we should be glad to co-operate with them; especially in the maintenance of the *status quo*.[8]

The Cabinet endorsed these views, and the same day (February 2) Hatzfeldt, on instructions from Bismarck, came to discuss the same question with Salisbury. He received the same general reply, the expression of England's desire to maintain the Mediterranean status quo, the likelihood that England's assistance would be available in the event of a French aggression against Italy, though not in the reverse case.

The negotiation was actively pursued between Salisbury, Corti and Hatzfeldt and led to the exchanges that took place on February 12 between England and Italy. The first Mediterranean Agreement contained the following provision:

> I. The status quo in the Mediterranean as well as in the Adriatic, the Aegean Sea, and the Black Sea shall be maintained

as far as possible. Care must be taken in consequence to watch, and if need be, to prevent any change, which, under form of annexation, occupation, protectorate, or in any other manner whatsoever, would affect the present situation to the detriment of the two Powers.

II. If the maintenance of the status quo becomes impossible, they shall so act that no modifications whatsoever shall occur except after a previous agreement between the two Powers.

III. Italy is entirely ready to support the work of Great Britain in Egypt. Great Britain in her turn is disposed, in case of encroachments on the part of a third Power, to support the action of Italy at every other point whatsoever of the North African coast districts, and especially in Tripolitania and Cyrenaica.

IV. In general, and to the extent that circumstances shall permit, Italy and England promise one another mutual support in the Mediterranean in every difference which may arise between one of them and a third Power.[9]

The precise, or perhaps imprecise, nature of the English commitment was accurately expressed in Salisbury's explanation to the Queen:

> The English despatch—which, of course, is the only one binding on this country, is so drawn as to leave entirely unfettered the discretion of Your Majesty's Government as to whether, in any particular case they will carry their support of Italy as far as 'material co-operation'.
>
> But, short of a pledge upon this subject, it undoubtedly carries very far the 'relations plus intimes' which have been urged upon us. *It is as close an alliance as the parliamentary character of our institutions will permit.*[10]

The following broader comment on policy, with which the letter to the Queen went on, is also worth quoting:

> If in the present grouping of nations, which Prince Bismarck tells us is now taking place, England was left out in isolation, it might well happen that the adversaries who are arming against each other on the Continent, might treat the English Empire as divisible booty, by which their differences might be adjusted, and, though England could defend herself, it would be at fearful risk and cost.

This, incidentally, suggests the reflection that Bismarck's gentle blackmail, the Continental League idea, was not entirely an invention of the future German Kaiser. The threat was not to be taken very seriously, but it remains true that Salisbury was desirous both of avoiding total isolation and any disturbance of the existing situation.

The Anglo-Italian agreement sufficiently expresses the fundamental aspect of British policy. The further exchanges that took place during the course of the year, involving Austria and Spain, and Italy again in December, need be no more than mentioned. They add little to the initial declaration of intent.[11] It may be noted, however, that the Treaty of the Triple Alliance was renewed on February 20, and that on that occasion Italy received from her allies a far stronger endorsement, especially of her imperial aims, than had been the case in the first treaty. She was assured of support in the event of taking action to resist French encroachments in either Tripoli or Morocco.

This of course Salisbury did not know, which gives all the more significance to the reservations expressed in the Anglo-Italian exchange.[12] The ambiguity was deliberate, and there is no denying that the Mediterranean Agreements were part of Bismarck's policy even though Germany was not a direct participant in them. The numerous threads of connections which had been and were being woven all ultimately led to Berlin.

Bismarck's preference for the avoidance of disturbance was entirely genuine, and so was Salisbury's, which is what made possible the convergence of the English and the German positions. The judgment that the Mediterranean Agreements represent the high point of English co-operation with the Triple Alliance is wholly justified; but this is quite different from saying that England had joined that combination. The favorable climate of Anglo-German relations persisted for a time and Bismarck cultivated it. The correspondence that he exchanged with Salisbury toward the end of the year is evidence of this, and he took the unusual step of communicating to Salisbury the text of the Austro-German alliance of 1879. It is also of interest that Salisbury's reply to Bismarck's lengthy analysis—in it Bismarck held out the bait of a closer connection with Russia if other "*puissances amies*" failed—was to a point tangential, ignoring certain hints and stressing instead the possibilities of choice open to England, which was not a demandant when it came to seeking the friendship of others.[13] We are touching here on a lasting and fundamental strand of British policy; it will reappear on a later occasion, when German policy was no longer directed with Bismarckian deftness.

A fair statement of the guiding lines of British policy was given by Salisbury on the occasion of a speech he delivered at Carnarvon on April 11, 1888. Among other things, he said the following:

> . . . what I call the neighbourly view of foreign politics extends beyond the mere controversies or disputes we may have with our neighbours. We must not only deal with them in a spirit of goodwill, recognising the necessity of concessions on the one side or the other, but we must also recognise that the members of every community have duties toward each other. We are part of what has been well called the 'federation of mankind.' We belong to a great community of nations and we have no right to shrink from the duties which the interests of the community impose upon us. There is all the difference in the world between good natured, good humoured efforts to keep well with your neighbors, and that spirit of haughty and sullen isolation which has been dignified by the name of 'non-intervention.' We are part of the community of Europe and we must do our duty as such.[14]

This was the very time when, the old German emperor, William I, Bismarck's long-term associate in the direction of German affairs, having died, there followed the brief interim of the three months' reign of Frederick III. The outlook of the new emperor differed in many respects from that of his Chancellor, but he was a dying man when he came to the throne, with the consequence that Bismarck was even less hampered in the making of decisions. The next German emperor, William II, displayed from the beginning the confused instability of his character. Bismarck remained in office, but the initial English reaction to the new German ruler was none too favorable. His anxiety to visit England was cause of both embarrassment and irritation—the visit eventually took place and passed off satisfactorily—but of more importance was a renewed German attempt to effect the

English alliance. In a long despatch to Hatzfeldt at the beginning of January 1889 Bismarck explained his case and the question was again broached to Salisbury on the occasion, in March, of Herbert Bismarck's visit to London. The alliance, defensive to be sure, was to be directed against France, and Bismarck considered that public knowledge of it would be a vaulable deterrent.

That nothing came of the suggestion is all the more significant. For if France was not especially bellicose, this was nevertheless the time when the agitation centering around Boulanger, reaching its climax, could furnish legitimate grounds for outside concern. The focus of French nationalist feeling was not Britain, but Britain was nonetheless somewhat disturbed by the growth of the French naval establishment, especially in connection with the Russian.[15] A naval Defense Act was enacted in March 1889 which provided for the building of ten battleships and sixty cruisers over the next four and a half years. In any event England would from this time adopt the two-Power standard: her naval establishment must match at least the next two largest ones.

The Anglo-German discussions resulted in a consolation prize, the quid pro quo by which Heligoland was ceded to Germany, in exchange for which Germany gave England a free hand in Zanzibar. This was in June 1890. By that time Bismarck was no longer in charge of German affairs and it will be convenient to deal with imperial matters and their repercussions in a separate section. To bring the story up to date we shall turn to French developments during the period in which the focus has so far been mainly British.

The French Escape from Isolation

First priority among the cares of French foreign policy went to the German question. We have seen the success of the efforts of Freycinet and Ferry, especially the latter, to shift the French interest away from the confining horizon of the line of the Vosges to the wider possibilities of empire. But it has also been pointed out that these efforts were always watched with suspicion by an important segment of opinion. The fall of Ferry after a minor Tonkinese setback had consequences which far exceeded the limited dimensions of the episode; it marked what may be described as the return of France to Europe. If Ferry's political career was not ended, his position among the directors of policy was in large measure destroyed. To be sure, Freycinet, also imperially minded, continued to play an important role. He was Prime Minister during virtually the whole of 1886 and occupied the war office from April 1888 to January 1893, resuming the prime ministership as well for two years, until February 1892, incidentally an illustration of greater continuity in France than the frequent changes of Cabinet convey at first sight.

Thus, if empire was not forgotten, the balance of interest and effort definitely shifted to Europe. One factor which weighed heavily on the considerations of French policy was the change in Bismarck's attitude, result of his conclusion that he would wash his hands of France. He would therefore continue more than ever to keep her isolated; the Mediterranean Agreements, which have just been discussed, are a measure of his success.

The two countries were embarking on an arms race. Bismarck's speech in the Reichstag in January 1887 is worth rereading; in it he acknowledged the pacific intentions of the French Government, but questioned the reliance that could be put on that fact in view of the past record of French behavior and opinion. He paid high homage to the martial capabilities of France, the degree of her power, and professed fear of what might happen if General Boulanger came to power. Bismarck had his way, while the French Chamber, on Boulanger's proposal—he was minister of war at the time—voted 80,000,000 francs for the improvement of arms. Bismarck's policy at this point is reminiscent of the view he had expressed to the emperor in 1875: "it is not necessary in order to preserve peace that France should feel confident that she will never be attacked under any pretext."[16]

The one cloud on Bismarck's horizon lay in the East. There is no denying that the Mediterranean Agreements, for all their genuine dedication to the preservation of the existing order, had an anti-Russian as well as an anti-French point, to the extent at least that those two countries were excluded from them; conversely, Russia's discontent over matters Bulgarian had anti-German overtones. To be sure, it is a long distance from the common condition of isolation to a combination of the isolated, even though Freycinet had sought to please St. Petersburg during the Bulgarian episode.

While Bismarck, despite his pretended alarm at the French situation, felt reasonably confident that there was little danger of a French attack, he also felt convinced that in the event of a Russo-German conflict French intervention could be counted on. Russian irritation, especially marked in the Tsar, did not seem to hold the likelihood of conflict. Nevertheless, albeit in an indirect way, Giers, who had succeeded Gorchakov at the Russian foreign office, thought it desirable to deny the possibility of a Franco-Russian alliance. His denial was put in these terms:

> What Russia wishes at present, is, on the one hand, the preservation of peace, and on the other, that of the European equilibrium. In order to reach this double goal, she must act first of all in such a way as to avoid any cause of conflict, *such as an alliance with France would be,* and then safeguard the equilibrium in question, should it be threatened nevertheless by the outbreak of a Franco-German conflict; and it would certainly not be by a rapprochement with Berlin that she would foster that purpose. In order for Russia to be able to play a preponderant role in the event of a Franco-German conflict, and in order to guarantee the European equilibrium should it be endangered, it is absolutely necessary that she should remain the unknown factor in the problem and that, without herself either encouraging or threatening anyone, she should give all cause for reflection.[17]

While this may be described as an attempt to put a good face on inescapable isolation, it may also be seen as accurately expressing at the time the Russian view of the merits of a French connection. The Reinsurance Treaty in June, a closely guarded secret, reflects the state of affairs at this juncture. But if stillborn is too strong a description of the fate of the Reinsurance Treaty, the fact remains that it bore little fruit.

The Russian ukase which forbade the purchase by foreigners of land in the western region of Russia dates from March 1887. It was in part expression of the influence on the Tsar of the Pan-Slav agitation and it created irritation in Germany, one manifestation of which was the decline of Russian securities on the Berlin exchange. This might have been but a passing cloud, but the treaty of June apparently did not succeed in allaying either the Tsar's or Germany's continuing irritation. One can easily understand Bismarck's annoyance at what appeared to him unwarranted obduracy on the part of Alexander III. Speaking in the Reichstag in February 1888, again on the subject of military reforms, he stressed the geographical position of Germany between Russia and France:

> He [God] has placed us next to the most bellicose, the most restless nation, the French nation; in Russia he has caused to develop belligerent tendencies which did not use to exist. We are therefore under pressure from two sides and driven to efforts which might not have been made.[18]

That year and the next the Franco-Russian relationship continued to develop. Flirtation seems the right word, for there was continued reticence on the Russian side in regard to political commitments. It was the merit of those involved on the French side not to press the suit too hard; supposedly emotional Frenchmen can be patient at times. While they persistently endeavored to cultivate Russian good will,[19] Freycinet was somewhat surprised, though very pleasantly, when the Russian military attaché, General Frederickz, broached the question of the purchase of 500,000 French rifles. When at a subsequent meeting, which seems to have been very friendly, Freycinet signified the favorable response of the French Government, adding, half joking half serious, *"seulement nous voudrions bien être assurés que ces fusils ne tireraient jamais sur nous,"* his interlocutor rejoined, *"Nous l'entendons bien ainsi, et nous vous donnerons toute garantie à cet égard."*[20]

The Russian attaché was hardly in a position to make political commitments for his government, nor was the ambassador, Morenheim, unless so instructed. But the transaction went through; it was not accompanied by any specific political commitments, the French resting content with its possible influence on the general climate of relations.[21]

This was also the time when the above-mentioned Russo-German financial difficulties led to Paris taking the place of Berlin in Russian financing. The French loan at the end of 1888, for 500,000,000 francs, the first of a long subsequent series, was greatly oversubscribed. The operation was repeated on an even larger scale within little more than a year. Money and guns have always carried loud voices, and it is proper to trace their role in the process through which the Franco-Russian alliance was eventually concluded; it is equally essential to bear in mind that the final result was not fated and that the steps leading to it were taken in the midst of a complex and fluid situation, the possibilities of whose development were at all points varied. The purpose of French policy was clear, and the patient skill of it deserves full marks for perseverance—a similar phenomenon will be observed ten years later, this time with England. France wanted to escape from isolation, more than ever, since she had shifted emphasis again to Europe; she was not yet reconciled to the abandonment of Egypt, the single greatest bone of contention with England, while distrust, of which the arms race was the manifestation, prevailed in the German direction. Russia was the logical candidate in her book; circumstances favored the connection, which, however, did not materialize for some time.

William II came to the German throne in June 1888. As already indicated, he was not long in giving evidence of the unstable quality of his character, of which his reign was to furnish so many other examples. The detailed advice which he conveyed to England on the score of strengthening her navy, or the manner in which he suggested that she deal with the Sultan,[22] to cite but incidental illustrations, made an odd impression on Salisbury. This was in 1891 and 1892, before which time more important things had happened in Germany.

It was not long after Willian II's accession to the German throne that relations began to sour between the old Chancellor, more than ever a difficult man, and his young master, so touchy on the score of his prerogatives. It was over the minor issue of holding in Berlin an international labor conference, to which Bismarck was opposed, that the final breach took place. It almost came to high words between the two, and Bismarck would not resign, but insisted on being dismissed. His comment on the title of Duke of Lauenburg, which was bestowed upon him by the emperor—"it will help me travel incognito"—adequately reflects his hurt pride. The passing of Bismarck from the scene of European politics was an event of the highest significance. The famous *Punch* cartoon about "dropping the Pilot" was apt, and so was Salisbury's comment, "an enormous calamity of which the effects will be felt in every part of Europe."[23]

The conference was held, and the Kaiser went out of his way to court the French[24]—he was a Francophile as he was a socialist—but on balance his efforts were of little avail. The comedy of errors connected with the artistic Berlin exposition in 1891 is another case in point. Again William II showed himself most appreciative of French art and French artists—he was an authority on that subject, too—and the occasion became tangled with a visit to Paris of the empress dowager, his mother. It was to be an incognito visit to be sure, though hardly secret. It was less than wise not to have given the French Government adequate warning of the projected visit and to allow hopes of political implications to be voiced in the German press in connection with it. The French Government was embarrassed, took all possible precautions to avoid incidents, but could hardly prevent immoderate comments on the part of some elements in French opinion.

Tempest in a teapot though the incident may have been, it took on a fair degree of significance, for William II felt insulted, and he was neither a moderate nor even a responsible character. To talk of mobilization, to tighten travel restrictions in Alsace, to berate the French ambassador in less than diplomatic language, was hardly a statesmanlike response. The combination of lack of reticence and of tact on the French side with well-meaning clumsiness on the German made an unpalatable brew. Matters were smoothed over but the total effect was to introduce a renewed degree of acerbity in Franco-German relations; the Kaiser was not cast for the role of jilted lover.

Freycinet, already in charge of the war office in previous cabinets, resumed the prime ministership in the same month that Bismarck was dismissed. This put him in an even better position patiently to pursue his persistent objective of establishing a formal connection with Russia, a goal to the achievement of which Germany made a substantial contribution. A major decision confronted her at this very moment, the issue of the renewal of the Reinsurance Treaty with Russia. Counsels were divided on the question and there were serious arguments both in favor of and against renewal. It suffices to register the final adverse decision, the prevailing of Holstein's view of the dangers of political bigamy. But the Russians were desirous of renewal, and there is a difference between the failure to reach an agreement and the abandonment of one which has existed; the latter case inevitably gives rise to suspicion as to the real cause of the abandonment, hence introduces a malaise in the atmosphere.

But this in turn did not mean an immediate Franco-Russian accord, for the question remained of whether and how far the interests of the two countries coincided. Leaving aside the factor of ideological difference—the godless French Republic and the autocracy of Holy Russia represented opposite poles of the European political spectrum—when it came to concrete interests the accent appeared to be on divergence. Isolation and discontent with the Mediterranean Agreements were essentially negative factors.

The same applied where England came into the picture. Both France and Russia met England in imperial competition but the locales of those encounters were widely separated, mainly Africa in one case, Asia in the other. Moreover, apart from the Egyptian perennial, there existed between England and France a real desire for accommodation, a tendency of which Ribot, the foreign minister, was himself an exponent and to which Freycinet was not unresponsive. In August 1890 precisely such an agreement was made, of substantial, if limited, scope.[25]

Germany stood in the reverse situation from England in French and Russian calculations respectively. While the German focus of French enmity and concern had been to a degree revived, Russo-German differences were still of relatively minor consequence, and Russia was certainly wholly indifferent to the issue of Alsace-Lorraine. Despite the failure to renew the Reinsurance Treaty, the tendency still ran strong in both countries which believed in the desirability of Russo-German friendship.

Nevertheless, the still fragile plant of Franco-Russian co-operation, even if at a relatively slow pace, seemed to develop. An outward manifestation of this was the visit of a French naval squadron to Russia, which was arranged in the spring, and took place in July 1891. The two weeks' stay of the French sailors in Cronstadt was a success, accompanied by many public and official manifestations. If some would raise their eyebrows at the picture of the Tsar standing at attention while the hated hymn of revolution was played,[26] this was all the more evidence of how far things had changed.

It is worth noting that, on its way back home, the French fleet paid a visit to Portsmouth, where it had been invited. That visit, too, went off well and can be seen as an expression of the delicately balanced state of relationships. As Salisbury wrote to the Queen in connection with that occasion:

> Though in the present state of Europe our interests lie on the side of the Triple Alliance, it is most important to persuade the French, if we can, that England has no antipathy to France, or any partisanship against her.[27]

The death of Lord Lytton in Paris, where he had been ambassador for many years, furnished the occasion for the expression of a genuine French manifestation of appreciation of his work.

But we may also speak of a vicious circle. For the budding Franco-Russian connection was influenced by the state of relations between England and the Triple Alliance. And a caution may be introduced at this point. It is no reflection on the work of scholarship in dealing with the question here under consideration to point to the distinction between analysis and reconstruction, based on a mass of subsequently available documentation on the one hand, and the circumstances of the time when things happened as they appeared to those immediately involved on the other. Treaties were mostly secret, and decisions were inevitably made on the basis of incomplete and inadequate information, impressions false or correct, and a good deal of guesswork on the score of intentions. Hence the vicious circle just mentioned.

For example, the visit of the French fleet to Cronstadt was obviously a deliberately intended public manifestation. But how appraise its precise significance? The existence of the Triple Alliance was known, but not the terms of its commitments. The French tried very hard to find out from the Italians precisely around this time—without success. Its renewal in 1891 was also known, but not the protocol which stated that:

> The accession of England being already acquired, in principle, to the stipulations of the treaty of this day which concern the Orient . . . the High Contracting Parties shall exert themselves . . . to bring about an analogous accession with regard to the North African territories of the central and western part of the Mediterranean, including Morocco. This accession might be realized by an acceptance, on the part of England, of the programme established by Articles IX and X of the Treaty of this day.[28]

It is not surprising that the French, and the Russians as well, in their ignorance of this qualification, should have attached greater weight than was warranted to Rudini's statement in the Italian Chamber on June 29, which gave an exaggerated and misleading view of the scope of the renewed alliance. The impression that England had virtually joined the Triple Alliance was confirmed by the Anglo-German agreement of the preceding June as a result of which Heligoland had been ceded to Germany. These cumulative impressions had the effect of strengthening the sense of isolation in both Russia and France, hence helped draw those two countries together. Their flirtation in turn—how serious was not known—helped tighten the Triple Alliance.

The favorable climate of the visit of the French fleet to Russia was soon followed by something more concrete. On August 27 Ribot and Morenheim, the French foreign minister and the Russian ambassador to France, respectively, exchanged letters in which the following appeared:

> 1. In order to define and consecrate the cordial understanding which unites them, and in their desire to contribute with one accord to the maintenance of peace, which is the object of their sincere wishes, the two governments declare that *they will confer on every question of a nature to threaten the general peace.*
>
> 2. In case this peace should actually be in danger, and especially in case one of the two parties should be threatened by aggression, the two parties *agree to come to an understanding* on the measures which the realization of that eventuality would make it necessary for both Governments to adopt immediately and simultaneously.[29]

The exchange was without a doubt a highly significant step, which gives a proper measure of the changing drift of relationships, and reference is often made to it as the date of the birth of the Franco-Russian alliance. So to describe the exchange is not wholly justified; the judgment is more accurate that:

> The letters of August 22, 1891 do not properly speaking constitute an alliance, but an agreement *sui generis* containing the seed of the more precise understandings which subsequent events or a clearer forecast of the future may cause the two contracting powers to make.[30]

The fact that the two countries were willing to make such a statement at this stage had in itself considerable significance, and the further development of their relationship may indeed be seen as a logical consequence of the first step. Yet that outcome was by no means an inevitable consequence in August 1891.

On the French side the purpose was steady, but it took another year before the Tsar's reluctance to put flesh on the skeleton of "consultation" could be overcome. The time was one of uncertainty in both France and Germany, the tone of whose relations did not improve. The Panama affair and the suggestion that Morenheim was implicated in irregularities irritated the Tsar and were calculated to confirm his view of the feeble and disorderly Republic. German maneuvers on the French border were a goad to touchy French sensibilities and the armament race showed no signs of abatement. It is in connection with the discussion of a military bill that the German Chancellor, Caprivi, emphasized the dangers of the war on two fronts:

> A rapprochement has taken place between Russia and France. It is impossible for us to abandon Alsace-Lorraine or to break our relations with Austria-Hungary. By strengthening our military forces we do not threaten Russia. Our only wish is to repel an attack should it occur. We are compelled to make provision for simultaneous war between two enemies[31]

were his words. The bill was adopted, even if not without difficulty. But the discussion of it, such statements as the one just cited by

Caprivi, and the bill itself, were hardly calculated to contribute to the mending of Russo-German relations; the vicious circle was not broken.

Caprivi's statement was not without foundation. Though the Franco-Russian exchange was of course secret, evidences of the rapprochement abounded. Even apart from such public displays as the visit of the French squadron to Cronstadt, statements made by Freycinet at the French military maneuvers in the autumn of 1891 constituted significant hints. As Ribot put it on the same occasion: "The result is a new situation for us."[32]

After the fall of his ministry in February 1892, Freycinet retained the war office in the succeeding ministry of Loubet, one reason being to insure continuity of the Russian negotiation: the Tsar preferred familiar faces, and the dicussion centered around the issue of military arrangements. On August 27, 1892, the Tsar's irritation having been overcome, and Giers having become convinced that the German connection—his own preference—could not be restored, a Franco-Russian military agreement was signed.[33] It specified the *casus foederis* in the event of a German or of an Italo-German attack against France or of a German or an Austro-German attack against Russia; mobilization of the Triple Alliance forces or of one of its members would result in French and Russian mobilizations; finally, the number of forces to be used against Germany was specified: 1,300,000 French, between 700,000 and 800,000 Russian. Needless to say, the convention was secret; interestingly, its duration was made contingent upon that of the Triple Alliance.

The tale is not quite finished. Freycinet, as just indicated, remained at the war office for some time, through a succession of ministries—three in a year—that reflected the impact of domestic scandals and divisions, not to mention that of anarchist agitation and deeds that flourished at the time. These changes somewhat interfered with the continuity of the Franco-Russian negotiation, though not to a substantial degree. In October 1893 there finally took place a return visit of the Russian fleet to Toulon. Whether in that city or in Paris the Russians were given convincing evidence of the popular enthusiasm that the connection with their country commanded. The recrudescence of Anglo-French colonial disputes, especially over Siam at this time,[34] was wholly satisfactory to Russia, in whose eyes the French alliance ought to have an anti-British quite as much as, if not more than, an anti-German focus. The Tsar gave his assent to the convention, something he was constitutionally empowered to do, to ensure its validity. French constitutional arrangements were different, the French President having no such powers. But there could be no question of a parliamentary debate on ratification. A bit of casuistry was resorted to, the contention that purely military arrangements fell outside the purview of parliament. In any case, on January 4, 1894, an exchange of notes between the two governments gave final validity to the 1891 convention implemented by the military one of a year later. Despite a possible legal flaw the Franco-Russian alliance had finally come into existence, to remain thereafter one of the important and fixed elements of European relations, the continuing fluidity of which must, however, be stressed.

Germany had naturally been watching the Franco-Russian flirtation with keen interest, and she had good sources of information in high Russian quarters, including the immediate entourage of the Tsar. On the French side, the easy relations which existed between Freycinet and the German ambassador, Münster, enabled them to discuss the situation with frankness. A fair sample is the conversation reported by the former after the visit of the Russian fleet to Toulon. To Münster's observation,

> Now that you are two, it will be very difficult for you to remain quiet. In your country they love war and you will draw the Russians in. . . . I believe in the peaceful policy of the government, but the nation is warlike

Freycinet insisted,

> What makes us sensitive and touchy as you say, is mainly the idea that we are thought to be weak and that insufficient account is taken of us. The stronger we shall be the less distrustful we shall be. Rest assured that our relations with you will become easier when we shall feel on a footing of equality. So long as we were facing the Triple Alliance our pride was constantly on the alert. We shall now be much less easily im-

pressed. As you can see, our understanding with Russia is a token of peace.[35]

The alliance with Russia was for France a very great accomplishment, ending as it did the long period of isolation in which Bismarck had maintained her but which did not long continue after his departure. The significance of the change is not less for the fact that there was little warrant in reading into the new situation any foreseeable hopes of righting the outcome of 1870; there were no French illusions on that score. That the alliance was defensive in intent, as was its counterpart the Triple Alliance, would be difficult to deny. But the Bismarckian system, the purpose of which was indeed to preserve the order and the peace of Europe on the basis of an overwhelming predominance of force in one quarter, had collapsed. No doubt Bismarck's was one way to keep the peace. But France had never been reconciled to that method; even apart from her specific territorial grievance, she regarded it as the very denial of equilibrium, hence as injurious to her interest.

Now Russia had come round to a similar view. She had no interest whatever in the French desire to recover Alsace-Lorraine, and the common anti-British interest in Asia offered but a thin basis of co-operation. Yet, in spite of these divergences, both countries had come to feel that, in view of other existing connections, their own would be a contribution to a more equable balance of forces. That is the ground on which they met, a common ground provided by Germany, as the terms of the military convention clearly indicate. Again we may quote a fair judgment or description:

> A contract by which France and Russia, recognizing their common interest in the preservation of peace and of the European equilibrium, undertake first to consult together for the preservation of this state of peace and of equilibrium (agreement of 1891), then to unite their forces to restore this equilibrium in the event that a third party should endanger it by an aggression against one of the two contracting parties.
>
> The military convention of 1892 specifies the technical conditions of the material collaboration which has been foreseen.[36]

This is not to say that Germany entertained any aggressive intentions. The problem was in a sense a more difficult and delicate one; it was already no less than that of adjusting the inescapable pressures created by the rate of growth of German power, which was becoming at least a potential threat to the established positions of others, hence was beginning to engender fears on their part. As to the merits of a preponderance of force on one side versus those of a more equable distribution of forces, all one can say is that both methods have so far proved to have been failures in the reckoning. We shall observe a somewhat comparable situation to that created by Bismarck for a time—the post-First World War French attempt to organize Europe—closer to our own day.

Lest, however, one fall into the fallacy of seeing in the developments of the following twenty years a non-existent consistency, before leaving the present subject a few more observations must be made about the state of European relations in 1894. The Franco-Russian exchange was followed within one month by the conclusion of a Russo-German commercial agreement which largely liquidated the quarrel going back to 1887. France and Italy, too, had got into a comparable dispute in 1888, which degenerated into a tariff war. While the mercurial Crispi was at the helm in Italy Franco-Italian relations reached a low point. No one outside of Italy felt regrets at his fall in 1891, and though he would come back for a time, the advent of Rudinì initiated some relaxation of the existing tension.

It was also at the beginning of 1894 that a Franco-German agreement was made which dealt with matters imperial, the Cameroons and the Congo, and represented a measure of common interest that may be called anti-British. This is a good place to return to imperial developments and to examine their impact on both Britain and France. Within just a decade they would furnish the occasion for a crucial and critical transformation in the mutual relations and the positions of both countries.

The Impact of the Revival of Imperial Activity (II)

The scramble for Africa, a major aspect of the world-wide imperial competition, had been well under way for some time.

That competition almost took primacy in the major European foreign offices, though it must never be forgotten that, in the last analysis, European relations *in Europe* were what mattered most. The struggle over distant scraps of often unmapped territory furnished, however, the stuff of novel problems, or gave older ones a new shape, and it sometimes gave rise to unexpected encounters and unforeseen alignments.

Broadly speaking, it may be said that the older established lines of rivalry, the Anglo-Russian and the Anglo-French, continued, for a time at least, to operate as they had in the past, lending validity to the belief in the permanence of certain relations. But the German intrusion into the imperial field was a new factor, to a much smaller extent the Italian, even the Portuguese in passing fashion. The ultimate consequence was eventually to produce, in place of the Bismarckian system, a different alignment of groups of rival Powers, of which the Franco-Russian combination was the first illustration. But in effecting the ultimate division of Europe into two rival camps, extra-European situations played an increasingly important role, far greater than they had in producing the Franco-Russian connection. In either case Germany may be regarded as the central factor, but our interest in German affairs is only relevant insofar as they impinge upon British and French.

The story of imperial activity and its impact is sufficiently known, and the purpose here is not to repeat it; it will be used in selective fashion, not even always chronologically, with a view to extracting from it elements relevant to our theme. For the sake of simplicity and of clarity of exposition it will be convenient to deal with its Asiatic aspects first.

The election of 1892 in England brought to an end Salisbury's first tenure of the prime ministership and his second sojourn at the foreign office. On balance he had served his country well; the judgment of his daughter's biography, kind and generous as it is, may be cited as a balanced and appropriate summation:

> Lord Salisbury looked upon his parliamentary defeat with a political equanimity which allowed free course to his sense of personal release. And so far as home affairs were concerned, he was right. It proved to be only a brief interlude in a command

of his fellow-countrymen's confidence which endured to the end of his life. But abroad its effects were less fugitive. His policy of "neighborliness," as he worked it, had secured for his country, a position of influence in Europe which was unique, in that it owed nothing to military preeminence or to that subtle manipulation of international jealousies, which was the chief weapon of Bismarck's genius. Its weakness as a principle of statesmanship lay in the extent to which it depended on his individual characteristics. It could not be passed on to a successor. Neither, as the event proved, could it suffer interruption without loss. That hidden familiarity with the hidden course of international happenings, to which his letters witness, owed something to a sustained intimacy with their development; the deference which he received was in part due to the extent to which his personality was identified abroad with the power which he represented. His exclusion from office, though it was only for three years, broke the charm on both sides. He never regained fully for himself, or for England, that mediatorial authority which through a process of unremarked growth attained its height during the years just recorded. In his last tenure of office there are successes in diplomacy to be recorded; but it was this Government which saw the zenith of his fame and achievement as a Foreign Minister.[37]

Even Bismarck had found cause to modify the appraisal he had made to the French representative, St. Vallier, at the time of the Congress of Berlin of *"ce clergyman laïque obstiné et maladroit."*[38]

Around 1892 it might appear that the just mentioned "mediatorial authority," or arbitral position, of England could be expected to be enhanced by the new situation of equilibrium created by the balancing of the Triple Alliance with the nascent connection between France and Russia, which in turn could lend all the more attraction to the asset of British isolation or at least independence. Yet we shall see how it was precisely out of the complications arising from imperial activity that the asset was lost. If the above-cited judgment of Professor Langer was premature in reference to the time it referred to, it seems fully warranted ten years later, around 1895.

Salisbury's succession went to the seemingly indestructible Gladstone, though signs of diminished vigor in him were apparent by this time—he was in his eighty-third year. In fact, in January

1894, he relinquished the prime ministership to Rosebery, who had been in charge of the foreign office, where his place was taken by Kimberley till the end of the Liberal administration in June 1895. The Liberals did not have a clear majority, retaining control by the grace of the Irish contingent; nor should the influence of the related issues of free trade and imperial preference, even if not yet active factors, be forgotten as elements in the general operation of British politics.

Salisbury had found the French difficult at times, but despite his occasional annoyance, he had steadfastly adhered to the policy of seeking accommodation with them. Toward French culture he was sympathetic and to France he went for the relaxation from his cares of office, though this should not be misread as a clue to his policy. Yet, insofar as one may speak of a measure of preferential inclination, Rosebery's was more marked for the right bank of the Rhine. On the French side, Freycinet and Ribot may be regarded as the counterparts of Salisbury in that they represented an orientation favorable to co-operation with England. In January 1893, Ribot's second ministry, as short-lived as his first—two months in each case—came to an end and the foreign office thereafter came into the hands of men—Devalle, Hanotaux—less favorable to the English orientation. The Russian alliance made for greater assurance, boldness, and independence and it is of interest that the year 1893 witnessed a crisis which, though not of lasting consequence, nevertheless fitted to perfection the newfound friendship of France.

The Siamese Crisis of 1893

Reference has been made more than once to the problem of India, the Northwest frontier, and the Anglo-Russian contest in Afghanistan. The persistent French advance in Indochina might raise a comparable situation in the Northeast. In 1885 a British protectorate was established in Burma. Siam now stood in a position somewhat comparable to that of Afghanistan, and the neutralized buffer while opposing any encroachment by a rival.[39] The issue came to focus on the British refusal to acknowledge a French claim to the left bank of the upper reaches of the

Mekong River, which the French had been hoping to use as an avenue of penetration into China.

The news of the appearance of two French gunboats at Bangkok and the delivery of a French ultimatum on July 13, 1893, created considerable excitement in London, while the press took up the issue with gusto on both sides of the Channel. Matters were hardly improved by the news of a French blockade and the unfounded report that the French had ordered British gunboats away. England could hardly put up with such behavior and there was talk of war; the clearing up of a misunderstanding saved everybody's face and the episode was reduced to its proper proportions.

Yet it took on greater significance than its small dimensions might seem to warrant. For Rosebery was embarrassed; if it should come to war, for which he had no desire, he wished to know the German position, which he found to be one of reticence. That position may be described as fear of being lured into pulling British chestnuts out of the fire and summed up in Caprivi's comment: "For us the most desirable opening of the next big war is for the first shot to come from an English ship. We are then certain of being able to enlarge the Triple into a Quadruple Alliance."[40] Such a hope represented a misunderstanding of the English position; Rosebery was satisfied with the French acceptance of a buffer state in Siam, and his German sympathies did not interfere with a sober appraisal of the British interest. He suggested to the Queen that she convey to her excitable grandson that "Germany is playing an extremely dangerous game"[41] and let the Austrian ambassador know that "if Germany were going to side with France in African questions, we must reconsider our position as regards our general attitude in Europe, most particularly in the Mediterranean and in the East."[42] The consequence of the episode was the feeling, especially strong on the German side, that Britain had yielded to fear; and this in turn may be regarded as a milestone on the long road of German misunderstanding which there will be other occasions to observe in the succeeding years, until they produced irretrievable consequences.

At the same time the isolation of Britain was proper cause for concern. The Siamese incident, especially as seen from India, fitted well the anti-British aspect of the Franco-Russian alliance, but that, too, was in part a misreading; for in the last analysis Germany, not England, was the real binder of that association. Nevertheless, the visit of the Russian fleet to Toulon, the anti-British tone of the French welcome to the Russians while the anti-German was soft-pedaled, the permanence of a Russian naval squadron in the Mediterranean, which would alter the balance of forces in that sea, gave point to the possible desirability of a closer English association with the Central European constellation. English influence in Constantinople seemed to be declining, and the result was a feeler toward Vienna, Austria on land and Britain on the sea being the two Powers whose interests most clearly coincided in the Balkans and at the Straits. At the end of January 1894 the Austrian ambassador reported Rosebery as saying:

> I assure you that I am absolutely determined to maintain the status quo in the Straits question, and that I would not recoil from the danger of involving England in a war with Russia; but I must tell you frankly that if France should take sides with Russia, it would be impossible for England to defend Constantinople against both powers; in any case we should be unable to allow our Mediterranean fleet to run the risk of a catastrophe by finding itself between the Russian and the French fleets. In such a case, we should require the assistance of the Triple Alliance to hold France in check.[43]

The outcome of this attempt may be described as the usual one. Austria would not, alone, make firm commitments. For one thing, the German connection had priority in her book, and Germany had by this time begun to develop an interest of her own in the Near East; rather than take a strong anti-Russian stance at the Straits she was still entertaining the possibility of disrupting the Franco-Russian alliance through the courting of Russia.[44] She would indeed gladly have welcomed England as an addition to the Triple Alliance, but only on the basis of concrete and firm commitments such as England would not make. Failing this, the factor of distrust of England prevailed, another very durable strand of German policy and an equally lasting obstacle to the formation of an Anglo-German connection.

We shall meet it again. As to the possibility that emphasizing England's isolation was the way to frighten her into joining the Triple Alliance, this was one of the worst, and also lasting, German misreadings of British power and psychology. The war scare of 1893 had in England what may also be called the normal, or usual, effect, that of increased naval appropriations, though it is well to bear in mind that the combined Franco-Russian establishment was still the main focus of English concern.

The Far Eastern Crisis: The Sino-Japanese War

Thus, by the middle of 1894, just as Rosebery had become Prime Minister, the negotiations between England and the Central European combination were abandoned and England's isolation confirmed. Evidence of this isolation could also be found in African developments, but before considering these we may turn to another manifestation of it which grew out of Far Eastern complications.

The salient local facts in the Far East were two: the decline, confusion, and impotence of the Chinese empire, reminiscent in many respects of the Ottoman situation, and the contrasting adaptation of Japan to the ways of the modern world, including those of power. The European interests involved were primarily the British and the Russian, the former above all commercial,[45] the latter more concerned with territorial expansion; Vladivostok, founded in 1860, did not answer the everlasting Russian search for access to warm water—it was icebound four months in the year. Far behind these interests were the German and the French, the former making progress in keeping with Germany's rapid commercial growth, while French attention was especially focused on Southeast Asia. The American interest in the Far East was also well established; it, too, was mainly commercial and like the British favored the integrity of China, being desirous of avoiding exclusion from any part of it by others. Japan, like Germany, was relatively a newcomer, but her geographical position gave her interest a particular point; there was a party in Japan which favored territorial expansion, pointed especially toward Korea, a land whose allegiance to China was again reminiscent of that of some Ottoman territories to the Sultan.

To make a long story brief it may be picked up at the point, in 1893, when small Chinese and Japanese contingents made their appearance in Korea. This was in keeping with existing agreements, but the refusal of the latter to depart, as the Chinese had done, until further demands were satisfied, led to a Japanese declaration of war against China in August 1894. The expectation that the Japanese would in the end be incapable of withstanding the sheer weight of the Chinese mass was soon to be belied.

Initially, both Russia and Britain were opposed to the Japanese operation, but there was ambiguity in the Russian position. For the common factor of territorial covetousness might in her case lead to a similarity of approach with Japan on the basis of an agreed division of spoils. However, the early Japanese successes induced in England a surprising volte-face, at the level of opinion especially. The anti-Russian component is here again reminiscent of the English reaction to the Near Eastern situation, in the seventies, for example.

The English proposal that the Powers agree on joint action was a reasonable suggestion in the circumstances, but it failed owing to the rejection of it by Germany and the United States. Russia was still hesitant at this point whether to associate herself with England in opposing Japan or whether to seek an accommodation with the latter. The prospect of Japan as a counter to Russia and the possibility that she could be an agent for the further opening of China also had attraction for England, where the view was expressed that:

> Instead of making attempts to maintain a status quo that exists no longer, let us see that when the situation is altered we do not lose by the alteration. We want a port and naval station far up the Chinese coast, a thousand miles north of Hong Kong, and with the consent of Japan we can get it. With that secured and China really opened to trade, we might regard the state of affairs in the Pacific with some equanimity.[46]

That the status quo had been altered was made amply clear by the signature in April 1895 of the Treaty of Shimonoseki, the registration of China's total defeat. Japan had rejected the moderating German advice to refrain from territorial claims on the mainland, demanding the cession of the Liaotung Peninsula with the base of Port Arthur.[47] The demand for Liaotung revived the possibility of joint Anglo-Russian opposition; as to the above-mentioned alternatives, they were closely discussed in Russian councils. One thing was important: Russia must not act alone in opposition and incur singly the enmity of Japan.

The result of consultations among the Powers was the conveying to Japan of opposition to her acquisition of Liaotung, which "would be a constant menace to the capital of China, would at the same time render illusory the independence of Korea, and would henceforth be a perpetual obstacle to the peace of the Far East."[48] This was a reasonable view, but the interesting thing is that the communication was sent by three Powers, Russia, Germany, and France, Britain being conspicuously missing. This needs a little explaining.

The Russian motivation is sufficiently clear. The German is most succinctly, if crudely, expressed in the Kaiser's later statement that "one must try to nail Russia to East Asia, so that she can concern herself less with Europe and the European East."[49] There was sense in such a policy, though it was perhaps not necessary for the Kaiser to conceal it in the following language to the Tsar:

> I shall certainly do all in my power to keep Europe quiet, and also to guard the rear of Russia so that nobody shall hamper your action towards the Far East. For that is clearly the great task of the future for Russia to cultivate the Asian continent and to defend Europe from the inroads of the Great Yellow race. In this you will find me always on your side, ready to help you as best I can. You have well understood the call of Providence and have quickly grasped the moment; it is of immense political and historical value and much good will come of it. I shall with interest await the further development of your action and hope that, just as I will gladly help you to settle the question of eventual annexations of territory for Russia, you will kindly see that Germany may also be able to acquire a Port somewhere when it does not *gêne* you.[50]

One is tempted to contrast this with the more soberly couched English acknowledgment cited earlier that Russian expansion in Central Asia fulfilled a civilizing mission; the Kaiser's form of language gives a strange ring to the charge of Albion's perfidiousness and sanctimony. To keep Russia away from Europe, to weaken, possibly disrupt, the Franco-Russian alliance were perfectly sound and legitimate aims of German policy. To a considerable degree a similar type of motivation had caused France to join the combination; she had relatively little interest in the Sino-Japanese affair, but she did not wish to find herself displaced as Russia's best friend and newly found ally. Actually, France exerted a moderating influence when some of the more belligerent Russian elements were anxious to use force in the Far East at this juncture.[51] The issue was resolved with Japan's acceptance of the Powers' suggestion in regard to Liaotung.[52]

The Russo-Franco-German combination was nevertheless an odd constellation which certainly had the effect of emphasizing the isolation of England. The English position in the Far Eastern imbroglio may be said to have paid good dividends eventually, but that was some years later and hardly an effective factor in current calculations. If the characterization of the tripartite combination as a "farce" is too strong[53]—it was effective after all—it is also true that the vision of an anti-British continental league—another of the Kaiser's pets, like the Yellow Peril—had little substance in it. The scramble for China which the Sino-Japanese conflict may be said to have inaugurated, would give rise to various issues and alignments; on some of these there will be occasion to touch later on.

It was just after the Far Eastern crisis had been resolved that the Rosebery administration was defeated, and that Salisbury came back, taking charge as before of both the prime ministership and the foreign office. During his last tenure he had to deal with the legacy of the foreign situation and the continued importance of foreign affairs. But it was not so much the now settled Far East which absorbed his attention as African and Near Eastern matters,[54] with which he had acquired ample familiarity before the Gladstone-Rosebery interlude. To these we shall now turn.

The Struggle over Africa

Since Salisbury was to play such an important role in the following years and we shall find him and England so often at the center of the story, it may be appropriate to quote at this point another judgment of the man and his place. The appraisal, incidentally, brings out the difference which has come to operate in our own century in the conduct of foreign, as well as of other, affairs of governmental concern:

> At his present age of 65 his blend of physical energy, experience and instructive judgment was at its maturest. His opinions were based on long experience, his intuitions were checked and his instincts guided and controlled. He could take his decisions rapidly and surely. The element of intuition was not then, as it is today, swamped in facts and figures. In the half century that has passed since his day knowledge has become so much more widespread and technical; statistics and exact information are broadcast daily; the masses are far more thoroughly coached in political matters. They are consequently more critical and less ready than in Lord Salisbury's time to accept guidance unquestioningly; the statesman's time is taken up in endless controversies and explanations. In these circumstances instinct withers; and leaders do not seem to feel they can rely on something within themselves. They ponder long over pros and cons. But in Lord Salisbury the old English preference of the man of action to think without verbal expression and to act without explanation was always strong. . . . Physiologists tell us that a man's familiar work comes to be directed by reflex action without conscious reference to his brain; and by this time Lord Salisbury's diplomatic decisions, like the touches of a master-musician on the keyboard, were made by instinct based on the experience of a lifetime.[55]

By 1895 the intense scramble for Africa had been under way for more than a decade, and one might also cite this other judgment of Salisbury's: "We only desire territory because we desire commercial freedom."[56] However that may be, England was fully involved in the process of gaining African territory, in which process she enjoyed the advantage of prior experience and practice. We must go back a little in time before resuming the tale in the mid nineties.

Much, though not all, of European activity in Africa was conducted on the basis of what is best described as "a shoe-string." Traders would establish coastal posts, ascend rivers, make treaties with local chieftains, and these activities would be the bases of exclusive claims to loosely defined and overlapping territories. Alternatively, some military men leading a handful of often native recruits would launch exploratory-conquering expeditions, plant the national flag, also make local treaties. It had been part of the purpose of the Berlin colonial conference to put some order into the process. But it was not long before scattered and unco-ordinated enterprises began to give rise to larger schemes, visions, or dreams, the scale of which was sometimes grandiose.

Gladstone's above-cited forecast of 1877[57] was becoming reality, and the name of Cecil Rhodes may serve as that on which to focus its effectuation. Businessman turned empire builder, he carried a long distance his vision of a South African empire. By 1889 he headed the just chartered British South Africa Company, whose rights of exercising governmental powers almost made it a state. The following year he was Prime Minister of the Cape Colony, the town of Salisbury was founded in future Rhodesia, and westward railroad building reached the Vaal River.

In 1888 the British East Africa Company had its charter extended to cover operations reaching an indefinite distance inland from the coast, where its activities had centered around Zanzibar, thus pointing to the sources of the Nile. With the well-established interest in the course of that river, the Cape-to-Cairo scheme is the simplest and best expression of the vision of British control over roughly the whole eastern half of the entire African continent.

The western side of it had not been neglected, especially around the mouth of the Niger River, where a protectorate established in 1885 was turned over the following year to the Royal Niger Company. But in the great western bulge of Africa the French were on the whole more active. Their methods put greater emphasis on military action and they did not make use of chartered companies, whose record for that matter did not prove altogether satisfactory and whose activities tended therefore to be brought under the more direct control of the home government. From the existing North African and Senegalese bases, then from the Ivory Coast, the upper reaches of the Niger and Dahomey, the French were converging on Lake Chad. They had also appeared on the banks of the Congo, and were pushing from the West toward the Nile. The small but important base of French Somaliland could suggest a grandiose vision comparable to the above-mentioned British. Frustrated at the mouth of the Nile, they might yet establish control of the upper reaches of that river.

But if the British and the French enjoyed the priority of an older imperial tradition, they were no longer alone in empire building by this time. Those had been right also who, like Lord Lyons,[58] had taken the view of inevitability in the German case despite Bismarck's early—and at the time authentic—disclaimer of interest in empire. The names of Luderitz, Peters, and Nachtigal are connected with what came to be the German establishments in Southwest Africa, in East Africa, and around the Bight of Benin. Under Peters' prodding especially, the idea began to take shape of a broad band of territory which, like the French though south of it, would span Africa from the Atlantic to the Indian Ocean.

The Portuguese and the Italians, too, entered the picture though on a minor scale. The former had long ago shown the way to other Europeans. Shorn of their Brazilian connection, but still established in Angola and Mozambique, they showed some intention of effecting, like the Germans, a transafrican junction of these two possessions. The Italians were, like the Germans again, latecomers in imperial activity and their ambitions were relatively modest. Their Eritrean colony, developed from the base of Assab, and their acquisition of Somaliland pointed to the encirclement, and the possible incorporation, of Abyssinia. This was the Crispian dream. The special case of King Leopold, then of Belgium, is known.

Attention may be called again to the varying motivations that prompted this outburst of imperial activity. Broadly speaking, it was a manifestation of the expansive energy and rapid growth of Europe herself. The argument of population pressure may be dismissed as a pretext; Black Africa was not suited to European settlement, and Italians flocked to America rather than to the deadly climate of the Red Sea. The economic urge has greater validity, deserves in fact priority of explanation. Britain was and had long been the world's leading trading nation; she was also wedded to free trade by this time, and the validity of Salisbury's statement takes on greater significance in the light of the failure of others to emulate the British example. The last two decades of the century witnessed a revival of the protectionist policy, Germany leading the way; the French Méline tariff dates from 1892, and others followed suit. We shall presently have occasion to observe the impact of this state of affairs on the British position. The special circumstances that prodded French activity, world power standing, an alternative to revanche, have been indicated. Finally, mention should be made of the link that became established between empire and the older factor of nationalism; Europeans took pride in the contemplation of the patches of color on the world map which indicated the extent of their respective empires; but this could also lead to domestic complications and cleavages, as the French case well illustrates.[59]

From what has just been said of the meeting and overlapping of interests one thing emerges clearly: the inevitable involvement of national policies, through the foreign and colonial offices especially. The extra-European locale of rivalries intruded at times an unexpected twist; the aftermath of Shimonoseki has been mentioned. Where Africa entered the picture, the Anglo-French relationship could, in fact to a point did, insert itself into the ancient tradition in which "hereditary enemy" had more validity than in the Franco-German relation. The Franco-Russian alliance had little significance in Africa, save to a point where it impinged upon Ottoman affairs. Bismarck, at least for a time, was an imperialist in France, though he was not unaware of the possibility of killing two birds with one stone. Italy, in whose case one may speak of a consistent pro-British orientation, could, from the British standpoint, serve as a counterweight to either French or German East African ambitions. In any case it is clear that the possibilities of alignments and combinations were numerous and varied, but it must also be borne in mind that agreement prevailed on the equal validity of imperial activity for all and that, within competition, the wish for accommodation was real—just as it often was in Europe herself. The usual recoil before the prospect of Ottoman partition may be cited as an illustration of this tendency.

In East Africa the British and the Germans met, but there

seemed to be room for both at first, though Zanzibar, where claims of the local ruler introduced certain complications,[60] was a point of contention. There was the additional question of how far claims to the hinterland could reach and be made good, and before long the region of the great lakes was involved. This meant several things. The eastern reaches of the Congo were involved, but more important was the everlasting problem of the Nile and its uncertain sources. Early in 1890, the great German explorer Karl Peters undertook an ambitious circuit which, taking him through Uganda, finally brought him out to the Red Sea. On his way he had entered into local agreements, bases for eventual German claims, but he was doomed to sad disappointment, for when he re-emerged to civilization he found that the European foreign offices had already dealt with the situation among themselves.

Several things had happened in the interval. While the Mahdi was achieving success in the Sudan, Emin Pasha (originally the Austrian Eduard Schnitzer) maintained his position in Equatoria. A mission, led by the explorer Stanley,[61] set out in 1888 to his "rescue"; the expedition bespoke Anglo-Belgian co-operation, or at least that of King Leopold, who joined in the financing of it with the head of the British East Africa Company, Sir William MacKinnon. The real purpose of the expedition was the control of Equatoria, and the so-called MacKinnon Treaty, though never formally ratified, was indication of the understanding: the Belgian Congo could extend to the west bank of the Nile, in return for which a strip of territory between Lakes Albert and Tanganyika would be British. The significance was obvious; it was an attempt to establish territorial continuity between the northern and the southern British possessions, or possessions to be.

Meantime, however, London and Berlin had had direct dealings of which it may suffice to say that their outcome was the cession to Germany by England of the island of Heligoland in exchange for receiving a free hand in Zanzibar. The treaty was concluded on July 1, 1890. It was an advantageous deal for England, for Heligoland had no longer any value for her. As Rhodes put it, it was "exchanging a suit of clothes for a trouser button"; but the location of the island, the prospective building of the Kiel Canal, and the German emperor's fondness for things maritime are what made it a satisfactory exchange for him.[62] At this point it is the East African aspect of the matter which is of interest; the Anglo-German agreement was but a step in a continuing story.

The Anglo-French declaration of August 5 is part of the story, though the scope of it was more far-reaching. For, forgetting about Zanzibar, the French received from Britain acknowledgment of their position in Madagascar and in addition a very generous interpretation of the limits of their sphere of influence in and around the Sahara. *The* [London] *Times* commented on Salisbury's "large liberality," which he defended with humor in speeches at the Mansion House and in the Lords. As he put it to the latter, having granted that a look at the map would indeed make the French claims appear extensive, "it is necessary to judge land not merely from extent but also from value. This land is what agriculturists would call very 'light' land, that is to say it is the desert of the Sahara."[63] There was truth in the statement, but it was also impolitic, and one can understand the note he received from Waddington, the French ambassador and negotiator: "No doubt the Sahara is not a garden . . . but your public reminder of the fact was hardly necessary. You might well have left us to find it out."[64]

The French were in no need to find out, for they had their eyes on more than the Sahara. The Ivory Coast and Dahomey were not desert, and they had established themselves in Gabon and on the right bank of the Congo. Pushing out from these territories and from Lake Chad, the above-mentioned plan was taking shape of reaching the Nile from the west, north of the Congo, through the present-day Central African Republic, to the Bahr el Ghazal. Thus one can see in this region, adjacent to Uganda, the convergence of four influences, British, French, German, and Belgian.[65]

In 1894 a British protectorate was established over Uganda, just after the conclusion, and, one may say, by way of compensation for the failure, of the Anglo-Belgian (really still King Leopold) treaty of May, which amounted to the implementation of the previously mentioned MacKinnon agreement.[66] The result may seem surprising, though it is less so in the context of the

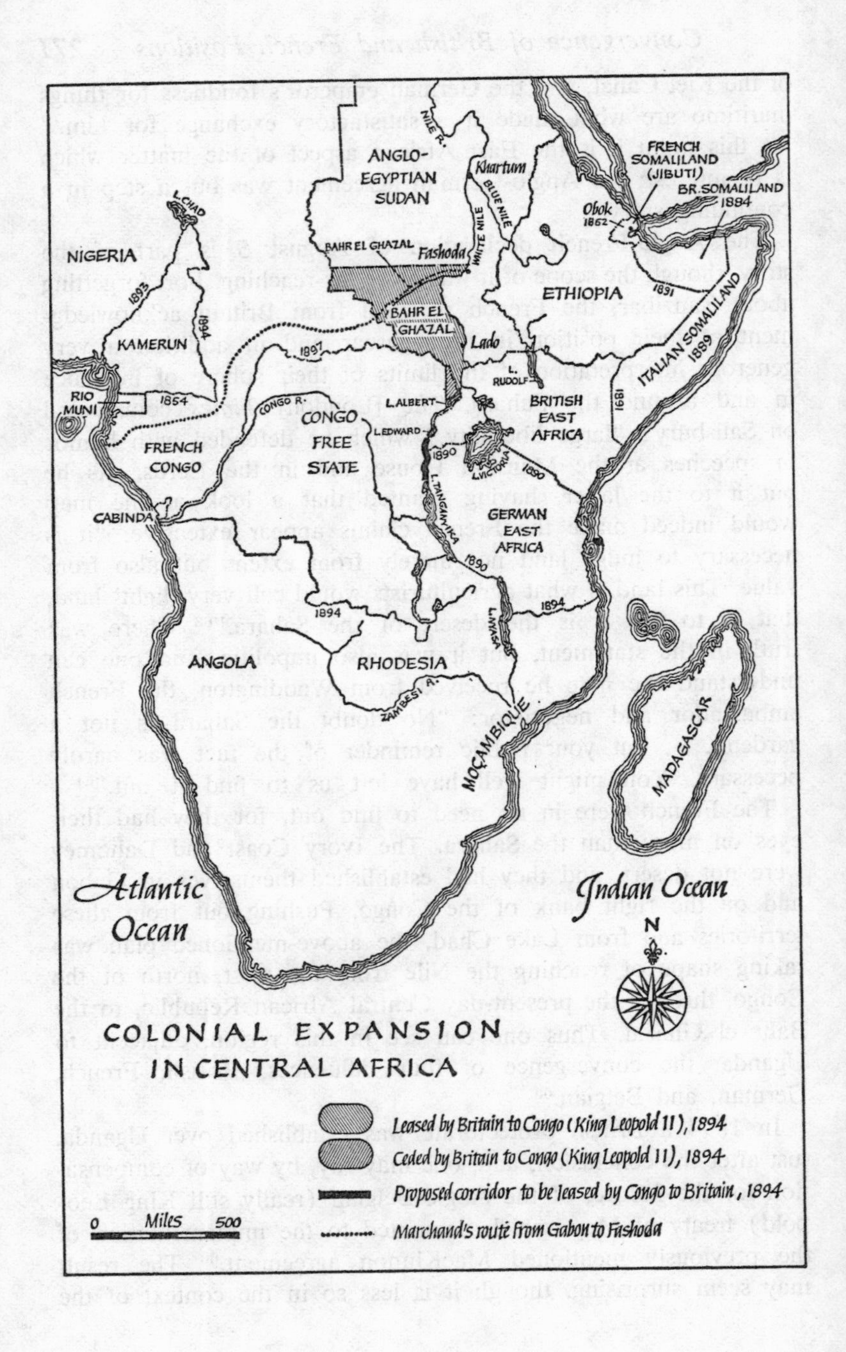
NILE R.
ANGLO-EGYPTIAN SUDAN
Khartum
BLUE NILE
WHITE NILE
FRENCH SOMALILAND (JIBUTI)
BR. SOMALILAND
1884
Obok
1862
L. CHAD
NIGERIA
BAHR EL GHAZAL
Fashoda
ETHIOPIA
1891
1893
1894
BAHR EL GHAZAL
ITALIAN SOMALILAND
1889
KAMERUN
1897
Lado
L. RUDOLF
RIO MUNI
1884
CONGO R.
L. ALBERT
BRITISH EAST AFRICA
1891
CONGO FREE STATE
L. EDWARD
FRENCH CONGO
1890
L. VICTORIA
1890
L. TANGANYIKA
CABINDA
GERMAN EAST AFRICA
1890
1894
L. NYASA
1894
ANGOLA
RHODESIA
ZAMBESI R.
MOÇAMBIQUE
MADAGASCAR
Atlantic Ocean
Indian Ocean
N
COLONIAL EXPANSION IN CENTRAL AFRICA
Leased by Britain to Congo (King Leopold II), 1894
Ceded by Britain to Congo (King Leopold II), 1894
Proposed corridor to be leased by Congo to Britain, 1894
0 Miles 500
Marchand's route from Gabon to Fashoda

other developments which have been indicated before.[67] The episode itself turned out to be a contribution to the state of these relations.

French opposition to the arrangement was foreseen and expected. In the important debate which took place in the French Chamber on June 7 words were not minced about the anti-French nature of British policy and its methods, words to which Hanotaux, the foreign minister, did not object. Britain wanted full control of the whole Nile to the exclusion of all others—hardly an exaggeration—though to insist on Turkish rights in the Sudan, an entirely distinct entity, especially in view of the position taken earlier by France, was rather a weak point. The acrimonious nature of Anglo-French exchanges left the British unmoved,[68] but a strong German protest was less expected. The German action mainly took the form of direct pressure on King Leopold, who in the end yielded to it, and to that which came from Paris, the outcome being the Franco-Belgian (Congolese) agreement of August and the abandonment of the Anglo-Belgian treaty by Britain.

Rosebery, under whose prime ministership these things happened, did not come out of the episode with much credit and was severely criticized at home, where some were reminded of the situation, exactly ten years before, under the last Liberal administration.[69] There was no Franco-German plot, but there had been considerable discussion between the two countries with a view to co-ordinating their policies.[70] The earlier conclusion, in March, of an agreement dealing with West African matters and leaving open the French route of westward expansion could be regarded in England as added food for thought on the score of the isolation of England. How far would Franco-German co-operation go?[71]

The Struggle for the Nile (II): Fashoda

That particular question had been answered when Salisbury returned to office a year later, yet the flurry of 1894 was but one episode in the continuing story of the struggle for control of the Nile, the closing chapter of which may conveniently be considered at this point.

The result of the events of 1894 may be described as a stalemate which left the fundamental issue of the control of the

Nile unresolved and the competition still open. Two days after the above-mentioned debate in the French Chamber that body voted an appropriation of 1,800,000 francs "for the defense of French interests in Africa"; Colonel Monteil, a French explorer and one of the active agents of French expansion in Central Africa, was put in charge of affairs in the upper Ubangi region. Delcassé, whom we shall meet again, another French imperialist, was undersecretary for colonies and had urged him on his initial voyage to the region. The French determination to secure access to the Nile cannot be placed in doubt; even the whole Egyptian question was not considered closed.

With the passage of time the likelihood of British withdrawal from Egypt was obviously becoming dimmer rather than closer to realization. Already in 1889 Salisbury had declared that "we shall pursue our task until the end," meaning the complete restoration of order, financial and other, in Egypt, a statement reinforced by the other that Egypt would not be abandoned "till she was capable of maintaining her own Government in the face of foreign and domestic foes." No less enlightening is the comment he added three years later to the newly appointed ambassador to Constantinople:

> If Egypt goes on improving as rapidly as she is improving now, the time will come when she will insist on being free from Turkey, or England, or anybody else. But I imagine that the result is some distance off; much too far to enter our calculations for the conduct of present diplomacy.[72]

In other words, for the foreseeable future, Britain would remain in control of Egypt. The above-mentioned stalemate of 1894 was not of long duration. Even before the return of Salisbury to office matters seemed to be coming to a head, mainly as the result of the persistence of France's Central African ambitions, the promotion of which may be chiefly ascribed to Hanotaux, apt representative of the colonial party and by personal inclination unsympathetic to a British orientation of French policy.

Debates in the French Chamber caused alarm in England, which was sounded by *The Times* among others, and led in turn to questions in the British Parliament. The prospect and the consequences of French control of the upper Nile, taking the British position from the rear and holding Egypt as hostage—this had been said in France—revived old visions of the Mediterranean as a French lake.[73] It was in reply to these forebodings that Sir Edward Grey, undersecretary for foreign affairs at the time, made the declaration that there was

> no reason to suppose that any French expedition has instructions to enter, or the intention of entering, the Nile Valley. . . . I cannot think that these rumours deserve credence, because the advance of a French expedition under secret instructions right from the other side of Africa, into a territory over which our claims have been known for so long, would be not merely an inconsistent and unexpected act, but it must be perfectly well known to the French Government that it would be an unfriendly act, and would be so viewed in England.[74]

This was strong and brave language, yet one might also wonder whether it was not possibly bluff; it was little use threatening France with a confrontation without taking into account both Germany and Russia. As events were to show, it was not bluff, and the subsequent unfolding of the tale is reminiscent of other Anglo-French confrontations, that between Palmerston and Thiers, for example.

The activity of de Brazza around the Congo and the work of Monteil farther east amounted to a co-ordinated plan, the final confirmation of which may be seen in the expedition on which Captain Marchand set out from Gabon in 1896. There was indeed concern in Paris, and attempts to clarify the meaning of Grey's declaration had not resulted in satisfactory explanations. The situation on the upper reaches of the Nile and the standing of various claims offered suitable grounds for legal disputation. Rosebery, too, was concerned; as he put it to the Queen, acknowledging that the French had never recognized the British claim, "we should not be on very strong ground if we had to rely on diplomatic action only."[75] There was opposition in the Cabinet as well.

He was also concerned about the difficulty and the cost of

dislodging the French, and things were not made easier for England by the visit of King Leopold to Paris in September 1895, during the course of which arrangements were made for the co-ordination of French and Belgian operations. More still, it was in 1896 that Crispi's imperial dream came to grief at Adowa. The collapse of the Italian position threatened the security of the approaches to the Nile from the East.[76]

On the English side the decision was made to reconquer the Sudan, a necessary preliminary operation designed to give legal contention the more solid backing of force. The task was entrusted to General Kitchener and initiated in the spring of 1896, just before Marchand started out on his trek. These were not yet the days of mechanized transportation and there ensued a relative lull.[77] Marchand reached the Bahr el Ghazal region in August 1897 but was held up for a time owing to local difficulties. By the end of the year, in connection with other Anglo-French African negotiations, Salisbury returned to the question of the Nile, firmly reasserting the position taken by Grey, informing Hanotaux that England did "not admit that any European Power other than Great Britain had a right to occupy any part of the valley of the Nile."[78] The use of the word "valley" is significant. Salisbury was now on stronger ground, for Kitchener had been making cautious but successful progress, until on September 2, 1898, he avenged at Omdurman the defeat of 1885. By that time Marchand had already hoisted the French flag at Fashoda, which he had reached in July and where Kitchener found him in occupation when he himself reached the place on September 19. While the two commanders behaved with decorum and tact, the confrontation had come in the sharpest fashion; it was now up to London and Paris.

Two statements may be juxtaposed which, between them, give a proper measure of the intensity and significance of the crisis. To Lord Cromer, Salisbury had written: "If we get to Fashoda, the diplomatic crisis will be something to remember and the 'What next?' will be a very interesting question."[79] Writing after the event, Freycinet made this appraisal: *"C'était bien de la guerre qu'il s'agissait. Durant cette période (depuis le mois de septembre 1898 jusqu' au mois de mars 1899) nous avons été à deux doigts des hostilités."*[80]

The first statement is also indication that Salisbury had foreseen and was prepared for the likely course of events; also, he himself kept the direction of them firmly in his own hands instead of delegating authority to others, as in Near Eastern affairs, for example. Not a belligerent man by nature, he had a year earlier, in March 1897, on his way back from France, where he had been convalescing, stopped in Paris to propose to Hanotaux the conclusion of a general treaty of arbitration, a proposal that had fallen on deaf ears. That he had thought matters out, if it came to a confrontation, is shown by the sealed instructions that he had sent to Kitchener, but which the latter was not to open until he reached Khartoum: Kitchener was to go to Marchand, but Khartoum would be held in order to maintain contact with Cromer in Cairo, and meanwhile another force was to march up the Blue Nile. Technically and legally, Kitchener was in Egyptian, not in British, employ.

The news of Omdurman reached Salisbury in France, at Schlucht in the Vosges, where he was vacationing though keeping in touch with affairs. He wasted no time in sending instructions to his ambassador in Paris. If Delcassé should touch upon the matter of a possible Marchand-Kitchener encounter, the ambassador, Sir Edmond Monson, was

> to point out to him that, by the military events of last week, all the territories which were subject to the Khalifa passed by right of conquest to the British and Egyptian Governments. Her Majesty's Government do not consider that this right is open to discussion.[81]

The "right of conquest" is an ancient one and universally acknowledged. Salisbury's position had the merit of clarity and it put the matter squarely up to Delcassé. The question might of course be raised of conquest of what and by whom. Past history offered many precedents of the clash of overlapping British and French claims, the final disposition of which had been settled by the test of force. Fashoda itself was an insignificant locality, but so had been many North American outposts at one time; what was ultimately at stake was far from small, the control of the Nile.

Delcassé was new to the office that he filled, having come to it at the end of June; the situation that confronted him, no less at home than abroad, was particularly delicate. Something will be said of it presently, but as he was destined to play so large a part in our story, this is a suitable place at which to introduce the man.

Representative of a southern constituency, the Ariège, he had early made a mark in the Chamber and this had in turn made him eligible for ministerial prospects. His first appointment was as undersecretary for the colonies, a subdivision of the ministry of the Navy at the time, in the second Ribot Cabinet of January 1893. He was an avowed and consistent colonialist, believing in the importance of asserting the French presence in the world, especially at a time when the great scramble for empire was being so vigorously pursued by others, and, interestingly, also believing in the possibilities of large economic development. A measure of his interest was his success in obtaining the creation of the colonial office as a separate ministry, a post which he assumed in May 1894 after a short interim out of office.

For a variety of reasons, mainly related to domestic politics, he was out of the government for the better part of the next four years, during which time he was one of the most active members of the navy committee of the Chamber. This interest fitted well his other, and he correctly believed that the nature and size of the naval establishment should be determined by the aims of policy, its imperial aspects in particular. He was also a staunch nationalist and republican, though he parted company with such men as Clemenceau on the manner in which French power should be used, even though for him, too, Germany remained the chief danger. It is all the more interesting that there was some opposition to his appointment to the foreign office in 1898 on the grounds of a too strong Anglophobia.

Anglophobe per se he was not, but he opposed the abandonment of positions and a policy of appeasement. His views may be judged from a statement in a speech in February 1898:

> A mistake has been made and we must hasten to recognize the fact. What is that mistake? It is in having sacrificed everything in order to balance the forces of the Triple Alliance. . . . You

can see how much security and confidence that mistake has given England in the achievement of her ambitions.

However, he did not propose

> to lend himself, in any fashion, to anybody's game by rousing French opinion against England, being neither an anglophobe nor an anglophile.[82]

Re-elected in a hotly disputed election in 1898—he had turned to the opposition—he found himself foreign minister just as the crisis, a legacy of previous governments and policies, especially that of which Hanotaux had been the promoter, was about to mature. The situation which he inherited was, to say the least, prickly. The clear determination of the British Government, firmly expressed by Salisbury, was backed in England by an outburst of jingoism, some expressions of which may seem startling. To give but one citation, which is, however, far from untypical:

> [The British people] were confronted with the fact that 'a friendly power' had, unprovoked, endeavoured to rob them of the fruits of their victories. They now realized that while they had been devoting themselves to great military operations, in broad daylight and in the eyes of the world, and prosecuting an enterprise on which they had set their hearts, other operations—covert, deceitful, behind-the-back—had been in progress in the heart of the Dark Continent, designed solely for the mischievous and spiteful object of depriving them of the produce of their labours. And they firmly set their faces against such behaviour.[83]

The provincialism of British arrogance and cant, descending to scurrilous expression, was only matched by its equivalent in France. It is an interesting illustration of the mood of the mid nineties, but it would be an unrewarding and thankless task to accumulate illustrations of it. To put it on the basis of "the right of conquest" was, if harsh, at least sounder; the facts of power *are* harsh and power is what counted. If French opinion was united in regard to England, it was otherwise rent in unusual bitterness. This was the time of the Dreyfus affair, on the impact of which there is no need to enlarge; *J'Accuse* had been penned by Zola at the beginning of the year. More important than opinion and feeling, though these might lead to rash action, was the more objective consideration of the concrete facts of power.

On the English side, if Salisbury was determined that England must have exclusive control of the Nile, and would in the last resort fight for it, war had no attraction for him. In France, Delcassé kept his head and came to the correct conclusion that France was not in a position to engage in war with England. This had nothing to do with the merits of imperial activity, even of the legal grounds on which British and French claims respectively rested; one is hard put to it to choose between the two on that score. As has been pointed out, Delcassé was a convinced imperialist; the legitimacy of imperialism, be it on the narrow ground of national interest or on the broader one of spreading the benefits of a more advanced civilization, was obvious and not open to question. He did not disapprove of French ambitions on the Nile or in Egypt, but he thought that French policy had been poorly conducted.

The objectivity of his appraisal is illustrated by some of the comments he wrote on the British Blue Book of October 9, 1898, and of which one example may suffice:

> . . . The truth is that all the governments which have been in office since 1882 have never been able to decide on any given course. Two policies were open to us: either to challenge England, in which case our whole foreign and naval organization should have been guided by that purpose, in other words secure for ourselves a sufficiently strong position in Europe and a powerful navy; or else, if such an attempt seemed to be above our possibilities of manoeuvre, to practice a policy of compensations, which were unquestionably due to us given our preponderant position in Egypt, the number of our nationals, the extent of our credits and the services which, since 1840, we have not ceased to render to that country. The choice was limited and the dilemma was brutal.[84]

This was both sound appraisal and clear thinking.

Despite some naval preparations on both sides of the Channel, the simple facts on the French side were two: the French fleet, even if second in rank, was not a match for the British; France would have to face Britain alone.[85] The rational conclusion could be one thing only: surrender. But it was not an easy operation, for Delcassé was caught between the fires of his own domestic opinion and of an even more than necessary British intransigeance, which, for a time at least, did little to provide him with a face-saving escape. England wanted to be quite sure that certain other matters were settled to her satisfaction before effecting any compromise with France.[86]

However, even in France, Delcassé was not alone, and we may speak of a pro-British party, meaning by this those in favor of pursuing imperial activity in agreement and through prior arrangements with England, instead of in challenging competition. Ribot may be described as such a man, but perhaps as important as anything was the decision, reached as early as September 21, to appoint Paul Cambon to the London embassy. This was made easier by the retirement of the incumbent, de Courcel, and it is very significant that Cambon's one condition was the adoption of an English orientation of French policy. Cambon was in Constantinople at the time, having previously served in Madrid. He had given proofs of his talents and belongs in the great tradition of French, in fact of all, diplomacy at its best. We shall meet him again, and observe the remarkable achievement that was contrived between himself and Delcassé in reversing the nature of the Anglo-French relationship; it took six years to accomplish the task.

The end of the Fashoda confrontation can be summed up briefly. Once France had decided to yield and Britain had clarified the situation to her own satisfaction, disposing of the attempted Belgian intrusion, then concluded with Egypt in January 1899 the agreement which established a condominium in the henceforth Anglo-Egyptian Sudan, she and France came to terms. The agreement of March 21, 1899, which established a line of demarcation between the English and French zones of influence, was not ungenerous to France; her exclusion from the valley of the Nile was all that Britain wanted.

Fashoda seems long ago, especially in the light of all that has happened since. It can indeed be looked upon as a small episode in a continuing story, yet the significance of it must be rated considerable. It inserts itself, for one thing, into the long record of Anglo-French imperial rivalry, of which, in some respects at least, it may be regarded as the close. The confrontation to which the name of a small Sudanese community is attached was the climax of a contest of epic dimensions, reminiscent of the eighteenth-century competition over much of the North American continent. Neither country was unaware of the stakes involved, and, allowing for changes in personalities and in mode of operation within either milieu, what is more striking is the consistency with which aims were pursued in both cases, through the alternation of Liberal and Conservative control in the one, through the bewildering frequency of governmental changes and in the face of violent internal dissension in the other.

As in earlier cases of comparable Anglo-French confrontation, one of the decisive factors had been the superiority of British naval power. France cannot help give priority to the land, and, in addition, the total balance of the relationship of power and resources had in the course of time appreciably shifted to the British advantage. The result in the end was the same, French defeat, for what else was Fashoda? No amount of French sophistry could conceal that outcome. There had been no war on this occasion though it was a close call for a moment. France acted wisely in refusing the ultimate test; her wisdom, if based on a correct appraisal of the balance of forces, did not conceal, either for her or for others, her defeat and the meaning of it in terms of power standing. Thus Britain had not been in need of continental allies, though her diplomacy was successful in insuring that in the event France also would have none. Full credit must be given to Delcassé's own diplomatic handling of the conditions which he inherited upon his advent to the Quai d'Orsay.

Defeat is never pleasing and can rankle. In the above-mentioned context of Anglo-French imperial rivalry the episode could be looked upon as one more lost round, perhaps retrievable in another. Certainly at the level of feeling the stress tended to be on continuity of outlook; the time which has passed since Fashoda, even the very present, can be used as evidence to confirm that the record is not wholly forgotten. But there is also the fact that 1898 was not 1763. Less than three decades before

Fashoda France had been worsted in the test of force by Germany, and the discrepancy of power between the two countries was by this time becoming quite apparent. Depending upon predilection, Frenchmen might debate which, between Britain and Germany, was better deserving of the designation of "hereditary enemy"; but one question was becoming inescapable: could France afford two such? To be sure, the Russian alliance remained as an anchor of French policy, but what use had it been at Fashoda, when the Russian advice had been to avoid letting matters get out of control?

In contrast, Britain could gloat over her success, and there were those who did, still basking in the sun of splendid isolation. Britain could feel that she was riding the top of the wave and contemplate with satisfaction the rapid and extensive spread of the patches of red on the world map. That this was illusion time has made clear, but there was in 1898 little reason to think that within less than a decade the two hereditary enemies would have joined hands, fundamentally for the reason of the growing similarity between their positions vis-à-vis the rest of the world. Before turning to an account of this extraordinary development a few other things must be considered first.

Britain and the United States

This heading may seem like an inopportune digression, coming after the questions which have just been discussed. But it will presently appear that it is not, for what we are considering is the extent, the position, and the evolution of British power, hence the accommodations that were demanded of it and which it made. That is why a brief discussion of the Anglo-American relationship is relevant at this juncture.

Britain's neglect and mishandling of her American colonies, following the eviction of France from the North American continent, had not had the expected effects. To be sure, a new nation, the United States, was born to independence, but Anglo-American commercial exchanges did not decrease as a result. The episode powerfully contributed to the British view of empire thereafter, stressing its commercial aspects; as late as Salisbury's time, in regard to the competition for the political control of extra-European territory, we find his above-mentioned plaint that the desire to avoid exclusion from the possibility of trade was at the root of Britain's imperial expansion.[87]

On the American side anti-British feeling long continued to flourish as a stock-in-trade of publicists and politicians. Yet one can properly attach greater importance to the Monroe Doctrine, proclaimed as early as 1823, and which can be interpreted as the expression of a fundamental, deep-rooted, and long-lasting community of interest; only in very recent years have the British begun to have doubts about the merits of the association in which they could for a long time regard themselves as the senior partners, a role which events have reversed.

Some contacts leading to friction there were. But during the course of the nineteenth century the boundary with Canada and the common interest in the possibility of an Isthmian canal were adjusted with what, in relative terms and in the general context of international relations, may be regarded as a modicum of difficulty. Even the Civil War found Britain eventually accommodating in the adjudication of the *Alabama* claims. The wisdom of English policy in not yielding to the temptation to grant the South recognition is also worth nothing. There was awareness in Britain of the vast possibilities of American growth; it would be best to accept it with good grace and to continue to cultivate American good will. This attitude, which may be regarded as a fixed component of British policy, has paid handsome dividends.

After the Civil War the promise of American growth entered into full and rapid realization. As the century neared its close America was no longer dependent on British protection, and the nature and conditions of the American growth, its energies largely absorbed by the task of filling an empty continent, had alone prevented the United States from becoming as active and important a participant in larger world affairs as its resources and power might have warranted. America could thrive in isolation, a condition of fact which was a natural blessing long before it became a doctrine and a distortion.

The primacy of domestic concern had not prevented the growth of American interest in foreign trade. New England whalers roamed the wide seas, and in the days of the *Clipper* the

American merchant fleet was second to the British alone. The American share in the opening of Japan is familiar. One may even speak of an American imperial attitude, but it was for a long time *sui generis,* akin in some ways to the Russian; just as the latter pushed into Siberia and Central Asia, *contiguously* to the initial core, so likewise the Americans went West, pushing aside when necessary the Mexican encumbrance.

However, as the end of the nineteenth century approached, there began to be indications that American imperial interest might be taking a shape similar to others. Captain Mahan was an American, whose famous *The Influence of Sea Power Upon History* (1890) might be regarded as a harbinger of things to come. Four episodes will be briefly cited, mainly with an eye on their bearing on the direction of British policy.[88]

The ill-fated Mexican intervention of the second French empire has been mentioned[89]; internal American difficulties alone prevented for a time the taking by the United States of a stronger stance of opposition, and the episode was liquidated shortly after the conclusion of the Civil War. It could after all be regarded as an infringement on the Monroe Doctrine, which, however, Britain did nothing in this case to uphold other than parting company with France when it came to action in Mexico itself.

Another Latin American country, Venezuela, had had a long-standing dispute with Britain over its boundary with British Guyana. The American Government had offered its friendly interposition as early as 1886; it was declined by Salisbury at the time. Following further unsuccessful negotiations between the two principals, the offer was renewed in 1895 in the form of a mediation proposal. The elaborate memorandum which was Kimberley's—the British foreign secretary at the time—reply is of interest largely for the rejoinder which in turn it evinced from the American secretary of state, again urging arbitration, but also containing the statement, which must have made strange reading in Salisbury's eyes, that "today the United States is practically sovereign on this continent, and its fiat is law upon the subjects to which it confines its interposition."[90] Shades of the British Navy being the reality behind the Monroe Doctrine! Salisbury took his time in replying, from July to November; he rejected arbitration again and denied the applicability of the Monroe Doctrine in the matter. However, the dispute did not degenerate beyond this point; the treaty of arbitration between Britain and Venezuela of February 1897 resulted two years later in an award favorable to Britain.[91] This success is far less significant than the more fundamental fact that, in an Anglo-American dispute, Britain had yielded. It was a logical, and not a very long step from this to the proclamation of the Roosevelt corollary to the Monroe Doctrine,[92] something not very far from the assertion of a United States protectorate over the entirety of the American continent, exclusive of the existing European possessions. This was in 1904, when Theodore Roosevelt was President, to whom imperialism was no strange concept.

No more than passing mention need be made of the Spanish-American War of 1898, an outgrowth of the Cuban revolt against Spain. The United States, largely unknown and ignored by many in the world when it came to matters of power and international affairs, gave a convincing demonstration of its power as well as of the fact that it was little different from others in its capability for manifesting jingoistic behavior. Cuba was liberated in the process, brought under an American semi-protectorate, and the Philippines were acquired as well as Guam. It is worth mentioning the contrasting behavior of the British and the German admirals at Manila when it came to the destruction of the Spanish fleet by the American.[93]

These last-mentioned developments, the acquisition of the Philippines especially, pointed to an increased American interest in the Far East, where as an aftermath of the Sino-Japanese War various European Powers were engaging in a scramble to extract concessions from China, reminiscent in some respects of the African situation, although small segments of territory only were involved in the Chinese case. The American position differed from the European in avoiding participation in the competition but in insisting instead on the preservation of China's integrity, equally open to the trade of all nations, a position comparable to the British in regard to the Ottoman Empire. This was the burden of Secretary John Hay's famous Open Door declaration in a note he sent on September 6, 1899, to the various interested governments, the British, the French, the

German, and the Russian. The participation of the United States in the relief of Peking at the time of the Boxer insurrection, in June 1900, was occasion for reassertion of the Open Door policy.

The last instance to be mentioned has to do with the Panama Canal. The Anglo-American interest in the possibility of an Isthmian canal had a long history and had been expressed in the 1850 Clayton-Bulwer Treaty, which registered a parity of positions. It was the same de Lesseps, so successful at Suez, who sought to reproduce that performance at Panama. The Panama Canal Company was launched in 1881, but a variety of circumstances, local physical conditions among them, brought the company to grief to the accompaniment of a parliamentary scandal in France. Following the failure of the French company, the United States evinced an interest in continuing the undertaking. A bill was introduced in Congress authorizing the American President to negotiate the acquisition of the necessary territory, and the conclusion in November 1901 of the Hay-Pauncefote Treaty disposed of any British claims, leaving the United States free to proceed alone in the matter, which it went on to do.[94]

The moral of the tale is clear, even leaving aside Joseph Chamberlain's impossible vision of an alliance of the Anglo-Saxon peoples.[95] It may be summed up in the observation that, with little exception, when dealing with the United States, around the end of the century British policy showed itself remarkably accommodating,[96] a fact for which it should receive full marks as giving evidence of farsightedness and wisdom. Yet, taking the wide world as a whole, these Anglo-American affairs were of relatively secondary importance by comparison with the issues involved in the close and keen competition in which the European Powers came into contact with each other. That is the reason why Anglo-American relations have been so briefly sketched, and we shall now return to the main arena of conflict.

BRITAIN, FRANCE, AND GERMANY

The fact that England had had her way at Fashoda and the intransigeance that Salisbury had manifested for a time even after the French surrender may be regarded as evidence of the degree of British power and of the self-confident assertion of that power. It is the purpose of the remaining sections of this chapter to show that this would be a false reading—these were no longer the days of Palmerston—and to examine the manner in which the recognition of the altered circumstances came to Britain and was eventually accepted by her. It is a tale long and tangled, much has been written on the subject, and here again the treatment will be selective, with a view to illustrating what seem to the writer the results of the evidence.

The control of the Nile, an established policy well before 1898, may be considered in connection with two other manifestations of British policy, in the Near East and in South Africa. When Salisbury resumed the prime ministership of England in 1895 Near Eastern affairs seemed a more immediately pressing issue than the sources of the Nile. The unregenerate Turk had contrived a new problem for the Powers to deal with, the massacre of its Armenian subjects initiated as early as 1894, a policy which, with only little exaggeration, had been described as genocide. The unfulfilled reforming provisions of the Treaty of Berlin, to say nothing of the conscience of Christian Europe, a fragile reed when considerations of power intruded, would be sufficient grounds for intervention of some sort, ranging from physical action to the traditional practice of ineffectual remonstrances.

That nothing was done for the Armenians is fair summation of the tale, although the matter was indeed considered by the Powers. It is equally fair summation to say that the fundamental reason for their inaction lay in their mutual suspicions, the fear that intervention by some while others abstained would give the latter an advantage in currying Ottoman favor. The various interests involved have been indicated before, to which the German must be added by this time. It was not long before Emperor William II, inveterate traveler and Germany's first salesman, would visit the Red Sultan, give him his autographed photograph, and seek to pose in Damascus as the protector of Islam.

These German actions were motivated by very real economic interests; the end of Bismarck's tenure is virtually coincident with the beginning of an active German policy of economic penetration of the Near East. The policy took clearest form in the securing of concessions for the building of Anatolian railways, what eventually came to be known as the famous Berlin-Baghdad scheme. Building was well under way in the nineties, and there is no necessity to point out that this German intrusion impinged upon older existing interests, mainly Russian, British, and French. There was toward the end of the decade the customary scramble for concessions.

Where Britain was concerned we may recall her well-established interest in the route to the East, be it in Egypt, more narrowly at Suez, or in the valley of the Euphrates. The British failure to participate in the construction of the railway section pointing to Baghdad was not an oversight like that which had allowed the French to build the Suez Canal. But these circumstances have a bearing on the just mentioned neglect of the Armenians. As early as the time of the Congress of Berlin Salisbury had explained his views of the future prospects of the Ottoman Empire[97]; the passing of twenty years gave him no cause to alter his opinion. Speaking in Albert Hall in May 1898, he expressed the following thoughts already cited in part:

> Nations may roughly be divided between the living and the dying. . . . For one reason or another—for the necessities of politics or under the pretence of philanthropy—the living nations will gradually encroach upon the territory of the dying, and the seeds and causes of conflict among civilized nations will speedily appear. These things may introduce causes of fatal difference between the great nations whose mighty armies stand threatening each other. These are the dangers, I think, which threaten us in the period which is coming on. It is a period which will tax our resolution, our tenacity and our imperial instinct to the utmost. Undoubtedly we shall not allow England to be at a disadvantage in any re-arrangement that may take place. On the other hand, we shall not be jealous if desolation and sterility are removed by the aggrandisement of a rival in regions to which our arms cannot extend.[98]

This to be sure was a statement prompted by Russian activity in the Far East rather than by the Ottoman situation, but on the score of "dying nations" Salisbury held similar views in the Ottoman and in the Chinese cases. England's arm extended to Fashoda, and certainly to the Straits. But the prospect of impending Ottoman demise naturally suggested the idea of how to arrange the succession without a major conflict; one obvious way to do this was a prior agreement on partition. The thought was still with him at this time and caused him to put out a feeler to St. Petersburg which might have led to the granting of Russia's traditional wish at the Straits. This was a large order indeed, but the death of the Turk, should it occur, called for grandiose plans. The idea of partition was not new at this time. As early as August 1895, on the occasion of one of the Kaiser's visits to England, Salisbury had thrown out hints to that effect. There was no response, for the Kaiser, prompted by his advisers, chose to read into the suggestion an instance of perfidious Albion sowing seeds of discord. The episode was a comedy of errors[99] and the outcome a momentary deterioration of Anglo-German relations. Thus Ottoman affairs went on as usual, punctuated by a passing rapprochement between Russia and Austria—the Balkans "put on ice" in 1897—and the episode of the Greco-Turkish War of the same year. The Powers could agree on rescuing the Greeks from the consequences of defeat, but their mutual suspicions reappeared when it came to dealing with Crete. There is no need to dwell on these events, and we may turn to the South African aspect of British policy.

The Boer War

The grand scheme of an all-British Cape-to-Cairo connection had been blocked by the Franco-German opposition of 1894. This did not mean a lessened British interest either in the North or the South. Having dealt with the Nile we may turn to South Africa, and this is the proper place to introduce Joseph Chamberlain. This typical representative of the rising industrial class had begun his political career in the local affairs of his native Birmingham, where his reforming administration helped coin the phrase "water and gas socialism." His Liberal affiliations were, however, put under too great a strain by Gladstone's attitude on the Irish problem. It was the first Home Rule Bill which, in 1886, caused a split in the Liberal ranks;

Chamberlain was one of the Liberal Unionists who dissented and helped the Conservative success in the following election while introducing a measure of confusion into the usual two-party system of Britain, since there were for a time, in addition, his own and the Irish groups.

Chamberlain was a nationalist, but not of the "little England" variety. Ireland could be considered an integral and hence inseparable part of the British Isles, but it was also not a far step from this type of reasoning—or emotion—to an enthusiasm for the whole empire. Chamberlain was also an imperialist if ever there was one and he finally found his proper home in the last Salisbury administration of 1895, in which he held the position of colonial secretary, still a relatively minor post but his own choice, somewhat to the surprise of the Prime Minister and of Balfour.[100]

Queen Victoria's Diamond Jubilee in 1897 may be described as just his "dish of tea," a suitable account of which and of Chamberlain's part in it may be found in Garvin's biography.[101] The presence of all the eleven colonial Prime Ministers[102] furnished occasion for the second Imperial Conference and for Chamberlain an opportunity to promote his cherished design of forging closer links among the members of the imperial community. With rather less flamboyance, Salisbury agreed; as he put it:

> We are undertaking a great experiment of trying to sustain such an empire entirely upon the basis of mutual goodwill, sympathy and affection. . . . It is the triumph of a moral idea in the construction of a great political organization which is the object and the effort in which we are all joined.[103]

Chamberlain, as fitted his background and his antecedents, set great store on the economic development of the empire, parts of which he felt had been neglected—Delcassé would have agreed with him. But he also felt concerned about the validity of the continued British adherence to the doctrine of free trade; should not Britain emulate others in seeking for herself a privileged position in the territories under her control? Such ideas were, in Britain, in advance of the time. Nevertheless, the course of the years since the formation of Salisbury's ministry tended to confirm the original estimate of Chamberlain as second only to the Prime Minister where it came to carrying influence in major policy decisions.

One particular aspect of imperial policy which held great appeal for Chamberlain was the federative idea. As he put it as early as November 1895:

> That empire . . . hangs together by a thread so slender that it may well seem that even a breath would sever it. . . . I remember on one occasion having been shown a slender, a frail wire, which a blow might break, and I was told that it was capable of transmitting an electrical energy that would set powerful machinery in motion. May it not be the same in the relation that exists between our Colonies and ourselves? And may not that thread be capable of carrying a force of sentiment and sympathy that will yet be a potent factor in the history of the world? . . . I am told on every hand that Imperial federation is a vain and empty dream. . . . Dreams of that kind which have so powerful an influence upon the imagination of men, have somehow or other an unaccountable way of being realized in their own time.[104]

There was one particular area where, on a more limited scale, a federative policy might be essayed, and this is where we rejoin the previous part of our story, the South African counterpart of Britain's policy on the Nile. It will suffice to recall by way of background the exiting Cape Colony, of which Cecil Rhodes was Prime Minister, the expanding activities as far as Rhodesia of his British South Africa Company, and the presence of the Dutch-derived Boer Republics of the Transvaal and the Orange Free State. Portuguese possessions abutted on these territories, and Germany had acquired an interest in East as well as in Southwest Africa. These are the main components of the tale.

The landlocked Boer Republics were enclaves of British territory, save for the possible access to the sea through Portuguese Mozambique. The discovery of rich gold and diamond deposits in the Transvaal had, among others, two effects: it brought in financial interests and a number of the usual type of adventurers,

Uitlanders as they were known. Both were primarily British and neither especially welcome to the agrarian, strongly religious Boers. President Kruger of the Transvaal was a fitting representative of this dour people. Garvin's characterization, "much allowance must be made for him, and a rudely-hewn grandeur belongs to his memory, but he was the father of war,"[105] seems appropriate.

An uncompromising and less than generous Boer treatment—in matters of taxation, for example—of the Uitlanders came into collision with the latter's demand for a voice in the affairs of the state, which could easily be elevated to a claim for the customary rights of free-born Englishmen. Leaving aside the rights and wrongs of the issue, there were ample makings of domestic trouble in the Transvaal, but the contiguity of the British possessions militated against its remaining purely domestic. This was the state of affairs when Chamberlain took charge of the colonial office. He was hardly the man to yield on British rights—or essential desiderata—and there is a measure of similarity between the Anglo-French relationship on the Nile, which Salisbury himself handled, and the Anglo-German in South Africa.

Anglo-German relations were not of the best at this point, what with Far and Near Eastern divergent approaches, not to mention the fact that Salisbury's view of the German emperor is best summed up by the phrase "he is false." Kaiser William's unstable disposition, easily given to suspicion, abetted by an irresponsible if fertile imagination, caused him to perceive possibilities of fishing in troubled South African waters. Some British problems, the friction with the United States over the Venezuela boundary dispute, for example, furnished him with a perfect opportunity. That in the end he made the worst of it was quite in character.

There is no space to go into details of the famous and picturesque Jameson Raid, an ill-contrived and foolish filibustering expedition in the closing days of 1895, which grew out of the above-mentioned Uitlander situation. It was an ignominious failure and ended in ridicule. But there was more than ridicule, for at one remove Cecil Rhodes was involved, and the prompt disavowal from London was not found convincing by all, not even in England.[106] At the time Chamberlain was fully exonerated, and his position was, if anything, enhanced, though this was to a point for other reasons.

It was on January 3, 1896, just after the failure of the Jameson Raid, that the following message was sent from Berlin by Emperor William II to President Kruger of the Transvaal:

> I express to you my sincere congratulations that you and your people, without appealing to the help of friendly powers [read Germany], have succeeded, by your own energetic action, against the armed bands which invaded your country as disturbers of the peace, in restoring peace and in maintaining the independence of the country against attacks from without.[107]

What it was proposed to accomplish by so sensational a gesture is not exactly clear. The Kaiser was ever torn between sentimentality and crafty planning, ever attracted by the grandiloquent and the sensational. To say that the Kruger telegram was a carefully calculated move of German diplomacy is putting it too strongly[108]; it can equally be argued that the Kaiser's advisers toned down his initial impulse. But there can be no doubt that the gesture was ill-advised, being a crude expression of the attempted German intrusion into South African affairs. It had, as might be expected, the effect of deflecting the focus of English popular attention away from Jameson and the Transvaal toward Berlin; there might be differences in England on the merits of Dr. Jameson's proceedings, there were none on the Kaiser's behavior. Minor as the incident was, it assumes significance, for it brings out one of the fundamental and lasting obstacles to the establishment of stable Anglo-German relations. This element is aptly expressed by Garvin:

> Then, and for twenty years after, the Germans laboured under one error that nothing could remove. They did not understand, and never yet have understood, the nature and power of political liberty:—that the British people when thoroughly moved is the master of its Government; that in crisis it has a will of its own; that while amiably or indolently inclined to mildness and concession in most foreign and Imperial complications, it is not

> cowed, but animated by extreme danger. Germany in her turn was amazed by an elemental outburst of British wrath and defiance.[109]

This touches on a fundamental aspect of the British mode of operation, the influence of which remains a constant factor, and the effects of which recur again and again. Whether British feeling becomes aroused in connection with a rightful cause or the opposite is another matter again; the common denominator remains the sense of external interference with its independence of decision.

The storm blew over and the aftermath of the incident need not detain us. But it is significant that Chamberlain expressed concern over the danger that President Kruger might unwisely seek to push his momentary advantage too far. For, if Jameson's methods were absurd, on the fundamental of British rights—or claims—in the whole South African region there was no divergence. As Chamberlain put it:

> I have done everything in my power to undo and minimise the evil caused by the late unwarranted raid by British subjects into the territory of the South African Republic, and it is not likely that such action will ever be repeated; but the state of things of which complaint has been made [the Uitlanders' grievances] cannot continue for ever.[110]

Taking a broad view, it is not unfair to say that, be it on the Nile or in South Africa, the basic British position was the same, the assertion of priority of control to the exclusion of others.

This was clearly expressed again in the debate in the Commons on February 13, 1896, when Chamberlain asserted:

> My conscience is clear. I have approached President Kruger in this matter as a friend to him and his Republic. . . . I will continue on behalf of her Majesty's Government to endeavour by every legitimate means to secure that justice [to the Uitlanders] which up to the present time has been denied. . . . I do not hesitate to say, it takes no prophet to predict, that sooner or later justice will be done.[111]

Or, as a member put it even more bluntly:

> We had now laid it down distinctly for all time that, as regards those foreign relations [of the Transvaal], Great Britain intended to remain the paramount Power having full control over such relations.[112]

Read Sudan for Transvaal and the identical statement could be made. The logic of empire and of imperial expansion is blatantly clear; we are reduced to a problem of power in the face of which, in the context of the time, the rights and claims of Sultan, Khedive, or Uitlanders vanish into insignificance, possible immediate causes or convenient pretexts.

Thus the seeds of the Boer War were planted. But there was a difference between the Nile and South Africa, although in either case the whole international situation had to be borne in mind; great as they were, the power and the resources of Britain had their limitations. An interesting illustration of this is provided by the conjunction of Salisbury's toying with the idea of letting the Russians have Constantinople with Chamberlain's considering the possibility of improving relations with France despite the Egyptian problem. As the latter put it to the former, "if we failed we would be no worse off; if we succeed we might deal with France afterwards without the slightest difficulty."[113] Some may be tempted to say "perfidious Albion"; where personal predilections toward Germany or France respectively were concerned the two men represented antithetic approaches; but both were Englishmen entrusted with the defense of the British national interest.

The difference between the Nile and South Africa was that in the case of the former France became directly involved, with the consequences that have been examined before. Germany did not become involved in comparable fashion over South African affairs but provided instead a highly interesting instance of a contrasting situation; it merits some examination.

In view of the uncertainties of the German position, her reticence at the time of the Anglo-French confrontation, it was obvious from the English point of view that it was preferable to deal with one thing at a time. That is one reason for Salisbury's continued intransigeance even after the French surrender at Fashoda. The agreement of March 1899 clarified and settled, for the time being at least, the Anglo-French relationship. The South African situation could now be attended to; the Boer War began in October 1899.

This manner of presenting the sequence of events constitutes to a point a distorting oversimplification; there was no carefully established time schedule, which may rather be seen as imposed by the inner logic of circumstances. Of the Boer War itself and its background little will be said. As in the case of the French on the Nile, the British had no predilection for war for its own sake; they would much have preferred peaceful accommodation, on the same condition, however, that they have their own way on what they considered essentials. Relations with the Transvaal did not improve after 1895. Kruger was hardly an accommodating man, and Milner, the British high commissioner in South Africa since 1897, was for his part determined. Some in the British Cabinet, having in mind the international situation as a whole during the intervening period, thought him too forward and intransigeant, but Milner was steadfast and had become convinced of the inevitability of the test of force. The re-election of Kruger to the presidency of the Transvaal at the beginning of 1898 boded ill for any possibility of compromise; appropriately, the meeting of the two men at Bloemfontein at the beginning of June 1899 ended in failure, over the perennial issue of the Uitlanders' rights. Actually, it was Kruger, deeply distrustful of the British, who took the initiative of a declaration of war.

The coalition of the Boer Republics pitted against the might of England may appear ludicrous, at least if the contest remained confined to the South African locale. It was. To be sure, the Boers enjoyed well-nigh universal sympathy, save in the British Empire, some members of which voluntarily contributed contingents; in this respect the position of Britain at the time in the eyes of the world brings to mind the later one of the United States in Vietnam. The Boers also earned widespread respect for their fighting ability[114]; the British were surprised at the extent of the effort they had to make and at the duration of the war. There was even a pro-Boer party in England, but in the end it counted for little and the war had on the whole the effect of exciting the national emotion. The inevitable conclusion, even if not until May 1902, was the Treaty of Vereeniging, which totally clarified the situation through the device of outright annexation.

The Boers, as just indicated, received no outside assistance. The French might read with satisfaction accounts of British setbacks, but they had just been put in their place, and Delcassé was a sensible man. German feeling, at the popular level, was also strongly pro-Boer, but German policy was quite a different matter. No Kruger telegram this time, but instead patronizing advice to the British from the irrepressible Kaiser on how to manage the war; it caused Salisbury considerable irritation. The contributions of German scientists to psychology do not seem to have helped the conduct of German foreign policy.

China and the Anglo-German Discussions

The expression "splendid isolation" is not of ancient vintage, dating from the mid nineties. By the time it was coined it expressed a condition that was disappearing, if it had not already passed, rather than existing reality. Salisbury did not think that England had guns enough to fight France and Russia at once, and we have seen the extent to which England sought to cooperate for a time with the Triple Alliance. The isolation of England when Salisbury resumed office and the increasing evidence that a major confrontation with France might be forthcoming over Central Africa raised the question again of the possible merits of some reinsurance. But Italy was set back in Africa, and Russia failed to show interest in Near Eastern rearrangements, preferring Balkan stabilization in agreement with Austria.

Germany was an uncertain quantity, clearly a success story of internal growth, but under leadership that was erratic, the Kaiser alternately torn between a strong desire for English friendship and unmeasured outbursts of frustrated dislike and suspicion. Germany's thriving economy made her increasingly a competitor of previously established England and she had also become an active participant in the world competition for empire. World politics and empire can hardly be divorced from naval power; even leaving aside the more grandiloquent forms of expression that might appeal to the Kaiser's propensity for display and his fondness for ships—"our future lies on the water"—there was behind these words the solid reality of Germany's economic rise and of growing German power.

The inherent threat contained in such a situation could be countered in two opposite ways: opposition, possibly nipping the danger in the bud; or accommodation. What talk there may have been abroad of preventive war in any quarter in those days—even the German attitude toward France—was not very serious, and the English preference is in general for compromise. The various power alignments, some of which have been indicated, might be transitory affairs, to be looked upon in the larger context of more lasting interests and established relationships, though of course circumstances might also bring lasting alteration in them. There is no secret in such thoughts, the natural stuff of statesmen's long-term contemplations; also the influence of tradition must be borne in mind. Anglo-French and Anglo-Russian differences were two such established traditions, as against which Anglo-German co-operation, in the heyday of French power especially, had also a long history. If the decline of French power could not be denied, France was still anything but negligible and evidently also entertained far-reaching imperial ambitions. This is not the analysis of a specific document penned in the foreign office, but a broad general outlook which, obvious as it may be, deserves consideration. It may be taken as the background of the attempt, three times renewed over three years, to put Anglo-German relations on a stable basis. It turned out to be a capital turning point and we must give it some consideration. The story has been told many times, it is the subject of an extensive literature,[115] and here again the emphasis will be on certain salient and especially relevant points and aspects.

As early as 1889, Herbert Bismarck, on a visit to England in connection with his father's feeler for an English alliance, reported of Chamberlain:

His friendship for Germany was never so sharply marked as in our conversation of yesterday. He said absolutely *Sine Germania nulla salus,* and insisted that on both sides we must devote our whole attention to remove all points of difference that might arise between the two countries in the future.[116]

When the possibility of an Anglo-German connection was revived in the second half of the nineties, it was fitting, from the standpoint of personal inclination, that the task of negotiation should fall to Chamberlain. Apart from the factor of age, which was beginning to tell on Salisbury, his relatively more pro-French predilection, and his intense dislike of the Germans pointed to this division of labor. It should never be forgotten, of course, that but limited importance should be attached to the qualifier "pro" in these matters; Salisbury, Chamberlain, and Balfour were first and foremost Englishmen. Chamberlain, in addition, despite what has just been cited, suffered from the handicap of German distrust; a meeting between him and Count Hatzfeldt, the German ambassador in London, in December 1897, seemed to confirm this German view, or prejudice.[117]

There were at this time various differences between England and Germany—West Africa, Samoa—but more important developments loomed in the Far East. In that quarter, however, it was the vigorous Russian activity that was the greater cause of English concern.[118] But, especially in retrospect, it may be said that most important of all was the looming adoption by Germany of an ambitious naval program. It is in connection with colonial differences with England that the Kaiser was prompted to write to his Chancellor, Prince Hohenlohe:

> Had we a fleet strong enough to enforce respect, the notice to terminate the old naval treaties would not have been given; our answer must be to keep in view a speedy and significant increase of our naval construction.[119]

The appearance of a naval party in Germany was both natural and logical, and there exists no law, national or divine, which endows England with an everlasting right to naval supremacy; it was rather again a question of resources and power, not forgetting will power. But if Germany was determined to become a major naval power, certain consequences followed which had to be faced.

Admiral von Tirpitz has properly been called the father of the German Navy; perhaps we should allow the German emperor the attribute of midwife. At any rate the German Reichstag enacted in March 1898 what is usually described as the first navy bill, an adequate description in the sense that it marked the deliberate launching of a new naval policy. Impulsive as the Kaiser might be, this was a carefully considered act of high policy; it was essentially a political act, for, pending the obviously distant day when the German Navy might by itself be capable of challenging the British, the growing German naval establishment could be used as a valuable bargaining asset.[120] One may read in this approach an element of blackmail, correctly so indeed, though care should be used in speaking of "blackmail" in diplomatic dealings.

In any case England was bound to be highly interested in the German decision. It may not be irrelevant to recall at this point Salisbury's above-mentioned "dying nations" speech of May 1898.[121] The reference was mainly directed to China and Turkey, but these were also the days when Latin decadence was a popular notion: Spain had given good evidence, the Italians had shown their capabilities at Adowa and its domestic aftermath; as to French decadence it is a very durable thing, to which one must admit that the current vagaries of the French domestic scene seemed to give particular point. It is enlightening to juxtapose Salisbury's speech with some suggestions Chamberlain sent to Balfour shortly before:

> . . . grave trouble is impending upon the Government if we do not adopt a more decided attitude in regard to China. . . . If only Lord Salisbury sees the peril and is prepared to meet it, I would rather leave to him the method than rush in with what may be impossible suggestions. But as the matter now appears to me I should propose:
>
> 1. To approach the United States officially and to ask an immediate reply to the question, "Will you stand with us in our policy?"
>
> 2. To approach Germany at the same time with the same question.
>
> 3. [Deals with the encroachment on China.][122]

Chamberlain was not one to bask contentedly in the contemplation of such a slogan as "splendid isolation"; he thought isolation a thing of the past and in the circumstances of the time more dangerous than splendid. The initiative of the attempt, the outcome of which might be an alliance, actually came from German quarters. While Salisbury was kept informed and remained sceptical, he gave Chamberlain a free hand and in his hands the discussion remained. The first meeting between him and Hatzfeldt took place on March 29, the discussion remaining confined to colonial questions, though this was merely an introduction to larger possibilities. As Chamberlain records it:

> I said that as far as I knew, there was no question between the two governments which affected any important interest, and they were all absolutely trivial in comparison with the great issues involving our relations with other nations. It seemed to me that on these greater issues the interests of Germany were really identical with our own.[123]

Hatzfeldt's report to Berlin conveys the impression, which fits the citation just given, of the prospect of Britain joining the Triple Alliance. The reply from Berlin was ambiguous, seeking to convey the impression that Germany was not the demandant, nor was she pressed for time. However, there was no delay and the two men met again on April 1. Chamberlain was quite frank and the discussion ranged wide. There were no further meetings for another three weeks, when Chamberlain had three more meetings with Hatzfeldt and with Eckardstein.[124] The difficulty, and the source of the failure, both at this time and later, already becomes apparent at this point. It must mainly be set to German misunderstanding, psychological in good measure, of the British, as well as to an exaggerated view of German power and of Britain's difficulties.

The difficulties existed—the Boer War and the Far East, where Russia was encroaching—but Britain was not, and above all did not feel, reduced to the position of demandant. For Germany to raise the issue of the reliability of England's parliamentary system[125] and to seek to extract concessions in advance as a token of British earnest was to miss the main point. As reported by Hatzfeldt himself:

> Mr. Chamberlain . . . developed in detail the view that if his hope of a mutual alliance with Germany must be renounced, it would be no impossibility for England to arrive at an understanding with Russia or with France. . . . As he had told me before he did not hold it advisable in dealing with us or others to settle the smaller questions by English concessions except in connection with a simultaneous general settlement.[126]

To which he [Hatzfeldt] added his own further confirmatory comment of the earnestness of Chamberlain's hardly veiled threat. To Hatzfeldt's observation that the occasion for an understanding might recur Chamberlain had commented: *"le bonheur qui passe."* Chamberlain may not have been a trained diplomat, as some of the Germans rather patronizingly thought; he was an unsensational and hard-headed businessman.

Salisbury was not surprised and hardly disappointed, only somewhat irritated at what seemed to him some of the pettiness of the German approach. To the above-mentioned reasons for the German hesitancy may be added a real fear of ulterior British motives, of getting Germany to pull British chestnuts out of the fire. There had indeed been a prior British attempt, unsuccessful as it turned out, to find an accommodation with Russia. But if it came to duplicity, the Kaiser knew how to overbid. The letter that "Willy" wrote to "Nicky" on May 30, 1898, may be quoted in part; among other things it reveals the Kaiser's nature and methods while providing some humorous relief:

> Dearest Nicky, With a suddenness wholly unexpected to me I am placed before a grave decision which is of vital importance to my country, and which is so far reaching that I cannot foresee the ultimate consequences. . . .
>
> About Easter a Celebrated Politician *proprio motu* suddenly sent for my ambassador and *à brûle-pourpoint* offered him a treaty of Alliance with England! . . . After Easter the request was *urgently* renewed but by my commands coolly and dilatorily answered in a colourless manner. I thought the affair was ended.

Now, however, the request has been renewed for the third time in such an unmistakeable manner, putting a *certain short term* to my definite answer and accompanied by such enormous offers showing a wide and great future opening for my country that I think it my duty to Germany duly to reflect before I answer.

Now before I do it, I frankly and openly come to you, my esteemed friend and cousin, as I feel that is a question so to say of life and death. . . . I am informed that the Alliance is to be with the Triple Alliance and with the addition of Japan and America, with whom pourparlers have already been opened! . . .

Now as my old and trusted friend I beg you to tell me what you can offer me and will do if I refuse. . . . [these italics mine][127]

This may be juxtaposed to the hope expressed by Bülow a few months later, on the occasion of Queen Victoria's forthcoming eightieth birthday:

I hope to God . . . that thus in full independence towards both sides, Your Majesty, on the eightieth birthday of Her exalted Majesty Queen Victoria, will be present as *arbiter mundi.*[128]

Nothing came of these brilliantly inept diplomatic maneuvers. The Tsar easily trumped his cousin's card with the rejoinder that he, too, had received tempting offers from England and that it was not for him to advise Germany where her best interest lay.

The ludicrous and crude German performance did to be sure make some contribution to the suspicion of Albion's perfidiousness, but, for the rest, there matters rested. One can hardly disagree with Garvin's judgment:

So William II and his counsellors—Bülow, brilliant but shallow and deceptive; Holstein, the complete logician arguing from false premises; Tirpitz, the inflexible sailor, who saw in his work for the future glory of the sea-service the soul of patriotism—these together began to break up on all sides the Bismarckian system to which the Hohenzollerns owed their empire.[129]

But all this is an aside, for Britain is our chief concern at this point. The fact that the Anglo-German negotiation had failed did not mitigate England's isolation, of which Chamberlain took a dim view. As he put it in a speech on May 13:

> All the powerful states of Europe have made alliances, and as long as we keep outside these alliances—as long as we are envied by all and suspected by all—and as long as we have interests which at one time or another conflict with the interests of all—we are liable to be confronted at any moment with a combination of Great Powers . . . We stand alone. . . .[130]

In other words, the Continental League was not a wholly empty fiction and Britain did not feel that she was *arbiter mundi.*

Chamberlain's observation to Hatzfeldt about the fleeting occasion, *le bonheur qui passe,* did not necessarily preclude the possibility that *le bonheur peut retourner.* The Boer War was carried to a successful conclusion, even if with the difficulty that has been indicated, and Germany did not seek to exploit the English embarrassment though she did not draw from it a favorable impression of English power; in the Far East the Boxer Rebellion, threatening to reopen the Chinese Pandora's box, was a source of renewed concern. The episode provided the occasion for a demonstration of unity by the Powers—an international expedition under the command of a German general. It also furnished, incidentally, some food for thought on the touted claims to the superiority of Western civilization—the behavior of the Western forces in Peking and the startling send-off of the Kaiser to the German contingent.[131]

The Anglo-German agreement of August 1898, a preliminary scheme for the partition of Portugal's South African possessions, should they come on the market as a result of Portugal's current financial embarrassment, may be seen as the small residue of the discussions which have just been related. It was also a misunderstanding, for the Treaty of Windsor a year later seemed to imply a different British view. Britain's intentions were not in either case evil designs, but the conjunction of the two agreements was a somewhat inept piece of diplomacy, well calculated to nourish the ever alert German readiness to suspect British duplicity.

British diplomacy has on occasion been strangely insensitive to the impact of its decisions upon others.[132]

But power remains power and may not be too choosey when it comes to bedfellows. Thus on two more occasions the attempt to establish an Anglo-German connection was renewed. They can be dealt with very briefly since the result was failure again, largely for the same reasons which had caused failure on the first occasion.

On November 20, 1899, the German emperor arrived in Windsor for a two-day visit. He was accompanied by Bülow who, like his master, had important discussions with Chamberlain. Broad general questions of policy were considered, as well as more immediate and concrete matters, Samoa for example; and Morocco was touched upon. The meetings seemed to create an atmosphere of euphoria, though it is not amiss to record Bülow's impression of his interlocutor as "the modern merchant, very definite, very shrewd, very unscrupulous, but withal very realistic; since he knows that without realism no business on a grand scale can be done."[133]

In the discussion with Bülow Chamberlain had touched upon the role of the United States, his appraisal of whose power and of the future consequences thereof can only be regarded as perceptive and prescient. His manner of promoting his project of a grand alliance was however less deft. For he chose to give public expression to his hopes in the second of the speeches that he delivered on November 30, to a Unionist lunch at Leicester, of which some extracts may be cited:

> The natural alliance is between ourselves and the great German Empire. . . . I cannot conceive any point which can arise in the immediate future which can bring ourselves and the Germans into antagonism of interests. On the contrary, I can foresee many things in the future which must be a cause of anxiety to the statesmen of Europe, but in which our interests are clearly the same as the interests of Germany, and in which the understanding of which I have spoken in the case of America might if extended do more perhaps than any combination of arms in order to preserve the peace of the world.
>
> . . . .
>
> I may point out to you that at bottom, the character, the main character of the Teutonic race differs very slightly indeed

from the character of the Anglo-Saxon (cheers) . . . and if the union between England and America is a powerful factor in the cause of peace, a new Triple Alliance between the Teutonic race and the two great branches of the Anglo-Saxon race, will be a still more potent influence in the future of the world.

I have used the word "alliance" sometimes in the course of what I have said, but again I desire to make it clear that to me it seems to matter little whether you have an alliance which is committed to paper or whether you have an understanding which exists in the minds of the statesmen of the respective countries. . . . An understanding, a determination to look favorably on the motives of those with whom we desire to be on terms of friendship—a feeling of that kind, cultivated, existing, and confirmed by all these three countries will I am certain be to their enormous advantage, and I believe, whether they think it themselves or not, will also be to the advantage of other nations.[134]

In Chamberlain's own calculations this was an olive branch—or a bait—to which he expected the German Chancellor to respond in kind, thereby putting the project on the ways. The result was a (to Chamberlain) unexpected anticlimax. Chamberlain was, after all, a responsible member of the British Government, next in importance to the Prime Minister alone; to speak publicly of "alliance," even with the qualifications indicated, was to have gone too far, to place the cart before the horse in the process of handling the relations among states, a process in which priority must be given to the more subterranean and quieter methods of diplomacy. This was especially indicated at a time when the policy that was being advocated ran counter to much popular feeling everywhere; world opinion was highly sympathetic to the Boers.

Even in Chamberlain's own country the response was rebuke, in which *The Times* joined, to say nothing of opposition and less sedate organs. Salisbury may have been failing but his stubborn adherence to "not isolation but independence" was considered sounder. The reaction was sharper abroad. There is little need to mention the French, but there was no enthusiasm in America. Worst of all was the German response. At the level of opinion, reflected in the press, sometimes descending to scurrilousness, there was little to choose between the German and the French. Bülow himself, in the Reichstag on December 11, elected to throw cold water on the idea, indulging in disparaging comments on the prospects of the British position.

Chamberlain was at once disappointed and angered. That there were reasons to suspect his candor may be granted—he was not blind to the possible effects on Russo-German relations of encouraging Germany to push toward Baghdad—but on balance there can be little question that Bülow had thrown away an opportunity; he thought himself very skillful but was instead merely too devious and clever: the Anglo-German relationship was undoubtedly changing and he thought Germany should push her advantage. A further expansion of her naval establishment would in time put her in a position where she could by herself present a serious threat in the home waters to a British Navy scattered over the world; Germany would then truly be *arbiter mundi.* Pending that future glorious day Britain would not be pressed too hard; the attempt to secure some small token concessions—again in Samoa—may be dismissed as ill-advised pettiness. Chamberlain was thinking in large terms, and he was also shrewd when it came to small matters. Subsequent incidents at sea in connection with the Boer War are also minor matters although they furnished Germany occasion to write irking notes in which the quality of overbearingness found full vent.

The course of the Boer War has been indicated. Britain was not so weak or decadent that she could not rise to the effort demanded, and initial setbacks had rather the effect of rousing the nationalistic emotion. The news of the relief of Mafeking in May 1900, shortly followed by the capture of Johannesburg, sent London "mafeking" in scenes of unrestrained, at times vulgar, jingoistic enthusiasm. The Commonwealth of Australia came into final existence in 1901. Perhaps the empire was anything but dying. The "khaki" election of 1900 reflected the mood of the British electorate.

That was also the year of the Boxer Rebellion, which raised in its train widespread possibilities of conflict over what many thought was the impending sharing of the Chinese inheritance. Russia was driving hard and once again Britain was looking for assistance in containing the Russian drive. Who but Germany or Japan could fill this role? A decision seemed all the more pressing as the possibility was not to be excluded of a Russo-German understanding.

These matters were discussed in the Cabinet with the outcome that Chamberlain, though he had had his fingers burnt, would try once more. A meeting was arranged at Chatsworth between himself and Eckardstein,[135] in which the usual arguments were repeated, Chamberlain warning that the alternative to failure was an understanding with the Dual Alliance. However, he went further than he had before, for he also held out the possibility of Britain joining the Triple Alliance; but, interestingly, reversing his earlier stand, he would approach that result in gradual fashion—the climate of opinion in both England and Germany was not suitable—dealing with specific issues first; Morocco was mentioned again.

Once more the German reaction was one of dilatoriness: let England's troubles increase—a better price could be commanded—and Holstein excluded the possibility of an accommodation between England and the Franco-Russian combination. His and Bülow's advice to the Kaiser was to let the situation mature, avoiding any show of eagerness, restraining the emperor's sound instinct on this occasion.

At this juncture, on January 22, Queen Victoria died, an event which brought much of Europe's royalty, the Kaiser for one, to London for her funeral. This furnished occasion for a long discussion between himself and Lansdowne; the latter was none too favorably impressed, mainly owing to the emperor's lack of balanced judgment. It is worth noting that William II's personal inclination had to be restrained by his own advisers. Metternich's report to the Wilhelmstrasse makes enlightening reading, revealing as it does the fundamental factor in the German estimate of the situation:

> I reminded His Majesty of yesterday's spectacle [the funeral of the Queen]. The military ranks stretched for miles. A muster of troops morally degraded, idiots, undersized and pitiable beings. The dregs of the population. With astonishment and affright we beheld yesterday that the English had reached the end of their military capacity.[136]

It is indeed quite true that recruiting for the Boer War had revealed shocking conditions in the physique of the English people and that a random gathering of the London populace does not make an impressive spectacle—the German equivalent would be better—but to equate such things, serious as they might be, with a catastrophic decline of Britain and her power is another matter again. Negotiations were continued for some months but there is no need to enter into the details of them. The result was the same as before, largely for the same reasons. This time one must say *le bonheur est passé,* for the failure of this third attempt marks a crucial turning point. Whether perfidious or sincere, Chamberlain's warning about possible alternatives was not an empty threat.

The Logic of Circumstances

A Parisian crowd would hardly have been a more impressive spectacle than a Londonian, and French decadence was far more widely accepted than British despite an impressive flowering of culture under the Third Republic. What is culture to guns?

Yet France was still a major Power. Despite Sedan and Fashoda her armed establishment was not to be ignored, while her considerable wealth was an instrument that her diplomacy knew how to use. The events and the negotiations that have just been recounted were closely watched by her and we shall now examine how she went about handling her own affairs. During the entire period under consideration Delcassé was in charge of the foreign office, insuring continuity of direction amid the vagaries of Dreyfus affairs and anti-militaristic and anti-clerical agitation in which good—or intransigeant doctrinaire—republicans could indulge to their heart's content. Of French domestic affairs some mention has been made before.

Additional Far Eastern Repercussions

Once Fashoda had been liquidated, but even before the dust had settled on the incident with the agreement of March 1899, Delcassé set about an examination of the French position in general. The fundamental fact was his correct appraisal of the possibilities of French power, from which the corollary followed that France could not afford the luxury of the simultaneous enmity of England *and* of Germany. From this in turn followed the conclusion that an accommodation should be sought with *either* one or the other while there was great concern lest an Anglo-German agreement develop. The negotiations between these two countries, which have just been described, were, needless to say, followed with both interest and anxiety in Paris; needless to say, also, the degree of control or influence that France could exercise on their course, if not entirely inexistent, was definitely limited.

For Delcassé, even the German possibility was not to be excluded a priori; for this there was some background in the Bismarckian policy at one time, but this prospect never reached the point of serious consideration. Cambon reported faithfully from London, but was hardly taken in by the Kaiser's show of personal cordiality.[137] Neither a genuine Franco-German accord, nor a Continental League, of which the former would have been a precondition for the league to have substance, were ever more than pipe dreams, even if the latter received some serious consideration in both Germany and England.

At the beginning of February 1899 an important meeting took place at the Quai d'Orsay, with the participation of the Cambon brothers and of Barrère, in which Delcassé reviewed the broad lines of French policy. The trio of French diplomats, representatives of French diplomacy at its most skillful, was to play a very important role in the coming years, especially Paul Cambon and Barrère. What emerged from the meeting was the following:

1. The Russian alliance should remain the cornerstone of French policy but needed adaptation to circumstances.
2. The Egyptian question was fundamentally an Anglo-French affair and should be treated as such; the attempt to internationalize it had been an unrewarding mistake.
3. The Franco-Italian quarrel should be liquidated and at the same time Spanish friendship cultivated.
4. The Anglo-French relationship should be normalized, a result that could be accomplished on the basis of fair equivalent compensations. The quarrel was counterproductive for France and time was not working in her favor.[138]

One can already see at this point the seed of the final outcome though it was hardly foregone at this stage. England was the master piece in the play but came as the last move. It is Delcassé's merit and chief title to fame, aided by duration of tenure and the mistakes of others, to have carried out the far-seeing plan to success. The operation as a whole might be described as a flanking operation where England was concerned.

Thus Russia came first. Delcassé was dealing with power and felt little concern for ideological differences. His comment on that score to an English acquaintance is revealing:

> In the present state of things the forms of government are an extraneous consideration and have nothing to do with the foreign policy of states, unless one wishes to undertake a crusade for the propagation of one's ideology. But that would be a terribly arrogant attitude toward the world, and toward the country it would be a deception because—and history shows it abundantly—whenever vis-à-vis the outside one is concerned with the propagation of a particular principle, instead of with the exclusive interest of the state, one is mistaken about the real vital interests and sooner or later one is victim of one's temerity.[139]

Muraviëv, the Russian foreign minister, had been in Paris in October 1898. Russia had little interest in Fashoda, but subsequent discussions led, in August 1899, on the occasion of a visit of Delcassé to St. Petersburg, to an exchange of letters which modified, or extended, the scope of the alliance to "the maintenance of the equilibrium among the European forces,"[140] and this was further strengthened in July 1900 with the signature of an agreement dealing in part with purely military preparations. The weakness of the Franco-Russian alliance lay in the divergence of the foci of interest of its participants: where France was looking at Africa, especially the southern Mediterranean, Russia was deeply involved in the Far East. England rather than Germany seemed to be the more likely candidate for the role of common enemy, hence all the greater significance attaching to the just mentioned agreements.

Delcassé was again in Russia in April 1901. France would assist with loans in large part to be used for the construction of strategic railways, but in the Far East her influence was used to moderate Russia's ambitions, seeking to dissuade her from the establishment of a Manchurian protectorate, a possible source of English as well as of Japanese opposition. Delcassé also had suggestions to make in regard to the Near East, the Baghdad railway and Persia; he was desirous of minimizing sources of Anglo-Russian difference—in Persia—though not averse to cultivating Russo-German ones—Baghdad—interestingly a point of convergence with English desires. England was ever in the background of his thoughts. As he put it to Cambon in the course of a general discussion shortly after his return from Russia: "So long as this quarrel is not ended, and ended once and for all, nothing will be assured and stable in Europe."[141]

The role of Japan must be mentioned again at this point. That country was the one interesting exception to what seemed the inescapable fate of Western dominance of the world. Without surrendering her cultural identity, she had adopted enough of the Western ways and techniques to have successfully maintained her independence. The Sino-Japanese War was a measure and justification of the course adopted by Japan, and it had brought her into the circle of the Powers involved in the future of China. This meant, as usual, the possibility of various rivalries and diverse alignments. Japan and Russia were contiguous to China, and Britain had long been established as the leading trading nation in the Far East, where, as in other quarters, Germany was a successful newcomer.

The European combination which had deprived Japan of some of the fruits of Shimonoseki was a carefully studied lesson in Japan; Britain had been the sole abstainer. As it apeared at the turn of the century, and especially after the Boxer Rebellion, that the collapse of China, leading to a possible partition, might be imminent, the tensions and the competition became more acute. The United States had declared its advocacy of the Open Door policy, a policy acceptable to Britain, who, however, would also entertain the possibility of defining spheres of influence for the various contenders.

Here as elsewhere the British preference was for accommodation. The compromise attempted by Salisbury at the beginning of 1898 had not succeeded, and the Russians seemed bent on extending their influence, of which Manchuria and Korea were the foci; they established themselves in Port Arthur. The Japanese, too, seemed to prefer the British approach, an agreement for a division of the spoils with Russia. We have seen the role that Germany played in Britain's Far Eastern calculations, the somewhat fanciful and loose dream which would have joined Britain, the United States and Japan to the Triple Alliance,[142] and the failure of the last attempt, in 1901, to reach an Anglo-German understanding. Britain had more freedom to choose than Germany believed to be the case.

It is interesting to cite what Chamberlain had written to Salisbury at the end of 1897:

> Talking of Allies, have you considered whether we might not draw closer to Japan? It seems to me that they are rapidly increasing their means of offence and defence, and in many contingencies they would be valuable Allies. They are at this moment much inclined to us and, being very sensitive, would appreciate any advances made to them. If we desired to take anything, and were to inform them beforehand, I imagine that we should be sure of their support. I do not suppose that a Treaty of Alliance would be desirable, but I should hope that an understanding might be arrived at which would be very useful. In any case they are worth looking after as it is clear that they do not mean to be a *quantité négligeable* in the East.[143]

The seed here planted was destined to prosper though it took five years for it to bear fruit. Chamberlain's approach to Japan in March 1898 proved abortive and for England Germany seemed more important.

The direct French interest in China, though it existed—the French had shared in the securing of concessions—was secondary to others; what mattered more was the indirect connection through the Russian alliance. In this respect the French efforts to exert a moderating influence on Russia have been mentioned. There were divergent counsels in the Russian milieu on how to deal with the Far East, but as negotiations with the Japanese dragged on inconclusively, the latter began to consider alternative possibilities to an agreement with Russia. In the middle of 1901, as it was clear that the last Anglo-German discussions were a failure, an Anglo-Japanese dialogue was initiated, and in November Prince Ito, one of the elder Japanese statesmen, went on a tour of the capitals of Europe to test the current climate. Paris, where Delcassé argued the case for a compromise accommodation with Russia, was hardly the most important stopping place.[144] London was the real goal of Ito's European journey, and Delcassé had no illusions about the trend of things, which he did not relish. As he put it:

> We must strive to avoid as long as possible a clash between Russia and Japan: it is necessary to prevent England from finding, in Japan, the soldier that she lacks in the Far East.[145]

The judgment was sound, for if England had difficulties, she was not an indiscriminate demandant, and a Japanese alliance might make her all the more reluctant to be accommodating with others—read France in this case.

But Delcassé's fears were soon realized. On January 30, 1902, the Anglo-Japanese alliance was signed, which was made public and ratified by Parliament. Piously endorsing the independence of China, it more pointedly acknowledged Japan's interest in Korea. There was in the alliance the customary provision for assistance to the ally in the event of its being involved in war with more than one Power. What this meant in effect was that the statement made by the French envoy to the Mikado (see note 144) took on the added validity of an English endorsement.

It was perhaps by way of asserting the French presence in the affairs of the world that, in October 1901, Delcassé decided on a gesture of firmness. A dispute with Turkey over debt payments led to the landing of a French force in Mytilene. Needless to say there was a flurry of excitement, and a debate in the French Chamber, but as Turkey gave in, the incident had no further repercussions.

The Anglo-Japanese alliance is an important landmark in the evolution of British policy and has been spoken of as marking the abandonment of isolation. In a sense that is obviously true; England *had* made an alliance in peacetime. But in another sense it may also be read as confirmation of the policy of independence in a more limited domain. Relieved in some degree of Far Eastern responsibilities, England would be all the freer to exercise her influence and her freedom of choice elsewhere, *in Europe,* for example. On an altogether different scale, the recent decision to abandon responsibility east of Suez comes to mind. Both instances represent a case of adaptation to circumstances in the light of a reappraisal of the possibilities of existing power.

France and Italy

Delcassé's concern was justified but he was not deflected from his course of liquidating all differences between his country and England. Before relating this climax we must pause to examine another aspect of his flanking operation, the Italian.

A parallel may be seen between the German desire to disrupt the Franco-Russian alliance and the French wish to detach Italy from the Triple Alliance; there was even in both cases the background of earlier affinity and friendly relations. But Italy felt weak and feared France's Mediterranean ambitions, a feeling that the French occupation of Tunis had confirmed. Crispi was none too stable a man and some of his peculiar fears were bogeys; the period of his prime ministership marked a low point in Franco-Italian relations, of which the tariff war begun in 1888 was one manifestation. Once Adowa had disposed of him there was in Italy some rethinking of a policy that was counterproducing. It was unrealistic to entertain any hopes in Tunisia, where the Italian position vis-à-vis France was even weaker than was the French in Egypt vis-à-vis England, and the tariff war proved more injurious to Italy than to France.

Delcassé, as indicated before, was in favor of normalizing relations and therefore welcomed a change of orientation on the Italian side. Crispi's successor, Rudinì, was free of anti-French phobia. A beginning of accommodation in regard to Tunis was made in 1896 and two years later a commercial treaty restored normal trading relations. The able Barrère was the French representative in Rome and it was not long before his patient skill reaped further rewards. For a long time Delcassé had had his eye on Morocco, where internal conditions made the likelihood of external intervention a not distant prospect.

Morocco, an independent country, but decadent and misruled, was equally open to all as the Madrid Convention of 1880 asserted. But in the context of the imperial activity of the day, and of geographical conditions, the primacy of the French interest in Morocco, contiguous to Algeria, was both legitimate and obvious. If anyone was in the way, it was England again, which indeed had commercial interests and some active agents in Morocco; Morocco had been discussed between herself and Germany in connection with the alliance negotiations. To bring Germany into Morocco would have been an invitation to trouble, although that would matter little had England joined the Triple Alliance; France might have been disgruntled, but she would have been impotent.

Italy, too, professed an interest in Morocco, though the opposite Libyan shore was a more serious focus of her hopes. She had in fact obtained a guarantee from her allies against possible French encroachment in Tripoli. The negotiations that went on between Paris and Rome against this background brought fruit in 1900. The agreement that was made in December between Barrère and Visconti Venosta, the Italian foreign minister, is one of the colonial quid pro quos characteristic of the time, a fair and reasonable way to conduct imperial activity, if such there is to be at all: each country gave a free hand to the other, Italy to France in Morocco, France to Italy in Tripoli. Needless to say, this could commit nobody else. However, the exchange had the important effect of voiding the Triple Alliance of part of its content while the climate of Franco-Italian relations had materially improved. The improvement continued—the naval fraternization in Toulon was further evidence of it—and could hardly be pleasing to Germany. Bülow's comment to Donna Laura Minghetti, reported by Barrère, has the ring of truth: "Italy will soon have to make a choice between marriage and concubinage (meaning us). The observation, divulged here, has caused great displeasure."[146] Bülow might, to be sure, have consulted Holstein on the subject of political bigamy.

Barrère's work was not yet done. If Italy could not be detached from the Triple Alliance, the next best thing from the French point of view was to obtain accurate information about the precise nature of her position in that combination. This is what was achieved in essence after another eighteen months of patient diplomacy. On June 30, 1902, Barrère and Prinetti, the current incumbent at the Italian foreign office, exchanged notes in which it was stated that

> In the case that France [Italy] were to be the object of a direct aggression on the part of one or more Powers, Italy [France] will maintain strict neutrality.
>
> The same will apply if France [Italy], in consequence of direct provocation, should find herself compelled in defense of her honor and security to take the initiative in the declaration of war. In this event the Government of the Republic [the Royal Government] shall have the duty to give previous information of its intention to His Majesty's Government [the Government of the Republic], thus permitting the latter to take cognizance that it is a case of direct provocation.[147]

To say nothing of the haggling that can surround the judgment on "aggression," the concept of "honor," honorable as it may be, introduced a great measure of flexibility in the making of a decision should the occasion arise. The best and most succinct appraisal of the significance of what Italy was doing is Poincaré's later observation, "Italy will decide," presumably on the basis of what she judged to be her best interest in the circumstances. That Italy was hedging was clear and was confirmed by her renewal of the Triple Alliance on June 28.[148] Not the least interesting aspect of the matter is the fact that Italy, weakest of the Great Powers, and ever a sensitive weather vane of the prevailing winds of the international climate, was expressing the judgment that the climate was changing, while herself by her action making a contribution to the change.

In any case, and limited as it might be, this was undoubtedly a feather in the cap of French diplomacy. Delcassé had cause to be pleased,[149] all the more as simultaneous negotiations with Spain in regard to Morocco were also taking a favorable turn. Perhaps the time had come to attempt the crowning achievement of settling the differences with England. But it takes two to make an agreement as well as to differ.

The Entente, Convergence of Diminishing Powers

The ground had already been prepared by the equally patient work of Cambon in London. Even before Salisbury finally resigned the prime ministership, Cambon reports him as saying:

> I have the greatest confidence in M. Delcassé and also in your present Government. But in a few months' time they will probably be overturned, and their successors will do exactly the contrary. No, we must wait a bit.[150]

Salisbury had seen Delcassé succeed Hanotaux. But change actually occurred in England rather than in France, where the Combes ministry lasted from June 1902 to January 1905 with Delcassé always at the foreign office. Roughly the same period is covered by Balfour's prime ministership in England (July 1902–December 1905) while Lansdowne had been at the foreign office since November 1900.

Cambon may be regarded as a permanent fixture in London, and since France, unlike Germany, was not, initially at first, interested in talking alliance but rather imperial differences alone, Chamberlain was also an important figure. Cambon's judgment of Chamberlain may be quoted:

> There is no doubt that Mr. Chamberlain has been disappointed on the side of Germany—having taken too seriously the friendliness of Emperor William and having spoken without sufficient thought of an Anglo-German alliance has produced in him a reaction in our favor. For my part I have confirmation of this—but it must not be forgotten that Mr. Chamberlain has no political principles, that he is the man of the present moment and that he changes opinion with an incredible facility; he is not in the least embarrassed by his own statements which he will deny with an astonishing readiness. He has a very correct sense of the necessities of opinion, all the changes of which he follows while seeming to direct them—hence his popularity.
>
> At the moment English opinion is very aroused against Germany; the Venezuela affair, in which England has been involved by the king, exasperates public feeling. Mr. Chamberlain will therefore adopt an anti-German policy. But he is a realist and would not

offer us anything save in fair exchange, if he was in the position to offer us anything.

The conversation reported by M. Lecomte should be taken note of and I believe that Mr. Chamberlain is sincere at the moment, but no reliance should be placed on declarations which may be carried away in the wind of the first current of public opinion, should that opinion alter its direction.[151]

The end of 1901, with the confirmed failure of the Anglo-German negotiation, may be regarded as the turning point; the Germans should perhaps have given greater weight to Chamberlain's frank warnings about alternative possibilities for England.

When Salisbury's final retirement gave Lansdowne a freer hand Cambon reminded him of the former's above-mentioned statement. The discussion was friendly, and various matters were mentioned which Cambon proceeded to list in a letter. There were numerous points of difference and many sources of friction, not least the running dispute over French fishing rights in Newfoundland, a legacy of the Treaty of Utrecht, as secondary an issue as it was permanent. The two countries had learned to live with such a minor irritant, to which neither attached great importance, but there was also little reason why it could be settled at this particular point, so firmly embedded had it become in their relations. It was one of the merits of the French approach that from the first it insisted on taking a large and collective view of the totality of differences; yielding by one country in one place might compensate for the other's concession in another, whereas a specific localized issue might be less tractable to adjustment.

Cambon may have exaggerated Chamberlain's subservience to the influence of opinion; that factor nonetheless was important, more broadly the various forces which, on either side of the Channel, made for a rapprochement. There were such forces in existence. The name of Sir Thomas Barclay, active in business circles, is an illustration; already in 1900 he had suggested the meeting in Paris of the British Chambers of Commerce. More importance attaches to King Edward VII himself. Constitutional monarch as he was, and not in any way desirous to overstep the bounds of his function, his personal inclination nevertheless fitted well the tendency that worked for accord, a tendency to which in his own case the Kaiser's behavior had doubtless made a contribution.

There is no space to go into details about the story of his visit to Paris in May 1903, the result of his own request. It was a delicate affair, for many in France had not forgotten Fashoda, and the popular reception was initially cool at best. But choosing to ignore any awkwardness, the tact and graciousness of his public addresses turned the visit into a great personal success. It was returned by President Loubet in July to the accompaniment of manifestations of cordiality.

The role of such things is worth mentioning but they are less causes than results, outward manifestations of the state of relations, which they may confirm but hardly in themselves create; the king's visit would not have taken place had not these relations been prospering. Delcassé had no wish to precipitate matters, and while he was perfectly willing to discuss Newfoundland fishing rights, his aim was far broader, Morocco being the prime focus of his interest. The occasion of the Loubet visit to London, during which Delcassé and Lansdowne laid the broad bases of a possible agreement, may be taken as the beginning of the closing phase of the negotiations. Gooch's summary is apt:

> Success was rendered less difficult by the very magnitude of the field of controversy. However impossible it might appear to settle particular issues in isolation, sacrifices might be tolerable as items in a balanced settlement. The diplomatic artists worked in large perspective, convinced that the removal of inflammable material would be worth more than the renunciation of this or that ancient claim or glittering ambition.[152]

Of such inflammable material the supply was abundant, from Newfoundland to the Pacific, by way of West Africa, Madagascar and Siam, not to mention the perennial of Egypt. This last seems to have been brought first into the discussion by Lansdowne, and Cromer was very anxious for a settlement of that particular problem. There is some humor in the fact that the relatively insignificant issue of Newfoundland seemed to be the most recalcitrant to composition, to the extent that Cromer was appealed to by a French representative in Cairo.[153]

In October 1903 a general arbitration convention was signed[154] and the trend toward complete agreement seemed clear, when a potentially disturbing cloud rose on the horizon. Tired of Russian dilatoriness and indecision the Japanese decided to cut the Gordian knot in unmistakable fashion. What happened at Port Arthur on February 4, 1904, was an early version of Pearl Harbor, a highly unorthodox procedure at the time. Britain's ally was at war with France's ally, clearly an awkward situation from the standpoint of the Anglo-French negotiations. Something will be said of the Russo-Japanese War and its impact in the next chapter, but the most significant thing at this point is that it had no effect on the Anglo-French discussion. On April 8, 1904, an agreement[155] was signed, the heart of which was the well-known Egypt-Morocco quid pro quo.

The British Government having declared its intention not to alter the political status of Egypt, the French in turn asserted that it would "not obstruct the action of Great Britain in that country by asking that a limit be fixed for the British occupation or in any other matter."

Reciprocally, the French Government declared that it had "no intention of altering the political status of Morocco," in return for which the British recognized "that it appertains to France, more particularly as a Power whose dominions are coterminous for a great distance with those of Morocco, to preserve order in that country, and to provide assistance for the purpose of administrative, economic, financial and military reforms which it may require."

The economic and financial rights of both countries remained unaffected, Britain adhered to the 1888 Suez Canal Convention, and both countries would oppose the creation of fortifications on the African side of the Straits of Gibraltar. Spanish rights in Morocco were acknowledged and were more precisely defined in a Franco-Spanish agreement of the following October.

Where Egypt and Morocco were concerned the writing on the wall was clear for all to see, and secret clauses attached to the agreements looked to the day when the inevitable would happen.

The agreement of April 1904, the Entente Cordiale, was received with well-nigh unqualified satisfaction in England, where the opposition in Parliament joined in voicing its approval. The French reception was more critical and Delcassé was attacked by various speakers in the Chamber. Hanotaux, whose own policy had been quite different, thought that "on the Nile, in China, Siam, Muscat, Constantinople, Egypt, Newfoundland, Tripoli, it is only retreat."[156] Deschanel thought that France had not made a proper bargain and should have proceeded with piecemeal negotiations instead of seeking a general settlement. Freycinet, who had been so involved in Egyptian affairs, was reconciled but sad.[157]

There was point as well as foresight in the critique of René Millet, former governor of Algeria:

> It is a retreat in good order. The error of twenty-five years ago perhaps rendered it inevitable; but why celebrate it as a triumph? We are not yet in Morocco, while England is in Egypt. We exchange rights for hopes. To hold Morocco we lack just a trifle—the consent of the Sultan. . . . It is impossible for France to undertake anything without knowing the inner mind of Germany. Of all pretensions the maddest would be to wish to isolate her. One does not isolate a strong Government—one exposes oneself to its resentment.[158]

However, there was general support for the policy of working in agreement with England; the motion of confidence in the government received 436 votes against 94. Needless to say, in the presentation before their respective parliaments, each foreign minister magnified his country's gains and minimized its concessions.

In retrospect, the consequences of the Entente Cordiale of 1904 are clear enough. At the time the arrangement fitted to perfection the English policy of reducing commitments, of which the Anglo-Japanese alliance was another example. But the Entente was no alliance in the British view, merely the negative elimination of certain sources of friction the better to be able to deal with others. To fight Germany for the sake of France in Morocco was very far from British thoughts, though there was an inevitable and implied anti-German point in the agreement. Chamberlain had spoken of Morocco to the Germans, but in the face of Germany's determination to proceed with her naval policy, if it came to a choice, the prospect of French naval bases in Morocco was preferable, or at least less undesirable, than that of German ones—especially if other sources of difference were being simultaneously eliminated.

The very fact that such a choice had to be contemplated was an implied admission of the diminished possibilities of British power. Yet England's diminution was not such as to place her in the category of demandant who would pay *any* price that might be asked for the sake of agreement. In this mistaken appraisal lay the fatal German error; German power was rising indeed, but Germany was not *arbiter mundi*. For the greatest land power to make a bid for a similar position at sea was to invite not only British opposition, but the possibility of a well-nigh world-wide coalition. However, we must not anticipate our story.

France on her side could not pretend to match unassisted either Britain or Germany, let alone the two together. The Russian alliance was therefore the sheet anchor of her policy. But there were elements of uncertainty in the Russian alliance. An alliance with Britain could, on balance, be more valuable than the Russian connection, though better still the two; however, Britain still generally adhered to Salisbury's view, except in the special case of the Japanese alliance, and despite Chamberlain's flirting with the possibility of the German. Full credit must be given to Delcassé and his able assistants for their undeviating persistence, the skill, suppleness, and moderation with which they went about their task, and for making use of opportunities, in part German-provided. Even if Delcassé had no more far-reaching aim than Morocco, he had acted with ability; he was continuing the sound policy of imperial expansion by way of compensation for the growing deficiency of native French power. That he was also running certain risks, as pointed out in the above-cited critique of Millet, for example, is undoubtedly true. The future would tell.

Britain and France were both Great Powers, but the difference between the two was appreciable and known to all in 1904. Yet, taking a long-term view of the evolution of power standing, it does not seem unfair to say that already at this time both Powers were converging toward a common defensive position vis-à-vis the rising power of others. The inner logic of their common situation, though not consciously expressed or fully realized, especially on the British side, should perhaps be regarded as the fundamental basis of their common interest that brought them together in the Entente Cordiale. In more homely language, whether they knew it or not, in the wide world of power competition, they were already in the same boat, in which they have in fact been ever since.

NOTES ON *Chapter VI*

1. Langer, op. cit., p. 48.
2. *CHBFP*, Vol. III, p. 245.
3. His previous administration from June 1885 to February 1886 had been too brief and had been followed by the equally brief return of Gladstone to the prime ministership till the following February. Rosebery was at the foreign office during this last interval.
4. See above, p. 222.
5. Salisbury to Lord Lyons, February 5, 1887. Cecil, op. cit., Vol. IV (1932), pp. 29–30. In addition to the Egyptian perennial, other sources of annoyance were French activity in Morocco and disputes over the Newfoundland fisheries and over Somaliland.
6. He exploited the episode in securing the passage of a new army bill.
7. Salisbury to the Queen, February 2, 1887. Cecil, op. cit., Vol. IV, p. 20.
8. Ibid., p. 21.
9. Pribram, A. F., *The Secret Treaties of Austria-Hungary,* 2 vols. (1920–21), Vol. I, pp. 95–97.
10. Salisbury to the Queen, February 10, 1887. Cecil, op. cit., Vol. IV, p. 24 (my italics).
11. The texts of all these exchanges may be found in the above-cited work of Pribram. It may be noted that the Anglo-Italo-Austrian exchange of December contained the following provision, which defined positions more sharply:

"Should the conduct of the Porte, however, in the opinion of the Three Powers, assume the character of complicity with or connivance at any such [cession of sovereign rights at the Straits or in Asia Minor] illegal enterprise, the three Powers will consider themselves justified by existing treaties in proceeding either jointly or separately to the provisional occupation by their forces, military or naval, of such points of Ottoman territory as they may agree to consider it necessary to occupy in order to secure the objects determined by previous treaties."

12. Germany, too, reserved a certain freedom of action through the qualification "according to the circumstances of the case," which appeared in Article IV of her separate treaty with Italy.

13. These exchanges are described and analyzed in Cecil, op. cit., pp. 72–77. Full texts may be found in *Die Grosse Politik der europäischen Kabinette,* Vol. IV.

14. Cecil, op. cit., Vol. IV, p. 90.

15. On the Franco-Russian situation, see below, pp. 245 ff.

In the middle of 1888 there had been a mild invasion scare in England. It was taken with sufficient seriousness to warrant the following appraisal by Salisbury in a minute to the Cabinet of June 29: ". . . the two departments [of defense] and Count Moltke agree in thinking that there are circumstances in which a French invasion may be possible, though the War Office think that the occurrence of requisite conditions is far more within the range of probability than the Admiralty are disposed to admit. But it seems to me sufficient for the Government that they agree to think it possible. Our stake is so great that full precautions must be taken against even a distant possibility." Cecil, op. cit., Vol. IV, p. 186.

16. Albin, P., *La paix armée, l'Allemagne et la France en Europe (1885–1894)* (1913), p. 252.

17. Ibid., p. 253 (my italics). The article in question appeared in the *Nord* on February 19, 1887. This newspaper was published in Brussels but known as a mouthpiece of Giers. The date is significant in view of the recent German and French armament moves.

18. Ibid., p. 260.

19. Examples of this could be multiplied, ranging from the lavish entertainment of visiting Russian grand dukes—the expression, *la tournée des ducs,* passed into the French language—to the reciprocal handling of an incident in French Somaliland and the co-operation of the French police in dealing with Russian agitators.

20. Freycinet, *La question d'Egypte,* pp. 374–75.

21. The somewhat humorous episode intervened in 1889 of the French exposition centered on the theme of the centenary of the revolution. This created considerable embarrassment and flurries of protocol for the monarchical governments, unwilling either to appear to endorse revolution or to slight France. Favorable comments on the exposition appeared in Russia.

22. Cecil, op. cit., Vol. IV, pp. 366–71. This went the length of an elaborate memorandum, sent in the spring of 1891 through the British embassy, which detailed the desirable [in the Kaiser's view] changes that the British ought to make in their naval establishment. As to the Sultan, he should be overawed by the unexpected appearance of British warships in Constantinople into acquiescing to British wishes in Egypt.

23. Cecil, op. cit., Vol. IV, p. 364.

24. A good description of the episode may be found in Albin, op. cit., pp. 200–2.

25. The quid pro quo involving French desistance in Zanzibar and a

corresponding British position in regard to Madagascar, as well as a British acknowledgment of the Saharan hinterland of Algeria.

26. The *Marseillaise* also happened to be the hymn of the Second International and was banned in Russia, the ban being lifted for the occasion of the French visit.

27. Salisbury to the Queen, August 22, 1891. Cecil, op. cit., Vol. IV, p. 395.

28. Pribram, op. cit., Vol. I, pp. 162–63. The treaty was dated May 6, 1891, but discussion for its renewal had been going on for some months. This single treaty, taking the place of the three treaties of 1887, incorporated in articles IX and X the earlier German guarantee of support in the event of Italy going to war against France to prevent an extension of France's North African possessions. Salisbury might have made some interesting observations on the wording of this protocol.

29. Albrecht-Carrié, R., *A Diplomatic History of Europe Since the Congress of Vienna* (1958), p. 211.

30. Albin, op. cit., p. 322.

31. Speech in the Reichstag on November 23, 1892. Cited, ibid., p. 354. It was in the summer of 1892 that Schlieffen was appointed to head the German general staff. The strategy for dealing with the war on two fronts was the reason for the military bill.

32. Freycinet, *Souvenirs 1878–1893*, p. 471.

33. Discussions at the military level had been going on for a considerable time, without hesitation on the French side, more tentatively on the Russian, though General Obruchev, the Russian chief of staff, was definitely a supporter of the French connection.

34. See below, pp. 259–62.

35. Freycinet, op. cit., pp. 504–5.

36. Albin, op. cit., p. 377.

37. Cecil, op. cit., Vol. IV, pp. 407–8.

38. Seton-Watson, *Britain in Europe*, p. 564.

39. See Curzon, G. N., "India Between Two Fires," in *Nineteenth Century*, August 1893.

40. Cited in Seton-Watson, op. cit., p. 572.

41. There is an element of comedy in the situation. Emperor William II was at Cowes when the report of the French order to the British gunboats was received. In his wonted emotional fashion, he was all for action, but was restrained by his advisers. The Italians, likewise apparently eager for action, were also giving restraining advice to their German ally. See Seton-Watson, op. cit., p. 572.

42. Ibid., p. 572. This relates to other developments, e.g., the Congo, considered below, pp. 270 ff.

43. Langer, William L., *The Diplomacy of Imperialism* (1956), p. 53.

44. The Russo-German commercial treaty dates from March 1894.

45. In 1894 England controlled 65 per cent of China's trade and her ships carried 85 per cent of China's exports and imports.

46. *St. James Gazette*, March 18, 1894. Cited in Langer, op. cit., p. 175.

47. The treaty also dealt with the islands of Formosa and the Pescadores, with Korean independence, and provided for an indemnity of 300,000,000 taels.

48. Germany, France, and Russia so expressed themselves in notes to Japan. Langer, op. cit., p. 186.

49. Seton-Watson, op. cit., p. 573. For an account of the entire episode, see also Brandenburg, E., *From Bismarck to the World War* (1933), Ch. III.

50. Cited in Langer, op. cit., p. 187.

51. A French loan was made to Russia in July.

52. It was a piece of ineptitude on the part of the German ambassador in Tokyo to have used comminatory language in presenting the German note, thereby incurring the main onus of Japanese resentment, which Japan showed she had not forgotten in 1914.

53. Langer, op. cit., p. 167.

54. American affairs, too, as in the case of the Venezuelan boundary dispute. For a discussion of these matters, see pp. 283 ff.

55. Kennedy, A. L., *Salisbury 1830–1903. Portrait of a Statesman* (1953), pp. 252–53. This, one must realize, is written in an English context. It goes some distance toward explaining more recent developments in the British milieu, as later chapters will show. For the rest, our century has witnessed ample evidence of action based on intuition, Hitler's being perhaps the most relevant, and disastrous, illustration.

56. Ibid., p. 207.

57. See above, p. 179.

58. *CHBFP*, Vol. III, p. 207, n. 1.

59. Nor can the missionary influence, though far weaker than the economic and the nationalistic motivations, be wholly disregarded. In a broader sense, the conviction that the spread of European influence was a beneficent factor was held by many with complete sincerity. The phrases "white man's burden" and *"mission civilisatrice"* are familiar enough. The connection between that aspect of the matter and the political led to a variety of complications and in some cases, at least, to a measure of unsavory cant and pretense. Yet, true as this is, it represents one limited aspect of the question only.

60. The British claim to a protectorate over Zanzibar, the claims of the Sultan of Zanzibar on the African mainland, which the British considered sustaining, and the beginnings of German activity overlapped.

61. Stanley's fame and his familiarity with Africa dated from the seventies, when he found Livingstone and subsequently explored the region of the sources of the Nile and the Congo River, this last exploration eventually leading to the organization of the Congo Free State under the sponsorship of King Leopold of Belgium. As to Emin Pasha, after his rescue he joined the German service until killed in Uganda in 1892.

62. Also, the population of Heligoland was German, though Salisbury was somewhat embarrassed when asked in Parliament whether their wishes had been consulted and had to reply that they had been ascertained "confidentially."

63. Kennedy, op. cit., p. 25.

64. Ibid.

65. The English agreements with Italy in 1891, centering around Abyssinia, were part of the same policy of protecting the approaches to both sides of the Nile.

66. There had been unsuccessful Franco-Belgian negotiations and what amounted to a westward race toward the Nile between the two.

The MacKinnon agreement between the Congo Government (King Leopold in effect) and the British East Africa Company acknowledged the northward course of the Nile from Lake Albert as far as Lado as the eastern boundary of the Congo State, in exchange for which a five-mile strip between Lakes Edward and Tanganyika was correspondingly recognized to the company. For a detailed account of the dealings between Britain and King Leopold, see Collins, Robert O., *King Leopold, England, and the Upper Nile, 1899–1909* (1968).

67. The Far Eastern situation, for example, and the state of continental relationships.

68. Hanotaux, Gabriel, *Fachoda* (1909), pp. 76–77, goes as far as asserting that the British ambassador threatened to hand an ultimatum which he had in his pocket.

69. This adds all the more interest to Rosebery's observation, in 1896, that some 2,500,000 square miles of territory had been brought under British rule in the course of the past twelve years, and to his further comment that English popularity in the rest of the world had not increased as a result. *CHBFP*, Vol. III, p. 218.

70. Langer's observation that "the first phase of the epic struggle for the Nile came to an end, but it left deep marks on the European alignment" (op. cit., p. 141) is an apt summation.

71. The British on their side had tried to establish an anti-French Anglo-German front, but there was irritation in Germany at what seemed too limited an English desire for co-operation. The question of Samoa also intruded at this point.

72. Salisbury to Sir Clare Ford. Kennedy, op. cit., p. 228.

73. See Langer, op. cit., p. 264. This may be set against the French statement that the British ambassador had had his attention called to *"la gravité des conséquences que pouvait avoir la camgagne du Soudan"* (Neton, Albéric, *Delcassé* [1952], p. 205, n. 1). Neither country was unaware of the doings and plans of the other.

74. Cited in Langer, op. cit., p. 265.

75. Ibid., p. 266.

76. The French-built railway from Jibuti to Addis Ababa, henceforth the chief outlet of Ethiopian trade, was opened in 1894, and French influence in Abyssinia, following the Italian setback, reached a high point with the conclusion of a treaty with Abyssinia in 1897. These operations were part of the larger French scheme to cut across the Nile.

77. There were other sources of tension, but they had to do with West Africa, where the British protectorate over Nigeria was established in 1895.

78. *CHBFP*, Vol. III, p. 253; also Langer, op. cit., p. 551, n. 29.

79. Langer, op. cit., p. 549.

80. Freycinet, *La question d'Egypte*, p. 413.

81. Kennedy, op. cit., p. 268.

82. Neton, *Delcassé*, pp. 156–57.

83. Churchill, W. S., *The River War*, 2 vols. (1899), Vol. II, pp. 311–12.

84. Neton, op. cit., p. 182.

85. Needless to say, British and French diplomacy were both active in Berlin, St. Petersburg, and Rome. The result of this activity was to confirm the isolation of France in the event of war. The Anglo-French clash was, naturally, wholly satisfactory to Germany, and it was even feared in

France that the Anglo-German agreement of 1898, looking to a possible partition of the Portuguese colonies, might be the prelude to a grander scheme of which the French empire itself might be the object.

86. In particular the clarification of the position of the Congo State in the upper reaches of the Nile, discussion of which went on with King Leopold in the autumn of 1898 and subsequently.

87. See above, p. 266.

88. For general discussions of American foreign policy we may refer to such standard treatments as Bemis, S. F., *A Diplomatic History of the United States* (1965), and Bailey, T. A., *A Diplomatic History of the American People* (1964). In particular on this period, Bradford, P., *The Great Rapprochement: England and the United States, 1895–1914* (1968). American foreign policy is only considered here for its peripheral connection with the British.

89. See Chapter III.

90. As a measure of the temper of the time we may cite Theodore Roosevelt's observation to Henry C. Lodge that "our peace-at-any-price men, if only they knew it, are rendering war more likely, because they will encourage England to persist; in the long run this means a fight. Personally, I rather hope the fight will come soon. The clamour of the peace faction has convinced me that this country needs a war." Cited in Garvin, J. L., *The Life of Joseph Chamberlain*, 4 vols. (1932–35), Vol. III (1934), p. 68, n. 1.

91. Meanwhile, in 1896, an investigating commission had been appointed by the American Congress at the request of President Cleveland, who had asserted the American obligation to support the findings of this unilateral body. In February 1897 a general treaty of arbitration was concluded between Britain and the United States, but it failed of ratification in the American Senate.

92. This was brought about by a dispute over debt collection in the Dominican Republic. Debts are legitimate enough obligations, and if the United States insisted on excluding the intervention of others it followed logically that an obligation developed upon it to intervene itself to insure proper order. The United States intervened in Santo Domingo, and subsequent cases of American intervention in Latin American states make an extensive roster.

93. The sending to the Philippines of a substantial German fleet, in view of the smallness of the German interest, gave rise to friction with the United States. The British squadron in contrast was careful to avoid any appearance of interposition between the American fleet and the Spanish. It was also in 1898 that the Hawaiian Islands were finally annexed by the United States and that Samoa was the scene of Anglo-American cooperation against Germany.

94. The "synthetic" revolution which resulted in the separation of Panama from Colombia and the American behavior in this connection, justifying President Roosevelt's later terse summation, "I took Panama," constitute an enlightening illustration of the ways of American imperialism, but this is not particularly relevant to the present discussion.

95. See below, pp. 306–7.

96. The issue of the Bering Sea fisheries and that of the boundary be-

tween Alaska and Canada, given importance by the discovery of the Yukon goldfields, were also settled amicably by arbitration.

97. See above, p. 190.

98. Kennedy, op. cit., p. 277. Russian encroachment in Manchuria could be contemplated with equanimity, but a prospective partition of China would find England prepared to claim her share.

In 1898 there was the further consideration, as Salisbury put it to his daughter, that "of course the Russians have behaved abominably and if it would be any satisfaction to my colleagues I should have no objection to fighting them. But I don't think we have guns enough to fight them and the French together." Ibid., p. 276. The essential fact was that Russia at this time was concentrating her attention and efforts on the Far East and was not desirous of becoming embroiled in Near Eastern complications at the same time. France on the whole followed the Russian lead.

99. Upon receiving different advice the Kaiser sought another meeting with Salisbury. The latter, thinking this a mere formality and having other commitments, failed to respond, a fact to which, not surprisingly, the Kaiser took great offense.

100. His standing in politics is indicated by the fact that he was offered his choice of posts, in particular the Home Office and the Chancellorship of the Exchequer. But he insisted on the Colonies, "in the hope, as he put it, of furthering closer union between them and the United Kingdom." Garvin, op. cit., Vol. III, p. 5.

101. Ibid., Ch. 54.

102. The federation of Australia did not come into existence until 1901.

103. Kennedy, op. cit., p. 300. Twentieth-century developments do not in any way detract from the British imperial vision at its best, any more than the demise of the Roman Empire reflects on its accomplishments.

104. *The* [London] *Times,* November 7, 1895. Cited in Garvin, op. cit., Vol. III, p. 26.

105. Ibid., p. 47.

106. The heated controversy, the trial, and the parliamentary investigation, the most controversial aspect of which was the role of Chamberlain in the affair, may be followed in Garvin, op. cit., Vol. III, Chs. 51, 52.

107. Langer, op. cit., p. 237.

108. This is the position taken by Albertini, L., *The Origins of the War of 1914,* 3 vols. (1952–57), Vol. I (1952), p. 82.

109. Garvin, op. cit., Vol. III, p. 93.

110. Chamberlain to Sir Hercules Robinson (the British representative in Pretoria), January 4, 1896. Ibid., p. 97.

111. Ibid., p. 107.

112. Ibid., p. 105.

113. Chamberlain to Salisbury, December 24, 1895. Ibid., p. 69.

114. The British were ill prepared for the guerrilla tactics to which the Boers resorted and in the end found it necessary to use a force of some 300,000 men. Some of the methods they adopted in dealing with the population earned them widespread opprobrium.

115. See Langer, op. cit., Ch. 22, and Albertini, op. cit., Ch. 2, sections 9 and 12.

116. Cited in Garvin, op. cit., Vol. III, p. 243, from *Die Grosse Politik der europäischen Kabinette, 1871–1914* (1922–27), Vol. IV, p. 406.

117. Garvin, op. cit., Vol. III, pp. 246–48.

118. The Russians were pursuing an active policy of expansion in the Far East, seeking to operate in agreement with Japan and in opposition to Germany at this point. In 1898 they obtained the cession of Port Arthur, the Germans having extracted from China the lease of Kiaochow.

119. Garvin, op. cit., Vol. III, p. 245, from *Die Grosse Politik* . . . , Vol. XIII, p. 34.

120. There was opposition to this decision in Germany, where some feared that Britain might "Copenhagen" the nascent German fleet. But those who argued in favor of taking the risk proved correct; as pointed out before, preventive war was not a serious factor in the thought and the policies of the time.

121. See above, p. 289.

122. Chamberlain to Balfour, February 3, 1898. Garvin, op. cit., Vol. III, pp. 251–52. One can clearly see here the seeds of later Chamberlain-sponsored developments.

123. Ibid., pp. 259–60. Garvin reproduces in full the five memoranda drawn up by Chamberlain as record of his meetings with the Germans. This, in connection with the exchanges that passed within the German milieu, as reproduced in *Die Grosse Politik* . . . , Vol. XIV, First Part, furnishes an excellent firsthand source of information.

124. Eckardstein was attached to the German embassy and close to the Kaiser, with whom he discussed the question in the interval. He was somewhat of a meddler and his interventions and reports did not help clarify the situation. An account of his activity may be found in Rich, N., *Friedrich von Holstein, Politics and Diplomacy in the Era of Bismarck and Wilhelm II,* 2 vols. (1965), Vol. II (1965), Ch. X.

125. Chamberlain envisaged no difficulty in obtaining parliamentary approval for a defensive alliance, to which secret clauses could be attached.

126. Garvin, op. cit., Vol. III, p. 275.

127. Ibid., pp. 287–88. From the correspondence between the Kaiser and the Tsar, often referred to as the Willy-Nicky letters.

128. Bülow to William II, August 24, 1898. Ibid., p. 291, from *Die Grosse Politik* . . . , Vol. XIV, First Part, pp. 339–42.

129. Ibid., p. 293.

130. Ibid., p. 282.

131. "There will be no quarter, no prisoners will be taken! As a thousand years ago, the Huns, under King Attila, gained for themselves a name which still stands for a terror in tradition and history, so may the name of German be impressed by you for a thousand years on China, so thoroughly that never again shall a Chinese dare so much as look askance at a German." Quoted in Bülow, Bernhard von, *Memoirs of Prince von Bülow,* 4 vols. (1931–32), Vol. I, p. 418.

132. The episode is reminiscent in some respects of that of the naval agreement of 1935 with Germany. See below, p. 477.

133. Cited in Garvin, op. cit., Vol. III, p. 505. Bülow's account of the German visit may be followed in his *Memoirs,* Vol. I, Chs. 19 and 20.

134. Garvin, op. cit., Vol. III, pp. 507–8.

135. Eckardstein was filling in for the ailing Hatzfeldt, whom he hoped to succeed in the London embassy. It should also be noted that Salisbury had just relinquished the foreign office to Lansdowne, who was less opposed to the alliance, and that it was hoped that advantage could be taken of Salisbury's prospective absence on holiday.

136. Amery, J., *The Life of Jospeh Chamberlain,* Vol. IV (1951), p. 151, from *Die Grosse Politik . . . ,* Vol. XVI, p. 296. The last volume of Garvin's above-cited work was written by J. Amery.

137. He reported as follows on February 6, 1901, at the time of the Kaiser's visit to England for Queen Victoria's funeral: "*. . . L'empereur d'Allemagne . . . me reconnut et m'appela avec une expression de familiarité cordiale: 'mon Cambon, me dit-il, je suis bien aise de vous voir et de vous dire que j'ai parlé de vous et que vous vous en apercevrez. Vous connaissez déjà mon sentiment pour votre pays; je considère la France comme indispensable à l'équilibre de l'Europe; il nous faut une France forte; je l'ai dit et, si vous avez quelque embarras, comptez sur moi, je vous prêterai mon concours mon.'*" Neton, *Delcassé,* p. 231.

Despite the ultimate sterility of the idea, it must be pointed out that Delcassé gave considerable thought to the possibility of co-operation with Germany, especially in exploiting the difficulties created for England by the Boer War. On this point, see Andrew, C., "France and the Making of the Entente Cordiale," *The Historical Journal,* X, 1 (1967), pp. 89–105.

138. Cited in Neton, op. cit., pp. 205–6.

139. Ibid., pp. 211–12.

140. Albertini, op. cit., Vol. I, p. 110.

141. Neton, op. cit., p. 246. An interesting sidelight is the Franco-German competition in courting Russia. This manifested itself in such things as the French resentment at the Tsar's presence at the German naval maneuvers in the autumn, a visit which took place to the accompaniment of impressive displays and of mutual declarations of friendship, conversely a source of German concern and annoyance.

142. See above, pp. 306–7.

143. Chamberlain to Salisbury, December 31, 1897. Garvin, op. cit., Vol. III, p. 249.

144. He had been informed by Lamsdorf of the Russian opposition to Japanese designs on Korea, the main focus of Japanese interest.

Delcassé's biographer reports the curious incident of the statement which the French ambassador in Tokyo, upon taking leave of his post, made to the Mikado: "*dans aucun cas, la France n'aiderait la Russie en cas de guerre avec le Japon.*" Neton, op. cit., p. 274.

145. Ibid., p. 274.

146. Cited in ibid., p. 224. However, Neton mistakenly makes Bülow, who had become Chancellor in 1900, still ambassador in Rome.

147. Albertini, op. cit., p. 129.

148. That is the reason why the Franco-Italian exchange was postdated November 1. There has been much controversy over the consistency of the two simultaneous commitments, which has been cited as an illustration of Italian duplicity, the phrase "the jackal policy of Italy" being used by some writers. A realization of the measure and the limitations of Italy's power would be a more balanced appraisal.

149. The changing nature of the Franco-Italian relationship was made clear by the exchanges of visits between President Loubet to Rome and King Victor Emmanuel to Paris, to the accompaniment of official amenities and popular demonstrations. While Germany had little cause to be pleased, Bülow passed off these manifestations with urbane quips.

150. Interview in *The* [London] *Times,* December 22, 1920. Cited in *CHBFP,* Vol. III, pp. 305–6.

151. Amery, op. cit., Vol. IV, pp. 205–6. This quotation is a comment written by Cambon of the report he received of a conversation between Lecomte, of the French embassy, and Chamberlain.

152. *CHBFP*, Vol. III, p. 309.

153. Neton, op. cit., p. 279.

154. A similar Franco-Italian agreement was concluded in December.

155. Albrecht-Carrié, *The Concert of Europe*, pp. 323–27. Other imperial differences were likewise liquidated, the French proving accommodating in Newfoundland and the British correspondingly generous in West Africa, but the various agreements dealing with these issues were made subsequently.

156. Cited in *CHBFP*, Vol. III, p. 316.

157. Ibid., p. 317.

158. From Hanotaux's preface to René Millet's *Notre politique extérieure, 1898–1905* (1905). Cited in *CHBFP*, Vol. III, p. 317.

PART THREE

In the Same Boat

(Since 1904)

VII

EUROPE'S CIVIL WAR, 1904–19

L'Angleterre y gagne [in the Entente] *que nous ne la tracasserons plus dans ce pays où 24 ans d'occupation l'ont enracinée. Elle paie largement cette quiétude, elle la paie au prix dont il y a un an encore, elle n'aurait même pas voulu entendre parler, et qu'elle repousserait peut-être énergiquement dans six mois. L'heure était propice. Je l'ai saisie.*

Delcassé to his wife, April 8, 1904

It has been well said that every country, if it has the option, would, of course, prefer itself to hold the power of supremacy at sea, but that this choice being excluded, it would rather see England hold that power than any other country.

Memorandum on the Present State of British Relations with France and Germany, January 1, 1907, by Eyre Crowe

A general association of nations must be formed under specific covenants for the purpose of affording mutual guarantees of political independence and territorial integrity to great and small states alike.

Point XIV of the Fourteen Points, January 1918

The developments covered in this chapter have been the subject of a very extensive literature. But the present treatment of the period will be relatively sketchy and brief, for that reason in part; but also because it is not our purpose to give a complete account of international relations but to confine ourselves to those aspects of them which concern the principals of our tale. Certain very important matters, the Bosnian annexation crisis for example, will thus be very summarily dealt with. Finally, what happened during this period may be considered as but the maturing of the seeds which had been planted by 1904, although the customary caution must be issued about the inevitability of historic development. The 1914 war was indeed the logical outcome of antecedent circumstances, but throughout the years preceding the war there was often doubt and unclarity about the individual position of particular states no less than about the climate of their relations. Nevertheless, in retrospect especially, it is fair to put stress on the factors of continuity and steadiness in the drift of the situation. Thus the war itself can be seen as the wholly logical transformation into an alliance of the Entente relationship of 1904; its course, and especially the plans made while it was being waged, as the continuation of well-established policies and traditions; its outcome as the misunderstood and misapplied attempt to proceed on the basis of these pre-existing traditions, a possibility of which the war itself had been the ultimate shattering. This approach indicates the natural divisions of the discussion into three parts: the ten-year prelude, the war itself, the false peace.

The Prelude, 1904–14

Morocco and Manchuria

These two countries are far apart, yet the connection between them is not far to seek. Russia was seeking to establish her influence in the former; England's opposition to further encroachment in China was the reason for the reinsurance, the lightening of her Far Eastern commitment, that was the meaning of the Japanese alliance. France had her eyes on Morocco; for the price of English acquiescence she had been willing to abandon her Egyptian hopes; since this last decision also amounted to an easing of the English position in that quarter, the Entente agreement had been reached. As pointed out before, the Egypt-Morocco quid pro quo could not dispose of the rights of third parties, though it implied at least diplomatic support of either participant in it for the other vis-à-vis such third parties should these attempt to assert rights or claims.

The virtual simultaneity of the outbreak of the Russo-Japanese War and of the conclusion of the Entente Cordiale has considerable significance. If one effect of the Anglo-Japanese alliance was to immobilize Russia's ally, England and France agreed in their desire to keep the conflict localized; it is enlightening to follow the parallel course of developments in the Far Eastern and the Moroccan quarters.

The war posed a dilemma for the Franco-Russian alliance, and Germany, needless to say, was on the alert for whatever opportunities might arise. Her first reaction to the Entente agreement was, officially at least, anything but unfavorable; in the Reichstag on April 13 Bülow said kind and approving words about the contribution to peace that it represented, and Delcassé for his part took ostensibly the position of dealing with Germany in complete openness: he explained to Radolin, the German ambassador, the nature of the Entente—a liquidation of disputes —and acknowledged France's special interest in Morocco while denying any designs on that country.[1] This French interest Germany was quite prepared to recognize, but French reassurances could be convincing only to a point, especially as it was not long before some knowledge of the secret part of the Entente agreement was acquired by Germany. It was natural that Germany should try to do two things: first, continue the efforts to disrupt the Franco-Russian alliance, or alternately and more improbably, to bring France into a grand continental combination; secondly, seek to find out the precise nature of the newly formed Anglo-French relationship, and, if it seemed too close, also disrupt it.

The embarrassment of France vis-à-vis Russia offered an opportunity to attempt the first course. As it appeared that the war was not going well for the Russians, the French embarrassment only increased. The decision to send the Russian Baltic fleet halfway around the world to the Far East gave rise to special awkwardness. The Dogger Bank incident[2] in October created considerable tension between England and Russia. The

French, needless to say, did their best to smooth things over; the incident eventually was passed off, but it was immediately followed by Russo-German discussions which led within a month to the drafting of a treaty of alliance. The treaty stipulated, among other things, in the original German version that

> If one [Germany or Russia] is attacked by a European Power, its Ally will help. The two allies, in case of need, will also act in concert so as to remind France of her obligations under the Franco-Russian treaty.

No clearer way could be devised to "put France on the spot," all the more so as in its strange odyssey the Russian fleet was receiving better assistance in coaling from German ships than in some of the French colonial possessions.[3] Though the Tsar was favorably inclined toward the German treaty, his insistence on the prior consultation of France, to which not surprisingly Germany objected, prevented the successful outcome of the proposal.

This is the point at which the connection with Morocco comes in. In December a French scheme of reforms was submitted to the Moroccan sultan. The weakening of Russia resulting from a continuing series of defeats correspondingly strengthened the German hand and a scheme was elaborated in the German foreign office which would serve to test the Anglo-French relationship. The reluctant Kaiser, in the course of one of his cruises, would pay a visit to the Moroccan sultan, thus giving outward notice to the world that Germany asserted equal rights in his country. Once the Kaiser, though unhappy, was let loose he posed in grandiloquent language as the protector of the sultan; this was the gist of his speech in Tangier on March 31, the opening gun of the first Moroccan crisis.

His gesture raised two questions. First, was Germany bluffing, and, if not, how far would she go in asserting an equal position in Morocco? Secondly, what position would England take? Sultan Abdul Aziz issued a call for a meeting of the signatory Powers of the Convention of Madrid of 1880, and thus the question of France's acceptance or refusal of the conference became the crucial issue. On the French side there had been talk, in the press and in the colonial party, of "French Morocco," while certainly the German position was in law fully justified, though the manner of asserting the claim was widely considered as an example of mailed-fist diplomacy.

Diplomacy of the more ordinary kind was also active at this point. For example, the Kaiser sent a message to President Roosevelt with a view to exerting indirect pressure on France.[4] It was difficult for France to refuse, yet to accept might be tantamount to undoing all of Delcassé's work in Morocco so far, his tactics having been to obtain a series of bilateral agreements with the various interested Powers. It could of course fairly be said that by neglecting Germany he had invited precisely the situation which had arisen. Many in France thought so; he found himself under severe attack in the violent debate in the Chamber on April 19. The Prime Minister, Rouvier, did not defend him with the utmost vigor; relations between the two, to use an understatement, were not of the best.

Delcassé was rather determined than rash. On the German side the prospect of an eventually French Morocco was no serious cause for objection, being indeed a logical result in the imperial context of the day. To be sure, Germany was entitled to some compensation, though when it would come to discussing the price, the French bargaining position would be all the stronger from having the prior assent of others. The crisis arose from the fact that the German tactic was to create abroad the impression that Germany might go the length of war in defense of the Sultan's independence, meaning her own claim.

Delcassé insisted that this position was mere bluff and that to yield to bluff was to invite further demands. Delcassé knew all about Fashoda, and it thus came to an appraisal or judgment and to a test of power. French efforts to "smoke out" Germany, in the form of finding out precisely what she wanted, were met by Bülow's deliberate attitude of "the Sphinx": the conference and nothing but the conference would do. Should calling the German bluff lead to the possibility of war, clearly the English position was crucial. Cambon was very active in London.

By no stretch of the imagination could the Entente agreement of 1904 be interpreted as an English commitment to go to war for the sake of French Morocco. But in view of the situation, the German attitude and methods seen in the larger context of European relations,[5] might England not agree to underwrite a calling of the German bluff? Was it not desirable for her to throw her weight into the balance to compensate for the disturbance of the equilibrium that was a consequence of the Russian defeat? This raises a particularly interesting point for the central theme of our discussion: the nature and the degree of clarity of the British position. This can be followed in detail in the documentary publications that have been made available. It may suffice to say that Lansdowne in a general way agreed with and supported the French position. His communication to Sir Francis Bertie, his ambassador in Paris, may be used as illustration:

> You are authorized to inform Minister for Foreign Affairs that we should be prepared to join French Government in offering strong opposition to such a proposal and to beg that if question is raised French Government will afford us a full opportunity of conferring with them as to steps which might be taken in order to meet it.
>
> German attitude in this dispute seems to me most unreasonable having regard to M. Delcassé's attitude and we desire to give him all the support we can.[6]

"All the support we can" is a loose expression. Delcassé may have been right in assuming that, if it came to the ultimate test of force, England would find herself compelled to join in the war, and somewhat later Bülow inquired from the British ambassador in Berlin, Sir Frank Lascelles, about the rumor of a British offer to France of a defensive and offensive alliance.[7] The possibility of British action was certainly not to be excluded, though Delcassé could hardly claim a firm commitment from England. To an inquiry from Cambon, "Can I write to Delcassé that if circumstances render it necessary, if for instance we have serious reason to believe in an unjustified aggression on the part of a certain Power, the British Government would be ready to concert with that of France on the measures to be taken?" Lansdowne replied, "Yes, you can. We are ready."[8] Upon Cambon's request for clarification in writing, Lansdowne had added:

> I am not sure that I succeeded in making quite clear to you our desire that there should be a clear and confidential discussion between the two governments not so much in consequence of some acts of unprovoked aggression on the part of another Power as in anticipation of any complications to be apprehended during the somewhat anxious period through which we are at present passing.[9]

One difficulty arose from divided counsels at the directing level in France. Cambon's and Delcassé's optimism where England was concerned was not shared by Rouvier, who, in a somewhat panicky fashion, took the German threat at face value and was himself opposed to an understanding with England.

Matters came to a head in France on June 6 in the course of a cabinet meeting at the Elysée. It was a highly dramatic session[10] in which Delcassé staunchly defended his policy and his assurance of English support. However, when it finally came to a vote, his was the only voice in favor of an uncompromising attitude. He did the only thing possible, tendering his resignation, thus bringing to a close seven years of continuous tenure and firm direction of France's foreign policy. Rouvier himself assumed the foreign portfolio.

This outcome was a major sensation. It had come in a sense to a personal test of wills between two men and the German Chancellor could claim that he had brought about the fall of the French foreign minister. It was no mean accomplishment, though the wisdom of Bülow's boasting is questionable; he contributed to the undoing of what he thought he had achieved.

For this did not turn out to be another Fashoda. Bülow did not proceed, as a more skillful diplomat would have, to make things easy for the accommodating Rouvier. To make a long story short it may suffice to say that, following France's yielding on the issue of the conference, the agenda for it was not agreed upon until the end of September.

During the interval a curious episode occurred, of which mention at least must be made. The Kaiser as a diplomat had no more tact or finesse than his Chancellor. On July 24, 1905, he and the Tsar were on their respective yachts at Björkö; in the course of a very friendly interview,[11] the Kaiser persuaded the Tsar, as a "souvenir" of their meeting, to sign the treaty which had been drafted the preceding October—and of which he happened to have a copy in his pocket! Having just inflicted a defeat upon France, that country would now, through the agency of her Russian connection, be dragged into the grand continental alliance. There is no need to dwell upon this futile and ill-conceived attempt, which foundered on the same rock as the original one, caused embarrassment to the Tsar when he had to withdraw, and created bad blood between the Kaiser and Bülow.

Of more importance are the concrete consequences of the German success over Morocco, which were two. The conference finally met at Algeciras from January 16 to April 7, 1906. Leaving aside the details of its sometimes difficult proceedings, the significant thing is that its final result, the Act of Algeciras, while it confirmed the parity of all in having access to Morocco, in effect strengthened the French position, for it gave international sanction to French action in the preservation of order in the country.[12] The shock was all the greater to Germany, who found herself, in the wake of her previous success, to a point because of that very success, essentially alone.

The other consequence occurred even before the opening of the conference. On January 10, 1906, Cambon called on Sir Edward Grey, the British foreign minister.[13] Enlarging on the danger of war, he asked if, in view of Britain's stake and of the deficiencies of French power, Britain could not supply 100,000 men to stand guard on the Franco-Belgian frontier should war break out. Grey pointed out that he could make no commitments unless assured of public support, but he thought there was point in Cambon's rejoinder that, especially since Grey thought such support was likely to be forthcoming, it might be desirable to have plans for it worked out in advance.

The result was the authorization which led to military discussions between representatives of the two countries, General Grierson for England and Colonel Huguet for France, the beginning of a long series to follow. The rather unusual fact may be noted that the Cabinet was not consulted, but only certain members of it apprised of the decision, the Prime Minister of course, Lord Haldane (war) and Asquith (exchequer). Also that the Prime Minister insisted that the discussions should have no binding effect on the governments.

Here in some ways were unexpected results that could hardly be pleasing to Germany. Yet the logic of them becomes very clear precisely if Germany is seen as the central mover. The 1904 Entente was in considerable measure the result of Britain's willingness to find an accommodation with France the better to be able to meet other commitments or looming dangers. Certainly in British eyes the Entente was not a positive anti-German alliance, yet the clearest source of potential danger *was* the rising German power; even apart from the factor of the German failure to seize the opportunity of establishing a connection with England around 1900—she had been England's first choice after all—the other manifestations of her rise, naval and commercial especially, were not ignored in London. France, more supple and less strong, had known how to seize the opportunity and the Entente had come into being.

The French would have preferred a more intimate association. Less powerful or clearer minded than the British, they entertained fewer illusions and hopes. By raising the Moroccan issue, and especially by the manner in which she proceeded to deal with it, Germany played into their hands. The apparent success of Bülow's bluff hoisted him on his own petard: having got rid of Delcassé, he procured the Act of Algeciras and tightened the Entente. Within a year of its conclusion that agreement, essentially of negative significance in British eyes at first, was beginning to take on a far more positive character, of which the military discussions were the best expression.

Delcassé or no Delcassé, and despite the turmoil, some of it even sordid, of French domestic affairs, the course of French foreign policy was quite steady; the permanence of Paul Cambon in London may be taken as an expression of this fact, as was that of Barrère in Rome. The Far Eastern setback suffered by the Russian ally was an embarrassment and, for a time at least, entailed a loss of position until Russia should have recovered.

All the more reason therefore to cling to the newfound British connection.

The British responded very handsomely. The fall of Delcassé as it appeared in England was an expression of both German aggressiveness and French weakness. Hence the need to throw the weight of British power in the scales in order to redress the threatened equilibrium. This is a fair appraisal of what happened, but it is also too rational and simple. For the process of British adjustment had in it an element of fumbling unclarity. The military conversations, authorized and known by only a few members of the Cabinet, while the Prime Minister insisted that they had no political implications, reveal the British position very nicely. The fumbling and the hesitation can also be regarded, not only or so much as characteristic of the British way and mind —to a point they were that—but as the manifestation of an automatic process of adjustment. The transformation that was the relative decline of British power was a process which had not reached the point and did not have the clarity that it had in the French case.

Hence the above-mentioned convergence of positions and the still dubious nature of the Anglo-French relationship. Seen in this light, and without advocating a deterministic interpretation or denying the role of individual men and of specific actions, any one of them anything but inevitably fated, one can yet speak of the influence of the deep forces and processes of change in shaping the long-term course of policies; it is certainly revealing to observe how little foreign policy was influenced by the intensity of French internal quarrels or by the substitution of a Conservative by a Liberal administration in England.[14]

An examination of the course of the Anglo-Russian relationship, which will now be considered, furnishes additional grist to this interpretation.

The Anglo-Russian Relationship and the Einkreisung

The similarity between the Anglo-Russian and the Anglo-French relationships, both characterized by intense imperial rivalry, has been pointed out before. In both cases the British position may be described as one of "reasonableness," if by this is meant the willingness to acknowledge the right of others to empire, with the proviso that they in turn accept the legitimacy of certain British desiderata, at which point their own view on the score of "reasonableness" might cease to coincide with the British. Mention has already been made of the British acceptance of Russian activity in Central Asia[15] and of Salisbury's passing conception of settling the Eastern Question after he had come to the conclusion that in supporting Ottoman integrity Britain had been backing the wrong horse.[16]

In the British imperial context, the South African and the Indian situations may both be regarded as illustrations of "defensive" expansion. But there is also the important difference between the two cases that, whereas in the former a definitive solution could be envisaged and was in fact effected—the Boer Republics were annexed—Russia presented an altogether different problem that could not be so easily and radically eliminated. The contest in Central Asia can be traced throughout virtually the whole of the nineteenth century; the defense of Ottoman integrity, especially that of the Straits, but also the control of Egypt and the Nile, may be regarded as the western flank of the British operation, the defense of the route to the East. To be sure, the East meant more than India, for the importance of the Chinese market had been growing, and with that growth the intensity of the competition of interests. Thus, across the whole breadth of Asia, from Constantinople to Peking, Britain and Russia met each other in ever closer contact; apart from the extreme western Ottoman end of this vast theater, the Far East—more specifically, the border region of Manchuria and Korea pointing toward the Yangtse area—Tibet and the Persia-Afghanistan complex were the specific points of contact and of contest. Some of this was analyzed in the memorandum drawn up on September 21, 1899, by Lord Curzon, Viceroy of India at the time.[17]

This was also the time when Britain's freedom of action was hampered by the embarrassment of the Boer War. The steady, one is tempted to say relentless, Russian expansive drive was proceeding in all sectors of the Asiatic front. But the successful conclusion of the South African episode and the making of the Japanese alliance, almost simultaneous events, had the effect of restoring to Britain greater freedom of action, soon manifested in greater assertiveness of position.

The central motive force of Russian expansion was the drive toward warm waters: the Straits, the Persian Gulf, Port Arthur were but variant possibilities, in addition by no means exclusive of each other. The renewed assertiveness of British policy is well exemplified by Lansdowne's declaration[18] of May 15, 1903, that

> Firstly, we should protect and promote British trade in the [Persian] Gulf. Secondly, we should not exclude the legitimate trade of others. Thirdly, we should regard the establishment of a naval base or a fortified port in the Gulf by any other Power as a very grave menace to British interests, and we should certainly resist by all the means at our disposal.

Here is a perfect illustration of the above-mentioned British "reasonableness" in combination with the clear and flat assertion of a *non possumus,* or perhaps better *non volemus,* when it came to certain matters. One is reminded of Grey's warning to the French shortly before Marchand set out on his Fashodan trek.

When juxtaposed to Curzon's statement a fortnight later that

> India is like a fortress with the vast moat of the sea on two of her faces, and with mountains for her walls on the remainder. But beyond these walls extends a glacis of varying breadth and dimensions. We do not want to occupy it; but we *cannot afford to see it occupied by our foes.* He would be a short-sighted commander who merely manned his ramparts in India and did not look out beyond,[19]

the shape of Britain's Indian policy becomes very clear. Curzon's royal progress through the Persian Gulf area later in the year was but an ostensible manifestation of it.

The status of remote Tibet might be described as unclear. It was the object of exchanges between Lansdowne and Beckendorff, the Russian ambassador in London, characterized by unwanted acerbity as well as by some humor in the similarity of the British and the Russian denials of aggressive designs while seeking to extend their respective influences in that land. With the expedition of Colonel Younghusband to Lhasa and the signature of an agreement in September 1904 the British scored a point.

The scoring was made all the easier by the current Russian embarrassment that was the war with Japan, an episode that gave rise to a number of disputes and incidents, of which the Dogger Bank affair was merely the most sensational. The Russo-Japanese War was a far more serious matter for Russia than the Boer War had been for England. The Tsar proved very accommodating in dealing with the Dogger Bank incident, but the most significant aspect of the situation is the fact that Britain did not seek to exploit Russia's difficulty beyond the point of taking advantage of the Russian weakness to come to an acceptable (to herself) accommodation.

To be sure, England remained completely loyal to her Japanese ally, and, in August 1905, she even took the step of extending the scope of the 1902 alliance, a fact best expressed in the following clause:

> Japan, possessing paramount political, military and economic interests in Korea, Great Britain recognizes her right to take such measures of guidance, control and protection in Korea as she may deem necessary, provided that they are not contrary to the principle of equal opportunities for the commerce and industry of all nations. Great Britain having a special interest in all that concerns the security of the Indian frontier, Japan recognizes her right to take such measures in the proximity of that frontier as she may find necessary for safeguarding her Indian possessions, a quid pro quo reinforced by the commitment of assistance of either member to the other should it be attacked by a single third Power.[20]

Both the Boer War and the Russo-Japanese War raised the perennial of the Continental League, a scheme at the center of which one always finds Germany. Britain did not like the Björkö project and appreciated Witte's role in blocking that arrangement. Witte became Prime Minister of Russia in October 1905, his task being the thankless one of liquidating the aftermath of the war with Japan after he had represented his country in the peace negotiations. Witte is largely and correctly associated with the economic modernization of Russia; a modern man himself and a realist, if he was not especially enamored of his French ally, he adhered to the French alliance, the value of which he appreciated, for the financial advantages it meant among other things. After 1905 Russia was more than ever in need of capital; in the loan that was launched in Paris in April 1906 there was English participation.[21]

The Liberal administration which took control in England at the end of 1905 was favorable to an accommodation with Russia, a tendency with which King Edward VII agreed, and which he did his best to assist.[22] The final outcome was the signature on August 31, 1907, of three agreements, which dealt respectively with Persia, Afghanistan, and Tibet.

The last-named, in which the suzerainty of China was acknowledged, was made into a buffer in which neither Britain nor Russia would seek to extend its influence. The independence of Afghanistan was recognized, though in effect the agreements pending between that country and England placed it within the sphere of British influence.[23] The most important part of the Izvolsky-Nicolson agreement dealt with the sharpest bone of contention, Persia, which—her integrity and independence, needless to say, were asserted—was divided into three zones, a Russian in the North, a British in the South, and an intervening neutral sector. The Straits and the Persian Gulf were not included in the agreement, but separate notes, a British one in April and a Russian in August, expressed respectively the British willingness to entertain changes in the régime of the Straits and the Russian acknowledgment of the preponderance of the British interest in the Persian Gulf.

A comparison of the Anglo-Russian agreement of 1907 with the Anglo-French Entente of 1904 is of interest. The reception of the former was far less enthusiastic than that of the latter, especially in England, where criticism was sharp on the score of what many considered an unsatisfactory bargain. Lord Curzon was particularly violent in his attacks, and Lansdowne though more moderate was also critical. On the Russian side, Witte was not entirely satisfied. But, on balance, the stress belongs on the similarity between the two sets of understandings. In both cases we are dealing with an imperial compromise, fundamentally not unfair to either participant; most important of all, in either case Britain had eliminated certain sources of friction, hence lightened the burden of her commitments. There was in the more recent instance no immediate counterpart to the Moroccan sequel, which changed almost immediately the character of the Anglo-French Entente, but neither was the Anglo-Russian relationship subsequently disrupted. The trend of relationships is well expressed in Gooch's words:

> Great Britain, for her part, having definitely sided with France, required the assurance of Russian support in face of the growing danger from Germany. Thus the removal of local frictions was followed, as had been the case with France, by diplomatic cooperation in various fields. The Anglo-French Entente and the Dual Alliance broadened into the Triple Entente, which confronted the Triple Alliance on the European chess-board. Though we were allied to no power except Portugal and Japan, and in theory retained perfect liberty of actions, we had now half unwittingly, but not the less irrevocably, thrown in our lot with France and Russia. It was this novel system of attachments which was to govern our policy in the coming years, and to determine its course in Persia, the Balkans and Morocco.[24]

To the word "irrevocably" one might take exception, but "half unwittingly" is entirely appropriate. Were we writing a general history of international relations, the center of the stage would belong to Germany, for it was she who insured the continuation of the course upon which these relationships had embarked, instead of procuring a by no means impossible alteration of their direction. France, of course, had good reason to be pleased, and she saw the picture in sharper outline. In the English case one is tempted to speak of an unconscious or automatic reaction of adaptation to the changing facts of power, a real and effective one nonetheless. Germany for her part had good cause for concern, which the talk of *Einkreisung* expressed. There was encirclement indeed, yet the emergence of the Triple Entente combination cannot be described as other than defensive; there was no plot to do Germany down, but rather fear of real or imagined German aggressive intent, a fear for which the German mode of operation gave grounds. As an illustration of this a letter from Grey to Theodore Roosevelt may be cited:

> . . . It [our policy] is not anti-German. But it must be independent of Germany. We wish to keep and strengthen the *Entente* with France, who is now very peaceful, and neither aggressive nor restless. She also plays the game fairly, and as long as she trusts one she is a good friend. The weak point is that she might some day have a scare that we intended to change. I think Germany has already tried more than once to make her imagine this.
>
> . . . .
>
> If . . . our *Entente* with France were to be broken up, France will have to make her own terms with Germany. And Germany will again be in a position to keep us on bad terms with France and Russia, and to make herself predominant upon the Continent. Then, sooner or later, there will be war between us and Germany, in which much else may be involved.
>
> It is in German diplomacy alone that one now meets with deliberate attempts to make mischief between other countries by saying poisoned things to one about another. It is the lees left by Bismarck that still foul the cup. The economic rivalry (and all that) with Germany do not give much offence to our people, and they admire her steady industry and genius for organization. But they do resent mischief making. They suspect the Emperor of aggressive plans of *Weltpolitik*, and they see that Germany is forcing the pace in armaments in order to dominate Europe, and is thereby laying a horrible burden of wasteful expenditure upon all the other Powers.
>
> The long and short of the matter is that, to secure peace, we must maintain the *Entente* with France, and attempts from outside to shake it will only make it stronger.[25]

Thus the initiative may be said to have remained in large measure in German hands; what Germany would do or not do, and not least important, how she did it, could determine whether all three of the relationships which between them constituted the Triple Entente—not an alliance be it noted—would prove lasting or ephemeral. That her own past relationship with either Russia or England might be restored was by no means excluded; even where France was concerned, the memory of 1870 no longer carried the vigor and the sting it had had for the generation which had lived through the episode. But fear feeds upon fear. With Russo-German relations, save as they bear incidentally upon others, we are not here concerned, but the Anglo-German relationship, apart from its being of crucial importance—England still rated first place in the world as a whole—is an essential part of our discussion. To it we must turn for a moment.

"Our Future Lies on the Water"

Where the sea and sea power are concerned, despite occasional lapses ending up in war scares, the epithet "unwittingly" hardly applies to the English behavior. For some time, since 1889, Britain had adhered to the two-power standard; the French fleet, second in rank, was a long distance behind and the two-power combination envisaged had mainly been a Franco-Russian. After 1904, and especially after 1907, things had obviously changed, for Germany had become instead the chief challenger.

The first German naval bill of 1898 has greater significance as the harbinger of a new policy than because of the actual increase of German naval power it envisaged. The English reaction was not one of alarm, although, as Germany persisted, some precautions were taken. Rosyth would be a first-class naval base and the First Sea Lord, Sir John Fisher, proceeded to reorganize and redistribute the fleet in 1904; the Japanese alliance and the state of relations with the United States made possible the reduction of South Atlantic and Pacific forces, hence a strengthening of the Home fleet. The first *Dreadnought* was launched in 1906.

John Fisher knew his mind and would not be deterred by niceties of law or protocol, as evidenced by his suggestion to King Edward "that we should 'Copenhagen' the German fleet at Kiel *à la* Nelson," and regretting "that we possessed neither a Pitt nor a Bismarck to give the order."[26] But this was early in 1908 and a purely personal view, by no means even remotely expressive of British policy, in spite of the position of its advocate.

For full five years instead, from 1907 to 1912, active negotiations intermittently went on, often carried out in a climate of friendliness; the high points of them at least must be recalled.

When the Kaiser was in England again in November 1907, he and Haldane, the secretary for war, discussed at length and in wholly amicable fashion the relations between the two countries. The Kaiser fully understood the English requirement to protect the "gate" of the Persian Gulf in connection with the construction of the Baghdad railway. But the English desire to bring Russia and France into the discussion put a stop to its further progress. The episode was rather in the nature of a passing clearing in the accumulating clouds. Fisher's own reaction has just been indicated.

A number of important things happened in 1908. The British were sincerely desirous of avoiding a race in naval building, though not at the cost of surrendering their own supremacy or of relinquishing their newly made French and Russian connections. But these being no more than a liquidation of differences did not exclude in British eyes the possibility of an understanding with Germany as well. In the reorganized Cabinet of April 1908 in which, under Asquith's prime ministership, both Lloyd George and Churchill held places, neither of these two men were moved by anti-German preconceptions, being more interested, especially the former, in matters of domestic reform.

Lloyd George could in fact, in July, argue the German case, in view of that country's position, before the Peace Society. He was perfectly capable of understanding Germany's fears and did not believe that the actions she took as a consequence of those fears implied any anti-English designs on her part. At about the same time Churchill foresaw no serious collision of interests anywhere in the world between the British and the German peoples, with whom he sympathized and whom "we wish well from the bottom of our hearts."[27] To be sure, the *Daily Telegraph* incident,[28] in October, a small enough thing in itself, may, because of the intensity of the storm to which it gave rise, be taken as evidence that, underneath the surface, uneasy suspicion prevailed.

The year 1908 was also that in which the Bosnian annexation crisis[29] began, which put a severe strain on the preservation of peace. Neither England, nor even France, offered Russia much support, with the consequence that Austria, thanks to Germany's backing in considerable measure, had her way. This situation lends all the more interest to the fact that it was in February 1909, at the approaching climax of the crisis, that the English royal couple visited Germany. The visit went off well, despite the Kaiser's touchiness, which led him to assert that he would rather go to war than submit to any outside pressure.[30] It is also worth mentioning that in Marienbad King Edward had a long and frank discussion with Clemenceau, the French prime minister at the time, who was outspoken in expressing his pessimistic views on the future. Clemenceau went on to explain the need for a substantial British land force to compensate for the deficiencies of the French.[31]

Thus the Anglo-German contacts were sterile of results, instead of which knowledge of an acceleration of German naval building prompted the First Lord of the Admiralty, MacKenna, to deliver a speech in the Commons on March 16, supported by another one by Balfour, which had the effect of producing a naval scare in England. A frightening picture was given of the rate of German progress, which England must match; the naval estimates, which Lloyd George and Churchill had opposed in the Cabinet, were passed. Bülow had turned down proposals for the limitation of the naval competition which was well launched by this time.

The Bosnian annexation crisis passed but the role played in it by Germany strengthened in many quarters the belief in German aggressiveness, hardly a contribution to the prosperity of an Anglo-German understanding. Nevertheless, while taking precautions, the British on their side refused to abandon the search for an accommodation; nor was there lack in Germany of those who also hoped for a composition of the dispute. The accession of Bethmann-Hollweg to the chancellorship in July 1909, when the Kaiser could no longer endure Bülow, was a favorable development; Bethmann-Hollweg himself believed in Britain's good will, and his appointment was well received in England. He was convinced of two things, the futility of the German efforts to disrupt the Franco-Russian alliance, and the importance that the British attached to the naval situation. An understanding was therefore all the more necessary lest Britain become more firmly involved with the Dual Alliance.

Thus negotiations went on, in which many participated, even

outside the upper and immediate circles of government. Albert Ballin in Germany and Sir Ernest Cassel in England, who had access to those circles in their respective countries and stood in comparable positions with respect to the rulers, were useful intermediaries. By 1910 the discussion began to take a more precise turn, of which Asquith gave an indication in a speech in Parliament in July,[32] as did similarly Grey in March 1911. Bethmann-Hollweg's reply in the Reichstag was, however, little encouraging when he said:

> I consider any control as absolutely impracticable, and every attempt in that direction would lead to nothing but continual mutual distrust and perpetual friction. Who would be content to weaken his means of defense without the absolute certainty that his neighbor was not secretly exceeding the proportion allowed to him in the disarmament agreement? No, gentlemen, anyone who seriously considers the question of universal disarmament must inevitably come to the conclusion that it is insoluble so long as men are men and states are states,[33]

a statement which, incidentally, has a very contemporary ring.

Domestic British issues, which led to the holding of two general elections in 1910, in January and in December, inevitably resulted in some slowing down of the Anglo-German discussions, but otherwise had no significant effect on their course; the naval problem was outside the scope of internal politics. In January 1911, Asquith appointed a Standing Sub-Committee of the Committee of Imperial Defence for "the coordination of Departmental Action on the outbreak of war."[34] Still hoping for the best, Britain would take no chances on lowering her guard.

Another incident, at the center of which Germany is again to be found, the Agadir crisis,[35] which occupied the second part of the year, also had surprisingly little effect on the discussions, though it led England to take from the first a very definite position, best expressed in the speech delivered at the Mansion House by Lloyd George.[36] The warning to Germany could hardly have been clearer, and it was correspondingly resented in that country. But the second Moroccan crisis was overcome before the year was out and the Anglo-German discussions went on.

Needless to say, as in the case of the Bosnian annexation crisis of 1908–9, the aftermath of the Agadir crisis could not but have an effect on the surrounding climate of international relations.

The climax of the discussions, leaving out innumerable details and statements, was reached with the famous Haldane mission, the visit of the British war secretary to Berlin in February 1912, the result of previous preparations, and itself intended to explore the ground and to pave the way for agreement at the highest level. The immediate background was perhaps not of the best, for on the German side the reaction to the Agadir crisis, largely under Tirpitz's prodding, had been the *Novelle*, a supplementary bill for increased naval appropriations; on the English side, it was somewhat less than tactful for the First Lord of the Admiralty to choose the day after Haldane's arrival in Berlin to deliver himself of a speech in which the contrast was pointed out between the necessity of a naval establishment for Britain, whereas the same thing was for Germany in the class of a "luxury."[37]

Nevertheless, the meetings between Haldane and Bethmann-Hollweg proceeded in an atmosphere of friendliness and understanding.[38] Each grasped the needs of the other's country, not omitting the factors of public opinion and of the pressure of their respective admirals; the exchanges of information were on both sides full and frank. Two points seemed to be fixed: Britain would maintain her supremacy whatever the cost; Germany would not alter her plans unless she could secure the price of a political counterpart. This is what provided the possibility of a solution, which the following formula, proposed by Bethmann-Hollweg, outlined:

I. The High Contracting Powers assure each other mutually of their desire for peace and friendship.

II. They will not, either of them, make any combination, or join in any combination, which is directed against the other. They expressly declare that they are not bound by any such combination.

III. If either of the High Contracting Parties becomes entangled in a war with one or more other Powers, the other of the High Contracting Parties will at least observe toward the Power so entangled a benevolent neutrality, and use its utmost endeavor for the localisation of the conflict.

IV. The duty of neutrality which arises from the preceding Article has no application in so far as it may not be reconcilable with existing agreements which the High Contracting Parties have already made. The making of new agreements which make it impossible for either of the Contracting Parties to observe neutrality beyond what is provided in the preceding limitation is excluded in conformity with the provisions contained in Article II.[39]

The meaning of this is quite clear: Germany would accept a measure at least of naval inferiority in exchange for a British commitment to neutrality in the event of a continental war. Germany had alliances in Europe, while Britain had none, save with Portugal, hardly a relevant matter. Omitting further details, fundamentally the political issue is the rock on which the negotiation, which went on for a while, was finally wrecked.

Kaiser William II and Tirpitz had participated in some of the discussions with Haldane. As Tirpitz saw it—the Kaiser essentially agreed—the whole attempt was a disingenuous English maneuver to do Germany down. On the British side the feeling was that a blanket commitment to neutrality was impossible; England might find it necessary to come to France's assistance, especially if Belgium should be involved, and this British reticence is to be considered in the light of the recent Bosnian and Moroccan crises. In any case failure was the outcome, and the judgment may be considered justified that this was so "because each side suspected the other of entertaining unavowed designs."[40] The English answer, introduced by a presentation of the First Lord of the Admiralty in the Commons on July 22, was an English version of the *Novelle,* a more convincing action than Asquith's hedging statement that "we cultivate with great and growing cordiality our special friendships; but they are in no sense exclusive. Our relations with the great German empire are at this moment . . . relations of amity and goodwill."[41]

This outcome of failure, even apart from the consequence of unfettered naval competition, could not simply put matters back where they stood before the issue had arisen, any more than the

1890 German refusal to renew the Reinsurance Treaty with Russia could put the situation back to 1887. Thus the further tightening of the Anglo-French connection may be regarded as the logical aftermath of the failure; it had two distinct aspects.

The more concrete one had to do with naval matters. The French in 1912 decided to concentrate their fleet in the Mediterranean in order to be able to deal with the combined Austro-Italian naval forces. The counterpart of this French action was the withdrawal of the main British Mediterranean fleet to concentrate it in home waters. The rearrangement was obvious for all the world to see and could hardly have been purely coincidental. There was in fact a British-drawn draft in the hands of Delcassé, back in the government as Navy minister.[42] But what is perhaps more revealing is that here was no more than the statement of a technical rearrangement, unaccompanied by firm political commitments. What would happen should war break out between Germany and France and the German fleet sail through the Straits of Dover toward a French coast denuded of any but land defenses?

The French, needless to say, would have liked some reassurance in the form of a more precise definition of the English position than they possessed so far. Cambon, who patiently pursued his work in London, was now urged by Poincaré, the French Prime Minister, to endeavor to obtain such a definition. Cambon found a sympathetic reception from Grey, but the best he could obtain in writing was an exchange of letters which stated as follows:

> From time to time in recent years the French and British naval and military experts have consulted together. It has always been understood that such consultation does not restrict the freedom of either Government to decide at any future time whether or not to assist the other by armed force. We have agreed that consultation between experts is not, and ought not, to be regarded as an engagement that commits either Government to action in a contingency that has not yet arisen and may never arise. The disposition, for instance, of the French and British fleets respectively at the present moment *is not based upon an engagement to cooperate in war.* You have, however, pointed out that if either Government had grave reason to expect an unprovoked attack by a

third Power, it might become essential to know whether it could in that event depend upon the armed assistance of the other. I agree that, if either Government had grave reason to expect an unprovoked attack by a third Power, or something that threatened the general peace, it should immediately *discuss* with the other, whether both Governments should act together to prevent aggression and to preserve peace, and, if so, what measures they would be prepared to take in common.[43] [my italics]

This is a good point at which to ponder on the operation and the evolution of British policy. To see the drift of the British position during the past decade there is no need of the hindsight that the passage of time has provided. There is no room to go into an extensive analysis of the *Memorandum on the Present State of British Relations with France and Germany,*[44] dated January 1, 1907, and drawn up by Eyre Crowe, senior clerk at the foreign office. It is a lengthy document, not wholly devoid of tendentiousness, but well worth rereading after sixty years. A brief quotation from it will suffice. Crowe considered it but natural

> that the power of a State supreme at sea should inspire universal jealousy and fear and be ever exposed to the danger of being overthrown by a general combination of the world. Against such a combination no single nation could in the long run stand, least of all a small island kingdom not possessed of the military strength of a people trained in arms.
>
> The danger can in practice only be averted on condition that the national policy of the insular state is so directed as to harmonise with the general desires and ideals common to all mankind, and more particularly that it is closely identified with the primary and vital interest of a majority, or of as many as possible of the other nations. Now the first interest of all countries is the preservation of national independence. It follows that England, more than any other non-insular Power, has a direct and positive interest in the maintenance of the independence of nations, and therefore must be the natural enemy of any country threatening the independence of others, and the natural protector of the weaker communities. . . . *It has been well said that every country, if it had the option, would, of course, prefer itself to hold the power of supremacy at sea, but that, this choice being excluded,*

> *it would rather see England hold that power than any other state.* [my italics]

From this broad view and a detailed analysis of the French and German records followed the conclusion that:

> A German maritime supremacy must be acknowledged to be incompatible with the existence of the British Empire, and even if that empire disappeared, the union of the greatest military with the greatest naval power in one State would compel the world to combine for the riddance of such an incubus.

Allowing for a measure of arrogance and cant in some of this statement, if one thinks without passion of the realities of power and of the manner of its exercise, much validity must be granted the contention of the italicized sentence. We are touching here upon a well-established and clearly understood line of policy. Since British power had diminished, at least in relative terms, Britain had made compromises and lightened her responsibilities; but naval supremacy she felt she could maintain. The German threat was at the time the clearest challenge, and though the first reaction was to meet it with the usual British "reasonableness," in the sense of that word explained before, ships would be built in sufficient number to maintain an adequate margin of superiority while Britain would persistently decline to make the political commitments that Germany demanded.

On this score there was perfect clarity, yet it is also the point at which unclarity appeared. For Britain *did* make other political commitments, however much Grey may have explained their limitations to Cambon. The view has come to be accepted in England that a better service would have been rendered to the preservation of peace—Britain's real wish and interest—by making her position clear instead of allowing others—read mainly Germany—to entertain false hopes and illusions. British power was striving to adapt itself to the changing relationships of the day, but the judgment that directed political decision was fumbling and reluctant of sufficient clarity. The involvement with France was becoming more intimate, but the degree of control that Russia could exercise on the course of affairs, through the

French alliance for one thing, was certainly not given adequate attention. There was point, if also oversimplification, to Lord Loreburn's observation that "in effect it left the peace of Great Britain at the mercy of the Russian court."[45]

The Anglo-French Convergence Bears Fruit

The focus of the discussion has been on British policy to the extent that it has for the reason that Britain still retained, in some degree at least, an arbitral position; also because that arbitral position, the range of freedom of maneuver, was narrowing. Britain was reluctant to acknowledge the change, hence the uncertainties and ambiguities of her position and her actions.

French policy was set upon a clearer course. Not that alternatives did not exist, and one may speak in the French case as well of a pro-German current, meaning by this that there were those in France who did not see a Franco-German clash as fated but entertained instead the possibility of some accommodation. In any case, however, there was on the French side adherence to the cultivation of the existing alliances and to the strengthening of the British connection.

Germany failed to exploit the possibilities of the British uncertainties. To repeat again, more than any other Power, she stands at the center of the story of the international relations of Europe, but our concern lies primarily with British and French policies and reactions. The increasing convergence of their positions, logical but not inevitable fruit of the Entente, is well illustrated by the developments which had their source in Mediterranean uncertainties. A brief survey of them will serve to bring out this just mentioned convergence.

THE RESTLESS BALKANS

Russia's everlasting desire to improve her position at the Straits lies at the root of the attempt which found expression in the loose understanding which Izvolsky and Aehrenthal, the Russian and Austrian foreign ministers, contrived at Buchlau in September 1908: in exchange for a not too clearly specified Austrian promise of support, Russia would give her consent to the formal annexation of Bosnia and Herzegovina by Austria. This last change would constitute but a relatively minor alteration in the existing state of things, although, for domestic reasons, it was of importance to Austria, which would thereby slam the door firmly shut on South Slav hopes; that is precisely why it represented a Russian concession of some substance. However, it was not an unreasonable approach to think that, if the two Powers most directly concerned could agree, the likelihood of Europe's consent to a modification of the Treaty of Berlin would be materially enhanced.

The status of the Straits was a more delicate matter, and it was fitting that Izvolsky should set about consulting others. But the Austrian precipitateness in proclaiming the annexation placed the whole question in a different context and set off a European crisis. That often told tale[46] will not be repeated here, where some aspects of the British and the French reactions alone will be retained.

Clemenceau was prime minister in France, whose views on Germany never underwent any change. He condemned the unilateral Austrian action as a breach of international obligations, which indeed it was, but did not think that the issue called for the recourse to force; a Balkan quarrel would not seem adequate justification of it in the eyes of French opinion. The calling of an international conference to examine the situation was his solution. Grey in London concurred in this view though he cautioned that there should be prior agreement on the agenda of the conference.

Izvolsky was disappointed at the feebleness of French support, of the even weaker one that he found in England, and was highly embarrassed by the dilemma in which he had, largely through his own carelessness, maneuvered himself. The conference was the only remaining Russian hope and became the issue around which the crisis unfolded. For Austria, strongly supported by Germany, proved recalcitrant; just as with France in the case of Morocco three years earlier, her preference was for bilateral agreements. The crisis lasted through the winter and was not resolved until Russia yielded in the face of strong German pressure; thus Austria was able to extract the maximum advantage from the episode when Serbia was compelled to make an abject declaration of acceptance.

The significance of the incident in the present context lies in two things. One is the close agreement between Britain and France in refusing to allow the Balkan quarrel to degenerate into a test of force that would involve them. The other, related to this first aspect, is that the test of force would have been one with Germany. This last country in fact emerges as the principal in the resolution of the whole affair, and her attitude had the effect of focusing Russian discontent even more on her than on Austria. Seen from London and from Paris it was the sort of behavior that helped create the image of aggressiveness and lent color to the strictures found in the above-mentioned Crowe memorandum. The state of Anglo-German naval rivalry at this time must be borne in mind as well.

The outcome rankled in Russia. The fact that she was still laboring under the impact of the war with Japan, her military weakness, and her domestic difficulties, had been contributing factors to her surrender no less than the lack of French and British support. That she should seek an opportunity for revenge needs no explaining. It was not very long in coming.

Russian diplomacy was active in the Balkan capitals, especially in Belgrade and Sofia. The conclusion of a Serbo-Bulgarian alliance in March 1912, especially in view of the well-established rivalry between those two countries, was undoubtedly a major success of Russian diplomacy.[47] To a point it had overreached itself and acted in irresponsible fashion, for, once unleashed, the Balkan states had it in their power to create a situation that the Great Powers might no longer be able to control.

The French reaction to this Russian activity was obviously of the highest importance, for the extent of French support might be crucial. That reaction may be described as ambiguous; it can be followed in the activity of Poincaré, the prime minister. Given his tendencies, his strong anti-German orientation, Poincaré set great store by the preservation, even the strengthening, of the Russian alliance. At the same time, Poincaré was of a highly legalistic bent and was not a rash man. Thus, while he gave Russia reassurances at first, he insisted that the problem was a Russian concern above all and on a strict interpretation of the terms of the alliance.[48] Not until his visit to Russia in August was he fully informed of the Balkan alliance, the aggressive intent of which was immediately apparent to him.

The result may be described as second thoughts on the part of both the French and the Russians. Although in the event of war in the Balkans qualified opinion leaned toward the expectation of a Turkish victory, war is ever uncertain, both in its course and in the nature of the larger complications to which it can give rise. In some respects a Turkish victory might be preferable even from the Russian standpoint, for the Powers might find it easier to agree and impose limitations upon the victor in that case than they would upon successful and overheated Balkan nationalisms.

Thus, counsels of prudence prevailed. Quite appropriately, the two major Powers most directly concerned, Russia and Austria, acting for Europe as a whole, made a *démarche* in Belgrade and in Sofia. When this turned out to be too late, war having broken out on a Montenegrin initiative soon followed by the rest of the Balkan states, Poincaré's earlier suggestion of a conference of the Powers may be regarded as the seed out of which the meetings that took place in London developed.

London was the appropriate place, for England was sincerely desirous of peace and the least involved of all. But it took some time for the Concert of Europe to get into action; for military developments overtook other possibilities. The quick and thoroughgoing victory of the Balkan allies was general cause for surprise, but, in the face of it, it would have been unrealistic to attempt to undo its effects.

Thus, two meetings took place simultaneously in the English capital in December: one of the belligerents, and one of the ambassadors of the Powers. The first registered with relative ease what amounted to the eviction of the Turks from Europe, save at the Straits themselves. The cession of territory *collectively* to the victors left open, however, the issue of its disposition, and this is where difficulties arose in the attempt to reconcile local wishes with the desiderata of the Powers.

Austria, with firm support from Germany, and from Italy as well in this particular matter, would under no circumstances allow Serbia access to the sea, although she no longer insisted on maintaining the territorial separation of Montenegro from Serbia, the Sandjak. Thus Albania was born,[49] to keep Serbia away from the sea, a solution which the Powers succeeded in imposing, though not without some difficulty, the last instance of the successful operation of the Concert of Europe.

Had the initial Russian-sponsored plan been put into effect, peace might have been restored to the Balkans. But in face of the Austrian opposition, deprived of more than diplomatic support from France and Britain, Russia drew back and even counseled moderation to Serbia. Unable to agree on a revision of the original scheme, mainly because of Bulgarian opposition, the Balkan allies fell out among themselves. Isolated against all—even Roumania joined in the fray—Bulgaria had to pay the costs of her unwise behavior.[50] But the Powers had their way in Albania, her frontiers and organization.

ENGLAND AT THE CROSSROADS

To the preservation of peace all may be said to have contributed, and the compromise reached was, from their standpoint, a triumph of moderation and reason. This judgment at least applies to the Great Powers. Of the British desire for peace there can be no question; the French stand was somewhat ambiguous. But it is not amiss to point out that this was the very moment when the two countries agreed on the redistribution of their fleets, surely an indication of increasing concordance. One must also bear in mind the domestic difficulties which hampered both.

In British politics the social question loomed large as well as that aftermath of it that was the Irish problem.[51] In France this was the time of a nationalistic resurgence, the *réveil national,* of which Poincaré's prime ministership, followed by his election to the presidency of the country in January 1913, was an apt expression. The three-year term of military service was enacted, designed to compensate for the deficiencies of French vis-à-vis German manpower, but it was bitterly debated and the opposition to it was not stilled and had not given up. Socialism was making headway in France, where there were those who did not view the Russian alliance with favor. Dislike of the Russian connection was likewise strong in Liberal quarters in Britain. It had been voiced in 1907 in a letter to *The Times* signed by a number of distinguished Liberals.[52]

Five years later a similar protest was addressed to Grey by the Manchester Liberal Federation,[53] this time on the score of the involvement with France over Morocco. The following quotation, inspired by the same spirit, is to the point:

> It [the supreme British interest] is *to have a navy which will be equal to any possible combination against us and a policy which will keep the probable combination against us to what we can meet without a gross inflation of expenditure on armaments.* Such a policy will necessarily be defensive and pacific. It will not regard this country as having a Providential mission to redress the balance of power in Europe. It will tend, as far as possible, to avoid entanglement in European quarrels.[54]

This statement illustrates to a nicety the British dilemma. It indicates, apart from the congenital Liberal bent, an awareness of diminished power and to a point even involves some contradiction. It was precisely because of this diminution of the British margin of power that the defense of the British interest no longer made possible the maintenance of an aloof arbitral position. Preservation of the European balance had been in the past the best defense of the British interest; but Britain had been driven to involvement with France and Russia precisely because of her inability to preserve that balance alone. The change was taking place in gradual fashion and was not consciously perceived; little wonder that British policy was hesitant and ambiguous, a fact well expressed in the above-mentioned exchanges between Grey and Cambon.[55] French policy was clearer on the whole, to a point because France had the advantage of an inescapably clearer consciousness of her own diminution.

Mention has just been made of the Moroccan problem; it again flared up into crisis in 1911. The tale may be regarded as a tragicomedy of errors, for France on the one hand was determined to extend her hold in Morocco, an outcome to which Germany on the other did not fundamentally object. Reasonably enough, Germany expected compensation. After Algeciras there had even been an attempt at Franco-German co-operation in

Morocco, but it had not succeeded. When in 1911 French troops went to restore order in Fez, in perfectly legitimate fashion, Germany quite correctly judged that the last chapter of Moroccan independence was about to close.

To compensation France, on her side, did not object. Naturally, she wanted to make it as small as possible, and equally naturally Germany wanted the most she could obtain, a proper basis for a compromise solution. But in the atmosphere of 1911 things went wrong, an outcome for which the responsibility lies in the main again at Germany's door. Kiderlen-Wächter's tactics are curiously reminiscent of Bülow's, and the crisis of 1911 bears a close resemblance to that of six years earlier. Dark threats, playing the Sphinx, frightening his adversary by dangling the possibility of war, were his method. This had the same effect as on the earlier occasion, with the consequence that, when a not unreasonable compromise was finally reached, in November 1911, it left behind it a trail of increased distrust and suspicion; most ominous of all perhaps, a more intimate Anglo-French connection.

There had been disappointment in England at the lack of support Delcassé had found in the French Government in 1905; France must be even weaker than had been thought, therefore in need of greater support than had been initially intended, hence in turn the military conversations. The English reaction to the Agadir incident[56] was remarkably prompt, a measure of Germany's too great success in conveying false impressions and raising the alarm. A warning by Grey on July 4 was followed, within less than three weeks, by Lloyd George's Mansion House speech, in which he asserted that

> If a situation were to be forced on us in which peace could only be preserved by the surrender of the great and beneficent position Britain has won by centuries of heroism and achievements, by allowing Britain to be treated, where her interests were vitally affected, as if she were of no account in the Cabinet of Nations, then I say emphatically that peace at that price would be a humiliation intolerable for a great country like us to endure.[57]

This declaration was cause for surprise in Germany, where it was seen as a gratuitous interference. It had been dictated in part by Britain's fear of a German naval establishment in Morocco and must be seen in the context of the Anglo-German naval rivalry. The Haldane mission, which has been discussed earlier, shortly after the settlement of the last Moroccan crisis was to bear no fruit.

The settlement of the Franco-German dispute left, to repeat, a train of deep suspicion in regard to German aims and methods. Squirm as she would, reluctant Britain, devoted to peace as she was, found herself increasingly in a similar position to France. France welcomed this, of course, and on the whole played her cards with skill.

The trail of interrelated events from the western to the eastern end of the Mediterranean has also been indicated before. The settlement of the Moroccan crisis, clear prelude to the French appropriation of that country,[58] induced Italy to collect her blank check in Libya. She declared war on Turkey in October, even before the final settlement over Morocco. Her action was unpopular with all for the good reason that a war involving the Ottoman Empire opened the door to too many uncertainties. Within a year Italy had her way, in part because Turkey thought it desirable to concentrate her forces to deal with the brewing Balkan storm.

The Balkan Wars, too, have been mentioned. The collective success of Europe, purchased at the expense of intensified Balkan discontent, had no morrow. Serbian feeling was deeply resentful of the humiliation inflicted by Austria, twice within four years, in 1909 and in 1913. The very fact of the successful war against Turkey, then against Bulgaria, and the elimination of the Turkish focus of Serbian irredentism, caused that emotion to concentrate exclusively on the Dual Monarchy. On June 28, 1914, the heir to the Austrian crown, Archduke Franz Ferdinand, fell victim to the pistol shots of young South Slav enthusiasts—assassins, heroic martyrs of the patriotic cause, as one may wish to call them.

A sensational incident to be sure, it yet need not have been more than that. Even when out of it the Austrian decision to settle scores with Serbia once and for all precipitated a European crisis, it could with reason be contended that the past record of crises overcome gave grounds for optimistic expectations. But, on the other hand, the succession, the acceleration of the tempo of crises, augured ill for playing with fire. The formal Austrian declaration of war against Serbia a month after Sarajevo precipitated feverish diplomatic activity that was this time destined to fail.

A whole library has grown out of the discussion of the crisis of July 1914 which there is no need to retail at this point.[59] It will suffice, by way of broad summation, to say that Russia took this time a firm stand. Germany, as she had done in 1908, likewise gave unwavering support to her Austrian ally; it was symbolically appropriate that, out of a Balkan quarrel and domestic Austrian difficulties, the first clash among major Powers should take the form on August 1 of a German declaration of war against Russia.

France, too, took a firm stand; rightly or wrongly, this represented a judgment on the since much debated issue of the validity of appeasement. Poincaré did not believe in the appeasability of Germany, which declared war on France on August 3. Involved in the Triple Entente in the manner that has been described, Britain was yet the least involved of all. It was therefore also appropriate that mediating proposals should mainly come from her; in the last days of peace Grey labored hard to bring about some compromise.

With war let loose on the Continent the situation was altered, and Britain was faced with the choice between participation and abstention. Grey explained this to Parliament on August 3 in a speech that gave little encouragement to those who opposed her intervention. The observations of a member of the House,

> Ay! do not let us forget that when we go to war against Germany we go to war against a people who, after all, hold largely the ideals that we hold. I do not mean the bureaucracy, I do not mean the military element, but the German civilisation is in many ways near the British civilisation. We think of their literature, we think of what they have done for progressive religious thought, we think of what they have done for philosophy, and we say that they are not the men we want to fight,[60]

were those of a voice crying in the wilderness.[61]

The War, 1914–18

For a long time before 1914 the socialistic doctrine had been making progress among the European masses, nowhere more than in Marx's native land itself. Socialists were opposed to war. Many hopes centered on the action of the Second International, which the governments correspondingly feared, should a conflict break out. On July 31, the French Socialist leader, Jaurès, was murdered, but there is little reason to believe that, had he lived, the course of events would have been other than it was. For Socialists, almost without exception, everywhere joined in the patriotic fervor that sent the soldiers singing to the frontiers; they were all, in their own eyes, embarking on the sacred and inescapable task of defense against aggression.

The war which had finally broken out was the logical outcome of the tensions and rivalries which had long been festering in Europe. With a qualification for Italy[62] the rival combinations of the Entente and the Central Powers were appealing to the arbitrament of force.

Of necessity, for the moment at least, military considerations took priority of place over politics and diplomacy. Better prepared and geographically advantaged, the Central Powers sought to capitalize on these assets to procure a prompt victory. The logical German plan was to destroy the Western force, the French, before the slower moving Eastern, the Russian, could take effective action; the British mattered relatively little at this point. Conversely, the Entente's best hope was to avoid this outcome, thus gaining time to mobilize its far greater potential, and in turn secure victory; here was a prime illustration of the difference between power in being and power in potential. The latter calculation proved in the end to be correct, but not until more than four years had passed and many things had taken place of which no one had dreamed in the days of 1914.

The story of the war has been told many times.[63] In keeping with our purpose, certain aspects of it alone will be retained or emphasized, those concerning primarily Britain and France.

France bore the full initial brunt of the German offensive, the plan of which seemed justified by the unfolding of events in

August. Despite a useful resistance, Belgium was soon overrun, the battle of the Franco-Belgian border was a German success, and the prize of Paris appeared within German grasp. But the French Army, though mauled, had not been destroyed. While the government fled to Bordeaux, imperturbable Joffre rallied sufficient force on the Marne for a stand in September, which, capitalizing on certain German errors, was successful. The fundamental aim of the German plan had been frustrated, a fact of capital importance, for it opened up unlimited possibilities, not least those in which diplomacy could find more ample scope.

While this was happening, the French had done two very understandable things. Though their Army in being was not initially numerically inferior to the German, they were, as they had been and would continue to be, obsessed by the consideration of their demographic inferiority. They pleaded with the British to send whatever reinforcements they could; the few British divisions that were sent proved a valuable asset in the early stages of the fighting. More importantly, the French urged the Russians to prompt action in order to relieve the pressure on themselves; the response, in the form of an invasion of East Prussia, even though it turned into the Tannenberg disaster, served the vital purpose of diverting some German force away from the Western theater, hence was an important contributing factor to the success of the Battle of the Marne.

Since the course and ultimate outcome of military operations, victory for one side or the other, or stalemate between the two, was bound to have a decisive influence on the political result of the contest, this is a good place to enter some considerations on what may be described as military diplomacy, meaning by this the use and distribution of the belligerent armies.

Of the Russians it may suffice to say that they enjoyed the usual advantages of space, weather, and numbers, while suffering from the deficiencies of backwardness in development, be it economic or political, decisive factors in the final reckoning. This condition put a premium on keeping open their lines of communication with their Western allies, a necessity which was to have a great influence on the attempted solution of the Eastern Question, as we shall presently see.

The surge of national feeling in Britain did not affect British calm at the governing level. While recognizing the magnitude of the task undertaken, the overall British approach to the war may be described as the classical. Depending on volunteers, which flocked in large numbers, for the land war, the main British contribution would, as usual, consist in naval power, control of the seas, which meant in turn keeping open the avenues of access to the wide world, the empire and the neutrals, with their unlimited resources, while denying the same advantage to the Central Powers.

The prospect of a protracted war put an obvious premium on the desirability of concerted action. That problem was minimal in the case of the Central Powers, and their eventual allies, Turkey and Bulgaria, for the overall direction of the war on their side remained to an overwhelming degree in German hands; a fact which, incidentally, goes a long way toward explaining their successes and their whole wartime performance. It was otherwise in the case of the Allies, among whom greater equality and notable divergences persisted which had their roots in a long past. To Russia the war opened the prospect of at least making progress toward the realization of her traditional ambitions, especially at the Straits, in turn a traditional focus of British opposition. France thought first of the undoing of 1870, more broadly of the elimination of the German menace; in more narrow and limited terms, the demands of manpower, hence contributions from additional allies, eventually loomed large in her considerations. Initially, the judgment is sound that "Russia had mainly striven to secure new alliances, England not to enlarge the circle of the existing ones, and France to extract the utmost from these."[64]

The German menace was common ground between Britain and France but with a marked difference of emphasis. That threat, in British eyes, was above all the one of naval and commercial competition; Britain took a broader world view than did France. She was not so certain that additional allies might not mean additional demands on her responsibilities rather than additional land forces, an aspect of things to which she was understandably less sensitive than France. And there were also points of Anglo-French rivalry, particularly in the imperial domain, although these did not loom large at first. Britain thought for a time that, while fighting a primarily naval war, she could proceed with business as usual in other respects.

As with any coalition, the most dependable cement of the Allies' combination was their common danger. This found expression in the common declaration of September 5, 1914, which pledged the three Entente Powers not to make separate peace; thereafter one may properly speak of them as "the Allies." There was point to this commitment, for doubts ever persisted in the West about the dependability of the Russian partner; the pro-German current, momentarily submerged, had never wholly died out in Russia, not least at the court itself.

The impressive performance of German arms, initially and on many occasions thereafter, made clear the desirability of co-ordination of the military action of the Allies. Discussions at the military level, passed on for decision to the political, from there returned to the military, made for modifications and delays which at times rendered plans obsolete or worse. Yet the military commanders themselves were no less jealous of their autonomy than their respective governments. Not until the breakthrough on the Italian front in November 1917 was a Supreme War Council organized, and it took the threat of disaster that was the German breakthrough on the British sector in March 1918 to procure the institution of a single command, given to General Foch. Kitchener and Robertson among the British had recognized the desirability of joint military planning, and the French had been its staunchest advocates, but the record of the attempts to overcome an obvious deficiency constitutes a long and disheartening tale, evidence of the bigoted obstinacy of national prejudice.[65]

It is difficult, for that matter, to separate the more limited aspects of this military diplomacy from the larger political motivation. Two things must here be borne in mind: the war aims of the various belligerents, and the fact that possession is nine points of the law. The military situation at the end of the war, at any point of its course in fact, could constitute a heavy mortgage on the shape of decisions and on the political outcome. The operation of these factors can best be examined under two distinct heads: the various interventions that took place, other than that of the United States; this last, because it was, like its effects, *sui generis,* quite different from any other, and which may be linked with the simultaneous occurrence of the revolution in Russia, and to the effects in turn of that convulsion.

The Interventions (Except the American), 1914–17

Faraway Japan had little direct stake in the European war itself, but her alliance with Britain was grounds for her intervention. Japan was interested in two things. In the more narrow and immediate sense, appropriation of the German position in the Far East; more broadly, extending her position in general in that part of the world. The first part of the program was easily accomplished and Japan never took an active part in the war in Europe.

There were other interests in the Far East, primarily the British, the Russian, and the American. From the beginning of 1915 Japan endeavored to extend her influence in China; her famous twenty-one demands in January of that year came close to the establishment of a protectorate, to which helpless China acceded in May. The Allies, too, eventually gave their consent to a development which in effect put the Japanese interest in competition with their own.[66] Russia was naturally concerned, but her own later difficulties led her to entertain even the possibility of the assistance of a Japanese contingent; however, nothing came of this idea.

Britain's concern was no less, for two reasons. Apart from her own large interest in China, the Japanese action was unfavorably seen by the United States, to the maintenance of good relations with whom Britain correctly attached great importance. Though there was no strong American reaction to the Japanese advance, a Japanese-American divergence was awkward from the point of view of the Allies.

In the war itself the Japanese intervention was thus a secondary episode. Not so the participation of Turkey, to which, however, it will be more convenient to return, since it was part of a much larger development, the issue of the whole Eastern Question, after dealing with matters Italian.

THE INTERVENTION OF ITALY

The war could offer Italy an opportunity to enhance her own position by furthering certain aims of her policy. Apart from the limited question of the *irredenta,* she had been seeking to extend her influence in the Adriatic, the Balkans, and the eastern Mediterranean in general. Having once declared her neutrality, she had obviously no stake in a victory of the Central Powers. Two roads were therefore open to her: continued adherence to neutrality; intervention on the side of the Allies. She would naturally expect a higher reward from the second course because of the greater cost it would entail.

No one was more grateful than the French for the initial Italian neutrality, which eliminated the need to man an Alpine front. Given the circumstances, it was unlikely that Italy would at a later point rejoin her former allies, but to join in the war at once against them might have seemed somewhat indecent precipitateness; Italian opinion, though divided in its sympathies, was on the whole quite content with neutrality.

It was impulsive Sazonov who entertained the thought of an immediate Italian intervention on the Allied side. His advances met no response from Rome, and little more in Paris or in London. Especially after the Marne, Italy, under the guidance of her Prime Minister, Salandra, and her foreign minister, Sonnino,[67] set about coolly examining prospects: what price for neutrality, what price for intervention? Negotiations were accordingly carried out, at times simultaneously, in Vienna and in London, the last a significant fact in itself, reflection of the traditionally common orientation of British and Italian policies, of the power of Britain, not to mention the justifiably greater confidence that secrecy would be better preserved in London than in Paris.

The Austrian negotiation did not prosper, despite the intromission of Germany's good offices, for understandable reasons if rather narrow considerations on the part of Austria. The Allies could be more generous, though a staunch Russian resistance was met in the protection of the South Slav interest on which the Italian impinged. But finally a compromise was reached, registered in the Treaty of London of April 26, 1915, and Italy went to war in May.[68]

To repeat, it is significant that London was the center of negotiations and Petrograd the chief center of opposition to the Italian demands. The French role was relatively secondary, France, like Russia for that matter, being highly interested in the asset of Italian manpower. It was England, appropriately, who furnished a loan—a paltry sum in retrospect—of £50,000,000. The disappointing results of the Italian intervention have been mentioned; another front was brought into existence, but the war went on as before.

BALKAN AFFAIRS

When Italy entered the fray the war had already spread beyond the circle of its initial participants. The British and the French were engaged in the attempt to reopen communications with Russia through the Straits, closed to them already in September. This situation opened the door to what seemed for a time, and in some respects turned out to be, a settlement of the Eastern Question, the fate of the whole Ottoman Empire. For convenience again, this will be dealt with under two heads: the European part, the Balkans; the Asiatic segment, Turkey proper and the Arab world. The two aspects, needless to say, were intertwined and chronologically overlap.

In Turkey, after the revolution of 1908 and the momentary hopes to which that revolution had given rise, the German influence became increasingly entrenched and remained so despite what was generally regarded as the setback of the Balkan Wars; the Turkish Army was being reorganized under German sponsorship—the Liman von Sanders flurry may be recalled[69]—although a British admiral was in charge of corresponding naval matters and some warships for Turkey were building in British yards.

A measure of the German influence was the treaty of alliance that was signed on August 2, 1914. The Turkish case was the reverse of the Italian: either neutrality or involvement on the side of the Central Powers; Turkish counsels, like Italian, were divided and diplomacy was active in Constantinople. The final push was provided by the incident of the bombardment of Odessa[70] in October, which prompted the Allies to take the initiative of a break.

Turkish power as such was no very great threat; the closure of the Straits was more serious. From this it was a natural step to the idea of reopening the passage, a proposal which found its most ardent advocates in Britain, Churchill being foremost among them. This imaginative conception raised a host of questions.

The whole Balkan situation for one. Thus, in view of the demands on Allied forces elsewhere, the asset of Greek participation would obviously be useful. But the Greek king, of pro-German leanings himself and a believer in German victory, was opposed to his country's intervention; it came to the resignation of his prime minister, Venizelos, who represented the pro-Allied current in Greece. Greece would of course have expected some compensation and this in turn raised the problem of Bulgaria. That country was, like Turkey, under the dominant influence of the Central Powers, nourishing grievances since the Balkan Wars against all her Balkan neighbors. The tale of Allied diplomatic activity in Greece, Bulgaria, Serbia and Roumania is long and involved.[71] It proved impossible to reconcile these differences between Bulgaria and her neighbors, despite promises of guarantee of territorial integrity and even an attempt to secure Greek and especially Serbian concessions. Something more will be said of this.

But, returning to the projected expedition to the Straits, an unexpected difficulty appeared. The scheme might have been thought to be welcome to Russia. Instead of this the dominant reaction, in view of Russia's inability to participate in the operation herself, was one of fear lest Western flags, mainly the British, but the Greek as well, be raised over Constantinople.

The outcome of this complication may well be called surprising, for it was the surrender by Britain of a position to which she had staunchly adhered for a century and at one time had even gone to war against Russia to defend. Here again it was appropriate that London should be the center of negotiations, although Paris was consulted. The memorandum that Grey received from Sazonov on March 5 proposed no less than the radical solution of the outright acquisition of Constantinople by Russia. Perhaps the most remarkable aspect of the matter is the relative ease with which Grey acceded to the Russian demand, a concession that must be seen as the result of doubts in regard to the steadfastness of Russia's purpose. Russia must be kept in the war at almost any price, and Grey took seriously Sazonov's threat of resignation,[72] with its implication of a possible change of political orientation in Russia.

Actually, it was France, where Delcassé was again foreign minister, which showed the greater reluctance and whose consent was not forthcoming until a month after the British.[73] Russia was prepared to respect the rights of others in Constantinople, but there certainly was point to the French observation that so radical a solution of the problem of the Straits raised the still larger question of the fate of the whole Ottoman Empire. And this is what happened in fact, for Pandora's box had been opened; a long negotiation resulted in a proposed solution of that problem. We shall return to it in a moment but will first briefly complete the story of Balkan affairs.

The projected Anglo-French expedition to the Straits was launched. As the Straits could not be forced by naval power alone, the Gallipoli Peninsula became a battleground. The Allies did not know how close they came to success and the result was failure and withdrawal. Whereupon they shifted their forces to Salonika at the "invitation" of Greece. That country, torn between rival factions, of which the king and Venizelos continued to be the chief representatives, was thereby placed in a wholly anomalous position, its "neutrality" at best highly qualified.

However, the Allied forces in Salonika remained inactive, while diplomacy was the opposite in Sofia and in Bucharest. Of the intricate story it will suffice to retain the outcome, although this must be mentioned. Russia was of course an active participant, but so were the Western Allies, France especially, less suspect than Russia in Roumania. In that country popular sentiment was generally pro-Western, again in contrast with the predilection of the king. With claims against both Austria-Hungary and Russia, Roumania was in a position somewhat comparable to Italy. Under Bratianu's leadership she kept hedging and haggling.

The idea of a Greek-Roumanian combination, making use of the Allied force in Salonika, was entertained more than once. It held the possibility, especially in view of the stalemate on the Western front, of taking the enemy in the rear. But, apart from the difficulty of resolving the Greek deadlock and of meeting Roumania's rather exorbitant demands and her tergiversations, there was always the problem of Bulgaria.

This was resolved in a sense when that country went to war in October 1915. The prize of Macedonia proved too tempting, which it was obviously easier for the Central Powers to promise than for Serbia voluntarily to surrender. Serbia was overrun and additional strains were placed on Greek neutrality when the remnants of the Serbian Army found shelter in Corfu, then were transported to Salonika.

Almost another year went by before, having secured her price from the Allies, Roumania joined them in active war, in August 1916. She had waited too long—an initially successful Russian offensive had turned into a near debacle—and she was largely overrun by Austro-German forces. It took even longer for Greece to make the same decision, in June 1917, a decision in the making of which the Allies, again mainly the French in this case, used more forceful arguments than the diplomatic.[74]

Except in the Greek case, and to a point in the Serbian, Russia was more directly concerned in Balkan affairs than were the Western Powers. Greece, despite the French action, was, for geographical reasons, of considerable interest to Britain, as she had been for a long time. What is worth noting in the Balkan situation is the degree to which the work of diplomacy, British and French like that of others, was subservient to military considerations. One is impressed by the relatively ineffectual role of diplomacy in bringing about interventions; Balkan decisions were far more influenced by the state of the war map and to an important degree by the views of dominant personalities in the various countries involved. In the case of the Balkan states in particular, Grey's judgment seems justified.[75]

At all events, in connection with the Balkan interventions a variety of commitments had been made, the justification of which lay in large measure in the necessities of war as they appeared at the time of their making. These commitments were clearly all of them mortgages on the future, in more homely language, chickens that would come home to roost. Because of the outcome of the war in Allied victory, they largely came to roost in London and in Paris, which is why mention of them has been made.

THE "SETTLEMENT" OF THE EASTERN QUESTION

Among the Balkan states Greece constituted an exception owing to her maritime position. The shrewd Cretan Venizelos had made his own the *megala idea,* the creation of a Greek empire centered on the Aegean through the adjunction to Greece of a section of the Anatolian littoral, especially around Smyrna; through the vicissitudes of more than two millennia much of the Greek character of that region had survived.

This was but one of the many claims, or hopes, to which the demise of the Ottoman Empire offered prospects of realization, following the first step on that road that was the Constantinople agreement of March 1915. Apart from the Greek design just indicated, four Powers had interests in the region, the three participants in the Constantinople agreement and Italy. This last, brought into the war as a consequence of the Treaty of London of April 1915, had not shared in the agreement, the two negotiatons, the Russian and the Italian, being conducted simultaneously but independently in London and Paris. However, the Treaty of London registered, if only in loose form, Italy's interest in the Near East.

It is of interest and significance that the plans for the eventual partition of the Ottoman Empire were in large measure Anglo-French plans. They fall under two heads, the Arab world and the rest.

The Turkish hold on the former[76] was loose and in some respects ill defined. The section of the Arab world bounded by the Red Sea, the Persian Gulf, and the Fertile Crescent presented a wide range of diversity; in some of it one may speak of a nationalistic sentiment, in other parts feudal conditions and rivalries prevailed. Either condition offered possibilities that it logically fell to the British, owing to their established positions on the periphery of the area, to attempt to exploit. The negotiations conducted from Cairo, and from Simla to some extent, led in 1915 to an understanding of sorts whereby the British undertook to support Arab independence under the leadership of Sherif Hussein of Mecca.[77]

It was the turn of the French to intrude by asserting their

claims in the Near East, centered particularly on Syria. A series of negotiations between London and Paris at the turn from 1915 to 1916, in which Sir Mark Sykes and Georges Picot were the chief representatives of their respective countries, led to the agreement which bears their names. The understanding was notified to Russia, where Sazonov's reaction, as might be expected, was that Russia should have a share in any partition of Asiatic Turkey. The final outcome provided for such a share in Armenia, adjacent to the Russo-Turkish border. This Russian zone abutted in turn on the French sector, which reached all the way to Palestine, this last to be placed under international status. The French had claimed it initially—it was but the southern extremity of the vilayet of Syria—but that would have brought them too close to Suez for British comfort. In addition, a zone of influence, reaching as far as Mosul, which it included, was also allotted to them, while a similar British zone in Mesopotamia extended from Baghdad to the Persian Gulf. The French had had to fight hard against both their allies, but in the end agreement was reached which, in terms of power balance, may be called a fair compromise.[78]

All this, interestingly enough, was done without consulting Italy. But the question she raised when she got wind of the scheme—"What about me?"—could only be answered by providing a share for her as well. This was found in Anatolia, the southern half of which, adjacent to the French zone and including Smyrna,[79] was allotted to her, together with an additonal adjoining sphere toward the Straits. As with the British at Suez, the Russians had no wish to see anybody else established too close to that sensitive area; here also the French had fought hard against making concessions at the expense of their own share. The meeting of the British, French, and Italians at St-Jean-de-Maurienne in April 1917 registered these compromise results.

The independent Turkey that was left, a fraction of Anatolia, may be regarded as an absurdity, an insult to Turkish national feeling, as in effect turned out to be the case. The aspect of these arrangements to be retained at this point is the fact that, because of the war, the three Powers which had dealt with the initial stages of the Eastern Question, almost a hundred years before, had finally contrived a solution of it, essentially on the basis of their mutual power relationships. The effect of changing conditions during the intervening period would not be long in appearing, but in any event the British and the French roles, and their competition in that part of the world were not finished; what has just been related is but a chapter in a continuing story.

The approach which led to the conclusion of the agreements just described was extended to the sharing of the German colonies, all of which were overrun in the course of the war.[80] There is no need to go into the specific details of their distribution beyond noting that they, too, were manifestations of the long record of Anglo-French imperial competition, amicably resolved in this instance.

One thing that should be noted is the factor of continuity of development. Having become fully aware of the importance of the nodal point of Suez, the British had steadily endeavored to obtain control of that passage. This they did with success, entrenching themselves ever more firmly in Egypt while at the same time expanding their interest in the region of the Persian Gulf; safety of communications, and the increasing importance of access to oil supplies, were the dominant motives. The war presented them with an opportunity to crown their work; this is the chief significance of the series of agreements which has just been described; in simplest form it seemed that the gap between Suez and Basra had largely been closed with the establishment of their pre-eminent influence in much of the Arab world. In their steady endeavor they had confronted French and Russian interests. As to the French, while it might seem that to a degree at least they were re-entering the Near East, it may be observed that in doing this they had had to contend with three other influences, the British, the Russian, and the Italian, to the first two of which they had had to make concessions.

THE IMPACT OF THE POLISH PROBLEM

Another instance warrants mention in which France was deeply involved. Poland was the initial battleground in the

East, and Polish national hopes had never died, for which there was sympathy in both Britain and France. These countries could hardly afford to intrude, however, in a situation that their Russian ally insisted on considering a domestic problem. Both Sazonov in Petrograd and Izvolsky in Paris made this quite clear to their French ally; as the former put it to Paléologue, the French ambassador in Russia: "Beware of Poland, it is dangerous ground for a French ambassador."[81]

But the fortunes of war furnished opportunities to the Poles. It was only natural that both sides in the war should seek to enlist Polish support, in doing which they adopted parallel policies, a measure of autonomy for part or all of Poland, though never complete independence. The vicissitudes of Polish affairs will not be dwelt upon beyond noting the similarity of the contending approaches of the Central Powers and of Russia. The Poles themselves thought in primarily Polish terms. While Pilsudski was for a time attracted by the German offer, there were those who thought of a return to the 1815 type of arrangement, a constitutional kingdom in personal union with Russia.

Britain and France were generally sympathetic to the cause of self-determination; for France especially it was the strongest basis of the claim to the recovery of Alsace-Lorraine. But the necessities of war, the never stilled doubts about the solidity of the Russian allegiance, and the French desire for future guarantee against the German danger, led to a Franco-Russian negotiation, which Doumergue went to Russia to conclude.[82] The result, at the beginning of 1917, was the agreement whereby either country underwrote in advance a free hand to the other in the settlement of its German frontier: Russia could have her way with Poland, as far as France was concerned, in exchange for which Russia would not object to an attempt to push Germany back beyond the whole course of the Rhine. The precise form that this arrangement would take remained unspecified—probably an independent buffer Rhineland state—but here was proof that the age-old French pursuit of "natural" frontiers had not been abandoned.

What Are We Fighting for?

THE INTRUSION OF AMERICAN POWER

The British and the French had entered the war in the conviction that they were defending themselves against German aggression. Beyond the first aim of survival the next question therefore was victory in conditions that would insure against the recurrence of the threat of German hegemony. The recovery of the lost provinces of 1871 was the clearest French hope; the British aim had no such precise territorial focus. Grey himself acknowledges that he entertained the possibility of a prompt restoration of peace if the initial German bid for victory was a failure.[83] We know what happened instead.

The Allies' diplomatic activity was thereafter largely dominated by the military necessities of the war though the far-reaching plans for Near Eastern rearrangements must not be forgotten. In the previous section the result of their efforts, the various interventions and the commitments that grew out of them, have been mentioned. Taken together these constituted a program of sorts for the future peace, an unco-ordinated plan, however, made up of bits and pieces, dictated by immediate circumstances as well as by long-established trends of policy.

Insofar as general principles existed, the British especially were well placed to contend that they were fighting for justice in general, for the rights of small nations as usual; the case of Belgium lent itself to this claim to perfection. There was little likelihood that the Germans would agree to any such program so long as they believed that victory would ultimately be theirs, and so long as the Allies adhered to the same view, there was clearly no meeting ground between the belligerent camps. That is the fundamental reason why the war lasted as long as it did and ended in total victory.

Vis-à-vis the world as a whole, the Western Allies especially enjoyed a certain advantage in that they could contend, allowing for the Irish qualification in the British case, that they were upholding the right of self-determination, which could in turn be linked, at least up to a point, with the broad democratic principle.

It was a simple fact after all that in Britain and France parliament was supreme whereas it was not so in Germany. It was likewise a fact that Germany contained various non-German groups and that Austria-Hungary was the very denial of the principle of nationality. These were real assets for the Allies, even apart from the merits of democracy and self-determination, for these principles represented the dominant trends of nineteenth-century historic evolution. In this context Russia was by way of being an embarrassment, though even she had taken the first hesitant steps toward constitutional practice after the 1905 revolution. The whole series of secret agreements could likewise be a source of embarrassment, which the British would defend apologetically on the score of necessity.[84]

Among the neutrals the United States stood in a position apart, both because of its past history and of its power. That power had had relatively little cause to play an active part in the game of power politics and imperial competition, the emphasis being on *relatively*. Certainly the United States was largely detached from the quarrels of Europe, as President Wilson very correctly put it; isolation was not so much a theory as a happy condition of fact. The power was there nevertheless, and the days of American innocence, such as it was, were about to come to an end. Lost innocence is not recoverable.

President Wilson was highly conscious of American power, not to say, which was more debatable and dangerous, of American moral superiority. Neither he nor the American people thought in terms of exploiting the war situation for selfish national advantage. If in the end America profited from the war in handsome fashion, in terms of economic and power position,[85] this was the unplanned result of circumstances; no one has argued that the war did not grow out of European quarrels, and the United States had nothing to do with the collective suicide of Europe.

It was entirely clear that the role of the United States could be of crucial importance, even though the phrase "arsenal of democracy" is of Second World War vintage and no one on either side of the ocean thought of American involvement in 1914 and for a long time thereafter. The initial reaction of the American President to the fact of war was, however, that he might play an important and useful mediating role between the belligerents. What hopes he entertained on that score in the early stages of the conflict were soon dashed by the irreconcilability of the contestants.

But while insisting and believing that America must remain outside the conflict, the hope of mediation persisted. It was the reason for the exploratory missions on which Colonel House went to Europe in the first half of 1915 and again a year later. He could only report back negatively, but his perceptive judgment is worth retaining, which he made at the very beginning of the war: "If the Allies win, it means largely the dominance of Russia on the Continent of Europe; and if Germany wins, it means the unspeakable tyranny of militarism for generations to come."[86] In passing, one will note the implied appraisal of power standing of the various belligerents. House's judgment may be juxtaposed to that of Paléologue on the score of the consequences of the Constantinople agreement of March 1915 for the future of the European equilibrium.[87] Finally, we may also cite House's somewhat premature, though ultimately correct, appraisal after his 1915 visit to Europe: "I have concluded that war with Germany is inevitable."[88] Wilson was not so convinced at this time, nor was the mass of the American people.

The chief significance of the United States in the war lay therefore in American resources, economic and eventually also financial. In dealing with the United States the Allies enjoyed two advantages which were corresponding disabilities for the Central Powers. Control of the seas gave the former an access to those resources which they could in turn deny to their enemies. This was no simple matter, however, and something more will have to be said of it in a moment. It naturally fell to the British to act as chief spokesmen and intermediaries for the Allies in Washington, in doing which the asset of common language, more broadly of the English derivation of American institutions and culture, was no inconsiderable factor. The French were less well known. Franco-American relations have been characterized by an emotive character, an alternation of often violent ups and downs. The Lafayette escadrille was American. The French nevertheless enjoyed at this time the asset of appreciable sympathy for their role in the war, and their ambassador in Washington, Jusserand, dean of the diplomatic corps, was an apt representative, in the best French diplomatic tradition. This was his appraisal of the American President:

> The accidents of politics have brought a president raised in the academic milieu, among books, in the midst of abstract ideas, fonder of meditating the written word than of talking with the witness, and who is intimidated by the necessity to take suddenly far reaching decisions.[89]

The British, not surprisingly, knew America better than did other Europeans. The general line of their policy may be described as one of accepting with good grace, if perhaps with mingled pride and some regret, the rise of America; instances of this have been cited before.[90] However, some serious problems arose in connection with maritime trade, the rules of which in time of war had not been fully clarified, despite the most recent attempt, the London Declaration of 1909.[91] A host of questions provided occupation for international lawyers, turned into sea lawyers in every sense of the word. In brief, and quite naturally, the opposing tendencies were on the British side to extend the range of the rights of belligerents while the United States insisted upon those of neutrals, so long at least as it itself remained neutral. These were the chief contenders, the French following the British lead, the neutrals the American.

Here also the Germans were at a disadvantage. Apart from the loophole of trade through such neutrals as Holland and the Scandinavian countries, their chief hope lay in denying Britain the supplies on which she was vitally dependent. Given the inferiority of their surface fleet, they resorted to the submarine weapon. But, clearly, a controversy over a detained ship or contraband is of a different order from one over the casualties of a ship sunk without warning. There was considerable tension in 1915, which induced Germany to yield to American representations and to relent on submarine warfare. All the while American industry and trade prospered from the demands of the Allies, creating an increasing American stake in the Allied cause, one not to be confused, however, with the crudely oversimplified legends about wicked bankers and merchants of death—was not the American farmer equally "wicked"? As late as 1916 President Wilson was re-elected after a campaign during which the most had been made of the slogan "He kept us out of war."

But, at the beginning of 1917, the Germans, seeing no way to ultimate victory despite their military successes, once more adopted for their policy the criterion which had caused them to invade Belgium in 1914, necessity is the higher law. They duly notified the United States that they would henceforth resort to the tactics of unrestricted submarine warfare. It was a calculated risk on their part, based on the assumption that the probable consequence, American intervention, would have no appreciable military effect. The first part of their judgment proved correct. Following a breach of relations in February and some exchanges, on April 6 the United States went to war. This intervention affected the future course of events in two ways. It insured for one thing the ultimate complete defeat of Germany and her allies; more importantly in the context of this discussion, it had a tremendous effect on the position of all the belligerents. Before dealing with this second aspect we must go back a little in time and briefly consider some other developments.

THE IMPACT OF WAR-WEARINESS

Reference has been made before to the nature of war aims, British and French in particular; they were shaped in large measure by the drift of circumstances and found expression in the above-mentioned series of secret commitments. The adaptation of policy to the change in conditions is what mainly concerns us here. The year 1917 witnessed the convergence of a number of seemingly unrelated, or even discordant, events.

It was in December 1916 that the Germans, unsure of the future, sought to capitalize on their successes, the latest of which was the overrunning of Roumania, to launch a peace offensive. The offer to discuss peace terms was hardly seriously meant—it carefully avoided specifics—but was important nonetheless for the appeal it could have to the war-weary masses everywhere. Neutral America was entrusted with the transmittal of the German proposal.

Interestingly, this was the cause of some annoyance to President Wilson, for the reason that to a point it cut the ground from under his feet. His own proposal that all the belligerents make a declaration of their war aims with a view to finding common ground could appear as an anticlimactic afterthought, even though it was not. In any case the necessity of furnishing some answer prompted the Allies to certain consultations, after which they formulated their reply. Disingenuous in part as it was, that reply reflected the above-mentioned advantages of their position in contrast with the German; to ask for the restoration of Belgium, for example, and to espouse the principle of nationality in broad terms amounted to calling Germany's bluff. The episode had no far-reaching consequences, but it was the first of a series which had the effect of emphasizing the ideological character of the war instead of that of a classical power struggle.

The Austrian attempt to reach an understanding does not belong in this category and will not be dwelt upon.[92] The same applies to the Pope's note of August, but two other events took on overwhelming importance.

From the standpoint of the struggle for power the year 1917 witnessed the defection of Russia, whose place in the conflict was taken by the United States. It was to prove a most worthwhile substitution for the Allies, yet for a brief time the two events worked to similar effect. The reaction of Socialists among the initial belligerents had resulted in the demise of the Second International. But Socialism was not dead, and as the struggle endured it showed signs of revival. The meetings that took place at Kienthal and in Zimmerwald in Switzerland, where representatives of both belligerent camps and of neutrals met, were small things though significant. Of far greater importance was the transformation that took place in Russia in March 1917. It was not unwelcome by the Allies, no longer embarrassed by the Russian autocracy, so long at least as the new constitutional régime kept Russia in the war, which it did while proclaiming its adherence to the commitments made by the tsarist government. But six months were enough to change things in radical fashion. Russia had in effect collapsed under the weight of an effort that her backwardness made it impossible for her to sustain. When, in November, the Bolsheviks swept away the moderate and ineffectual reformers, they constituted by a minute fraction of the Russian mass. But they did have the support of that mass in its desire to withdraw from the struggle; the Army "voted with its feet" by going home. Consistent Marxists that they were, after appealing to all without distinction, former allies and enemies alike, to end the war on the basis of "no annexations or indemnities," but finding no response to their appeal, the Bolsheviks proceeded to make their own peace, in fact a total surrender.

The lack of response to their pleas showed that among the other belligerents the governments retained sufficient control; yet this was no proper measure of the real response. The appeal of the Bolsheviks and their disclosures of the doings of wartime diplomacy served to emphasize the need to clarify war aims, especially among the Western Allies, who had suffered an enormous setback and must now continue the war without Russia, at least pending the still problematic day when the American potential would have become effective fighting power.

THE AMERICAN ROLE IN THE FINAL SHAPING OF WAR AIMS

Where they themselves were concerned the Bolsheviks had for the moment merely yielded to the inescapable fact of defeat. If they made little distinction among the rest of the belligerents, all capitalist states, the Russians had ostensibly espoused at least eventual democracy and certainly self-determination. These were principles that the British and the French had endorsed, even if some of their commitments, made public by the Bolsheviks, raised certain awkward questions. But America's hands were unquestionably clean and President Wilson need not indulge in any squirming in order to explain the American purpose. Thus for a time the influences of Wilson and Lenin worked to the same general effect. But as the Russian influence at the level of states disappeared as a consequence of the Russian defeat and of the chaos that engulfed the country thereafter, America was left alone in the position of political leadership based on real power.

The result of these circumstances, as just indicated, was to create pressure on the Allied leaders to clarify their purpose, a pressure made all the greater by the fact of war-weariness.

The French had stood fast at Verdun, but there were mutinies in the French Army in the year 1917, the end of which saw near disaster on the Italian front. To talk of victory was very well but had a hollow ring. Could victory be achieved, and if so, at what price and to what purpose? The letter of Lord Lansdowne which appeared in the *Daily Telegraph* at the end of November expressed the mood of discouragement—or reasonableness in another interpretation. While agreeing that "reparations and security" were both desirable, he was sceptical of the first in a conflict the prolongation of which could only "spell ruin to the civilized world"; he was willing therefore to settle for security, and proposed, though in general terms, a program which he thought could constitute an acceptable basis of negotiations. To that end, according to him, it should be made clear:

1. That we do not desire the annihilation of Germany as a Great Power;
2. That we do not seek to impose upon her people any form of Government other than that of their own choice;
3. That, except as a legitimate war measure, we have no desire to deny to Germany her place among the great commercial communities of the world;
4. That we are prepared, when the war is over, to examine in concert with other powers the groups of international problems, some of them of recent origin, which are connected with the question of "the freedom of the seas";
5. That we are prepared to enter into an international pact under which ample opportunities will be afforded for the settlement of international disputes by peaceful means.[93]

The English origin and the nature of this proposal should be noted in passing: no territorial issues were specifically mentioned, while stress was put on the economic aspects of the future. Translated into concrete terms, this program might easily produce something not very different from the Bolshevik-advocated peace without annexations or indemnities; it would be difficult to reconcile with the distinction, especially emphasized in American quarters, between the German leadership—Prussian militarism—and the good German people.[94]

The British Government did not feel that it could ignore the mood of which Lansdowne's proposal was one of the expressions. Lloyd George, who had displaced Asquith in the prime ministership a year earlier, was a far more vigorous and determined war leader than his predecessor; his problem was to reconcile the continued pursuit of Britain's war aims with the growing desire for an end of the conflict. This he attempted in a speech which he delivered to the Trade Unions on January 5, 1918. It was a very important declaration and a fair indication of where Britain stood and of what she thought could be achieved. The following quotation will suffice to give an indication of the degree of precision to which Lloyd George could arrive:

> The first requirement always put forward by the British Government and their Allies has been the complete restoration, political, territorial and economic, of the independence of Belgium, and such reparation as can be made for the destruction of its towns and provinces. Next comes the restoration of Servia, Montenegro and the occupied parts of France, Italy and Roumania. We mean to stand by the French democracy to the death in the demand they make for a reconsideration of the great wrong of 1871. We shall be proud to fight to the end side by side with the new democracy of Russia. But if her present rulers take action which is independent of the Allies, we have no means of intervening to avert the catastrophe which is assuredly befalling their country. Russia can only be saved by her own people. We believe, however, that an independent Poland, comprising all those genuinely Polish elements who desire to form part of it, is an urgent necessity for the stability of western Europe.[95]

Here were some definite things even if considerable room was left for maneuver and final implementation. The impending defection of Russia was in some respects a godsend, since it made possible a reopening of the whole Eastern Question as the settlement of that problem had been arranged in the above-described agreements.

Thus the belligerents, Britain at least, were taking a great step toward a possible compromise. But the contenders were still too far apart and nothing came of Lloyd George's proposal, reduced to an appeal to British and to world opinion; for one thing, the German command had still not abandoned the hope of victory for its arms. In addition, Lloyd George's speech was superseded by a not very different American declaration three days later, Wilson's famous Fourteen Points. Here is a prime example of the role of power, for in the fact of American power lies the reason for the role destined to be played by the American statement. The Wilsonian program evoked little response in Germany at the time, but from all the Allies came assent, even if it was in some cases mere lip service.

We shall not reproduce this often quoted charter of the future, of which it is enough to extract the main points. The complete espousal of the principle of nationality was, for the short term, the most important; less so were such general principles as advocated in phrases like "open covenants, openly arrived at" or "freedom of the seas"; for the longer-term future, the last of the Fourteen Points, the advocacy of an association of nations to create order where anarchy had hitherto prevailed, had great potential significance. It was Wilson's own and most cherished contribution.[96]

Meanwhile the war went on, and American power made possible another thing, the total victory of the Allies. Germany had miscalculated again; not only was the American potential effectively mobilized, but German submarines failed to prevent its conveyance to Europe. In the face of this fact, and after the failure of their 1918 offensives on the Western front, the German command came to the rational conclusion that an end should be put to the war, a task for the accomplishment of which they "rediscovered" the civilian government, on whose shoulders the responsibility for the delicate operation could be unloaded.[97]

Some very interesting things happened at this juncture. The Fourteen Points were likewise "discovered" in Germany, and on the basis of their promise the German Government approached the American, not the Allies, be it noted. Although America insisted on calling itself an "associated," rather than an "Allied," Power, clearly Wilson must secure from the Allies a mandate to act as their spokesman. An extremely important discussion ensued, the climax of which occurred at the turn from October to November, when the Allied leaders met with Colonel House to consider the question. The discussion centered around the precise meaning of the Fourteen Points; it was a close and even heated debate, but American power—the dangled threat of separate action—prevailed in the end. Thus, with two relatively innocuous reservations, one British (freedom of the seas) and one French (the precise scope of restoration), the Fourteen Points became the basis of the future peace.[98]

The first step was the conclusion of an armistice, a technical military question, which was arranged and took effect on November 11.[99] It was tantamount to a total German surrender, thereby creating another ambiguity. For the victors had it in their power to deal with their enemies as they wished, but at the same time they were of their own free will—or at least under American prodding—committed to the Fourteen Points. The factor of American power had been responsible for this outcome. How far the American program could be reconciled with the aims of the power relationships of Europe, which traditional diplomacy had written into the series of wartime commitments, was a large question indeed. Would these aims, especially those of the British and the French, merely be swept away and disregarded, superseded by a new order that would insure impartial justice for all? The least that could be said is that the role of British and of French diplomacy had been notably minimized as a consequence of the American intrusion into the conflict. It was not difficult to foretell that the issue would constitute one of the central problems of the making of the peace, a process in which the influence of power relationships was shortly to appear, and which we shall now proceed to examine.

The Peace

The task of making peace after the First World War was an immense undertaking, vastly more difficult than it had been a hundred years before. The fundamental reason for the difference lay in the changes that a century had brought about, the most important of which may be summed up as the spread of democracy, the rising of the mass in a broad sense. The slogan, appropriately of American coinage, "to make the world safe for democracy," was adequate summation of the change; but in it could also be found a warning, for it was the expression of dangerous hopes and illusions. The war had been fought by the peoples, and their expectations were understandably high, demagogically encouraged at times. Lloyd George's phrase, "a world fit for heroes to live in," was irresponsible promise; such a world may have been deserved, but how would the damage of war be made good save by more sweat and hardship? This should of course be the lot of the guilty, but none acknowledged guilt in their own eyes, with the consequence that universal consensus on the desirability of a peace based on justice became in concrete terms translated into violent disagreement and bitterest frustration. Without expatiating on the psychological climate of 1919, one must never lose sight of it as the background against which the peace was to be made—or attempted. The irreconcilability of various national expectations is too obvious to need more detailed explanation. The psychological factor just alluded to was of special importance in the democratic countries, the victors—they held genuine elections after all—but one must not forget that Germany, too, had undergone a revolution of sorts, got rid of her Kaiser, and adopted a new democratic constitution. Had not the "good"—as good as others anyway—German people been told that the Allies had no quarrel with them, but only with their wicked Prussian, militaristic masters?

The decision to reverse the procedure of 1815 of negotiating the peace with the participation of the defeated enemy meant that the main decisions were essentially in the hands of three Powers, more narrowly of their chief representatives, Wilson, Lloyd George, and Clemenceau, the Big Three of 1919.[100]

Wilson, representing American power, could not be ignored, nor did he mean to be. His ambitions were high and his intentions pure, too pure perhaps, though it is undeniable that America, confident in her strength, sought no advantage for herself, in which respect she was in a category apart. Wilson was highly aware of the moral superiority of his standing, himself little acquainted with or interested in the details of European quarrels, which he tended to view with Olympian detachment. His approach to these problems was simple, bordering on naïveté: he would depend on the advice of a large staff of competent and disinterested—qualities which indeed they possessed to a high degree—"experts"; as he put it to them on one occasion: "Tell me what's right, and I'll fight for it." The question "What is truth?" had been heard by another Messiah. The idiosyncrasies of the American President did not make him the best of negotiators or diplomats. Clemenceau's double-edged reference to Wilson's "noble candor" is worth recalling.[101]

Lloyd George was certainly energetic and able, though his knowledge of the foreign domain was, like Wilson's, scant. He was genial as well, but also mercurial, endowed with perceptive political antennae, hence too responsive to the shifting winds of opinion, which he was not above manipulating and exploiting. Undependable therefore to a degree, he had definite ideas about what constituted the British interest. Old Clemenceau, the strongest personality of the three, was disillusioned and cynical; "the tiger" was his nickname in French politics. A cultured man, admirer of old Greece, intelligent and sharp-witted, he could be ruthless; like many Frenchmen, who have no especially high regard for their own kind, he was yet a sincere patriot and, like Lloyd George, had clear notions on the score of the national interest; but he was also realistic and understood power well.

Tardieu, Clemenceau's right-hand man, gives a vivid description of how these men, who held the fate of much of the world in their hands, worked together:

> The tone was conversational, no pose, no show. Orlando spoke little. It was a dialogue of three—an astonishing contrast of natures the most opposite one could meet or conceive. The dialogue was at times tragic in its grave simplicity; at times almost gay—always direct and sincere. That one duped the other is a legend. From beginning to end they discussed with a profound desire to agree. Wilson argued like an academician who criticises a thesis, sitting upright in his armchair, developing his ideas with the clarity of a didactic logician. Lloyd George discussed like a sharpshooter, with sudden cordialities and equally sudden explosions, his knee in his hands, armed with prodigious indifference to technical arguments, drawn instinctively toward unexpected courses, dazzling in verve and inventiveness, responsive only to the great permanent reasons of solidarity and justice, in constant apprehension of Parliamentary repercussions. Clemenceau's dialectic, instead of being built on syllogisms like Wilson's, or exploding like that of Lloyd George, proceeded by massive affirmations, often animated by fascinating emotion.[102]

Since our concern lies with Britain and France, it is primarily the role of these two countries that will be examined, but no attempt will be made to relate the full tale of their respective records; a selective treatment will suffice to bring out the policies of the two countries and the behavior of their representatives.

The French Position and the French Problem

During the war France, like Britain, had made certain commitments, either out of inescapable necessity or in order to further certain interests, as in the Near East, for example. These could hardly, however, be called a co-ordinated program of war aims. Insofar as such a program existed, it was largely induced by the effort that the war had entailed.[103] To this there was one concrete qualification; the recovery of the loss of 1871 was always taken for granted once the war had begun, though by itself that question would hardly have led France to take the initiative of hostilities. However, the performance of German power produced an overwhelming desire to guard against the recurrence of a confrontation. The legitimacy of this wish was generally acknowledged by others, the question being how to give it satisfaction. Security, more than anything else, was *the* peace aim of France.

The French endeavor to achieve security had two aspects, the territorial and the military; there was in addition the determination to collect compensation for the damage suffered in the war. The territorial issue centered on the disposition of the left bank of the Rhine. Foch[104] and many others insisted that German power must be confined to the other side of that river. Little time was lost over the possibility of outright annexation, to which both Wilson and Lloyd George were adamantly opposed. As the latter put it, "At my first visit to Paris my strongest impression was the statue of Strasbourg in mourning. Do not let us make another Alsace-Lorraine."[105] It was a telling argument, especially if one espoused the principle of self-determination, and the Russian Revolution had deprived the Franco-Russian agreement of 1917 of whatever weight it might otherwise have carried.

There was a second line of defense. The Rhineland might be detached from the main body of Germany and erected into one or more independent buffer states; there were even those enthusiasts in France who envisaged a return to the fragmented Germany of pre-1871. That possibility, too, ran counter to the right of self-determination, for the making of Germany had been in the trend of historic development. But the strategic argument was not to be lightly dismissed. There were many, sometimes even heated, discussions among the Three, especially between Wilson and Clemenceau[106]; Wilson was even rumored to have threatened to leave the conference at one point. His argument that the future League of Nations would provide for the security of France, as of everyone else, was too divorced from existing reality to carry much conviction.

The stalemate was finally broken through a compromise. The Rhineland would remain German, but it would be demilitarized, as well as a fifty-kilometer band on the right bank of the Rhine[107]; in addition, it would be occupied for a number of years. Most important of all, the United States and Britain entered into treaties with France whereby they promised her assistance in the event of a renewed German aggression. Here was a fair and imaginative Anglo-American contribution; in the deficiency of French power unassisted, the combined power of the English-speaking countries was clearly worth untold divisions and more than the limited strategic asset of the line of the Rhine.

Because of the importance of this document, the subject of a regrettable tale in the reckoning, the full text of the Anglo-French treaty warrants quoting:

> Article 1. In case Articles 42 and 43 of the treaty of peace with Germany, neutralizing the Left Bank and fifty kilometers on the Right Bank, may not at first provide adequate security and protection to France, Great Britain agrees to come immediately to her assistance in the event of any unprovoked movement of aggression by Germany.
>
> Article 2. The Treaty will only come into force when the corresponding Treaty with the United States is ratified.
>
> Article 3. The Treaty must be submitted to the Council of the League of Nations and must be recognized by it as consistent with the Covenant. It will continue in force till, on the application of one of the parties, the Council agrees that the League itself provides sufficient protection.

Article 4. The Treaty shall before ratification be submitted to Parliament and the French Chamber for approval.

Article 5. The Treaty shall impose no obligation on any Dominion unless approved by the Parliament of such Dominion.[108]

Some observations will be made in a moment in regard to the British role in this affair. At this point, where France was concerned, it is enough to point out that, even apart from the implied control that any alliance connotes—no foolproof definition of aggression has yet been devised—this particular treaty was a one-way arrangement. It was not in reality an alliance but a unilateral guarantee given by one state to another, an expression therefore of dependence in some degree at least, of the guaranteed on the guarantor. No clearer acknowledgment could be found of the limitations of French power, an entirely correct appraisal. However, as Clemenceau also correctly pointed out, America especially was far away, whereas Germany was next-door. This is the hinge where frontier, military, and political considerations joined.

For the rest, France endeavored to weaken Germany in all possible ways. Germany was to be disarmed, and where it came to the frontiers of Germany elsewhere, France tended to support the most anti-German positions, as in the Polish case, for example, just as she was opposed to the Anschluss of Austria or to any revision of the existing south German border with the future Czechoslovakia.[109] A measure of contradiction was involved at this point, for though no one advocated the "pastoralization" of Germany in 1919, a weak Germany would be less capable of paying Reparation than a strong and prosperous one. France wanted *both* security *and* Reparation, though security came first. Germany was saddled with an enormous, though in 1919 unspecified, liability. Generally speaking, with a few notable exceptions,[110] the economic thinking that went into the settlements of 1919 was of remarkably low quality. We shall return to this in connection with an examination of the British position.

The British Position

We may now turn to a consideration of the aims of British policy and of the manner in which it was attempted to implement those aims.

As befitted the great imperial Power that was Britain these aims did not have so narrow and limited a scope as the French. British thinking ran mainly along lines of trade and empire, and for Europe of restored equilibrium. However, the wartime German performance had made a deep impression on Britain as well as on others. Lloyd George's too great preoccupation with the domestic bases of his own position induced him to call a general election in December 1918. The famous khaki election has been rightly adjudged an illustration of the less desirable aspects of democratic politics and in the reckoning was not a wise move. It was too easy in the circumstances to capitalize on the nationalistic emotion with such slogans as "Hang the Kaiser." The British electorate handsomely endorsed the wartime coalition and Lloyd George naturally led the British delegation in the peacemaking. The following characterization of him is apt:

> No Plenipotentiary ever approached the supremely difficult task of rebuilding a world in ruins with a less perfect equipment of precise knowledge; but he learned quickly, and he brought a fresh mind to the bewildering array of problems which confronted the peacemakers.[111]

His nimbleness of mind, which appeared to some as unreliable fickleness, soon had occasion to manifest itself, and this is a good place to say something of Reparation. The validity of the concept was not questioned in any Allied quarters, and the Germans themselves did not expect to escape what they would have called an indemnity. The question was how much should and could Germany pay; the "should" and the "could" might be quite different. The long discussions that went on among the Allies and the Americans are not recommended reading as a model of high-level economic thinking.

The French had financed the war largely through borrowing, contracting huge debts, both domestic and foreign, a behavior that was irresponsible to a degree.[112] Especially as the prospects of victory became clearer, the idea that Germany would pay it all became highly attractive. It was the French who, in the pre-armistice discussion of the Fourteen Points, had insisted on an interpretation of Point VIII that would set no limitations on the meaning of "restoration."

The French are no less attached to money than the British, but when it comes to public finance it is not unfair to say that the management of the latter gives evidence of a higher degree of soundness and responsibility in the orthodox sense. Their own wartime performance was evidence of this, but Britain, too, had come out of the war saddled with a large burden of debt, some of it incurred in order to finance her allies. It might be expected that from London, the financial capital of the world, would come a better understanding of the implications of Reparation, an international financial operation of huge dimensions, than from Paris or even from 1919 New York.

It is all the more interesting to recall that the British insisted on the inclusion of pensions in the Reparation bill, a position which could only serve to swell its dimensions. The reason is not far to seek, for this demand would have the effect of enlarging the British share in Reparation; apart from casualties and sunken ships, and the important but more-elusive-of-measurement factor of trade losses, Britain had nothing so concrete to present as the physical devastation of northern France.[113]

Thus in this matter a dilemma comparable to that which confronted the French was met by the British, though for different reasons. Britain was more sensitive than France to commercial considerations; a restored Germany, not saddled with a huge indemnity, was a desirable prospect for British trade. The essence of the British dilemma arose from the fact that Germany had been at once her greatest competitor and her best customer.

The problem of the disarmament of Germany was simpler, based on the unanimous belief in the German responsibility for the war. Here again, however, it is interesting to observe that the British was the greater insistence of the small size—100,000 men—of the Army that Germany should be allowed to maintain. The influence of their own domestic experience, a regrettable one in this case, had the effect of forbidding conscription in Germany; the French felt much less enthusiastic about a professional Army.

In this rather confused state of affairs, second thoughts, in the form of the influence of traditional British interest and thinking, were not long in asserting themselves. The consequence was that, as early as the end of March, Lloyd George produced the famous Fontainebleau memorandum, of which some passages follow:

> The maintenance of peace will depend upon there being no causes of exasperation constantly stirring up the spirit of patriotism, of justice or of fair play. To achieve redress our terms may be severe, they may be stern and even ruthless, but at the same time they can be so just that the country on which they are imposed will feel in its heart that it has no right to complain. . . .[114]

Without pausing to reflect on the inherent naïveté of the hope that Germany would find "ruthless" terms acceptable because they were "just," we may proceed with further quotation:

> . . . I am, therefore, strongly averse to transferring more Germans from German rule to the rule of some other nation than can possibly be helped. I cannot conceive any greater cause of future war than that the German people, who have certainly proved themselves one of the most vigorous and powerful races in the world, should be surrounded by a number of small States, many of them consisting of people who have never previously set up a stable government for themselves. . . .

One hears echoes of a long line of British thought, the belief in Anglo-German affinity, not to say common superiority. The debate in the Commons of August 3, 1914, may be recalled.[115] But why, then, hang the Kaiser? More sensibly, perhaps, Lloyd George believed

> That the duration for the payment of reparation ought to disappear if possible with the generation which made the war.

One important consideration was the fear of Bolshevism, to which Germany, if driven to despair, might turn.[116] Having expressed this view, Lloyd George went on:

> From every point of view, therefore, it seems to me that we ought to draw up a peace settlement as if we were impartial arbiters, forgetful of the passions of the war. This settlement ought to have three ends in view. First of all it must do justice to the Allies by taking into account Germany's responsibility for the

origin of the war and for the way in which it was fought. Secondly, it must be a settlement which a responsible German Government can sign in the belief that it can fulfill the obligations it incurs. Thirdly, it must be a settlement which will contain in itself no provocations for future wars, and which will constitute an alternative to Bolshevism, because it will commend itself to all responsible opinion as a fair settlement of the European problem.

Finally, on the subject of disarmament:

> To my mind it is idle to endeavour to impose a paramount limitation of armaments upon Germany unless we are prepared similarly to impose a limitation upon ourselves. . . .
>
> . . . .
>
> . . . Unless we secure this universal limitation we shall achieve neither lasting peace, nor the permanent observance of the limitation of German armaments which we now seek to impose.

The lengthy Fontainebleau memorandum calls for some observations. Allowing for certain inconsistencies in behavior on the part of its author, read in the light of retrospect, the chief impression that emerges is rather that of a statesmanlike approach. More important is the fact that it represented a return to the fundamentals of British policy, a detached reasonableness and sanity instead of the yielding to passion.

With this approach there were, however, two difficulties. One was the fact that such an attitude was easier to maintain when British power was such as to insure Britain full confidence in her arbitral position. This, in 1919, was no longer the situation, for Britain was in a very real sense, even if with certain differences, fundamentally in the same defensive position as France.

The other difficulty was not an especially British one, though Britain had been in the forefront of the democratic movement. That movement, the rise of the masses in general, has already been alluded to; it created a psychological and political climate in which the limited, but sensible approach of pure power relationships was impossible. The people are more easily moved by ideas and emotions. One must resist the temptation to embark upon a discussion of one of the most fundamental dilemmas of our time, which has seen simultaneously the continuing rise of the mass and the intensification of the crudest uses of power.

Pascal's phrase, *"qui veut faire l'ange fait la bête,"* comes to mind, which was nowhere better illustrated in 1919 than by the curious performance in connection with Reparation. Putting it on a moral basis, as the memorable Article 231 of the Treaty of Versailles did, the famous "war guilt" clause led to untold controversy and to disastrous result. It was in large part an American contribution, a fact that makes for sobering reflection.

But to return to our main topic, when the Germans presented extensive objections to the terms of the treaty, of which the text was given to them at the beginning of May, Lloyd George was thrown into near panic. What if Germany refused to sign the treaty and gave herself over to Bolshevism instead? Even Wilson grew tired of Lloyd George's everlasting gyrations; the treaty eventually stood.

Some Other Issues

There is neither room nor necessity to go into all the issues, whether concerned with Germany or not, that arose in connection with the peace settlements. But two or three of these may be mentioned as illustrative of similarity or difference between the British and the French reactions.

Vis-à-vis both Japan and Italy, Britain and France were bound by definite commitments. In both cases American opposition was encountered which could be justified on the basis of the principle of self-determination; in the case of Japan, in addition, her designs on China impinged on American interest. A serious problem was thus raised, that of the validity of self-determination versus that of the sanctity of treaties.[117]

Britain and France took the same position of attempting to dodge the dilemma by acknowledging the validity of both principles. While they urged the Italians to accede to American wishes, and even made some efforts to effect a compromise, they would not deny the validity of their signatures. This is how the Italian problem developed in 1919 into an Italo-American dispute which prevented a solution of it, at least until Wilson had passed from the political scene and the American people had washed their hands of the quarrels of Europe. Here, too, was an interesting case of power relationships. Clearly, Italy did not have the power to coerce America into withdrawing her veto; but also, apart from that veto, how could America coerce Italy into acquiescence in the Wilsonian point of view? The Japanese, maneuvering with greater skill than the Italians, contrived to extract American assent to their desires.

The colonial problem was on the whole resolved with little difficulty. The Fourteen Points were sufficiently loose on that subject to make it possible for a compromise to be achieved by introducing the Anglo-American concept of mandate; as a consequence, the German colonies and parts of the Ottoman Empire were allotted in accordance with the wartime inter-Allied agreements, save where the Russians, who had excluded themselves, were concerned. But instead of becoming outright possessions, in keeping with the practice of earlier wars, they became mandates, meaning that the title to them formally passed to the League, which in turn appointed "mandatories" for the territories concerned. Thus the concept of trusteeship was formally and legally introduced into the imperial domain. Precisely what the effect and the significance of this would be the future alone could tell.

The Treaty of Sèvres, which dealt with the Ottoman Empire and was not signed until August 1920, was destined to a peculiar fate. The part of it dealing with Turkey proper never really came into effect owing to the successful revival of Turkey under the leadership of Kemal. Britain was not involved in this, save temporarily at the Straits, where hers was the chief force in occupation. The liquidation of the claims on Turkey—French, Italian, and Greek—did not occur without some Anglo-French friction, but that story will be touched upon in the next chapter.[118] So will, likewise, the continuing Anglo-French rivalry over the Arab Near East; already in 1919–20 France experienced some difficulty in securing British and American acquiescence to her Syrian and Lebanese mandates, owing in part to a degree of Arab opposition.

The League of Nations has been mentioned several times. It may be put without reservation to America's, more specifically to Wilson's, credit to have attempted to give body to an ancient dream of mankind. In theory none could object; in practice some very relevant questions could be asked.

Sceptical Clemenceau did not think that Utopia could be so easily realized, but there were many in France who responded to the Wilsonian hope. Nevertheless, even the most pro-League sentiment in that country insisted that if the League was to have reality it must be possessed of effective and dependable power. The logic of that conclusion was difficult to refute, but it ran into the traditional and congenital British and American reluctance to undertake commitments of uncertain future scope. The result was an unfortunate evasion. The Covenant of the League, as it emerged in 1919, was essentially an Anglo-American document, example of the parallel thinking and ground that the two peoples shared to the exclusion of others, example also of the isolation of France among the Big Three. The French position, to be sure, then and later, drew much support from other land Powers; but the two most powerful states happened to be the English-speaking naval Powers. Perhaps this did not matter very much, for, as it happened, America repudiated the League, refusing to ratify the Treaty of Versailles *because* the Covenant was part of it, an outcome full of irony since that arrangement had been insisted upon by Wilson himself precisely to insure that none could escape from the world organization. The League was as a consequence a crippled child from birth. Its operation, the use of and the attitude toward it of the British and the French, its ultimate demise, also belong in the next chapter.

All in all, the nature of the peace might be thought not unsatisfactory to Britain and to France, to the former especially. She had, as usual after a war, emerged with large imperial acquisitions; the German Navy, especially after Scapa Flow,[119] was no more; and Russia was in chaos. But there were also doubts and problems, some of which were not immediately apprehended in the flush of success. The appraisal given by Gooch, although written three years later, may be quoted:

> The British empire emerged from the titanic struggle with a large accretion of territory, and with the German Navy at the

> bottom of the sea; but Britain is burdened by debt, and her best European customers are temporarily ruined. The Balance of Power has ceased to exist; for the French supremacy on land is as unchallenged as British supremacy at sea. The Triple Entente, like the Triple Alliance, has disappeared. In a new world, where familiar landmarks have been swept away by the raging tempest, British statesmen have discovered that the highest interests and the abiding prosperity of their country are bound up with the vitality and authority of the one operative organisation for the preservation of Peace—the League of Nations. [120]

Even this judgment would not be long in being tested, as will shortly appear.

The French reaction was from the beginning rather one of dissatisfaction and disillusionment. It is enlightening to reread the debate on ratification which took place in the French Chamber from August 26 to October 2.[121] Tardieu, who defended the treaty, had to fall back on making the most of what concrete advantages France had secured, and there were indeed some: the occupation, the demilitarization of the Rhineland, German disarmament, and Reparation. There were those in France, mainly drawn from the Marxist Left, who thought the treaty too harsh.[122] But the chief criticism came from those who stressed the inadequacies of the guarantees it provided for the future security of France. Without any great sense of either enthusiasm or elation the French Chamber ratified the Treaty of Versailles. But a good measure of the prevalent French feeling may be gathered from the results of the general election that took place in the following November. The Socialists, among whom the tendency to conciliation was strongest, saw their numbers reduced from 102 to 68[123]; the overwhelming bulk of the "blue horizon" Chamber, counterpart of its khaki equivalent across the Channel, was the expression of the predominant, strong nationalistic emotion.

The League as a concept, as already indicated, had found considerable support in French opinion, even in parliamentary quarters. As early as July 1917 a "ministerial commission of study for the Society of Nations" had been created, in which Léon Bourgeois was appropriately active.[124] Bourgeois was active again in 1919 in defending the French view of the League, but the result that had emerged was undoubtedly a feeble reed and an untried instrument. Possibly in the course of time teeth might be put into the League, but pending that day no one in France thought it an adequate guarantee of security. The Anglo-American guarantee, on the other hand, could be an unqualified source of reassurance. Unfortunately, as luck would have it, the Franco-American treaty never even reached the point of debate on the floor of the American Senate. The consequences of this could not but be considerable; they go a long way toward explaining much that happened in the subsequent unfolding of French foreign policy, not to mention the state of Franco-American relations. The 1960s are not the first time that these have been disturbed.

We shall not attempt a critique of the merits and failings of the German peace of 1919. The Treaty of Versailles was to be the object of much subsequent criticism in many quarters. The outcome of another war may be cited as evidence of how mild, by comparison and in many respects, it was. But it suffered from the fundamental vice of ambiguity, which was the result of the compromise that it represented between irreconcilable hopes and tendencies. The judgment of the French historian Bainville may suffice as summation: *"une paix trop douce pour ce qu'elle a de dur."*

In a situation that was at best uncertain, how Britain and France proceeded to make the worst of even what possibilities and opportunities they had will be the subject of the next chapter in our story. It is a perfect illustration of failure of adaptation, in comparable though different ways.

NOTES ON *Chapter VII*

1. Neton, op. cit., pp. 312–13.

2. The strange and incredible mistaking by the Russians of British trawlers for Japanese gunboats and the shelling of these by the Russians with some loss of life.

3. The British were taking a rather rigid view of the rights of neutrals and belligerents, an additional source of embarrassment to the French, torn between conflicting loyalties.

4. The result was indeed an American urging that France accede to the holding of a conference, combined, however, with assurances of support for the French position. As might be expected, Delcassé was attempting to

interpose French mediation in the Russo-Japanese War, to which in some respects he attached greater importance than to the Moroccan situation. Cf. Anderson, Eugene N., *The First Moroccan Crisis, 1904–1906* (1930), p. 245; Albertini, op. cit., Vol. I, p. 158; Andrew, Christopher, *Théophile Delcassé and the Making of the Entente Cordiale* (1968), Ch. XII.

5. Russia's defeat, with the consequent disorganization of her military establishment, plus the domestic political and social turmoil that was a consequence of her defeat, made Russian power ineffectual, hence correspondingly resulted in a weakening of the Franco-Russian combination.

6. Lansdowne to Sir F. Bertie, April 22, 1905. *British Documents on the Origins of the War, 1898–1904,* Vol. III (1928), pp. 72–73. On the bases for Delcassé's reliance on British support, in part as a result of "indiscretions" on the part of various British service chiefs, see Andrew, op. cit., pp. 279 ff.

7. *CHBFP,* Vol. III, p. 343.

8. Albertini, op. cit., p. 155.

9. Lansdowne to Cambon, May 25, 1905. *British Documents . . . ,* Vol. III, p. 78.

10. A description of it, as well as of some of the *dessous* of French politics and of certain intrigues, may be found in Neton, op. cit., pp. 345 ff. See also Andrew, op. cit., Ch. XIV.

11. The Kaiser's account of the meeting that he sent to Bülow (*Die Grosse Politik . . . ,* Vol. XIX, pp. 458–65) is recommended as highly entertaining reading, but also as an appalling illustration of the sort of hands the fate of Europe was in. Albertini's judgment on the episode seems the most apt: "To such a man (William II) was entrusted so great a part of the destinies of the world! Those who served him—Bülow at their head—many times asked themselves whether he was of sound mind, and whether he should not be put under restraint, but they never dared to do this. They dared not, because, whether brilliant or dull-witted, they all, with the exception of Bismarck, were courtiers before they were statesmen." Albertini, op. cit., Vol. I, p. 160.

12. Apart from reasserting the open door principle for Morocco, the conference of Algeciras was mainly concerned with arrangements for the preservation of order in the country, in doing which a special position was recognized to France and to Spain, and with providing supervision for the finances of Morocco.

13. In December 1905 the Liberals were returned to office, the prime ministership being by Campbell-Bannerman while Grey succeeded Lansdowne at the foreign office. This change in the Cabinet resulted in no change in the direction of foreign policy.

14. The military conversations between Britain and France continued uninterruptedly and were supplemented by parallel Anglo-Belgian discussions.

15. See above, p. 263.

16. See above, pp. 289–90.

17. *CHBFP,* Vol. III, p. 319.

18. One should not forget the German role in these matters, the most concrete manifestation of which was the Baghdad railway project, which was cause for much diplomatic activity. Nevertheless, despite the importance of this factor, it may, *relatively* speaking, be described as tangential to the larger issue, which is why it is slighted in the present discussion.

19. *CHBFP,* Vol. III, p. 326, n. 1.
20. Ibid., pp. 336–37.
21. There was some questioning of the wisdom of this action in England on the plea that it would tend to strengthen the hand of the conservative forces. The first Duma, which met in May, was shortly dismissed, in July, and Witte himself had been dismissed in May. Campbell-Bannerman's undiplomatic, if sincere, comment on these manifestations of reaction, *"La Douma est morte, vive la Douma!,"* ruffled Russian tempers, but only in passing fashion, another illustration of the primacy of power considerations and relationships over ideological.
22. On his way back through Paris from the peace negotiations in Portsmouth, New Hampshire, Witte received an invitation to visit King Edward. Although he felt unable to accept it without the Tsar's authorization, he conveyed the answer that he would use his influence to promote friendly relations with England.
23. The recalcitrance of the Emir delayed, but only for a time, the ratification of the agreement.
24. *CHBFP,* Vol. III, p. 366.
25. Cited in Trevelyan, G. M., *Grey of Fallodon* (1937), pp. 131–33.
26. Lord Fisher, *Memories* (1923), pp. 18–19.
27. Both Lloyd George and Churchill are cited in *CHBFP,* Vol. III, pp. 389–90.
28. In the course of an interview with a British journalist the Kaiser had expressed himself too freely about the Boer War, contrasting popular German reaction with his own (he had even offered advice on how to conduct the war). Poor co-ordination in responsible German quarters resulted in the publication of the interview in the *Daily Telegraph,* with the consequence of producing a domestic storm in Germany and of arousing feeling in England.
29. This crisis, originating in Ottoman and Balkan affairs and initially from the Austro-Russian relationship, is dealt with later on. See below, pp. 362–64.
30. King Edward proceeded to visit Emperor Francis Joseph at Ischl. His efforts to enlist the Austrian ruler's help in moderating the German naval program if anything backfired.
31. The issue of conscription in England was raised in the Lords by Lord Roberts in a speech on November 23, moving "that the defense of these islands necessitates the immediate provision of an army so strong in numbers and so efficient in quality that the most formidable nation would hesitate to attempt a landing on these shores." The motion was carried in the Lords but the voluntary system continued to be adhered to.
32. *CHBFP,* Vol. III, p. 435.
33. Ibid., p. 346.
34. Ibid., p. 437, n. 1.
35. The Agadir crisis is treated later on in this chapter, pp. 368 ff.
36. See below, p. 368.
37. *CHBFP,* Vol. III, p. 457.
38. The accounts of the two principals, which are in essential agreement, can be followed in their respective recollections: Haldane, R. B. H., *Before the War* (1920), pp 72–81, and Bethmann-Hollweg, T. von, *Betrachtungen zum Weltkriege,* 2 vols. (1919), Vol. I, pp. 50–57.
39. Haldane, op. cit., p. 79.

40. Gooch in *CHBFP*, Vol. III, p. 465.
41. *CHBFP*, Vol. III, p. 467.
42. *Documents Diplomatiques Français*, 3e. série, Vol. III (1931), Doc. 420.
43. Grey to Cambon, November 22, 1912. Ibid., 3e. série, Vol. IV (1932), pp. 536–37; *British Documents . . .*, Vol. X, Part I (1938), pp. 614–15.
44. The entire memorandum may be found in *British Documents . . .*, Vol. III (1928), pp. 397–420.
45. *CHBFP*, Vol. III, p. 469.
46. An account of this episode may be found in Albertini, op. cit., Vol. I, Chs. IV, V. Detailed studies of it are Schmitt, B. E., *The Annexation of Bosnia* (1937) and Nintchitch, M., *La Crise bosniaque (1908–1909) et les puissances européennes*, 2 vols. (1937). The proclamation of complete Bulgarian independence and the Young Turk revolution introduced additional complications.
47. The thread is clear that runs from the Moroccan crisis of 1911, through the Italo-Turkish War, to the Balkan Wars of 1912–13. Turkey's involvement with Italy was obviously a tempting opportunity for the Balkan states to settle scores with the Ottoman Empire.
48. A good account of the episode is in Albertini, op. cit., Vol. I, Chs. VII, VIII. Poincaré's own version is found in his memoirs, *Au service de la France. Neuf années de souvenirs*, 10 vols. (1926–33), Vol. II (1926), Chs. II, VI, VII.
49. That an Albanian nationality exists may be granted, but whether the conditions prevailing in Albania were suitable to the organization of a state is another question again.
50. The Treaty of Bucharest, which settled the last Balkan War, was a purely intra-Balkan affair.
51. The two were quite distinct, but the Parliament Act, which was an outgrowth of the former, may be regarded as a link between them, since as a consequence of it the Lords' opposition to the Irish Bill could be expected to be overruled.
52. From *The* [London] *Times* of June 11, 1907. Cited in Joll, op. cit., pp. 207–9.
53. Ibid., pp. 210–11.
54. Spender, J. A., *The Foundations of British Policy* (London, 1912), p. 56. Cited in Joll, op. cit., p. 212.
55. See above, pp. 359–60.
56. By way of conveying the assertion of equal rights, on July 1 Germany sent the gunboat *Panther* to Agadir, ostensibly for the protection of German interests and nationals.
57. Cited in Albertini, op. cit., Vol. I, p. 331.
58. The French protectorate over Morocco was established in March 1912 and the agreement about the Spanish zone was implemented simultaneously.
59. The fact may be taken as a suitable recognition of the significance of the episode as marking the end of an epoch. Among the many works that could be mentioned it may suffice to cite Albertini's, already referred to *The Origins of the War of 1914*, 3 vols. (1952–57), particularly Vols. II and III, which are entirely devoted to an analysis of the July crisis itself.

60. Cited in Joll, op. cit., pp. 228–29.

61. The statement is particularly worth citing nevertheless because it expresses a deep and persistent trend in British thought and feeling, one that goes a long distance toward explaining certain aspects of British policy and to which there will be occasion to return in later pages (see Chapter VIII).

62. Italy declared her neutrality on August 3 on the correct, if legalistic, plea that Austria had not fulfilled the terms of the alliance; more broadly, a matter of interpretation and judgment, on the contention that her allies were the aggressors. In effect, she, too, was continuing the hedging policy which had been hers for some years.

63. Convenient treatments are Falls, C., *The Great War, 1914–1918* (1959), Liddell Hart, B. H., *The War in Outline* (1936).

64. Pingaud, A., *Histoire diplomatique de la France pendant la grande guerre,* 3 vols. (1937–40), Vol. I, p. 105. This work, written by an official of the French foreign office who had access to information, is a valuable source, especially for the dealings with the smaller nations.

65. Examples could be multiplied, of which the failure of the expectations raised by the Italian intervention is a good illustration. The Italian action came too late to capitalize on the benefits of an initially successful Russian offensive, while the Serbs, disgruntled by the advantages promised Italy, sulked in their tents. There are many others.

66. The participation of China in the war on the side of the Allies, which took place in 1917, was one way to counter Japanese ambitions, for it would have the effect of giving China a voice in the final settlement.

67. The foreign minister at the outbreak of war was San Giuliano, but he soon died and after a short interim Sonnino took charge of the office, which he retained through the signature of the treaty of peace with Germany.

68. Italy was to acquire the *irredenta* and rather more (the Brenner frontier, Istria, and northern Dalmatia), a predominant position in the Adriatic, and she was also given a somewhat loose promise of imperial compensation.

69. General Liman von Sanders, in charge of this reorganization, was put in command of the Constantinople garrison, but this appointment was withdrawn when other Powers, especially Russia, protested.

70. This was done by the German cruisers *Goeben* and *Breslau,* which, in August, had escaped to the shelter of the Sea of Marmora, whereupon they were "sold" to Turkey though retaining their German commanders and crews. They "escaped" into the Black Sea and created the incident in question.

71. It may be followed in the previously cited work of Pingaud, *passim.* Also, Miller, W., *The Ottoman Empire and its Successors* (1966), Ch. XX, and in Howard, H. N., *The Partition of Turkey; A Diplomatic History, 1913–1923* (1931).

72. Grey of Fallodon, Viscount, *Twenty-Five Years, 1892–1916,* 2 vols. (1925), Vol. II, p. 188.

73. Pingaud, op. cit., Vol. I, pp. 247 ff.

74. Endless and inconclusive discussions were cut short by an ultimatum of the French envoy and the landing of French troops near the capital. The result was the abdiction of King Constantine, the return of Venizelos to power, and the intervention of Greece in the war.

75. "Anyone . . . may well ask how it was that Allied diplomacy, or rather want of diplomacy, did not lose the war." Grey, op. cit., Vol. II, p. 159.

76. This refers to the Asiatic portion of the Arab world only, the North African section being totally under British, French, and Italian control.

77. This was also in part at least designed to counter the attempt of the Sultan to capitalize on his position as religious head of Islam by proclaiming a Holy War against the enemies of Turkey.

78. This division might be thought inconsistent with the Anglo-Arab understanding, and much controversy arose subsequently which, in altered form, is unresolved to this day. There was imprecision in the MacMahon-Hussein exchanges, and the British made it clear to the Arabs that the claims of their allies, the French in this instance, would have to be considered. It was also the British who, in November 1917, issued the since famous Balfour Declaration, another hedging and ambiguous statement, the seed out of which modern Israel and its attendant problems have grown.

79. As a consequence of their continued neutrality the Greeks had missed their opportunity where Smyrna was concerned, but only for the moment.

80. Again this was mainly an Anglo-French understanding, Italy being excluded, though Japan participated in the division of the German possessions in the Pacific, and Belgium was to obtain a share of German East Africa (Ruanda-Urundi).

81. Pingaud, op. cit., Vol. III, p. 268. Likewise Izvolsky reported to Sazonoff: "I told him [Cambon] in the least uncertain terms that such an idea was totally unacceptable to us, for Russian public opinion would never consent to transferring the Polish question to the international domain." Ibid.

82. The French wished to recover the frontier of 1814, rather than that of 1815 or 1870, meaning the incorporation of the Saar. The rest of the left bank of the Rhine was so unquestionably German that its outright annexation was not considered, but the possibility of a return to the pre-1871 fragmentation of Germany was. Cf. Pingaud, op. cit., Vol. III, pp. 298–302.

83. Grey, op. cit., Vol. II, p. 161.

84. Ibid., Ch. XXV, *passim*. Balfour was to take a similar position. It should also be pointed out that the validity of self-determination was thought of primarily in European terms and did not at this stage extend to the imperial domain.

85. Already before the United States entered the war its favorable balance of trade had grown from $435,000,000 in 1914 to $2,674,000,000 in 1916. Corresponding increases occurred in the production of wheat and of steel, for example, the war having the effect of inducing a boom in the American economy. Cf. Renouvin, *Histoire des relations internationales*, Vol. VII (1952), p. 60.

86. House to Wilson, August 22, 1914, House, E. M. *The Intimate Papers of Colonel House, arranged as a narrative by Charles Seymour*, 4 vols. (1926–28), Vol. I (1926), p. 285.

87. Pingaud, op. cit., Vol. I, p. 256.

88. House, op. cit., Vol. I, p. 442.

89. Jusserand to Berthelot, January 1, 1917. Pingaud, op. cit., Vol. I, p. 225, n. 1.

90. See above, p. 285.

91. An outgrowth of the second Hague Conference, this declaration generally restated existing maritime law, putting added emphasis on the rights of neutrals. The declaration failed of unanimous ratification and an American proposal during the war that belligerents voluntarily abide by its provisions was not accepted by them.

92. It was the result of the death of Francis Joseph in November 1916. This brought to the throne the less committed figure of Charles I, but more important were the weaknesses and the difficulties of the Dual Monarchy. The attempt took the form of approaches to the French Government but never really "got off the ground."

93. [London] *Daily Telegraph*, November 29, 1917. Cited in Joll, op. cit., pp. 237–38.

94. This distinction could easily be interpreted as an invitation to revolution in Germany, as a reward for which a "soft" peace would be obtained. It contributed much to the subsequent confusion and controversy that developed around the terms of the German peace.

95. *CHBFP*, Vol. III, p. 522.

96. The idea had a long history behind it, but its formal sponsorship by the head of the most powerful state warrants the attribution of fatherhood to the American President.

97. Here lies the root of the unfortunate legend that the German Army was never defeated and that Germany was tricked into surrender by her enemies on the one hand, stabbed in the back by unpatriotic elements at home on the other.

98. The discussion can be followed in detail in Mermeix (pseud. Gabriel Terrail), *Les négociations secrètes et les quatre armistices* (1919), and in Rudin, H. A., *Armistice 1918* (1944).

99. The Italian case presented a more difficult problem. The handling of it and the consequences of the evasion that was resorted to may be followed in Albrecht-Carrié, R., *Italy at the Paris Peace Conference* (1938). That situation, while an interesting case study of power relationships, falls outside the scope of our treatment. The German armistice was the last, having been preceded by others, with Bulgaria, Turkey, and Austria-Hungary, in that order.

100. Japan had little interest in matters European, and Italy to a large extent behaved like a Power with limited interests, concentrating too narrowly on her own problems, and letting the Three make the decisions about Germany, *the* main problems of the peace.

101. It was doubled-edged because the French *candeur* is usually incorrectly translated as "candor." The French word carries the connotations of innocence and naïveté, the English, those of open-mindedness and honesty. Clemenceau knew English well.

102. Cited in *CHBFP*, Vol. III, pp. 528–29. This statement, incidentally, is a more balanced and sober description than the far better known and more sensational, but also highly distorted one, given by John M. Keynes in *The Economic Consequences of the Peace* (1920).

103. The discussion induced at the end of 1916 by the German "peace offer" and the American inquiry about the war aims of the belligerents had not really elucidated the question. The contemporary (February 1917) Franco-Russian agreement was likewise vague. The motion unanimously

voted by the French Chamber is characteristic of the temper of the time: France expected "the liberation of the invaded territory, the recovery of Alsace-Lorraine and the just reparation of damage." As to Clemenceau, his general attitude was well summed up in his phrase *"Je fais la guerre."*

104. His memoranda of November and January, his appearance before the Supreme Council in May, were expressions of his efforts to make his views prevail, in which endeavor he was unsuccessful.

105. *CHBFP*, Vol. III, p. 530.

106. See Mermeix (pseud. Gabriel Terrail), *Le Combat des Trois* (1922), and Mantoux, P., *Les délibérations du Conseil des Quatre* (*24 mars–28 juin 1919*)*: Notes de l'interprète*, 2 vols. (1955).

107. The issue of the Saar may be regarded as a footnote to the larger one of the disposition of the German Rhineland, although it was the object of a separate and intense controversy. The French claim to the frontier of 1814 was opposed by both Wilson and Lloyd George; no one, not even Clemenceau, seriously argued that the Saarlanders were not German. Here, too, a compromise was achieved: ownership of the Saar coal mines would pass to France, under the head of Reparation, while the territory itself was placed under League administration for a period of fifteen years, when a plebiscite would be held to determine its national allegiance.

108. The text of the British treaty may be found in Cmd. 221 (1919). It was similar to the Franco-American treaty, except that the preamble made clearer the one-sided character of the British guarantee, as evidenced by the following introductory paragraph:

> Whereas there is danger that the stipulations relating to the Left Bank of the Rhine contained in the Treaty of Peace signed this day at Versailles may not at first provide adequate security and protection to the French Republic . . .

Articles 42 and 43 of the Treaty of Versailles established the demilitarized zone on the right bank of the Rhine as well as on the left bank.

109. This does not invalidate the intrinsic merit of these positions, but they undoubtedly fitted well the larger French purpose.

110. Keynes was the most outstanding. While his criticism was well founded and may be said to have been proved correct in the event, it is enlightening to compare the treatment of Germany after 1919 with that of the post-Second World War, in particular to consider the Soviet attitude and behavior where reparations were concerned.

111. Gooch in *CHBFP*, Vol. III, p. 326.

112. It was a French writer, Gaston Jèze, who expressed the judgment that "France's financial policy during the great war will remain a model of how not to do things; a worse financial management is difficult to imagine." Cited in Duroselle, J.-B., *La politique extérieure de la France de 1914 à 1945* (mimeographed course of lectures at the Sorbonne, 1965), p. 68, where a balanced analysis of French wartime finance may be found.

113. The outcome of these circumstances was that the total of Reparation was not written into the treaty of peace. Germany was required to make certain immediate payments and to deliver certain quantities of goods, and a commission was set up to examine her liability and the manner of its discharge, a task which it took another two years to accomplish.

114. This and the following quotations from the Fontainebleau memorandum are taken from Joll, op. cit., Doc. 50, where it is reproduced in part.

It is interesting to set the Fontainebleau memorandum side by side with Grey's observations on the situation at the end of 1916 (Grey, op. cit., Vol. II, pp. 131–33) as an illustration of a persistent British outlook.

115. See above, p. 370.

116. This factor is brought out in lengthy detail in Mayer, A. J., *Politics and Diplomacy of Peacemaking. Containment and Counter-Revolution at Versailles, 1918–1919* (1968), a valuable but badly proportioned study.

117. Italy had not committed herself to the acceptance of the Fourteen Points save insofar as they concerned Germany, and Japan had not participated in the pre-armistice discussions.

118. See below, pp. 431–34.

119. Pending decision of its disposition the German Navy was interned at the British base of Scapa Flow. There it scuttled itself, a fact which gave rise to some unjustified, but understandable, suspicion of British connivance.

120. *CHBFP*, Vol. III, p. 538.

121. As well as the report of August 5 of the committee on the peace, of which Barthou was *rapporteur*.

122. Thus Albert Thomas asserted that instead of concentrating on the weakening and the division of Germany, "we should lean on those elements in Germany with whom an understanding is possible, we should put our dependence on democratic Germany."

123. This is all the more significant in view of the progress of Socialism as a result of the war. The strength of Socialism, as well as of labor agitation in general, had been manifest earlier in 1919.

124. He was the author of a work entitled *Pour la Société des Nations*, which had been published in 1910.

VIII

THE COMMON FAILURE, 1920–39

Mais les textes diplomatiques ne valent que par la volonté qu'on a de s'en servir.

J. Paul-Boncour, *Entre deux guerres,* Vol. III, p. 44

Si vous aviez fait avancer 200,000 hommes, vous auriez rendu un immense service à tout le monde.

Pope Pius XII to the French ambassador, March 16, 1936

A quarrel in a far-away country [Czechoslovakia] between peoples of whom we know nothing.

Neville Chamberlain, September 27, 1938

Traditional European diplomacy offered a choice of two types of peace policy. One consisted in building up unquestioned preponderance of power on the side of the defenders of the established order, and in equipping them with the means of coercion necessary to prevent a successful revolt. This meant holding the lid down on the boiling kettle of European unrest and dissatisfaction. It was this conception . . . which, on the whole, appealed to the French as best fitted to meet the requirements of their security. The other strategy called for a removal of the causes of revolt in order to eliminate the chances of an explosion. This meant taking the new order merely as a starting point in a process of continuous adjustment, intended eventually to produce a new and more generally satisfactory settlement. Britain, by virtue of her geographic position, her interests, and her outlook on European affairs, was drawn toward this alternative, although not without certain important reservations. There was obviously little hope of reconciling two such divergent courses.

A. Wolfers, *Britain and France Between Two Wars,* p. 5

The last of the above quotations is a fair summation of the fundamental cause for the common failure of British and of French policies in the dreary interval of fumbling that constitutes the record of the long armistice. Either policy might conceivably have succeeded, but both were doomed unless pursued with determined consistency, and most of all if not supported by adequate power, not excluding the willingness to make use of that power. One may doubt that such power existed, but there can be no question that the will was deficient; will is a component of power no less than the more easily measurable expressions of it, guns, ships, and economic resources. Britain and France vis-à-vis the rest of the world had for some time been suffering a diminution of place, increasingly brought to a common defensive position. That was the real meaning of their initial association, the Entente of 1904; the logic of circumstances had brought them into the same camp in the Great War. The fact of victory had not really altered that common defensive aspect of their positions. Joined in a common purpose, they might—though even this is far from certain—conceivably have brought the world back to some orderly equilibrium. Neither alone could do it; to oppose each other was to invite common disaster. Yet this is what they did with precisely that ultimate consequence, however much at certain points of time outward appearances might seem to point to positions of different standing. The process was a tortuous one, which it is the purpose of the present chapter to trace in its main lines.

The Divergence of British and French Views

From the formation of the Entente Cordiale to the outbreak of war in 1914 the increasing convergence of the British and the French interests has been made clear. The persistence of the threat contained in the rise of German power, compounded by the heavy-handed methods of German diplomacy, had insured the transformation of the Entente into the wartime alliance. The war had indeed given rise to certain differences, even pointed to certain divergences rooted in past rivalries, but the effectiveness of German power had insured the persistence of its prime purpose, the defeat of the German bid for hegemonic power.

That result was accomplished in 1918 and registered in the treaties of peace of the following year, that of Versailles above all. But the process had been accompanied by unexpected events, of which the two most significant were the Russian collapse and Revolution and the American intervention, to which the disintegration of the Habsburg Empire may be added. Thus the Europe of 1919 was very different from that which had been reconstituted a hundred years before at Vienna.

One important difference between the two cases, fruit of a century of economic and social evolution, was the far larger place that must be given to the masses, because of their common expectations and claims in the socio-economic domain and because of their exacerbated national emotions. Defeated, chaotic, and impotent as she may have been, kept outside the pale of the peace settlements, Russia nevertheless was an important factor in the calculations of all, the standard-bearer in the eyes of much of the mass of the egalitarian hope of social justice. World revolution was frustrated after the war but social unrest could not with impunity be ignored. It is significant that the last section of the Treaty of Versailles is the charter of the International Labor Organization, a provision of which there had been no counterpart at Vienna.

The feelings and hopes of the masses, from whom such sacrifices had been demanded during the war, made themselves felt in other ways as well, mainly two, which in some respects were inconsistent: exacerbated and intransigeant nationalisms on the one hand, hence often belligerent vis-à-vis each other; an immense revulsion toward the fact of war, best reflected in the appeal of the slogan "the war to end all wars" and in the intense, if short-lived popularity of the Messiah come from across the ocean. These factors weighed heavily on the nature of the settlements, yielded to or exploited by the makers of these settlements, at times even against their better judgment.

But there was another aspect of the Europe of 1920 which stood in contrast with that of 1815. The makers of the settlement of Vienna represented the same constellation of Powers that had existed in 1789; France was one of them, under the general suspicion of all to be sure, yet acknowledged as a necessary and legitimate member of the European family of nations—or states.

Not so in 1920. For one thing, the European family had proved incapable of resolving its problems without the intervention of the American newcomer, whose role henceforth, be it active or passive, would inevitably be of paramount importance to all. The passing of the European age had begun. But, even within Europe, an unnatural distortion had taken place among the normal constellation of her traditional components. The Dual Monarchy was no more, gone past retrieving. Russia and Germany were in their different ways reduced to total impotence, but, despite their losses, territorial and other, their identities were preserved; sometime in an unpredictable future they would have to be reintegrated into the European complex.

The propulsion of the United States into the position of greatest Power in the world had been too sudden for the American people to absorb it in the form of accepting the responsibilities inherent in their newly revealed position. It would take another world war to accomplish that result; on the earlier occasion their reaction was one of disappointment and frustration and they gave themselves up to the view that they had been mistaken in not adhering to the advice of their first President not to mix in the quarrels of Europe, and to the comforting illusion that in their moral superiority they could return to the undisturbed cultivation of their own garden. The return to "normalcy," meaning that to isolation, was the genuinely overwhelming desire of the American people, to which they gave expression in their choice for President in 1920 and in his two successors, the trinity of Harding, Coolidge, and Hoover.

A distraught and disorganized Europe must fend for itself. For the moment Europe meant two Powers, Britain and France.[1] The war had, in different ways, inflicted very severe damage on both, but in both the pre-existing social and political structure had survived unscathed. Victory had in fact redounded to its credit, a fact of particular significance in the French case, where the Third Republic seemed now established beyond the reach of the attacks of its detractors.

If the central issue of the war had been the German problem, the question was whether that problem had been solved or not. In the immediate sense it undoubtedly had, registering the formalization of German impotence. But what of the future, ten or twenty years hence? Despite their concrete gains, imperial and others, and even without the wisdom of hindsight, it might be argued that the British and the French interests still coincided in the long term, and not vis-à-vis Germany alone for that matter. In fact both countries asserted their devotion to the alliance.

But here a divergence also appeared very shortly. The removal of the German danger made it easier for the traditional differences which its rise had submerged to reassert themselves, in the imperial domain, for example, as we shall presently see.[2] More important was the attitude toward Germany herself.

Where Britain was concerned, the weight of tradition seems to have been the greater influence in coloring the current view of things. Though awareness of relative diminution of power existed, the final outcome of the war for Britain could be seen as inserting itself as an episode in a continuing record. The experience was old and hallowed by repeated success which had identified the defense of the British interest—and of the liberties of Europe—with the preservation of the continental equilibrium. Britain had for centuries successfully opposed, and in the end defeated, the hegemonic ambitions of any one continental Power. She had resisted Philip II's Spain, Louis XIV's and Napoleon's France, and now most lately Wilhelmine Germany. At Vienna in 1815 Castlereagh had been a staunch defender of France's place in Europe: to diminish France unduly would have defeated Britain's basic purpose, which was not France's defeat per se, but the preservation of an equilibrium of which France was a necessary and essential part.

It might well be contended that the inadequacy of French power had been acknowledged for quite some time before 1914 by Britain. Nevertheless, given the European vacuum of power, where Germany was so severely fettered, might not French power be uncomfortably large if unchecked? The restoration of German power—within adequate limits to be sure—was desirable to the proper functioning of Europe. This is an eminently reasonable view, open to one qualification only, to which no answer could be forthcoming at the moment. Would Germany be content with an "adequate" place among nations, or would the restoration of her power all the sooner lead to a recurrence of her hegemonic bid?

It is important to realize that Britain did not deeply feel a consciousness of fundamental danger. This would point to the value of the 1815 precedent, when Britain had supported France, yet at the same time set great store by the continuation of the Quadruple Alliance.[3] Should it come to the worst, Britain, the chief backbone of the alliance, was capable of dealing with French power. The merit of this approach lay in minimizing the possibility of German discontent as a spur to renewed aggression; the flaw lay in the fact that in the First World War Britain had no longer been *the* backbone of the coalition. The United States had been needed.

This way of looking at the German problem was further reinforced by the dilemma born of commercial considerations. The destruction of German naval power may have been clear gain; but to wreck the German economy was a different matter, best summed up in the above-mentioned observation that Germany was at once Britain's greatest rival and most valued trading partner.

Why not, therefore, as in 1815, allow Germany place and recovery, while still maintaining the alliance with France? The fact is worth repeating at this point that the treaty of guarantee to France, contemporaneous with the German peace, had been made contingent upon the implementation of a similar American commitment. In the last report Britain did acknowledge the superiority of American power.

The result had been frustrating for France, by whom the English alliance was indeed much desired. But here a difficulty intruded from the different view of things, at once more realistic and more intractable, that was taken by France. Unlike Britain, France had known the experience and the taste of defeat. The 1918 victory was welcome, and France correctly felt that she had made a generous—indeed a too costly—contribution to its achievement; but the victory was no cause for either undue elation or for unwarranted illusions. The opposite, in fact, was the case and the French reaction is characterized by an almost pathological obsession—justified as it may have proved in the reckoning—with the persistence of the German danger.

"Security" therefore became the untiringly reiterated slogan, expression of well-nigh unanimous consensus, for which French policy would strive, and security meant above all reinsurance against a recurrence of the German threat. Here of course a dilemma might present itself to France as well, who wanted to collect reparations for the losses sustained; a weak Germany might be less capable than a prosperous one of meeting her financial obligations. The tendency was for a time to ignore the dilemma; but if prosperity meant strength for Germany, at no point was there hesitation in choosing the priority of weakness. Here was a built-in source of divergence between the French and the British outlooks, the order of priorities being precisely reversed.

If the wish for security commanded universal support in France, this left the question open of the means by which to achieve it. The attempt to try a variety of means, or several of them together, and the debate on which to choose, lies at the heart of French policy throughout the long armistice. The peace had made Germany weak—specifically, she was disarmed —and clearly she could be no danger for some time. But the French were sufficiently realistic to understand the probable impermanence of the treaty provisions—Clemenceau thought that he had done well if he had made his country safe for a generation. More dependable arrangements were needed to compensate for the long-term and fundamental fact of the inferiority of the potential of French power.

From Alliance to Opposition

Among the means that France sought to enlist, and the one that in fact she pursued with the greatest persistence, was the British connection. The failure of the 1919 Anglo-American guarantee did not diminish the desire for a continuation of the British alliance, and it is worth examining the attempts that were made until 1923 to formalize such a relationship.[4] It takes two to make an alliance, and the story therefore impinges quite as much on British as on French policy.

Something has already been said of the divergent approaches of the two countries to the problem, which therefore became one of finding ways to reconcile or compromise these differences.

At the end of 1921 Briand was in charge of both the prime ministership and the foreign office in France, his English counterparts being wartime Lloyd George and Lord Curzon. Following a visit of the last-named to Paris the discussion of an alliance was opened in London, where Briand and Lloyd George met later in the month. The circumstances of the moment and the personalities are worth noting. Of Lloyd George enough has been said in an earlier connection[5]; as to Curzon, he may be seen as the embodiment of the British imperial tradition. Stiffness rather than flexibility was characteristic of him, and his outlook was unduly affected by his own Indian experience. Briand was a very supple man, adept at compromise, and he felt a deep revulsion toward war; but in the last analysis Briand was French and shared the French concern for security.

This was the time of the Washington Naval Disarmament Conference, which met in that city from November 1921 to February 1922, and at which Briand had represented his country in the opening stages with disappointing results. For the conference was in some respects a hard lesson in the realities of power, and France had been compelled—unfairly as she thought—to accept an unsatisfactory ratio for her naval power.[6]

The Anglo-French discussions thus were not conducted under the most favorable auspices.[7] As to Lloyd George, he set great store by general economic revival for all, an expression of the concern for British trade. He met Briand in Cannes to discuss his far-reaching plans; the more limited, though not unrelated, issue of an Anglo-French alliance is what is of interest at this point.

The two exchanged lengthy memoranda[8] explaining their respective countries' positions, and finally on the twelfth Lloyd George brought forth a concrete proposal, which was as follows:

> Art. 1. In the event of direct and unprovoked aggression against the soil of France by Germany, Great Britain will immediately place herself at the side of France with her naval, military and air forces.
>
> Art. 2. The High Contracting Parties reassert their common interest in articles 42, 43 and 44 of the Treaty of Versailles, and

will consult together should any breach of them be threatened or any doubt arise as to their interpretation.

Art. 3. The High Contracting Parties undertake further to concert together in the event of any military, naval or air measures inconsistent with the Treaty of Versailles being taken by Germany.

Art. 4. The present treaty shall impose no obligation upon any of the Dominions of the British Empire unless and until it is approved by the Dominions concerned.

Art. 5. The present treaty shall remain in force for a period of ten years, and shall, if approved by both parties, be renewable at the end of that period.[9]

This text merits close analysis, for it discloses unvarying fundamentals of the British position, and discussion at this point will save later repetition. The French critique and the French counterproposals[10] were the work of Poincaré, who succeeded Briand in both the latter's capacities at the end of the month,[11] and who was to retain office until May of the following year. The advent of Poincaré to power in France was symbolically appropriate, for his whole previous record, before, during the war, and at the peace, had been the expression of the intransigeant approach in dealing with Germany, who in his view understood the language of force alone. If his horizon was unquestionably limited, Poincaré was devoid of neither forcefulness nor ability; in him Curzon was to find his match, and perhaps rather more than his match.

It will be noted in the above-cited text that Britain would undertake to resist a "direct and unprovoked" aggression against the soil of France, but that she went on to make a distinction between this and a breach of Articles 42, 43, and 44 of the Treaty of Versailles. The second case would merely call for consultation (shades of 1936!). Also, the Dominions were not to be involved, evidence of the British attachment to the evolution of the imperial structure, and the duration of the alliance was set at ten years. As before 1914, Britain acknowledged the inadequacy of French power alone; the judgment that "what had to be safeguarded was not only the integrity of the Low Countries but the independence of France herself"[12] still held, or, as it was to be put by a later prime minister, the Rhine was Britain's frontier.[13]

Poincaré objected, quite logically, on two scores. The purpose of the demilitarization of the Rhineland was to leave Germany open to French action, an action which might be necessary in the event of a German initiative in the East. It was precisely such a move that was the more likely and the probability of which would be enhanced if Germany could feel assured of British passivity in that case. Thus France might find it necessary to take the initiative against Germany, and any German action which induced this result should be considered in the category of "indirect" aggression. The precedent of Sadowa being the prelude to Sedan was trotted out again. The attempt to distinguish between a German move toward the East or the West was a dangerous fallacy, and a British guarantee of French soil was essentially superfluous, for a German attack in the West would probably induce British opposition, treaty or no treaty with France.

The exemption of the British Dominions from involvement was the only unquestioned provision of the British proposal, but there was relevance to pointing out the deficiency of the initial ten-year duration of the treaty, the period during which the likelihood of its necessity was small. Thirty years was suggested instead.

Finally, it is of interest to observe that there was also objection to the unilateral formulation of Article 1, which had the effect of putting France in the category of a "protected" state, a humiliating position. Britain needed France as much as the reverse and the treaty should be one between equals. This is a secondary point but a significant one nonetheless. Britain in fact did not fully recognize the parity of positions, but felt as in the past that her own remained arbitral to a degree; France on her side, in 1922, especially under Poincaré, was bent on asserting her power as equal to the British. That tale is not yet ended.

The formal assertion of parity and the extension of time were not stumbling blocks, but the possibility of Britain's involvement in the instability of East Europe most definitely was. The logic of the French contention was undoubtedly strong, but there was also suspicion that France might abuse her position to establish an undue place for herself and thereby involve Britain in action inimical to the British interest.

To all intents and purposes this is the end of this particular story. Many people on both sides of the Channel acknowledged the fundamental community of interests between the two countries, but it proved impossible to give this broad recognition the concrete form of a treaty.[14] To France the inevitability of involvement with Eastern Europe was inescapably clear; that she was in some respects in the same boat as France, as she had been before 1914, Britain might admit, but in that boat there was no room for Poles and Czechs. Britain was torn between the Continent and other associations; she would go as far as the Rhine but no more. France would therefore proceed with the implementation of a continental policy—she had been doing this for some time—without England if necessary, all the more so in the absence of England. We shall presently observe the implementation of her search for security, that ever constant factor, but mention must be made, briefly at least, of some specific developments which at the time exacerbated the Anglo-French relationship and made Britain more than ever feel that she was better off free of the fetter of involvement with France. The absence of the pressure of a common danger gave all the more scope to placing emphasis on difference. The wartime Anglo-French duet showed every indication of turning into an Anglo-French duel.

THE END OF THE ALLIANCE

The scenes of the contest were two, Germany and the Near East; they will be dealt with in that order. The inner contradictions of French policy where Germany was concerned had no need to wait for the evidence of the failure of that policy in order to be perceived by many, by the British not least. The inadequacy of the economic thinking which went into the Reparation section of the Treaty of Versailles has been mentioned before. Considerations of morality and justice, the precedent of 1871, became irrelevant in face of the dimensions of the German obligation. Keynes' critique,[15] which time was to prove justified, dates from 1920; in simplest form, Germany could only discharge her debt if she built up so huge a favorable trade balance as to cause serious injury to her creditors, at least within the confines of a capitalist, money economy. But the French chose to adhere to the emotional appeal which had initially prevailed. They wanted a weak Germany; they wanted her to pay as well. In their view her failure to do so was merely confirmation of unrepentant ill will which must be broken by coercion.

There is no need or room to go into the early record of the story,[16] the negotiations and the haggling which led to the initial settlement of London in 1921, Germany's early difficulties, all leading to the climax of 1922. *"L'Allemagne paiera"* was the simplest French approach, of which the just mentioned advent of Poincaré in place of the more accommodating Briand, promised enforcement. The test came at the end of the year, when the Reparations Commission was confronted with two French questions[17]: was Germany in default? Was her default willful? The first was answered unanimously in the affirmative—facts are facts—but on the second the British member parted company with his French, Italian, and Belgian colleagues.

Despite the lack of unanimity the French decided to take the law into their own hands. The occupation of the Ruhr, the only kind of language Germany understood in Poincaré's book, was the form that the French action took. The small Belgian participation, and the reluctant token Italian representation, all the more emphasized the French character of it, which made it an isolated test of force between Germany and France. The record of the episode is sufficiently known[18]: the German opposition in the form of passive resistance, the great inflation, and finally the German surrender in the face of Poincaré's determination.

In 1923 Germany alone did not have the means to resist French power and therefore must submit to a second defeat. The English behavior is highly instructive at this point. There were loud protestations in England at what was widely considered an abuse of power by France, but there were no more than verbal urgings from the government—the Germans were disappointed—and the French had their way. But it is also not surprising that the image of French power should have been a cause for concern, one calculated to insert itself into the classical British tradition of balance. This same French resoluteness manifested itself at the Genoa Conference[19] in April–May 1922, for the failure of which France was largely blamed in England —"Wrecking the Entente—Premier's Threat to France," ran a headline in *The* [London] *Times* of May 7. Little wonder that the negotiations for an Anglo-French alliance should not prosper in such circumstances, but it is no less revealing, and a measure of the British estimate of British power, that British opposition should have remained as weak as it was.

In the absence of the United States as an active participant, Britain and France were the two Powers that mattered. The long-term prospects of Germany and others, so central to the concerns of French policy, were in the British case overshadowed by more immediate cares about the state of the economy.[20] There were in British eyes other issues besides the European, important as these may have been, and we may pause at this point to give some consideration to the empire and the sea, the related fundamental bases of British power.

There may have been regrets in Britain at the passing of naval supremacy, but no inclination to contest the greater potential of the United States. In this respect the sensible nineteenth-century policy merely continued, and what happened in 1922 may be seen as an extension of the British retreat, of which the pre-1914 withdrawals from the Pacific, the Caribbean, and the Mediterranean are earlier illustrations. America and Britain shared the desire to reduce the burden of armaments, in which respect it may be pointed out that their positions differed little from that of others, the French, for example. The similarity lay in the fact that all wanted to retain a position of supremacy for themselves, the difference in that between the land and the sea.

Mention has already been made of the Washington Naval Conference of 1921–22. Britain readily acquiesced in parity with the United States, a position all the easier to take from the extreme unlikelihood of a clash between the two and from what would have been the futility of engaging in competition with America. The reality of a common Anglo-American front was thereby emphasized, for which the basic community of interests was more dependable insurance than formal treaties of alliance. But deference to the superiority of American power, and the desire to maintain the American connection, also took the form of the arrangements that dealt with the Far East.[21] The outcome was undoubtedly a successful assertion of American wishes and constituted a measure of retreat for Japan, but most significant of all in the present context, Britain relinquished her 1902 alliance with that country. Japan was hardly pleased, and she felt humiliated, but the validity of Britain's tacit choice was to be demonstrated in another twenty years.

The Far Eastern community of English and American interests may be said to have had its counterpart in a similar community of English and French interests in Europe. But here the historic background was less favorable and the element of concern about the extent and the use of French power intruded. The difference over Germany has been indicated, to which the Ruhr episode had given sharp focus. But the tale of traditional imperial rivalry, the presumable settlement of which had been the basis of the 1904 Entente, experienced a recurrence now that the common German threat had been at least momentarily eliminated.

ANGLO-FRENCH RIVALRY IN THE NEAR EAST

The circumstances of the war had placed the French at a disadvantage where matters imperial were concerned. The Western front had inevitable priority in the allotment of their resources and it was natural that the British share should be the larger in the conquest of the German holdings and in the Near Eastern theater. The wartime agreements, expression of the balance of interests and of forces, have been examined in the preceding chapter, as well as their registration in the peace. The attribution of the German colonies was source of no appreciable difference, but it was otherwise in the Near East, where the French experienced difficulty in establishing control in their allotted share.[22] The Arabs, be they nationalists of Western style or feudal chieftains, agreed in their desire for independence. To the ambiguous wartime promises made to Sherif Hussein by the British was added the Anglo-French declaration of November 11, 1918, that promised liberation from Turkish control to the subject peoples of the Turks. Between that date and the signature of the Treaty of Sèvres in August 1920 there was restlessness in the

Arab Near East. Faisal, second son of Hussein, contrived to erect under his rule an Arab kingdom in Syria. He was in Paris during the Peace Conference to present his case and got as far as obtaining the promise of an inter-Allied mission to Syria. Owing to French and Italian refusal, with which the British went along, the mission was inauspiciously reduced to its American members, Doctors King and Crane. Honest, but less than tactful in proceeding independently of the Allies, the King-Crane mission reported that the Syrian Arabs wanted independence. Barring this, an American mandate was their preference, the British were their second choice, but in no case the French. The report, as might be expected, was shelved.

These activities were calculated to feed French distrust. The idea died hard in France of British plotting to evict them totally from the Near East. While there was no such plotting, the suspicion was fed by the work and behavior of certain individuals; the famous Lawrence of Arabia was certainly enamored of the Arabs and definitely not pro-French; he went as far as feeling that his own people had betrayed the Arabs. Also it should be pointed out that the British held views that were at once more flexible and of more far-reaching scope than did the French. While the latter, in consonance with their own colonial tradition and practice, wanted firm control, at least a protectorate in a limited area, the former could envisage a far looser arrangement which would still secure their paramount influence in the entire Arab world. From this standpoint a French presence was at least inconvenient. Given this set of circumstances, Anglo-French differences need no further explaining.

It was unfortunate, in addition, that in part owing to a failure of communication, the French established themselves in Syria in 1919–20 through military action. Faisal, whom the Syrians undoubtedly wanted, was evicted from Syria. The meeting at San Remo in April 1920 confirmed France's title to the Syrian and Lebanese mandates and this was written into the Treaty of Sèvres.[23]

This state of affairs must be seen as a continuation, or a resumption, of the nineteenth-century Anglo-French rivalry in that part of the world. The record of it so far had been of gradual French retreat, of which the renunciation of Egypt had been the last and most important manifestation. English control of Egypt, become a protectorate in December 1914, was not called into question.

As pointed out before, in terms of empire, the outcome of the war, where Britain was concerned, appeared as inserting itself to perfection into the classical tradition. Britain obtained control of some former German colonies, but most of all, through mandates or alliances, she seemed to have secured predominance in the Near East, the intervening region between the Mediterranean and her Indian possession. Yet this accomplishment, which marks the high point of a long-established trend, soon appeared to be ashes, for it almost immediately became a turning point, beginning of the process of retreat of empire. The unexpected turn of events in the reduced Turkey of the Treaty of Sèvres may be called the catalytic agent of reversal.

Already before the signature of that treaty, Mustapha Kemal, defying the Sultan, had set about building the new Turkey, resuming the long-frustrated attempt to introduce that country into the modern world. His ultimate success may be attributed to two causes, in addition to his own abilities. One was the fact that nationalist Turkey, while intensely nationalistic,[24] genuinely renounced empire; the Arabs must be left to their fate, in which Turkish interference was scrupulously eschewed. The Treaty of Sèvres was reality for them; for Turkey proper it was a meaningless scrap of paper.

The other reason for Kemal's success may be described as the war-weariness of the Allies, unwilling or unable to exert sufficient force against him, to which must be added their rivalries. Britain stood alone at Chanak[25] in October 1922, deserted by the French and the Italians, her request for Dominion assistance coolly received by the latter. For the rest, the luckless Greeks were also left to their fate—and their doom—finally sealed at Smyrna. The French and the Italians had been allotted spheres of influence in Anatolia. For the retention of these they would not fight in earnest; the Italians were first in adopting a policy of accommodation with Kemal, hoping to retrieve by this method some of their influence in the Near East; the French soon followed their example.[26] It is no great exaggeration to describe the Greco-Turkish War as an Anglo-French contest at one remove, in part on the French side retaliation for the course of events in the Arab world.

There was nothing for it but for Britain to cut her losses. As Bonar Law put it in *The Times* on October 6, "We cannot act alone as the policemen of the world."[27] Lloyd George's policy had failed—his tenure of office came to an end shortly thereafter—and the Treaty of Lausanne in July 1923 registered the formal recognition of the new Turkey; Curzon's skillful negotiation could not alter the fundamental fact. This turning point in British influence in the Near East was further emphasized by the fact that negotiations had been in progress since 1922 for a revision of the status of Egypt, the beginning of another long story of retreat in the Near Eastern quarter.

In the context of Anglo-French relations at the turn from 1922 to 1923—the Near East and the Ruhr—the discussion of an alliance may appear like an exercise in futility. Indeed it was, and there was point to the British insistence that differences between the two must first be settled despite the French assertion that they were peripheral and should not interfere with the more fundamental issue that was the German problem.

THE FRENCH ORGANIZATION OF EUROPE AND THE LIMITATIONS OF FRENCH POWER

The French Security System

Poincaré was the man to assert French power. In accord with Britain, preferably and if possible, but without her if need be, France would proceed with the organization of her own security. Power may be resented, but it also commands attraction and respect. It is of interest to note that the Italians exemplified precisely this; sharing the British view on the whole as they did, their policy in the Near East and toward Germany followed nevertheless in the French wake.[28]

Here we come to a fundamental aspect of the whole European scene, where on the Continent French power was for the moment the only organized reality. The abandonment of the Anglo-American guarantee was understandably, and not unjustifiably, resented by France. It was an invitation to search for alternative solutions. For these there was ample material at hand owing to the simple fact that a number of European states shared the French wish to preserve the advantages that they had reaped from the outcome of the war, the German defeat, the Russian collapse, and the demise of the Austro-Hungarian empire.

From the French point of view the first alone of these elements really mattered; the Russian collapse had been regrettable and the destruction of the Habsburg empire was irretrievable. They were, however, inescapable facts to which adjustment was necessary; like it or not, France cannot adopt a policy of isolation in Europe. It is out of these circumstances that developed the French organization of Europe. It is the usual experience that the victors become conservative defenders of the status quo which registers their advantage. Consequently, be it vis-à-vis Germany and for her own protection, or elsewhere lest dangerous revisionist precedent be created, France would become the defender of the existing state of things everywhere.

This policy found expression in the conclusion of a number of treaties designed to deal with this state of affairs, the three great problems with which Europe was confronted, the German, the Russian, and the Danubian.

The peace had not restored the neutral status of Belgium, which the German action in 1914 had destroyed. The reality of French power could be a more concrete and dependable guarantee for Belgium than unreliable promises, while the asset of Belgium, in terms of geography and resources, if small compared to France's own, was by no means negligible. This is sufficient explanation of the conclusion of a Franco-Belgian alliance, which took place in September 1920.[29]

The case of Poland was more complicated and contained more far-reaching implications. Reborn after more than a century of alien rules, Poland had equal cause to fear her two potentially powerful neighbors, between whom she might be hard put to make a choice, especially as both entertained irredentist grievances against her.

The common Franco-Polish interest vis-à-vis Germany was obvious and fitted into the traditional French policy of enlisting support in Eastern Europe against whatever Power, Habsburg or Hohenzollern, might dominate the center. A Franco-Polish alliance came into existence in February 1921, which proclaimed the dedication of both countries to the preservation of the peace of Europe and their common interest in the maintenance of the existing treaties; it provided for concerted action in the event that *either or both* should be the object of an unprovoked aggression.

The Russian factor could not be ignored at this point. Russia had been France's ally and represented a good deal more than Poland. But Russia was gone, and in addition the ideology to which her government was dedicated professed world revolution as one of its aims. In the Bolshevik view, France, because of her organized power, was the most objectionable defender of the existing social order. France correspondingly feared the Bolshevik infection, and, once intervention in Russia had failed, would become the defender of Europe against the spread of the virus. This was the policy of the *cordon sanitaire,* earlier version of the American one of containment, in which Poland played the role of kingpin.[30] The range of French commitments may already be noted at this point, but there were more to come.

Three states in Central Europe were beneficiaries of the demise of Austria-Hungary. In 1921, in the form of three bilateral agreements involving Czechoslovakia, Roumania, and Yugoslavia, the Little Entente came into existence. Its aim was the prevention of Habsburg restoration and most of all opposition to Hungarian nationalist revindications.[31] France had no quarrel with Hungary, with whom in fact she had at one point been even sympathetic during the peace negotiations. But, as mentioned before, France feared the precedent of successful revisionism in any quarter, and therefore was inclined to endorse the conservative aims of the Little Entente.

It took some time before formal links were established between herself and that grouping. In 1924, 1925, and 1927 treaties were concluded between France and Czechoslovakia, Roumania, and Yugoslavia respectively. The first of these had a German focus, the second fitted into the policy of the *cordon sanitaire;* as to Yugoslavia, she had a bone to pick with Italy, both on irredentist grounds and because she feared that country's further ambitions.[32]

The French organization of Europe, or French security system, deserves some critical examination. The greatest source of strength of it, one that should not be minimized, lay in the authenticity of the common interest shared by the participants in the system. Without a doubt for the near future, so long as Germany and Russia would be impotent, but for the longer term as well, when that condition would no longer obtain, the totality of resources, manpower, economy, and wealth contained in the collectivity of its members represented an impressive amount. It could be a comforting exercise in Paris to indulge in the simple arithmetic of adding Polish, Czech, and other divisions to those which the French Army could produce.

But here also was the source of possible weakness and flaws. For in order to insure its effectiveness, this collectivity must operate in unison. If France could envisage with satisfaction the diversion of German force that an eastern Polish front would entail, the reverse was even more true. France might indeed save Poland from destruction, but in the last analysis, Poland could hardly save France unless that country was capable of furnishing the more substantial effort. France in other words must be prepared to take the initiative of action to assist Poland—and others—should they be the ones to be primarily endangered; she could not merely rest content to rely on *their* assistance when she herself would be threatened.

During the decade of the twenties this was largely a hypothetical question, yet one which it did not need the wisdom of hindsight to foresee the possibility of its eventually arising. Some things were very clear, the fundamentally defensive attitude of the French people, their revulsion toward the fact of war, the lack in short of an aggressive will. Poincaré to be sure did possess such a will, and was indeed considered by many, outside of France but even in France to a point, as having an excess of it; the episode of the Ruhr could be cited as evidence. But how long would Poincaré, and the tendency which he personified, last? The element of will thus appears to be all-important in the situation. Should French will falter, the whole network of alliances would not be worth the paper it was written on. We shall presently see the effects of the lack of French will.

But there was more, which may be put under two heads: the allies of France themselves, the other Great Powers. Foreign policy and military power are not abstractions divorced from the concrete bases of power, among which the importance of economic factors need hardly be stressed. France's allies, with the exception of economically well-balanced Czechoslovakia, were primarily agricultural producers, and they all faced the problem of creating orderly economic and financial conditions for themselves, of finding markets and sources of supply for their needs. In this respect, Germany, not France, was their more natural connection; it is the sense in which Central Europe "belongs" to, or at least with, Germany. In the financial sphere alone could France be of substantial assistance, as in fact she was. Despite the severe losses she had suffered herself, France was still wealthy; she could and did make considerable loans to her Eastern allies, as she had earlier to Russia; the fundamental motivation was the same, before 1914 and after 1920.[33]

France thus found herself in the position of having undertaken to organize the major part of continental Europe outside the Soviet Union. The system was designed to thwart German, but also Russian, revisionist aims, the abandonment of which could hardly be expected on the part of these countries. One consequence of it was to induce a measure at least of Russo-German co-operation, as Rapallo[34] prematurely announced. The fact that a new ideology had taken over the control of Russia had here divergent effects: it reduced the possibility of accommodation on the one hand; on the other, it tended to strengthen the bond between France and her Central and Eastern European allies, all of whom had strong anti-communist régimes. But this condition also had the effect of impeding internal reforms, at least of slowing them down, of thus increasing the domestic social and political strains in the countries of mid Europe, hardly a source of reliable strength.

Italy was not yet a revisionist state. But Italy was very dissatisfied with the peace. More important perhaps than the specific grievances that she nurtured—the substance of these was rather small—was the fact that the outcome of the war had robbed her of the best asset of her foreign policy, the balance of power. Italy viewed with a jaundiced eye the seemingly dominant position of French power, and France on her side, not needing Italy for the moment, tended to be somewhat cavalier in her treatment of that country.[35] There was one common real interest between the two, the preservation of the independence of Austria, but for the rest Italy was resentful of the predominance of French influence in Danubia, which she had hoped would be her own preserve after the demise of the Dual Monarchy.

This more than ever put Italy in the British camp. As we have seen, Britain was torn between the willingness, born of the acceptance of the long-term desirability of the French alliance, to work with France, and the current feeling that French power was at once too great and abusively handled.

The preceding considerations show the magnitude and the risks of the task undertaken by France, faced with the probably irreconcilable opposition of Germany and of Russia, with the more qualified one of Britain and of Italy. One may be tempted to draw a comparison between the post-First World War French system and the earlier one created by Bismarck. The similarity of the association of satisfied powers desirous to preserve the status quo—Russia was only qualifiedly so in Bismarck's time—should not conceal the great difference. Bismarck himself could be on good terms with all the Great Powers, except France, for whose isolation he successfully strove; but equally important, Bismarck, if genuinely a man of peace after 1871, would not recoil before the use of force if needed. The emphasis therefore is on contrast between the prevalent mood of Bismarckian and Wilhelmine Germany and the France of post-1919. Put in another way, Bismarck had operated from a position of strength, France was operating from a position of weakness, whatever appearances might be.[36]

Are There no Alternatives?

COLLECTIVE SECURITY, A TALE OF FUTILE SEARCH

Poincaré's policy was not without its critics in France, where some even had dubbed him *Poincaré-la-guerre.*[37] If he had stood up to Curzon, to the latter's discomfiture, and if he had forced a new German surrender, these successes did not conceal some shortcomings of his policy. The Ruhr episode gave rise to some violent feelings in Germany but it also had a clarifying effect, of which the advent to power of Stresemann was the manifestation.[38] Stresemann was a patriotic German, wholly dedicated to the restoration of his country's position, but Stresemann also understood the realities of power. For the moment at least, the association of German weakness with Russian impotence was a counterproducing policy. The connection need not be broken—as in fact it was not—but Germany must come to terms with the West, meaning primarily France, especially in the absence of more effective British support.

On the French side, if German will had been broken, the concrete results of the occupation were meager at best. There was alarm in France at the fall of the value of the franc,[39] especially in the light of what had happened to the German mark, nor was the widespread condemnation abroad of French behavior without impact at home. The general election of May 1924 was a success for the Left, the Cartel des Gauches, and a repudiation of Poincaré. Edouard Herriot, leader of the Radical Socialist party, that bulwark of the Third Republic, succeeded Poincaré as both Premier and foreign minister in June.

Four months earlier Ramsay MacDonald had become the first Labour prime minister of Britain, likewise taking charge of the foreign office. The change in England was more narrowly a response to the domestic state of the economy[40] and MacDonald's position was less secure than Herriot's owing to the fact that he led a minority government dependent for its existence on Liberal support.

These nearly simultaneous changes augured a possible change in orientation, though hardly a sharp about-face, in the foreign policies of the two countries. The new combination in England was if anything more inclined toward sympathy for Germany than its predecessor. Curiously in a way, the outlook of British Labour in general may be described as more parochial than that of its Conservative opponents, yet at the same time more responsive to the "collectivist," or "Messianic" approach to international problems such as the League of Nations, or better, the ideal of the League of Nations, exemplifies. More "traditionalist" Conservative opinion in England had evinced marked scepticism of the Wilsonian gift to mankind, just as had its counterpart, the Right in France. The conjunction of Herriot and MacDonald might be the prelude to a fresh attempt, rooted in a liberal, conciliatory, internationalist approach, to extricate Europe from the morass of the German problem. Western-oriented Stresemann might help. This is what came to pass in a sense, though not quite in the way that might have been expected after the Chequers meeting of Herriot and MacDonald in June.[41]

We must go back a little at this point. We shall not repeat what has been said of the 1919 discussions,[42] out of which the Covenant emerged, beyond recalling the French caveat: the League in brief would be acceptable to France provided it had teeth. Since inevitably such an institution must begin with the world as it is at a particular point of time, the status quo created by the war must be its base. The League, therefore, must be an element in the defense and preservation of the existing situation, though this did not preclude sincere devotion to the new ideal as a substitute for the old ways of power politics and alliances on the part of an appreciable section of French opinion, broadly speaking, the liberal Left.[43] But even that opinion would not relinquish the shadow of hope for the substance of solid guarantees; quite consistently, also, it insisted on the indivisibility of peace and on the value—or the danger—of precedent. As Herriot himself put it in the Senate on July 11, 1924, *"Une fois le premier détail de l'architecture tombé, tout l'édifice tomberait lui-même."*[44]

In Geneva, where the League came to have its home, the French position had stressed the necessity of giving precision and force to the loose language of the Anglo-American Covenant. The debate was moreover linked with the related one on disarmament, for many felt that the destruction of Germany's armed force was but a prelude to that desirable precedent being followed by others. The division of opinion was sharp and clear between those who saw security as a precondition to disarmament and those, more trusting, who would have reversed the causal relationship between the two. It was not so much a question of which was right as of different geographical conditions and consequent historical experiences, land powers versus sea powers to a large extent; in concrete terms between French and English. The logic, if also the hopelessness, of the French contention may be granted, as shown by subsequent discussions of the issue since, and by the reversal of the American stand, for example, now that the United States feels deprived of the traditional assets of the protection of the sea, naval power, and distance.

No attempt will be made to follow the lengthy, to a large extent dreary and futile, Genevan discussions, or the multitude of projects to which they gave rise. They have been rehearsed often and in many places.[45] But, briefly, two or three episodes must be mentioned. It was in 1923 that a Draft Treaty of Mutual Assistance, an extended form in a sense of the French attempt to obtain the insurance of a British alliance, was presented to members and non-members of the League. It received very wide support, but, ironically, it fell to MacDonald to reject it in the following July,[46] thereby killing a possibility that could not be realized without British endorsement. On the score of assuming problematic commitments of unpredictable range the British attitude was one of widespread reluctance that transcended party lines.

But in part owing to the internationalist—even if somewhat theoretical and abstract—bent of British Labour, in part because of the exertions of some able representatives of the smaller Powers, such men as Beneš of Czechoslovakia and Politis of Greece, it proved possible to bridge Anglo-French differences. This was done in the Geneva Protocol, which produced the imaginative solution to the definition of aggression of equating that recalcitrant concept with the refusal of arbitration, or of the verdict of arbitration, to which all would commit themselves. The Protocol was unanimously endorsed by the Assembly of the League in October.

It was again Britain's turn to default, for the Conservative administration to which the Labour government gave way after the election of the same month,[47] was at once more and less sympathetic to foreign entanglements. The broad internationalistic outlook did not appeal to it, and indeed there was validity in the consideration of the extent of Britain's responsibilities, especially in the light of the lack of universality of the

League; a more limited assumption of responsibility, such as the 1902 alliance with Japan or the 1904 French Entente represented, was more congenial ground. Whatever the differences with France may have been, there was willingness to acknowledge that the safety of the Rhine frontier was a direct British interest. This is the seed out of which Locarno was born.

The new British Government was again headed by Stanley Baldwin, who may be characterized as endowed with both shrewdness and slothfulness. The following, if perhaps unduly gentle, is not an unfair portrait of the man who was to fill such an important part of the British political scene between the wars:

> The strength of his position came from the fact that he was not an out-and-out Conservative, but a moderate, representing himself as the plain man, a man of sanity, without art or guile, a countryman puffing slowly on his pipe and (so the cartoonists would have it) gazing pensively at his pigs. He seemed to represent Old England, and his speeches, reflecting on love of country and countryside, underlined this, just as his indifference concerning foreigners—later a handicap—confirmed it. In spite of appearances, however, he proved himself the ablest politician of the day, and in a crisis fully the master of events.
>
> Yet his power and ability came from his apparent lack of them; people trusted him—and they did trust him—because he appeared to be *not* a politician, but the plain man in politics. And in part this was true: his policy was to have no policy; he never had a plan ahead of a gathering crisis. He hated coming to decisions, and to do so made him physically nervous, so that his hand would twitch. He was in fact a very sensitive person, behind his bovine mask. When in doubt, he preferred to do nothing, hoping that things would settle themselves. He admitted that he was a lazy man. . . . In a crisis he would withdraw to his sanctum; or if it was acute, go to bed. . . .
>
> In the Cabinet Baldwin seldom gave a lead. . . . In keeping with this spirit was his devotion to the House of Commons, and his friendliness and accessibility to all members (except the intellectuals whom, characteristically, he had great contempt for); Labour members, in particular, trusted him and liked him in private. And this because, essentially, his policy was that of the moderate trade unionist; to prevent the spreading of the class war, to lower

the temperature, to achieve as he put it in his moving speech in parliament in March 1925, "peace in our time." Who in England did not want that? Here lay his strength, and his weakness; he would not fight for what he believed, particularly against his own party, until a crisis came upon him, and he tired easily. In both his public and his private character there was much that was endearing; but he lacked the touch of greatness, content to follow events, not to master them.[48]

Foreign affairs were in the hands of Austen Chamberlain, not as strong a personality as his father, Joseph. It fell to his lot to pronounce the funeral oration of the Geneva Protocol, which he did in Geneva in March 1925. This position was consistent with the general Conservative reluctance toward commitments of broad and indefinite scope. Chamberlain nevertheless was sensitive to the awkwardness of having been the instrument that deceived widespread hopes. This fact, together with his own general Francophile inclination, in combination with the Conservative preference for limited commitments, resulted in the contribution he made to the assuagement of hopes he had himself frustrated.

He had to deal with a new French government, for Herriot had been brought down in April[49]; but this had little effect on the direction of France's foreign policy, which in fact entered a period of unusually stable continuity. Briand came to the foreign office, a place he was to retain for almost seven years, through a succession of French governments, some of which he headed himself. The case of Briand brings to mind the earlier one of Delcassé, and the quip, made in connection with the instability of French governments in comparison with the greater stability of the British, that it is preferable to have a number of governments which adhere to a consistent policy than to have a durable government without a policy. Allowing for the facetiousness of the remark, where foreign policy is concerned it remains true that, within broad limits, France was embarking on a period of greater continuity than Britain.

In the unfolding of French foreign policy this is a highly important interval. Ending in failure as it did, it represents nevertheless a French attempt to find an alternative to the policy of mere coercion. How and why it failed the following pages will endeavor to show.

THE SPIRIT OF LOCARNO

The circumstances of 1925–26 seemed favorable to a novel approach. Even the episode of the Ruhr occupation, like a burst abscess, had had a clarifying and in some ways a not unhealthy effect. Out of it came the Dawes Plan, a restored German currency, and Stresemann the "Westerner." Britain's return to the gold standard at the pre-1914 parity of the pound was intended as a manifestation that the impact of the war had been successfully absorbed, and the American debt had also been funded.[50] France was about to do the same, and she, too, would succeed in stabilizing the franc, albeit at only one fifth of its prewar value. The less intransigeant Left was in control.[51]

There is no need to dwell on the background of negotiations, the origins of which can be traced to 1922. It is fair to describe them as an Anglo-German initiative.[52] The discussions began in earnest in February 1925 and were mainly, on the French side, conducted by Briand. They made sufficient progress during the course of the year to make possible the famous meeting that took place in the pleasant surroundings of Locarno in October, when a number of instruments were signed.[53]

The most important of these was the so-called Rhineland Pact, which involved the acceptance by Germany of her frontiers with France and Belgium. The acceptance was reciprocal, and the integrity of these frontiers was guaranteed by Britain and by Italy. There was more—which was to be highly significant ten years later—for the demilitarization of the Rhineland (Articles 42 and 43 of the Treaty of Versailles) was equally guaranteed.

Here was obviously a large German concession, the kind no French government would make after 1871. The guarantee fitted well the British willingness to assume a definite and limited commitment; it had been reiterated in a British foreign office memorandum of February, which expressed the opinion that it was "a necessity of British and, therefore, of imperial defense to reach some understanding with France and Belgium which may entail a guarantee on our part that these territories shall not fall into other hands."[54] The stress must be put on "limited commitment," for there was no counterpart in the East to what was being done in the West. Germany refused to undertake a similar commitment in that quarter, meaning that she did not renounce—in fact by indirection reasserted—the validity of her revisionist aims in that region. She would, to be sure, eschew the use of force, as evidenced by the arbitration treaties between herself on the one hand, Poland and Czechoslovakia on the other, which formed part of the Locarno network. Even more, the Franco-Polish and the Franco-Czech alliances were reaffirmed.

Here was clearly an ambiguity, possibly left for the future to resolve. The guarantee of the Western frontier may be seen as the equivalent of an Anglo-French alliance. Even if it was couched in such form as to soothe German feeling, since, theoretically, Germany was guaranteed against French aggression quite as much as the reverse, it was difficult in actual fact to conceive of a situation where Britain would be brought to use armed force against France. But what of the possibility that France should take the initiative in defense of her commitments to her Eastern allies? It was improbable that Britain would consider this a case of French aggression, but would she judge it the reverse within the meaning of the Rhineland Pact?

The simple truth is that Britain was returning to the past, the uncertainties of pre-1914 and of July 1914, and enhancing her arbitral position. France and Belgium she would indeed defend—her own clear interest was involved—and her abstention might be a brake on the possibility of French action. There was no need of the hindsight of 1936 and 1938 to foresee such possibilities in 1925, and they were realized in France.[55] Nor should the collective note to Germany by which the other Powers, in view of her disarmed condition, gave a satisfactory (to her) interpretation of her obligations under Article 16 of the Covenant, be overlooked.

Much therefore would depend upon future German intentions and behavior, obviously unknown quantities in 1925. If Germany on her side made the very substantial contribution of *freely*, rather than by *Diktat*, accepting many remaining disabilities, she undoubtedly also achieved a great success, the recovery of respectability and standing among states, a fact of which her admission to membership in the League in 1926, a corollary of Locarno, was the clearest registration.

Where France was concerned we are touching upon a most fundamental problem of her foreign policy. The German danger was the great French obsession; France had endeavored to deal with it through suppression, at best a difficult position to sustain for an indefinite time, especially in the face of widespread criticism abroad, the unfavorable tone of much of world opinion. Might true reconciliation with Germany be the answer?

Here we come to another difficulty. Disarmed and impotent though she was at the moment, Germany still contained great potential and as a consequence she remained the central problem of Europe, as she had been before 1914. From the standpoint of finding her proper place among nations, the war had undoubtedly been a grievous setback. What view did the German people take of their rightful position? Mention is relevant at this point of the two legends which had gained widespread currency in Germany, both of them designed to exonerate the "honor" of the German Army, or at least the honored place that the military had filled in the German record: that of Allied treachery in the armistice negotiations, followed by a peace in which they had supposedly broken their pledges; that of the stab in the back from German weaklings at home, Socialists and their ilk.

Yet it was precisely these elements which had set up and organized the Weimar Republic. Despite subsequent setbacks, they still carried much weight.[56] Like the rest of the German people they agreed on the "iniquities" of Versailles, the Ruhr and the consequent catastrophic inflation. Stresemann was not one of them, but from them his moderate, Western-oriented policy derived its main support. The redress of grievances they wanted but aggressive intent was not part of their program. They might well be content with a "reasonable" and legitimate place for Germany, and, above all, if satisfactory economic conditions could be restored and maintained in the country, the German problem might yet be capable of solution. There was much to be said for giving encouragement to the liberal tendency, the Left in general, which did exist in Germany.

To this the French could make a large contribution, and the policy for which Briand stood might be the harbinger of better times. But it must also be expected that, once embarked on the path of concessions, more would have to be yielded; the very granting of some could not but be an encouragement to the demand for more. This Briand understood, but the question was, how much and how fast? To say nothing of the nationalist opposition in France, even the liberal Left did not feel that it could gamble French security. Herriot had abstained in the vote on the Ruhr occupation in the French Chamber, and he did not believe that France should act in isolation from Britain, but that did not mean he was willing to relinquish the solid guarantees that France held in the form of Germany's disarmament or the Rhineland occupation; nor would he give up reparations. In defending Locarno before the French parliament Briand had laid stress on the value of these same solid and concrete guarantees which remained in French hands; Locarno did not render obsolete the Treaty of Versailles.

He was willing enough to make further concessions and even to overlook German breaches of the disarmament provisions of the treaty of peace, and he loyally supported Germany's candidacy to League admission, using the occasion of her accession for one of his most impressive and successful flights of oratory in Geneva. His speech was very well received, a fact which constitutes an accurate reflection of a widespread outlook in 1926. For this was the heyday of the League, which many hoped and felt might become a reality and supersede the dreary and outdated game of power rivalries.

Could France have made a *grand geste,* wiping the slate clean of discriminatory advantage, and thereby hoping, through this evidence of trust, to earn Germany's friendship and gratitude? One is tempted to mention Konrad Adenauer at this point, but we shall meet him later, after much more will have happened. The prospect may have been attractive, but actually the deed could only have been done by a France sufficiently strong, reliant on her own power, instead of by one aware of a fundamentally weaker position. We cannot know what the effects of such an attempt would have been: perhaps a peaceful, reconciled Germany; but perhaps also one more quickly resuming the old path. In fairness, it could hardly be asked of any responsible French statesman, however starry-eyed he might be, to incur the risks of such a gamble, not to mention the fact that, had one tried, he certainly would not have long retained his office. Given the long-term relationship of forces, Germany and others, too, must make a contribution to French and to general security.

The League of course might be an answer, and there was for it a substantial current of support in France. But the perennial problem recurred of how to make a League guarantee sufficiently credible and foolproof so that it would be a dependable substitute for one's own means of defense. French efforts to do this, quite logical in their approach, nevertheless took, in the eyes of many, the color of an attempt to enlist the rest of the world, the League members at least, in the protection of France. And one may say, why not? Should not the League become an automatic world coalition in support of any victim of aggression, France or anyone else? At which point the difficulty recurs of defining aggression, and of the willingness of some, France not excluded, to undertake uncertain and unlimited commitments.[57]

The same sort of difficulty bedeviled the everlasting discussion of disarmament, the French position ever a variation on the theme "We shall gladly disarm as soon as and to the extent that we feel secure." The French insistence on measures of control and on measurable criteria for the estimate of power, in being and potential, ran into the difficulties which still beset such discussions at present. Some thought it insincere pretext for the preservation of a hegemonic position.[58]

There is no need to dwell at length on this dreary record of impotence. Briand, who supported the League, had other ideas as well. Speaking before the Assembly of the League on September 5, 1929, he assumed the sponsorship of the concept of European union.[59] He was entrusted with the task of pursuing his scheme, and the following May he produced a lengthy memorandum outlining in detail his ideas. Here was an imaginative approach, a prescient realization that the age of Europe's civil wars had been superseded. Of it it will suffice to say that the replies that came were disappointing, full of reservations and doubts; the proposal was in effect politely pigeonholed. By 1930 and 1931 the urgent preoccupations of Europe were others.

Some other things had happened by this time which, though seemingly of not overwhelming importance at the time of their occurrence, are nonetheless revealing of the direction of French policy. French criticism of Locarno has been mentioned. But the Poles, for example, had reservations as well. To the extent that their alliance with France was mainly looked upon by them as reinsurance for their own protection, what incentive would be left for France to come to the assistance of Poland once the aims of her own security were achieved? Even the reassertion of the alliance as part of the Locarno network of agreements did not completely set Polish qualms to rest.

These received added confirmation from subsequent developments in France. As Stresemann kept pressing for additional concessions, the rewards of Germany's "good" behavior, Briand was not unwilling to make some. The settlement of German reparations that was the Dawes Plan was an incomplete arrangement which set no terminal date for their payment. Following the conclusion of the agreements which funded the various wartime debts to the United States, the debtors, who were creditors of Germany on the score of reparations, won their point of establishing at least a de facto connection between the two sets of obligations.[60] This was one fundamental result of the Young Plan, which set for reparations the terminal date of 1988 and came into effect in May 1930. The German concession—such was the German view of it in Germany—was matched by a French one in the form of agreeing to an advanced termination of the fifteen-year occupation of the Rhineland, a quid pro quo[61] which might be interpreted as confirmation of the continuing relaxation. Actually it was not; rightly or wrongly, France did not feel sufficiently secure.

The termination of the occupation did not affect the demilitarization clauses of the treaty of peace with Germany. It made a difference, nevertheless, whether or not the Rhineland bridgeheads were in French hands, especially in the event of needed French action against Germany, say in support of Poland. This did not pass unnoticed in France, the words of whose war minister, André Maginot, may be cited:

> There is no doubt that, on the day when, as a result of the withdrawal of our troops, our northeastern frontier will be deprived of the protection given it by the barrier of the Rhine, it will be indispensable that this frontier, which will remain open, be assured of a new protection by means of a strong defensive organization.
>
> No one in France would understand it if the evacuation of the Rhineland ahead of the established schedule should not be immediately accompanied by provisions for the defense of, our northeastern frontier.[62]

These words were spoken in the Chamber in connection with the request for credits for the *organisation défensive de la frontière*. The debate took place in the closing days of December, although the project had been under study for some time, just after the evacuation of the second zone of occupation and six months before the advanced evacuation of the third and last zone. Thus the Maginot Line came into existence, a highly impressive defensive accomplishment indeed.

What better evidence could be cited of the lack of aggressive French intent? But also what better way to raise doubts among France's Central and Eastern European allies about the reliability of French purpose? Of the value of the Maginot Line as a base from which to launch an attack one can only take a sceptical view; and what would be the sense of a purely defensive war fought by France in assisting Poland or Czechoslovakia? France's protestations of pacific intent were in fact a far more accurate expression of her real mood and desires than the often accepted interpretation of militaristic and hegemonic intent. Perhaps it would be more accurate to say that France could not make up her mind, for neither would she face the implications of being content with her own safety, regardless of what else might happen in Europe; it would take some years before it came to that. At any rate the credits were voted, the Maginot Line was built, and the implications of it were not lost on France's allies. At the very least, and ironically, the strengthening of French defense implied a serious weakening of the French security system.

Thus Briand's long tenure of the foreign office falls into two very distinct parts. The first half of it, to 1929, was the heyday of success, when the "spirit of Locarno" was abroad. His efforts were undoubtedly sincere to liquidate the aftermath of the war, to reintegrate Germany as a respected and respectable member of the community of states. In retrospect they may appear naïve and futile. Without a doubt they failed, but one must guard against the easy wisdom of hindsight and as a consequence fail to understand the mood and the spirit which prevailed in Europe and the world for a brief span of years.[63] They constitute an attempt that was anything but ignoble, or in the context of the day wholly unrealistic and doomed a priori. The failure became increasingly clear during the last years of Briand's tenure of office, and he died shortly after relinquishing it a sad and disappointed man. Something will have to be said of how and why things went wrong, of how men of good will were unable to control forces of which they had but an imperfect understanding. However, before doing this something more must be said about the concerns of British policy and the manner in which Britain attempted to deal with them.

British Fumbling in the Twenties

This subject has been covered in part, and we have seen the British opposition to certain French policies and actions, especially when these seemed to interfere with the British predilection for an equilibrium of power. But the divergence between the two countries must be kept in proportion; however much they might disagree, the probability of armed conflict between them remained well-nigh unthinkable. French power might be overinflated, for the moment at least, and in need of some curbing, but fundamentally the thought was accepted in Britain that her frontier was on the Rhine. Where the difficulty lay, a serious shortcoming indeed, was in the reluctance to acknowledge that, since Germany was a unit and bordered on France as well as on Poland, it was futile to pretend that the connection between

Western and Eastern Europe could be ignored. The result was the typical ambiguity of Locarno, which restored in some measure Britain's arbitral position, yet failed to answer certain questions, just as they had been left unanswered before July 1914.

In any case, during the twenties Britain failed to assert a strong leadership. Much of the discussion, of the German danger, for instance, was obviously theoretical for the moment. Why seek to fetter the future in a too rigid mold instead of trusting to pragmatic flexibility? This made it all the more possible to concentrate on two things, domestic affairs and extra-European developments.

Of the former it will only be said at this point that the difficulties which had confronted Britain already before the turn of the century now existed in accentuated form. They were in part the result of the prior start in industrial development, which, initially an advantage, was now turning into a handicap in the competition with more recently risen rivals, among whom the United States, Germany, and Japan stood in the forefront. The war had in addition seriously upset the delicate balance—imports, exports, the financial role of London in the world, returns of the carrying trade and those on foreign investment—of the British economy. Britain continued to grow, but at a slower pace than others, which meant in effect a relative decline. The return of the pound to the prewar gold parity in 1925, largely a matter of prestige and standing, has been generally adjudged a mistake which impeded the restoration of a proper trade balance; it was strongly opposed by some, Keynes, for example, at the time it was done. Half depressed and half prosperous, Britain jogged along, her attention absorbed in debate about unemployment, the fate of depressed industries and areas, the problem of wages and of the proper degree of responsibility of the state for social services. These matters, rather than foreign affairs, constituted the substance of British politics; the parliamentary debates do not reflect the concern for security so often found among the French; no such concern was felt in Britain.

The state of the economy nevertheless impinged on foreign affairs. Nineteenth-century Britain had become wedded to free trade and empire. The merits of the first were now questioned by some, but the tradition was still too strong and the power of the sacred cow could not yet be successfully challenged. For their Safeguarding of Industries Act, a measure of protection, the Conservatives were rebuked in the election of December 1923, as a result of which the first Labour prime minister of Britain came to power.

The liberal free trade tendency had had its counterpart in the liberal approach to the evolution of empire. Here there was continuity unchallenged, but the war had an impact on this evolution as well. Whether or not it be true that Britain exploited the Dominions, the relationship with them had undoubtedly been profitable. In some respects it was reversed, the Dominions now being desirous to maintain the benefits of their British connection. This meant in concrete terms that they were anxious to retain a monopoly of the British market, a large importer of food products and other raw materials. Tariffs Britain would not yet adopt at this point, and the discussions initiated at the conference that met in London in 1921 turned to constitutional issues. The outcome deserves no more than passing mention, for it merely confirmed the existing tradition. These constitutional matters were again taken up at the Imperial Conference of 1926 and the new relationship of the Commonwealth was finally defined in the Statute of Westminster of 1931. Balfour's definition of the collectivity is apt as "autonomous communities within the British Empire, equal in status, in no way subordinate to one another in any respect of their domestic or internal affairs, though united by a common allegiance to the Crown, and freely associated as members of the British Commonwealth of Nations."[64]

Here, too, was an experiment "noble in purpose," but in the present context the significance of it is not of great substance. It was still possible to believe, or to hope, that the method adopted—unrestricted freedom of evolution—would maintain the reality of a world-encompassing community. Yet the attachment of the Dominions to the prerogative of independence is also worth noting; it was probably irresistible in view of their growing maturity and of the decreased position of power of Britain herself. Here the role of the American impact must be mentioned, a fully emancipated dominion itself in a sense, but one which had achieved such dimensions of power as to overshadow the parent. It is very significant that at the Washington Naval Conference of 1921–22 the weight of the Pacific Dominions, Australia and New Zealand, conscious of the relative extents of British and American power, was used to induce Britain's acceptance of American preferences.[65] Lloyd George's bombast about the maintenance of Britain's naval supremacy had better be quietly forgotten. Canada, likewise, next-door to the United States, would fall increasingly in the wake of that country. For the rest, if the Dominions were desirous of cornering the British market for their own products, they were not loath to seek elsewere the satisfaction of their needs for manufactured products.

The empire proper therefore consisted of the rest of directly controlled British territory, still an impressive total. In it India stood in a special position. In economic terms, for example, she was no longer the privileged market of Britain's cotton mills and she appeared to some as a liability rather than an asset. Politically, the demand was increasingly being asserted for self-government; it dated from before the war, and the Indian National Congress was its chief spokesman. India had been promised "responsible government," though not full independence, in 1917. The judgment seems apt that the British "did not produce a Lord Durham for their Indian empire,"[66] in contrast with what they had done for Canada almost a century before. British dilatoriness, as it seemed to the Indians, resulted in resistance, of which Gandhi, that saintly and shrewd politician, became the embodiment. The suppressive methods that were tried seemed ill suited to cope with his weapon of non-violent illegality, and for that matter they were enforced with a lack of conviction. For a long time discussions led nowhere, but they were evidence of the loss of the determination which had been such an important factor in building the empire. Yet possibilities of accommodation were not entirely closed, and the significance of the Indian case was capital, for it meant a test of the possibility that the association of peoples that was the Commonwealth might be extended to include peoples of non-British descent.

The apparent success that was the establishment of a dominant position in the Middle East has been mentioned.[67] The just indicated uncertainties connected with India tended to detract from the importance of the Middle East as an avenue of communication, but on the other hand that region, not least because of its petroleum resources, was assuming greater importance in its own right. The early difficulties centering around Turkey have also been indicated. There were others as well, for the status of Egypt was unsettled. Anglo-Egyptian negotiations foundered on the issue of the control of the Sudan, which the British would not relinquish. They remained in Egypt, including Suez, but it was fairly predictable that the Egyptian question would not "go away" and could not be indefinitely kept unresolved. In Egypt, as elsewhere in the colonial world, European control had by this time been highly successful in implanting the seed of European ways, not least the nationalistic virus. This was very marked throughout the Arab world, where the French were confronted with a comparable problem, especially in their Tunisian and Moroccan protectorates.[68]

The protection of the Suez passage had been one of the reasons for the British establishment in Palestine. The dragon seeds contained in the wartime Balfour Declaration were barely beginning to sprout at a time when Jewish immigration was not very significant. But the seeds had been planted; with the harvest they would eventually yield the next chapter will deal.

Ireland, be it in terms of numbers or resources, is a small thing compared with Britain, and the early nineteenth-century fears of an inimical Ireland certainly belonged to the past. But the fact that she was part of the United Kingdom gives Irish developments a special significance. Whether the British experience in Ireland falls within the imperial context or the domestic may be left open to question. It is without a doubt a case *sui generis* that rather stands in contrast with the rest. The importance of it on the eve of 1914 need not be repeated[69]; Home Rule and the whole Irish problem had been put on ice for the duration. Needless to say the question re-emerged after the war.[70] It was not a pleasant, not to say very creditable, passage, of which it may suffice to observe that it constitutes a blot on an otherwise generally generous and pliant record; it caused many people in Britain to contemplate in discomfort the unexpected means of suppression that were resorted to in Ireland. The later French performance in Algeria comes to mind.

To be sure, the British had shown themselves quite capable of ruthlessness on other occasions, as witness the Boer War. But, allowing for the contemporary criticism of that performance, the mood of 1921 Britain was not that of 1899. Lloyd George called into play all his ingenuity and his wiles and indulged in an amount of double-talk and squirming unusual even for him. He should not nevertheless be deprived of the credit for having solved the thorny problem. The solution, stemming from the agreement of December 1921 and the Government of Ireland Act of the following year, was radical and simple. Granting Ireland, with the exception of Ulster, a status similar to that of Canada, was to a point an ambiguity that both sides could accept. It was tantamount in effect to granting the Irish complete control over their subsequent fate; despite the prolongation of trouble and violence among the Irish factions for a time, the bases of pacification, even of future amicable relations, had been laid.

The reason why this record of imperial evolution has been mentioned is because of the significance it assumes in the context of this discussion, primarily concerned with the facts and the behavior of power. Leaving aside the knowledge that the unfolding that another thirty years has brought, and putting oneself in the ambience of the twenties, some things nevertheless seem clear. It could indeed be contended, as in fact it was, that the liberal evolution of the empire was continuing in traditional fashion, adapting itself with characteristic British tolerance and flexibility, if one takes a broad view of the entire development. But even in that optimistic interpretation, it would have been hard to deny the influence of centrifugal forces. If these were given scope, be it in the Dominions of British derivation, in Ireland, or elsewhere in the empire proper, this was undoubtedly in part at least because of the changed position of British power. It matters little whether the emphasis be put on a weakened economy or on the prevalent mood of postwar British opinion and feeling, a psychological factor. Are not the two related after all, each at once cause and effect of the other?

The consequence, however, was a vicious circle or a snowballing effect. If Australia and Canada were beginning to feel the attraction of the pull of American power, it was in simple form because of the relative power of the United States compared with that of Britain. But the very fact that they responded to this new attraction had the inevitable effect of loosening and weakening the totality of the power that could be enlisted under the British label. To this there was no remedy unless a substitute could be found. The subsequent discussion will endeavor to analyze the manifestations of the continuing search for position in accord with the fundamentally altered facts of power, and to make some assessment of the degree of success, or the lack of success, of that search.

An Excursion into Unreality, 1929–33

In his memoirs Churchill makes the following observation:

> It is difficult to find a parallel to the unwisdom of the British and weakness of the French Governments, who none the less reflected the opinion of their Parliaments in this disastrous period.[71]

This quotation may well serve as summation of the following section.

The Impact of the Depression

On June 30, 1930, the last of the French troops moved away from the German Rhine. The trust of Germany that this gesture implied should be grounds for German gratitude and promote further reconciliation. So thought, or hoped, those in France who had favored the move, the more liberal elements, with Briand at their head. To these the German answer was a disappointment as it came in the shape of the results of the Reichstag election the following September. Prior to it there had been in that body an insignificant group of twelve members of the National Socialist German Workers Party, Nazi for short, the lunatic fringe that any democracy can afford; after the election of 1930 the twelve became 107, still lunatics perhaps, but hardly a fringe. This result was not specifically intended as a pointed reply to the French gesture of conciliation, for all that it had been contended in Germany that French concessions had come too late and had been too small to have the desired effect. The German people at this time were more concerned with other matters, the state of their economy for one, though undoubtedly the most had been made of the argument that all their woes had their roots in the iniquity of the *Diktat* of Versailles.

The League of Nations had originally been intended as an institution of universal scope. It was far from being that in 1930 and the world was anything but united. Yet in a sense it was, in the sense at least of the interdependence of the members of the community of nations; political and economic developments could not be isolated in the scope of their repercussions. Though we are here primarily concerned with British and French affairs, these cannot be understood save in the large context of world developments, about which therefore something must be said, if only very sketchily and by way of general background.

This is not the place to enter the debate on the origins of the Great Depression,[72] which may be broadly attributed to the failure to restore a proper equilibrium between productive capacity and that of consumption. The delicate balance of international trade and financial interconnections which had grown up before 1914, and which the war had disrupted, had not really been restored. Much of Europe's economic recovery was the result of illusions, which the flow of American capital for one thing had done much to sustain. To blame it all on the Wall Street crash of October 1929 is a simplistic view, yet the event and the date are appropriate symbols.[73]

Without taking a narrow Marxist and deterministic view, it is nevertheless difficult to deny that the Great Depression lies at the root of much that happened during the decade of the thirties, especially its opening years, and that it made on the minds of a new generation an impression quite comparable to that of the Great War itself on their fathers. It will make for convenience of treatment and clarity of exposition to consider its consequences in the case of three countries, Germany, Britain, and France. The reason for considering the German case at this point is the same as in Bismarck's and in William II's time; Germany lies if anything more than ever at the center of other developments, the initiator to which others reacted, the leader in the *Totentanz* about to begin.

Whatever the shortcomings and the weaknesses of the Weimar Republic, the central fact remains of the fragility of the roots of German democracy. As it has been put, perhaps the German people have lacked the experience of an authentic revolution, which their ingrained tendency of subservience to authority—any authority—makes it difficult in their case to enact. Their simultaneous devotion to ideas, theories, and abstractions lies at the root of the inability of the forces of the moderate and liberal Left to put aside their ultimately petty differences in the face of a threat that was to overwhelm them all, not excluding the Communists, who, equally dedicated to an ideology, thought that in chaos they perceived the dawn of their own proximate success.[74] A state cannot function without a budget, and if Social Democrats and Center Christians insisted on being doctrinaire, there was nothing for it but to resort to presidential government, for which in its wisdom the Weimar Constitution had made provision in the famous Article 48. But an emergency that lasts becomes a new condition. Repeated popular consultations of the electorate, too many of them, offered no solution other than the continued rise of the Nazi representation. Disoriented as they were, with unemployment rising to 6,000,000, the memory of the great inflation still fresh, the German people flocked to the promise of easy nostrums. The Center and the Left, both moderate and extreme, on the whole held their ground, but, as just indicated, failed to unite. Here in brief lies the heart of the story of which the end point was the appointment of Adolf Hitler to the position of German Chancellor on January 30, 1933.[75] The iniquitous peace, the wicked French, not to mention racial extravaganzas, were an easy, if also cheap, appeal; at any rate Germany would soon be great again. Within another three months, having suppressed some of the opposition, the Reichstag, through an Enabling Act, made Hitler unquestioned master of the Reich.

These ominous events did not evoke across the Channel, nor even more surprisingly across the Rhine, the reaction that might have been expected. The English, like the Germans, had troubles of their own; if the impact of the depression, measured by unemployment, for instance, was less severe in Britain than in Germany, it was severe enough. Characteristically British, and in significant contrast to the German, the British reaction to the emergency was union. The National Government was organized in August 1931. A month later it acknowledged the emptiness of Churchill's accomplishment of 1925; the pound went off gold, left free to find its own level. Given the place of Britain in world trade and finance, this confession of impotence was a momentous event which had world-wide repercussions; many countries followed the British example, and the event may also be seen as a step in the process of the displacement of London by New York, of Britain by America.

Where German affairs were concerned the British reaction was mixed, and a source of some confusion, especially among the Left. For it was in that quarter that dislike of Nazism and all that it stood for was most marked, but it was also the one in which sympathy for the German grievances, real and imagined, was strongest. One avenue of escape was to put faith in the League and in disarmament. The by-election in East Fulham in October 1933, just after Germany had quit the League, may be cited as a significant illustration; the majority of the government, which had been 14,000, was turned into one of 5,000 for the opposition, pacifist feeling playing an important role in the shift.[76] But the preceding year Austen Chamberlain had expressed the view that "the less we hear of the sanctions of the League, the stronger its moral authority will be, and unless its moral authority be strong, whatever the sanctions are they will not prevent war."[77] We shall see in a moment the efforts of Arthur Henderson[78] in the latter domain in Geneva and the British reaction to Far Eastern complications. Something must first be said of the situation in France.

In that country the elections of 1928 had brought to power the seemingly inconsistent combination of the team of Poincaré and Briand.[79] However, where foreign policy was concerned, as we have seen before, it was Briand who mattered; Poincaré and the Right did not interfere with the policy to which Briand was dedicated, although he was attacked by them in parliament.[80] For a time, but only for a time, France indulged in the satisfaction of contemplating her relative immunity to the depression, of which Tardieu unwisely boasted. The nature of the well-balanced French economy was the source of this pleasing condition, but in time the depression came to France as well, even though its impact was much milder than in Germany, Britain, or the United States. There was nevertheless unemployment, not to mention partial employment, and the outcome, registered in the 1932 election, was the return of a Left majority, similar to that of eight years earlier.[81] Once more Herriot was prime minister. This amiable man, sincerely devoted to the Third Republic, a practical compromiser above all, was not made of the stern stuff that an emergency calls for.[82] The four-year period of the 1932 legislature in France is of crucial importance; the uncertainties which beset the country found reflection in an unusual degree of governmental instability; eleven ministries fill the interval.

The fundamental reason was domestic. The soundness of the franc and the stubborn defense of its new parity, attempted through an orthodox policy of deflation, were difficult to reconcile with the demands of the mass. The outcome was the near explosion of 1936, the advent of the Popular Front, but the situation was complicated by the impact of foreign developments, mainly those across the Rhine. The rise of Nazism in Germany might be expected, because of its aggressive nationalistic content, to arouse the opposition of the French nationalistic Right. Since, for other reasons, Nazism was equally anathema to the Left, the result might be expected to be a unifying effect. Actually, the opposite was the case and both the Right and the Left were split, to the ultimate greater glory of Nazidom. This needs a little explaining.

It was among the Left that the chief support of a policy of reconciliation with Germany was to be found. If there was no counterpart in the French Left of the "guilty conscience" complex that so affected British attitudes, the tendency toward tolerance and understanding was strong, even in the face of certain German excesses; the way to counter the Nazi appeal might be further concessions rather than a return to the suppressive policy of Poincaré; this could be the best way to encourage the German Left. Yet this approach was qualified by the unwillingness to gamble French security, as Herriot, for one, repeatedly made clear. Thus the French Left was uncertain and torn in its approach to Germany, in the opening years of the thirties at least. The League it tended to support, but was in this respect quite clear that the League must have power.

The Right, too, could accept a strong League though its attitude in this respect was the more limited and cynical one that saw in that institution a mere adjunct to France's alliances, otherwise feeling little respect for the more starry-eyed, in its own view unrealistic, outlook of sincere supporters of the League as a *substitute for* rather than an *adjunct to* French power. But the Right was also divided. Nationalistic though it might be, its conservative inclination where matters domestic were concerned made it not altogether unresponsive to the Nazi outlook on other scores, as it had been to the Fascist for that matter. The Nazis' insistence on posing as the defenders of civilized Europe against Bolshevik barbarism, more narrowly the defense of property rights, was among other things a skillful gambit which had not a little appeal to the property owning class everywhere. From this it might be but a step to considering an accommodation with the new Germany, even if we are still a long distance from the slogan "Rather Hitler than Blum," and the later appeasement which will be considered presently.

At any rate there was in France considerable, if unco-ordinated, ferment, of which that classical French phenomenon, the appearance of *ligues*[83] was a manifestation. One illustration, the most sensational, will suffice. It was on February 6, 1934, that there was rioting in Paris; the immediate motivation of it lay in domestic problems again, but the incident created the impression of the possibility of a coup and showed the depths to which France was divided, as well as the bitterness of her divisions. The government fell, and her political leaders were sufficiently frightened to organize a version of union government that embraced nearly the whole range of the political spectrum, under the leadership of the conservatively innocuous Doumergue. The divisions of Britain never achieved the sharpness of those of the French, but, as indicated before, their fundamental nature was of a similar kind. However, in Britain the government was stable; still under the National label, and under the prime ministership of MacDonald, after the election of October 1931, it was, to all intents and purposes, a Conservative government.[84]

British and French Policies

This is the general background against which the operation of British and French policies must be considered. One more element may be added, especially marked in the British case, the strength of pacifist feeling. The East Fulham by-election of October 1933 has been mentioned. These were the days of the Oxford Oath,[85] a sensation and a scandal to a point, hardly a proper expression of the feeling of the mass of the English people, one which yet may be put in juxtaposition to the riots of the following February in Paris. Support for the League, of which the Oxford Oath was to a point an expression, was very strong in England. It was registered in massive fashion in the Peace Ballot two years later, which to a point also revealed a weakness and an inconsistency, for some who would put all their trust in the League would balk at using force in its behalf. Bluff is a dangerous tool in international relations. Outright pacifist feeling did not command comparable support in France, but revulsion against war in general, an overwhelmingly pacific mood, was also ingrained among the French people. The fond delusion of "peace at any price" was to come a little later.

Against this background then we may proceed to examine foreign policy in both countries. The year 1931 produced a major test, the first real one, for the League.[86] Of Japan's Far Eastern ambitions it may suffice to say that, after the frustrating experience of the Washington Conference of 1921–22, Japan had been biding her time.[87] The time seemed ripe in 1931, when Japan embarked on the path of imperialist aggression in Manchuria. China appealed to the League, and all that need be retained of the episode is the successful Japanese defiance of the world organization. This success was in some degree at least insured by British action, or rather refusal of action, in the sense that such action alone *might* have insured success for the League.

This was not sheer perversity, for Britain's reticence rested on solid ground, perhaps best expressed, although not until three years later, by Baldwin. "Never," said he, "so long as I have any responsibility in governing this country, will I sanction the British Navy being used for an armed blockade of any country in the world until I know what the United States of America is going to do."[88] Even if one grant that here was in part a convenient pretext, the fact remains that the United States was not a member of the League, as was not either the Soviet Union at this time. Nevertheless, here was a body blow to the organization, for Japan merely quit the League and collected her loot. It is all the more interesting to note the above-mentioned enthusiasm for the League in Britain, *subsequent* to the Manchurian episode. Who could retain faith in the League after such an experience? At best one might derive some comfort from the consideration that the League was essentially a European institution, that the Far Eastern test was hardly fair, and that it might yet prove effective within the European milieu.

Manchuria meant little to the French, save possibly again as a precedent, and they did not attempt to play a significant role in the affair. In 1931 two other problems had for them greater significance, one involving the League, but not the other, the proposed Austro-German customs union and the Hoover moratorium.

The second was a direct consequence of the world's, more particularly Germany's, economic distress. It was in response to President Hindenburg's appeal that the American President, Hoover, issued the proposal that bears his name, a one-year suspension of payments on all international obligations. This had one good result, the end of that hopeless undertaking that was the collection of German reparations. But there were some undesirable effects as well. The French were understandably irritated, in view of their large stake in reparations, at not having been properly consulted. They accepted the moratorium, but when a year later the United States insisted on the resumption of payments on its own debts—reparations had been virtually abandoned meantime—they defaulted on their obligation. There is little need to explain the American reaction to this action.

That reaction seemed all the more justified as the French were hardly in financial straits at the moment; in 1931 they had accumulated nearly one fourth of the world's gold. The power of that commodity is not to be denied, and that power was used in exercising pressure on the makers of the Austro-German agreement. It was less than deft on their part to present the proposed customs union as a contribution to economic recovery at large; to the French it immediately brought visions of the nineteenth-century Zollverein. The issue came before the League and was referred to the Hague Court for adjudication; was the union consistent with the terms of the treaties of peace and of subsequent Austrian commitments? The answer of the court was "no"—by a vote of eight to seven—which suggests, without impugning the integrity of the judges, that the fact that French, Italian, and British judges are members of those respective nationalities is not a meaningless consideration. France and Italy felt at one on the score of the Anschluss.[89]

Something has been said on various occasions of the mooted problem of disarmament. A preparatory commission had been appointed in 1926 and after it had labored for six years a disarmament conference formally opened in Geneva in February 1932. Tardieu presented a French plan characterized by the usual French approach to the question, which the advent of Herriot to office in June did not substantially modify; on the score of the connection between security and arms the French position may be described as essentially one of national unanimity.[90] MacDonald would have been more amenable, for he felt on the whole that, in this as in other matters, it was French obduracy which prevented the restoration of normal relations with Germany; his meetings with Brüning and with the American Secretary of State, Stimson, were barren of results. If the British position had in it the elements of a gamble, the quite logical position of France was also wholly sterile of results.

From this point on, the subject of disarmament may be disposed of very briefly. Germany was growing impatient and she had a useful talking point in her demand for *Gleichberechtigung:* disarmed as she was, she did not seek arms for herself, but merely the end of discrimination, which could be achieved by others imitating her. The question therefore was, could Germany be trusted or not? and the French answer was still "no." The answer may have been justified, especially in the light of the momentary wave of Nazi success, but it was by itself insufficient unless accompanied by a willingness to enforce the still valid terms of the peace. It seemed futile in any case to prolong the shadowboxing, and there was in fact clarification before long. In September Germany withdrew from the disarmament conference; she was momentarily brought back thanks to a weasel-worded declaration which both she and France could accept, a fact which in itself was evidence of its lack of meaning; there are limits sometimes to the usefulness of diplomatic verbal subterfuge, however skillful it may be.

Once Hitler was in power uncertainty did not persist very long. In October 1933 Germany withdrew from the disarmament conference as well as from the League. Following the above-mentioned episode of the sixth of February in France, in the new French Cabinet the foreign portfolio fell to Barthou. A brief and temporary chapter of French foreign policy was opened. One of his first acts was to put an end to the futile pretense; that was the meaning of his note to Germany of April 17, which may be said to have written *finis* to the attempt to reach an understanding in regard to disarmament: France would fend for herself and rely on her own means of defense. There was much to be said for a realistic approach based on a frank acknowledgment of the facts of power—provided the consequences of that position were understood and accepted and the proper conclusions implemented. This Barthou would have done, and we shall presently examine what may be described as the last French attempt to organize and assert the leadership of Europe. Before doing this, however, mention must be made of another episode which is highly revealing of the tendencies of both British and French policies at this time.

Mussolini's Four-Power Pact

MacDonald, though by this time largely dependent on Conservative support, was personally attached to the hope of disarmament. He and his foreign minister, John Simon, were in Geneva in March 1933, bearers of a British proposal, the details of which there is no need to explain. In Geneva the British ministers received an invitation from Mussolini to go to Rome to discuss a plan of his own.

It should be noted at this point that the Fascist régime in Italy had emerged from its formative period and seemed solidly established in control. Italy, Fascist or other, chafed at French "hegemony" and while she had no desire to replace it by another, she welcomed the possibility of a return to a more equable equilibrium of power. From her standpoint, and even apart from the Nazi compliment of imitation, advantages could be derived from Germany's resurgence. More broadly, it could be contended that the sterility of French policy called for a realistic substitute which would grant Germany her due. As often in the past, the fundamental aims of Italian policy coincided with those of the British.

In addition, Mussolini, who always took pride in his "realism," had little but contempt for the Genevan institution; as early as 1928 he had proclaimed himself an advocate of treaty revision. Here might be a point of difference with the British, especially where the League and MacDonald were concerned. In any case the British ministers went to Rome, where Mussolini presented his plan. It was realistic indeed: there were four Powers that mattered in Europe, Britain, France, Germany, and Italy—Russia was still beyond the pale; possessed of power, it was correspondingly their responsibility to insure the orderly functioning of Europe, if necessary by "inducing" others to accept their decisions. The concept was hardly an original one, none other than that of the Concert of Europe. Granting that the Concert had broken down, and that it was a denial of the hopes centered in the League, the proposal was not one to be lightly dismissed, especially if the impotence of the League were acknowledged. In any case the British response was not unfavorable and this was conveyed to the French by MacDonald and Simon on their way back to London.

For France here was a clear dilemma. It could be pointed out to her that the Four-Power directorate contained an implicit reinsurance against certain German demands; any such, if excessive, or for that matter any unreasonable or aggressive position taken by any member of the Four-Power constellation, would tend to produce an automatic coalition of the other three; was not this, at worst, a watered-down Locarno? The difficulty lay in the fact that, in her everlasting search for security, France wanted *both* Anglo-Italian support *and* her Eastern alliances. No one would suggest revision at her expense, save possibly in the imperial domain, but in Europe revision clearly meant changes in the Eastern frontiers.

It is all the more interesting and significant that the initial French reaction to Mussolini's proposal was not one of outright opposition; that might have meant the loss, or at least the weakening, of British and Italian support. But where France's

Eastern allies were concerned the choice was simple and clear; they understandably refused to pay the price of a problematic peace in Europe. The Little Entente made this quite clear and proceeded to tighten its bonds; Poland did not feel otherwise. Needless to say, and quite properly from their point of view, supporters of the League everywhere were up in arms against a recrudescence of the wicked ways of power, while France's allies wasted no time in making their position known to her.

These matters were extensively debated in France[91] and a way out was found. It was left to the skill of French diplomacy —which, technically, performed well on this occasion—to say "no" in effect while ostensibly saying "yes." The document that was signed in Rome on June 7 at best saved Mussolini's face, but he entertained no illusions as to what had happened. Revision could indeed take place, but only within the ambit of the League. What need was there to reassert Article 19 of the Covenant at this juncture?

The outcome may be interpreted in two divergent ways. It was ostensibly a victory of the forces of conservation and of those which supported the League. But perhaps greater significance attaches to the initial French reaction; if one considers the succession that goes from Locarno, through the Maginot Line, to the Four-Power proposal, it is not difficult to perceive a process of retreat in which French security became increasingly confined to France alone. The lesson was not lost on France's Eastern allies.[92] Under the impact of German resurgence the climate of Europe was radically changing.

THE LAST FRENCH ATTEMPT TO ORGANIZE EUROPE, AND ITS INCONSISTENCIES

Barthou, who took charge of the Quai d'Orsay in February 1934, was a peppery little gentleman entering his seventies who may be characterized as belonging to the Poincaré school.[93] He set about doing two things, simple in conception, less so in execution: he would reassert the validity of the existing system, the alliances; he would also extend their range. Like a traveling salesman, he set about a tour of the capitals of Eastern Europe. It is perhaps significant that the reception he met, in Poland especially, was definitely more enthusiastic at the popular level than at the official.

Britain and the Franco-Soviet Treaty

In regard to two major European states which stood outside the French system, in fact looked askance at it, Russia and Italy, Barthou's efforts were primarily directed toward the former. To be sure, France had been the chief advocate of the *cordon sanitaire,* but the realities of power often find little difficulty in overcoming ideological differences when confronted with the requirements of the national interest. On the Soviet side two things had happened with the passage of the years. One was a de facto stabilization. Both sides, Communist Russia and the capitalist states, had been proved wrong in their common initial assumption that they could not coexist; they were in fact doing so; Soviet Russia had been recognized by most other states and commercial relations had been resumed. On the Soviet side it was possible to think of "socialism in one country" and, without abandoning the ideal of world revolution, to put it off to some indefinite future; much could happen meantime.

The other thing, a related aspect of the hope of world revolution, was a revised estimate of the German situation. Nazism, the rise of which had been contemplated with a measure of equanimity by the Soviet leadership, might be the last gasp of a dying capitalism; in actual fact it was becoming entrenched and before dying might do unpleasant things, to Russia especially. Be it on the score of fear of Germany, or on that of preventing the feared capitalist coalition, a common interest was emerging between the Soviet Union and France. In terms of ideology the situation between the two countries had been reversed; but the Tsar's dislike of the godless Republic had not prevented the conclusion of the Franco-Russian alliance forty years earlier, the name of whose cement had been Germany.

But here Britain intruded, to whom the prospect of such an alignment was uncongenial, in part because it would tend to close the door to the reintegration of Germany into the European comity, a prospect which she had not abandoned. Thus British influence may be regarded as decisive in the shape of the proposal that finally emerged. Rather than a simple bilateral agreement, an arrangement similar to Locarno would be contrived in the East, hence the name Eastern Locarno: the Soviet Union, Poland, Germany most of all, but some others as well, would join in a common guarantee of all the existing frontiers. The structure would in addition be reinforced by a Franco-Soviet treaty of mutual assistance which would have the effect of linking the two Locarnos, since it would involve Russia on the Rhine in the same way that France was to be involved in the East.

Barthou discussed these matters with Litvinov, the Soviet foreign commissar, in Geneva[94] in May. He went to London in July to explain, or "sell," the idea to the British, and it is of interest to note the British reaction, expressed by Sir John Simon: "We made it entirely plain from the beginning, whatever may be the interest and the encouragement which this country may be prepared to offer in this new pact, we are not undertaking any new obligations at all."[95] He also insisted on the "reciprocal" aspect of the obligation assumed by all the participants, Germany for one, seeking thereby to minimize any anti-German aspect of the arrangement.

The whole attempt may be described as confusion and hedging, and in fact one may well wonder that such a scheme was ever contemplated. For it clearly ran into insuperable difficulties. How could Nazi Germany be expected to endorse such a plan, let alone conceivably come to the assistance of Poland in certain circumstances, when even Stresemann had refused to declare himself satisfied with Germany's Eastern frontier? In Polish eyes the prospect of Russian assistance was, to put it mildly, a mixed blessing. In fact, the French refusal to choose between Russia and Poland, translated into the attempt to drive the Russo-Polish team in harmony, may be regarded as the most glaring flaw in the whole proposal. Little wonder it failed, owing to Germany's refusal for one—British pressure proved of no avail in overcoming Germany's resistance. But Poland, too, refused. One may indeed sympathize with her in the horrible dilemma of having to choose between Russia and Germany; it was in January 1934 that she had concluded a non-aggression pact with Germany, rather an expression of her doubts about the dependability of her French connection than the result of ideological sympathy with Nazism or of Colonel Beck's personal pique.[96]

But there was a residue from the attempt. In December, a purely Franco-Soviet Pact was agreed upon, which was described in the French Senate as a "return to the traditional equilibrium of our diplomacy."[97] Even so, the hedging character of French policy is apparent, an aspect of it registered in the protocol which declared that

> The common intention of the two governments being not to contradict in any respect, through the present treaty, the commitments previously assumed toward third states by France and by the U.S.S.R. in accordance with published treaties, it is understood that the provisions of the present treaty may not receive an interpretation which, being inconsistent with treaty obligations assumed by one of the Contracting Parties, would expose it to sanctions of an international character.[98]

In other words France reasserted the prior validity of Locarno, meaning by this that, in the last resort, Britain retained a power of veto on her action. This was even more clearly brought out in the Chamber debate on ratification, when the rapporteur for the foreign affairs committee, explaining the above statement, stated that

> In her desire to remain faithful to the Locarno agreements, as she undertakes to do by the protocol of the treaty, France should make certain that the guaranteeing powers, Britain and Italy, understand in the same way that she does the conditions of aggression and attribute the whole responsibility of it to the same state.[99]

This was further confirmed by Sir John Simon's earlier statement in the Commons that

> The terms of the prospective Franco-Russian pact, so far as they are known to us . . . are, we are assured, such that all its provisions will be subordinated to the operation of the Locarno Treaty.[100]

On this understanding Britain was willing, even if only with a modicum of enthusiasm, to endorse the Franco-Soviet treaty.

France on her side was quite correctly taking the position that under no circumstances would she part company with Britain. The resulting arbitral position thus given to Britain entirely suited her book. It did not necessarily run counter to Baldwin's statement that "when you think of the defense of England you no longer think of the chalk cliffs of Dover; you think of the Rhine,"[101] or to Austen Chamberlain's assertion that "it has been a cardinal principle of British policy in all times, and under all Governments, that we could not allow the Low Countries to be dominated by the greatest military power of the day."[102] But the fundamental ambiguity persisted which had been characteristic of Britain's pre-1914 policy; one is reminded of the gist of Grey's caution to Cambon: if the circumstances warrant, Britain's power would be thrown in the scales. But who would be judge of the circumstances, and what if France, because of her Eastern involvements, should act, then find herself hard pressed? The French reticence vis-à-vis the Russians, growing out of such considerations, was not lost on them.

The Italian Card and the Abyssinian Imbroglio

Despite the inner contradictions of French policy manifested in the attempt to enlist in its camp *both* Poland and Russia, there was point to the Soviet alliance; should it come to the worst, Poland might be let go for the sake of the greater Russian power. A similar reasoning, and a corresponding deficiency, applied to the Italian case, for it meant in this instance an effort to attach *both* that country and Yugoslavia to the chariot of French policy. In the Italian case, moreover, a more sympathetic view might be expected from England, where, be it Churchill or MacDonald, the ideological aspect of Fascism seemed little obstacle to co-operation.[103]

The attempt to play the Italian card was not so much Barthou's as his successor's, Pierre Laval. That unsavory character, who came to an appropriately ignominious end,[104] yet had a policy that was neither wicked nor absurd. The reason for his assumption of the foreign office, a post which he retained until the beginning of 1936,[105] was the fact of Barthou's demise, when he fell victim to the bullets that were primarily directed to King Alexander of Yugoslavia in Marseilles in October 1934.

The visit was intended as part of Barthou's effort to put new life into France's old alliances.

Prospects for a rapprochement with Italy were not entirely devoid of substance. Despite the initially favorable response to Hitler's accession to power, Mussolini took without hesitation a determined stand when a coup in Vienna, which resulted in the murder of the Austrian Chancellor, Dollfuss, prematurely attempted to bring that country within the orbit of Berlin. When it came to the defense of Austria's independence a genuine common interest with France was involved; there was no need of either country paying a price to the other to enlist its support.

It was in pursuit of this Italian policy that Laval went to Rome in January 1935. His visit seemed highly successful since it was announced on the seventh that all outstanding differences between the two countries had been liquidated. There was agreement over Austria, and, for the rest, in concrete terms the differences were relatively small. It was nevertheless somewhat surprising that after so many years of bickering Italy should now be satisfied with the small coin that was an enlargement of the collection of deserts that had been the result of her imperial activity so far.

The answer lay in one word, Abyssinia, which was undoubtedly the object of a bargain, the precise nature of which may, however, never be reliably documented.[106] Italy ever contended, like Germany, that she was entitled to a proper place under the sun, meaning empire. The story of her interest in Abyssinia had a long background, and Mussolini decided to pick up the thread where it had been left after the Crispian failure of forty years before. To be sure, there was now the difference, and the awkward fact, that Abyssinia, like Italy herself, was a member in good standing of the League; but Mussolini, ever contemptuous of the Genevan institution, decided that the time was propitious for flouting the League. In the short term his judgment was correct.

We shall not attempt to retrace the course of the tragicomedy of errors that was the Abyssinian imbroglio.[107] It will be enough to say that the League, when appealed to, was only capable of giving renewed evidence of its impotence. What after all was the League but Britain and France? United, they might have carried others and the day; divided, they could only stultify the organization without gaining the benefits of the alternative that would have consisted in giving evidence of effective leadership and power, to whatever uses these might be put. Actually, they did not differ as much as seemed to appear, as the Hoare-Laval scheme in December conclusively demonstrates. That plan was in effect a device for the surrender of Abyssinia, but its premature disclosure gave rise to a loud outcry in England, which was compelled to abandon it, while Samuel Hoare resigned. The League had had no choice but to find for Italian aggression, a decision followed by the voting of sanctions. Laval was put in an awkward position, mainly concerned with preserving the newly found Italian friendship, and did his best, while paying collective security lip service, to hinder and minimize the effect of sanctions.

Under the spur of an indignant public opinion[108] Britain was a strong advocate of sanctions while remaining highly concerned lest the enforcement of these bring her into an open clash with Italy. Thus, instead of fundamental agreement between Britain and France, what appeared was wide and violent discord, reaching the point of undignified vituperation on the French side.[109] Actually, there was little to choose between the two: France would willingly annex the League when it served the limited purpose of her protection against Germany. She could not do this while protecting Italy by advocating ineffectual sanctions, and thus she fell between two stools and in the end would have neither the League nor Italy. Britain could be very sanctimonious about sanctions, which in this case might serve to prevent Italy from establishing a position in Africa that she regarded as injurious to concrete British interests.

Why should the rest care if the two mainstays of the League took such a limited view, incapable of rising above the promotion of narrowly conceived national interest? Quite justifiably they felt deceived and learned their lesson: the League had better be forgotten and each one for himself should seek as best he could to insure his own safety by coming to terms with the power that mattered and knew its own mind. The Abyssinian episode was in effect the death of the League. As to Britain and France, their ultimate fundamental interest coinciding, they could contemplate the wreck of what between them they had wrought; in a curious way their policies indeed were alike.

No doubt a case could be made for a "realistic" approach to the facts of power, an outlook not uncongenial to Laval. The German answer to the above-mentioned note of April 1934 was just a year in coming. It took the form of the decrees of March 16, 1935, which openly re-established German armed force. The meeting of the other three Locarno Powers at Stresa was a proper response; it took place in that city in mid April[110] and delivered itself of the evasive declaration that

> The three Powers, the object of whose policy within the framework of the League of Nations, find themselves in complete agreement in opposing, by all practicable means, any unilateral repudiation of treaties which may endanger the peace of Europe, and will act in close and cordial collaboration for this purpose.[111]

The League, too, was brought into the picture as a consequence of a French appeal. On April 7 the Council found that

> Germany has failed in the duty which lies upon all the members of the international community to respect the undertakings which they have contracted, and condemns any unilateral repudiation of international obligations.[112]

In brief, Hitler and Mussolini were both gambling correctly on the common unwillingness of Britain and France to take any effective action.

Anglo-French Divergences

It is both enlightening and relevant to mention at this point an incident or episode, of minor dimensions in itself, yet highly revealing of the trend of British policy no less than of its mode of operation. On June 18, 1935, Sir Samuel Hoare, the British foreign secretary, and Ribbentrop, the German ambassador in London, exchanged notes which registered the agreement that

> the future strength of the German navy in relation to the aggregate strength of the Members of the British Commonwealth of Nations should be in the proportion of 35:100.[113]

Leaving aside the trust that could be placed in German promises, a subject not yet so clear at this time, the British contention that here was a contribution to the limitation of German armament—submarines were excluded—which would otherwise proceed in unregulated fashion, can only seem feeble, even if sincerely meant. The French chose to emphasize the factor of Britain's unilateral endorsement of a modification of the treaty of peace, a matter in which they had a right to be consulted. They were both dismayed and incensed, and the step augured ill for Anglo-French co-operation. The incident is a good illustration of differences in outlook and methods and of what may be called the occasional British absent-mindedness—rather than wicked calculation—in taking the interests and feelings of others into proper account.[114]

Those who would could take comfort in, as well as take at face value, Hitler's reassurances that he was only bent on redressing legitimate grievances, but had no intent beyond that, and in the consideration that a satisfied Germany would be a positive contribution to the general peace. If the appraisal were correct they would be justified; appeasement per se is no crime, but the most enlightened of behaviors in the proper circumstances.

The German and the Italian actions, related and so usefully meshed, though not yet as the result of planned co-ordination, inflicted a severe blow to the hope that collective security might prove an effective substitute for the time-honored and traditional operation of the politics of power managed by the sovereign state. The advent of Anthony Eden to the British foreign office, a dedicated supporter of the League and of collective security, is best interpreted as a lag in the process of unwilling British adaptation to the changing conditions, of which a resurgent Germany was the most concrete manifestation. Neville Chamberlain at the exchequer and Churchill in the political wilderness stood for different approaches.

Their reading of the situation led them to highly different conclusions. The former, Austen's half brother, was inclined to recoil before the use of force and proceeded on the assumption that, if only treated with tolerant understanding, Hitler's Germany could be reintegrated into the peace-loving community of Europe. Churchill had never recoiled before the use of force; he had come a long way from the days, ten years earlier, when he had taken an unfavorable view of the French alliance, and was now agitating for the strengthening of the British military position.[115] But Churchill had achieved a reputation for being somewhat irresponsible and erratic, if at times brilliant; his voice carried very little weight at this time. The general election of 1935 in Britain, when support of the League was so central an issue, introduced an element of confusion and weakness in the operation of foreign policy. Eden replaced Hoare and Chamberlain was already carrying considerable weight in the inner councils of the state—he was generally regarded as Baldwin's successor, which he became in fact in March 1937. These men were symbols of divided counsels.

Greater clarity and a more resolute attitude might have been expected in France. Laval may, to a point at least, be seen as Chamberlain's counterpart, meaning by this that his outlook was not beclouded by ideological predispositions; even at the cost of Abyssinia he would seek to enlist Italy's support, and if he would thus seek reassurance against the German danger he was not averse to the removal of certain German grievances. His behavior in connection with the Saar plebiscite in January 1935 is evidence of this.[116]

Likewise, also to a degree, Paul Reynaud in France may be seen as the counterpart of Churchill in England. Generally associated with the Right, but of an independent cast of mind, he agitated vigorously at this time, both in and outside parliament, for an increase, but above all for a reform, of the French military establishment along the lines advocated by a prescient but still obscure army captain. De Gaulle's *Vers l'armée de métier* was published in 1934; it makes to this day fascinating reading with its accurate description of the Battle of France of 1940 six years before the event.

Some appropriations for rearmament there were in France, but essentially Reynaud's pleas, like Churchill's in England, fell on deaf ears. It is significant and revealing that one of the criticisms into which the *armée de métier* ran was that it was undemocratic. The above-mentioned impact of foreign ideologies in France, the culmination that was the events of February 1934, had elicited the response that was to become the Popular Front. The Popular Front was patriotic in the French Jacobin tradition,[117] but it was primarily concerned with the social question, which the impact of the depression was making more acute.

The Popular Front, though hardly by an overwhelming endorsement, won the election of May 1936, whereupon the government of Léon Blum set about instituting a program of social and economic reforms and reversing the deflationary policy of preceding governments. In retrospect, the reforms seem mild enough and even belated; no one is nowadays exercised over the welfare state, but the effect in 1936 France was an exacerbation of feelings, frightened conservatism thinking it saw the specter of Bolshevism in control. The enthusiasm of British Conservatives for the French Popular Front was at best qualified. Its leader was a convinced Socialist and a gentle enough person; he was also a highly civilized man, a product of French culture at its best. For that very reason perhaps he would have been better left to the pursuits of literary endeavors than to the harsher game of politics, especially in the circumstances of the time.

Almost immediately upon his assumption of office Blum found himself confronted with the necessity of an agonizing reappraisal, the source of which lay beyond the Pyrenees. This will be dealt with in a moment, but some consideration must be given first to the legacy which was his as a consequence of events on the Rhine just before he became Prime Minister. We are referring to what is perhaps the most crucial event of the long armistice, the resumption in the international domain of the leadership of Britain—to the greatest damage of all, not least herself in the end.

FRANCE SURRENDERS LEADERSHIP TO BRITAIN

From the Rhine to the Pyrenees

On March 7, 1936, the ambassadors of the Locarno Powers were called to the Wilhelmstrasse, where they were handed a memorandum, of which it will suffice to quote the following passage:

> The Locarno Rhine Pact has lost its inner meaning and has ceased in practice to exist. Consequently, Germany regards herself for her part as no longer bound by this dissolved treaty. The German Government are now constrained to face the new situation created by this alliance, a situation which is rendered more acute by the fact that the Franco-Soviet Treaty has been supplemented by a Treaty of Alliance between Czechoslovakia and the Soviet Union exactly parallel in form. In accordance with the fundamental right of a nation to secure its frontiers and ensure its possibilities of defence, the German Government have today restored the full and unrestricted sovereignty of Germany in the demilitarized zone of the Rhineland.[118]

Immediately following this declaration, Hitler conveyed the same news to the Reichstag while German formations were marching into the forbidden zone, a step taken in disregard of the judgment of his own military advisers; at this stage German force was not yet a match for the French. But Hitler's intuition was proved right. The French prime minister, Sarraut, uttered brave, but also empty, words, for the divided counsels of the French Government—interestingly, the military were more cautious than some of the civilians—resulted in the evasion that was an appeal to the League. The appraisal of Paul-Boncour is correct that

> The members of the Council, whether indifferent or neutral, reassured by our forbearance, no longer fearing a conflict in which they might have been involved, since our initial abstention made it possible to believe that we ourselves had shelved that possibility, showed little eagerness in finding a solution.[119]

If France would not defend herself, why should others undertake the task? There is little need to explain the reaction of the Poles and other French allies; as Paul-Boncour reports it:

> Boncour, how can you expect us to believe that France will come to our defense, after we have observed how little concern she has shown for what affects her directly?[120]

What better justification could there be for the Nazi-Polish pact?

Of course the English were consulted. English "reasonableness," of which Chamberlain was the foremost exponent, could understand the validity of German troops marching on German soil; another German grievance was being removed—who but the legalistic, intransigeant French were responsible for its being done in so awkward a fashion?—and this was therefore, in the last resort, and if one took a sufficiently broad and understanding view, a contribution to the restoration of normality, hence to real peace. The British advice was of caution and inaction, behind which France was only too willing to find the shelter of pretext for her own behavior.

It is difficult to imagine that, had the French taken action, there would have issued from Britain anything more serious than disapproving noises—if that. The reality of the matter was the French abdication, which, whether welcome or regretted, was clear to all. The registration of it in the Belgian withdrawal from the alliance was a clear indication of how the wind was blowing; France and Britain acknowledged it a year later by releasing Belgium from her obligations.

The French organization of Europe had collapsed. Where could Europe look for alternative leadership? Germany was only too ready and willing to assume the guidance, but the nature of her regime made her the last possible choice if some other could be found. Would Britain take up the burden?

It was logical and proper in the circumstances for France herself to accept such a British leadership if it should be forthcoming. The reassertion of the Locarno bonds in April was unconvincing, and more significance attached to the formal abandonment of sanctions against Italy in June; yet, Locarno or no, the fact remained that more than ever Britain and France were in the same defensive position vis-à-vis the revisionist Powers, Germany, Italy, and Japan.

One of the reasons often given for Hitler's choice of date for the Rhineland coup and for the abject French surrender is the fact that this took place on the eve of a French general election. There is point to the charge if not valid justification of France's supine behavior. France had after all a responsibility to herself; she had been the architect of a system for Europe, she was possessed of considerable power, and could not hide behind English skirts. In any case this was the legacy with which the Popular Front government of Léon Blum found itself saddled in June. There was little prospect of the Rhineland coup being undone, and very soon occasion appeared for additional confirmation of the French surrender.

On July 17, 1936, General Franco raised the standard of revolt in Spain. Spanish coups were no novelty, and had usually worked themselves out beyond the barrier of the Pyrenees without causing foreign repercussions. But this time it was different, mainly for two reasons: the coup was neither a complete success nor a total failure and it divided Spain in two, launching her upon civil war; even that might have remained confined to the limits of Spain had Italy not become involved from the start. From the Italian standpoint this was to prove a capital, in the reckoning a fatal, decision. Following the success of her Abyssinian adventure, blown up to undue proportions by the intrusion of the League, Mussolini had initially declared that Italy was satisfied. Had she really been such, she might then have joined the ranks of the *beati possidentes* and thrown the weight of her influence against the rest of the discontented have-nots. But she elected otherwise, at which point it is only fair to point out that the behavior of the British and the French throughout the episode was calculated to make credible what otherwise might have been but empty talk about decadent democracy. The revulsion against the fact of war in those two countries was indeed profound; what could they gain from it for that matter? But then the question was, what was the limit to which their concessions would go, or was there possibly no limit to the extent of these concessions? Here lies the key to the Italian mistaken judgment which led that country to throw in her lot with Hitler, more immediately, to interfere in Spain. For a small price a significant advantage might be gained, which would put Italy in a position to play more effectively the game of blackmail, vis-à-vis France especially.

In any case Italian assistance to the rebel forces in Spain was forthcoming from the very beginning. The legal government of Spain was a popular front coalition somewhat similar to the French; it might be expected that the French Government of Léon Blum would evince sympathy for the brother Spanish régime; and so it did. However, France was in the throes of enacting her new social legislation, beset by strikes of unusual dimensions, and by an unusually violent division of political sentiment. That is essentially the reason why Blum was loath to exacerbate these divisions, possibly risking importing the civil war into France. The other dominant consideration in the eyes of the French Government was the position of Britain. In that country, sympathy was very limited for the popular front government of Spain. For France it was essential above all that, whatever happened, she do not part company with Britain and find herself isolated; the Soviet Union was too far away, and for that matter too close co-operation with her could have the effect of accentuating French internal divisions and of increasing the British reluctance to stand by France.

This is the background of the French proposal, made to Britain and to Italy, on August 1, for the "rapid adoption and rigid observance of an agreed arrangement for non-intervention in Spain." Blum's own declaration on foreign policy on June 23, in which he had endeavored to minimize the role of ideologies in foreign relations, could be seen as a forerunner of his proposal, but the significance cannot be overemphasized of its French origin. It was the clearest expression of the desire to maintain accord with Britain, whose reaction was indeed wholly favorable; thus the non-intervention committee was born.[121] It was entirely appropriate that the committee should sit in London, the nearest thing to an authentically neutral capital. We shall not dwell upon the operation of the farce—the word is not too strong—that the committee proved to be. But even such pretense might be of use, if it could serve the purpose, as in the last resort it did, of enabling the Fascist Powers to have their way in Spain while maintaining the fiction of agreement among all and thus avoiding an extension of the conflict. It took three years for the Spanish agony to come to a conclusion, during which time much happened.[122]

Of these happenings, where British policy is concerned, two chief aspects are worth considering, which are not unrelated. Britain wanted to avoid war but she was not prepared to surrender uncritically her interest. The question therefore reduced itself to that of how to deal with the aggressive Powers, Germany and Italy. The neat and rewarding dovetailing of the activity of these two countries was bound to suggest that it might achieve even greater effectiveness for planned co-ordination; this was the meaning of the formation of the Rome-Berlin Axis—the term was Mussolini's—in November 1936. Britain's reaction may be described in simplest form as an attempt to break the Axis, the means she used by the one word appeasement.

That word has fallen into bad repute, in large measure because of the failure of this particular attempt. This is wholly unwarranted, for nothing is more sensible than to appease the appeasable; to make concessions on the other hand to that whose appetite is unlimited is futile or worse, for it only has the effect of increasing the demand for concessions and of ultimately putting the would-be appeaser in a worse position eventually to meet the test of resistance. A judgment is obviously implied at this point; an easy one in retrospect, when the consequences have been revealed, but one open to greater uncertainty before they have unfolded. No doubt the inexcusable lengths to which Britain went in pursuit of that policy were largely influenced by the moral climate of Britain at all levels.

In the attempt to break the Axis Italy might seem the more likely prospect. That is the reason why, to put it in simplest form, Britain was willing to pay the price of Spain if she could find accommodation with Italy. This is the meaning of the gentleman's agreement between the two in January 1937, the failure of which did not prevent a new attempt in April 1938. Chamberlain may have been misled, but there is no denying the steadfastness of his purpose, in pursuing which he was even willing to part with his foreign minister[123]; Halifax took over from Eden in February 1938. This is one place where criticism of Chamberlain seems warranted: he was so sure of himself that he was willing to assume the direction of the foreign policy domain, which was hardly his own. It is nevertheless also revealing to note the determined British attitude in the matter of "pirate" submarines in the Mediterranean; they promptly disappeared when Britain took a definite and uncompromising position.[124] Perhaps there might be limits to British concessions; in dealing with Italy, Britain yet insisted on insuring the protection of her position in the Mediterranean and the Red Sea.

With Germany things might be a little more difficult. The questionnaire that Eden sent to that country in May 1936 was hardly a skillful move; it elicited the indignant reply that might have been expected: Germany was not on probation. But there was no end of the visits of British statesmen to Germany. To cite but one, the account of the friendly interview between Hitler and Lloyd George in Berchtesgaden on September 4, 1936,[125] makes reading which is at once revealing and distressing. Lloyd George was no longer a power in England but he still represented an important current of opinion. Many other instances could be mentioned, and there is no need to dwell on declarations of foreign policy at home and in Geneva, futile and empty exercises in beating the air or practicing the policy of the ostrich.

France had nothing to offer. Beset by internal difficulties of an economic nature, which even the devaluation of the franc and adherence to a mistakenly orthodox financial policy did not succeed in alleviating, she meekly and supinely followed England. There is irony in such a declaration as her foreign minister made in the Chamber on December 4, 1936:

> In the first rank there is England, with whom, as Mr. Eden pointed out in the House of Commons, our relations are at once close and cordial.
>
> It would be difficult to remember a time when they have been better.[126]

To put it bluntly, this was sham. Should it come to the worst, of course Britain and France would be together. But the worst might be avoided, and Chamberlain's policy was directed to that end through a policy of concessions, to which France should make a contribution, and on whom pressure might be put to procure agreement with the English view. Agreements with Italy were bilateral, and therefore tended to create the impression that British and French interests in the Mediterranean were not necessarily identical.

This divergence, under the spurious cloak of ostensible agreement, received confirmation at the time of the Austrian Anschluss, in March 1938. Mussolini did not react this time, having by now become a prisoner of the Axis rather than an equal partner in it; he was content with the untrue statement of approval and satisfaction that earned him Hitler's gratitude.[127] Neither did anybody else react—how undo a *fait accompli?*—and in England there was much tolerant understanding, accompanied by wishful hope, for the removal of yet another legitimate German grievance.

The Anschluss was occasion for France's reassertion of her treaty obligations to Czechoslovakia, the clearly marked next victim. It was also cause for a French inquiry of England, and Chamberlain's answer on March 24 in the Commons was unexceptional:

> France has informed us that she would not allow any interference with the independence of Czechoslovakia; we do not have the same commitment as France with that country; but we have commitments to France and it is unlikely that we should be able to remain outside the conflict.[128]

Quite so, but one could read between the lines and look under the surface. Might not France be induced to adopt a "reasonable" policy of concessions, in the doing of which some gentle British pressure might help, and thus avoid the need of calling Britain's obligations into play? Appeasement was no English monopoly, and there were already at this time those in France, such men as Flandin, for example, who felt that German rearmament, the remilitarization of the Rhineland, had in effect voided Locarno of its meaning, hence that a different orientation of policy was called for.

There was logic in this interpretation, but it also contained the seed of the fatal mistake of French policy. If it is improbable that island Britain could divorce herself from continental events, such a hope was even more absurd for France. To renounce a policy for Eastern Europe, which meant in effect giving the green light to the realization of the old dream of Mitteleuropa, was suicide for France. The value of the English alliance was thereby enhanced, and it was a correct conclusion to see in it the last resort of an ineluctable necessity. But this need not imply abject surrender. There was point in foreign minister Delbos' statement in the Chamber on the occasion previously cited that

> I wish to declare, in the name of the government, that likewise all the forces of France, on land, at sea and in the air, would be spontaneously, immediately used for the defense of Great Britain, in the event of an unprovoked aggression.[129]

The probability of an attack against England without one on France was small, but the fact remains that the position of both countries was in a fundamental sense equally threatened, therefore that England needed France quite as much as the reverse. This is the basic condition of which France failed to make use, by asserting a position of equality and demanding an equal voice in joint counsels. To retain the English connection by meekly underwriting British decisions was easy enough, but it was unnecessary, and in the end disastrous, surrender. The specific turning point, the concrete act of this surrender, was the failure to react to the remilitarization of the Rhineland and the initiative of proposing non-intervention in Spain. Both were French decisions, and it would be unfair to blame England for them, thereby attempting to exonerate France from her own responsibilities. This, however, makes the fact of surrender all the clearer, for the desire not to part company with England was in both cases an important factor, even if also a convenient pretext. What explanation of the French behavior may be found in the divisions of French opinion has considerable validity; it is not a justification, however, but rather an apt registration of the malady of France.

The Fruits of English Leadership

THE END OF CZECHOSLOVAKIA

Such divisions had no counterpart in the British body politic, though in a way it, too, was sick. English democracy was functioning, whatever may be said of the 1935 election, and there is little question that Chamberlain in the second half of the thirties was an authentic representative of the prevalent mood of public opinion; insofar as it registered to the impact of foreign affairs that mood was almost one of peace at any price.

It was not long before there was occasion to test the mood. Hitler's by now familiar tactics of declaring that his latest coup was his last—until he discovered the need of another—were taken at face value. It is an incontrovertible fact that some three million Germans in the Sudetenland and along the Austrian border had been included in the Czechoslovakia that emerged from the war. The reasons for this decision, historical, strategic, and others were far from devoid of validity, but clearly also here was a ready-made issue if Germany chose to make one out of this condition. Agitation among the Sudeten Germans began shortly after the advent of Hitler to power, before which time there had been rather little.

Following the Anschluss, it was not long before the problem was brought to the fore. The Nazi aim was a clear-cut solution, no less than the incorporation of the Sudeten Germans into the Reich, a solution the strategic implications of which could hardly be overlooked, especially in view of the fundamental nature of the Nazi régime, not to mention Bismarck's dictum that he who controls Bohemia controls Central Europe.[130]

No attempt will be made to repeat the story of the Czech crisis of 1938, which has given rise to such an extensive literature.[131] Only some aspects of it will be considered, those which, consonant with the orientation of this essay, illustrate the British and the French reactions. The mission that Lord Runciman undertook in Czechoslovakia and in Germany in August 1938 clearly showed one thing, the British interest in the problem. That interest was not primarily concerned with Czechoslovakia, as the often quoted remark of Chamberlain about "a quarrel in a far-away country between people of whom we know nothing"[132] clearly indicates. The humble acknowledgment of ignorance may be praiseworthy; for the prime minister of Great Britain to own such in a matter where he was prepared to play a major role might cause some raising of eyebrows. What Chamberlain was intent upon was the preservation of peace; as he put it in the House on July 26, just before Runciman was about to set out:

> If only we could find some peaceful solution of this Czechoslovakian question, I should myself feel that the way was open again for a further effort for general appeasement—an appeasement which cannot be obtained *until we can be satisfied that no major cause of difference or dispute remains unsettled*[133]

rather an ambitious program and a measure of Chamberlain's uncritical illusions.

The crisis continued to unfold under the guidance of the by now familiar Hitlerian tactics. His speech at the close of the Party Congress at Nuremberg on September 12 was the opening gun of the last phase of it. But sophisticated English reasonableness would not be put off by a foreigner's excesses of language. It was undoubtedly desirable to maintain accord with France but this was not a very difficult thing to do. According to the testimony of Paul-Boncour, who refused the foreign ministry in the Daladier ministry organized in April, the abandonment of Czechoslovakia was already sealed.[134] Though with a heavy heart and entertaining few illusions, Daladier did not feel that a halt could be put to the German progress in mid Europe; Georges Bonnet, who agreed, took charge of the Quai d'Orsay. To be sure, after the Rhineland abdication and the policy adopted in the Spanish Civil War, it would have been difficult to wrest leadership from England, where Chamberlain pursued a steady course, uninhibited by qualms about the merits of appeasement. The common policy of the two countries found expression in the communiqué that was issued in London on September 18 after the visit of the French ministers to that city:

> After a full discussion of the present international situation, the representatives of the British and French Governments are in complete agreement as to the policy to be adopted with a view to promoting a peaceful solution of the Czechoslovak question. The two Governments hope that thereafter it will be possible to consider a more general settlement in the interests of European peace.[135]

The question was no longer whether or not to defend Czech integrity and the terms of the treaty of peace, but how to induce Czechoslovakia's surrender without Hitler having the satisfaction of war. In this endeavor Chamberlain would stop at nothing, and it is difficult to withhold a degree of admiration for his singleness of purpose, however much one may condemn and bemoan the willful obtuseness of his understanding. Putting aside all pride, he flew to meet Hitler in Berchtesgaden first, later in Godesberg. It was just before that second meeting that Chamberlain gave out the statement that

> A peaceful solution of the Czechoslovakia problem *is an essential preliminary to a better understanding between the British and the German peoples;* and that is the indispensable foundation of European peace.[136]

This is highly revealing. What mattered Czechoslovakia, or Central Europe for that matter, if Germany and Britain could agree? And what role, but one of acquiescence, could then fall to France? Behind it all, there was of course the usual assumption, sole possible justification of his policy, that Germany was seeking no more than her legitimate own.

Hitler did not make things easy, raising his bid between the two meetings with Chamberlain, and after Godesberg matters looked dark. It came to mobilizations, but at the eleventh hour Hitler yielded to the entreaties of his Italian compeer, who despite his bombastic, but only verbal, support, did not want war—not yet at least. Thus the Munich meeting took place, which saved the peace. In the face of a virtual ultimatum, not so much from her enemy, as from her supposed friends, France and Britain, Czechoslovakia accepted her dismemberment.[137]

The method had been rough and perhaps even more the subsequent implementation, which already hinted at what trust could be put in the Anglo-French guarantee of the reduced Czechoslovakia. But, if one takes a broad view, what more had been done than the redressing of a not illegitimate German grievance? Of course, if one took the view that this was but one step in the implementation of the program outlines in *Mein Kampf,* the operation was merely futile sacrifice. One might indeed go one step further and agree that mid Europe "belonged" to Germany, to do there as she pleased, after which she might embark on further Eastern adventures, leaving the decadent Western democratic possessors of empire alone. The naïveté of such hopefulness hardly needs to be pointed out. The exclusion of the Soviet Union at Munich was significant, nor was the lesson lost upon her. Here was the Four-Power Pact of 1933, in its original version, in action.

Yet it is relevant to quote the joint declaration issued by Hitler and Chamberlain on September 30:

> We, the German Führer and Chancellor and the British Prime Minister, have had a further meeting to-day and are agreed in recognizing that the question of Anglo-German relations is of the first importance for the two countries and for Europe.
>
> We regard the agreement signed last night and the Anglo-German Naval Agreement as symbolic of the desire of our two peoples never to go to war with one another again.
>
> We are resolved that the method of consultation shall be the method adopted to deal with any other question that may concern our two countries, and we are determined to continue our efforts to remove possible sources of difference and thus to contribute to assure the peace of Europe.[138]

Even without the light of retrospect, such optimism on the part of Britain seems unwarrantedly sanguine. To allege doubts about the dependability of Russian action and military power was not wholly without warrant, as was the contention that Britain needed time to rearm. These factors must be balanced against the very great concrete losses. Even the Czech Army alone was a far from negligible asset. But it must also be adduced that the enthusiastic reception that Chamberlain received in England on his return from Munich, when he waved the peace-in-our-time scrap of paper, is an accurate indicator of the prevalent state of opinion in that country. He was an adequate expression of it; Britain is a democracy after all. There is also point to the argument that, in dealing with other states, ideological differences should not interfere; but this can be fallacious when part of an ideology implies aggressive intent, a condition with which democracy is often at a disadvantage in dealing. Churchill judged it with more accurate terseness, who said: ". . . it must be recorded with regret that the British Government not only acquiesced but encouraged the French Government in a fatal course."[139]

Daladier, who entertained fewer illusions than Chamberlain, but was also a weaker and more indecisive man, somewhat to his surprise was also welcomed in France, where the bulk of opinion was as loath to face war as it was in England. Yet there was a difference between the two countries. For France, unlike England, had definite treaty obligations to Czechoslovakia; her welching on them can hardly be described as other than abject pusillanimity, and, needless to say, was a severe blow to her standing. There were critics of Munich in France, as there were also in England, but they were few and hardly representative of the prevailing mood.

Toynbee's facetious summation of Chamberlain's policy may be cited, which introduces incidentally a lighter note in a dreary record:

> We may think of him as a Victorian Midland English business man, who, in walking to his office one morning along the well known street that he has trodden hundreds of times before, suddenly finds himself face to face with a tiger. Knowing, as he does, that man-eating carnivores have not been bred in Mercia since the Interglacial Age, the good man persuades himself that, in spite of its sinister appearance, the quadruped confronting him must be a masquerading local donkey that will be unable to resist a carrot; so he courageously holds out a carrot to the monster. The next minute the creature demonstrates by killing and mangling a passing child, that its appearance corresponds to its real nature; and this horrible spectacle moves the man to change his policy. After a moment of hesitation, he arms his free left hand with a policeman's truncheon; but he goes on holding out the carrot in his right hand; for, in spite of having witnessed the tiger's damning 'kill,' he is unwilling to abandon all hope of the creature's turning out to be a donkey even now. So he continues to proffer the carrot, and assures the beast (as if it could understand human speech) that the truncheon that he now holds in his left hand is intended strictly for self-defense and is, in fact, too feeble a weapon to be used for aggressive purposes.[140]

England had been civilized for a long time, but this had not prevented her from using force in the defense and promotion of her interest; if the present policy was proof of civilization, it must be decadent civilization, as the mid Europeans were wont to assert, placing the accent on the adjective. To quote Churchill again, as he put it in another connection: "All these [the delusions of the supporters of the coalition] constituted a picture of British fatuity and fecklessness which, though devoid of guile, was not devoid of guilt, and . . . played a definite part in the unleashing upon the world of horrors and miseries which, in so far as they have unfolded are already beyond comparison in human experience."[141] The case of France was not radically different.

WHOM THE GODS WOULD DESTROY . . .

Yet even decadent British civilization was not perhaps quite ready to surrender if only it could be made aware of a direct threat to itself. This was the effect of what, from another standpoint, was but a logical consequence of Munich, the final destruction of Czechoslovakia. On March 15, 1939, German troops were in Prague while Bohemia-Moravia was made a German protectorate and Slovakia went its separate satellite way.

Using the pretext of the dissolution of the Czechoslovak state as creating new conditions which relinquished Britain from her guarantee to the mutilated creation of Munich—this was Chamberlain's first reaction—was hardly a noble or courageous stance, but two days seemed to suffice to remove the scales from his eyes. Speaking in Birmingham on the seventeenth, while still defending his previous actions, he also stated:

> . . . while I am not prepared to engage this country by new unspecified commitments operating under conditions which cannot be foreseen, yet no greater mistake could be made than to suppose that, because it believes war to be a cruel and senseless thing, this nation has so lost its fibre that it will not take part to the utmost of its power in resisting such a challenge if it ever were made. For that declaration I am convinced that I have not merely the support, the sympathy, the confidence of my fellow-countrymen and countrywomen, but I shall also have the approval of the whole

British Empire and of all other nations who value peace, indeed, but also value freedom even more.[142]

Even the first sentence of this statement did not hold true for long: exactly two weeks later, on the thirty-first, speaking in the Commons, Chamberlain had this to say:

> I now have to inform the House that . . . in the event of any action which clearly threatened Polish independence, and which the Polish Government accordingly considered vital to resist with their national forces, His Majesty's Government would feel themselves bound at once to lend the Polish Government all support in their power. They have given the Polish Government an assurance to this effect.[143]

The further statement that

> I may add that the French Government have authorized me to make it plain that they stand in the same position in this matter as do His Majesty's Government,

has a slightly odd ring. The Franco-Polish alliance had never been officially denounced, however unconvincing it may have been by this time. This is merely added confirmation of the extent to which France had surrendered her leadership to England, a more acceptable prospect after all than a surrender to Germany.

It is a somewhat unusual procedure in diplomacy for a state to issue a unilateral guarantee to another without request from the latter, though the Anglo-Polish relationship was eventually regularized, and one cannot but pause before the curious performance of British policy. From Hitler's point of view, either Britain was changing the rules of the game that she had played at Munich, or else this was innocuous bluff, perhaps intended for domestic consumption. At any rate he would not be deterred from the pursuit of his long-dreamed-of plans, recently given more concrete formulation in the famous Halsbach memorandum.[144]

The familiar round of grievances and claims, now directed against Poland, the non-aggression pact with whom was denounced, was clear indication of the direction of the next German move. We shall not tarry on the German-Polish exchanges, which followed what might be described as their "normal" course in the circumstances; nor on the strange triangular playing for position among the Western Powers, Germany and the Soviet Union, pursued in lackadaisical fashion by the first. They failed to overcome Soviet suspicion, whose demands they could hardly meet for that matter, the whole episode eventuating in the *coup de théâtre* that was the Nazi-Soviet Pact of August 23, 1939. Once the partition of Poland had been arranged between the two, Germany lost no time in moving; without the formality of a declaration of war Poland was invaded on the first of September. The Second World War had begun.

If the British Navy could contribute little to the defense of Paris in 1914, what could it do for Warsaw twenty-five years later? But the surprising, to some unconvincing, change that the German occupation of Prague had induced in Britain, was real. It fell to the same Chamberlain, the embodiment of appeasement, to declare war against Germany. Following desperate last-minute negotiations, and finally an ultimatum, this was done on September 3. Chamberlain, a well-meaning and honest enough man according to his limited lights, kept his word. It was very late in the day, but perhaps it was necessary to have gone through the performance of attempted appeasement in order to procure the consensus of the British people. The price was to prove very high.

Interestingly, France followed suit some hours later. The fact is significant, for the French purpose was at this point less solid than the British. That an article should appear in the French press under the title "Why die for Danzig?" is a measure of how far the malady had gone in France; as if the issue were Danzig! Yet there was logic in the judgment that, after the renunciation of Munich, and in the face of the Nazi-Soviet Pact, here were poor grounds and occasion for the test of force. Bonnet's efforts were directed toward finding some accommodation, even at the cost of Poland's yielding.

But this would also have been futile, save in the hope of an eventual Nazi-Soviet clash, in which case the Western Powers instead of the Soviet Union could have been in the position of *tertius gaudens*. These are idle speculations. War had come which would complete the unfinished business of 1919, for Britain and for France among others.

BALANCE SHEET OF THE LONG ARMISTICE

What emerges from the dreary record of British and French fumbling during the long armistice?

The two countries had found themselves in alliance during the First World War, a conflict which in the most fundamental sense had its roots in the German problem, meaning the problem of finding some adjustment between the demands of the growing German power and other established positions. Insofar as the purpose of the war had been the defeat of the German bid for power, the war had been a success. But the ensuing peace was a failure, mainly for two reasons.

Not so much because of the actual terms of the peace settlement, though no doubt some of the specific provisions of the Treaty of Versailles were unwise. The American-inspired Article 231, the famous "war guilt" clause, for example, represented a well-intentioned effort, but also a gratuitous insult calculated to furnish a perfect tool to later German propaganda; the principle of Reparation in itself was wholly justified and Germany fully expected to have to pay for her defeat.

But this much-controverted article goes to the root of a deeper difficulty. The First World War had been a war of peoples in a way that no preceding conflict had been; exacerbated national feelings must be given satisfaction, a fact expressed to perfection by Lloyd George's exploitation of it in the khaki election of December 1918, though he himself knew better. The statesmen who made the peace were neither particularly wicked men nor especially lacking in intelligence; but they were the representatives of the popular opinions upon which they depended for their tenure of office, and therefore far less free than their predecessors of 1815 to take a calm and dispassionate view of things.

The second difficulty lay in the fact that, again in contrast with 1815, the very fabric of Europe had been destroyed with the collapse of three of her major components. Austria-Hungary was gone beyond retrieving, and Russia was not in a condition to participate in the affairs of Europe, save by way of promoting universal revolution, hardly a suitable basis for discussion or compromise. Germany to be sure remained as an organized entity; she might conceivably have been treated as France had been in 1815.

Initially, this was not possible for the reason just alluded to, the democratic factor, the intensity of popular nationalistic emotions. Later on, as passions became cooled, this might have been conceivable, and indeed this may be said to have been the broad trend of British policy. But here lay also the fundamental flaw of that policy, for Britain failed to appreciate the fact that she was still fundamentally in the same defensive position as France, no longer the arbiter of the destinies of Europe. Like France she was a satisfied Power, anxious to keep her own, like France sincerely desirous of peace, though unlike France she would have entertained certain modifications of the status quo, especially if these did not affect her own interests. To a degree she felt tied to France, in the sense that she agreed that her own frontier was now on the Rhine. But she sensed no immediate danger, and her fear, induced by traditional thinking, of the magnitude and abuses of French power led her to take a stance of opposition to French policy.

The consequence was to make France the jealous and intransigeant guardian of the new status of Europe. This was an absurdity because the France of after 1919 was not possessed of adequate power, not least of the will, for such an undertaking; the result was that she, a victor, remained obsessed with her security and fearful of the precedent of change anywhere. French policy during the whole of the long armistice may be described as an illogical inconsistency. To assert power when no effective opposition existed may be described as a policy which amounted, to use the French phrase, to *enfoncer une porte ouverte*. What concessions France made were indeed, from the German point of view, too little and too late. But it would have been both unfair and unreasonable, and impossible behavior on the part of French statesmen, simply to have adopted a policy of complete trust of Germany and the abandonment of guarantees. This could only have been conceivable if France, with her own means, had felt herself a match for Germany; she correctly felt she was not. Germany must therefore be kept impotent. It is always dangerous, and the source of unwonted tensions, when the weaker finds himself in a position to dominate the stronger.

To be sure, one should not overlook the impact of the unexpected calamity that was the Great Depression, both in Germany and in France. But this is hardly a satisfactory explanation for the strange abdication of France during the thirties. France still had important assets after all, and these she simply threw away; again it may be said that her leadership was accurate reflection of the malady of the French body politic.

The one correct judgment that France made was the decision not under any circumstances to part company with England. This necessity was rather better understood in France than across the Channel, and the aberration of British policy is cause for little less wonder than that of the French. The persistence in the policy of appeasement, well intentioned as it may have been, on the part of the British leaders, was, as in the French case, expression of the illness of the British nation. For France supinely to follow British leadership after 1936 indeed procured agreement but was not the road to salvation for either.

The divergent outlooks of the two countries, their "conflicting strategies of peace," have been well analyzed by Professor Wolfers, and we may refer to the quotation at the head of the present chapter. It might be put this way: from about the turn of the century Britain and France found themselves in a broadly similar position, in the same boat; they rowed together for the first twenty years, until 1919; but for most of the next twenty they pulled in opposite directions and the boat drifted without a competent steersman. After a fashion they pulled together again after 1936, but the misguided command was overwhelmingly British. The methods that they used after the First World War in the attempt to meet the challenge of a new set of circumstances proved equally inadequate for both countries.

Britain and France were unquestionably together in September 1939. But war is ever full of surprises. Like the First, the Second World War unfolded in wholly unforeseen fashion. Once more, to be sure, it accomplished its initial purpose of defeating the renewed German bid for world power, but so much happened in the process, that both France and Britain found themselves faced with another entirely new set of conditions.

The next, and closing, chapter of this tale will trace these vicissitudes and show the degree of divergence which, for a time at least, seemed to place the two in entirely different categories, yet in the end put them still in the same boat, a craft, however, of wholly different construction from that in which they had been for the preceding forty years.

NOTES ON *Chapter VIII*

1. Italy, because of her power and of the strain that the war had put on her resources and her political institutions, counted for relatively little. She was soon to embark on the Fascist experiment and it was some years before circumstances enabled her again to play a significant role.
2. Particularly in the Near East. See below, p. 431.
3. It was even secretly renewed in 1818 at the Congress of Aix-la-Chapelle.
4. These may be followed in the French Yellow Book: *Documents Diplomatiques: Documents relatifs aux négociations concernant les garanties de sécurité contre une agression de l'Allemagne* (*10 janvier 1922–7 decembre 1923*) (1923), and in *Cmd. 2169, Papers Respecting Negotiations for an Anglo-French Pact, France, No. 1* (1924).
5. See above, pp. 396 ff.
6. What rankled especially was the parity with Italy, which France, not unjustly, felt was open to similar considerations as applied to the American-Japanese relationship. But in Washington France found herself isolated and yielded to pressure. The United States and Britain were mainly interested in their mutual relationship and in the Japanese position and evinced little interest in the French contention. On the significance of the Washington Conference for Britain, see pp. 430–31.
7. As early as 1919 (in the Lords on July 24, for example) Curzon had made no secret of his revisionist approach to the Treaty of Versailles.
8. *French Yellow Book,* Docs. 23 and 25.; *Cmd. 2169,* Docs. 34, 35.
9. *Cmd. 2169,* Doc. 38.
10. *French Yellow Book,* Docs. 23 and 25.
11. Briand's fall was due to his being considered too amenable to British suggestions. Summoned to Paris by the President, Millerand, to furnish explanations, he attended a meeting of the Cabinet and defended his policy in the Chamber. Without waiting for a vote he then resigned.
12. Lord Strang, *Britain in World Affairs* (1961), p. 283.
13. Baldwin, in a speech in the Commons on July 30, 1934. Cited in Wolfers, op. cit., p. 229, n. 2.
14. The discussion may be said to have petered out, especially on the British side, the French desire for a British connection being stronger than the reverse.
15. *The Economic Consequences of the Peace* immediately created a sensation. Sound as it was, Keynes' critique to a point defeated its own purpose owing to the style of his attacks, and even rendered a disservice to the cause of sound economic thinking which he advocated.

It is superfluous at this writing to call attention to the disastrous consequences of the famous "war guilt" clause (Art. 231 of the Treaty of Versailles). By introducing a moral approach to an essentially economic and political issue it mainly succeeded in breeding controversy and fostering confusion.

16. It may be followed in detail in the work of Weill-Reynal, E., *Les réparations allemandes et la France,* 3 vols. (1948), especially in Vol. II, *L'application de L'état des payements, l'occupation de la Ruhr et l'institution du Plan Dawes, mai 1921–avril 1924.*

17. The specific nature of the default mattered less than the fact that it was used by France as the occasion for a showdown.

18. Cf. n. 16. See also the *Survey of International Affairs 1920–1923* (1927), pp. 186–203.

19. This is the meeting in preparation for which Lloyd George had met Briand at Cannes. Germany and the Soviet Union had both been invited to the conference, of which Lloyd George held hopes of laying the bases of European economic recovery.

20. See Mowat, C. L., *Britain Between the Wars 1918–1940* (1955), Ch. III, and Taylor, A. J. P., *English History 1914–1945* (1965, Ch. VI).

21. The Four-Power Treaty of December 13, 1921, dealing with the Pacific, and to which, interestingly, France was but reluctantly admitted; and the Nine-Power Treaty of February 6, 1922, dealing with China.

22. See below, p. 433.

23. It may be added that, in December 1918, an agreement between Clemenceau and Lloyd George yielded the Mosul area to British control in exchange for a promise of British support for French mandates in the Near East. The cession was criticized in France, although no oil had yet been found in Mosul. Where oil was concerned, France made an advantageous agreement with England in December 1919, in consequence of which she fell heir to the German share (25 per cent) of the Turkish Petroleum Company, the future Iraq Petroleum Company.

24. Allowing for the qualification that Armenians and Kurds had no separate existence in the Turkish nationalist book.

25. Having ousted the Greeks from Anatolia, the victorious Turks turned toward Constantinople, but wisely opted in favor of avoiding an armed confrontation with the British force at the Straits. An armistice concluded at Chanak was the result, which made possible subsequent peaceful negotiations.

26. The Italians gave up their zone of Adalia in June 1921. The French, after some military reverses in Cilicia, came to terms with Kemal in the Franklin-Bouillon agreement of October 1921, as a result of which Kemalist Turkey even obtained French war matériel.

27. Taylor, op. cit., p. 192.

28. Albrecht-Carrié, R., *France, Europe and the Two World Wars* (1961), pp. 134–35.

29. Belgium would have liked, in fact preferred, an English guarantee as well, and there were in fact subsequent Anglo-Belgian discussions with that end in view. Their course and their ultimate failure parallel the abortive attempt to conclude an Anglo-French alliance.

30. The Treaty of Versailles had only settled the Western boundaries of Poland. In the East it came to war between Poland and the Soviet Union, a war of far-ranging vicissitudes, in the course of which France

offered some assistance, and which was concluded by the Treaty of Riga in March 1921, as a result of which the Russo-Polish boundary remained fixed until 1939.

31. Austria had no such aims, the problem in her case being that of the Anschluss, the possibility of union with Germany.

32. A connection between Poland and the Little Entente, especially with Czechoslovakia, would have been a logical extension of this network of alliances, but it ever remained a missing link owing to Polish-Czech differences, particularly over Teschen.

33. A fact confirmed by the conditions often attached to the loans, in which the building of military power was often emphasized.

34. Both the Germans and the Russians had been invited to participate in the conference that met in Genoa in April 1922. They used the occasion to conclude a bilateral agreement at Rapallo, which, while it normalized their mutual relations, had the effect of arousing the suspicion of the other Powers.

35. Although it may be doubted that anything could have been done by France, so long as she was the dominant Power on the Continent, to bring Italy genuinely into her camp.

36. It may be pointed out in fairness that in a sense France had little choice, for, short of abdication, she cannot not have a European policy. The chief mistake, and corresponding responsibility, of Britain and the United States, lay in their gross misreading of the situation. The best way to restore more healthy conditions in Europe and to curb the abuses of French power, real or imagined, would have been deliberate involvement, one aspect of which would have been the allaying of the French obsession with security, which would in turn have facilitated the normalization of the German position.

37. This rather referred to the controversy raging around the issue of responsibility for the outbreak of the war in 1914. No doubt, while Poincaré hardly had sought to precipitate war, he was clear in his own mind that Germany could only be dealt with by opposing force rather than by seeking compromise, and consequently assumed an intransigeant posture in support of Russia.

38. Stresemann became Chancellor in August 1923 and proceeded to dismantle the futile policy of passive resistance. He subsequently retained the foreign office alone, from November 1923, when the new Marx government was formed, until his death in October 1929.

39. The franc fell from 19.92 to 27.20 to the dollar during the first ten weeks of 1924. This was also the time when the question was under discussion of the repayment of the war debt to the United States and of the connection between that obligation and German reparations, an issue on which France and the United States took opposite positions. The futile and hopeless debate, largely on moral grounds on both sides, will not be gone into in this discussion. It accomplished little beside creating irritation, bad feelings, and mutual recriminations. The two positions, from the standpoints of their respective assumptions, are equally justified, and there could be no common ground between them so long as the two sides adhered to these irreconcilable assumptions.

40. The election of 1923 was taken as a repudiation of Conservative policy, particularly in the matter of protection.

41. The meeting was the prelude to the implementation of the Dawes Plan, which had already been essentially accepted by Poincaré.

42. See Chapter VII.

43. This was well brought out, for example, in the debate in the French Chamber in connection with the advent of the Clemenceau ministry in November 1917.

44. Cited in Wolfers, op. cit., p. 19.

45. They can be followed in Zimmern, A., *The League of Nations and the Rule of Law, 1919–1935* (1936); Rappard, William E., *The Quest for Peace* (1931); Walter, F. P., *A History of the League of Nations,* 2 vols. (1952).

46. The normal British reluctance to undertake commitments of uncertain scope was reinforced by the even greater reluctance of the Dominions to involve themselves in the affairs of Europe.

47. The government had been brought down as the result of Liberal desertion.

48. Mowat, op. cit., pp. 196–97.

49. As in the British case, this was purely the result of domestic, in this case financial, affairs.

50. The return of the pound to the prewar gold parity was largely Churchill's work, not one of the accomplishments generally regarded as contributing to his standing of prestige, though not an empty gesture in the light of Britain's position in world trade and finance.

51. The stabilization of the franc, for the performing of which operation Poincaré was brought back to office, resulted in the curious duality represented by the team Poincaré-Briand, which lasted for three years. Under its guidance France pursued a conservative domestic, especially financial, policy in combination with a liberal foreign policy.

52. Locarno had been credited to a German initiative going back to 1922. This is correct to a point, though even at that time Britain had played a role in the suggestion, and in the end it was British willingness which made Locarno possible.

53. The final signature took place in London on December 1, after which ratifications promptly followed.

54. Wolfers, op. cit., p. 216, n. 16; also, p. 258, n. 10.

55. This is brought out in the debate in the French Chamber on March 1, 1926 (Wolfers, op. cit., p. 260, n. 12), in such works as Fabre-Luce, A., *Locarno sans rêves* (1927), and in the contemporary discussions in *l'Europe Nouvelle,* among others. It is analyzed in Albrecht-Carrié, op. cit., pp. 167–72.

56. The election of Hindenburg to the presidency of Germany in 1925, to succeed the Socialist Ebert, was cause for concern to the liberal and democratic forces in and outside of Germany. Yet it must also be remembered that the election was a close one.

57. A good discussion of this point may be found in Wolfers, op. cit., especially Chapters V, X, and XXI.

58. The discussion of the issue of disarmament may be followed in the works of John W. Wheeler-Bennett, particularly *Disarmament and Security Since Locarno, 1925–1931* (1932), and *The Pipe Dream of Peace: the Story of the Collapse of Disarmament* (1935).

59. Like the League, this was hardly an original idea, but the formal

sponsorship of it by a Great Power was. See Albrecht-Carrié, R., *One Europe* (1965), pp. 221–28.

60. This contention was never formally accepted by the United States though it was to receive added de facto validity from the Hoover moratorium of 1931. See below, p. 465.

61. It may be considered as Stresemann's last achievement, for if he did not live to see it actually implemented, he together with Briand, was the chief architect of it. He died on October 3, 1929, shortly after a last appearance in Geneva, where he had supported Briand's scheme for European Union.

62. Cited in Wolfers, op. cit., pp. 74–75, n. 9.

63. The Kellogg-Briand Pact of 1928, in retrospect a perfect example of an exercise in futility, becomes understandable as an expression of the mood of the time.

64. Taylor, op. cit., p. 253.

65. One may see here an illustration of the centrifugal effects of the decline of British power, a factor the influence of which has continued to operate with increasing force.

66. Taylor, op. cit., p. 153.

67. See above, pp. 433–34.

68. The agitation of the *Destour* movement in the former and of the *Istiqlal* in the latter may be regarded as the seeds eventually destined to flower into the full independence of the two countries.

69. See Chapters VI and VII.

70. The Irish situation remained essentially quiescent during the war although the Easter Rebellion in 1916 momentarily confronted Britain with an uprising, with which, however, she dealt with determination.

71. Churchill, W. S., *The Second World War,* Vol. I, *The Gathering Storm* (1948), p. 60.

72. Among the many discussions of the world economic crisis, a convenient reference is Hodson, H. V., *Slump and Recovery 1929–1937. A Survey of World Economic Affairs* (1938).

73. Just as the death of Stresemann at the same time is apt symbol of a turning point in the political climate of European relations.

74. The presidential election of 1932 did to a point produce a merger of the liberal forces, which were successful to the extent of re-electing Hindenburg. The casting of that embodiment of the old imperial Germany in the role of bulwark of German constitutionalism and democracy—he was aged eighty-five in addition—may be taken as an indication of the parlous state of German democracy.

It is worth noting that, in December 1933, the Executive Committee of the Communist International declared that "the question of how soon the rule of bankrupt capitalism will be overthrown by the proletariat will be determined by the successful work of the Communist parties." Cited in Joll, James, *Intellectuals in Politics* (New York, 1960), p. 31.

75. The setback suffered by the Nazis in the election of November 1932 and the shady dealings of some members of Hindenburg's entourage, von Papen and von Schleicher in particular, become in this context secondary incidents.

76. It is aptly characterized by Lord Strang as "a movement of political irresponsibility." Strang, op. cit., p. 313.

77. In the House of Commons on March 22, 1932. Cited in Wolfers op. cit., p. 326.

78. Henderson was foreign minister in the second Labour Government, that took office in June 1929. In the National Government his place was taken by Lord Reading, who was in turn succeeded by Sir John Simon in October, to continue in that capacity until June 1935.

79. This was because of Poincaré's success in stabilizing the franc in 1926.

80. The debate on foreign policy that took place in November 1930, as a result of which the Tardieu ministry was overthrown, is enlightening. The Right had attacked Briand's policy but voted for the government, while the Left, favorable to it, did the opposite. The intrusion of domestic issues accounts for this reversal.

81. The contrary view may be taken that a Left majority is the expression of normality. This to a point is true, for there was not in France in 1932 a deeply felt sense of crisis, but rather discontent with the policy of the Right in domestic affairs.

82. This characteristic lends irony to the fact that he was overthrown in December on an issue of principle, that of honoring the French obligation in the matter of the debt to the United States. Once German reparations had been virtually liquidated at Lausanne in July, in response to the American insistence on the resumption of payments after the expiration of the Hoover moratorium, France defaulted on her debt.

83 For a discussion of the French malaise and its manifestations, see Albrecht-Carrié, *France, Europe and the Two World Wars,* pp. 242–53.

84. The attraction of the "Union" label was difficult to resist. The major part of the Labour party refused to adopt it, the consequence being that the party was temporarily wrecked and could offer no effective opposition.

85. A resolution, passed by a substantial majority at the Oxford Union in February 1933 that "this House will in no circumstances fight for its King and Country." Cf. Mowat, op. cit., p. 422.

86. The Italian action in Corfu in 1923 may be regarded as having been an earlier test, but the impact of that episode had largely evaporated in the subsequent atmosphere of euphoria, when the "spirit of Locarno" and pro-League sentiment prospered.

87. An oversimplification to a point, but one not unjustified in the present context.

88. Speech in Glasgow on November 23, 1934, at which time Baldwin was Lord President of the Council. As Zimmern put it, "of the two leading sea-powers, who together could have provided a police-power for civilization, one was out of action and the other determined at all costs to deny or ignore the responsibility." Cited in Wolfers, op. cit., p. 326, n. 14.

89. Germany and Austria announced their abandonment of the scheme two days before the verdict of the Hague Court was forthcoming.

90. The French were indeed fertile in making proposals and suggestions, which it would be unrewarding to attempt to analyze in detail, the central issue remaining the one indicated before, an impasse out of which no way could be found.

91. In the Chamber on April 6, May 30, and June 9; in the Senate on May 4. The relevant texts may be found in the French foreign office publication, *Pacte d'Entente et de Collaboration paraphé à Rome le 7*

juin 1933 (1933). See also Jarausch, H. K., *The Four Power Pact 1933* (Madison, Wis., 1966).

92. This was all the more so as the mood of Germany in 1925 and in the years immediately following was very different from that of the Nazi Germany of 1933. The German reaction to the Four-Power Pact proposal had been one of hesitant caution.

93. He had been Poincaré's right-hand man on the Reparation Commission at the time of the Ruhr and of the Genoa Conference in 1922. His sharp exchange with Sir John Simon in 1934 in Geneva on the score of Germany and disarmament was only in keeping with his straightforward, intransigeant attitude.

94. The Soviet Union was not a member of the League at this time, but it was as a consequence of these discussions that she became one, being admitted in September by the overwhelming vote of 39 to 3.

95. In the House of Commons on July 13, 1934. See Wolfers, op. cit., pp. 274–75.

96. That such a factor intruded is not in doubt. Beck manifested his annoyance by not meeting Barthou upon the latter's arrival in Warsaw, a gesture of retaliation, for he himself having felt slighted on the occasion of a visit to Paris.

97. By the chairman of the foreign affairs committee on December 18. See Wolfers, op. cit., p. 137, n. 9.

The pact was finally ratified in May 1935, but it is of interest that, already two years earlier, the Chamber had expressed itself *unanimously* in favor of the conclusion of an agreement with the Soviet Union. The bases of rapprochement between the two countries may in fact be traced to 1931 and to the signature of a non-aggression pact in November 1932, following the return of Herriot to the prime ministership.

98. *Documents on International Affairs, 1935* (1936), Vol. I, p. 118.

99. Cited in Wolfers, op. cit., p. 139, n. 11.

100. On May 2, 1935. *Documents on International Affairs, 1935*, Vol. I, p. 118.

101. See above, note 13.

102. Chamberlain, A., *Down the Years* (1935), p. 166.

103. We have seen MacDonald's favorable response to the Four-Power Pact proposal. Churchill, like Austen Chamberlain, had been able to say kind things about Mussolini, with whom both entertained not unfriendly relations.

104. He was tried and executed in 1945 because of his wartime policy of collaboration with Germany. The trial was largely a farce, yet the verdict may be regarded as a case of poetic justice, if not of justice unqualified.

105. He continued at the foreign office when Flandin succeeded Doumergue in November 1934 and after Flandin's fall the following June, when he himself became prime minister as well.

106. In the subsequent dispute that arose, Laval and Mussolini gave divergent interpretations of what had been agreed upon, but no written evidence has been forthcoming. Cf. Albrecht-Carrié, R., *Italy from Napoleon to Mussolini* (New York, 1950), p. 243.

107. It can be followed in the *Survey of International Affairs, 1935.*

Also in Mandelstam, A. N., *Le conflit italo-éthiopien devant la Société des Nations* (Paris, 1937).

108. This was the time of the Peace Ballot and of a general election in November, when support of the League was endorsed by the government. The Hoare-Laval scheme, propounded immediately after the election, naturally raised some doubts about the sincerity of the election pledges.

109. Certain organs of the French press—the weekly *Candide* is a good illustration—certainly exceeded the bounds of both fairness and good taste. For the British reaction to the Abyssinian imbroglio, see Vaucher, P., and Siriex, P.-H., *L'Opinion britannique, la Société des Nations et la guerre italo-éthiopienne* (Paris, 1936).

110. It was preceded by British, French, and Italian protests to Germany immediately after the issuance of the German decree, as well as by ineffectual scurryings of British ministers to Berlin, Moscow, Warsaw, and Prague. See *Documents on International Affairs, 1935,* Vol. I, pp. 64–80.

111. Ibid., p. 82. The qualification "of Europe" is significantly double-edged, for this was the time when the Abyssinian issue was in the making and Italian military preparations were openly under way. That particular problem, interestingly, was not dealt with at Stresa.

112. Ibid., pp. 98–99.

113. Ibid., p. 142.

114. One is reminded of Macmillan's performance in December 1962–January 1963, which in that case brought prompt retaliation in the form of the French veto of the British application for membership in the Common Market.

115. His parliamentary speeches and his memoirs, especially the volume entitled *The Gathering Storm,* bear ample witness to this.

116. As provided in the treaty of peace, a plebiscite was held in the Saar to enable it to decide its future allegiance. There could be little doubt of the answer, but in view of the nature of the Nazi regime and of the strength of Catholic and Socialist feeling in the Saar, a third alternative, continuation of the status quo, was proposed. Laval gave it little encouragement and the plebiscite resulted in an overwhelming vote in favor of reunion with Germany.

117. The Franco-Soviet Pact, expression of the about-face of Soviet policy, made it possible for French Communists, in contrast with the earlier behavior of their German counterparts, to join other parties of the Left and to endorse French rearmament.

118. *Documents of International Affairs, 1936* (1937), pp. 43–44.

119. Paul-Boncour, *Entre deux guerres,* 3 vols. (1945–46), Vol. III (1946), p. 38.

120. Ibid., p. 39.

121. In accordance with a British suggestion the committee was enlarged to include Germany, the Soviet Union, and Portugal.

When Blum had visited London he had been advised by Eden to be cautious in the matter of selling arms to Spain. But it must also be acknowledged that there was opposition to this in France as well, even in Left quarters. The situation is brought out in Blum's testimony before the commission that investigated the responsibility for the events leading to the war and for the wartime policy. Assemblée Nationale, Première législature, Session de 1947, *Les événements survenus en France de 1933 à 1945,* 2 vols. (n.d.), Vol. I, p. 215 ff.

122. The monographic literature on the period is very extensive. A summary of the developments in the international situation during the period may be found in Albrecht-Carrié, *A Diplomatic History of Europe Since the Congress of Vienna,* Ch. XII; also, Duroselle, J.-B., *Histoire diplomatique de 1919 à nous jours* (1953), pp. 220–66.

123. His behavior in dealing with the Italian ambassador, Grandi, taking sides against his own foreign minister, was, to say the least, unusual, and a source of surprise and rancor to Eden.

124. Attacks on neutral shipping were widely believed to be the action of Italian submarines. Following orders issued by the British Admiralty in August, at a French suggestion a conference met at Nyon. Despite the absence of Italy, an agreement was eventually reached with her, assigning her a patrol zone, whereupon the "piratical" attacks ceased.

125. It may be found in Gilbert, M., *The Roots of Appeasement* (New York, 1966), Appendix 2, pp. 197–211.

126. *Documents on International Affairs, 1936,* p. 275 (my translation).

127. "Benito, I shall never forget it," ran Hitler's telegram of relieved appreciation to Mussolini, to which the latter is reported to have commented, "Neither shall I."

128. Cited in Paul-Boncour, op. cit., Vol. III, p. 84. For a discussion of Chamberlain's speech, see *Survey of International Affairs, 1938,* Vol. II (1951), pp. 74–76, where emphasis is placed on the reticence of the British attitude.

129. On December 4, 1936, in the Chamber.

130. The destruction of the strategic possibilities of defense of Bohemia is what must be borne in mind, by comparison with which the Sudeten issue was little more than a useful pretext for the fulfillment of the larger purpose. It took a mere six months after October 1938 to clarify the status of Bohemia.

131. Apart from numerous subsequent treatments, such as Namier, L. B., *Europe in Decay, A Study in Disintegration 1936–1940* (1950) and Wheeler-Bennett, J. W., *Munich, Prologue to Tragedy* (1948), it may be followed in the account in the *Survey of International Affairs, 1938,* Vols. II, III (1951, 1953).

132. Broadcast speech of September 27, 1938. *Documents on International Affairs, 1938,* Vol. II (1943), p. 270.

133. Ibid., p. 168 (my italics).

134. Paul-Boncour, op. cit. pp. 96–101.

135. *Documents on International Affairs, 1938,* Vol. II, p. 213.

136. On September 22, 1938, before emplaning for Godesberg. Ibid., p. 225 (my italics).

137. Hungarian demands and even Polish in Teschen followed the Munich settlement, which dealt with the German claims alone.

138. *Documents on International Affairs, 1938,* Vol. II, p. 291.

139. Churchill, W. S., *The Gathering Storm* (1948), p. 251.

140. *Survey of International Affairs, 1939–1946,* Vol. X, *The Eve of the War, 1939* (1958), p. 41.

141. Churchill, op. cit., pp. 69–70.

142. *Documents on International Affairs, 1939–1946,* Vol. I (1951), p. 71.

143. Ibid., p. 126. A similar guarantee was extended to Roumania and to Greece on April 13.

144. On November 10, 1937, before his military and naval advisers and his foreign minister, von Neurath, Hitler had given a specific outline of his future plan of action.

IX

EPILOGUE: SINCE 1939

I have not become the King's first minister in order to preside over the liquidation of the British Empire.

Churchill, 1942

The interesting question is not why ordinarily the British do not want to become Europeans, but why exceptionally they sometimes talk and behave as if they do. If the history of world events is looked at as a whole during the years of progressive unification, it can be seen that the periods in which the European idea made some progress in British political thinking are those of disappointment, alarm and setback in other parts of the world.

C. M. Woodhouse, *British Foreign Policy Since the Second World War*, pp. 223–24

Since 1945 the international status of France, which collapsed, has been much the same as that of Britain, which held out alone.

E. Wiskemann, *Europe and the Dictators, 1919–1945*, p. 221

Fundamentally, the foreign policy of Vichy was an attempt at adaptation to new circumstances. . . . Consequently, there was, despite superficial fluctuations, a remarkable continuity in French foreign policy, particularly vis-à-vis Germany.

A. Hytier, *Two Years of French Foreign Policy*, p. 358

She [France] feels that a misunderstanding of her rights or an affront to her dignity would be not only an injustice but, perhaps more important, an error.

De Gaulle in Algiers, November 3, 1943

The point has been made in the preceding chapter that the fundamental cause for the breakdown of peace in 1939 lay in the failure of the First World War to produce conditions of stability in its final outcome; the unfinished business of 1919 must therefore be picked up where it had been left off. Perhaps the reason for the failure must be attributed to the enormity of the task of adaptation to the novel circumstances, social and others, of our century. The Russian Revolution, the emergence of American power, may be seen as dwarfing to the level of Balkan pettiness the long-standing quarrels of the great European states.

It is not our purpose to discuss such matters, even if it is necessary to bear them in mind lest one achieve a distorted sense of importance and proportion and because they are the larger framework within which our principals operate. We are concerned with a more limited aspect of things. Certainly, as also pointed out before, one aspect of the First World War was the resistance to the German bid for power. That bid had only been momentarily defeated and its renewal bore sharper features in 1939 than in 1914.

From this standpoint, the Second World War, like the First, was successful in accomplishing its purpose, even though, like the First again, its ultimate outcome and much that happened in its course overshadowed the limited aspect of its initial urge. Coming down to our circumscribed theme of the impact of changing conditions on British and French power, the period of the last three decades divides itself into two very unequal segments: that of the war itself, prolonged perhaps for a short time thereafter; the subsequent one of at least relative peace. We shall survey both in succession, bearing in mind that the second, much longer than the first, is too close to us to define with significant clarity its chronological divisions. Through both there runs the common theme of search in adaptation to rapidly altering conditions, but also, owing to these very circumstances, a marked contrast between Britain and France. As usual, our treatment will, to a point at least, be selective.

The War (1939–45)

What was done in 1945, in setting up the structure of the United Nations, is revealing and worth bearing in mind. In the Security Council five Powers were placed in a special position through the possession of the veto, a fact in which one may see a legacy of the situation existing in the League of Nations, or even an extension of the earlier concept of the Concert of Europe. But there was now the difference that, whereas in the earlier situations the appanage of Great Power status corresponded roughly at least to reality, the arrangment of 1945 did not. The United States and the Soviet Union were clearly in a category by themselves, superpowers, as they have since been called. French and Chinese power in being was non-existent in 1945. Taking a long-term optimistic view, a case could be made for expecting that the realization of the Chinese potential would someday put China effectively in the category of the great; this could turn out to be prescient farsightedness.

The French case seemed rather more dubious. Granted that some French recovery might be expected, the potential was limited at best. The reasons for including France among the great were two. One was historical, France's past record of importance; the other was the fact that it was still felt that Europe lay in considerable measure at the heart of world developments—the war had unquestionably arisen out of European differences—hence that there should be some representation of continental Europe in the inner circle of power. Germany in 1945 was hardly a possible candidate for the post, which therefore fell to France, perhaps one might say by default.

Britain stood in a position by herself. Her wartime performance and role had made her one of the Big Three; she had stood at the center of direction and her voice had carried considerable, if somewhat diminishing, weight in the making of decisions. The war itself had also served to emphasize the contrast and the separation between Britain and all the rest of the Continent, save Russia, like herself a peripheral European Power. Certainly in 1945 in terms of power standing the stress was on contrast between Britain and France. Yet that image was misleading, and the whole story of the postwar may be summed up as one which was to show Britain as belonging in the category of the second-rank, or middle, Powers, closer to France in effect than to the superpowers. The two are perhaps still in the same boat.

Britain and France Together

In 1939, more exclusively than in 1914—Russia was now neutral—French power, the French Army in the last analysis,[1] was the chief weapon of the West. For the long term, should there be one, Britain's naval power and her imperial potential could tell, but hardly at first. What had been true for twenty years was now clearly brought out, the fact that Britain needed France as much as the reverse was true.

The burden would presumably therefore fall at first mainly upon France, especially as Poland was disposed of with expedition, when Germany gave in that country a telling demonstration of the new possibilities of mechanized warfare. There were many who felt unconvinced by the Anglo-French declaration of war in fulfilment of their obligation to Poland, especially after the destruction of the latter, which the Western Powers had observed while themselves remaining inactive. Even apart from the legacy of mistaken appeasement, facts are facts; how would the Western Powers restore Poland? Could they not, having gone through the motions of satisfying honor, plead the excuse of inescapable reality?

Hitler indeed thought that they might. It cost him little to assert that he had no quarrel with the British or the French; his speech of October 6 could be interpreted as a peace offer. But the answer given to it by Chamberlain six days later meant what it said. Slow as they may have been in their reaction, the British people had finally awakened and their purpose was clear; the restoration of Poland was but incidental to the larger task of defeating German aggression in general. For that same reason, no consideration will be given to various other attempts, the intromission of neutrals, the Low Countries, the Vatican, or the exploratory mission of the American undersecretary of state, Sumner Welles, in February–March 1940, reminiscent of Colonel House's First World War visits to Europe; nothing came of any of them. These attempts were in part prompted by the curious course of hostilities, the "phoney war" as it has been called; for some months after the fall of Poland the belligerents stood inactively facing each other across the Franco-German frontier.

If the stalemate was to be broken, someone sometime must take the initiative of action. Germany was not likely to be starved into surrender by the weapon of the blockade, nor was the war at sea to have that effect on Britain. The war at sea was nonetheless important, not for that reason only, but because of its impact on neutrals, chiefly the United States.[2]

That country was generally sympathetic to the Allied cause, but American opinion at all levels was still overwhelmingly conditioned by the reaction to the experience of the First World War; "the quarrels of Europe are not our quarrels" succinctly sums it up. The curious legislation that was the Neutrality Acts was the concrete expression of the pathetic, if understandable, hope of the American people that they could immunize themselves from the affairs of the rest of the world. There were some in America who saw things in a different light, the President himself, for one, but his leadership must be cautious; he had not insisted in the face of the strong reaction to his "quarantine" speech of 1937 in Chicago.[3]

The winter of 1939–40, while the "phoney war" was quiescent in the West, witnessed an episode of which passing mention at least must be made because of its wider impact, especially on the two countries with which we are concerned. Despite the Nazi-Soviet Pact and the subsequent "correct" behavior of the Soviet Union, which had reaped some concrete fruits from a new partition of Poland, there was little love lost or trust between the makers of that piece of cynically expedient diplomacy. The Russians were anxous to secure the defense of their Western frontier, extending their control toward the Baltic. Having obtained concessions from the small Baltic states of Lithuania, Latvia, and Esthonia,[4] they went to war against the more intractable Finns.

The world in general was full of sympathy and admiration for the heroic resistance of the Finns, but in the end, though with more difficulty than might have been expected, the Russians had their way. Considering the circumstances, the terms they imposed on Finland seemed surprisingly mild; they were designed to insure better protection for Leningrad. In the process the Soviet Union got itself expelled from the League, a futile gesture, yet a significant one from the standpoint of British and French policy.

These two Powers attached considerable importance to the stopping of the iron ore supplies that Germany was receiving from the mines of northern Sweden; the cutting of the supply routes, from Norwegian Narvik or through the Baltic, was a question of blockade and involved their relations with the Scandinavian states. The intrusion of the Russo-Finnish War into this situation raised the possibility of assistance to Finland, which in turn led to the problem of transit through Norway and Sweden. Interestingly enough, the French seem to have been more anxious than the British to go to the assistance of Finland. There is no need to go into the resulting exchanges, which were fruitless owing to the anxiety of the Norwegians and Swedes to maintain their neutrality. In retrospect the British and the French may be grateful for the Scandinavian refusal of co-operation.

The situation took another turn. Within less than a month of the conclusion of the Russo-Finnish War, Germany cut the Scandinavian Gordian knot. On April 9, 1940, Denmark was overrun in one day and successful landings were effected in Norway. The Norwegians resisted and the Allies went to their aid. They failed, and by June finally withdrew from the last foothold of Narvik. This was a not insignificant setback, be it in terms of the failure of British sea power or in the value of the possession of Norway for purposes of sea and air warfare. In addition much else had happened meantime.

In France, the more determined Reynaud had become Prime Minister on March 22, a change which presumably bespoke a more vigorous prosecution of the war. It was suitable that the community of British and French purposes should find expression in the joint declaration of March 28, which stated that

> The Government of the French Republic and His Majesty's Government . . . mutually undertake that during the present war they will neither negotiate nor conclude an armistice or treaty of peace except by mutual agreement.

They undertake to discuss peace terms before reaching complete agreement on the conditions necessary to ensure to each of them an effective and lasting guarantee of their security.

Finally, they undertake to maintain, after the conclusion of peace, a community of action in all spheres for so long as may be necessary to safeguard their security and to effect the reconstruction, with the assistance of other nations, of an international order which will ensure the liberty of peoples, respect for law, and the maintenance of peace in Europe.[5]

The Collapse of France—Britain Alone

This statement of common intent was not long in being sorely tested—and found wanting. The Scandinavian episode was but the prelude to the real war, the beginning of which was the launching of a German attack against the West. A modification of the German plan of 1914 called this time for the overrunning of both Belgium and Holland.

The course of military operations is sufficiently known. Dutch resistance quickly subsided, the Belgian lasted somewhat longer, but the breakthrough in the Ardennes followed by the German dash to the sea, had the effect of isolating the whole British Expeditionary Force and a section of the French Army, both of which were pushed into the sea. After a brief pause the Battle of France began on the Somme; very soon it turned into a disastrous rout. By mid June the effective fighting arm of the Western coalition, the French Army, had been broken beyond retrieving.

This raised a question for each of the Allies, that of adherence to the just cited declaration of less than three months before. At this point the two parted company: France sued for a truce, Britain elected to fight on. The reasons for the difference and the manner of the parting merit some notice; the future consequences were considerable.

That France was defeated was an undeniable fact. The question therefore was for her of making a decision based upon an appraisal of the probable future course of events. There were two opposite views in France. Though defeated, France still had important assets, her fleet and her empire, both of them beyond at least immediate German reach. She could, therefore, her government taking refuge either in London, as the Norwegian and the Dutch had done, or in Algeria, continue in the war with Britain, letting the Germans rule and use metropolitan France. Such a decision could only be predicated on the assumption of ultimate German defeat, which would restore France and in the fruits of which she would share.

The opposite view held that, without the asset of the French Army, Britain would be incapable of achieving victory. Either of two things would then happen: Britain herself might be defeated, or a stalemate would ensue which might lead to some Anglo-German accommodation, some of the price of which France herself, now helpless, might furnish.

Neither view was irrational, let alone traitorous. The judgment in fact that Britain would be incapable of achieving victory may be regarded as anything but unreasonable and was widely shared abroad. To be sure, there might be another possibility, the extension of the war to include some neutrals. Among these, two alone were significant, the United States and the Soviet Union. There was no reason in June 1940 to foresee the intervention of the latter; as to the United States, it may suffice to recall Reynaud's pathetic appeal to the American President for the supply of "clouds of airplanes."[6] Apart from the fact that these were non-existent at the time, given the temper of the American people, the reply could be one thing alone to Reynaud's cry in the wilderness.

Thus the second view prevailed, of which the accession of Pétain to power in replacement of Reynaud was the outward expression. Pétain secured an armistice and France was militarily out of the war. The domestic vagaries of the French body politic, the suicide of the Third Republic, the accession of Pétain to the position of Head of the French State, with constitution-making powers, his semi-mystical views about the French need of atonement as a preliminary to restoration, the whole internal tale of the Vichy régime, important as it is to bear in mind their influence, do not in themselves belong in these pages.

Foreign policy does. Within the assumptions just stated there were still the two possibilities indicated of German victory and of a stalemate. Both had their advocates in France. Broadly speaking, it may be said that Laval was the outstanding exponent of the first, while Pétain, more cautiously, was inclined to reserve the future. In any case the problem was how to make use of the remaining French assets; control of them had better be retained in French hands until that future was less clouded.

The British for their part acknowledged that the course of events absolved France of the commitment not to make a separate arrangement, but they, needless to say, were anxious lest the remaining French assets, the very respectable fleet, above all, should fall into German hands. They dared not press the French too hard, while naturally remaining sceptical about French reassurances in regard to the fleet.[7] Similar considerations applied where the Germans were concerned; they, too, dared not press too hard lest the fleet be turned over to Britain. The outcome was the compromise whereby the French fleet remained in French hands, though immobilized under German and Italian supervision—on June 10 Italy had entered the war against both Britain and France in order to be an active participant in the expected, or at least hoped-for, kill.

But at this point something unexpected happened, the significance of which seemed relatively small at the time, yet, as events turned out, was to have considerable effects in the future. During the 1930's a youngish French officer had written a short essay dealing with the Army and the war of the future. His modern and prescient views made him a prophet without honor in his own country, where the prestige of victory in the last war redounded to the credit of aging generals—Pétain for one—and the ways of the past. Captain de Gaulle's views had a better reception in Germany, which proceeded to give a telling demonstration of their validity at the expense of France herself. Among political leaders in France, Reynaud had stood out as an exception in seeking, but failing, to have de Gaulle's views accepted by parliament.[8]

Now become a two-star general, de Gaulle had just been given a minor post in Reynaud's wartime Cabinet.[9] He served as go-between in some of the exchanges between London and Paris in the crucial days of June. On the seventeenth he flew back to London from Bordeaux with General Spears in the British plane which had brought them to France the preceding evening. He was not to see his country again for four years.

As already pointed out the question of how to deal with France was a poser for the British Government. Confronted with the French plea for an armistice, a move of still uncertain outcome, its reaction was to encourage what forces of resistance there might be in France. General de Gaulle on his side was opposed to surrender. The result was that he was allowed the use of the B.B.C. for the famous appeal which he made to the French people on June 18. The text of it is worth citing:

> The leaders who, for many years past, have been at the head of the French armed forces, have set up a Government.
>
> Alleging the defeat of our armies, this Government has entered into negotiations with the enemy with a view to bringing about a cessation of hostilities. It is quite true that we were, and still are, overwhelmed by enemy mechanized forces, both on the ground and in the air. It was the tanks, the planes, and the tactics of the Germans, far more than the fact that we were outnumbered, that forced our armies to retreat. It was the German tanks, planes, and tactics that provided the element of surprise which brought our leaders to their present plight.
>
> But has the last word been said? Must we abandon all hope? Is our defeat final and irremediable? To those questions I answer —No!
>
> Speaking in full knowledge of the facts, I ask you to believe me when I say that the cause of France is not lost. The very factors that brought about our defeat may one day lead us to victory.
>
> For, remember this, France does not stand alone. She is not isolated. Behind her is a vast empire, and she can make common cause with the British Empire, which commands the seas and is continuing the struggle. Like England, she can unreservedly rely on the immense industrial resources of the United States.
>
> This war is not limited to our unfortunate country. The outcome of the struggle has not been decided by the Battle of France. This is a world war. Mistakes have been made and there has been untold suffering, but the fact remains that there still exists in the world everything we need to crush our enemies some day. To-day we are crushed by the sheer weight of mechanized force hurled against us, but we can still look to a future in which even greater mechanized force will bring us victory. The destiny of the world is at stake.
>
> I, General de Gaulle, now in London, call on all French officers who are at present on British soil, or may be in the future, with or without their arms; I call on all engineers and skilled workmen

from the armament factories who are at present on British soil, or may be in the future, to get in touch with me.

Whatever happens the flame of French resistance must not and shall not die.

To-morrow I shall broadcast again from London.[10]

And so he did, to the following effect:

> Frenchmen must now be fully aware that all ordinary forms of authority have disappeared.
>
> Faced by the bewilderment of my countrymen, by the disintegration of a Government in thrall to the enemy, by the fact that the institutions of my country are incapable, at the moment, of functioning, I, General de Gaulle, a French soldier and military leader, realize that *I now speak for France* [my italics].
>
> In the name of France, I make the following solemn declaration:
>
> It is the bounden duty of all Frenchmen who still bear arms to continue the struggle. For them to lay down their arms, to evacuate any position of military importance, or agree to hand over any part of French territory, however small, to enemy control, would be a crime against our country. For the moment I refer particularly to French North Africa—to the *integrity* of French North Africa.
>
> The Italian armistice is but a clumsy trap. In the Africa of Clauzel, Bugeaud, Lyautey and Noguès, honor and duty strictly enjoin that the French should refuse to carry out the conditions imposed by the enemy.
>
> The thought that the panic of Bordeaux could make itself felt across the sea is not to be borne.
>
> Soldiers of France, wherever you may be, arise![11]

Thus was born the Free French movement. De Gaulle's were indeed brave words, but they were clearly also a call to rebellion, for there could be little question of the legality of the government of Marshal Pétain, whatever one might think of its quality and behavior. It was, incidentally, likewise entirely legal that de Gaulle should subsequently have been tried—*in absentia*—and sentenced to death. And it may also be noted that there was initially in France virtually no response to his appeal. With few exceptions, the military leaders elected the option of obedience to legitimate authority; the mass of the French people, in their distress, put their trust in Pétain, to whose fatherly figure they looked for protection, appreciating his refusal to abandon them.

To challenge the legality of the state is in essence a revolutionary act, which in the end success alone can justify; from this standpoint, de Gaulle in 1940 was behaving no differently from Lenin in 1917. Such behavior also constitutes an act of faith, and in both cases one may see the deep conviction born of dedication to a cause, combined again in both cases with a shrewd understanding of the facts of power. At certain crucial turning points in the life of nations the act of faith itself can be a vital component of power—even the only one perhaps for a time.

If one thinks of the democratic West as a whole, which, among major Powers would include the United States, Britain, and France, the last may be regarded as the advanced post of defense, be it from the standpoint of resisting the encroachment of the totalitarian view or from the more limited one of checking the initial thrust of German armed force. In the prosecution of war an advanced post may even be deliberately sacrificed, but the simile breaks down when applied to a whole nation, which, whatever its vicissitudes, does not suddenly die.

What matters, therefore, in the context of this discussion, is the manner in which the entity France was reacting and seeking to adapt itself to the changed circumstances, and one perceives at this point the three lines of thinking which have been mentioned before. The assertion of the ultimate solidarity of the three leading democracies, whatever the current incertitudes of American policy might be—de Gaulle's position; the acceptance of Germany's victory as foregone—Laval's assumption; the more guarded and hedging tendency which did not see the future wholly clear—Pétain's inclination. The last, Pétain's Vichy, was what counted most for the moment.[12]

Pétain did not believe in an eventual British victory, and there was even resentment on his part, the feeling that the advanced post had not been adequately supported. This was clearly brought out in his harsh and rather exaggerated reply to Churchill in the last days before the end in France. To Churchill's reminder of the German breakthrough in March 1918, a situation which had been redressed, Pétain retorted:

> Yes, the front was re-established. You, the English, were done for. But I sent forty divisions to rescue you. To-day it is we who are smashed to pieces. Where are your forty divisions?[13]

In any case the French collapse raised many problems for Britain. If behind France there was still Britain, what was there behind Britain save the United States, a highly problematic quantity? For the time being Britain must decide alone, and the possibility was not to be excluded that she might before long find herself in the same position as France. As early as May 20, Churchill wrote to President Roosevelt in these terms:

> . . . our intention is, whatever happens, to fight on to the end in this island, and, *provided we can get the help for which we ask*, we hope to run them [the Germans] very close in the air battles. . . . Members of the present Administration would likely go down during this process should it result adversely, but in no conceivable circumstances will we consent to surrender. If members of the present Administration were finished and others came in to parley amid the ruins, you must not be blind to the fact the sole remaining bargaining counter with Germany would be the Fleet, and if this country was left to its fate by the United States no one would have the right to blame those then responsible if they made the best terms they could for the surviving inhabitants. Excuse me, Mr. President, putting this nightmare bluntly. Evidently I could not answer for my successors, who in utter despair and helplessness might well have to accommodate themselves to the German will. . . .[14]

The possibility suggested bears rather close resemblance to the actuality over which Pétain was shortly to preside in France. But it was not tested in Britain. In that country, Churchill had finally replaced Chamberlain on May 10; his advent to power, given what he stood for and his personality, was eminently apt; just as his predecessor had been the adequate embodiment of the spirit of appeasement, so now Churchill was the proper personification of the spirit of resistance.

The evacuation at Dunkirk of the remnants of the B.E.F. had

been the endpoint of a major military disaster; it was also a moral victory, to which Churchill gave stirring verbal expression. Given the decision to fight on, two things were immediately paramount for Britain, her relations with France and those with the United States.

Of the first something has already been said, in which the fate of the French fleet and of the French empire were the stakes. The armistice provisions for the fleet were unsatisfactory to Britain. How far could the French be trusted despite their declarations that the fleet would rather be scuttled than used against Britain, especially in view of the means of pressure that the Germans possessed? Yet it might be unwise to antagonize Vichy too far, though Vichy on its side was anxious to avoid a total break, a situation which made for caution on both sides. Conversely, the British assertion of the intention to restore France, even if taken at face value, was obviously dependent on the course of events and on the final outcome of the war.

De Gaulle and the Free French represented a card in this situation. Clearly, Vichy must deny him any status lest it deny itself, while on the British side the foreign office cautioned about being "careful not to ride two horses at the same time."[15] On August 27 a measure of recognition was granted the Free French in an exchange of letters between Churchill and de Gaulle. There had been some, though very limited, response to the latter's appeal when the Chad territory, the Cameroons, and some scattered island possessions had joined the Free French movement, which Britain would regard as administering these territories in trust.

It is in this context of mutually suspicious reticence that Anglo-French relations must be seen, as well as a number of episodes of which mere mention will suffice. The British attack upon and their destruction of a part of the French fleet at Mers-el-Kebir at the beginning of July, when it refused to surrender or to sail away to the West Indies; the more amicable arrangements that took place in British ports and in Alexandria; the fiasco that was the attempt on Dakar in September; recriminations over the blockade, and a number of others.[16] Perhaps the most serious encounter was that which took place in the Near East, where in view of the concessions granted by Vichy to the Germans in the use of air facilities, the British felt that Syria and Lebanon must be removed from Vichy control. In June–July 1941 Frenchmen fought Frenchmen when British and Free French forces ousted those of Vichy in that quarter.[17]

No doubt the German failure in the Battle of Britain in the summer of 1940 raised the prospect of a long war. Like the Marne in 1914 this was a negative success, and how Britain would ultimately win was not apparent. Nevertheless this was an inducement to Vichy to persist in the policy best described as *attentisme;* even avowed French promises of collaboration with Germany did not change this. France would not make formal peace, nor allow herself to be dragged into an open clash with Britain, holding out to Germany the bait of her resources to counterbalance Italian and Spanish claims on her North African possessions that Hitler kept in abeyance. As late as 1942, Churchill could feel that

> the Vichy Government had to pay its way from week to week with its German masters and that they had not done more than was absolutely necessary to stave off a complete German occupation. They had endured Oran, Dakar, Syria, and Madagascar, the British blockade and British air raids with the least possible show of anger.[18]

Nevertheless, any possibilities of French action were severely circumscribed by the fact of defeat, and the emphasis must remain on contrast between the British and the French positions. Britain's standing was high, who held the fort alone, while the opinion voiced by Marshal Smuts in 1940 that "France is gone in our day and perhaps for many a day" corresponded more closely to the prevalent view of France abroad. France in the world carried but little wieght and her future at best was dark.

As indicated before, the stalemate that resulted from the German failure in the Battle of Britain produced a situation comparable to that which had developed in the First World War after September 1914. To a far greater extent than in the earlier conflict Germany was in control of the Continent between Russia and Spain. The quality of Italy's performance made that country little more than a satellite and a laughing stock; there is no need to go into the details of Central European and Balkan realignments and re-shufflings. It was Britain against Germany; even in North Africa, where the war ranged into Egypt and Libya, the direction of operations was finally taken over by the Germans.

But in contrast with the First World War there were now two major neutrals, the Soviet Union and the United States, whose action might break the stalemate. Where the latter was concerned, an unresolved ambivalence was characteristically expressed in the debate that went on, with little sign of resolution, over the question of whether or not the country had a stake in the outcome of the war, or, to put it differently, what was the significance for the United States of a possible German victory? How would it affect the national interest?

Stated in this form, the answer of the administration was that it would be detrimental. But the conclusion drawn from this view was not the decision of belligerency. The presidential election of 1940 is enlightening, when President Roosevelt decided to break the unwritten two-term tradition; it is reminiscent of the 1916 election, when the slogan "He kept us out of war" was used to good effect in Wilson's campaign. The question therefore reduced itself, from the American point of view, to how to give maximum help to Britain while still remaining neutral; "all help short of war" is a fair description of American policy at this point.

Britain banked heavily on American aid, and Churchill kept driving home the significance of a German victory for the United States. While the Battle of France was still raging, he wrote to Lord Lothian, his ambassador in Washington:

> If Britain broke under invasion, a pro-German Government might obtain far easier terms from Germany by surrendering the Fleet, thus making Germany and Japan masters of the New World. This dastard deed would not be done by His Majesty's present advisers, but if some Quisling Government were set up it is exactly what they would do, and perhaps the only thing they could do, and *the President should bear this very clearly in mind.* You should talk to him in this sense and thus discourage any complacent assumption on the United States' part that they will pick up the

> *débris* of the British Empire by their present policy. On the contrary, they run the terrible risk that their sea-power will be completely over-matched. Moreover, islands and naval bases to hold the United States in awe would certainly be claimed by the Nazis. If we go down Hitler has a very good chance of conquering the world.[19]

This makes clear the awareness of Britain's dependence on American resources and assistance. The canard propagated by some American historians[20] that President Roosevelt deliberately maneuvered his country into the war need not be seriously discussed. But without going such lengths, it is also undeniable that the drift of American policy was clear within its outward irresolutions. As early as November 1939 the existing neutrality legislation had been modified to repeal the embargo on the sale of war matériel. Still mindful of the *Lusitania* and the wicked bankers, America insisted that the belligerents must use their own ships and pay cash, "cash and carry" as the arrangement was known, which attempted to reconcile profitable business, sympathy for and aid to the Allied cause, and avoidance of the risks of involvement.

The creation around the American continent of a 300-mile zone in which hostilities were forbidden, the decision to refuse the acknowledgment of any transfer of territory on the American continent among non-American states, were hardly neutral acts, especially when seen in the light of the fall of France and the just cited warning conveyed by Churchill through Lord Lothian. The French collapse came as a shock to America and was calculated to bring home the meaning of the Western European barrier for her own protection. The preamble of the stillborn Franco-American treaty of 1919 might have been profitably read at this point, which stated that a German aggression against France

> would be and is so regarded by the Treaty of Versailles as a hostile act against all the Powers signatory of that Treaty and as calculated to disturb the Peace of the world by involving inevitably and directly the States of Europe, and indirectly, as ex-

perience has amply and unfortunately demonstrated, the world at large . . .

Prescient words!

Even "cash and carry" was not without its serious limitations; the cash would soon run out and the carrying was subject to severe losses from the submarine warfare. Especially after France was gone, Britain, in order to stand at all, would need more help. All aid to Britain short of war was the answer, of which the clearest manifestation was the destroyer-bases deal in September 1940: in exchange for the handing over of fifty overage destroyers to Britain, the United States secured long-term leases of bases in British territory in the western Atlantic and in the Caribbean. It was a bold and imaginative act, especially on the eve of an election. It could indeed be presented as a measure useful in the defense of the Americas, but the implication was also inescapable that Nazidom was a threat to the United States.

The convergence of Anglo-American interest was becoming increasingly open, if yet only tacitly avowed, and the forging of common links went on. Canada was a belligerent, but this did not prevent the creation, in August 1940, of a Permanent Joint Board of Defense between her and the still neutral United States. Britain was clearly America's first line of defense, just as France had filled that role for Britain; should Britain go down, America was committed to resist any attempt at German encroachment in the New World. Yet this possibility might never be tested, either because Germany would fail, or because, even if victorious in Europe, she would draw back from challenging America. Thus the American hedging ambiguity continued. This was the meaning of the re-election of Roosevelt in November 1940, an endorsement of his policies, as well as of his promise that "your boys are not going to be sent into any foreign wars."

This endorsement strengthened Roosevelt's hand and increased his freedom of maneuver, of which he soon made further use. It was in March 1941 that was enacted that imaginative stroke of genius that was Lend-Lease: America, by now the arsenal of democracy, would place her resources at the disposal of any state the defense of which, upon the President's decision, was deemed essential to America's security.[21] To say the least of it, this was a rather unusual kind of neutrality, though one must recognize that our time has been fertile in giving unwonted flexibility to the concept.[22]

The intertwining of British and American policies cannot be overemphasized; it had a long background, the war brought it into sharp focus, and we shall have occasion to observe the confusing consequences of the survival of its tradition where Britain is concerned.[23] Still a further manifestation of it was the meeting of Roosevelt and Churchill at sea off Newfoundland in August 1941, when the Atlantic Charter was born.

It is interesting to compare this very loose and vague declaration of general principles with its more precise First World War counterpart, the Wilsonian Fourteen Points. It is worth noting, however, that the Atlantic Charter was an Anglo-American statement whereas the Fourteen Points, eventually endorsed by others as they may have been, were a purely American pronouncement. The British association is important and there was special significance to it, coming as it did on the morrow of the involvement of the Soviet Union in the war. Little wonder that Britain's "special link" with the United States should be hard adying as a myth. It was not a myth in 1941.

The Intervention of the Soviet Union and the United States

Between Hitler and Napoleon the differences are many, mainly those to be associated with the ideological content of the French Revolution and progressive modernization in contrast with that of the Nazi aberration. But there is also similarity in the aspect of the episodes associated with their names if one regards them as pointing to the unification of Europe. In 1941, from the Pyrenees to the Vistula, Europe, with few exceptions, was under Nazi control. But the two peripheral states of Europe, Britain and Russia, the former especially, have traditionally been antagonistic to such unity for the simple reason that they have regarded it as creating the threat of a Power of too large dimensions, hence inimical to their own safety and interests. Just as eventually the two united in resisting Napoleon's France, so once more they were brought together by the common threat that was now Hitler's Germany.

In both cases the conjunction was effected as the result of an initiative of the internal European Power; in June 1941 Hitler started out on Napoleon's road to Moscow. Fatal as the step was to be in both cases, it was yet a logical one, for the staunchest core of opposition was in both cases Britain rather than Russia. To dispose of the British resistance it seemed necessary to secure one's rear.

There was a difference this time, however, which in simplest form may be put in the observation that the power of Britain in 1941 was no longer, at least in relative terms, the power that had been hers in Napoleon's time. In terms of power standing it was America that was the real heir to Britain, reluctant as she may still have been to acknowledge the fact. But the circumstances of the war, the role that Britain had been playing in it, to a point concealed and falsified the reality; ostensibly, in August 1941, Britain was in a position of parity with the United States in asserting the general principles that must serve as the bases for the future organization of the whole world. It is also significant that Russia, already in the same belligerent camp, was not associated in the initial declaration of the Atlantic Charter, though this should not be extended into seeing her exclusion as a deliberate attempt to keep her from having a voice in the eventual shaping of the final settlement.

The Soviet Union had been suspicious of all. She had through the years increasingly pursued the narrow defense of the Russian national interest, putting on ice, though not abandoning, the more Messianic aspects of world revolution. The prediction that capitalistic rivalries were bound to result in clashes among capitalistic states had been realized, and the Nazi-Soviet Pact could even be interpreted as a stroke of genius that allowed, even assisted, the clash to occur while Russia, uninvolved, could enjoy the comfortable position of uncommitted bystander. France by collapsing had frustrated Russian calculations of a long and exhausting land war.

But the conclusion was not that Russia must now intervene. Events in France moved too fast for any possibility of action, and Russia contented herself with some extension and consolidation of her position on her Western borders. Britain, needless to say, would have welcomed Russia's intervention. More modestly,

Sir Stafford Cripps went on a special mission to Moscow, where he arrived on June 12, near the climax of the French disaster. He met with little success, for the Russians were playing their cards very close to their chest; besides, who knew what would happen to Britain or what accommodation she might reach? Even after prospects had been altered by the Battle of Britain, the Russians refused to depart from their non-committal position.

Here we rejoin the earlier tale of the stalemate of 1940–41, the period of the inconclusive consolidation of the Nazi control of Europe leading to Hitler's decision to launch operation Barbarossa, the invasion of Russia. Perhaps over-crafty, hence suspicious of craft, or even suspecting craft where there was none, Stalin seems not to have taken to heart various warnings, some from Churchill himself, of the impending German attack. For their lack of adequate preparations the Russians would have to pay dear. But what is of greater significance in the present discussion is the British reaction, which was immediate and unhesitant. It is best expressed in Churchill's own words in his broadcast of June 22:

> The Nazi régime is indistinguishable from the worst features of Communism. It is devoid of all theme and principle except appetite and racial domination. It excels all forms of human wickedness in the efficiency of its cruelty and ferocious aggression. No one has been a more consistent opponent of Communism than I have for the last twenty-five years. I will unsay no word that I have spoken about it. But all this faded away before the spectacle which is now unfolding. . . .
>
> . . . .
>
> I have to declare the decision of His Majesty's Government—and I feel sure it is the decision in which the great Dominions will in due course concur—for we must speak out now at once, without a day's delay I have to make the declaration, but can you doubt what our policy will be? We have but one aim and one single, irrevocable purpose. We are resolved to destroy Hitler and any vestige of the Nazi régime. From this nothing will turn us—nothing. . . . Any man or state who fights on against Nazidom will have our aid. . . . That is our policy and that is our declaration. . . .

. . . .

This is no class war, but a war in which the whole British Empire and Commonwealth of Nations is engaged. . . . *It is not for us to speak of the action of the United States, but this I will say: if Hitler imagines that his attack on Soviet Russia will cause the slightest divergence of aims or slackening of effort in the great democracies who are resolved upon his doom, he is woefully mistaken.* . . .

. . . .

He [Hitler] wishes to destroy the Russian power because he hopes that if he succeeds in this he will be able to bring back the main strength of his Army and Air Force from the East and hurl it upon this Island. . . . His invasion of Russia is no more than a prelude to an invasion of the British Isles. He hopes, no doubt, that all this may be accomplished before the winter comes, and that he can overcome Great Britain *before the Fleet and air power of the United States may intervene.* . . .

. . . .

The Russian danger is therefore our danger, *and the danger of the United States,* just as the cause of any Russian fighting for his hearth and home is the cause of free men and free peoples in every quarter of the globe. . . .[24]

Three things emerge from this statement. First priority went to the destruction of the German bid for power; this did not mean that the shape of the future was to be ignored, but the necessities of war came first. From this followed the second, the unquestioning acceptance of the Russian partnership, although one might foresee the possibility of some difficulty in reconciling the opening and the closing phrases of Churchill's declaration. However, *for the time being,* those differences must be put aside, so long at least as survival came first. Would the Russians adhere to this view? Finally, the close identification of the British and the American interests could easily cause the raising of some eyebrows in the United States. But it must also be pointed out that there was implied the need of American intervention, which in turn implied the acknowledgment of the deficiencies of British power. If the common purpose, defined as the defeat of Germany, could be successfully accomplished, it did not take great perspicacity to foresee future problems aplenty.

The event was to prove justified Churchill's prognostication in regard to the United States. Mention has already been made of the Atlantic Charter, and of the significance of that declaration, vague and guarded as was its content. The importance of Britain in the American scheme of defense was fully recognized in Washington. As early as November 1940, when the outcome of the Battle of Britain had been made clear, a memorandum to President Roosevelt from Admiral Stark, the Chief of Naval Operations, contained the following passage:

> I believe that the continued existence of the British Empire, combined with building up a strong position in our home areas, will do most to assure the *status quo* in the Western Hemisphere, and to promote our principal national interests. . . . I also believe that Great Britain requires from us very great help in the Atlantic, and possibly even on the Continents of Europe and of Africa, if she is to be enabled to survive.[25]

Discussion of the American position between the President, the Secretary of State and the defense departments finally led to the following directive by the President on January 16, 1941:

> That we would stand on the defensive in the Pacific with the fleet based on Hawaii; that the Commander of the Asiatic Fleet would have discretionary authority as to how long he could remain based in the Philippines and as to his direction of withdrawal—to the East or to Singapore; that there would be no naval reinforcement of the Philippines; that the Navy should have under consideration the possibility of bombing attacks against Japanese cities.
>
> That the Navy should be prepared to convoy shipping in the Atlantic to England, and to maintain a patrol off-shore from Maine to the Virginia Capes.
>
> That the Army should not be committed to any aggressive action until it was fully prepared to undertake it; that our military course should be very conservative until our strength had developed; that it was assumed we could provide forces sufficiently trained to assist to a moderate degree in backing up friendly Latin-American governments against Nazi inspired fifth column movements.
>
> That we should make every effort to go on the basis of continuing the supply of materiel to Great Britain, primarily in order

to disappoint what he [the President] thought would be Hitler's principal objective in involving us in a war at this particular time, and also to back up England.[26]

One should not lose sight of the fact that the United States was looking in two directions and that, in some respects, its foreign policy had been more active in the Far Eastern theater than in the European. Japan's ambitions had been clear for quite some time, the aim of which was dominance of an enormous area, the awkwardly named East Asia Co-Prosperity Sphere. There were European interests of long standing in the Far East, among which the Russian and the British had first place. The fact of war had opened new possibilities for Japan; endeavoring to avoid a clash with Russia, she had taken advantage of French impotence in Indochina[27] and she had induced Britain to close for a time the Burma Road, the avenue of assistance to China.

The United States observed this Japanese activity with disfavor, and relations between the two countries became increasingly unfriendly. While the American preference was undoubtedly for peace, there was little indication of any willingness to make such concessions as the existing aggressive and expansionist leadership of Japan would have found acceptable. The possibility of an armed clash was therefore no alien thought in governmental circles in the United States, as the above-cited directive clearly shows. But when Japan cut through the Gordian knot of irreconcilability between her own and America's aims through the device of a surprise attack on the Hawaiian base of Pearl Harbor, where telling damage was inflicted on the American fleet, surprisingly caught unprepared, she simultaneously cut through the Gordian knot of the unresolved American debate about America's relation, if any, to the European war. Interestingly, the Germans and the Italians obliged and furthered the clarification by taking the initiative of declarations of war against the United States. The world was clearly split between two sharply defined hostile camps, with the sole qualification that Russia and Japan remained at peace with each other.

The United States was inadequately prepared, and, especially after the crippling blow of Pearl Harbor, not in a position to stem the Japanese advance in the Pacific or into the British and the Dutch possessions in Southeast Asia. British interests in that quarter were considerable, but what forces Britain had in it fared ill; her resources, already strained to the utmost, would not permit the diversion of a major effort away from the European and Near Eastern theaters, a fact which was to have considerable repercussions in the future. But it is very significant that, again in keeping with earlier decisions, and despite the shock to American opinion that was Pearl Harbor, and the intense emotion to which it gave rise, the American Government did not allow itself to be deflected from the view that the European war must have priority. Even before Pearl Harbor the Soviet Union had been made eligible to the benefits of Lend-Lease.

Churchill's reaction to these events was understandable and fully justified:

> No American will think it wrong of me if I proclaim that to have the United States at our side was to me the greatest joy. I could not foretell the course of events. I do not pretend to have measured accurately the martial might of Japan, but now at this very moment I knew the United States was in the war, up to the neck and in to the death. So we had won after all![28]

Well, not quite won, or at least not for some time to come. In actual fact the entrance of the United States into the war initiated the period of the nadir in Allied fortunes. But the resources of America, immune at home behind the barrier of two oceans, were equal to the task.

Until there were signs that the military situation would be redressed, priority of attention must obviously go to that aspect of things, leaving political considerations to the future, though sight must never be lost of the fact that the military face and course of the war itself becomes an important element of the eventual political outcome; it is a concrete measure and demonstration of the power available.

Two weeks after Pearl Harbor Churchill went to Washington, where he, with Roosevelt and the Russian ambassador, Litvinov, proceeded to organize and to co-ordinate the prosecution of the war, confirming that Germany was the chief enemy.[29]

A year did not elapse from Pearl Harbor before the high tide of Axis and Japanese successes had passed and begun to recede, even though it would take the better part of another three years before it would be fully swept back. It will suffice to mention a few places and dates: the battles of the Coral Sea and of Midway, in May and June 1942 respectively—they were entirely American-Japanese encounters—showed the recovery of American sea and air power, product of the resources of American industry; at Stalingrad the Germans failed and by November the Russians, despite their frightful losses, passed to the offensive, never to lose the initiative thereafter. Almost simultaneously, at El Alamein, the British likewise launched an offensive, which broke the back of the Axis power in North Africa; while this was happening sixty miles from Alexandria, on November 8 an Anglo-American armada effected landings in Morocco and in Algeria. What resistance there was did not significantly interfere with that operation; by the following May the Axis forces had been totally cleared out of North Africa.

The War After 1941

BRITAIN ONE OF THE BIG THREE

From the end of 1942 ultimate Allied victory was secure, but the war still had to be carried on, hence military considerations remained of capital importance. However, since it was no longer a matter of sheer survival, increasing attention could be given to plans for the future.

That future was in the hands of the Big Three, more narrowly three men, Roosevelt, Stalin, and Churchill. As in the First World War, America was the most detached Power, though the American involvement and contribution in the material sense were far more substantial in the Second World War than in the First. Not only was the war with Japan overwhelmingly an American enterprise, but in the Mediterranean and in Europe as well the American contribution assumed vast and increasing proportions. Concrete American interests were involved, in the Far East especially, but the broad focus of American interest lay in the organization of the future, one aspect of which was of course the relationships of power, Soviet power especially.

The Soviet Union and Britain tended to think in somewhat narrower and more classical terms of power. Stalin wanted as much as he could get for the future security of Russia; he could hardly be expected to relinquish the gains derived from the time of his collaboration with the Axis, whether or not these would fit the principle of self-determination. There was, in addition, another potent tool in the Soviet armory, the ideological.

Communism still held a broad appeal for large masses of people; and it is even surprising to observe the degree to which Communist parties loyally continued to adhere to the leadership of Moscow despite the Kremlin's expedient gyrations. From condemning, and even to a point sabotaging—in France, for example—the "imperialist" war, after June 1941 Communists became ardent patriots and played a leading role in the resistance movements everywhere. To put an illustration in extreme and simple form, what if Communism, in say Yugoslavia or Poland, should manage to achieve control, then opt for admission in the Union of Soviet Socialist Republics? The outcome could easily insert itself into the initial hopes and predictions, put on ice for a time, of world revolution. The timing had perhaps been somewhat wrong, but had not the broad contention that capitalist states were bound to fall out among themselves been realized? In a sense, therefore, Soviet aims might be regarded as unlimited.

Of course they could not be loudly proclaimed while Russia remained highly dependent on America's material assistance, but it is significant that relations between the Soviet Union and its allies were ever strained and tinged with suspicion, especially on the Soviet side. The long controversy over the opening of a second front is revealing in this respect, allowing that it was true that Russia had suffered terrific losses and was carrying the heaviest burden of the land war. Stalin's understanding of power was crude to a degree, well expressed in his alleged retort to the consideration of the Vatican's influence: "How many divisions does the Pope have?"

Such possibly unlimited aims would hardly suit American and British purposes. Here a distinction must be made between the two which, in somewhat simplified form, may be expressed by saying that where it came to the relationships of power, the American President was relatively an amateur, the British Prime Minister a professional. Both agreed upon the necessity of a second front and had a very difficult time explaining to Stalin its continued postponement and the choice of the indirect Mediterranean route at first.

Again, to resort to some simplification, the American President tended to think too much of the approach of domestic American politics when operating in the very different domain of the international. Churchill in this respect was closer to Stalin; he set great store, for example, by the value of physical occupation of specific territories, of agreement on spheres of influence, as illustrated by his interest in the Balkans and the rough division of influence in them which he contrived with Stalin after the meeting in Moscow in October 1943.[30]

The British war aims may be said to have been chiefly two, related aspects of the larger one that was the preservation of the British position; the defeat of Germany, as of Italy and Japan, was their precondition. For the rest, as Churchill himself put it, he proposed to maintain the integrity of the British Empire,[31] a warning in part directed at the uncritical American propensity to favor the independence of all peoples, colonials included; in addition, and as usual, the balance of power in Europe was desirable, which meant opposition to too great an extension of Russian influence, under whatever auspices, national, ideological, or both, this might be attempted.

This is what explains the protracted and at times acrimonious discussions over the future of Poland. The Polish case was especially delicate for Britain—it was the initial cause of the war, after all. The Polish government-in-exile, first in Angers, then in London, naturally stood for the reconstruction of Poland. But Russia was adamant and eventually withdrew recognition from that government in favor of the puppet one set up in Lublin. The story of the Warsaw insurrection of 1944 and of Russian passivity on that occasion is familiar.

Yugoslavia is another case in point, where rival organizations fought against the Axis and with each other for control. The gradual shift of British support to the Communist-led faction of Tito can only be interpreted as an expression of the desire to have a valid voice in the outcome. But Churchill failed in the attempt to convince Roosevelt of the desirability of a Balkan invasion.

Greece could be cited as well, a country where Britain, as always, was especially sensitive to the establishment of an influence other than her own.[32] There will be occasion to return to the Greek situation because of the great importance that it was to assume in 1947.[33]

These indications will suffice to suggest the general line of British policy and the manner in which Churchill strove to secure its aims; no attempt will be made to consider all the situations and issues, from Italy to the Far East, in which this policy found expression. The sum total of its endeavors appears most clearly in the discussions for the termination of the war itself and of plans for the longer-term future. These discussions took place at two levels: in the three-cornered exchanges between Washington, London, and Moscow, what might be called routine diplomacy; at summit meetings, where the supreme war leaders met each other face to face. The high points of this activity alone will be examined.

The year 1943, following the eviction of the Axis from North Africa, saw Italy invaded. The Allied plan to a degree miscarried, for the "soft underbelly of the Axis" proved to be a craggy mountain road; Italy was a battleground for the following two years. Nevertheless, an important result was accomplished, for the Fascist régime collapsed and the successor government of General Badoglio concluded an armistice with the Allies. What is most important to retain in the present context in connection with the Italian situation is that it was essentially dealt with by the Western Allies, Russia doing little more than acquiescing in their decisions, even if with reluctant suspicion at times. This fitted into the Churchillian approach of creating a de facto equilibrium of power.

Needless to say, such things tended to feed Russian distrust, the problem being to maintain a proper balance between that factor and the desirability of adhering to the common purpose of the war. If the writing on the wall was already clear in 1943, the war nevertheless was far from finished. There were during

1943 many exchanges between Washington and London, and the above-mentioned Moscow conference in October may be seen as an attempt to co-ordinate their result. In Stalin's eyes the second front had first priority, but the steady advance of the Red Army gave increasing point to the drawing up of concrete plans, especially in the matter of Russia's future Western frontier. The poser that Poland presented has been alluded to.

The American-sponsored Four-Power declaration[34] and Eden's proposal of a European Advisory Commission were both accepted. They were broad statements of aims of policy that stood in need of more specific definition. This was one of the purposes of the meeting that took place in Teheran a month later, the first which brought the Big Three together.

Relations between Roosevelt and Churchill had been easy and candid. Apart from the factor of personality this was an adequate expression of the large area of common ground that existed between the two English-speaking Powers, the special Anglo-American relationship. But there were also differences in orientation and stress, America tending to set greater store by the future organization of the whole world, Britain to put more weight on the concrete. This is where the factor of power intruded, for if Churchill and Stalin spoke the same language of power, this made at once for clearer understanding and for greater divergence between the two. In the final analysis, America also had concrete views on specific problems, the German, for example.[35] The consequence was that Churchill found himself in the position of having to acquiesce in the face of American-Soviet agreement. Britain had already become too dependent on American assistance to be able to afford the luxury of an independent stand, to attempt which would have been merely ineffectual. Poland, too, was much discussed in Teheran, inconclusively on the whole; the best that Eden could do upon returning to London was to advise the Poles to be accommodating with the Russians. But in general the meeting in Teheran unfolded in an atmosphere of geniality.

The war went on toward its appointed end during 1944. The Normandy invasion in June finally gave Stalin satisfaction. Inevitably, it raised the problem of France, but since French affairs are a major part of our discussion that issue will be deferred for the moment. We shall not dwell, either at this point or later, on the meeting at Dumbarton Oaks in the autumn of 1944, prelude to the establishment of the United Nations the following June, for the reason that, save peripherally, that topic has but little bearing on our central theme. More important was the real prelude to the end, the much controverted meeting of the Big Three again that took place at Yalta in February 1945.

First of all it may be noted that France was not present at Yalta. In 1945 France could not, by any stretch of the imagination, be considered in the category of the Great. Nevertheless, in view of the fact that Germany and her fate was the most important item on the Yalta agenda, the omission of France may be regarded not so much as an injustice as a mistake, the price of which would appear in the future. Churchill understood this, but the facts of power were clear; France's own power at the time was very small and England's power was not sufficient to secure representation for her in the face of Russo-American opposition. There is no need to dwell on the detail of the arrangements that were made for the division of Germany into zones of occupation,[36] nor upon those which mainly concerned Russia in eastern Europe. Whether the reason be the state of health of the American President, or a dose of naïveté on his part, the fact remains that agreement was obtained on the basis of an evasion—some would prefer to call it a fraud.

Russia's concern with her security was both legitimate and understandable. But, given the nature of the Russian system and its methods, what could be the meaning of "friendly" bordering states, whose "freely" elected governments would have to be "democratic"? The Red Army was in possession or shortly would be. Whether the evasion could or should have been avoided does not concern us here. But this much may be said: the power of America, its armed establishment and its economy, on which others depended, was not brought to bear on the situation[37]; Britain was not possessed of such power.

The last phase of the German war can also be omitted. In contrast with 1918 Germany was this time overrun, and at Potsdam in July 1945 once more the Big Three[38] met to implement their earlier decisions. There were reciprocal recriminations at Potsdam, but the facts of power were crudely asserting themselves. The Russians were heavy-handedly having their way in the East, save in Yugoslavia, whence they shortly withdrew, leaving the presumably dependable Communist régime of Tito in control, and in Greece, where British armed force was used to resist a Communist takeover.

Despite Hiroshima and Nagasaki American power still did not assert itself as it might have in 1945. An equilibrium of sorts was being established; across the middle of Europe ran a line of demarcation largely based on the fact of effective occupation. Though badly strained, Russo-American agreement persisted, in the face of which Britain was impotent. Britain was still, ostensibly and formally, one of the Big Three. But were there really three? The ripening of the seeds of British decline will be traced in the concluding section of this chapter. Before proceeding to a survey of the last twenty-five years, our own time, we must go back a little to give some attention to the record of the French reaction and adaptation to the circumstances up to 1945.

FRANCE: THE TRANSFORMATION FROM PÉTAIN TO DE GAULLE

Certain things emerge from the record of the first three years of the war which has been described so far. The positions of Britain and France after June 1940, and especially after the Battle of Britain, at first sight appeared to be highly contrasting. While this was largely correct in the immediate, it nevertheless concealed some points of similarity which the future would bring out.

Churchill was well aware of how thin the margin of success had been. Indeed, had it not been for certain German errors, the resort to improvisation in the face of an unexpected, because in their eyes unreasonable, British determination, things might have gone otherwise. Churchill, as has been indicated,[39] did not exclude the possibility of failure. He himself was prepared to move the government to Canada, thence to continue the fight; but he understood that in that event a situation might develop in Britain herself not very dissimilar from that which existed in France. It would be rash to assert that the possibility of a British Quisling or Pétain must be totally excluded, though fortunately this never came to the test.

Churchill's own reaction was the sound one of instilling courage into his own people—perhaps his greatest claim to fame and to their gratefulness—to mobilize British resources, all the while banking heavily on the American card. The Germans and the Japanese rendered Britain an enormous service by forcing, not only the United States, but also the Soviet Union into the British camp. Russia fared ill at first and for some time America could do but little on the battlefield. The effect of their participation was nonetheless to diminish the importance of the British role. Britain was one of the Big Three, justifiably so, because of her record so far, but henceforth only one, and we have already observed the growing diminution of her role and influence.

The French case was ostensibly different. France *was* defeated and Pétain *was* the ruler of France. Despite the remaining assets of her fleet and empire she was rather a pawn than a director of events. The difference between Britain and France in assessing the future had deep historical roots. The British outlook was broader, taking a correct view of the conflict as one of world dimensions; the French, Pétain's in particular, focused on the more parochial aspect of it as an episode in the long Franco-German contest. To France, Britain, the broad wide world across the oceans, thus became secondary and incidental.

Pétain's patriotism is unimpeachable. Apart from the limitations of his personal outlook, in matters military no less than social, his age also became a factor. He fell under the influence of other men, mostly Laval, whom he disliked personally. The judgment of a sympathetic critic may be cited:

> When Laval asks of him something that he does not wish to do, the first day he throws him out; the second day he listens to him but refuses; the third he questions him and the fourth he yields.[40]

The physical deterioration of Pétain, even the dimming of his mental processes, became increasingly marked as time passed. Relations between the two men were not easy, and there was even a period, from February 1941 to April 1942, when Laval was out of office while Darlan took his place.

But the shared belief in German victory was the common ground of these men. For a variety of reasons[41] they also shared a strong anti-British bias. Laval is the most important of the three characters. An unattractive personality, he was an intelligent man, not an unpatriotic Frenchman according to his own lights, but altogether cynical in his approach.

On the assumption of German victory Laval would go very far. After the German attack on Russia he could deliver himself of this judgment: "I hope for a German victory because otherwise Bolshevism will prevail everywhere."[42] His ignominious end in 1945 may be seen as a case of poetic—hardly of legal—justice, yet if one set him beside Sir Samuel Hoare, for example, the stress might well be on similarity rather than on difference.

His opinion, expressed in 1943, is also worth mentioning that "we must be on the side of the victors; if the Allies are the victors, de Gaulle will be the man of the occasion; if the Germans win, he, Laval, will have served the country well."[43] At worst this was cynical clarity, but it also shows an adequate appreciation of the possibilities of maneuver to which French power had been reduced. The later cartoon comes to mind which showed de Gaulle and Adenauer laying a wreath on Laval's grave over the caption, "He was too early for his time."

The fundamental mistake of all these men, apart from the erroneousness of their basic assumption, lay in their belief in the possibilities of collaboration with Germany, as a result of which France could still have an adequate place in Europe. The extent of their illusion is well brought out by the meeting between Pétain and Goering in December 1941. The latter was astonished at the demands of the former, to the extent of exclaiming: "Monsieur le Maréchal, who are the victors this time? You or us?" Hitler had no concern, apart from the sweets of revenge, other than extracting from France the utmost for the purposes of his war.

The result was a series of increasing and on the whole unreciprocated concessions amounting to a policy that such epithets as "mean" or "abject" best describe. The only saving reservation was the fact that, in the last resort, Vichy France would not make formal peace, nor allow itself to be dragged into war against Britain, thereby therefore to some extent at least reserving the future.

Even such freedom of maneuver as Vichy France still possessed lost its meaning after the Allied landings in North Africa. The whole country fell under German occupation and the fleet was scuttled while the rest of the empire passed under Free French and Allied control. Totally impotent and deprived of any bargaining counters, the story of metropolitan France thereafter is that of an impotent wraith and may be left out of our considerations. Yet, interestingly enough, France had not disappeared but rather reassumed a place in the Allied coalition.

The theory of the shield (Pétain) and the sword (de Gaulle) has been advanced as explanation of the French wartime record. Certainly not the result of calculated plan, the theory has validity as descriptive of the complementary roles of the two men.

The British, or Churchill's, reaction to the collapse of 1940 had a double aspect. For the short term, the war, avoid the fleet and the empire being used against Britain; for the longer future, France must somehow be restored and play a commensurate role as a necessary part of the European community, the traditional British policy vis-à-vis all continental states. This meant a cautiously suspicious treatment of Vichy and a hesitant acceptance of de Gaulle, ever keeping on guard against the risks of riding two horses at one time.

De Gaulle's appeal of June 18, 1940, had found initially very little response among the French.[44] Yet, two days earlier, Churchill had been impressed by de Gaulle's understanding of the British refusal, so often criticized in France, of the futile sacrifice of the British Air Force in the Battle of France. Even if in pain and anger, de Gaulle could understand Mers-el-Kebir. The initial merit of de Gaulle was to accept the validity of the British view of the war as a conflict of world-encompassing dimensions, in which the Franco-German confrontation was but an episode.

Clearly, however, whether because of its exiguous dimensions or because of the existence of Vichy, the Free French movement could not be granted recognition as representing France; it obviously did not. To put it briefly, de Gaulle's steady aim was to secure precisely such a position; his ultimate success in this endeavor shows his quixotic romanticism to have had sounder foundation than the seemingly more realistic appraisal of such men as Pétain or Laval.

Save in this sense, de Gaulle was anything but a romantic. Deprived of means, financed by the British, he was aware of his complete dependence. Nor was he free of suspicion of Britain and her motives. His reaction to these circumstances was to assert all the more vigorously and with colossal gall that *he* was France, to be treated with the deference due an equal; in this lies the key to his tactics. Churchill, rather a more romantic character himself, was attracted by such absurd magnificence, his admiration for which caused him to bear, with equanimity and humor in general, the burden of the cross of Lorraine. As he put it:

> He had to be rude to the British to prove to French eyes that he was not a British puppet. He certainly carried out this policy with perseverance. He even explained this technique to me, and I fully comprehended the extraordinary difficulties of his problem. I have always admired his massive strength.[45]

We shall not attempt to survey the record of the Free French during the first two years of the war. It dwindles into details in the larger context, but one observation should be made at this point. In British eyes, if France, whether Vichy or Free, retained a measure of importance, America had properly much more. America's French policy may be said to have opted for Vichy, whither Admiral Leahy was sent as ambassador. It was a rational policy which, however, in contrast with the British, suffered, to put it most succinctly, from the shortcoming of a preconception that tended to write off France, any France, in the future. As to the Free French movement, be it Roosevelt or Cordell Hull, they thought it represented nothing, which was nearly correct at first; hence de Gaulle's claims could be dismissed as unimportant quixotry, delusions of grandeur, and a nuisance. His most concrete achievement was a degree of irritation.[46] Granting that there was bigger fish to fry than France, this attitude, most of all the persistence in it long after there was any justification for it, must be set down as a serious shortcoming in the statesmanship of the American President. The more opportunistic Russians showed greater flexibility; initially contemptuous, after June 1941, the Russians discovered all sorts of merits in Free France.

The North African landings in November 1942 opened an entirely new chapter in the story. By that time some sections of the French empire, Equatorial Africa and some island possessions, had rallied to the Free French movement. A year earlier, in December 1941, de Gaulle had created a French National Committee, a government in potential, but still with no international standing. The adherence of French North Africa, whether by conquest or consent, and the complete occupation of France by the Germans could offer an opportunity for the transfer of recognition by others. This was indeed the hope of the Free French, but at this point a tangled, in some of its aspects sordid, episode intervened, of which mention must be made.

It is significant that the Free French had no prior knowledge of operation Torch, the North African landings. This was the result of an American decision, to which Churchill reluctantly agreed. De Gaulle's reaction needs no explanation—he was in the Near East at the time. The intrigues that went on around the figures of Darlan and Giraud constitute one of the less successful American exercises in diplomacy. It took an ultimatum from Churchill to de Gaulle to bring the latter to Morocco and indulge in the "comedy," as he called it himself, of an amicable meeting with Giraud.

However, de Gaulle, in the last analysis a political more than a military man, could play politics with the best. Had it not been for American support, Giraud, an honest man but a political innocent, would have been eliminated from the scene far sooner than he was. The operation took a year. In June 1943 a French Committee of National Liberation (CFLN) was finally organized in Algiers, an awkward bicephalic body in which the two generals held equal positions. By December Giraud was reduced to the role of military commander only and soon thereafter was removed from that post. It took another year, to June 1944, before the committee was transformed into the Provisional Government of the French Republic. But American opposition persisted, even after the Normandy landings, and the Provisional Government did not receive de jure recognition until the end of October.[47] Some of this is detail which may seem of minor interest and importance. The reason it is mentioned is because the American attitude, persisted in long after there was justification for it, and in which it is difficult not to see the smallness of personal pique on the part of the American President, was to have lasting effects. This unnecessary performance can best be described as regrettable.

The persistence of the American attitude had failed to keep up with the course of events. Reference has been made to the fact that the German attack on Russia produced an about-face in the Communist attitude everywhere. French Communists, reverting to their 1935 position, could now serve best the Soviet cause by being patriotic Frenchmen once more, an attitude congenial to many. In France as elsewhere the Communists played a major, highly effective, and creditable, role in the resistance, which they in fact endeavored to annex.

The American intervention and the course of events after November 1942 gave a great fillip to the French Resistance; de Gaulle's appeal of June 1940 could be unearthed and responded to. But this did not go without creating the problem of an internal struggle for control of the liberation movement. This was a domestic French problem in the main, of which it will suffice to say that here also the Provisional Government in Algiers managed to become accepted by all the various French tendencies.

However useful the French Resistance, it would be idle to pretend that the liberation of France was not essentially the work of the Anglo-American coalition. De Gaulle had been kept out of the initial Normandy invasion, but when he landed in France he acted as the head of a totally independent French Government in making administrative decisions; plans for an Allied military government of France had best be set aside. It was a gracious Allied gesture to let the liberation of Paris be in its final stages a French deed, a case of intelligent understanding. When General Koenig's tanks arrived and the German forces had locally surrendered, in the great surge of emotion that moved the crowds along the Champs Elysées, the towering figure of General de Gaulle led the march as the fitting symbol of a France reborn.

His courage, his determination, his arrogance had paid. When the final German surrender was signed at Rheims on May 8, 1945, a French representative was present along with the American and British—the Germans were appalled. In large measure owing to British insistence, France was to share in the occupation of Germany on an equal footing with the Big Three.

Yet one should not confuse shadow with substance. Of French power in being there was in 1945 virtually none. What French military formations existed—they had been growing but were still almost insignificant in comparison with those of the Big Three—were wholly dependent on alien, mainly American, equipment. The French economy was at a virtual standstill, and here also France was in a position of dependence, again mainly on America. When it came to the giving of assistance, America could be very generous, to France as to others; but this was a very different thing from the willingness to recognize a special place for France in future councils. The attitude of the American President tended to be noncommittal, rather inclined to look upon France as another piece of ravaged Europe which, like others, must of course be restored, lest chaos and possibly the Communist influence prevail. The reluctance to grant full recognition to the Provisional Government and its head, to turn over to them full control of domestic affairs, are indications of the American estimate of the measure and possibilities of French power.

The Soviet attitude was not very dissimilar, with two important qualifications. Russia herself had undergone tremendous suffering and losses, far greater in fact than had France. That French distress should leave Russia insensitive was only natural, and there could be no question of Russia giving material assistance when she herself was still in need of the benefits of American bounty. As to the possibility of chaos in France, this might fit very well Russia's political aims. Stalin had made friendly gestures, more friendly than the United States toward the Provisional Government; he had even concluded an alliance with de Gaulle in 1944. But that did not preclude on his part the most realistic, and crudest, approach in regard to French power; he and Roosevelt had agreed in excluding any French participation in the Yalta discussions.

The British took a different, and far more sensible, view, based on the realization that if either chaos or Communism, or the latter as a consequence of the former, were not to prevail over the whole continent of Europe, France must have an important place and voice in the future. Who else could fill that role? In this condition lay one of the main assets of the French position, a negative asset, however. The war had been a very severe drain on British resources and power, a condition in part and to a point concealed by the position of at least ostensible parity that Britain held in the councils of the Big Three. But Britain, too, was highly dependent on America, and among the members of the dominant triumvirate the fiction of equality was being subjected to increasing strains. In the endeavor to retain as much of her position as possible Britain must more than ever bank on the asset of the American connection.

Nevertheless, between Britain and France, the principals in our tale, in 1945 the emphasis appeared to be on contrast rather than on similarity of position. Britain still had a large place in world councils; she must try to retain that place, or as much of it as possible. France had virtually none, her problem was to climb back from the depths of 1940 and to recover what place she could.

Despite the stress on difference, the accident of wartime performance, the importance of which could certainly not be ignored, yet introduced a measure of distortion. Perhaps in a deeper sense the emphasis should be placed on the fact that, vis-à-vis the rest of the world, Britain and France were still, as they had been for quite some time, essentially in the same boat. The observation made twenty years later by a perceptive student of European affairs, "Since 1945 the international status of France, which collapsed, has been very much the same as that of Great Britain, which held out alone,"[48] might be taken as the theme of our closing pages, in which we shall attempt to sketch how this has come to pass.

THE CONTINUING SEARCH FOR POSITION

The literature on contemporary affairs is vast and the rate of its proliferation tends, if anything, to increase. We know at once too much and too little. A far greater amount of documentation is currently made available than used to be the case; the labors of the future historian will in all probability in certain instances add but little to our knowledge. At the same time, much—how much we cannot know—remains unrevealed that will eventually provide material for reappraisal—and for innumerable doctoral dissertations.

To attempt a final assessment would be rash, if for no other reason than because of the lack of perspective. Yet it is not impossible, on the basis of the available information, leaving aside complexities of detailed operation, let alone the hidden springs of motivation and the tortuousness of performance, to detect certain trends and to reach some tentative conclusions.

This will be done by delving into the record in selective fashion. Selection, inevitable in any case, implies judgment, which some would prefer to call bias. Ranke's ideal of perfect objectivity is no longer the fashion, but its validity remains as an approximation to be striven for. The best that one can do is to plead honesty of purpose and openness of mind; if these be granted, the reader then must be the judge of the validity of the accomplishment and of the merit of the contribution.

These things are said by way of clarification and to explain the manner of approach. From the mass of known facts some threads will be picked out to illustrate some trends which in the writer's judgment insert themselves in the theme of continuity in the search for position within the context of shifting circumstances. For the sake of simplicity of exposition within the limits of available space, it has been thought desirable to deal separately with the two principals in our tale. What inevitable repetition may be thereby involved has for its compensation greater clarity of presentation; the repetition will be minimized by dealing, with avowed arbitrariness, with certain developments under either the "British" or the "French" rubric, though obviously many of these developments concern both.

The Continued Decline of Britain

In dealing with the British case, rather than telling the story in chronological fashion, it will be presented under three distinct heads, corresponding to the three large circles of British interest: relations with the United States, the devolution of empire, the relationship with Europe. The three of course operate simultaneously and interact upon each other; separating them will make possible a clearer dissection.

THE "SPECIAL RELATIONSHIP": BRITAIN AND THE UNITED STATES

It was in the midst of the Potsdam conference, the Far Eastern War still unfinished, that Attlee took Churchill's place in the discussions. The British people had returned to office the Labour party, with an unexpectedly large majority to boot. This was not so much a repudiation of the wartime leadership of Churchill as an expression of the fact that, the war ended, the focus of their preoccupations had shifted to domestic concerns.

The judgment that "there was a deep nostalgia for the past and a tacit assumption that the world owed the British people a living as a reward for having stood alone"[49] is only true in part. It may be taken as reflecting a loosely felt attitude vis-à-vis the outside, but in effect many in Britain would have rather forgotten the rest of the world. Though no such phrase had been used as Lloyd George's promise in the 1918 khaki election of a world fit for heroes to live in, an expectation of that nature was abroad in the hope of a better world in the future.

The transition was smooth and the Labour government indeed proceeded to enact a program of social legislation; the shift was rather of emphasis than of kind. Labour had been part of the wartime coalition and Churchill was by no means a diehard reactionary in regard to the social question. To cite but one illustration, the Beveridge *Report on Social Insurance and Allied Services* dated from 1942. In addition, the war itself had inevitably enlarged the domain of state control and regulation. No revolution was entailed in continuing the practice, nationalizing coal, for example, and extolling the virtues of planning.

Nor was there any marked reversal in the domain of foreign policy, where, under Bevin's direction traditional lines were generally adhered to. Yet Britain, more than any other country, is dependent on the outside, trade in the last analysis, for the existence of her people and for the conditions of their existence. The United States was more capable of adopting an independent policy and in that country the desire was strong, as in 1919, for a return to "normalcy." As on the earlier occasion, the huge American war machine was dismantled with alarming alacrity[50] in response to the pressures of popular demand. Interestingly, there was a reversal of the traditional American and British attitudes to free trade, in which America now found greater appeal, whereas control was of necessity more emphasized in Britain.

Britain could not ignore such things as her burden of debt, the loss of her foreign assets, or the balance of trade. The abrupt American termination of Lend-Lease in August 1945 came as a shock to Britain no less than to others. By way of compensation, an American and a Canadian loan at the end of the year were intended to tide Britain over the immediate difficulties of postwar readjustment. How much of an illusion this was did not take long in appearing in the rate at which the loans were used up, while the effects of the severe winter of 1946–47 emphasized the fragility of the British economy; the pound was devalued in September 1949. Meanwhile America came to the rescue again. The Marshall Plan was a general salvage operation directed toward Europe as a whole rather than toward Britain in particular. It came into effect in 1948 and was one of the most enlightened foreign policy operations ever designed by any country, but where Britain was concerned it is important to note that it had the significance of emphasizing the similarity, rather than the difference, of the distress that Britain shared with others.

The appointment of General Marshall to the American secretaryship of state in February 1947 may be taken as the indication of a change in the orientation of American policy, a change that was largely a reaction to the policy of the Soviet Union. However much that country had suffered from the war, she displayed no lack of vigor in the pursuit of an aggressive policy of expansion. Asserting an increasingly tight control in the Eastern countries of Europe, those where the presence of her armies made such an operation easy, she looked farther afield for opportunities. The existence of very large Communist parties in France and in Italy in particular, where Communists participated in the governments, gave sharp point to the possibility of a Communist Europe, where the feebleness and the vacuum of power constituted an invitation to the intrusion of Soviet influence. This the United States would not allow to happen, and the Marshall Plan in this context may be seen as an anti-Soviet operation. Such in fact it was, even though this detracts not a whit from its validity or from the element of simple generosity that it represented on the part of the American people.[51]

But, to repeat, the effect was to show the limitations of the power of Britain, unable by her means alone to stand up to the Russian pressure on the Continent. Only America could undertake that task, in which Britain at most could assist. Thus the world came to be divided in two, the United States and the Soviet Union, in a category apart from all others, leading in their train whatever clients or satellites would willingly accept, or could be coerced into accepting, the leadership of the two superpowers, as they came to be known.

The primacy of American power had long been acknowledged by Britain. Baldwin's declaration in 1934[52] that he would never allow the use of the British Navy for blockade operations until he knew what the position of the United States would be, may be cited as an illustration among many of a line of British policy firmly and consistently adhered to.

The elaboration of the treaties of peace with what were regarded, properly on the whole, as secondary German satellites, Italy, Hungary, Roumania, Bulgaria, and Finland, was finally completed by February 1947. It had given rise to protracted discussions, in the case of the Italo-Yugoslav border in particular. Of that episode it will suffice to say that it served to sharpen the division of Europe in two, and the antagonism between America and Russia, while bringing out the small mediating role that Britain could exercise.

Yet the American reaction was somewhat slow in developing;

Churchill's Fulton speech,[53] in which he sought to shake American lethargy, coining the "iron curtain" phrase, evoked little response. An abrupt change was about to take place, which was of the highest importance where Britain was concerned.

The determination on the part of Britain to prevent the extension of Communist control to Greece has been mentioned; it meant keeping armed forces in Greece. But in February 1947 the conclusion was reached in London that, whatever the consequences of failure in Greece might be—and they could easily extend to the entire eastern Mediterranean—British resources, meaning by this the state of the British exchequer, were no longer equal to the task. Britain would withdraw her forces from Greece.

The American response was immediate and dramatic. It was the so-called Truman Doctrine, the clear declaration that the United States would resist the extension of Soviet control in both Greece and Turkey.[54] A clearer case of British surrender would be difficult to imagine. Interestingly enough, the transfer of position, which was effected with smoothness and a lack of recrimination, all took place within the English-speaking family, within Anglo-Saxondom, as some would rather put it. Seen from another angle, the long-established British policy of cultivating good relations with America was proving itself justified. But this is a misleading interpretation, for, however much common ground they might have, the two countries were distinct states and America was making its own decisions. To be sure, one could go a step further and read the event as the manifestation of a change in relations in which Britain was destined to become a subservient client, a tool of American policy, but such a relationship had never been in the mind of the directors of British policy. Yet the fact of demotion stood clear for all the world to see.

The partnership, as some preferred to call it, was in any event not a relationship of equality but undeniably one of dependence, as the unfolding of events was to show. The German problem, the fate of Germany, was one of the touchstones of American-Soviet relations. The country was divided into four zones of occupation,[55] with the city of Berlin, a beleaguered island in the Soviet zone, under quadripartite rule. In 1948, the Russians, ill-advisedly as it turned out, thought to evict the Western Powers from Berlin by virtually severing its connections with the West. In the American response that was the air lift, the means that eventually defeated the Russian attempt, Britain gave loyal assistance. Here was undoubtedly a common interest.

But for the rest the leadership in shaping policy toward Germany was American, in which Britain acquiesced. Thus was first created Bizonia, a fusion of the American and British zones, the German currency was rehabilitated, and eventually the Federal Republic was born, gradually to become one of America's most trusted allies.

Changes in the direction of American policy could at times be abrupt and show a modicum of regard for British sensibilities. In the desire to recreate force in Europe, America engineered the North Atlantic Treaty Organization (NATO), a quite authentic expression of the common desire that united the free countries of Europe and the United States in resisting Communist encroachment. But, unafraid of Germany herself, America could perhaps too easily overlook the distinction between Germany and her recent European victims. The proposal to create a European force in which Germany would participate led to lengthy discussions. When in the end the European Defense Community was defeated by the French, Eden could play the mediating role of savior by proposing an alternative solution acceptable to all.[56]

Some crumbs of comfort—they were little more than that—could likewise be derived from the feeling that it was Attlee's precipitate visit to Washington in 1950 which stayed America's hand, which it was feared might unleash the nuclear weapon when the war was going badly in Korea.

The Korean episode will not be discussed; it had the effect of strengthening the American desire, just indicated, to rebuild the power of Europe. Another aspect of this same wish was the American endorsement of European integration in general, meaning Western, or free, Europe of course—more will be said about this, too, later on.[57] This was largely at first a French idea, which aroused a minimum of interest, even some sneers, in Britain. America had no hesitation in indicating her preference and in urging Britain on a path on which Britain did not wish to embark at this stage.

The Suez episode in 1956 served, among other things, to bring out very clearly certain aspects of the Anglo-American relationship. Sufficient has been said in other connections of the nature of the British interest in the Middle East and of the particular place of the Suez Canal in the British scheme of things. That interest was at once political, strategic, and economic, with increasing weight on the last-named aspect owing to the growing importance of oil, of which the Middle East as a whole was the chief supplier to Britain. The American interest had a different emphasis. American companies had developed a substantial stake in Middle Eastern oil, of which, however, America was totally independent for her own needs. The broad American interest in the region was politico-strategic, part of the policy of containment of the Soviet Union which must be held at the Greco-Turkish barrier and prevented from establishing a foothold in the Arab world and the Mediterranean, precisely what the British interest had been for a long time.

There is no little irony in the fact that the immediate origin of the Suez crisis may be seen in the American action of withdrawing the offer of credit for the building of the Aswan Dam. The Egyptian response took the form of nationalizing the Suez Canal, and from this action, after a period of futile tergiversation, was born the Anglo-French decision to resort to the use of force.[58] Yet the American reaction in turn to the Anglo-French operation was both prompt and sharp; it produced what may seem like the ludicrous spectacle of the United States joining its chief rival, the Soviet Union, in condemning two of its NATO allies in the United Nations. Britain and France yielded in the face of such pressure. Whether the American position was the result of high-minded adherence to principle, whatever the cost, or an instance of political naïveté, it could not have been taken had not American power been such in comparison with that of its allies that it could proceed on the (correct) assumption of their complete dependence. It was a sad occasion for Britain. Quite naturally, given the knowledge of American views, and despite the Aswan episode, Britain had proceeded with her plans without informing the United States. But the sharp American rapping of British knuckles did not disrupt the Atlantic alliance, all of whose members, like Britain herself, were far too dependent on American power and good will to be able to indulge in policies of which America disapproved or to part company with America. The Suez episode had a very sobering effect on Britain; needless to say, the humiliation endured left behind it a train of resentment.[59] The American behavior in the whole affair, whatever may be said of it on other scores, had at the very least been impulsive and cavalier, giving a minimum of thought to some of its long-term implications and consequences.

But long past were the days of Arabi Pasha and the pill must be swallowed. Of the British action this also must be said, that it was ill contrived and that it, too, was based on an inadequate consideration of the facts and the relationships of power. There is little reason to question that, in purely material terms of armed power, the combination of Britain, France, and Israel was more than adequate to deal wth Egypt—Israel showed that she could do this alone. But power does not only consist of guns; having embarked on a course, of which some measure of American condemnation was predictable, the British will failed.

This is a good place to say something of the general problem of defense in the case of Britain, for it, too, illustrates the nature of the relationship of dependence on the United States. Britain had fully shared in the wartime development of the atomic bomb, but the cost of the undertaking and of its subsequent development was beyond her resources; even though she possessed some nuclear armament, she was no longer in a class with the two superpowers in that domain,[60] and the United States was not eager to continue the wartime co-operation, instituting instead the restrictions of the MacMahon Act in 1946.[61]

In his book *British Foreign Policy Since the Second World War*,[62] Woodhouse gives an excellent analysis of Britain's defense policy through a study of the annual series of Defense White Papers to the end of the fifties. Nothing could be more apt than the following quotation from the 1948 White Paper:

> The United Kingdom, as a member of the British Commonwealth and a Great Power, must be prepared at all times to

> fulfil her responsibilities not only to the United Nations but also to herself. For this purpose, the first essential is a strong and sound economy, with a flourishing industry from which to draw the strength to defend our rights and fulfil our obligations.[63]

This puts the finger on precisely the right place, for the simple fact is that Britain did not have the adequate economic base to support the rank of first-class Power. It would take us too far afield to rehearse the not very inspiring record of steady British retreat. The abandonment of Blue Streak, the American promise of weapons for British submarines, the giving up of the too costly TSR2, are all milestones on the road of which the last step at this writing has been the radical decision to withdraw British forces from East of Suez. It may have been a wholly sensible decision, fully in keeping with the economic possibilities of Britain; it is difficult to imagine a clearer acknowledgment of the retreat of diminishing power.

The reaction of the United States toward such developments has been ambivalent. For the United States, if willing to condemn Britain in 1956 and if generally sympathetic to the liquidation of the British Empire, has been driven to realize the usefulness to itself of positions held by Britain, East of Suez among other quarters. Discussions have been many over a long period about who was to foot the bill, a share of which at least the United States has been willing to assume. The British withdrawal from the Far East and from the Indian Ocean may be seen as the logical end point of the line of development that began with the ANZUS Pact, the first in which America ostensibly took Britain's place in Commonwealth defense affairs.

Reverting to the point made in the above-cited Defense White Paper of 1948, a word may be appropriate about the state of Britain's economy. Britain, like others, recovered from the war, in part owing to American assistance. Britain, in contrast with continental Europe, had suffered less physical destruction; but this in some respects resulted in the disadvantage of a less up-to-date plant. Conditions were, however, very different from what they had been after the First World War, when unemployment had been the great nightmare; Britain enjoyed instead full employment and a rising standard of living for the mass.

But this presumably satisfactory state of affairs was itself a source of difficulty. Without following closely the details of the ups and downs of the British economic scene, it may be said in general terms that Britain experienced, especially after the 1950's, during which she enjoyed the advantages of devaluation, increasing difficulties with her balance of trade, the problem of paying her way in the world. This has given rise in turn to the phenomenon of "stop-and-go" operation of the economy, a spurt of activity with inflationary overtones, the result of which is a growing deficit in the balance of trade, followed by an attempt to redeem this condition through the institution of restrictive measures, wage freezes, income and price controls, for instance.

This bespeaks instability and has had repercussions on the position of the pound, a matter of very considerable moment, for if London is no longer *the* financial capital of the world, it still retains much of the place which, through free evolution and natural development, it had achieved in the nineteenth century. To maintain such a position without a strong and stable currency seems in the nature of an acrobatic act that cannot be indefinitely sustained.

The United States has been sympathetic and desirous, as in the matter of defense, that Britain should maintain her position lest its own burden of responsibility be increased. Assistance in one form or another, loans from the United States or the International Monetary Fund, are expedients that can be useful for a transitional passage; they are not ultimate or permanent solutions. Pressure has been accumulating for some years, roughly during the past decade. Matters came to a head taking the shape of a new devaluation of the pound in November 1967. That, too, can be no ultimate solution, and Britain—the rest of the world, too, America included, owing to the still large place of Britain in the world's financial operation—is struggling with the problem.

THE DEMISE OF EMPIRE

The picture drawn so far has been mainly in dark colors. While there are redeeming aspects in the British domestic scene, it does not seem unfair to say that the reliance on the United States, the special relationship, such as it has been, has not had any particular usefulness as far as preserving the British position of power. But that position was due not only or so much to the resources of the British Isles,[64] which are scant, as to the fact that Britain had become the heart and center of an empire which had come to cover nearly one quarter of the planet. That domain, now become Commonwealth, was still essentially intact in 1945.

Like many British institutions, the imperial structure of which Britain is the heart is not characterized by the simplicity and neatness of orderly rational construction. In this very fact many would see its merit, an example of the British pragmatic genius for flexible adaptation. Its history and evolution bear the imprint of the liberal attitude which allowed increasing scope to the desires of its constituent members. The commercial importance of this world-encompassing network cannot be overemphasized; it lay at the heart of Britain's economic and financial power, which in turn made it possible for Britain to assume the chief burden of imperial defense.

There was a converse aspect to this relationship, best expressed in the fact that in the two world wars the totality of resources of the British imperial complex had been available to Britain, be it in economic or military terms. If the relationship could be preserved, it could constitute the basis of an enormous power aggregation, of benefit to all its members, and fully in a class with the two superpowers. Conversely, if it could not, the separate members, Britain herself for one, would be demoted to a position ranging from second rank to insignificance.

It has become almost bad form to perceive any merit in the imperial process; the Marxist interpretation and the British nonconformist conscience in some of its manifestations can join hands at this point. Leaving aside that interesting aspect of the question, something must be said here of the sad and regrettable, not for Britain alone, failure of certain hopes.

The so-called White Dominions had achieved a considerable degree of autonomy, having become masters of their own foreign and economic policies. British as they were in the main,[65] they naturally tended to think primarily in terms of their immediate concerns, even if these might seem at times provincial in their scope. The attraction of American power, military and economic, was irresistibly strong in Canada, however much some Canadians might regret it. Nevertheless it was undeniable that in the case of Canada the United States was increasingly filling the place of Britain, be it from the standpoint of defense or economy. Even in matters primarily imperial, the problem of the dependent parts of the empire or British action in the Middle East, the Canadian position could at times be closer to the American than to the British.

The change was even more marked in the cases of Australia and New Zealand. Highly sensitive, for reasons of geography if for no others, to the pressures issuing from Asia, fearful of the threat to their racial purity, they were especially aware of their dependence. The fact that the Pacific war had been an overwhelmingly American enterprise, Britain incapable of resisting the onslaught of Japan in Hong Kong or in Singapore, assumes great significance at this point. Australia and New Zealand thus drifted increasingly into the American orbit, a fact that was finally and clearly registered in the ANZUS Pact of 1951, a defensive alliance in the Pacific between Australia, New Zealand, and the United States, in which Britain was not even a participant.

India was a case by itself, where the desire for independence had for some time developed roots; it was in many ways the most important test case. Simple coercion was out of the question after 1945, but when India achieved independence in 1947, in the awkward form of two states, India and Pakistan, high hopes still persisted. For both remained within the Commonwealth, even if the precise meaning of the association remained to be defined and tested.

States have a regrettable way of behaving like states. Even if one overlooked the tragedy that accompanied the process of separation—time might soften that memory—the relations between India and Pakistan were not and have not since been of the best. Both countries nevertheless continued to attend meetings of the Commonwealth Prime Ministers in London. India, because of her dimensions, aspired, under Nehru's leadership, to a world role, a fact which to a point put her into competition with Britain herself and with an emerging China, though this last aspect was persistently denied in India for a time.[66] Leaving aside the intricacies and the ambiguities in which these conflicting desires have involved India, two particular aspects of Indian policy may be mentioned for their value as illustrations.

India, quite naturally, was sympathetic to the similar desire for emancipation of other dependent peoples in the Commonwealth. This led her to assume a leadership of sorts, insofar as she played a role *within* the Commonwealth, of the non-white elements in that association; hence various stresses, of which more in a moment. Secondly, she concentrated on the issue of Kashmir and her relationship with Pakistan, which by way of reinsurance gave signs of an increasingly Chinese orientation. It came to a brief war in 1965, the very thing for which the Commonwealth, if it had any significance, might be expected to provide mediatory services. One cannot emphasize too much the significance of the fact that mediation was indeed provided, but that it took place in Tashkent rather than in London. What meaning had the Commonwealth association?

Indian sympathy for the agitation of other colored peoples for independence has just been mentioned, an agitation of which the most important focus was in Africa. Ghanaian independence led the way in 1957, since followed by the emergence to a similar position of others, which there will be no attempt to enumerate. Most of these newborn states retained their Commonwealth membership, with the consequence, among others, that the majority of that membership became colored.

Here was a paradox, for if the British have on the whole dealt with fairness with their colored dependents, have indeed rendered them many services, the British feeling of racial distinctness has remained strong and as a consequence has rankled. Out of this an unexpected situation arose. The treatment of the Boers after they had been defeated, the granting of Dominion status to South Africa before the decade after the war was out, may be taken as an illustration of Britain's liberality in matters colonial. Many Boers loyally accepted the British connection—Marshal Smuts comes to mind—but some did not, and eventually the more reactionary tendency prevailed among them, which, controlling the state, embarked on a policy of sharp racial discrimination, apartheid, reminiscent of the American doctrine of "equal but separate" status, the main emphasis being on "separate." British liberalism, directed to the Boers, had forgotten the non-white element, some four fifths of the population.

The result was awkward. On the one hand, Britain had no control over domestic South African legislation, nor did she wish, for commercial reasons in part, to attempt any coercive measures. In the climate of our day avowed racial discrimination is a capital sin. The United Nations could only resort to unimplementable verbal condemnations, but within the circle of the Commonwealth, where by this time the majority of members were no longer white, it came to a sharp break in 1961. In face of the strong condemnation of South Africa's racial policy, that Dominion, become meanwhile a republic, decided to abandon the Commonwealth. Whatever the merits or faults of racial discrimination, one thing stood out inescapably: the divisive factor had proved stronger than the forces of cohesion. What could be the meaning of the Commonwealth after that?

The racial issue was likewise at the root of the Rhodesian problem, where, however, for constitutional reasons, Britain still had supervisory rights. Rhodesia's Unilateral Declaration of Independence in 1965 was, in simplest terms of existing law, plain rebellion. But Britain, whether she could or not, would not resort to force despite the exhortations of some members of the Commonwealth.[67] A successful breach of the law is deplorable; such a breach, accompanied by proclaimed defiance, is worse, for it devalues the law. The same question as before may again be asked about the meaning of the Commonwealth.

Nor have the attempts at what would seem the very sensible federative approach met with any success. In Malaya, the Caribbean, in East and Central Africa, around Aden, they have all failed. Even in Nigeria, held up for a time as a model, the effort to preserve unity led for a time to civil war. The simple fact of racial distinction and feeling, whatever one may think of it on other grounds, would be idle to deny.[68] There is much to be said for not allowing in Britain the development of the racial situation that plagues the United States; hence the wisdom of a restrictive policy of immigration where Asians and Africans are concerned.[69] But once more, then, what meaning has the Commonwealth?

There is good reason to bemoan the failure of what seemed at one time a possibility full of promise, but the simple fact is that the Commonwealth has failed; as a reality it is no more. One is reminded in some ways of the post-First World War French security system and of the vicious circle that was its fundamental flaw. What gave that system validity was French power rather than the enhancement of that power through the asset of Polish and other divisions. When French power itself abdicated, the whole system collapsed. Without pushing the parallel too far, it remains true that Anzac and Indian divisions had been of service to Britain, but as power weakened at the central core, as Britain was no longer capable of assuming the main burden of providing defense and insuring cohesion, the centrifugal forces asserted their disintegrating effect. To the extent that the United States has taken over from Britain the chief responsibility of defense, this may be useful to such countries as Australia, for example; for Britain it merely emphasizes demotion.

Britain is left with bits and scraps, often more in the nature of headaches and nuisances than assets; a large number of mini-states may conceivably join the United Nations and reduce that institution to absurdity.

Independence need not of course mean the severance of commercial connections, so important an element in the British position of power, and it is sometimes pointed out that the British economic stake in India has rather grown than decreased since that country became independent. But against this two factors militate. One is the diminution of Britain's own resources, the availability of British capital for use abroad, especially in the face of rising competition, not least the American, but others as well. The other is the fact that the new independent states tend to assert a greater independence in economic policy as well. Their actions may not always necessarily be of the wisest; they are the inevitable consequence of the assertion of the prerogative of sovereignty in all domains.

The story would not be complete without some mention of the Middle East. The position that Britain had secured for herself in that part of the world at the end of the First World War has been indicated[70]; it fitted to a nicety the long record of Britain's imperial growth. The fragility of the accomplishment was not long in appearing, but despite such things as the long-drawn-out squabble with Egypt, the sprouting of the dragon's teeth sown in Palestine, the qualified relinquishment of Iraq in 1930, the Middle East was a useful British base of operation during the Second World War; El Alamein is only sixty miles from Alexandria.

By the time the war ended Arab nationalism was a well-established element in the situation that must somehow be come to terms with. It was largely a negative emotion in the sense that the unity of the Arab world was then, as it still is, a myth which had what reality it possessed only in its opposition to alien influence, meaning British in the main. Britain encouraged the formation of the Arab League in 1945, but she and Egypt were unable to agree on a renegotiation of the 1936 treaty, which Egypt demanded.

The entire situation was complicated by the intensification of the Jewish problem, meaning the continued, though in part impeded, immigration of Jews into Palestine. In their efforts to escape the poisoned atmosphere of Europe the Jews enjoyed sympathy in many Western quarters, but the Arabs could not see the merits of having to furnish compensation for the sins of Christendom, an awkward argument to answer. At any rate the tension grew, the creation of a Jewish state being the most authentic focus of Arab unity, and the British were caught on the horns of a dilemma largely of their own making.

It was a truly impossible situation, until, not knowing what to do, the British acknowledged their failure as they had in Greece a year before. However, in 1948 it was the United Nations rather than the United States that was called upon to deal with the impasse. The decision to partition Palestine is secondary to the fact of the sanctioning of Israel. The result was war, in which Israeli determination and competence got the better of far vaster but equally less competent Arab numbers. Thus Israel was born, endowed with absurd frontiers, but unrecognized by the Arab states, who would accept no more than a truce and an armistice line. The British had largely extricated themselves but certainly had not enhanced their position in the Middle East.

In the vote in the United Nations the United States and the

Soviet Union found themselves in accord, a fact which corresponds to the increasing involvement of both states in the region. The nature of their respective interests has been indicated before.[71] Meanwhile the Anglo-Egyptian discussion continued and Egypt went her way to depose King Farouk, after a short interlude Colonel Nasser emerging in control. An agreement of sorts was reached in 1954[72] on the two chief items of controversy: for the Sudan Egypt acknowledged the right of self-determination. The details regarding the Suez Canal need not be specified; they amounted to another step in the process of British retreat, though still not total eviction, from Egypt. The Baghdad Pact in 1955, which linked Turkey, Iran, and Pakistan with Britain, deserves no more than passing mention. It was part of the American attempt to close the ring around the Soviet Union, which lends all the more interest to the American refusal formally to join in it, and was grist to the mill of those who contended that Britain was increasingly accepting the subsidiary role of an agent of American policy.

The picture of amicable relations between Egypt on the one hand, the United States and Britain on the other, in 1954 was misleading; the condition was also short-lived. We regain at this point the previously mentioned events of 1956. The conflict at the root of which was the Suez Canal, more immediately the American action about the Aswan Dam, merged at this point with the other standing issue that was the very existence of Israel. The French were involved in the nationalization of the Suez Canal and had the additional grievance of Egyptian encouragement in the developing Algerian situation.[73]

Actually, it was Israel which took the initiative of hostilities—the Arabs made no secret of their determination to eradicate Israel in the most literal and total sense. Israel was militarily highly successful, until the British and the French—we shall not go into the issue of collusion—intervened under the ostensible but unconvincing pretext of separating the belligerents. We shall not repeat the ignominious end of the adventure where the British and the French were concerned. The blow to British prestige was severe, and if to speak of British eviction would be overstating the case at this stage, certainly the burden of Western influence in the Middle East was shifted to America. This was well shown in 1958, when it was a primarily American initiative that prompted a brief intervention in Lebanon, accompanied by a British one in Jordan, and the proclamation of the Eisenhower Doctrine.[74]

A substantial British interest remained in the Persian Gulf and in southern Arabia. It may suffice to say that the passing of another decade has seen a further diminution of influence in that quarter as well. The difficulties centered on Aden and the attempt to set up a federation of South Arabian sheikdoms were a repetition of what had by this time become a familiar pattern. The federative attempt proved to be a failure in this case as in others, and Aden has been relinquished, Britain taking the above-mentioned radical decision to abandon further responsibilities east of Suez.

All these developments may be regarded as a sensible adaptation to inescapable conditions. Whether or not they be so, it would be difficult not to see in them a diminution of place. The insufficiency of British power lay at the root of Britain's renunciation, but the abandonment in turn itself constituted a diminution of power, for the British position in the world, more than that of any other state, rested on empire.

When one contemplates the long imperial record of Britain one is tempted to think of history being undone. Starting out as a not especially important or powerful island off the continent of Europe, Britain at one point launched on the broad seas of the world. It would be carping to deny that, as human affairs go —they seldom go without the manifestation of a large dose of man's inhumanity to man—it has been a magnificent story. But that story seems to have come to an end and Britain may again be primarily an island off the coast of Europe, though hardly an insignificant one. In closing the examination of the decline of the British position some consideration will be given to the question of her relations with Europe.

BRITAIN RETURNS TO EUROPE

We may recall Disraeli's judgment a century ago that Britain was more Asiatic than European, and Churchill's more recent one that between the continent of Europe and the high seas

Britain would always opt for the latter. But the high seas option seems to have proved a failure, be it in the form of cultivating the special American connection or in that of keeping the empire together as a significant force. What, then, of the European possibility?

In a very real sense Britain had saved Europe, however much additional assistance may have been needed to carry the operation to ultimate success. Despite her relative detachment and her unique position Britain had always been an important, sometimes a major, factor in the affairs of Europe. Yet insularity remained strong in Britain and the feeling that Europe was other. In the course of a speech delivered at Columbia University in New York in 1952 Eden could assert the view that "[that] the United Kingdom should join a federation on the continent of Europe . . . is something which we know, in our bones, we cannot do."[75] But two years later Dean Acheson's perceptive estimate was that "Britain has lost an empire and not yet found a role."[76] And this other judgment may also be cited:

> The interesting question is not why ordinarily the British do not want to become Europeans, but why exceptionally they sometimes talk and behave as if they do. If the history of world events is looked at as a whole during the years of progressive unification, it can be seen that the periods in which the European idea made some progress in British political thinking are those of disappointment, alarm and setbacks in other parts of the world.[77]

Given the nature of the political structure of Britain, the deep-rooted and widespread feeling of the British people in regard to Europe must ever be borne in mind. Nor did the difference between the approaches of the two chief political parties amount to more than one of shade; if Labour tended to be more parochial and isolationist in general, the Conservatives were traditionally wedded to the balance of power; European alliances, be they Russian or French, were not uncongenial to them, but their primary function was the preservation of the liberties—the divisions in a different reading—of Europe.

The fundamental facts at the end of the war were two: one was the weakening of the British position which the wartime relationship had already brought out; Britain had lost her unique arbitral position. The other was the distinguishing fact that, of the European belligerents other than Russia, Britain alone had not known defeat. The rest, between the Channel and the Vistula, constituted, as it has been put, "the club of the defeated." Even the German defeat, however impressive the German wartime performance may have been, was undeniable this time.

This situation had divergent effects. On the one hand it served to emphasize the distinctness of Britain; on the other it placed Britain—like Russia—in the position of being able to assert leadership in Europe. If one adds to this the consideration that Europe had given the final and convincing demonstration of the catastrophic futility of her quarrels, the effect of the war may be seen as creating a community of position and interests among Europeans, especially vis-à-vis the outside. Whether that element would prove the stronger against the exacerbation of national feelings that the war itself had induced, the future alone could tell.

In any case it made very good sense for Churchill, the elder statesman now free of the responsibilities of office, to speak in glowing terms of the prospects of European unity, as he did in 1946 in Zurich; he did so again at the Hague in 1948 and in Strasbourg before the Council of Europe[78] two years later. Even Bevin, who was in office, produced some favorable noises on the score of the merits of European unity.

But this was not enough. What Britain might and should have done, capitalizing on the asset of her prestige, was to take the active initiative of leadership in concrete proposals. That Britain had difficulties of her own, domestic and imperial, is true, but her inaction nevertheless showed a failure of imagination. It is not an unreasonable speculation that in the chaos that prevailed in the prostrate Europe of the time—Britain was, whatever her difficulties, functioning in organized and orderly fashion—British leadership could have asserted itself and been accepted. The simple fact is that, whether Labour or Conservative—the Conservatives were returned to office in 1951 under Churchill again—the British people and their leaders did not wholly believe in European integration. To contend that Britain could only co-operate with a Socialist Europe, as the Labour pamphlet on

European Policy did, or that national sovereignty must remain sacrosanct, as Churchill and Eden insisted, was in fact to resort to evasive subterfuge. In any case such opportunities as there may have been of British leadership in organizing Europe were allowed to pass. It was a lost chance from Britain's own point of view, for at the time Britain could almost have "annexed" a willing Europe, in the sense at least that her leadership could have been both asserted and accepted. The high seas, the empire, and the weight of tradition proved to be too strong an attraction.

At this point, in 1950 to be precise, another avenue seemed to open. We shall analyze in greater detail, in the next section dealing with French policy, the initiative known as the Schuman Plan, out of which grew the European Coal and Steel Community (ECSC). The chief significance of it at this juncture consists in two aspects of it. First is the fact that this limited initiative was thought of by its originators "as a step in the federation of Europe." Secondly, and more important, is the fact that Britain was invited to join. May 1950 was the crucial moment, the passing of which may be followed in an official British paper[79] among other places. Jean Monnet and Robert Schuman were both in London to plead the case, but it was found impossible to agree on methods of procedure. Another opportunity was lost, but the passing of it was for a time neither regretted nor was its significance understood in Britain. The mid fifties, especially after the termination of the Korean War, seemed a period during which improving economic conditions helped nourish the illusion that Britain, with her overseas connections, could recover and go it alone. There was not a little scepticism of the prospects of the ECSC, not to mention some sneers, sometimes directed toward the "Black International."[80]

The Suez episode was cause for second thoughts on the capabilities of Britain alone, but it had no effect on the movement of continental integration. The Treaty of Rome in 1957 brought into existence the European Common Market, the little Europe of the Six. Britain remained unbelieving, even though the paler rival that was the European Free Trade Area (EFTA), joining Britain and six minor and peripheral states, was organized by way of some response.

But as time passed the Common Market proved an unexpected success while Britain's difficulties continued unresolved. Macmillan, who had succeeded Eden after the Suez fiasco, could in 1957 assert that "most of our people have never had it so good."[81] There was truth in this statement, intended for electoral purposes in part, but in the same speech he had also pointed to the unresolved problem of rising prices, and in fact a deflationary policy was shortly adopted. This is what finally led him in 1961 to apply for British membership in the Common Market; in the failure of other possibilities, Europe might yet provide salvation.

The negotiations that were carried on in Brussels were laborious and they were watched with a variety of feelings in different quarters. They were brought to an abrupt end when, in January 1963, the French President, in the course of one of his biannual press conferences, declared a veto on the British application. The precise reasons for this act have been much debated,[82] but the broad basis of his objection must be acknowledged to have been correct: Britain was not ready, Britain was not yet European. Whether from this it followed that Britain ought to be excluded is another question again.

At any rate it is true that Macmillan had not succeeded in convincing his own people, in Britain itself, any more than he had succeeded in evoking a response with his famous, as well as highly appropriate and timely, "winds of change" speech in Capetown in 1960. The French veto of January 1963, especially the brutal manner of it, created a sensation. That fact is less important, however, than the mood of the British people. Until the veto came, those who believed in the desirability of Britain joining Europe, for the sake of both Britain and Europe, were rather less concerned with the likelihood of her being rejected than with the possibility that Britain herself, if accepted, might be the one to decline.[83] Needless to say, the blow to British pride was deeply resented, but otherwise no British tears were shed.

This left the British problems, both that of her economy and of her place in the world, unresolved. The economic situation, plus the natural process of erosion that accompanies a long tenure of power—the Conservatives had been in office since 1951—resulted in the Labour victory of 1964, though the closeness of the outcome, a margin of three votes in Parliament, was indication of the perplexities and lack of conviction of the electorate. The new Prime Minister, Harold Wilson, belonged to that section of Labour that had been sharply anti-European. Confirmed in office in 1966, with a comfortable majority of about 100 this time, his new tenure seemed to initiate a period of rapid disintegration. In the face of mounting economic difficulties, a steadily adverse balance of payments among them, if Labour insisted on adhering to orthodox financial methods as it did, the choices were very limited. There was irony nonetheless in the picture of a Labour government imposing a wage freeze and finding as a consequence of such measures more difficulty in keeping its own following in line than in dealing with the smirks of the opposition.

The drop in the popularity of the government was catastrophic. But this could be a transient phenomenon. What is of greater significance is the conversion of Labour to the European solution, with the consequence that all three political parties[84] in Britain stood committed to it. This is an odd situation, for it cannot be claimed that, despite some change, the prospect of joining Europe has captured the imagination of the British people, whose main reaction to it is one ranging from passive indifference to fatalistic resignation.

The realization of the failure of the Commonwealth has only recently begun to penetrate the British consciousness at the popular level. As to the United States, there are many in Britain who have come to feel, and resent, a relationship which to them appears as one in which Britain is increasingly the assenting tail of the American kite. Thus Europe may appear as a lesser evil, but not the enthusiastically accepted promise of redemption, a life buoy of possible salvation in the midst of a sea of troubles. The undesirable aspect of this attitude is that it constitutes a position of weakness; seemingly left without alternatives, Britain's position of demandant lends itself to exploitation.

Which brings us to the French situation and to the relationship with France, for it is the Fifth Republic which has stood out most adamantly against the admission of Britain into Europe. We shall return to this in our closing pages, following an examination of the French record to parallel that which has just been made of the British.

Where Britain is concerned the picture may seem dismal. In many ways it is, though it would be rash to write off the capabilities of the British people and their inner resources. It is no exaggeration to say, however, that the course of British power has since the war been on a path of continuing decline and that Britain has not yet found her place as a state among states.

The Qualified Recovery of France

The fundamentals of the French position and problem in 1945 have been indicated at the close of the first section of the present chapter. While the needs of domestic reconstruction must have priority, the future position of France as a state among states would inevitably be affected by immediate developments, the unfolding of which could not wait for the recovery and the reordering of either France or others. The wartime leader, General de Gaulle, was especially sensitive to the foreign policy aspect of the situation; considering the means at his disposal, he had already achieved not inconsiderable success.

But the paucity of the means persisted, as well as certain unknowns, the most important of which was perhaps the American position. The dimensions of American power were not a subject for debate, but the use to which that power would be put was less clear. A quarter of a century before, American power, no less overwhelming in relative terms, had very shortly opted for withdrawal. Similar pressures were now again at work in the American milieu, which resulted in a distressingly rapid dismantling of the American war machine. Possession of the atom bomb might compensate in part for this dismantling, but there were many areas and situations where atom bombs could be of little use, while the physical presence of classical armed forces might make a crucial difference. There was this time no substantial French Army, as there had been in 1919, for use in Eastern Europe, for example; insofar as a role was to be performed, in Greece, for example, it devolved on Britain, whose resources were strained and who must also look to her domestic reorganization. These circumstances gave enormous importance to the nature of the Russo-American relationship and to the continued dependence of all on America's bounty. Lend-Lease was abruptly terminated in 1945.

Circumstances likewise placed severe restrictions on the operation of French foreign policy. In a sense, just because de Gaulle was so beholden to Britain and to America, he was all the more suspicious and desirous of asserting independence from them, in which fact must be seen the normal operation of the factor of ingratitude in the relations among states, which in the last resort must depend upon relationships of power. On the score of the Communist ideology de Gaulle entertained no illusions, ever regarding it as an alien element in the national body; yet at the same time he attached qualified importance to it, looking upon it as a passing phenomenon in comparison with the more lasting factor of the national reality and interest, be it Russian or other. Whatever place France had in European affairs she owed to British and American insistence, the former especially, but this did not prevent his attempting to play the Russian card. His refusal of a British pact and of a meeting with Roosevelt in Algiers on the latter's return from Yalta[85] were manifestations of this desire to assert independence. Yet it also appeared that the Russian card did not pay very well if one considers that the Franco-Russian Pact of December 1944 preceded the Yalta meeting.[86]

Here there was room for difference, for a strong case could be made for the continuing fundamental identity of the French with the British interest. Many would take this view in France, but where de Gaulle himself was concerned his wartime experience had caused him to be impressed, in fact overimpressed, by the importance of Britain's "special link" with America, an impression which could indeed be substantiated by many British statements and acts. This element deserves special mention because of the role it was to play again under the Fifth Republic. We shall return to this later on.

Given the existence of the wartime régime in France and the emergence of a Provisional Government in Algiers, the institutional situation must be normalized in the country. This was the task of a constituent body elected for the purpose. It failed at first, but, partly out of weariness, in October 1946 the French electorate endorsed a second attempt.[87] Thus the Fourth Republic was born, but already at the beginning of the year de Gaulle had given up his office. If he would not resort to the illegality of a coup, neither would he remain save on his own terms. It will be convenient of examine French developments under the rubrics of the two successive régimes which have held sway in the country, the Fourth and Fifth Republics.

THE FOURTH REPUBLIC

The new legality was destined to a brief existence, a mere twelve years. Largely a replica of the Third Republic, it was a system no longer suited to the exigencies of a new time, hence its eventual collapse under stresses which it proved itself incapable of absorbing; it was often an object of derisive comment both at home and abroad while it lasted, though there has been increasing acknowledgment of some very notable accomplishments that took place under the Fourth Republic.

The tortured course of French politics since the Great Revolution, the inability of the French people to emulate the British example of stable flexibility in adaptation to change, while it must ever be remembered, does not belong in these pages. Nevertheless a few brief observations are necessary about the French milieu during the fifties.

One of the fundamental elements in the decline of the French position had been the demographic factor. Whether in advance of or behind other nations, France was in this respect the exception, having achieved virtual stability of numbers for three quarters of a century. Now this began to change, exceeding the normal postwar phenomenon of a momentarily rising birth rate. The fact alone need be registered, explanations of it, that of socioeconomic policy, for example, being none too convincing. What is significant about it are two related aspects. The sheer numerical rise, roughly from forty to fifty millions within the span of a quarter of a century, important as it is, is less so than the change in the age structure of the population; the French are now, like others, a young people instead of being one of the oldest; correspondingly, the change in the psychological climate, at once cause and effect, cannot but have profound repercussions.

Needless to say, it would be absurd to credit the reversal

in the demographic picture to the Fourth Repbulic as such and it is only mentioned at this point because the radical break with what had in France become a tradition occurred while that régime prevailed. While politics and parties reverted in the main to the model of earlier practice, furnishing food for jibes and feeding disrespect for outworn institutions, some fundamental changes were taking place in the society.

The administrative structure of the French state was strong and of generally high quality, but in many respects France was, among developed countries, relatively undeveloped and backward, much of her potential unused. This was especially marked in the economic and financial domains. In the latter, what can only be called loose practice continued, inflation was allowed to run its course, the franc fell from 50 to 350 to the dollar between 1944 and 1949, and that was not the end of its downward course, a record which stands in marked contrast with the British, German, and others. France for a time was repeatedly in the position of the beggar seeking, cap in hand, outside assistance.

From 1945 to 1958 the deficit of her balance of payments has been calculated at $11,000,000,000. Yet there was in a sense some method in this seeming irresponsible madness,[88] most markedly different from the austerity of Britain, in contrast with which it achieved better results for the economy as a whole. There was after the war in France, as elsewhere in Europe, strong pressure for the extension of the domain of the economic activity of the state, and the nationalized sector of the economy was appreciably enlarged.[89] But this was done in measured fashion, the result being a combination of state and private enterprise where, however, overall planning and direction were the most significant aspects. In France, where economic thinking and practice had been relatively backward, there appeared a competent team of planners, already organized during the war, who were given free rein.

The effect was to begin to insert France into the modern world of economics. Although much still remains to be done to this day, the significant fact is that of change in attitudes, matching the corresponding one in the demographic domain, probably not unrelated phenomena, with common psychological roots; the war had in this respect the salutary effect of shaking loose the fetters of a too rigid static structure. Much of this change went on relatively unperceived, partly because it was undramatic, reflected in unflamboyant statistics, partly because greater attention was commanded by the more visible aspects of chaotic politics. But if the "German miracle" was more widely advertised, the change in France had perhaps even greater significance because it meant launching upon a novel path and breaking with tradition, whereas the German case rather meant continuity after a temporary break.

The Fourth Republic thus may be credited with having laid the solid and dependable bases of the recovery of France. Against this background we may turn to the consideration of the external policy of France under that régime, although it is well to bear in mind that the departure from office of General de Gaulle, for whom foreign affairs ranked first, had the effect of altering the order of priority given to them and to domestic problems respectively. As it has been put, "For the Fourth Republic foreign policy no longer constitutes the single fundamental preoccupation. For twelve years the simplifying factor of a nationalist ideology will be missing. . . . foreign policy will henceforth be inseparable from the domestic ideological struggles."[90]

In any case in the foreign domain the fundamental problem was also that of recovery, but the course of the war had placed it in a wholly novel context. During the war de Gaulle had striven to maintain the position of France. Hostilities just ended, the guiding lines of his policy may be expressed in the trinomial: independence, preservation of the empire, position or status in general. His Russian policy must be regarded as an attempt to counterbalance the (to him) too dominant Anglo-American influence. It hardly paid off and even he must bow before the realities of power: France was admitted to participation in European arrangements, in the making of which her voice carried but little weight, as witness her exclusion from Yalta and from Potsdam; even such share as she had, she owed to British and American influence in the main, the former especially, in whose eyes the recovery of French place fitted into the traditional policy of European balance. Here was cause for combined gratitude and irritation.

The advent of the Fourth Republic, with Bidault at the foreign office, introduced a more flexible approach to the conduct of foreign policy. But in any case this was secondary to the fact that the dominant consideration for all was the sharpening confrontation between the two superpowers. The turning point was 1947, when the Truman Doctrine was notice to the world that the United States would not return to isolation but instead assume the burden which had become too heavy for Britain to carry in the Middle East. In the face of this confrontation, and given her weakness, what could France do but align herself with the Western camp? The eviction of the Communists from participation in the government took place in May 1947.[91] The launching of the Marshall Plan in 1948, the successful defeat of the Berlin blockade, were clear indications of the American position; the signature of the North Atlantic Treaty Organization (NATO) Pact in March 1949 was the logical climax of that policy, most simply stated as the American guarantee of the independence of the Western European states against any Russian attempt at encroachment. From one standpoint NATO was an old-fashioned military alliance based on the common interest of the participants in it. In actual fact, because of the disparity of power, it amounted to a unilateral American guarantee of the rest; the continued independence of Western Europe *was* an American interest.

The two major rivals faced each other across the middle of a divided Germany,[92] the Western part of which was under American, British, and French occupation. Clearly, from the standpoint of defense, the integration of this Western German zone, especially in view of its economic potential, was a desirable asset. To a degree, therefore, it may be said that the reorganization and the rearmament of Western Germany were at least implied in seed in NATO. But here a problem arose. For if such a prospect was acceptable, indeed desirable, from the American point of view, to Britain to a lesser degree, it raised understandable fears among the continental states.

For France in particular it gave new body to the old problem of security. How France attempted to deal with the situation constitutes one of the major aspects of her policy.

The Problem of Germany and the Construction of Europe.

There has been occasion in the preceding chapter to discuss the French obsession with security after the First World War. Changed as the context may have been by the Second, the issue had lost none of its sting or urgency. Well before war had broken out again General de Gaulle had made his own the classical French approach to the problem:

> This protection denied her by nature France, in the course of centuries, has sought to secure through diplomatic means. Others may have sought mainly the domination of the seas, the exploitation of distant lands, free outlets, the unity of a scattered race; what obsesses us is the security of our hexagon. To create a political system which could prevent our neighbors from injuring us, sums up, for a thousand years, the schemes conceived and the treaties concluded by France.[93]

The arrangements made at Potsdam were satisfactory to de Gaulle, who favored the creation of a permanently fragmented Germany. After the clear breakdown, in 1948,[94] of any hope of quadripartite agreement in regard to Germany, the rehabilitation of Western Germany was undertaken, mainly under American auspices. Though she dragged her feet, France did not have the power to prevent this development. The milestones in the process were the institution of a new currency—the Berlin blockade was the Russian answer to this—and the Washington agreements of April 1949, from which, out of the merged Western zones of occupation, finally emerged the Western Federal Republic, still subject to certain disabilities to be sure.[95] The debate in the French parliament on the recommendations made at a meeting in London of the Powers concerned in regard to a new status of Germany was at once measure of French fears and of French impotence; ratification was obtained on June 17 by the margin of 297 to 289 votes.

The logical consequences were not long in appearing in the form of a decision of the Atlantic Council that Germany should participate in the defense of the West. This was in September 1950. The prospect of the additional asset of a number of German divisions was highly attractive to the American military chiefs, especially as the United States was carrying the main burden of the Korean War initiated in June. But a Pandora's box had been opened. Before dealing with that issue and its resolution, an oblique and imaginative French approach to the German problem had been launched.

Four months before the just mentioned decision on German rearmament, on May 9, 1950, the French foreign minister, Robert Schuman, threw out a bombshell in the course of a press interview. Among other things, he read a statement drawn up by Jean Monnet and his team:

> Europe will not be made all at once, nor through a comprehensive construction; she will first be made through concrete undertakings which will create a de facto solidarity. The gathering of the European nations requires that the century old opposition between France and Germany shall be eliminated. The action undertaken must concern in the first place France and Germany.

To this end the French Government proposed

> to place the totality of the Franco-German production of coal and steel under a common authority in an organization open to the participation of the other European countries.

This was to be accomplished as follows:

> through the pooling of the basic productions, the institution of a new High Authority whose decisions shall bind France, Germany and the countries that shall adhere to it, this proposal will create the first concrete bases of a European federation indispensable to the preservation of peace.[96]

Here we find the convergence of several trends. The desirability of peace may be taken for granted, but the dependable establishment of it through the sudden creation of certain institutions that would inaugurate a rule of law among nations belongs in the domain of Utopia; even revolutions have not succeeded in making a tabula rasa of the past. The dream of a united Europe belongs in the same category. It is a noble ideal, with ancient roots, but it has run into the reality of rival diversity, most concretely expressed in the vitality of the nation-state, fundamental aspect of the history of modern Europe, of the whole modern world in fact. It is equally true that the result has been collective suicide, of which the twentieth-century conflicts, originating in Europe, have been the expression. The world, or even Europe alone, contains far more than Germany and France and their quarrels, yet, in view of the impasse which had been reached in the relationship between those two countries, the time was perhaps ripe for a resolution of that particular problem.

The initiative proposed by Schuman may be regarded as a form of the defense of the French interest. Weaker in potential than even Western Germany alone, France enjoyed nevertheless certain advantages, while Germany suffered corresponding disabilities, fruits of her recent record, on which the former could seek to capitalize. But the merit of Schuman's proposal lay in the fact that, instead of seeking to capitalize on these advantages in the form of freezing controls, it offered Germany the counterpart of the hand of reconciliation. The scheme in this respect represented the acknowledgment of the failure of earlier French policy, that of the interwar in particular. Here was in a way the *grand geste* which the victorious France of 1919, obsessed by fear, had been incapable of making. To Germany it could have considerable attraction, be it in the form of the liquidation of an unrewarding past and an unproductive quarrel, or in the more limited one of promoting the German interest, the type of policy pursued by Stresemann. The Second World War had had the clarifying advantage of producing in the final reckoning the undeniable defeat of both countries.

There might be risks involved, especially for France. Might not the greater economic weight of Germany make her eventually the dominant partner in the association? But, against this, the scrambling of the economies, of which that of the coal and steel industries might be but the prelude, might eliminate that danger by making difficult the purely national control of the basic necessities of war. Thus one must stress in particular the two elements in the Schuman Plan that were the opening offered to others and the more distant view of European federation; because initially more modest, the proposal was in this respect more realistic than Briand's larger European Union of twenty years before. There were understandable hesitations in both Germany and France, especially on the part of the specific interests more immediately involved. But there was on the French side the official authority of the foreign minister, to which the German Chancellor, Konrad Adenauer, responded in kind.

Thus was eventually born the European Coal and Steel Community (ECSC), formally organized in the treaty of April 18, 1951. We shall not go into the intricate details of this elaborate instrument[97] beyond pointing out that, whatever might be said, it undeniably encroached upon the hitherto sacrosanct attribute of national sovereignty, in which fact lay precisely the great hope of the European federalists. It is worth mentioning, however, that Jean Monnet, one of the prime movers of planning in France, was likewise one of the chief architects of the Schuman Plan. Also, that in the debate in the French parliament in December ratification was finally secured by a vote of 376 to 240, the bulk of the opposition coming from the Communist deputies and the Gaullist representatives. Both judged rightly from their respective points of view that the treaty was a setback for Soviet influence as well as for national sovereignty.

The ECSC grouped six European states, Italy and the three Benelux countries in addition to the initial two. The absence of Britain is the most striking fact, and thereby hangs a tale.

It was Mendès-France who stated in the French Assembly, though in a different connection,[98] that "an axiom of French policy is never to part company with Great Britain," giving expression to a fundamental aspect of that policy in our century that has been alluded to more than once in these pages. It was Churchill who, speaking in Zurich in 1946, had stated that "the first step in the resurrection of the European family must be the association between France and Germany," adding that Britain and the Empire "must be friends and guarantors of the new Europe."[99]

Reference has been made to the possible opportunity of a British leadership in bringing Europe together at the end of the war and to the British failure to seize that opportunity. France took a different and sounder view in considering Britain as primarily European. Schuman's press declaration of May 1950 and his attempt to enlist Britain's interest in his proposal have also been indicated. Actually, the British inclined to a sceptical view of the prospects of the scheme; their prudent lack of imagination on this occasion caused them to miss another opportunity as well as it caused Europe to miss it. The Six, important as they were, did not constitute Europe, although the possibility existed that their enterprise, if successful, might eventually become a core of attraction for the rest. The consequences of this British timidity were to weigh heavily upon the future, as we shall presently have occasion to see.

The Schuman proposal was not a substitute for German rearmament, which, however, it would situate in a different context. If the ECSC was acceptable to France, German rearmament raised instinctive objections and fears. The result was the search for a compromise between these objections and American desiderata. Protracted negotiations ensued until an involved French proposal was accepted for the organization of a European Defense Community (EDC), the heart of which was the participation of a German contribution without the formation of an autonomous German armed force. Even this unpromising hybrid solution was the source of much questioning in France, where approval of it was repeatedly put off, to the increasing annoyance of others. Leaving aside the intricate details of these discussions, to make a long and tedious story short[100] it will suffice to say that in August 1954 the government of Mendès-France put an end to French tergiversations by submitting the EDC treaty to the French Assembly; it went down to defeat by a vote of 319 to 264, the majority being furnished by the combination of traditional nationalist elements, Gaullists included, and Communists.

There was irony in this final outcome. From Britain, which had refused the firmer commitment that France had been asking, Anthony Eden saved the day. On the one hand Britain committed herself more firmly to the maintenance of her forces on the Continent, on the other Germany would join NATO and contribute to it a purely German force. Having wrecked her own proposal France accepted these alternative arrangements, though the parliamentary vote in December was close—287 to 260. Germany followed suit two months later, having achieved another step on the road to the recovery of position. It may be mentioned in passing that there was substantial opposition in

Germany to German rearmament and that Secretary Dulles' talk of "agonizing reappraisal"—meaning an implied threat to bank on Germany *instead* of France—did not help the case of EDC in the latter country. But in the last resort France had been incapable of blocking German rearmament. French power, such as it was, in 1954 was subjected in addition to severe tests in the imperial domain. We shall turn to these in a moment but at this point will pursue the evolution of the French position in Europe in general.

The French defeat of EDC had caused dismay in Germany, not least to Chancellor Adenauer, a man sincerely devoted to the cause of Franco-German reconciliation. Here a curious and unexpected phenomenon must be registered, the altered tone of the Franco-German relationship after the Second World War, not only or so much at the official level of governments, but at the grass roots as well. It has been suggested by way of explanation that the inevitably close and numerous contacts that the German occupation of France entailed, allowing for all their harshness and unpleasantness, on balance had the effect of convincing each people that the other was also essentially made up of human beings. However that may be, there is no denying the fact that in the main the French attitude toward Germany after 1945 was not informed with the deep and all-pervading feeling of hatred that was characteristic of the period after 1918, not at least in any comparable degree. Among the young especially, contacts have been amicable and numerous, and certainly the numbers of those crossing the Rhine in an easterly direction constitutes an innovation.

At all events the experiment of the ECSC seemed to prosper. The proponents of it, mainly French, had thought of it as a first step toward the more ambitious goal of a politically united Europe. Consequently, they did not rest on their laurels. In October 1955 Jean Monnet launched the *Comité d'action pour les États-Unis d'Europe* and published in the same year *Les États Unis d'Europe ont commencé,* while Robert Schuman gave expression to the synthesis in which Christianity and socialism joined in the democratic ideal. Here was French leadership at its best, which found a wide response abroad, though such views were by no means monopolistically French. It was in fact a

Benelux initiative and a Dutch memorandum which led to the meeting in Messina in June 1955 of representatives of the six members of the ECSC. Under the chairmanship of Henri Spaak, the Belgian foreign minister and himself a convinced European, a committee set to work. Its report, ready the following April, finally led to the conclusion of the Treaty of Rome, signed on April 25, 1957, which launched the European Economic Community, the little Europe of the Six, on its course of further integration, economic first, but in the eyes of its makers another step on the path of political integration.

The debate in the French Assembly is revealing of the dominant trend at this point. The Socialist leader, Guy Mollet, aptly summed it up in his declaration that

> My profound conviction . . . is that the integration of Germany into a larger European whole, which will have authority over her as well as over the other participating states, can alone provide a durable solution of the German problem.[101]

Incapable of dealing alone, because of insufficient power, with a possible resurgence of the German threat, France was essaying the policy of "dissolving" Germany into Europe, with the implied corollary of her own dissolution as well. It should be noted, in addition, that this novel approach also implied a drift away from the dependence on alliances so characteristic of the interwar period. The existing alliances were not abandoned or denied, but in American eyes the Russian danger had first priority and in countering it Germany took on the guise of an ally. It was consistent therefore that the United States should favor the policy of European integration. So long as things remained unchanged America and Europe could continue joined as they were in NATO, but the possibility also existed that a relaxation of tensions in the Cold War could in turn produce stresses in the Atlantic Alliance. These would indeed develop though only at a later period.[102]

From the American standpoint the larger the European entity the better, hence the tendency to favor the entrance of Britain into Europe.[103] But Britain, having voiced the desirability of the liquidation of the Franco-German quarrel, was still holding back when it came to joining Europe. It was in May 1953 in the Commons that, during the discussion of EDC, Churchill himself had declared: "We are not members of the EDC and we have no intention of being integrated in a federal European system. . . . We are with them but not among them."[104]

When the demise of the Fourth Republic took place in 1958 the Common Market was launched. Before closing the story of that régime something must be said of its imperial policy.

The French Union.

The choice that faced the Third Republic between revanche and empire in the closing decades of the nineteenth century has been discussed before. The imperial option had paid. As it was put in the Consultative Assembly in May 1945, "without the empire France would only be today a liberated country. Thanks to her empire France is a victorious country."[105] Two world wars had had the inevitable effect of discrediting the standing of Europeans among their dependent peoples and of accelerating the growth of the consequences implied in the very process of transferring European ways to the African and Asiatic worlds. During the Second World War, save in the Middle East, France had experienced no difficulties on the score of the allegiance of her overseas possessions, even despite the divisions between Vichy and the Free French.

General de Gaulle himself could easily have made his own Churchill's statement about the liquidation of the empire. He was responsible for the re-establishment of French rule in Indochina, even though in a sense that meant a reconquest. But the French imperial milieu could not remain immune to the pressures for independence which were making themselves felt in all colonial empires. The question was how to deal with them. Certain salient episodes of the story will alone be retained.

If one compares the long-term British and French imperial records, it may be said that, in general, the French have dealt with native populations with rather better success than their British rivals. But this has ceased to be the case in the twentieth century, although when it comes to ultimate results and to the influence retained by either Power in its former domain the outcome remains an open question. In both cases the record has been one of devolution and abandonment, a process which the more flexible and looser British structure has made less bloody and painful.

For the strongly centralist character of the French state at home had been transferred to the imperial domain. One aspect of the *mission civilisatrice,* French version of the white man's burden, had been to turn African Blacks and others into Frenchmen. This had been done with considerable success but had only affected a very thin layer of France's dependent populations; and just because of the success of the endeavor, the infusion of the French revolutionary principles also trained the cadres of possible rebellion. The solution of the dilemma thus posed could be found in complete integration, but this, if carried to its logical conclusion, would have had the effect of creating a community of some 100,000,000 in which the French of France would have been a minority, or, as it was put, France would have become a colony of her colonies. The dilemma has been well expressed by Grosser:

> The only policy which makes it possible to combine the centralizing and the liberal tendencies is that of assimilation. And the consequences of assimilation soon appear unacceptable. One is thus led to seek accommodation with either centralism or with egalitarian liberalism. It so happens that it is more tempting and easier to cheat with a moral principle than with a political and administrative tradition.[106]

Perhaps not very surprisingly the French balked at this point; when it comes to racial feelings, the difference between the French and the British, though it exists, is rather one of degree than of kind. Also, there is no point in denying the problem arising from the difference in degree of development, economic and other, between the European milieus and those of many of their dependents.

Thus, in dealing with the problem of empire, the Fourth Republic was confronted with the rigidity of centralized structures, to which must be added the fact of the weakness resulting from defeat and demotion, in part a psychological element. The result was a hybrid compromise. We may leave out the details of the attempted solution that was the French Union,[107] for it may be regarded as essentially stillborn. It made possible for a while the access of African Blacks to parliament and even to ministerial positions in Paris, but in the last resort it involved but little relaxation of the central controls. Given time for quiet evolution, there might have been promise in the essay, but time was not granted, the result being a policy of unresolved confusion, lacking consistency and attended by some grievous mistakes in addition.

What amounted to the final ousting of the French from the Levant, where political control at least was concerned, has been dealt with before.[108] The Far East, Indochina, early became a major problem. Following the ousting of the Japanese, the French missed an opportunity to come to terms with the local nationalist movement under the leadership of Ho Chi Minh. The latter's visit to France in 1947 convinced him of the futility of any attempt at compromise and the consequence was war. The complete Communist control of China from 1949, the Korean War in 1950, had the effect of inserting a limited colonial operation into the larger context of the Cold War. American material assistance was insufficient to turn the tide and remained limited short of direct American involvement. On the French side the war was but half-heartedly pursued amid the welter of domestic politics. It was an unpopular war that aroused a minimum of interest in France, whose conscript Army was never used in Indochina. With the climax of Dien Bien Phu in May 1954 the end had come and negotiations were already under way by that time.

A new French Government in June assumed the task of liquidation. It was led by Mendès-France, a consistent critic of the operation, who, with skill and luck, managed to effect a less unfavorable compromise than might have been expected in the circumstances. Laos and Cambodia emerged as distinct entities while the remainder, Vietnam, was partitioned on the Korean model. These details matter relatively little in the present context, the significant fact being the ouster of France from Southeast Asia. Increasingly, her place in that quarter would be taken by the United States, but thereby hangs a different tale, which is outside the bounds of our concern.[109]

It was the same Mendès-France who laid the bases of the liquidation of the French position in North Africa, but it would take several years before that sorry tale would be brought to a close. In the Maghreb the situation was complicated by the fact that, while Tunisia and Morocco were formally protectorates, Algeria was constitutionally assimilated to metropolitan France; Algeria was moreover in part a colony of settlement, some 10 per cent of its population being made up of Europeans, many of whom were also authentically Algerians.

It could not be expected that the whole of French North Africa would remain immune to the ferment at work in that Arab world, even if French schemes of full assimilation in the case of Algeria had been pursued with greater vigor and consistency. In any case rebellion broke out in Algeria in 1954. It had inevitable repercussions in the adjoining Tunisian and Moroccan protectorates, but in their case matters were settled with at least comparative ease with the acknowledgment of their full independence in 1956.

Meanwhile the Algerian rebellion went on, which France seemed unable to subdue despite the fact that she sent to Algeria the major part of her armed forces. Tangled in a seemingly hopeless struggle, her influence elsewhere was correspondingly reduced, and her contribution to NATO in Europe was heavily drawn upon. The war was also an embarrassment to France's allies, especially the United States, torn between the desire to maintain the Western alliance and the sympathy for the liquidation of colonial empires in general.

The climax of the Suez episode in 1956 has been mentioned. Where France was concerned her interest in the Suez Canal was secondary to her irritation with Egypt as the chief center of agitation for Arab independence and of encouragement of the Algerian rebellion. Whether the toppling of Nasser would in the long term have made any difference to the outcome in Algeria may well be doubted. From a limited and immediate standpoint there was logic in the Suez undertaking, but there was none in the manner in which it was carried out. For the French and the British not to have sought American approval in advance was the only possible course, since American disapproval could be taken for granted. The only thing to do was to face all with a quick *fait accompli,* disregard expected condemnation, and proceed from there to the intricacies and delays of diplomatic action.

The American condemnation may have been more prompt and severe than expected, but the spectacle of the United States joining the Soviet Union against its own allies was also unconvincing as a permanent stance. French determination would seem to have been somewhat stronger than British, but in the end France yielded too. For both countries there stood revealed before the whole world the spectacle of their impotence; their positions of privilege in the Security Council of the United Nations certainly did not correspond to the realities of power. For both it was inexcusable levity to have embarked on the operation without adequate prior thought of its effects or determination to face the foreseeable consequences, as in all probability they could have done with impunity.[110] At the level of national power, more seriously perhaps at that of will, both had ignominiously failed and stood revealed in their nakedness. The stresses introduced by the episode in the harmony of the Atlantic Alliance were likewise part of the aftermath.

For the rest of her colonial domain, in Black Africa and in Madagascar, the Fourth Republic faced no major crises though there also the seeds of change were ripening.[111]

The failure of Suez hardly improved the situation in Algeria. In contrast with the Indochinese war, that in Algeria had deep repercussions in France herself, until it began to affect the operation of the body politic. Not without some justification, the Army felt increasing bitterness and dissatisfaction at a succession of defeats for which it held the politics and the politicians at home responsible. Increasingly also, the European settlers in Algeria, or some of them at least, showed signs of taking matters into their own hands. The result was a conspiratorial situation, until amid the seemingly irresponsible game of musical chairs of short-lived governments the danger of a military coup emerged. In the middle of May 1958 a new and impotent government was considering how to deal with the prospect of civil war.

A *deus ex machina* saved the day at this point and made possible an orderly transition. From his retreat in Colombey-les-deux-Eglises, whither he had withdrawn since 1946 and had been writing his memoirs, General de Gaulle had been following events with attention. Despite his failure to play a successful political role through his organization of the movement known as the *Rassemblement du Peuple Français* in 1947, he enjoyed the asset of unimpeachable patriotism and complete dedication to the national cause. Everything that he had ever said went to confirm the view that he was a believer in a French Algeria. It was thus wholly natural that his name should be put forward by those elements, the potentially rebellious generals and the European Algerians, who held such a view. Feeling unsure of its ability to control the situation, the existing government acquiesced. Whatever share in these events de Gaulle himself may have had—a controverted point, still and perhaps forever—the least that can be said of him is that he played his cards with a cool head and with masterly skill. Only at the eleventh hour did he make known his availability, with the consequence that he assumed power on his own terms and totally free of commitments.

The transfer of power was effected in wholly constitutional fashion, so that, as in 1940, the thread of legality was not broken. De Gaulle simply became head of the government under the existing constitution, but in actual fact the Fourth Republic, much like the Third, had signed its own death warrant, even if it took a while longer to enact fundamental constitutional changes. It is therefore appropriate to consider the last part of our story under the heading of the Fifth Republic.

DE GAULLE'S FIFTH REPUBLIC

The return of de Gaulle to power was genuinely and overwhelmingly welcome, be it by frightened parliamentarians or by a disoriented and divided opinion. Yet it was also the result of a misunderstanding and a mystification, as will presently appear. The judgment is apt that "on the 13th of May 1958 . . . many rose against legality in the name of the nation. They believed that they could deal with the problems that the Fourth Republic had been incapable of resolving by changing men and institutions. That was to be their greatest illusion."[112]

By way of broad introductory generalization it may be said that General de Gaulle was dedicated to the restoration of France's position in the world. But this was a loose concept and ideal in need of more specific definition. On this score two things may be added. His wartime record and performance were evidence of his capacity to adopt long-term views as well as of his broad understanding of the nature of power, in which material and concrete assets played a role that did not exclude that of ideas, of moral and psychological considerations. He had convincingly shown his ability to manipulate these assets. His methods may be described as a mixture of romantic vision with the coolest understanding and calculations, a rare combination which has often led astray his detractors no less than his admirers.

In May 1958 there was in France a concrete problem that demanded immediate action; it was no less than the threatened collapse of the state precipitated by the inability to deal with the Algerian imbroglio. This last, short of an immediate and total abdication, could not be resolved by any sleight of hand. It will be convenient therefore to examine the record of the Fifth Republic under the heads of the reform of the French state, the solution of the Algerian dilemma, more broadly the problem of empire, then the longer-term issue of restoring the French position in the world at large. These to be sure were not unrelated activities, all the while interacting upon each other, and the first two will be dealt with together.

The Reorganization of the French State and the Imperial Problem.

Constitutional rearrangements can be dealt with briefly. While a fundamental necessity and a precondition, they fall essentially outside the purview of our purpose. Mention of them is nevertheless a prerequisite to an understanding of the others.

On June 1 General de Gaulle became Prime Minister and two days later parliament granted him full powers, limited to six months for metropolitan France. New constitutional arrangements were also to be enacted and these came into effect as a result of the popular referendum which took place on September 28. At the beginning of 1959 General de Gaulle became at once President of the Republic and of the French Community, France and the empire.

Whether and how far the new constitutional arrangements represented a significant innovation in France was a question that the future alone could answer. Important as they are in themselves, constitutions depend for their real significance upon the manner in which their provisions are used. The view that the régime of parties had proved inadequate commanded widespread acceptance. As an alternative France had more than once in the past turned to a strong man for her salvation, although one notable aspect of this particular transition was the fact that it had been effected without resort to violence, the threat of which had been sufficient to procure its enactment within the framework of legality. The Fourth Republic, like the Third, had died the quiet death of abdication. Conceivably, the new régime could evolve into a replica of the familiar Bonapartist experience; it might also turn into a presidential régime somewhat along the lines of the American democracy; finally, nothing very significant might happen. One thing was clear: there was without a doubt a strong personality at the head of the state, one that was neither afraid to use power and to assume responsibility, nor lacking in definite views and ideas; one in addition capable of cold calculation and possessed of maneuvering skill.

The events of May 1958 and the state of the French economy, that of French finances especially, raised some doubts about the launching of the European Economic Community (EEC), the Common Market, all the more as during the year 1958 the ECSC had been experiencing certain difficulties. Among the Six, France constituted in fact the most serious question mark. These doubts were soon put to rest. No attempt was made to undo or restrict the experiment, while domestic fiscal rearrangements, of which the devaluation of the franc by 20 per cent was the most radical, made possible adherence to previous plans, and the Common Market was soon to prove an unexpected success.

Precisely what de Gaulle's ideas on the score of the Algerian problem were at the end of 1958 and the schedule of their evolution remain unknown quantities. He inspired confidence in all at first, not least among the Moslem population of Algeria. But, to make a long and involved story short, it will suffice to say that he came to recognize before very long that he must deal directly with the leaders of the rebellion. This was no easy task, complicated as it was by the fact that he must first educate French opinion to the necessity of at least drastic rearrangements; and all the while the war went on. The more limited problem of the Army was not the least difficult aspect of the situation, for de Gaulle found himself in the anomalous position of having been brought to power by those elements least inclined to yielding while his task had become that of performing an operation of abandonment.

Little wonder that he has been accused of betrayal, quite correctly in a sense, by those who found him doing the opposite of what they had expected of him. With the Army he dealt with ruthless firmness, putting down the threatened "insurrection" of the generals in April 1961. Plots and attempts on his life made little impression on him, while he could on the other hand capitalize on the increasing weariness of the French people gradually brought to realize by the demands of the war that to insist that the Algerians, other than the 1,000,000 Europeans, were French was a denial of reality.

Negotiations with the insurrectional government, the *Gouvernement Provisoire de la République Algérienne* (GPRA), were likewise protracted and difficult; initiated, broken, resumed, until the Evian accords of March 1962 broke the impasse. The referendum of January 1961 had already indicated that the French people in their overwhelming majority were ready to acknowledge the inevitable, and the final outcome was confirmed in another referendum in April 1962. By September an independent Algeria came into existence and was admitted the next month to membership in the United Nations.

The new state was in many respects a French creation; the large section of the Sahara included in it had never been part of anything that could be called Algeria save in French administrative arrangements. Incidentally, the desert was in many ways the most valuable Algerian asset, for important deposits of oil and of natural gas had recently been discovered in it. A massive exodus of Europeans took place, a loss to the new state. By the criterion of material interest alone, independence was a setback and the economic condition of Algeria has in considerable measure been a record of deterioration.

Yet connections between Algeria and France were far from being wholly broken, even though the rights and guarantees retained by France in the Evian accords have to a large extent been honored in the breach. The French reaction has been to turn the other cheek while continuing to provide substantial aid to Algeria, whose political orientation has been increasingly toward Moscow. The reason for this meekness has been political; it is part of the calculated policy of endeavoring to retain influence in what has come to be called the Third, or non-aligned, World, one of the manifestations therefore of the effort to restore the French position in general.[113]

The referendum of September 1958 was also designed to provide the bases for reconstructing the entire French Community. Would or would not the overseas members of that community retain their association with France? The answer was overwhelmingly "yes," 9,200,000 to 600,000, save in Guinea, which as a consequence was cast adrift.[114] Within less than two years the bases of the association had to be revised and loosened, its constitutional foundations becoming more contractual. Largely on the basis of formerly existing French administrative divisions, French West Africa, French Equatorial Africa, and Madagascar gave rise to fifteen independent states, all of which became members of the United Nations, France being left, like Britain, with a few scattered tatters of empire under her direct control.

Here was imperial devolution with a vengeance, more radical in its outcome than in the British case, for there was no pretense of any Commonwealth. In neither case, however, was the result total abandonment. The British situation, the continuing disintegration of the Commonwealth, has been discussed.[115] The French method was different and the efforts to retain continued influence have chiefly taken two forms. One is that of economic and financial assistance. Proportionately to her resources, on a per capita basis or as a part of her GNP, France has contributed substantially more than any other state, about three times as much as the United States, to the underdeveloped world. The tendency has been to decrease the dimensions of that contribution, which has diminished from 1.5 per cent of the French GNP to about .8 per cent over the five-year period ending in 1967.

The other aspect of French policy has been to put great emphasis on the cultural domain, possibly a more lasting investment. Some 40,000 Frenchmen are scattered, mainly throughout the former French empire, largely as teachers, paid by France, in an effort to meet the great demands of increasing scholarity from the lowest to the highest levels. In keeping with the French centralist tradition, the links between such a place as the University of Dakar, for example, and Paris remain very strong.

Finally, it must be noted that the French assistance to the underdeveloped world has been almost exclusively directed to the Francophone community and that France has insisted on bilateral arrangements instead of an international pooling of aid. Whether this be neo-colonialism, as some would have it, or not, it undoubtedly represents a calculated attempt to maintain a place for French influence throughout the world, hence is in essence a deliberate political operation, though not necessarily a condemnable one for that reason.

That attempt has reached far beyond the limits of the former French empire, and France has shown aspirations to some position of leadership of the whole non-aligned world. In this she has met with a measure of success, partly because of the internal nature of the régime of the Fifth Republic, an attractive model for some, partly because she has asserted an increasingly independent position vis-à-vis the United States, another tendency appealing to many other countries. That French prestige rose during the past decade of Gaullist rule would be difficult to deny.[116]

THE ASSERTION OF INDEPENDENCE AND THE RECOVERY OF POSITION

Thus we come to the closing section of our tale, the attempt to pursue an independent policy. The operation and the manifestations of this attempt may be observed under two distinct but related headings, which may conveniently be labeled Europe and the Atlantic. An extensive literature has come into existence which touches upon aspects of our concern. Considerations of space alone would prevent a survey and an analysis of it; we must be content with confining the present discussion to an examination of the issues and trends in which French policy has been involved during the past decade.

One of the merits that must be granted President de Gaulle, as already indicated, is his ability to take large and long-term views of events. Two fundamental instances may be mentioned. The technical transformations of weaponry and the general recovery of Europe have called for a rethinking of the relationship established between Europe and the United States, more narrowly the terms of the Atlantic Alliance; the conditions of the 1960's were different from those of the preceding decade. Likewise, the emergence of China has created new stresses in the Communist world, more specifically in the form of the Sino-Soviet divergence; and this again, in combination with the Russo-American nuclear equilibrium has tended to create at least a measure of rapprochement between these two states.

From these fundamental circumstances many other things have followed: a diminution of the Russian threat to Western Europe, a diminished credibility of the American guarantee, a shifting of the American interest toward Asia (the containment of China as of Russia twenty years earlier), and a loosening of the Soviet control over its Western satellites.[117] Within this broad background many other issues have unfolded, be it in the Near East or in Africa, for example. There is nothing specifically French about such observations, but de Gaulle elected, in his own inimitable style to boot, to capitalize on them, often in sharp form and in more trenchant fashion than others. His thought was made quite clear in the statement that

> it is wholly natural that, in the event of a conflict, America should see her own survival as her chief objective and should therefore consider the time, the extent and the manner of her nuclear intervention in terms of this natural and overriding necessity. That is one of the reasons why France is endowing herself with her own nuclear armament. It follows that important modifications impose themselves on the French government in regard to the conditions and the manner of our participation in the alliance since that organization is based on integration, which is today no longer valid for us.[118]

Or again the following year:

> So long as the ambitions of the Soviets and the nature of their régime hold over the free world, on both sides of the Atlantic, the threat of a terrible conflict, France is in danger of destruction

> and of invasion, without being assured that her American allies, themselves directly exposed to death, would be capable of sparing her that risk.[119]

He did not wait for the final enactment of constitutional changes in France or for the liquidation of the French imperial problem to begin to press his views. As early as September 24, 1958, less than four months after his return to power, he sent to the American President, General Eisenhower, a personal memorandum[120] the central point of which was the assertion of a claim to parity for France, the setting up of a tripartite directorate in which France would have an equal voice with the United States and Britain. Omitting details, the subsequent discussion of this claim resulted in its final rejection. For France to claim an equal voice with the United States in world affairs may seem absurd in view of the disparity of power; but there was increasingly less differential if one thinks of her position in comparison with the British, a vanishing legacy of the war. Despite the fact that de Gaulle failed to formulate concrete proposals, that the rejection of his claim, even if it was seemingly preposterous, was a wise move may be regarded as an open question.

For the French request was accompanied by the implied threat of an alternative, the adoption of an independent policy. The threat was not an altogether empty one as subsequent events were to show. One aspect of it was the disruption of the Atlantic Alliance, a policy which has since been consistently pursued, beginning with the withdrawal of French naval forces from the NATO command, through the refusal of the establishment of launching pads for missiles on French territory, to the eviction from France of the NATO command and of the American military establishment. The creation of an independent nuclear force —a decision going back to the Fourth Republic, be it noted— the *force de frappe,* is another manifestation of the same policy of independence.

Considering the extent of French resources, there could obviously be no possibility of France achieving a level comparable to the American or the Russian in the domain of weaponry. She might, however, reach the British level, and Britain or her side had not abandoned nuclear weapons. Despite criticism of these policies in both Britain and France, the possibility was never realized of the two countries merging their nuclear efforts or the more imaginative one of *both* giving the example of abandoning the pursuit of what some would call a chimera. Yet power being what it is, it would be difficult to deny that membership in the nuclear club, even at the very low level, gives added weight to those possessed of nuclear weapons. The implied consequence of unchecked proliferation is another matter again, but it was wholly logical for France—as for China—to refuse adherence to the non-proliferation treaty that the United States and the Soviet Union contrived to produce in 1967. This last achievement, granted all its merits and desirability, could nevertheless easily take on the color of an attempted Russo-American hegemony, the seeds of which it undoubtedly contained. Even among the other signers of the treaty there has been much reluctance and doubt; German hesitations, among others, are well known.

The chief asset of French policy may seem negative, in large measure, to use a harsher term, blackmail, the standard weapon of the weak; the phrase "jackal policy," an unfair characterization, has been used to describe Italian policy over an extended period. To part company with NATO might not mean a catastrophic diminution of security, in the assumed persistence of the umbrella of American protection; it implied nonetheless the necessity of rearrangements and of a rethinking of the significance and role of the Atlantic Alliance, not necessarily a bad thing in view of the changing conditions, of which the French position was as much reflection as cause.

Yet de Gaulle's policy was not merely negative and destructive. While desirous of independence, he insisted on the validity and the permanence of the American alliance; as he put it in 1965, "So long as the solidarity of the Western peoples will seem to us necessary for the eventual defense of Europe, our country will remain the ally of its allies."[121] Thus he unhesitatingly endorsed President Kennedy's handling of the Cuban missile crisis in 1962, even if pointing out that he had not been consulted. The question thus became, what was the content and meaning of independence, a path along which France alone could not go very far. The answer was an attempt to establish a position of representative leadership for a great deal more than France. This doggedly pursued policy, attended by a measure of success, to establish such a position in the underdeveloped world, the former French empire in particular, has been indicated.

Could a comparable result be accomplished in Europe? Here we must distinguish between two aspects of the same problem, which may be called that of the construction of Europe on the one hand, hence in the present context the French attitude toward Euorpe and European integration; on the other hand, the American position, more specifically the Franco-American divergence.

The launching of the European idea through the concrete realizations of the ECSC and the EEC, in which the Fourth Republic had played an important role, has been discussed. De Gaulle's views on these questions were of a somewhat different nature from those of the pro-Europeans. Of Europe he often spoke indeed, but to him it was ever *l'Europe des états,* one in which the national state remained the irreducible reality, to the dissolution of which into a federal structure he remained adamantly opposed. He has also, on various occasions, spoken of Europe as extending from the Atlantic to the Urals, a phrase the implications of which were both far-reaching and unclear.

The United States, going back to the days of the Marshall Plan, had been favorable to European unity on as broad a basis as possible. In its view the Common Market was a desirable development, which, however, should be enlarged through the inclusion of Britain above all, likely prelude to the addition of several other states as well. In 1962, on July 4, President Kennedy held out the prospect of interdependence, an association on the basis of equality between the United States and a united Europe, two entities of comparable dimensions of power, which could then, as equals, discuss the implementation of their common interests. There is no need to consider at this point the larger possibility of an Atlantic community. Europe in any case could be an equal partner and carry an equal voice in decisions, matters of defense, for example.

This approach was essentially rejected by France, very shortly in dramatic form. Britain's economic difficulties, the too heavy cost of ballistic engines, led to a meeting in Nassau between her prime minister, Macmillan, and President Kennedy. The meeting was rather improvised, its implications inadequately thought out in advance, and the agreement which it produced was clear expression of the dependence of Britain on the United States in matters of defense.[122]

This was precisely the sort of relationship to which de Gaulle objected. He resented as well the exclusiveness of the Anglo-American meeting, calculated to confirm his belief in the special relationship that Britain was endeavoring to maintain with the United States. In the circumstances, the subsequent American offer of similar arrangements to France took on the color of an afterthought, almost that of insult added to injury.

It was especially unfortunate that the Nassau meeting, which took place from December 18 to 21, 1962, should have followed by a few days a visit of Macmillan to de Gaulle. Britain was at this time knocking for admission at the gates of the Common Market in Brussels, where negotiations to that end had been going on for some time. These were laborious and their success remained in balance. The divided state of British opinion and the persistent traditional sense of otherness where Europe was concerned have been indicated before.

Irritated by the succession of events in December—Macmillan's visit to Rambouillet and the Nassau meeting—de Gaulle used the occasion of a press conference on January 14, 1963, to voice France's veto to the admission of Britain to the Common Market, a thing which he did in addition in unnecessarily haughty, humiliating, and brutal terms. There was much consternation abroad, but the Common Market operated under the unanimity rule. To say that Britain was not yet adequately European was hardly an exaggeration; whether it followed from this that it was wise to exclude her is a different question again. Her exclusion at any rate did not impede the successful progress of the EEC, to which her admission, for good or ill, would undoubtedly have given an altered character.

Here was precisely the real issue, for behind the circumstances of the episode lay a more serious consideration. For the Six were not equal, Germany and France standing out among the rest. Germany may have carried the greater economic weight of the two, but owing to the disabilities, results of the Nazi record, under which she still labored, she was adhering to a policy of at least relative effacement, content with the hope that the recent past would gradually become forgotten. The result was therefore to give France a place of primacy in the association, a place to which the intrusion of Britain would have constituted a challenge.[123]

A change of emphasis became evident in the orientation of French policy, of which Germany became the focus. The solution of the German problem, the "dissolution" of Germany into Europe, of which the ECSC had been the first manifestation, was not abandoned, but a different twist was given to it, which might be expressed as the attempt to create a Paris-Bonn Axis. Chancellor Adenauer had found General de Gaulle highly congenial, and an authentic link of understanding developed between the two men. De Gaulle's visit to Germany in September 1962 was an outstanding success, and the highly complimentary expressions that he used in addressing the German people fell on gratefully receptive ears. Despite the fact that the French rejection of Britain was a disappointment to France's partners among the Six, it is significant that it was almost immediately followed by the conclusion of a Franco-German treaty of co-operation.[124] This was a long way from the position voiced by Mendès-France in the French National Assembly ten years earlier that "it is an axiom of French policy never to part company with Great Britain."

But if there was genuine satisfaction in Germany at the extended French hand of reconciliation, Germany found herself at the same time placed in an awkward dilemma. For the French insistence on independence and the consequent deterioration of the Franco-American relationship contained the possibility of facing Germany with having to make a choice between the two, the last thing that she wanted. Although France was proceeding with the development of her nuclear armament,[125] clearly the American arsenal alone carried credibility. The awkward American proposal of a Multilateral Force (MLF), a clumsily contrived attempt to integrate the NATO forces in some respects reminiscent of the French version of EDC, was opposed by the French and eventually even by the British. It was quietly dropped, having meanwhile given rise to some French discontent over the German endorsement of it.

Thus, the Franco-German treaty of friendship, if not entirely stillborn, failed to produce any substantial fruits. A Franco-German core was the logical base of a Western European combination. Without Britain Europe may perhaps still be conceived, but without *both* France and Germany the concept of European unity is totally devoid of meaning, although the prospect of a joint dominance of the two held little attraction for the rest. So long as he remained in office, until 1963, Chancellor Adenauer made every effort and many concessions in an attempt to give substance to the Franco-German relationship. So did others among the Six for the sake of avoiding the disruption of the association, which to a point France sought to exploit and dominate. At the same time the rift between France and her partners has also been overstated on occasion. It is quite understandable, for example, that, given the productive capacity of French agriculture, France should seek to maximize the possibilities and benefits of the large market of the Six; this represents no more than a legitimate and wholly normal promotion of the national interest, in which respect France is hardly unique.

If the particular association with Germany proved politically disappointing,[126] other cards might be played. General de Gaulle never deviated from the view that the Yalta arrangements were a mistake and an injustice, an American one in the main, the effects of which should be undone. He was also a firm believer in the national reality as a stronger and more durable element than any ideology. The Soviet Union might stress the ideological factor, but in the last resort mainly for the promotion of the Russian interest; de Gaulle hardly ever referred to the Soviet Union, nearly always speaking of Russia instead, and the French Communists he had contemptuously dubbed "separatists."

There was considerable validity in this view, to which the Russo-Chinese split gave added point. But long before that split occurred, Tito in Yugoslavia had succesfully asserted the heresy of a "national" Communism. The events of 1956 in Eastern Europe, most markedly in Hungary, all pointed in the same direction. Nor was the Soviet Union itself immune from the gathering winds of change, especially after the startling speech of Khrushchev at the Twentieth Party Congress in that same year. The very fact of economic success liberated forces the accent of whose demands was on consumer goods and greater freedom of expression. The *embourgeoisement* of the Communist milieu caused it to put a new emphasis on goals in large measure reached long ago in the more economically advanced Western democracies, while Russia was still relatively backward, even in comparison with some of her satellites, Czechoslovakia, for example.

This trend, in combination with that of social reform in the capitalist world, might be thought to lead to a convergence of positions and policies in the context of which ideological difference would tend to vanish, or at least lose much of its sting. Such was indeed the case, yet it could also be contended that the past half century had witnessed a steady spread of the area under Communist allegiance. Was not de Gaulle perhaps right in asserting the more lasting validity of the national entity?

The result of this evolution was a relaxation of tensions while new ones were created resulting from confusion. The phenomenon of socio-political convergence and the technical progress of weaponry had the effect of creating common ground between the United States and the Soviet Union. If the two can agree, either in positive terms, or even in the more negative ones of relenting on their dedication to mutual destruction, the credibility of the American guarantee to Europe would be thereby diminished; who could expect the United States to act differently from others in giving first priority to its own interest, and might not that best be insured through direct understanding with the Soviet Union? The younger, more intransigeant, and "purer" Communism of China began to speak of Russo-American collusion. Doubts about the dependability of the American purpose were by no means exclusively French.

Of such an evolution it was possible to take an optimistic view. The division of the world into two blocs centered around the United States and the Soviet Union, the Cold War, was seen by many as an unhealthy, undesirable, and transitory situation, for which polycentrism could offer the alternative of greater flexibility. But polycentrism could operate in both camps. The successful assertion of heretical tendencies in the Communist world could be welcomed in the free. That world is less rigidly united and controlled, but in it, too, the fact of the overwhelming American weight, American hegemony as some called it, was resented in varying degrees. In the French case in particular one must bear in mind the importance of the factor of resentment induced by certain American positions. It is well illustrated by such a statement as the *"Lettre aux Américains,"* which appeared in *Figaro* after the Suez episode:

> In the eyes of three hundred million Arabs you have humiliated us before a Nasser. . . . Perhaps you believe that after all the worst risk you are taking is to have to take our place. There are those in France who think that you do not find this prospect altogether uncongenial. But be careful. It would be a mistake to seem, this time again, to prove them right. . . . You might be wrong in banking too heavily on our need of you. For that need is reciprocal. We cannot break the Atlantic front, but nor can you. . . .
>
> One cannot deny a still proud old people what constitutes the only future worthy of its past without risking provoking in it, possibly against its own interest, unpredictable emotional reactions.[127]

It was de Gaulle who elected to give the resentment its sharpest expression, and here it is well to bear in mind that, allowing for the peculiar form he gave to his actions and utterances, he was the spokesman for far more than himself; even some of his critics fundamentally agreed, be it at home or abroad. As between the Soviet Union and France, especially de Gaulle, it would be idle to speak of love lost or illusions. From the Russian point of view France's disruptive activity within the Western alliance could only be welcome; de Gaulle was royally received in the Soviet Union although he reaped little more than this unexpensive reward. His flirting could, among other things, serve as a means of pressure on the German Federal Republic. Of perhaps greater significance was his encouragement of the assertion of independent position on the part of the satellite countries of Eastern Europe; his visits and his speeches in Poland and Roumania struck a responsive chord at a widespread level, whatever Gomulka may have felt it necessary to answer.[128]

To assert that the German problem is essentially a European question that should be settled primarily by Europeans, and that in such a settlement the Soviet Union is entitled to a voice, is a tenable position, especially if one assumes two things. First, the increasing convergence of the American and the Russian interests; secondly, the abatement of the Russian threat to Western Europe.

To speak of Europe from the Atlantic to the Urals is not very convincing. Such an agglomeration is open to the same criticism that applies to the combination of the United States with a number of European states, the inevitable dominance by one member of the association. The Soviet Union, to be sure, if only for geographical reasons, is European in a way that the United States is not, but one should not exaggerate the role of the ocean as a factor of separation, especially in our day of easy and rapid communications and transportation[129]; there is also the fact that Russia's participation as a major factor in the affairs of Europe is relatively recent and that she, like Britain, has traditionally played a peripheral role in those affairs.

We may return to Britain for a moment. To put it in the bluntest fashion, Britain has returned to the status of a European island; the decision to withdraw from east of Suez and the impotence in playing a significant role in such African developments as have taken place in South Africa, in Rhodesia, or in Nigeria attest to this conclusively. It was logical in the circumstances for Britain to seek to join Europe, though regrettable that the attempt should appear as a resort of desperation, a decision *in extremis* when all else had failed, thus weakening her bargaining position.

The result was in essence the same on the second attempt: a French veto, though one expressed in less decisive form. The French objections, stressing technical considerations in the main, had considerable validity, amounting to the contention that, before joining Europe, Britain must put her own house in order. It has in fact been argued that, had the verdict been other, the result would merely have been the initiation of protracted negotiations in which Britain would have been confronted with a largely united Six instead of with French opposition alone.[130] However that may be, and granting that many difficult questions remained to be solved, one could argue just as well that the best approach to their resolution was to undertake the discussion of them. Thus the validity of the French objections is less important than the fact that circumstances furnished a convenient pretext for covering the real motives of the opposition.

These were political in their essence, and one arrives at the seemingly paradoxical conclusion that the reasons for the British application and for the French refusal were in considerable measure based on kindred political considerations in both cases. The purely economic factors are real indeed, but, for the reason indicated before of the disabilities under which Germany continues to labor, among the Six, France held a position of preeminence, one at least of *primus inter pares.* This was not necessarily unacceptable to the rest, though naturally irksome, especially in view of the uncertainties that surrounded Gaullist aims. France might conceivably aspire to the role of spokesman for a restricted Europe, but hardly more than that, if even that. It is possible at any rate to interpret the policy of de Gaulle as an attempt to "annex" Europe in a sense, even if without aggressive intent.

The intrusion of Britain would challenge that position of primacy, such as it may be, a position for which Britain herself could be a candidate, more acceptable than France to some others, if primacy there must be. It could in any case serve to restore British standing in the same manner that Britain's exclusion served the French. Thus we are brought back to a classical situation, one in which the relationships among three states, Britain, France, and Germany—the dominant factor in the international life of Europe (Russia always excluded)—remain paramount. Of the three, Germany carries the greatest potential weight, but for reasons that will not be repeated cannot at present be a candidate for leadership. To attempt to capitalize on this situation by creating a Franco-German combination in which France has a dominant role constitutes a dangerous gamble for two reasons: it runs into the opposition of others for one thing; it is acceptable to Germany, insofar as it is, only so long as German disabilities continue, which to be sure is likely to be for some time. Conceivably, the time might last long enough to establish a de facto condition that would achieve permanence; but it is also easy to imagine that, if and when German disabilities are removed, Germany could become the dominant partner in the association, which would be an odd result for French policy to have achieved. The pre-1914 situation comes to mind, when, had there not been the accident of war, Germany was by way of peacefully achieving the dominance of Europe.

Since the war France has made an unexpected recovery, the solid bases and the reality of which have been explained. To have achieved rough parity with Britain is no mean accomplishment, when one thinks of 1940 and 1945. De Gaulle, whatever the ultimate outcome of his career may be, has rendered his country services that can neither be denied nor undone. Not least, he extricated it from the imperial impasse, to a point snatching victory from defeat. Capitalizing thereafter on accomplishments that were not of his making, he succeeded in restoring to the French people a sense of self-respect, a most desirable achievement after the humiliation they had suffered. For a nation to have a sense of purpose, even a sense of mission, is no ignoble aspiration, any more than it is for an individual to take a serious and high view of the significance of his existence. That is how the great accomplishments of mankind have been achieved, even though a high price has sometimes been paid owing to the perversion and abuses which are the reverse side of the coin of the possibilities contained in the human condition. Prophets, artists, and conquerors are wont to hitch their wagon to a star; their fate is often that of Icarus and, to change metaphors, at times the pure metal fails to be separated from the baser dross.

To return to more mundane and immediate considerations, the caution that has been issued about the tentativeness of appraising the recent past, the course of the last quarter of a century, has even greater validity when applied to events that still carry the smell of fresh printer's ink. Mention of these nevertheless is warranted.

This is especially true of the French scene, for the "reign" of General de Gaulle came to an end in May 1969; the passing from the active scene of his strong personality is a landmark, suitable occasion at least for some tentative reflections. The British scene by contrast has presented a landscape of continuity. Whether the restrictive measures initiated by the Labour government will achieve their intended purpose of economic redressment is a subject of open debate, unaffected by the recent verdict of the British electorate. So likewise the problems with which Britain has been contending; her relationship to Europe, the legacies of imperial devolution, be they Rhodesia, Nigeria, not to mention diminutive Anguilla, continue to hang in the balance. It does not seem rash to predict that it will be some time before Britain finds her place in the world. Those who seek inspiration in the model of Sweden, not to mention that of the Irish Republic, even in the unlikely and undesirable event of their proving correct in the ultimate reckoning, will have to wait for quite some time.

In the French case, perhaps in keeping with a less calm political tradition, outward occurrences have been more sensational, though their lasting effect may be less so. One of the boasts of the Gaullist régime was the strength of the French financial position, the solidity of the franc. The form it took of exalting the place of gold and of uttering unkind remarks about the solidity of the dollar was not devoid of solid bases, but turned out to be little more than a passing and futile irritant. The French economy does not have sufficient weight in the world to assume the burden of such challenges.

Another boast was the large increase in the student population of France at the upper levels of education. That claim was wholly justified, yet it provided the occasion for exposing the weakness of both boasts. Things might have been easier for the régime if the increase in the student population had been smaller, or if, alternatively, adequate provisions had been made for the care of the increased numbers. The stresses of inadequate conditions were at the root of the student revolt in May 1968, precipitated by some insignificant incidents, as such things often are. Here was in other respects a manifestation of the well-nigh universal unrest of the young, the abler and the more thinking especially. The spectacle of the Sorbonne for some weeks in May–June 1968 was proper source of astonishment, and it even caused some to think back to 1848. For the revolutionary impulse seemed to be strong, characterized by extravagant aims rather than limited grievances—these existed too—and the students sought the alliance of the workers. The response of 10,000,000 strikers was misleading, the workers remaining highly suspicious of the bourgeois students, and one could find humor in the spectacle of the Communist leadership, become a conservative force, straining to maintain control of its troops by leading them from the rear.

There was irony, too, in the fact that General de Gaulle was absent on a visit to Roumania, expounding his customary views. He only curtailed his visit by one day, but his return at first did not alter the impression of stunned passivity and lack of reaction on the part of the government. The situation was saved by the calm behavior—and the physical stamina—of the prime minister, Georges Pompidou. By the time, on May 30, de Gaulle addressed the nation in his more wonted style, his uncompromising stance in favor of order had the support of a large mass of frightened bourgeois, many of whom had initially shown no special disfavor toward the gaiety of student rebellion. The ensuing parliamentary election, in June, confirmed the popular reaction in the form of endorsing Gaullist candidates, who as a consequence enjoyed in the National Assembly an overwhelming majority, an unprecedented situation in French democracy.

But the events of May–June left behind them considerable wreckage. The university was to be thoroughly reorganized through modernization; very large wage increases granted to the workers raised problems for the French economy as well as questions about the stability of the franc. The crisis of November 1968, when a devaluation was widely expected, passed; de Gaulle's pride would not allow devaluation. But this was no more a solution than had been King Canute's stand. The drain on French reserves, though at a less dramatic rate, did not cease; within a year the Bank of France's hoard of nearly $7,000,000,000 had melted to about half that figure.

In the spring of 1969 General de Gaulle sought a fresh endorsement of the French people in a new referendum. He elected to make a stand on the odd combination of two totally unrelated issues: decentralization through the setting up of twenty-one regions was one, a most desirable aim in overcentralized France; the other was a reform, virtually the abolition, of the Senate. The two were in addition combined in a lengthy and intricate statement calculated to discourage would-be readers of it. The French electorate rejected the package, whereupon General de Gaulle resigned, as he had said that he would in the face of such an outcome; de Gaulle's Fifth Republic was after all not a dictatorship. The manner of his exit seemed a peculiar anticlimax, though it has also been interpreted as a purposely contrived defeat. Still quite vigorous at seventy-eight, his return to the political scene is definitely in the domain of the improbable, even if one remembers Hindenburg and Pétain.

The ensuing presidential election brought, on the second balloting,[131] Pompidou to the presidency—he had been dismissed from the prime ministership in the interval, another source of much speculation. Not unfairly, the verdict has been interpreted as expressing the wish of the French electorate to have Gaullism without de Gaulle, which in turn raises the question of the meaning of the observation. The "Europeans," in France as elsewhere, have taken heart again. Time alone can tell whether a gradual change will be gently effected that will lead to a fundamental reversal of French policy, in the matter of the British application for membership in the EEC, for example, or whether, again in gentler fashion, the basic fact of opposition will remain. At best, many concrete problems will have to be resolved, and the observation that Britain must put her own house in order is no less valid in the case of France. An unexpected—at the time of its occurrence—and neatly contrived devaluation of the franc by some 12 per cent in August 1969 is but a step among many that will have to be taken. A period of uncertainty is indicated for the future, the near future at least.

The weakening of the French position produced by the events since 1968 likewise put a brake on the effort to restore France's influence in the world. The effort could hardly be expected in any case to be pursued with the same vigor, let alone the same style, after the departure of de Gaulle. But, allowing for circumstances and personal idiosyncrasies, the fundamentals of power remain, whatever the correct appraisal of them may be. The recovery of France has been substantial; constitutional changes and the trend toward modernization are not in the nature of passing accidents or personal whims.

The desire to assert an independent policy ranked high among

Gaullist aims. The appeal of it continues no less, in France as elsewhere in Europe. One aspect of its attempted implementation was France's rapprochement with the Soviet Union, whose threat to the West had supposedly reached the vanishing point. This remains largely true despite the episode of the occupation of Czechoslovakia by the forces of the Warsaw Pact allies in August 1968. That high-handed performance was in the last analysis an expression of the dilemma which confronted the Soviet Union in the face of the pressure for liberalization, at home no less than among its satellites. The episode was understandably a setback to efforts at rapprochement with the Soviet Union, whether originating in the United States or in the European West. The clumsy Soviet action has not solved the problem to which it was directed, and the pressures have continued to exist, as witnessed by domestic Soviet developments, by such things as the Roumanian stance, and by the state of Sino-Soviet relations, or by the meetings of groups of representatives of Communist parties in Moscow and in Bucharest; the unity of the Communist movement has perhaps even poorer prospects than the reunion of the Christian churches. From the standpoint of the relations among states it is more important to stress the similarities with 1956. Hungary then, Czechoslovakia twelve years later, were in the last analysis tacitly acknowledged as belonging in the Soviet domain. Within that understanding, attempts at accommodation have been persisted in, as witenssed by the continuing Russo-American discussion in the domain of armaments, for example.

The ineluctable fact remains that France is of the West, as is Britain. For both, finding their place and role in that West, in the world for that matter, remains a search, to a degree attended by what might be called an attenuated survival of classical rivalries and methods. The war created circumstances which seemed suitable for a clean sweep of the superseded rivalries of Europe, and for a time it seemed that a united Europe might be born. England, best situated to assume the leadership of such a movement at one point, proved incapable of overcoming the weight of her own past. Then, in perhaps more measured fashion, largely from France seemed to emerge the needed leadership. In many European hearts the initiative struck a responsive chord; here one could see France at her best insofar as she stood for the universalistic tradition of the equality and brotherhood of man. But France, too, largely for internal reasons, which have been explained, failed to persevere in the undertaking. Her savior in 1958, whether because he, too, was incapable of rising above the limitations of his own past conditioning, or whether because he correctly judged that a too ambitious and precipitate undertaking was doomed to failure, undoubtedly put a brake on the unifying tendency. The following judgment is adequate summation, which fits the British case no less well than the French:

> Any French foreign policy in the postwar period is fatally caught in the contradictions of a nation formerly mistress of its destiny and capable of exerting a profound influence on that of the world, but which finds itself today too burdened by history to be content with being Switzerland, yet at the same time finds its economic and military capacity too limited to enable it to play an arbitral role on the world scene.[132]

Whether or not there had been an occasion when the part of wisdom would have been to seize fortune by the forelock, the occasion was missed. Thus the travail of Britain and of France, of all Europe, indeed, outside the Soviet Union, in this respect continues. The forms that it will take, and what shape the results to which it may lead, remain in the lap of the future.

Conclusion

We have traced the record, over a century and a half, of two states, the intention being, through selective illustration, to bring out the manner in which they have endeavored to defend and promote their national interests through the use of what power they had at their disposal. From the unfolding of our tale the reader may draw certain conclusions about the operation and the management of power. It seems appropriate, in closing, to summarize some of the factors that emerge.

Britain and France have been states in a world of states. The shortcomings or merits of the state as an institution have not been a subject for discussion in this treatment; it has been taken as a condition of fact, as obvious as it is fundamental: the sovereign national state for some time has been, and still is, the reality of the world's political structure. Our principals have realized that condition for quite some time, ahead of many others, in this respect leading the way; much that has happened and is still happening represents the effort of the entire human race to organize itself in accordance with this model.

Like any living thing, the first care of the state is survival. But not in a state of immobility; growth or expansion are attributes of life until decay overtakes it. Thus it may be said that the state is naturally aggressive, manifesting this characteristic through the use of its power and the endeavor to enhance that power. But here a qualification is needed, for two reasons: first, this aggressiveness, a life force, does not operate in blind, wholly unregulated fashion; those in charge of the national interest have generally been—certainly in the case of the two states under consideration and in the period chosen—civilized men, and a large part of their problem has been that of reconciling the conflict between the cruder urge of power and some rule of law. That is how honorable individuals come at times to adopt devious and even brutal methods. Secondly, there are the constrictions imposed by the limitations of existing power, the complex resultant of a multitude of factors, some of them concrete, material, and measurable, others of a more elusive nature. This has been pointed out.

As we look back over our tale some things emerge, both similarities and differences, in the methods adopted by the two states.

The most important difference stems from a fact of nature—or geography. Island Britain, once she had discovered the possibilities of the sea, even if rather late, used them to excellent effect. Not to mention the impact of this condition on the issue of defense and on the development of institutions, it made for a largeness of outlook denied to others. Disraeli was quite right in asserting that Britain was more Asiatic than European in his time. Hence the detachment and moderation, even if read at times as perfidy by others, that Castlereagh, for example, could display at Vienna in dealing with the archenemy France.

But this points to a fundamental question in the operation of

British power. For Castlereagh's position was only tenable so long as there was adequate power to sustain it. Such power Britain possessed in his time and for some time thereafter, long enough for a tradition to take root. A similar approach to the problem of Germany after a century had passed no longer served; instead of helping Britain it contributed to obfuscating confusion and to much trouble for all, Britain included. The problem Britain faced in the effort to adjust to diminishing power has been a major thread in our theme; we shall return to it in a moment. It may be pointed out that meanwhile another tradition developed which grew out of Britain's imperial endeavors. Castlereagh may have been France's best defender at Vienna; this did not interfere with the acquisition of further imperial positions. Even the Dutch Cape and Ceylon were retained; to be sure, they had been for moment in law—or perhaps better, legalistically—French possessions. Britain in her strength could afford to be logically inconsistent or ruthless, even to make some mistakes, so long, as Gladstone put it, as they were "the follies of a strong man."

Continental France was denied the advantage of Britain's island position, and de Gaulle's judgment[133] is essentially sound. The pursuit of "natural boundaries," meaning primarily the Rhine, in other words, security of her frontiers, constituted, perhaps to an unwarrantedly exclusive degree, the first care of French policy. France was not blind to the possibilities of empire, but could not or would not invest in that enterprise sufficient resources to parallel the British performance. It was Britain in fact that mainly stood in her way. Be it in 1763 in North America and in India, or on the Nile in 1898, Britain could be wholly intransigeant and carry out her desire. The French horizon as a consequence remained narrower than the British; in sharpest form the contrast may be expressed as that between Churchill's "appeal of the wide ocean" in one case, the obsession in recent times with the blue line of the Vosges in the other.

The existence of this last condition in France was expression —even an exaggerated expression—of the decline of French power. And this points to a significant difference in the manipulation of power between Britain and France. The imperial tradition was sufficiently strong in France for some to take the position that, despite 1870, the peace of Frankfort, and an increasingly powerful Germany, France should participate in the late nineteenth-century scramble for empire. But it is also significant that Delcassé, one of the chief advocates of colonialism, took a limited view of empire; rather than look to the whole world as Britain did, he saw Indochina and even Madagascar as bargaining counters, thinking that an extension of France from North Africa to the Congo was a goal more commensurate with the possibilities of French power. In this as in other endeavors the point has also been made of the different use made of the factor of culture as such in the British and the French cases; it was far more deliberate and conscious in the second.

The Third Republic did remarkably well in the imperial domain, thereby compensating to a point for other deficiencies of French power, demographic and economic. But this was not sufficient, and France strove to escape from the isolation in which Bismarck succeeded in keeping her so long as he lasted. The policy of eastern alliances, Turkish, Swedish, Polish, Russian in turn, is an old tradition in France, even in the heyday of her power. Britain felt otherwise. She felt, quite rightly for a long time, that the best defense of her own interest lay in preserving an arbitral position, which meant in turn eschewing the commitment of her power until a concrete situation had arisen, at which point she would proceed to tip the scales in the direction she found most advantageous to her interest.

But British power, too, declined, in the sense at least of a diminution of the margin of its primacy. The response bears similarity to the classical French: a search for alliances. But it was an ambiguous response: the Japanese alliance could be interpreted as confirming the traditional arbitral British detachment from the continent of Europe. Within a mere two years the Japanese alliance was followed by the Entente Cordiale; the ambiguity of that commitment from the British standpoint has been brought out in our discussion. Not surprisingly, Britain was reluctant and slow in adjusting to the changing facts of power and to her correspondingly changed position.

The difficulty was compounded by what, paradoxically, may be described as the disadvantages of victory, whereas France had the benefits of defeat. It was too easy, if perhaps not very excusable, for Britain to read 1918 as a modern edition of 1588, 1763, or 1814. French decline had been far clearer, which made for clearer thinking, and the victory of 1918 was for France but brief cause for elation; it did not eliminate or even diminish the obsession that was the wish and the search for security.

The deficiencies, to say no more, of British and French policies between the two world wars have been discussed at length. They represented in both cases a failure of adaptation to changed circumstances and a mismanagement of power. The French position may be seen as an impossible one, French power being inadequate to the task it had set for itself, even if this is no justification of the poor handling of what power there was. The British failing is perhaps even worse.

Yet this also brings out another element in the operation of power which affected both countries in crucial fashion. An important factor in the conduct of foreign policy is the organization of its operation, meaning the loci of control and direction, the structure of the foreign office and of the foreign service. Without entering into details about a subject that by itself would warrant a substantial volume, it may suffice to say that control remained in the hands of remarkably few individuals, preferably of aristocratic origin, especially in Britain—the French milieu was more egalitarian, where members of the Third Estate, such as the Cambon brothers and Barrère, proved far superior to their contemporary counterparts of noble extraction.

We are touching on a fundamental problem of our time, consequence of the steady rise of the mass, that of the operation of foreign policy, especially in a democratic milieu. Palmerston, Disraeli, Thiers for a time, or the Duc de Gramont could make fiery speeches that elicited a ready response from an easily aroused opinion. But that condition has been changing with the passing of time. National emotion was still sufficiently powerful in 1914 to sweep away the Second International. But anti-militarism had already become very strong in France, while in Britain the Boer War had given rise to much criticism, had almost proved a traumatic experience. Palmerston had been a fire-eater, Gladstone and Salisbury were not. The last two, however, did not recoil before the possibility of war, even if they strove to avoid it. Likewise in France, if after 1870 no politician could publicly express willingness to underwrite the Treaty of Frankfort, the leaders of the Third Republic were for the most part sober and realistic men; Déroulède and Boulanger proved to be bubbles.

The revulsion against war received an enormous impulse from the experience of the First World War. Britain and France are democracies. If the ultimate direction of foreign policy continued in both countries to remain in very few hands, it could not help reflect the dominant mood. The French abdication of 1936 and the subsequent British appeasement may be adjudged abject; undoubtedly they were mistaken. Yet it would be difficult to contend that such men as Chamberlain and Daladier were not authentic expressions of the prevalent mood of their day. This has been called decadence, which in a sense it is, certainly in the context of the harsh realities of power. The point has been made in our discussion that for some time Britain and France have been in the same boat in more senses than one.

In the face of disaster, realized in one case, threatened in the other, Churchill and de Gaulle saved or retrieved the situation, even if in wholly different fashions. At the end of the Second World War Britain stood in a very similar position to that of France at the end of the earlier conflict; for both the victory was ashes. What then to do with victory? All of Churchill's rhetoric and determination furnished no answer to the inescapable necessity of adaptation of injured and diminished power. Again the weight of tradition proved a handicap; neither empire nor the sea supplied an answer, and Britain is still searching for her place among nations.

The case of France is similar but also different. Again, defeat turned into an asset. France has recovered to a point of rough parity with Britain. De Gaulle's achievement, apart from possibly durable constitutional reform and the liquidation of the empire, has been the restoration of a sense of self-respect to his people. His manipulation of sometimes almost nonexistent power was highly skillful and to a degree successful, but some of his other essays rather served to reveal the limitations of that power. His, like Churchill's, performance showed the importance of the role of individuals at certain points of time. They showed likewise that for the longer term the totality of the national resources counts for more. France, too, is searching for her proper place among nations. The fundamentals of physical conditions and material assets, plus the weight of a long history in both cases, have shaped the different forms in which the two states have been and are pursuing the everlasting goal of protecting and enhancing their respective national interests.

NOTES ON *Chapter IX*

1. Britain had introduced conscription in 1939 and her Army was of excellent quality, but of small dimensions by comparison with those of the continental states.

2. The position of the United States and the resulting Anglo-American exchanges are reminiscent of the period of the First World War prior to the American intervention, despite the self-imposed restrictions of the American Neutrality Acts.

3. His tentative suggestion of "quarantining" the aggressive Powers, easily identifiable at the time, had aroused a storm of protest.

4. In September–October 1939, Lithuania, Latvia, and Esthonia were forced to sign non-aggression treaties with the Soviet Union, allowing in addition the use of naval bases and the stationing of Soviet troops in their territories. This was a preliminary to their virtual absorption, which took place in August 1940, following petitions of newly elected parliaments in the three countries.

5. *The* [London] *Times,* May 29, 1940. Cited in Hytier, A., *Two Years of French Foreign Policy, Vichy 1940–1942* (1958), p. 19.

6. For Reynaud's appeals to President Roosevelt of June 10 and 14, see his useful, though awkwardly titled, *La France a sauvé l'Europe,* 2 vols. (Paris, 1947), Vol. II, pp. 295–96 and 330–31.

7. Woodward, Sir Llewellyn, *British Foreign Policy in the Second World War* (1962), pp. 68–73. Also, Hytier, op. cit., pp. 25 ff.

8. An interesting and prescient preview of what turned out to be the Battle of France can be found in de Gaulle, Charles, *Vers l'armée de métier* (1944 edition), pp. 166–95.

9. As undersecretary for national defense, but not until the cabinet reshuffle of June 6.

10. De Gaulle, Charles, *War Memoirs, The Call to Honour, 1940–1942* (1955), *Documents,* pp. 11–12.

11. Ibid., pp. 12–15.

12. While Pétain and Laval agreed in thinking that the war was lost, there was a shade of difference in their outlooks, Pétain entertaining the greater illusions where it came to dealing with the Germans.

13. De Gaulle, op. cit., p. 71.

14. Churchill, *The Second World War,* Vol. II, *Their Finest Hour* (1949), pp. 50–51 (my italics).

15. Woodward, op. cit., p. 75.

16. Hytier, op. cit., pp. 51–69, 83–90; Woodward, op. cit., Ch. V.

17. The Near Eastern complications grew out of the coup of Reshid Ali in Iraq. In order to support the new régime, Germany obtained concessions from Vichy for the use of Syrian air facilities, a contravention of

the armistice terms. It is significant that the chief proponent of the pro-German attitude was Admiral Darlan, who for a time superseded Laval as Pétain's foreign minister. The anti-British tradition, not surprisingly, finds some of its strongest representatives in the French naval establishment. For the rest, the incident is an episode in the long story of Anglo-French rivalry in the Near East. See Hytier, op. cit., pp. 108–11.

18. Woodward, op. cit. p. 113. The foreign office seems to have taken a less optimistic view, more convinced of French defeatism. In May 1942 the British landed in Madagascar to insure against its use by the Japanese.

19. Prime Minister to Lord Lothian, June 9, 1940. Churchill, op. cit., p. 355 (my italics).

20. As a good example of this interpretation may be cited Tansill, C. A., *Back Door to War, the Roosevelt Foreign Policy 1933–1941* (1952), especially Chapters XXV and XXVI.

21. By ostensibly pooling resources on a basis of reciprocal lending, the ground was cut from under the possibility of any controversy arising such as had bedeviled the relations between the United States and the Allies over the debts contracted by the latter during the First World War.

22. An additional stretching of the concept, or practice, of neutrality may be seen in the occupation of Greenland by American, Canadian, and British forces following the overrunning of Denmark by the Germans and the severance of the connection between Iceland and Denmark.

23. See below, pp. 549–57.

24. Churchill, *The Second World War,* Vol. III, *The Grand Alliance* (1950), pp. 331–33 (my italics).

25. Cited in Butler, J. R. M., ed., *Grand Strategy,* Vol. II (1957), p. 423, from Langer W. L., and Gleason, S. E., *The Undeclared War* (New York, 1952), p. 222.

26. Butler, ibid., p. 424.

27. France allowed Japanese forces in Indochina, and Japan also "arbitrated" a territorial dispute with Thailand—in the latter country's favor.

28. Churchill, op. cit., pp. 291–93.

29. It is from this meeting that issued the Declaration of the United Nations, similar to that of the Atlantic Charter, but joined in by twenty-six states at war with the Axis. Under the circumstances, this was a relatively innocuous gesture, certainly by comparison with the military necessities of the moment.

30. Woodward, op. cit., pp. 291–93.

31. In a speech in Parliament during the course of a debate on India.

32. When Greece was attacked by Germany in 1941 Britain diverted forces from the North African theater to assist her. Likewise after the defeat of Germany, British forces were the mainstay of the Greek opposition to the threat of a Communist takeover.

33. See below, p. 553.

34. The participation of China, and the absence of France, in this declaration may be noted, which fitted the American view of the respective future prospects of the two countries.

35. The discussion of Germany at Teheran is of little more than historic interest, largely an academic exercise in retrospect. No decisions were

taken in regard to Germany other than setting up a Three-Power European Advisory Commission.

36. Germany was initially divided into three zones of occupation, in addition to a section assigned to Polish administration. Subsequently, a zone was carved out of the American and British ones for occupation by France.

37. The continuing war with Japan and the prospective role of Russia in it was a factor in the situation.

38. As a consequence of a British election, resulting in a Labour victory, Churchill's place was taken by Attlee in the middle of the Potsdam conference. The change had no material effects on British policies.

39. See above, pp. 521, 524–25.

40. Lucien Romier in *Figaro*. Cited in Duroselle, op. cit., p. 323.

41. The Ethiopian episode for Laval; the lack of support in the war for Pétain; naval antagonism, more specifically the Mers-el-Kebir encounter, for Darlan.

42. Cited in Duroselle, op. cit., p. 335. The fear of Bolshevism, before, then, and since, was hardly a monopoly of Laval's.

43. Ibid., p. 330.

44. At the end of July the Free French forces amounted to some 7,000 men.

45. Churchill, *Their Finest Hour*, p. 451.

46. The tempest in a teapot that was the St. Pierre and Miquelon affair is an illustration. In December 1941 Admiral Muselier, on orders from de Gaulle, landed in the islands and organized a plebiscite, to the profound annoyance of the United States, which had been endeavoring to establish a modus vivendi with the Vichy régime.

47. Despite the advice of others, including General Eisenhower, President Roosevelt initially favored the establishment of a military administration for liberated France rather than turning over that administration to the Provisional Government.

48. Wiskemann, E., *Europe and the Dictators, 1919–1945* (1966), p. 221.

49. Woodhouse, C. M., *Post-War Britain* (1966), p. 18.

50. The monopoly of atomic weapons, however, compensated in considerable measure for the dislocation of the classical military establishment.

51. After a momentary hesitation the Soviet Union opted against participation in the American proposal and even turned its face against it.

52. In a speech in Glasgow in November 1934. Cited in Northedge, F. S., *British Foreign Policy; the Process of Readjustment 1945–1961* (1962), p. 26.

53. A speech delivered on March 5, 1956, at Westminster College in Fulton, Missouri, whither Churchill had been invited by President Truman.

54. The concrete form of the action was a request to Congress, which was immediately granted, for an appropriation of $400,000,000 for assistance to Greece and Turkey.

55. Apart from the section under Polish administration and the half of East Prussia under Russian. These areas were to all intents and purposes severed from Germany and integrated into the Polish and Soviet states respectively.

56. See below, p. 582.

57. See below, pp. 579–85.
58. Where the French were concerned there was in addition the motivation deriving from their involvement in the Algerian war, the rest of the Arab world, Cairo in particular, giving encouragement to the rebels.
59. The Suez episode also had internally divisive effects, for an important segment of British opinion disapproved of the British action.
60. After the Soviet Union embarked on the development of nuclear weapons. She produced her first atomic explosion in 1949.
61. Legislation which placed restrictions on the sharing of relevant information with other Powers.
62. London, 1962.
63. Cited in Woodhouse, *British Foreign Policy Since the Second World War* (New York, 1962), p. 79.
64. Although it was initially. The existence of abundant supplies of coal and iron in close proximity with each other, in combination with British inventiveness, had made Britain for a time *the* workshop of the world, and she enjoyed during that period the advantage of priority of development.
65. Canada contains an important—about one third of the total population—French-speaking element. In South Africa the British component is roughly comparable to that of Dutch derivation, but the two together make the total white population less than a quarter of the total.
66. The rivalry was already incipient at the time of the Bandung meeting, in 1955, though outward agreement could be maintained by stressing the anti-imperialist plank.
67. Britain joined in the imposition of economic sanctions advocated in the United Nations, but instances of the success of such sanctions are difficult to find.
68. The tendency to think of racial prejudice as an appanage of the white people derives from the virtual monopoly that they have had in the imperial domain in recent times. But this is highly misleading. With the emergence to independence of most of the imperial domain, instances are multiplying of intolerance and discriminatory practices among non-white groups.
69. The precipitately enacted legislation of February 1968, when East African Indians were seeking to exert their right as British subjects to go to England, can only be regarded as a manifestation of panic, a hardly warranted one at that.
70. See above, pp. 432–34.
71. See above, p. 555.
72. In 1951 Egypt abrogated the still not renegotiated treaty of 1936 and ended the condominium of the Sudan.
73. See below, pp. 587–88.
74. Essentially another move in the policy of containment of the Soviet Union, specifically in the Middle East, in this instance in the form of a promise of military and economic assistance to those Arab states that might request it. This was the basis for the American intervention in Lebanon in 1958.
75. Strang, *Britain in World Affairs* (1961), p. 356, n. 3.
76. Woodhouse, *Post-War Britain*, p. 49.
77. Woodhouse, *British Foreign Policy* . . . , pp. 223–24.
78. Despite Churchill's advocacy of European unity and his assertion

of British interest in Europe the nature of the link that he envisaged between the Continent and Britain was never made explicit by him.

79. Command 7970. Miscellaneous No. 9 (1950). "Anglo-French Discussions regarding French Proposals for the Western European Coal and Steel Industries." May–June 1950.

80. The Black International referred to the dominance of Christian, particularly Catholic, democracy in France, Germany (Adenauer), and Italy (De Gasperi), a bogey especially unpalatable to certain Labour circles.

81. In a speech in July 1957.

82. The visit of Macmillan to Rambouillet in December 1962, followed by the Nassau meeting with President Kennedy, conveyed to de Gaulle an impression of duplicity and profoundly irritated him. The real motivation of his veto seems, however, deeper. See below, pp. 599 ff.

83. See, for example, Albrecht-Carrié, R., "To a British Friend: Are You in Europe?" *Journal of International Affairs,* XVI, no. 1 (1962), pp. 18–27.

84. The Liberals have always been in favor of Britain joining Europe, but they carry little weight in British politics.

85. Roosevelt's invitation to de Gaulle to meet him in Algiers was not intended as a slight, but was rather the result of pressure of work and the condition of his health, this last a factor unknown to de Gaulle.

86. It may be said to have paid better at the domestic level, however, for the Communists, participating in the government, gave loyal co-operation where it came to matters of economic reconstruction.

87. It is important to bear in mind that the constitution of the Fourth Republic was adopted by a minority vote, when one considers the very large proportion of abstentions, almost equal to the opposition vote and to that in favor of the constitution.

88. Which for that matter was not inevitable. A plan for the stabilization of the franc, proposed by Mendès-France in 1946, was rejected, largely for domestic political reasons.

89. For a discussion of this, see Einaudi, Mario, et al., *Nationalization in France and Italy* (Ithaca, N.Y., 1955), Part II.

90. Grosser, A., *La IVe. République et sa politique extérieure* (1961), p. 35.

91. De Gaulle's association with the Communists was a matter of tactics and of expediency and should not be misread as his entertaining any illusions on their score. He had steadfastly refused to allow them to control certain key ministries, and the same policy was adhered to after his departure from office.

92. Even though the process proved a laborious one, by 1947 treaties of peace with the rest of the European enemy countries were concluded, with the exception of Austria, with whom peace was not made until 1955. No formal peace has been made with Germany, which has instead emerged as two separate and functioning states, the Federal Republic in the West, and the Democratic Peoples Republic in the East.

93. De Gaulle, *Vers l'armée de métier* (1944 ed.), pp. 17–18. The work was first published in 1934.

94. Any prospects of reaching Four-Power agreement in regard to Germany were shattered after the meeting held in London in February 1948. Following that meeting the Western Powers and the Soviet Union went

their separate ways in their treatment of their respective zones of occupation.

95. The Western Powers retained certain supervisory rights and the French claim to the Saar remained in abeyance.

96. De Carmoy, Guy, *Les politiques étrangères de la France 1944–1966* (1967), p. 97; Grosser, op. cit., p. 234.

97. For a discussion of it see Diebold, W., Jr., *The Schuman Plan; a Study in Economic Cooperation, 1950–1959* (1959).

98. In 1954, during the debate on the European Defense Community.

99. He reverted to this theme on a number of occasions. See above, note 78.

100. A brief account of it may be found in Grosser, op. cit., pp. 239–46.

101. De Carmoy, op. cit., p. 119.

102. One should bear in mind the impact of the Korean War, which could be interpreted as a diversion of American interest toward Asia, and the entirely different case of the Suez episode in 1956, which found the United States and the Soviet Union at least momentarily united in opposition to Britain and France.

103. Economic considerations also militated in favor of American support of European integration.

104. De Carmoy, op. cit., p. 112.

105. Cited in Grosser, op. cit., p. 27. Allowing for overstatement, it remains true that the empire had enabled France to play a larger role in world affairs than she would have otherwise.

106. Grosser, op. cit., p. 250. Herriot expressed fear of the consequences of assimilation carried to its logical conclusion in the debate on the constitutional structure of the empire in August 1946.

107. See Williams, Philip, *Politics in Post-War France* (1954), especially Part III, "The Constitution."

108. See above, pp. 522–23. The somewhat ambiguous promises made by the Free French during the war should be borne in mind.

109. The American involvement was part of the policy of containing Communist expansion. SEATO, organized in September 1954, was the Far Eastern counterpart of NATO in the West. France was a participant in it, but SEATO was never to achieve great significance.

110. Russian condemnation could be taken as foregone, and so could American opposition; the United States was not taken into the confidence of the British and French while they were making preparations for the Suez expedition. Given the obvious circumstances, a judgment had to be made about the probability of either or both the United States and the Soviet Union implementing their opposition with more than verbal condemnations or threats.

111. There was a rising in Madagascar in 1947 but it was ruthlessly suppressed, to the tune of some 100,000 casualties, effectively, however, for the time being.

112. Grosser, op. cit., p. 396.

113. This was clearly expressed by the secretary of state for Algerian affairs in a speech on November 4, 1964: "Algeria is also and above all the 'narrow gate' through which we penetrate into the Third World. A disagreement between France and another North African state is merely a bilateral issue. A dispute with Algeria would have repercussions beyond the

limits of Franco-Algerian relations and would risk ruining the efforts of our diplomacy in the whole world." De Carmoy, op. cit., p. 292.

114. The discrepancy between the Guinean verdict and others raises the question of the significance and validity of the vote, reflection in turn of the conditions of the milieus in which it was cast. The outcome in the case of Guinea, under the dominant influence of Sékou Touré, induced a French reaction that may appear peevish, but was also designed as an object lesson in the consequences of rejecting the French connection.

115. See above, pp. 557 ff.

116. This remains true despite the events of 1968. These are commented on below, pp. 605 ff.

117. The Soviet occupation of Czechoslovakia in August 1968, designed to put an end to Czech deviationism, appeared as a reversal of this process. But while this is the case in the immediate sense, the leaven of the forces in the Communist commonwealth has not been destroyed.

118. Press conference of July 29, 1963. De Carmoy, op. cit., pp. 335–36.

119. Television address of April 16, 1964. Ibid., p. 367.

120. The actual text of the memorandum is not available, but sufficient is known of it to make discussion possible. See, for example, the analysis in Schoenbrunn, David, *The Three Lives of Charles de Gaulle* (1966), p. 295–300. Schoenbrunn has had access to the document.

121. Press conference of September 9, 1965. De Carmoy, op. cit., pp. 367–68.

122. At the end of 1962 the United States decided to abandon the development of Skybolt, undertaken in collaboration with Britain. As compensation for the effect of this decision on Britain's defense plans, she accepted the American offer of Polaris missiles.

123. While this is not the only consideration, and the validity of the questions raised in the purely economic domain should not be underestimated, the political aspect of the British application remains the dominant factor. See below, pp. 605–6.

124. It was Germany who insisted on the formality of a treaty, which as a consequence was hastily drawn up.

125. The first French nuclear explosion took place in the Sahara in 1961 and further legislation for the development of nuclear weapons was enacted in the autumn of 1963. The first thermonuclear test occurred in the Pacific in 1968 and additional ones are planned.

126. This disappointment, such as it was, has not seriously interfered with the fundamentally altered tone of the Franco-German relationship which has been described earlier.

127. Thierry Maulnier in *Figaro*, January 9, 1957. The point is not whether this judgment was sound or not, but that it may itself be regarded as an expression of the emotional reaction against which it cautions.

128. It was an easy thing for Gomulka to hint at the uselessness of the prewar alliance with France. Ceausescu in Roumania in 1960 adopted a more cordial, if also guarded, attitude. The ferment at work in the Soviet Union's satellites, recently most marked in Czechoslovakia, is what led to the occupation of that country by forces of the Warsaw Pact in August 1968, but the questioning has not been stilled. See below, pp. 610–11.

129. Even in olden times the Mediterranean has been a link rather than a barrier compared with the Alps, for example.

130. It has been pointed out that the picture of differences between France and her five partners in the Common Market was in some degree at least a distortion, for the five could find satisfaction in a situation which, behind the shelter of French opposition, enabled them to pose safely as favorable to the acceptance of Britain. The contention is not devoid of some truth.

131. No candidate achieved a majority in the first round of the election, in which the Communist candidate came third with 21 per cent of the popular vote. The position taken by the Communist leadership, advising its followers to abstain on the second balloting—an instruction widely obeyed—was an important factor in the final outcome. The French Left continues badly divided and as a consequence ineffectual.

132. Grosser, A., *La politique extérieure de la Ve. République* (1965), p. 7.

133. Cited above, pp. 578–79.

BIBLIOGRAPHY

In view of the time span covered in this essay and of the nature of the treatment, no attempt will be made at an exhaustive bibliography. The great documentary collections, which have been and are being currently published, such as the *British Documents on the Origins of the War* or the *Documents Diplomatiques Français,* although referred to on occasion, are consequently not listed. The same applies to such a useful publication as the Royal Institute of International Affairs' *Survey of International Affairs* and its companion *Documents,* and to the relevant volumes of such collective undertakings as *The New Cambridge Modern History* and the French collection *Peuples et Civilisations.* When cited, the authors or editors of such collections or series have not been indicated. The titles given below represent a selection of the books which have been found useful. The list consists of some general treatments, plus in the main of monographs, biographies, and memoirs, and makes no pretense at completeness.

ALBERTINI, LUIGI. *The Origins of the War of 1914,* 3 vols. Oxford, 1952–57.

ALBIN, PIERRE. *La paix armée, l'Allemagne et la France en Europe* (1885–94). Paris, 1913.

ALBRECHT-CARRIÉ, RENÉ. *Italy at the Paris Peace Conference.* New York, 1938.

———. *A Diplomatic History of Europe Since the Congress of Vienna.* New York, 1958.

———. *France, Europe and the Two World Wars.* New York, 1961.

ANDERSON, EUGENE N. *The First Moroccan Crisis, 1904–1906.* Chicago, 1930.

ANDREW, CHRISTOPHER. *Théophile Delcassé and the Making of the Entente Cordiale*. New York, 1968.

ASHLEY, EVELYN. *The Life and Correspondence of Henry John Temple, Viscount Palmerston*. London, 1879.

BAILEY, THOMAS A. *A Diplomatic History of the American People*. New York, 1964.

BARRACLOUGH, GEOFFREY. *An Introduction to Contemporary History*. New York, 1964.

BELL, HERBERT C. F. *Lord Palmerston*, 2 vols. London, 1936.

BEMIS, SAMUEL F. *A Diplomatic History of the United States*. New York, 1965.

BERGER, ERNST E. *Die grosse Politik Delcassés. Frankreichs Kampf um die Vorherrschaft in Europa*. Berlin, 1939.

BERNARD, AUGUSTIN. *L'Algérie*. Paris, 1930.

BETHMANN-HOLLWEG, THEOBALD VON. *Betrachtungen zum Weltkriege*, 2 vols. Berlin, 1919.

BINDOFF, STANLEY T. *The Scheldt Question to 1939*. London, 1945.

Bismarck, the Man and the Statesman; being the Reflections and Reminiscences of Otto, Prince von Bismarck, 2 vols. New York, 1899.

BLAKE, ROBERT. *Disraeli*. London, 1965.

BONNET, GEORGES. *Défense de la paix*, 2 vols. Paris, 1946–48.

BRADFORD, PERKINS. *The Great Rapprochement: England and the United States, 1895–1914*. New York, 1968.

BRANDENBURG, ERICH. *From Bismarck to the World War*. London, 1927.

BUCKLE, GEORGE E., ed. *The Letters of Queen Victoria*. Second Series, 3 vols. London, 1926; Third Series, 3 vols. London, 1930–32.

BÜLOW, BERNHARD VON. *Memoirs of Prince von Bülow*, 4 vols. Boston, 1931–32.

BUTLER, JAMES R. M., ed. *Grand Strategy*. London, 1957.

CAMBON, PAUL. *Ccorrespondence*, 3 vols. Paris, 1940–46.

The Cambridge History of the British Empire, 8 vols. in 9. Cambridge, 1929–59.

The Cambridge History of British Foreign Policy, 3 vols. Cambridge, 1923.

CARMOY, GUY DE. *Les politiques étrangères de la France 1944–1966*. Paris, 1967.

CECIL, ALGERNON. *British Foreign Secretaries, 1807–1916*. London, 1927.

CECIL, LADY GWENDOLEN. *Life of Robert Marquis of Salisbury*, 4 vols. London, 1921–32.

CHAMBERLAIN, AUSTEN. *Down the Years*. London, 1935.

CHURCHILL, WINSTON S. *The River War*, 2 vols. London, 1899.

———. *The World Crisis*, 4 vols. in 5. London, 1923–29.

———. *The Second World War*, 6 vols. Boston, 1948–53.

CLOUGH, SHEPARD B. *France, A History of National Economics, 1789–1939*. New York, 1939.

———. *European Economic History*. New York, 1968.

COCHERIS, JULES. *La situation internationale de l'Égypte et du Soudan*. Paris, 1903.

COLLINS, ROBERT O. *King Leopold, England, and the Upper Nile, 1899–1909*. New Haven, 1968.

COURT, WILLIAM H. B. *A Concise Economic History of Britain*. Cambridge, 1964.

CROMER, EVELYN BARING, LORD. *Modern Egypt*, 2 vols. New York, 1909.

DANGERFIELD, GEORGE. *The Strange Death of Liberal England*. New York, 1935.

DESCHANEL, PAUL. *Gambetta*. London, 1920.

DIEBOLD, WILLIAM, JR. *The Schuman Plan; a Study in Economic Cooperation, 1950–1959*. New York, 1959.

DUGDALE, BLANCHE E. C. *Arthur James Balfour*, 2 vols. New York, 1937.

DUROSELLE, JEAN-BAPTISTE. *La politique extérieure de la France de 1914 à 1945*. Mimeographed course of lectures at the Sorbonne, Paris, 1965.

———. *Histoire diplomatique de 1919 à nous jours*. Paris, 1953.

EDEN, SIR ANTHONY. *The Memoirs of Anthony Eden*, 3 vols. Boston, 1960, 1962, 1965.

EUBANK, KEITH. *Paul Cambon, Master Diplomatist*. Norman, Okla., 1960.

FABRE-LUCE, ALFRED. *Locarno sans rêves*. Paris, 1927.

FALLS, CYRIL. *The Great War, 1914–1918*. New York, 1959.

FREYCINET, CHARLES DE. *La question d'Egypte*. Paris, 1905.

———. *Souvenirs 1878–1893*. Paris, 1913.

GARDINER, ALFRED G. *The Life of Sir William Harcourt*, 2 vols. London, 1923.

GARVIN, JAMES L. *The Life of Joseph Chamberlain*, 4 vols. London, 1932–35, 1951. (Vol. IV by Julian Amery.)

GATHORNE-HARDY, GEOFFREY M. *A Short History of International Affairs*. New York, 1950.

GAULLE, CHARLES DE. *Vers l'armée de métier*. Paris, 1934.
———. *War Memoirs*, 5 vols. New York, 1955–60.
GILBERT, MARTIN. *The Roots of Appeasement*. New York, 1966.
GOOCH, GEORGE P. *Before the War. Studies in Diplomacy*, 2 vols. London, 1936–38.
GREER, DONALD M. *L'Angleterre, la France et la révolution de 1848*. Paris, 1925.
GRENVILLE, JOHN A. S. *Lord Salisbury and Foreign Policy: The Close of the Nineteenth Century*. London, 1964.
The Greville Memoirs, see Strachey.
GREY OF FALLODON, VISCOUNT. *Twenty-Five Years, 1892–1916*, 2 vols. New York, 1925.
GROSSER, ALFRED. *La IVe. République et sa politique extérieure*. Paris, 1961.
———. *La politique extérieure de la Ve. République*. Paris, 1965.
GUÉRARD, ALBERT. *Napoleon III; a Great Life in Brief*. New York, 1955.
GUICHEN, EUGÈNE DE. *La guerre de Crimée (1854–1856) et l'attitude des puissances européennes*. Paris, 1936.
GUIZOT, FRANÇOIS. *Mémoires pour servir à l'histoire de mon temps*, 8 vols. Paris, 1858–67.
HABAKKUK, H. J., and POSTAN, M., eds. *The Cambridge Economic History of Europe*. Vol. VI in 2 parts: *The Industrial Revolution and After*. Cambridge, 1965.
HAIG, ROBERT M. *The Public Finances of Post-War France*. New York, 1929.
HALDANE, RICHARD B. H. *Before the War*. New York, 1920.
HALIFAX, LORD. *Fullness of Days*. New York, 1957.
HALLBERG, CHARLES W. *The Suez Canal. Its History and Diplomatic Importance*. New York, 1931.
HAMILTON, LORD GEORGE. *Parliamentary Reminiscences and Reflections, 1886–1906*. London, 1932.
HANOTAUX, GABRIEL. *Fachoda*. Paris, 1909.
HEINDEL, RICHARD H. *The American Impact on Great Britain*. Philadelphia, 1940.
HENDERSON, GAVIN B. *Crimean War Diplomacy and Other Essays*. Glasgow, 1947.
HERTSLET, EDWARD. *The Map of Europe by Treaty*, 4 vols. London, 1875–91.
HODSON, HENRY V. *Slump and Recovery 1929–1937. A Survey of World Economic Affairs*. New York, 1938.

HOUSE, EDWARD M. *The Intimate Papers of Colonel House, arranged as a Narrative by Charles Seymour,* 4 vols. Boston, 1926–28.

HOWARD, HARRY N. *The Partition of Turkey; a Diplomatic History, 1913–1923.* Norman, Okla., 1931.

HUREWITZ, JACOB C. *Diplomacy in the Near and Middle East,* 2 vols. Princeton, 1956.

HYTIER, ADRIENNE. *Two Years of French Foreign Policy, Vichy 1940–1942.* Geneva, 1958.

JENKINS, ROY. *Asquith.* London, 1964

JOLL, JAMES. *Britain and Europe, Pitt to Churchill, 1793–1940.* London, 1950.

JORDAN, W. M. *Great Britain, France and the German Problem 1918–1939.* London, 1943.

JULIEN, CHARLES A. *Histoire de l'Afrique du Nord.* Paris, 1931.

KENNEDY, AUBREY L. *Salisbury 1830–1903. Portrait of a Statesman.* London, 1953.

KEYNES, JOHN M. *The Economic Consequences of the Peace.* New York, 1920.

KINDLEBERGER, CHARLES P. *Economic Growth in France and Britain, 1851–1950.* Cambridge, Mass., 1964.

KNAPLUND, PAUL. *Gladstone's Foreign Policy.* New York, 1935.

———. *The British Empire, 1815–1939.* New York, 1941.

LA GORCE, PIERRE DE. *Histoire du Second Empire,* 7 vols. Paris, 1896–1905.

LANGER, WILLIAM L. *European Alliances and Alignments.* New York, 1931.

———. *The Franco-Russian Alliance.* Chicago, 1930.

———. *The Diplomacy of Imperialism.* New York, 1951.

LANNOY, FLEURY DE. *Histoire diplomatique de l'indépendance belge.* Brussels, 1930.

LIDDELL HART, BASIL H. *The War in Outline.* New York, 1936.

LLOYD GEORGE, DAVID. *War Memoirs of David Lloyd George,* 6 vols. London, 1933–36.

———. *The Truth About the Peace Treaties,* 2 vols. London, 1938.

MACMILLAN, HAROLD. *Winds of Change 1914–1939.* London, 1966.

———. *The Blast of War, 1939–1945.* New York, 1968.

———. *Tides of Fortune, 1945–1955.* New York, 1969.

MANDELSTAM, ANDRÉ N. *Le conflit italo-éthiopien devant la Société des Nations.* Paris, 1937.

MANTOUX, PAUL. *Les délibérations du Conseil des Quatre (24 mars–28 juin 1919): Notes de l'interprète,* 2 vols. Paris, 1955.

MARDER, ARTHUR J. *The Anatomy of British Sea Power.* New York, 1940.

MARRIOTT, JOHN A. R. *The Eastern Question.* Oxford, 1940.

MAYER, ARNO J. *Politics and Diplomacy of Peacemaking. Containment and Counter-Revolution at Versailles, 1918–1919.* New York, 1968.

MEINECKE, FRIEDRICH. *Geschichte des Deutsch-Englischen Bündniss Problems, 1890–1901.* Munich, 1927.

MERMEIX (pseud. GABRIEL TERRAIL). *Les négociations secrètes et les quatre armistices.* Paris, 1919.

———. *Le combat des Trois.* Paris, 1922.

MIDDLEMAS, KEITH, and BARNES, JOHN. *Baldwin: A Biography.* London, 1969.

MILLER, WILLIAM. *The Ottoman Empire and its Successors.* London, 1966.

MILLET, RENÉ. *Notre politique extérieure, 1898–1905.* Paris, 1905.

MONTEIL, P. L. *Souvenirs vécus. Quelques feuillets de l'histoire coloniale.* Paris, 1924.

MONYPENNY, WILLIAM F., and BUCKLE, GEORGE E. *The Life of Disraeli, Earl of Beaconsfield,* 6 vols. New York, 1913–20.

MOON, PARKER T. *Imperialism and World Politics.* New York, 1926.

MORIER. See Wemyss.

MORLEY, LORD JOHN. *Life of William Ewart Gladstone,* 3 vols. New York, 1903.

MOWAT, CHARLES L. *Britain Between the Wars 1918–1940.* Chicago, 1955.

NAMIER, LEWIS B. *Europe in Decay, a Study in Disintegration 1936–1940.* London, 1950.

NETON, ALBÉRIC. *Delcassé.* Paris, 1952.

NINTCHITCH, MOMTCHILO. *La crise bosniaque (1908–1909) et les puissances européennes,* 2 vols. Paris, 1937.

NORTHEDGE, FREDERICK S. *British Foreign Policy; the Process of Readjustment 1945–1961.* London, 1962.

PALLAIN, GEORGES. *Ambassade de Talleyrand à Londres 1830–1834.* Paris, 1891.

PARRY, ERNEST J. *The Spanish Marriages.* London, 1936.

PAUL-BONCOUR, JOSEPH. *Entre deux guerres. Souvenirs sur la IIIe. République,* 3 vols. Paris, 1945–46.

PENSON, LILLIAN M. *Foreign Affairs under the Third Marquis of Salisbury.* London, 1962.

PHILLIPS, WALTER A. *The Confederation of Europe.* London, 1920.

PINGAUD, ALBERT. *Histoire diplomatique de la France pendant la grande guerre,* 3 vols. Paris, 1937–40.

POINCARÉ, RAYMOND. *Au service de la France. Neuf années de souvenirs,* 10 vols. Paris, 1926–33.

PRIBRAM, ALFRED F. *The Secret Treaties of Austria-Hungary,* 2 vols. Cambridge, Mass., 1920–21.

RAMBAUD, ALFRED. *Jules Ferry.* Paris, 1903.

RAPPARD, WILLIAM E. *The Quest for Peace.* London, 1931.

RENOUVIN, PIERRE. *La politique extérieure de Th. Delcassé.* Paris, 1962.

———. *Histoire des relations internationales. Le XIXe. siècle,* 2 parts. Paris, 1954, 1955. *Les Crises du XXe. siècle,* 2 parts. Paris, 1957, 1958.

RICH, NORMAN. *Friedrich von Holstein, Politics and Diplomacy in the Era of Bismarck and Wilhelm II,* 2 vols. Cambridge, 1965.

ROBIQUET, PAUL, ed. *Discours et opinions de Jules Ferry,* 7 vols. Paris, 1893–98.

RONALDSHAY, EARL OF. *The Life of Lord Curzon,* 3 vols. London, 1928.

RUDIN, HARRY A. *Armistice 1918.* New Haven, 1944.

SCHEFER, CHRISTIAN. *La grande pensée de Napoléon III; les origines de l'expédition du Mexique (1858–1862).* Paris, 1939.

SCHMITT, BERNADOTTE E. *The Annexation of Bosnia.* Cambridge, Mass., 1937.

SCHOENBRUNN, DAVID. *The Three Lives of Charles de Gaulle.* New York, 1966.

SCHUMAN, FREDERICK. *War and Diplomacy in the French Republic.* New York, 1931.

SENIOR, NASSAU WILLIAM. *Conversations with MM. Thiers, Guizot and Other Distinguished Persons,* 2 vols. London, 1878.

SETON-WATSON, ROBERT W. *Britain in Europe, 1789–1914.* Cambridge, 1937.

———. *Disraeli, Gladstone and the Eastern Question.* London, 1935.

SPENDER, JOHN A. *Life of Herbert Asquith, Lord Oxford and Asquith.* London, 1932.

STEEFEL, LAURENCE D. *The Schleswig-Holstein Question.* Cambridge, Mass., 1932.

STRACHEY, LYTTON, and FULFORD, ROBERT, eds. *The Greville Memoirs,* 8 vols. London, 1938.

STRANG, LORD. *Britain in World Affairs.* New York, 1961.

TALLEYRAND. *Mémoires du Prince de Talleyrand,* ed. by Duc de Broglie, 5 vols. Paris, 1891–92.

TANSILL, CHARLES C. *Back Door to War, the Roosevelt Foreign Policy 1933–1941*. Chicago, 1952.

TARDIEU, ANDRÉ. *The Truth About the Treaty*. Indianapolis, 1921.

TAYLOR, A. J. P. *The Struggle for Mastery in Europe, 1848–1918.* Oxford, 1954.

———. *English History 1914–1945*. New York, 1965.

———. *The Italian Problem in European Diplomacy 1847–1849.* Manchester, 1934.

TEMPERLEY, HAROLD W. V. *England and the East: The Crimea.* London, 1936.

———, ed. *A History of the Peace Conference at Paris,* 6 vols. London, 1920–23.

———, and PENSON, LILLIAN M. *Foundations of British Foreign Policy, 1782–1902*. Cambridge, 1938.

THIERS, ADOLPHE. *Discours parlementaires de M. Thiers,* publiés par M. Calmon, 16 vols. Paris, 1879–89.

[LONDON] *Times. The History of the "Times,"* 4 vols. in 5. London, 1935–52.

TREVELYAN, GEORGE M. *Grey of Fallodon.* New York, 1937.

VANSITTART, LORD. *The Mist Procession. The Autobiography of Lord Vansittart.* London, 1958.

VAUCHER, PAUL, and SIRIEX, P.-H. *L'Opinion britannique, la Société des Nations et la guerre italo-éthiopienne.* Paris, 1936.

WALTER, F. P. *A History of the League of Nations,* 2 vols. New York, 1952.

WATT, D. C. *Personalities and Problems; Studies in the Foundations of British Foreign Policy in the Twentieth Century*. London, 1935.

WEBSTER, CHARLES K., ed. *British Diplomacy 1813–1815: Selected Documents Dealing with the Reconstruction of Europe*. London, 1921.

———. *The Foreign Policy of Palmerston, 1830–1851,* 2 vols. London, 1951.

WEILL-REYNAL, ETIENNE. *Les réparations allemandes et la France,* 3 vols. Paris, 1948.

WEMYSS, ROSSLYN. *Memoirs and Letters of the Right Honorable Sir Robert Morier,* 2 vols. London, 1911.

WHEELER-BENNETT, JOHN W. *Disarmament and Security Since Locarno, 1925–1931*. New York, 1932.

———. *The Pipe Dream of Peace: the Story of the Collapse of Disarmament*. London, 1935.

———. *Munich, Prologue to Tragedy*. New York, 1948.

WILLIAMS, PHILIP. *Politics in Post-War France*. London, 1954.

WILSON, ARNOLD T. *The Suez Canal*. London, 1939.

WISKEMANN, ELIZABETH. *Europe and the Dictators, 1919–1945*. London, 1966.

WOLFERS, ARNOLD. *Britain and France Between Two Wars*. New York, 1940.

WOODHOUSE, CHRISTOPHER M. *Post-War Britain*. London, 1966.

WOODWARD, ERNEST L. *Great Britain and the German Navy*. New York, 1935.

WOODWARD, SIR LLEWELLYN. *British Foreign Policy in the Second World War*. London, 1962.

ZIMMERN, ALFRED. *The League of Nations and the Rule of Law, 1919–1935*. New York, 1936.

INDEX

CANADA
NORTH
AMERICA
NEWFOUDLAND
ST. PIERRE & MIQUELON
GREAT BRITAIN
IRELAND
FRANCE
Atlantic Ocean
Pacific Ocean
BERMUDA (BR.)
BAHAMAS (BR.)
GIBRALTAR
MOROCCO
FRENCH WEST AFRI
BR. HONDURAS
JAMAICA (BR.)
BR. WEST INDIES
GUADELOUPE (FR.)
MARTINIQUE (FR.)
TRINIDAD & TOBAGO (BR.)
BATHURST
SIERRA LEONE
FRENCH GUIANA
BR. GUIANA
GOLD COAS
WASHINGTON (BR.)
FANNING (BR.)
CHRISTMAS (BR.)
JARVIS (BR.)
MALDEN (BR.)
STARBUCK (BR.)
MARQUESAS IS. (FR.)
MANIHIKI IS. (BR.)
TUAMOTU ARCH. (FR.)
SOCIETY IS. (FR.)
COOK IS.
AUSTRAL IS. (FR.)
PITCAIRN (BR.)
DUCIE (BR.)
SOUTH AMERICA
ASCENSION (BR.)
ST. HELENA (BR.)
TRISTAN DA CUNHA (BR.)
GOUGH (BR.)
FALKLAND IS.
SOUTH GEORGIA
SOUTH ORKNEYS (BR.)
SOUTH SHETLANDS (BR.)
THE WORLD
AFTER WORLD WAR I